Beer of Broadway Fame

Beer of Broadway Fame

The Piel Family and Their Brooklyn Brewery

ALFRED W. McCOY

excelsior editions
State University of New York Press
Albany, New York

Cover Credit: Brooklynpix.com; B. Merlis and R. Gomes, *Brooklyn's East New York and Cypress Hill Communities.*

Published by State University of New York Press, Albany

© 2016 State University of New York

Excelsior Editions is an imprint of State University of New York Press

For information, contact State University of New York Press, Albany, NY
www.sunypress.edu

Production, Jenn Bennett
Marketing, Fran Keneston

Library of Congress Cataloging-in-Publication Data

McCoy, Alfred W., author.
   Beer of Broadway fame : the Piel family and their Brooklyn brewery / Alfred W. McCoy.
      pages cm
   Includes bibliographical references and index.
   ISBN 978-1-4384-6140-3 (paperback : alk. paper)
   ISBN 978-1-4384-6141-0 (e-book)
   1. Piel family.   2. McCoy, Alfred W.—Family.   3. Piel's Beer (Firm)—History.
4. Breweries—New York (State)—New York—History.   I. Title.

TP573.5.A1M35 2016
663'.309747—dc23   2015036570

10 9 8 7 6 5 4 3 2 1

For Those Piels Who Brought the Family Business
into the Third Generation

Frederick Lange

Gerard Piel

Margarita Piel McCoy

Contents

List of Illustrations

Images

Photo Gallery: The Piel Family

Figures

Map

Tables

Acknowledgments

The fifteen years spent researching and writing this book were an extraordinary voyage of discovery, not of a distant land or into a long-forgotten past, but of something as close as my own family. This book started as an antiquarian project, morphed into a social history, and wound up in my preferred scholarly terrain, the shadowy netherworld of covert operations. Instead of the roster of names and dates that are the stuff of most genealogical histories, I found a hidden past of espionage, state surveillance, family intrigues, and personal betrayals.

Every history stands or falls upon the quality of its documentation, and this one is certainly no exception. The feasibility of the entire project rested upon the care that many Piel family members took with inherited papers and photos that became warp and weft for weaving this history. I am grateful, more than I can say, to the third-generation Piels for this invaluable service—including, Marie-Luise Kemp for preserving her parents' photos; David Piel, who wrote up memorable anecdotes that liven several chapters; Mark Piel, who found family papers and rare photos; Rollo Lange who shared memories; Daniel Piel who sent photos; and, particularly, Eleanor Jackson Piel for sorting out the Piel brewery's papers in a musty Brooklyn storage locker; and her husband Gerard Piel who believed deeply in this project and supported it generously with time, personal papers, and professional contacts.

Although Gerard's older brother William Piel, Jr., a renowned litigator, died before I started this research, his name was sufficient to open the voluminous Piel Bros. records at the Wall Street law firm Sullivan & Cromwell, counsel to the brewery for a full quarter-century. My long day-into-night reading of piles of these files in Conference Room C on the thirty-fourth floor of 125 Broad Street, as liveried waiters served coffee and clerks delivered stacks of immaculate photocopies, remains one of the most memorable events in a decade's research.

A descendant on matriarch Maria's side of the family, Christian Heermann, transcribed family letters from the old German *fractuer* handwriting and shared his histories of the Heermann Hof, Maria Piel's ancestral home at Herne in North Rhine–Westphalia. But, above all, I am grateful to my mother Margarita Piel

McCoy for both the childhood stories that inspired this project and her invaluable interviews throughout the long years of research and writing.

The Piels of my own fourth generation were both helpful and critical—helpful with the research and critical of the time it took me to complete this demanding project. I am grateful to Tommy Kemp for access to family artifacts stored at his farm in northern Maine; Weezy Kemp Ringle and Steve Ringle for help with the photography and genealogy; Bia Piel, for introducing me to the literature on therapy for families in business together; Jonathan Piel, who kindly shared media contacts in connection with the Bruno Bettelheim story; Tony Piel, who both provided documents and defended me before the family as other writing projects claimed my time; and, above all, Olga Lange, for her careful curating of family papers and meticulous scanning of the many photos stored at her Lake Parlin cottage. My eldest son Matthew drew the genealogy and the brewery's organizational chart, skillfully rendering both complexities visually comprehensible. Finally, my sister Margarita Candace Ground typed many of the lengthy oral history transcripts and cast a critical eye over the manuscript's penultimate draft.

Several long-time employees of the family's firms were generous with their expertise, including Leonard Lazarus who was counselor to the Piel family for over sixty years, as well as the key advisers to the current family business M&G Piel Securities, accountant Jerry Salomone and financial adviser Harvey Ross.

Beyond the family, colleagues at the University of Wisconsin–Madison were quite helpful, including Matt Gildner, who did research in the U.S. National Archives; Maureen Justiniano, who scanned many of the 1,600 images collected for the project; Judy Vezzetti, who did genealogical research during breaks from her duties as the chair's secretary in the History Department; Anne Bailey and Marta-Laura Suska, who finished some challenging German translations; Erin Hardacker, who edited an early draft and compiled the bibliography; and Nancy Mulhern, the knowledgeable Government Documents Librarian at the Wisconsin State Historical Society, for searches into nineteenth-century beer production and the records of the Senate Internal Security Committee.

Elsewhere Zeph Stickney, archivist at Wheaton College, Norton, Massachusetts, sent documents about Mathilde Lange's career as a faculty member; while school archivists Ruth Quattlebaum and Emily Tordo provided the records for the ten Piel family members who attended Philips Andover Academy. In Europe, Martin Lengwiler and his researcher Cemile Ivedi conducted archival research in Zurich, Switzerland; my wife's uncle, David Hove, recruited these researchers; and, finally, Bernd Volkert found sources about the Lange and Heermann families in Berlin libraries.

In the search for photographs, curators were unfailingly cooperative, including Louisa Watrous, archivist at Mystic Seaport, who provided a photo of the Piel Bros. brewery; Nilda Rivera, licensing director, Museum of the City of New York, who sent a photo of the old Piel Brewery; Alla Roylance and June Koffi, helpful librarians at the Brooklyn Collection, Brooklyn Public Library, who facilitated access to their superb photo archive of the borough's rich social history; Tad Bennicoff, archivist at the Smithsonian Institution, who assisted with the evocative portrait of Dr. Mathilde Lange; and Barry Lewis, editor of the *Sunday Record* in Middletown, New York, who kindly gave permission for use of the 1971 photo of Dr. Lange. Private collectors were particularly helpful, notably Don Bull of The Virtual Corkscrew Museum who generously donated a copy of his photograph of Gottfried Piel; and Brian Merlis, a local historian of Brooklyn's neighborhoods, who found the rare photo of the Piel brewery workers, circa 1900.

Every writing project reminds me of my gratitude to Bob Cluett, who taught me a love for this craft at a small Connecticut boarding school and later wrote an exemplary history of his own New York family, *The Gold of Troy*, that served as a model for this project. My friend and fellow Southeast Asia historian David Chandler shared a privately published history of his elite New York family, providing valuable cultural insights into the city's old Anglo aristocracy. Closer to home, my wife, Mary McCoy, gave me sensible counsel about family concerns at key points in the text, and her father, Professor Edward Pixley, advised me about the conclusion.

Once I finished a first draft of the manuscript, I was fortunate to encounter skilled editors who lent their talents to the realization of this project's potential. I am particularly grateful to Gwen Walker at the University of Wisconsin Press for extraordinary editing that produced a coherent narrative and inserted these Piel particulars within a wider U.S. social history. When I sent draft chapters to several prospective publishers, Michael J. McGandy, senior editor at Cornell University Press, read the draft introduction and offered an important suggestion. Once I had introduced myself as a "privileged observer" on page one, I had to reappear, he said, at strategic points in the narrative—advice that I have followed, hopefully not to a fault.

After the book found a home at SUNY Press, staff there were enormously helpful, including press co-director James Peltz who supported the project; acquisitions editor Amanda Lanne-Camilli who shaped the book's final form; her associate Jessica Kirschner who moved the book assiduously through the many demanding steps toward publication; and Jenn Bennett who efficiently supervised the actual production. Needless to say, I alone am responsible for any errors or omissions.

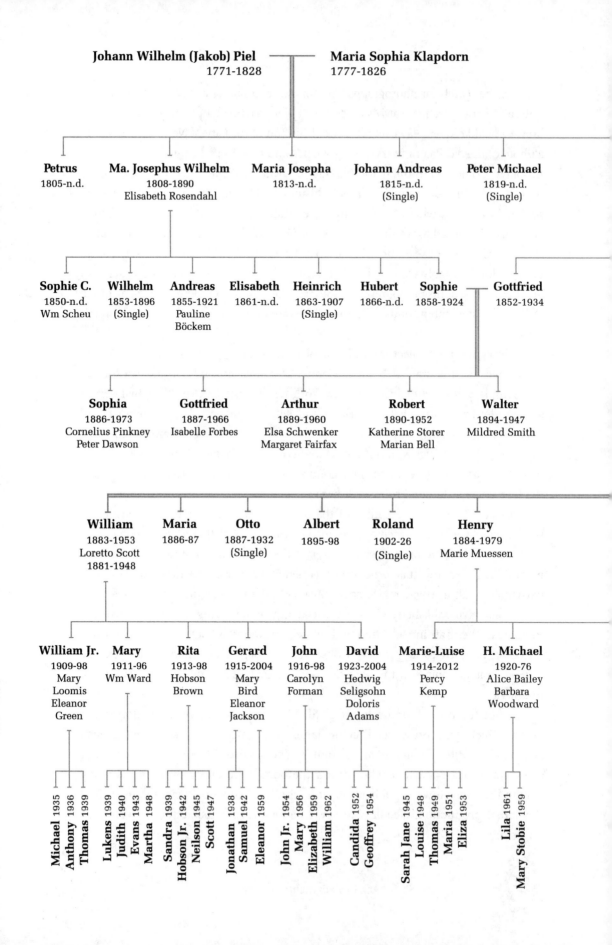

Johann Wilhelm (Jakob) Piel
1771-1828

Maria Sophia Klapdorn
1777-1826

Petrus
1805-n.d.

Ma. Josephus Wilhelm
1808-1890
Elisabeth Rosendahl

Maria Josepha
1813-n.d.

Johann Andreas
1815-n.d.
(Single)

Peter Michael
1819-n.d.
(Single)

Sophie C.
1850-n.d.
Wm Scheu

Wilhelm
1853-1896
(Single)

Andreas
1855-1921
Pauline
Böckem

Elisabeth
1861-n.d.

Heinrich
1863-1907
(Single)

Hubert
1866-n.d.

Sophie
1858-1924

Gottfried
1852-1934

Sophia
1886-1973
Cornelius Pinkney
Peter Dawson

Gottfried
1887-1966
Isabelle Forbes

Arthur
1889-1960
Elsa Schwenker
Margaret Fairfax

Robert
1890-1952
Katherine Storer
Marian Bell

Walter
1894-1947
Mildred Smith

William
1883-1953
Loretto Scott
1881-1948

Maria
1886-87

Otto
1887-1932
(Single)

Albert
1895-98

Roland
1902-26
(Single)

Henry
1884-1979
Marie Muessen

William Jr.
1909-98
Mary
Loomis
Eleanor
Green

Mary
1911-96
Wm Ward

Rita
1913-98
Hobson
Brown

Gerard
1915-2004
Mary
Bird
Eleanor
Jackson

John
1916-98
Carolyn
Forman

David
1923-2004
Hedwig
Seligsohn
Doloris
Adams

Marie-Luise
1914-2012
Percy
Kemp

H. Michael
1920-76
Alice Bailey
Barbara
Woodward

Michael 1935
Anthony 1936
Thomas 1939

Lukens 1939
Judith 1940
Evans 1943
Martha 1948

Sandra 1939
Hobson Jr. 1942
Neilson 1945
Scott 1947

Jonathan 1938
Samuel 1942
Eleanor 1959

John Jr. 1954
Mary 1956
Elizabeth 1959
William 1962

Candida 1952
Geoffrey 1954

Sarah Jane 1945
Louise 1948
Thomas 1949
Maria 1951
Eliza 1953

Lila 1961
Mary Stobie 1959

DESCENDANTS OF JAKOB PIEL,
SHOWING FOUR GENERATIONS IN AMERICA

Compiled by Paul Piel, 276 West 11th St.,
New York City, N.Y. June 4, 1957

Updated by Stephen B. Ringle, 2000
Designed by Matthew F. McCoy, 2015

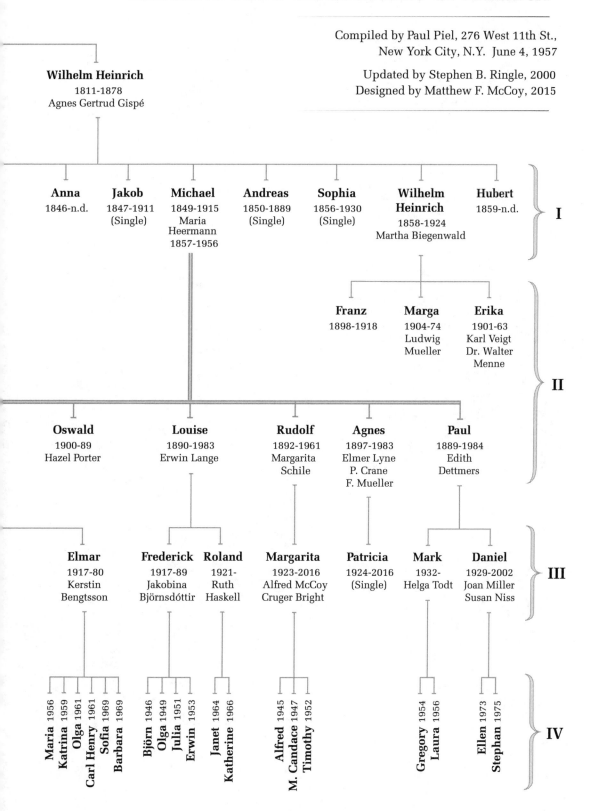

Wilhelm Heinrich
1811-1878
Agnes Gertrud Gispé

Anna
1846-n.d.

Jakob
1847-1911
(Single)

Michael
1849-1915
Maria
Heermann
1857-1956

Andreas
1850-1889
(Single)

Sophia
1856-1930
(Single)

**Wilhelm
Heinrich**
1858-1924
Martha Biegenwald

Hubert
1859-n.d.

I

Franz
1898-1918

Marga
1904-74
Ludwig
Mueller

Erika
1901-63
Karl Veigt
Dr. Walter
Menne

II

Oswald
1900-89
Hazel Porter

Louise
1890-1983
Erwin Lange

Rudolf
1892-1961
Margarita
Schile

Agnes
1897-1983
Elmer Lyne
P. Crane
F. Mueller

Paul
1889-1984
Edith
Dettmers

Elmar
1917-80
Kerstin
Bengtsson

Frederick
1917-89
Jakobina
Björnsdóttir

Roland
1921-
Ruth
Haskell

Margarita
1923-2016
Alfred McCoy
Cruger Bright

Patricia
1924-2016
(Single)

Mark
1932-
Helga Todt

Daniel
1929-2002
Joan Miller
Susan Niss

III

Maria 1956
Katrina 1959
Olga 1961
Carl Henry 1961
Sofia 1969
Barbara 1969

Björn 1946
Olga 1949
Julia 1951
Erwin 1953

Janet 1964
Katherine 1966

Alfred 1945
M. Candace 1947
Timothy 1952

Gregory 1954
Laura 1956

Ellen 1973
Stephan 1975

IV

1

The Piel Family

The door was locked and the rambling old house was deserted. So I punched out a glass pane, reached in, and opened the back door. Maybe I shouldn't have. But it was the only way I could get in.

The corridor was dimly lit by the faint sun of a cloudy summer's day in northern Maine. Stepping over the broken glass into that corridor, I was aware of everything—my steps, the filtered light, the objects around me. Even now, nearly fifty years later, I can still recall every minute of my hour in that house back in the summer of 1968. For I wasn't just breaking into a house. I was breaking into my family's past.

Along that corridor were small, sparse rooms with single brass bedsteads clean and ready for a summer staff long gone. At the end, off to the left, the kitchen seemed abandoned in the middle of a meal. Great steel pots were stacked in a sink filled with grease-covered water. Plates had been left on the dining room tables. The anteroom at the front of the house was, by contrast, immaculate. Even in the faint light, the colors of the old Turkish carpet still glowed. Upstairs, there were more bedrooms with more brass bedsteads. Everything else had been cleaned out.

Climbing the last flight of stairs, I came into an attic that ran the length of the house. At both ends were small dormer windows. Streams of daylight showed a bare wooden floor stripped clean of the clutter from better days.

Beneath a shaft of light at the far end, I saw a single piece of furniture, a small chest of drawers. As I approached, there was a letter lying on that bureau. The handwriting had the distinctive left-hook angles of my mother's hand. It was written in the blue ink she always favored. On the back, it was signed Margarita, my mother's name. Clipped to the back was a small snapshot. I pulled open the drawers, looking for more papers, other photos. Nothing. These were the only papers in the dresser, in the entire attic, in the whole house.

The photo showed the front veranda with five women seated comfortably, smiling into the camera across the span of three generations. At the center, I could recognize my mother's grandmother Maria Piel, the matriarch then in her eighties, seated on a chaise lounge, hands knitting a sweater, white hair pulled back into an austere bun. Seated on the railing was my mother's older cousin, Marie-Luise. To her left on the railing was Mother herself, just seventeen and radiant, wearing a white dress, saddle shoes, and her hair long with the gentle curls of the early 1940s. Seated to the right were two of her grandmother's German relatives.

That letter was a formal thank-you note, gracious and chatty. "Dear Grandmother," it began, "I want to thank you for the wonderful time I had in Maine. I enjoyed every minute of it—you've no idea how much I think of Lake Parlin thru out the year & just being there is wonderful."

As I went down the stairs and retraced my steps through those corridors, I glanced about for other letters or papers. There were none. A half-century's clutter had recently been cleaned out to prepare the property for sale to a real estate speculator.[1]

Finding that letter and photo churned emotions I still cannot describe. It was, to say the least, an unsettling coincidence. Why just that letter in this enormous house with dozens of empty rooms, lying, almost waiting for me on that bureau? Adding to this eerie aura, just a few years after my visit this house, which had stood for nearly a century, burned to the ground.[2] If I believed in such things, I would call it fate, an invitation, even a summons.

The photo's smiles and the letter's genteel prose resonated with the wondrous tales my mother had told me, as a child, of her larger-than-life family, their Brooklyn brewery, and this grand estate up in the Maine woods. Back then I suspected my mother was embellishing a bit to make a good story better. But even her most fabulous tales had a kernel of truth that later provided me with important leads for writing this history.

There was her mother's uncle Willy Schmidt, the gunrunner, who started a revolution in Haiti to better sell rifles to both sides at a hefty markup. Visiting a sugar plantation in Brazil, he ran off one night with the planter's wife, horses and hounds in pursuit through the moonlight. Uncle Willy brought Consuela back to New York, where he moved her in with his wife and children. Since there were just so many slots in the family crypt, the real competition between the two women was to die first and claim the burial spot. Then there was Uncle

Erwin, a U.S. diplomat in Turkey during World War I who was sent home for trying to get America into the war—on the side of Germany.

Mother's best and, frankly, most imaginative stories were about her father's parents, the saga of their migration to America and the fabulous life they lived in their adopted land. Grandfather Michael Piel had been the strongest man in his village back in Germany, so strong he could lift a loaded hay wagon on his back. So strong that, when he struck his stepfather for hitting his mother, the man was crippled for life. Michael fled to New York, one step ahead of the law. There he built a successful brewery and sent ample funds back home to pay for his beloved Maria's migration to America.[3]

But, said Mother, her imagination now in full flower, Maria had taken vows in a Catholic convent. So her family split the cash with the mother superior who told Maria that it was God's will for her to go to America and marry Michael Piel. Their brewery was so successful that Michael and Maria soon had a mansion in Manhattan, an ocean-going yacht with dinner service embossed with the ship's name *Meridrud*, and a summer estate up in Maine with a retinue of servants, tutors, and musicians. There, Mother said, ladies in their white gowns would repair to a gazebo for strawberries and cream to chat while a small orchestra played invisibly in the woods nearby.

Even so, Grandmother Maria was bedeviled by the sin of leaving the nunnery, breaking her marriage vows to Jesus, and marrying Michael Piel. The specter of eternal damnation haunted her household. She extracted daily confessionals from her children. Most of them later refused to have anything to do with religion. So in the fading fall light, as our car twisted through the Pennsylvania hills toward the Catholic convent where Maria was spending her last years, Mother told us that we two, me then nine and my sister just seven, were the few among her dozens of descendants being raised in any church. Great-Grandmother was ninety-seven and growing frail. The ghosts were gathering. Seeing us, Mother said, would soothe her fears.

For reasons never explained, our own family never vacationed at that estate up in Maine. I only knew of it from Mother's stories—enchanting stories that portrayed the past as a wondrous place full of extraordinary events and adventurous characters that made me, without thinking much about it, grow up to become an historian. So, with my profession's love of paper, I saved that letter and photo, putting them in an album that I carried with me through moves to Asia and Australia and back again to America.

In 1998, some thirty years after my visit to Maine, the family business marked its centennial, though brewing beer had given way to managing money. At a meeting of the board of directors, I suggested a short history might be in order. Everyone looked at me, the family's only historian. So I started this project by recording my mother's memories of her family, their Brooklyn brewery, and those summers up in Maine. Mother recalled that, in later years when times turned tough for the brewery, her father ran a poultry breeding business, shuttling chicks between rented barns on Long Island and a hatchery on a hill behind the big house in Maine.

Though it wasn't all that relevant, I turned our interviews to that long-ago visit in the photo, sometime in the summer of 1940. "Well," said Mother into the tape recorder, "I remember I went up with my father, it was hot, and my mother said 'why don't you go up to Maine with Daddy,' who was going up for his chickens, 'and stay up there a while.' It was a long day's drive to get from Boston to Lake Parlin and I was not invited to stay over. I stayed overnight, I think, and went home the next day with Daddy. I don't remember the reason. *Tante* Louise was busy or there just wasn't room for me. 'What? In that barn!' My mother was really livid. It didn't faze me because it's family. And I don't know what was behind all that."[4]

Some months after that interview, one of Mother's many cousins gave me all the business's surviving papers, which had been deposited in a storage locker after the Brooklyn brewery was sold in the 1960s. Midst those boxes filled with eighty years of mortgages, contracts, and corporate minutes was a sworn statement, signed by Mother's father and dated July 1940, just a few weeks after that unfortunate visit to Maine.

"Know all men by these present that I, Rudolf A. Piel," my mother's father had written, "in consideration of the sum of One ($1.00) dollar . . . paid by Maria Piel of Lake Parlin, Jackman Station, Maine . . . do hereby . . . sell and convey and forever quit claim unto said Maria Piel, her heirs and assigns forever all of his right, title, estate, and interest in . . . [a] certain lot or parcel of land situated in . . . Lake Parlin Farm, and owned by Maria Piel."[5]

Put simply, Mother's father was signing over his piece of land on the family estate to his mother Maria for a dollar. In a second document, he reserved "all my rights in and to approximately ten poultry range shelters . . . which are now on said Lake Parlin Farm, and which are my property and are to be returned to me." Her father was taking his poultry equipment and leaving the family estate at Lake Parlin, forever.[6]

A few years ago when I began writing these words, I telephoned Mother to make sure the photo and letter were indeed from that visit in the summer of 1940. To prod her memory, I summarized her father's legal declarations, documents she had never seen. After mulling it over for a few minutes, Mother added some missing details. By then, her father's chicken coops on a hill behind the big house created an incessant noise and horrible smell that detracted from the efforts of Grandmother Maria and her daughter, Mother's *Tante* Louise, to run the Parlin farm as a fancy inn for travelers on the road to Quebec City.

But Mother was now nearly ninety. She just didn't remember writing that letter or seeing the photo. So, recalling her uncanny memory for clothes, I asked her if she could remember what she was wearing seventy-three years ago during that summer's day in 1940.

"It was a white dress, with red lines that came together to make a pattern of squares," she said.

"Hmm," I replied. The old black-and-white snapshot only showed the dress as a whitish blur. "What about the cut of the dress?"

"There were buttons down the front," she said.

Right. "What about the collar?" I asked.

"It was a shirt collar," she said. Right again.

"What about the sleeves?" she now asked me. "I believe they were either half- or three-quarter length."

"Half," I replied, "just above the elbow."

"Yes," she said, "that's the dress I wore for that visit."[7]

So during that day at Lake Parlin there must have been a bitter family fight. Though my Mother had expected to stay for the summer, the next day she got in the car with her father and did not return for many years. And that breach never healed. For the next fifteen years, her father never saw or spoke to his mother again until she died in 1956 at the age of 99.[8] Now I knew the reason why our family never visited Lake Parlin.

During my decade of research into this family history, turning up a wealth of documents in New York, Washington, Düsseldorf, and Zurich, the fables faded, replaced by some uncomfortable truths. The titans of family legend touched earth. The outlandish, often amusing characters of my mother's childhood stories became a bit too real as I learned the details of their complex, compromised lives.

With success and affluence had come bitter sibling rivalries over the brewery of the sort that often occur inside a family business. Some of these maneuvers were ruthless. The anger among the family lasted for years. Compounding these conflicts, the family's assimilation from Germans into Americans was extraordinarily painful, marked by state surveillance, accusations of treason, and personal betrayal.

Slowly I learned a hard truth that had somehow eluded me for forty years as a professional historian. The past is a dangerous territory.[9] Family history is not just some genteel diversion for elderly retirees. Asking questions runs the risk of unexpected, even unsettling answers.

Three Generations

Even knowing all that I now know about them, there is still something interesting about my mother's family, these Piels. They were not powerful, with generals or politicians whose doings supposedly changed the course of history. They were not really rich, although they built a business that sustained them for several generations. Once famous for their beer and its advertising, they are now largely forgotten.

1.1. Lake Parlin, Maine, Summer of 1940 (left to right): Margarita "Peggy" Piel; Marie Luise Piel; "Grandmother" Maria Piel; "Agi" Heermann; Maria Heermann.

Yet these Piels lived their lives grandly for three generations, as if actors in some unfolding family saga. They were intense, overblown, almost operatic. They did everything that everyone else did. But they did it just a bit more passionately, as if a skein of madness that ran through their lineage infected them all. For over a century, they had sufficient capital to finance ambitious ventures, lifting them above the daily grind for more adventurous lives. Yet they were never wealthy enough to join the ranks of the idle, uninteresting rich. Even at their peak of prosperity on the eve of Prohibition, they were never beer barons, more like beer baronets.

Some of their pursuits were self-indulgent—hunting or fishing relentlessly, dabbling in the arts, collecting kitschy German paintings or costly vintage violins. But their careers were often exceptional. Innovative industrialist. Brilliant litigator. Pioneering publisher. And they built things. A brewery that became one of the biggest in America. A scientific publishing company that reached four continents in a dozen languages. And, above all, a family business that has survived, at this writing, for more than 130 years.

Two brothers, Gottfried and Michael Piel, arrived in America from Germany over a hundred years ago, started a brewery in Brooklyn, and struggled to survive midst relentless competition that could easily have crushed their upstart venture. By the 1880s, New York was already the brewing capital of America, with more breweries producing more beer than any other city, including Milwaukee or St. Louis. Through quality and innovation, Piel Bros. grew from Brooklyn's smallest brewery in 1884, making just 850 barrels, into the sixteenth-biggest brewery in America producing over a million barrels by 1952. During Madison Avenue's golden age in the 1950s, Piels tried to compete with the national brands by creating "soft sell" advertising for its famously funny "Bert and Harry" beer ads.

By the 1960s, however, New York's regional brewers could no longer match the vast advertising budgets of the big Midwest brands that were fast becoming national conglomerates. For not only was New York the nation's premier market, producing and consuming more beer than any other, it was also the most parochial. Unlike the Midwest shipping brewers Anheuser-Busch, Miller, or Pabst, New York's biggest, whether Ehret in the nineteenth century or Ruppert and Rheingold in the twentieth, were usually absorbed in their own regional market, making them vulnerable to national consolidation. By 1976, the Piels' plant was demolished, leaving rubble where their model brewery once stood. Brooklyn's last brewers, Rheingold and Schaefer, also closed, leaving New York City without a brewery for the first time in more than 300 years.

Though their company had survived both Prohibition and Depression to become, under its second generation, one of the country's biggest brewers, Piel Bros. had faded like all the rest—like all the thousands of German breweries once found in cities across America. After the business was sold in the 1960s, the cousins of the third generation managed the proceeds prudently, supplementing their incomes from professional careers for the next half-century. Through it all, a family of German farmers became middle-class Americans.

But there is much more to the Piels' story than this simple, synoptic narrative. The history of the family and their business brushes up against many of the forces, large and small, that have shaped New York and the nation for more than a century.

By tracing this company's changing fortunes from rapid growth in the Gilded Age, through the travails of Prohibition, to the relentless competition from national brands after World War II, we can explore the economic forces that erased over 2,000 family-owned regional breweries from cities across America and ended all brewing in New York City for several decades. And by intertwining the history of this company with the intimate story of its family, we can weave some disparate strands—ethnic assimilation, economic change, and state surveillance— into the tapestry of a rising metropolis and a changing country.

Above all else, the story of the Piel Bros. brewery illustrates the tensions embedded in that commonplace term "family business." Combining "family" with "business" creates a company riven by an underlying contradiction between the irrational intimacies of any family versus the rational demands of the modern marketplace. As psychologists and consultants have learned recently through voluminous research, the fusion of family and business must be carefully managed to avoid corrosive conflicts.

To capture this clash between family and business found inside every family firm, this history operates simultaneously at two levels: the corporate and the personal. Thus, each chapter of this book moves between the Piel households, where emotional tensions were usually suppressed, and their brewery, where these personal issues were fully expressed—a destructive pattern often found inside a family business.

These tensions introduce a twist into every chapter of this history, with commercial success at the brewery unleashing divisive emotions inside the family. Among the dozen surviving children of the family's second generation, childhood resentments grew up to become boardroom battles that contributed to the brewery's slow decline and ultimate sale. Throughout the three generations chronicled in this book, these conflicts drive the history of the Piels and lend some larger significance to their story.

In the folk wisdom of many societies worldwide there is a recurring belief that any family enterprise experiences a similar cycle of rise and decline. "There are but three generations in America from shirt sleeves to shirt sleeves," industrialist Andrew Carnegie observed famously in his 1886 book, *Triumphant Democracy*. Compared to Britain, wealth matters far less in America where, he said, "it is much more easily acquired and, what is more telling, much more easily lost," bringing families back to the worker's symbolic shirt sleeves by that third generation.[10]

Carnegie's maxim seems a translation, into the American vernacular, of an old Lancashire proverb: "There's nobbut three generations atween a clog and clog." That English wisdom resonates with the old Italian saying, "dalle stalle alle stelle alle stalle" ("from stalls to stars to stalls"). Writing in the fourteenth century, the historian Ibn Khaldun observed a three-generation cycle in the life of Arab dynasties, from the hardened desert warrior who captures the crown to his effete grandson who loses it. More recently, the head of the U.S. Family Business Council observed that, in this world of accelerated change, "it just makes sense that family businesses might only last 50 to 60 years on average."[11] Indeed, as they struggle through transitions from founding patriarch, to a sibling partnership and, finally, to a consortium of cousins, only 10 percent of America's family firms survive to the third generation.[12]

But there are more basic reasons for this three-generation cycle. After the third generation, with new marriages complicating kinship and diversifying genes, the family's coherence, shared identity, and common attributes are rapidly diluted as first cousins become second or second once removed. For many if not most of us, our lived experience of family is often just that—three generations. With luck, we are born into a family circle with parents and grandparents. As elders fade and children appear, we in turn become parents, then grandparents, sustaining that succession. Without much reflection, this three-generation cycle is often what many mean when they speak, conversationally, of "family."

Beyond that tight family circle, personal choice and particular experience shapes what or even whether we think about those distant cousins. Anything beyond three generations means the clear ties that bind a family business dissolve into a spreading pool of ever-more-distant cousins. Anything beyond the clear bounds of nuclear family necessarily involves imagination. Cultural invention thus determines how whole societies consider kinship, whether patrilineal, matrilineal, or bilateral. Among human kind's many creations, family is thus uniquely paradoxical in its Janus-faced character—enduring and ephemeral, fixed and fluid, real and invented.

Let us consider that basic tool of genealogists and family historians, the "family tree." It usually shows a stylized lineage descending from two founders without antecedents, our very own Adam and Eve, and then grows branches that represent three, four, or even five generations. Yet we should use these trees cautiously, aware they are an illusory cultural convention that denies our biological reality. For even among first-generation Piels, no Piel was ever more than half a Piel. To state the obvious biological fact that family trees often ignore, every child is the product of two families, one depicted in that lineage and the other's ancestry often ignored.

We do not descend neatly down the branches of a single family tree. We move through a vast, spreading web of kinship impossible to depict visually and difficult to grasp conceptually. A more appropriate metaphor might be an hourglass with myriad grains, or genes, moving through each human body from countless antecedents to infinite descendants. Beyond three generations, our ancestry grows almost exponentially in complexity, blurring family ties, blending us into all humanity, and complicating any human institution, whether business or monarchy, built upon such shifting foundations.[13]

So it is not too surprising that the Piels' brewery founded by two jealous brothers in the 1880s would be sold by their feuding children in the 1960s, leaving a legacy of conflict for the cousins of the third generation. Even the most prominent family firms have had similar experiences. In their inveterate infighting, the Piels of New York have revealing parallels with better-known family firms in cities worldwide—the Agnellis of Turin, the Krupps of Essen, the Binghams of Louisville, the Pritzkers of Chicago, and the Bronfmans of Los Angeles. The fusion of blood and business can, in some instances, foster stable management over the span of several generations. But often this same combination produces bitter struggles for assets or corporate control—something seen in recent years among the Agnelli, Bingham, Bronfman, and Pritzker families.[14]

Managerial Revolution

Apart from these endemic personal conflicts, there is a broader economic trend of corporate consolidation that has influenced the course of family businesses in America—a change particularly evident in the brewing industry. At the peak of U.S. economic power after World War II, mainstream American scholars, exemplified by Alfred Chandler's Pulitzer prize-winning study *The Visible Hand*, celebrated the country's "managerial revolution" that replaced family firms with modern corporations. Starting in the mid-nineteenth century, "entrepreneurial or family capitalism" yielded, in sectors requiring funds for growth, to "financial capitalism." As both family- and financier-controlled firms expanded after the 1880s, they needed the skills of professional managers who had first appeared in the railroads. During the 1920s, "new accounting, budgeting, and forecasting methods were becoming normal" at major firms such as DuPont, General Electric, and General Motors. Through the sum of these changes, Chandler argues, "managerial capitalism soon replaced family or financial capitalism."[15]

Economist John Kenneth Galbraith popularized this idea in his famous 1958 book *The Affluent Society*. Tycoons such as Rockefeller, Morgan, and Hearst were, he said, "the undisputed masters of the business concerns they owned" until the 1920s. Although their sons and grandsons might still have the wealth, "the power implicit in running the firm has passed to professionals," that is, "the professional manager or executive."[16] Indeed, by 1963, none of the top 200 non-financial companies were still privately owned, whether by families or individuals.[17]

By the 1970s, large corporations seemed so dominant in the U.S. economy that federal policymakers tried to protect the "little guy" by fostering small businesses, often family firms, "as vibrant sources of renewal." Over the past forty years, similar tensions have recurred in the mature market economies of Japan, South Korea, and the United Kingdom, where large corporations remain prevalent through a mix of market advantage and state support (the ten largest firms produced 79 percent of South Korea's GDP in 2011). Meanwhile, governments struggle for strategies to assist the welter of small, often family-owned firms (4.8 million in the UK, 4.3 million in Japan), leaving large corporations with professional management dominant in the world's more dynamic economies.[18]

Yet examined more closely, the shift to the managerial corporation, long celebrated as a hallmark of U.S. economic history, was less common and more complex than this literature imagined. Absent any explanation, Chandler and Galbraith apparently assumed that, through sheer force of market rationality, the managed corporation not only superseded but somehow erased the family business.

Even at the start of the twenty-first century, however, family firms still comprised over 80 percent of all U.S. companies and a full third of the Fortune 500 roster. At a time when family business was supposedly superseded, the *New York Times* business section carried three contrary reports in a single week, April 2015, about family fights at the apex of global capitalism. A first-generation proxy battle pushed the chief executive's ex-wife off the board of Wynn's Resorts, operator of a half-dozen leading Las Vegas casinos. Struggling to fulfill his father's legacy, the second-generation chief executive of Comcast failed to acquire Time-Warner in the century's biggest telecommunications bid. The chairman of Volkswagen, the founder's grandson, was ousted after bitter wrangling among third-generation cousins for control of the world's largest auto manufacturer.[19]

Through such conflicts, however, only 30 percent of family businesses survive into the second generation and less than 10 percent into the third. Specialists have argued that this poor succession rate is "caused when the business system and family system overlap," producing disputes as "family members act out the intense personal and interpersonal issues of the family agenda in their behavior in the family's business." Such volatility in an essential sector that accounts for 40 percent of the U.S. economic activity and nearly half its employment is a significant problem, for both individual families and the wider community. So intractable and important are these issues that there are, at this writing in 2015, family business therapists practicing in every major U.S. city, specialist journals publishing hundreds of articles, and special courses at leading business schools. The Center for Family Business at Northeastern University is devoted to solving "complex interpersonal and family business issues." Similarly, the program for Families in Business: From Generation to Generation at Harvard University offers a week-long seminar, with a registration fee of $39,000, teaching "practices that drive high performance . . . and healthy family relationships."[20]

Clearly, Chandler and Galbraith overstated their argument. The managed corporation eclipsed, but did not erase the family business. We need to correct this literature's predetermined causality with case histories, trying to understand the mix of interpersonal pressures and macroeconomic trends that pushed individual family firms toward professional management and entire industries toward consolidation.

Through a rare combination of business and family documents covering a full century, the Piels provide an apt cameo of these changes. Indeed, their brewery suffered from many of the "unique problems" that psychotherapists have since found inside family-owned companies. The father founder is often a "larger-than-life figure" who blocks development of "healthy conflict negotiation skills" among his heirs. Working in the family firm "may impede the child's ability to establish independence." Sibling rivalries among the founder's children can "transfer into the business arena" where "disputes become intensified and confused." The Piel businesses studied here, a brewery and a mutual fund, follow this literature's typical three-generation progression: first, domineering patriarchal founders; next, a troubled sibling partnership; and, finally, an effective consortium of cousins. Through their close parallels with this generational pattern, the Piels allow us a century-long perspective on the personal tensions that therapists have only recently identified inside contemporary family firms.[21] In sum, the study of this single brewery can illuminate both the creativity of family businesses and their endemic personal conflicts—offering insight into the micro-level dynamic driving the macroeconomic change studied by Chandler, Galbraith, and others.

As the history of Piel Bros. demonstrates, the terms "family business" and "corporation" are not mere words or static categories. They are dynamic social formations with the power to shape both individual identity and collective behavior. Corporations are, of course, impersonal institutions, created by law and governed by rules that merge diverse employees into a cohesive organization. Each family business, by contrast, bears the idiosyncratic imprint of the individuals who created it. Family firms can inspire enormous dedication and self-sacrifice as their founders struggle throughout the day and decades to build a company that expresses their creativity and secures their children's future. Yet families, with all their irrational intimacies, also nurture slights, hurts, and jealousies that can spill into their business as the second or third generations succeed parents and grandparents. Although Carnegie, Ibn Khaldun, and sages across the centuries are probably right about that three-generation cycle in family fortunes, the actual dynamics, as the history of Piel Bros. illustrates, are more complex and more contingent upon social context than they might have imagined.

As a company that was born at the peak of family-owned business and died midst corporate consolidation, Piel Bros. exemplifies sweeping changes in both the brewing industry and the wider U.S. economy. Between 1850 and 1914, foreign, largely British, financiers invested $3 billion in American industries—ironworks, railroads, and factories—that remade a pastoral land of farms and plantations into an industrial nation of smoking factories and steel-ribbed cities. By 1890, technological innovation had transformed brewing from a traditional craft into an efficient industry—raising annual production at the biggest breweries from just 8,000 barrels in 1860 to 800,000 by 1895. With the exception of a few giants such as Anheuser-Busch and Pabst, however, brewing largely resisted the U.S. "organizational revolution that gave rise to . . . vertically integrated, bureaucratically managed corporations" in other consumer industries such as cigarettes, canned meat, flour, soap, or sugar. Among the thousand plus breweries operating in 1917, only two, Anheuser-Busch and Schlitz, ranked among the country's top 278 corporations.[22]

The Piel brothers founded their Brooklyn brewery at the dawning of America's great industrial age in the 1880s when consumer goods benefited from technologies that cut costs and expanded sales. The U.S. brewing industry was in the midst of rapid expansion through refrigeration, pasteurization, and mechanized malting that was revolutionizing this ancient craft.[23] Hence Michael Piel, with a flair for innovation in food processing, founded his new model brewery at Brooklyn in 1883 with novel methods that balanced quality and a quest for industrial efficiency.

Starting in the 1920s and accelerating after World War II, financiers expanded U.S. corporations into conglomerates that produced the country's iconic brands, mass produced and mass marketed through network advertising—first on radio, later on television. As "previously separate spheres of industrial, commercial and bank capital are now brought under the common direction of high finance," wrote former German finance minister Rudolf Hilferding about finance capital, "the masters of industry and of the banks are united in . . . the elimination of free competition . . . by the large monopolistic combines."[24] But not for beer, at least not at first.

Beer and Brewing

Both the character of beer and its ambiguous status in America made brewing the last major consumer industry to be consolidated and heavily capitalized. Beer is mankind's oldest manufactured beverage, dating back 6,000 years to the ancient Egyptians. Though time alone should have allowed its mastery, beer's complex, still mysterious microbiology makes brewing capricious. Unlike rum from fermented sugar, wine from grapes, or grain alcohols such as scotch and sake, beer is susceptible to spoilage. This delicacy kept its distribution localized within the ambit of the brewery and beer wagon until the late nineteenth century.[25]

Reflecting their British origins, colonial Americans drank Scotch-style whiskey or, as a secondary choice, English-style ales served warm and often bitter. After the 1840s, however, a tide of German immigrants introduced their cool, smooth-tasting lager beers, which soon supplanted hard liquor as the nation's summer beverage. Between 1850 and 1860, the number of U.S. breweries tripled to nearly 1,300. Meeting the swelling demand required a massive harvest of winter ice from rivers and lakes. Once pasteurization and refrigeration allowed long-distance shipping in the 1880s, there were other problems. Sunlight spoiled the shelved beer until brewers introduced tinted bottles. Tin cans cut shipping costs for condensed milk, fish, fruit, and countless consumer products. But beer's chemistry reacted to the metal, precipitating unpotable salts, until vinyl coating was perfected in the mid-1930s. Beer also has an aura of authenticity—evoking the craft, land, and waters of a particular place—that resisted commodification.[26]

Even as these problems were being solved, the spreading temperance movement stigmatized beer, making major banks reluctant to invest and slowing the consolidation that came to almost every other consumer industry in the Gilded Age. Moreover, the "managerial revolution" of the 1920s coincided with the Prohibition of all alcoholic beverages, stalling any modernization of the nation's breweries for nearly fifteen years.[27]

Once Prohibition was repealed in 1933, change and consolidation came to brewing with extraordinary force. With limitless capital and lavish advertising, the rising national brewers—Anheuser-Busch, Miller, Schlitz, and Pabst—cut costs and expanded markets, undercutting long-established regional companies and unleashing a relentless consolidation. In little over a half-century, hundreds of family-owned breweries were amalgamated into national and then transnational conglomerates. In 1962, when Piels was finally sold to a larger company, the top 200 industrials, many of them conglomerates, controlled 56 percent of all U.S. manufacturing.[28]

By the turn of the twenty-first century, brewing had become the most concentrated and globalized of all consumer industries, largely controlled by just two transnational conglomerates. And these two were among the 35,000 transnational corporations that dominated world trade, many of them funded by a financial sector which produced nearly half the profits in the entire U.S. economy.[29]

A few figures can illustrate the transformative impact of finance capital on the brewing industry. At the peak of the industrial age in 1900, all of America's 1,816 breweries had a combined capitalization of $415 million that was, when adjusted for inflation, still only 17 percent of the $52 billion that a multinational conglomerate paid for just one company, Anheuser-Busch, in 2008.[30] By 2012, two transnationals, the Belgian InBev and London-based SAB Miller, controlled nearly 80 percent of U.S. beer sales and over 200 brands in 42 countries worldwide.[31]

In this almost Darwinian process, regional brewers like Piels bought out local breweries until the national brands swallowed them all—disgorging the family's third generation into the ranks of America's striving middle class. At the same time that it transformed the brewing industry, the rise of finance capital also reached deep inside the Piel family, rupturing personal relations and nearly ripping the family apart. Not only was their brewery extinguished, but the process was painful as once-close siblings responded to these relentless market pressures with bitter infighting over the future of their family firm.

Family and the State

Beyond this central problem of economic change, the experience of the Piel family also reveals a great deal about two broad themes that, though secondary in this study, are nonetheless central to the country's modern history: the forced assimilation that virtually erased German American identity from public life in New York and cities across America during World War I; and the impact of U.S. internal security on private lives, starting in that same period and reviving during the Cold War.

The Piel family's fortunes were shaped, to a remarkable degree, by the growing strength of the U.S. state, both its regulatory powers and its covert surveillance. Starting in 1919, the federal prohibition of alcohol meant hard times for the Piels, just as its repeal in 1933 gave the family prosperity midst the Depression. During World War I, moreover, the creation of the country's first internal security apparatus subjected the second-generation Piels, along with many prominent German Americans, to pervasive surveillance—stigmatizing the entire family and slowing their acceptance into New York society. A generation later during the Cold War, several family members found themselves fighting accusations of "disloyalty" within a spreading fog of state surveillance that enveloped their private lives for nearly twenty years. Looking back, it seems both surprising and significant that this clandestine dimension of U.S. state power intruded so forcefully and so frequently into the lives of an ordinary American family.

This internal security apparatus also played a central role in the forced assimilation of German Americans. For decades, scholars have pondered the conundrum that the country's largest ethnic group is also its least visible. In 1910, Germans were the nation's most numerous foreign-born, with a proud presence of

German-language newspapers, churches, civic groups, and beer gardens. A century later, German was still the largest ancestry given in the U.S. Census—cited by 58 million Americans in 1990, 43 million in 2000, and 50 million in 2010. Yet any visible display of German ethnicity has been utterly erased through what one scholar has called the country's most "spectacular case of collective assimilation."[32]

The U.S. government achieved this accelerated assimilation through a raw coercion that has generally eluded historians. Although created to protect the home front during World War I, Washington's internal security apparatus also became a powerful engine for breaking German American identity. Compounding the pressures of mass conscription and formal proscription of alien loyalties, wartime counterintelligence enveloped German Americans in a suffocating surveillance.

This sudden flight from German identity prompted scholar Russell Kazal to ask "where did they go," what kind of Americans did they become, and what were the consequences of their assimilation for this country? Some historians argue that German Americans sought cultural refuge in a "monolithic whiteness," an American nationalism, or mass consumerism. "When looking for answers to large questions," Kazal suggests, "it sometimes helps to dig in small places." For him such a small place is Philadelphia, where he finds a German American retreat into a generic ethnic identity as "old stock" Europeans.[33]

Yet we might find other answers if we look in still smaller places, inside a single family. The Piels' experience suggests this cultural response to forced assimilation was not found in any broad communal identification, such as white or old stock European, but instead in a retreat into family, its affluence and acceptance becoming the strongest marker of personal identity. German heritage has thus become a minor inflection, along with class, college, or profession, in a multifaceted Americanized persona.

So, we might say that the Piels were ordinary in an extraordinary way. Their story is more than the usual immigrant saga of overcoming adversity to achieve success, though they certainly did that. Their history, across the span of three generations, reveals much about the making of the country's middle class and much more about the changing character of a rising city and its brewing industry.

Family History

Through the exploration of these three broad themes—ethnic assimilation, state surveillance, and, above all, economic transformation—this book attempts to reconcile the disparity between the universal importance of family in human history and the parlous state of its study. There is, of course, a seemingly irreconcilable conflict between social history that, in searching for general trends, reduces individuals to the norm versus family history that emphasizes, even celebrates, unique attributes. Indeed, many of the prominent civic associations based on lineage—the Daughters of the American Revolution, Holland Society of New York, Mayflower Society, or United Daughters of the Confederacy—are inherently exclusive.[34] The whole field of family history, encapsulated in those quasi-fictional family trees, is an exercise in drawing boundaries for exclusion, saying we are somehow different, we are in some way better.

Yet there is nothing more universal than family. With the exception of foundlings or orphans, the entire human community is founded upon some form of family. Through child rearing, shared labor, and inheritance, family is arguably the single most important human institution across cultures and centuries. Clearly something so central, so literally seminal, for human history merits serious study.

At the dawn of the twenty-first century, millions of Americans were actively engaged in some form of family history. Yet the scholarly yield from this massive effort seems somehow slight.[35] Almost all these histories are privately published or circulated exclusively among family members. Offering a possible corrective, the few professional historians who write about individual families usually treat their subjects, unless particularly prominent, as exemplars of larger trends.[36] That, in essence, is what I have tried to do in this history of the Piel family and their brewery, embedding this method within the text of every chapter.

Complicating matters in my case, historians, unlike creative writers, usually strive to suppress any personal feelings that might bias their role as detached interpreters of the past. The complexities of treating the intimate history of any family redouble when historians try to write about their own ancestors with the same objectivity demanded for more distant scholarly topics, such as my own earlier work on elite Filipino families.[37] The discipline, as an essay in a leading journal explained, has long harbored "the fear that an autobiographical project may destabilize the professional historian's hard-won authority as a reconstructor of the past." In recent decades, however, historians have embraced their position as privileged observers and started venturing into this forbidden terrain. Indeed, recent work on historical memory has subverted the old standard for objectivity, now requiring, argues Pierre Nora, that the historian "acknowledge the close, intimate, personal liaison he maintains with his subject. Even more, to proclaim it, to meditate on it, to make it, not the obstacle, but the means of his understanding."[38]

So instead of the historian's usual self-effacing stance, found in countless academic monographs, I will, when relevant, presume to the first-person pronoun and intrude into the narrative. If objectivity, elusive under the best of circumstances, is not possible in such autobiographical projects, then accuracy and understanding seem not just substitutes but, in a sense, even sterner standards. Writing such intimate history thus presents unique challenges, forcing me to set aside the ingrained loyalties and antipathies found in any family, and struggle for balance, particularly in treating the boardroom battles among relatives. Instead of glossing over these bitter, often demeaning personal disputes, their insertion in a wider social context, as tensions endemic to almost any family business, seems to allow a more even-handed approach.

This problem of balance begins with the kind of documentation available for the century of family and corporate history covered in this book. For the first twenty years after their arrival in 1883, the Piels were building a business, with little time for personal letters or company records. Absent direct, detailed documentation, I had to recover fragments of their past from scattered sources— census records, building permits, insurance maps, residential directories, and trade journals. Then, through the artifice of historical narrative, I tried to make all that mute data somehow sing through the first two chapters of this book. Writing about this more distant past from such standard sources resonated comfortably with the kind of "objective" historical research I was trained to do.

After the brewery's incorporation in 1898 brought the family modest wealth, the trickle of data becomes a torrent of more intimate information—voluminous corporate minutes, hundreds of personal letters in German and English, thousands of photographs, a thousand pages of diaries in tight copperplate penmanship, and several oral histories, one reaching seven hundred pages. While psychiatrist and historian David Musto needed years to tease out the elusive traits of the famously reserved Adams family of Massachusetts, the Piels were not shy about expressing their rivalries and resentments.[39] Indeed, the word intimate cannot begin to describe the passionate interior lives revealed in the rich fund of Piel family papers. Love/jealousy, loyalty/betrayal, self-sacrifice/bitter resentment, sibling rivalry/incestuous longing are just some of the dueling emotions that spring from these pages. From chapter 3 onward, therefore, the tenor of my writing changes from an impersonal forensic reconstruction of times past into a self-portrait of lives in full. As these chapters move toward the present, involving my grandfather then my mother and their family fights, I tried for balance by seeing events from multiple perspectives, trying to present all sides.

Yet this wealth of family documentation also carries an embedded bias, exemplified by a Piel family tree compiled by matriarch Maria's middle son Paul. As a trained artist, Paul used perspective to lead the viewer's eye to a fundamental difference between the two brothers who founded the brewery, Michael and Gottfried Piel. On the left side of this family tree we see Gottfried and his wife Sophie, shown clearly as first cousins, begetting five children who all married without issue—a withered branch without fruit. On the right side, by contrast, the marriage of Michael and Maria, Paul's own parents, multiplies many times over to a second generation with seven surviving children, a third with fifteen, and a fourth with forty-six—a strong trunk with many flowering branches.

Interviews with family members confirmed this interpretation. "According to Paul," recalled his nephew Gerard Piel, "Grandmother [Maria Piel] thought that that was a proper rebuke from the Lord for the almost incestuous marriage of Gottfried to the mother of all those sons and that one daughter. That they were all sterile and not begetters of children."[40] When we peel away its artifice, this family tree reveals the ingrained infighting that makes the Piels' business history often seem the sum of such conflicts. And it exemplifies the almost primal bias that makes a balanced account of this family, or any family, so difficult.

For a family historian such as myself, who requires generational continuity as the prerequisite for writing, the failure of Gottfried's children to reproduce also raises complex issues, emotional and analytical. Their extinction breaks the three-generation cycle, creating a disconcerting void in family memory. By their extinction, the Gottfried Piels indicate the importance of family not only as the repository of human memory, but also as the vehicle that moves humanity from past to future. Without descendants, there are no family stories, no collective memory. Without heirs, treasured heirlooms become estate sale bargains. The photos from Michael's side of the family show, in countless gestures captured within the camera's frame, parents handing on their assets, emotional and material, in a cycle of continuous renewal. By contrast, the album of one of Gottfried's children, Walter Piel, saved serendipitously by an in-law after his suicide, has photos without captions—Walter as a pilot in World War I, Walter at a fishing camp in some woods. Instead of the joy of recognition, these images seem a sad artifact of memory without meaning, a past without a future.

Though allowing a remarkably frank look at the lives of Michael Piel's descendants, these rich sources thus incline us to tell the story from their perspective, privileging management over labor, family over society, and one lineage over another. Indeed, the passing of Gottfried's children without issue has erased any written or oral record of their perspectives on the family's endemic feuds.

Throughout a decade of research, I tried to correct this bias by mining every possible source—newspapers, archives, and court records. But time had worked its relentless winnowing and all this documentation could supplement but not supplant the family's own records. In the end, my only corrective is to admit the limitations of my sources and treat them accordingly.

Conclusion

Looking back over the last century, this family's history raises, at the broadest level, almost unanswerable questions about the price we have all paid for our country's prosperity. By seeing the nation's past through the prism of its smallest unit, the family, we can grasp more intimately, more fully, the impact of sweeping social change upon individuals, their communities, and, by inference, the country as a whole.

The rise of corporations and conglomerates not only erased a family business, but also reached deep inside individual lives, translating the grand sweep of economic change into the personal pain of family feuds, business disputes, and lifelong animosities. The surveillance that seemed so imperative in time of war, became, at the familial level, personal betrayal, ruined reputations, and blighted lives. Not only did the state security formed during World War I accelerate the assimilation of the country's largest ethnic group, it also forced a wrenching cultural change inside individual families.

This history thus traces the interaction between an immigrant family and powerful institutions, corporate conglomerates and the national security state, whose sum has shaped contemporary American society. The deeper meaning of our collective experience can become more meaningful at this microcosmic level. By studying a century of tumultuous change through a single family, we can understand more fully what that history might have meant for the people who actually lived it. Through the lives of these three generations, we can gain a fuller sense of what has happened to so many of us during the past century of this country's unprecedented prosperity. As we will see in the chapters that follow, this history of the Piel family and their Brooklyn brewery can thus serve as a cameo of our collective experience in a burgeoning metropolis and a changing America.

2

_____

Brooklyn Brewery

Just months after they arrived from Germany, three immigrants named Piel, two brothers and a cousin, bought an abandoned brewery in the remote East New York section of Brooklyn. In December 1883, the *Brooklyn Daily Eagle* reported that "the old Lanzer Brewery . . . has been purchased by the Piel brothers, of this city, for $30,000." It was "being fitted up with all the modern brewing appliances," with production set to start on New Year's Day. After the completion of the Brooklyn Bridge that May, the entire district of East New York was, the paper said, poised for prosperity. Apart from the new bridge to Manhattan, the area had good rail connections out to Long Island, west into Brooklyn, and south to Coney Island.[1] Beyond East New York, the city of Brooklyn was already the country's fourth-largest industrial center and its biggest port, handling more tonnage than New York and hosting the nation's largest naval shipyard.[2]

Even so, the Piel Bros. brewery was a fragile enterprise that, by all rights, should have failed. The old Lanzer Brewery was little more than a ruin: windows smashed, equipment antiquated. For superstitious local residents, the small, brick building seemed cursed by a succession of gruesome suicides. Brooklyn also had one of the most crowded beer markets in America, with some forty local breweries selling direct to "tied saloons" they controlled through loans or mortgages. In their first year, Piel Bros. brewed just 850 barrels of beer, with each barrel, under U.S. tax law, holding 31 gallons. Midst the rapid expansion and rising capitalization of the city's big brewers, there really should not have been a second year. But the Piels soon found their niche by making a better tasting beer.

Against enormous odds—tough competition, a later boycott of their product initiated by rival brewers, and spreading prohibition—they not only survived but even prospered. Within little more than sixty years, those 850 barrels grew to a million and Piel Bros. became the sixteenth-biggest brewery in America. As a family business, one of the toughest obstacles they faced in this struggle for success was each other: first, the founding brothers who became bitter rivals; and, then, their children who fought long and hard for control of the company. Despite all the external pressures and internal problems, the Piels' brewery became an exemplar of that extraordinary energy from the millions of emigrants who crossed the Atlantic to build America's cities, factories, and farms in the late nineteenth century.

Migration to America

In the midst of this mass migration, the *S.S. Belgenland*, a 3,600-ton, single-stack steamship, landed at New York from Antwerp on September 22, 1882, with a passenger list identifying Gottfried Piel and his cousin Wilhelm Piel as German merchants. Unlike the thousand passengers traveling "steerage," they were among the hundred plus who had enjoyed the comforts of "saloon" class.[3] Gottfried, just 30 years old, soon established himself as "an export merchant in New York."[4] Seven months later, Michael Piel, then 34, landed at New York to answer his brother Gottfried's call "to found with him in East New York . . . a typically German brewery, to be conceived on modern and scientific principles."[5]

In this country's national mythology, our immigrant ancestors landed at Ellis Island bearing their worldly possessions in cloth bundles, tired, hungry, and poor, yearning to be free. The founders of the Piels' brewery sailed first-class to New York with their money yearning to make more money. Challenging that oft-repeated myth, the Piels were among the many immigrants who came with sufficient capital to start a business, purchase property, or homestead a farm. Indeed, merchants represented up to 12 percent of all German male immigrants in the nineteenth century. The major European capital exporters—Britain, France, and Germany—followed that flow of immigrants by investing mainly in North America.[6]

The Piels were part of that great surge of European immigration that brought over five million Germans to the United States between 1848 and 1914. This wave crested during the 1880s when nearly 1.5 million Germans arrived in America, representing 28 percent of all immigrants during that decade. Not only did the Piels land at the peak of this human tide, but they settled in New York, home to the country's largest concentration of Germans. So many, in fact, that this city had become "one of three capitals of the German-speaking world, outranked only by Berlin and Vienna." During the 1850s, many of the early immigrants had clustered in an area of Manhattan's Lower East Side dubbed "Kleindeutschland," or Little Germany, where their distinctive shops, theaters, and beer gardens made them a visible presence. By 1875, German Americans accounted for a full third of New York City's population, spreading out to Yorkville on Manhattan's Upper East Side and to Bushwick in the still independent city of Brooklyn.[7]

Brewing beer in Brooklyn was both a challenge and an opportunity. By 1880, the New York metropolitan area produced nearly a quarter of the country's beer, with Manhattan's fifty-seven breweries making over 1.5 million barrels annually. As the site of thirty-nine breweries, Brooklyn alone brewed another million barrels, rivaling Chicago, Milwaukee, and St. Louis. This was a thriving but highly competitive beer industry whose large plants and cut-price distribution could readily crush a small, upstart firm. Since most of the breweries in the New York area were already making the German-style lager beer, Piel Bros. would have to do something different, something better, to survive.[8]

Despite the industry's size and success, New York's breweries, unlike the big Midwestern brands, were still largely family enterprises focused on their own metropolitan market. Even as late as 1900, only seven city breweries were joint stock companies. In short, New York was still a market where a fledgling firm could find a niche. Instead of building a large, mechanized plant like many of their competitors, Piel Bros. started small, emphasizing quality, clientele, and family management with all its strengths and weakness. Unlike the bigger local companies that sold their beer through tied saloons, the Piels would make their brewery a resort destination, selling direct through their banquet hall and beer garden to drinkers drawn, by their superior product, from all over Brooklyn.[9]

The Piel Brothers

To start their business in the early 1880s, the Piel brothers brought considerable entrepreneurial skills as managers of rural businesses, farms, and small factories in Germany's Rhineland. The elder Michael had trained as a *brewmeister* in Dortmund. The younger Gottfried was a businessman who saw opportunity in that abandoned building. Together in their first year of operation, 1884, Piel Bros. started out as Brooklyn's smallest brewery, with limited capital and a local clientele—a modest foundation for what later became a modern enterprise.

Looking back, the key to the firm's survival in these difficult years was the assets the brothers brought with them from Germany—sufficient capital to start the business, the skill to brew a quality beer that would stand out in the crowded Brooklyn market, and, above all, contrasting personalities that somehow complemented each other in their boundless determination to succeed.

The two brothers, though just three years apart in age, seemed polar opposites in ways that would later roil their family firm and transmit tensions deep into the second generation. Michael was taciturn yet passionate, physical yet inventive, an engineer with a taste for the arts, a dynamo driven to create, collect, and build. He embraced physical danger, first on the battlefield, later as a hunter of moose, bear, and bobcat. Raised on a farm, Michael could make anything grow, whether wheat, hay, hothouse tomatoes, or indoor flowers. Yet he also had a feel for machines, quickly mastering the operation of any new tool, whether centrifuge, refrigeration, or motorcar. With a height of six feet two inches and a powerful frame, he had the raw physical reserves to work fifteen-hour days for fifteen years to build a business.

Gottfried was, by contrast, a dandy who sported fine clothes, a talker fluent in three languages, and an urbanite who preferred a round of golf to shooting bear. Short, slope-shouldered, and pot-bellied, he looked best in a tailored suit. Rather than plunging into the plant to tinker like Michael, Gottfried was a front-office manager, familiar with balance sheets, finance, and corporate etiquette. Gottfried married money; Michael married for love. If Gottfried was a thoroughly conventional man, then Michael was a thoroughgoing iconoclast—a decorated German veteran who left Germany, a baptized Catholic who rejected religion, and a traditional brewmaster who yearned for industrial innovation.

In their new business venture, far more challenging than they might have imagined, the Piel brothers compensated for limited capital with their considerable skills—Gottfried's entrepreneurship and, above all, Michael's knowledge of brewing. Born in March 1849 at Stofflen, Düsseldorf, on the edge of Germany's industrialized Ruhr region, Michael was descended from farming families "whose members successively aimed to expand their patrimony of tillable lands," and who had acquired a large farm at Mörsenbroich just outside the city. There, Michael spent his youth learning "the arduous discipline of farm labor from sun-up to sun-down." At the age of 18, he started his compulsory military training with the Kaiser Alexander First Grenadier Guard Regiment at Berlin. Although he had already completed his required service when the Franco-Prussian War started in 1870, he rejoined his unit and saw action at Paris and Gravelotte where the

2.1. Gottfried Piel, Düsseldorf, circa 1890. (Photo by Arnold Overbeck, Konigs-allee 43, Düsseldorf. Credit: The Virtual Corkscrew Museum)

Guards suffered staggering casualties. Though Michael never mentioned it, eighty years later his grandchildren would find an Iron Cross decoration among his wife's personal effects.[10]

Stimulated by his exposure to urban life in Berlin, Michael returned to the family's Mörsenbroich farm after the Franco-Prussian War bent on modernization—developing a new breed of bees, inventing a prize-winning centrifuge for honey extraction, and turning to brewing as "offering the best opportunity for his talent of applying machinery to natural processes." Fascinated by "the new science of modern refrigeration," Michael had just completed a brewing apprenticeship "in the old-style subterranean cellars at the breweries of Dortmund, Westphalia," when his younger brother summoned him to New York.[11]

In the months before his departure, Michael became entwined in a situation that could have complicated his emigration. During a visit to his mother's family farm at Herne some 50 kilometers from Düsseldorf, Michael was working in a field when a young woman named Maria Heermann happened to look down from her window in a neighboring farmhouse. There she saw him "in his six

2.2. Barn with prayer lintel above the door, Heermann Hof, Herne, North Rhine Westphalia, Germany, 1937. (Photo by Frederick Lange)

foot height, grain sack over his shoulder, rhythmically striding and tossing his arm over the ready fields." Maria's life at the Heermann Hof was "hard and demanding," offering her a bleak future. For four centuries her family had worked this land as bonded "serfs" of the barons von Romberg. In 1853, just four years before Maria's birth, the Heermanns had caught the spirit of the Ruhr's industrial capitalism and began contesting their servitude, winning free title, under the Prussian agrarian reform, to their ancient farm's 60 acres. Though she was the firstborn, the farm must, under law and custom, pass intact to the eldest son. If any but the heir stayed on the land, they must remain chaste and chattel, living their lives as bachelor farmer or maiden aunt. As a farm girl, Maria did hard physical labor in the fields and was not educated for any profession.[12]

Today that old farm has become "Hof Waning," advertised on the Internet as a "green oasis" with manicured grounds and elegant spaces to assure the success of your sit-down dinner for thirty or your wedding party of sixty. When I visited in 2004 at the invitation of Frau Waning, this farming district had become a small rural island surrounded by the Ruhr's concrete grid of rails, roads, canals, and cities—making it impossible to imagine the isolation and desperation of life choices here a century ago.[13]

Back in the 1880s, life on that land was harsh. The property had a typical Westphalian house barn, a single structure with a wide entrance at one end for cattle and horses, and separate door at the other for the farmer's residence. The long winters kept farmers and animals inside together, with dank air and the hard labor of hauling feed and manure. The barnyard was a sea of deep mud after every rain. Spring and summer brought long hours of sowing and harvesting. Men could find work down the Ruhr's coal mines that burrowed relentlessly beneath these fields; but for women the only life was on the land.

Marriage was Maria's escape from a life sentence of endless, unrewarded toil. She had no dowry of land or capital to make a marriage. Her mother, Agnes Holtz, daughter of a well-to-do family, had died when Maria was 10, cutting her childhood short. Two years later, her father, then almost 60, married a much younger woman from an established family in nearby Recklinghausen. The stepmother sent Maria, "with whom she did not get on very well," to study with the Catholic nuns in the next town of Castrop for the finishing needed to marry her off to a nephew. Michael's sudden appearance disrupted those plans.[14]

Their passion evidently produced problems. According to a biography written by their eldest son, Michael supposedly married Maria at Bochum, Westphalia, on March 19, 1882. That date was, however, a fabrication, a fiction to allow a proper fourteen months before the birth of their first child at Verviers, Belgium, on May 10, 1883.[15] This was a necessary fiction since the Heermann's family history reports Maria "was heavily pressured by her stepmother to go to a nunnery in Belgium for the birth because she was not married."[16] Yet an extract from Bochum's church records, found in family files, states that "brewer Michael Piel from Bilk and Maria Heermann from Oestrich were married on March 29, 1883 (honestly)"—that is, in the eighth month of Maria's pregnancy.[17]

To sort through this tangled tale, chronology can help. First, in August of 1882 when days were warm and wheat high in the fields, offering both privacy and comfort, Maria conceived out of wedlock. Next, on March 29, 1883, Maria, now eight months pregnant, reportedly married Michael at Bochum's Catholic Church. She either left for Belgium after the wedding, or she traveled 350 kilometers back-and-forth from Belgium to Bochum. Either way, it seems an improbable journey, in that conservative period, for a pregnant woman well into her third trimester. Or, just maybe, somebody paid a parish clerk to record a wedding that never happened. Then, only eighteen days later on April 17, Michael Piel sailed from Antwerp aboard the *S.S. Switzerland* and reached New York on

2.3. Maria Heermann Piel, circa 1890.

April 29. On May 10, four weeks after his departure, their first child was born in Belgium. Four months after that on August 24, the *S.S. Belgenland* arrived at New York from Antwerp with a passenger identified as "Mrs. Maria Piel," age 26, carrying her infant son. Whether they were actually married or that certificate was a costly convenience, their premarital relations were a transgression of divine law punishable by hellfires that would, in later years, bedevil the Piel family.[18]

Sacrament aside, theirs was a union of passion and ambition. Baptized Catholic in a Protestant nation and raised on farms engulfed by the Ruhr Valley's industrial boom, Maria and Michael were both tempered from childhood by hard physical labor and stringent social custom. Living at the outskirts of the free city of Düsseldorf, the Piels were affluent farmers who worked simultaneously to expand their lands and diversify into industrial production. By contrast, the Heermanns, born in a pocket of rural tradition midst the Ruhr's heavy industry, had spent centuries as peasants bonded to the land by obedience to a feudal lord and a Catholic bishop. While the Heermann farm had just 60 acres in the Ruhr Valley, the Piels owned 200 acres at Mörsenbroich, numerous parcels around Düsseldorf, another large farm on the city's south side, and some businesses.[19]

2.4. Michael Piel, circa 1890.

The Piel's Mörsenbroich farm would eventually be erased by Düsseldorf's expansion. But the Heermanns' Westphalian homestead stands even today with a stern inscription, adapted from the 127th Psalm, carved deep above the barn door by Maria's grandfather in 1821: "God the Father protect this house and all who go in and out. If the head of the house does not work, then the workers' labors are useless."[20]

While Michael was secular, scornful of priests, and at his best with animals, plants, and machines, Maria, who was eight years younger, clung to faith and family, filling her house with children, relations, and servants, and her mind with saints, prayers, and fears. Yet, in the end, both were members of large farming families with limited resources. While Maria was dispossessed as a daughter, Michael was the second son among six siblings whose elder brother would work the family farm and whose own temper created complications. "His father was a strict disciplinarian who sometimes chastised his children physically," Michael's grandson recalled. "One day when they were walking across the field together, Michael's father raised his cane to strike Michael and Michael took this cane out of his hands and broke it over his knee and handed the pieces back to his father. When they got home that night, Michael's father said to Michael's mother 'Michael has to go' and Michael went." With little land or capital to bring to their union, Maria reportedly told Michael "he wouldn't be able to do anything much in Germany. They would not be a success and they had to go to America."[21]

If that story is correct, then Maria—penniless, eight-months pregnant, and either unmarried or recently married—had the confidence to dispatch Michael overseas just weeks before the birth of their first child. Ultimately, the spark between them transcended all these differences and difficulties, sending them across the Atlantic to America and joining them there in a struggle for all the wealth, liberty, and leisure denied them back in Germany.

Arriving in America

Through a fortuitous coincidence, Michael and Maria arrived in New York at a time when fortunes were to be made by brewing German-style lager beer. Unlike the warm, bitter, easily spoiled English ales that dominated U.S. brewing for its first two centuries, German lager was, said one expert, "a more palatable beer, lighter both in body and in alcohol content, and possessing a sparkling quality." Since lager's distinctive yeast sinks to the bottom of the vat and only ferments when cold, the resulting brew was more resistant to spoilage and often served cool from the brewery's ice-chilled cellars. Once lager was introduced by German immigrants in the 1840s, these attributes proved ideal for consumers in America's long, hot summers and for commercialization via long-distance shipping.[22] Over the next thirty years, U.S. brewers also experimented, adapting a new style of lager beer from Pils, Bohemia, by adding corn or rice as adjuvants to create a "light-bodied, low-alcohol, . . . translucent brew" with a rich, foamy head—in short, a distinctive, American-style Pilsner that would prove overwhelmingly popular.[23]

Between 1850 and 1890, the country's annual consumption of beer, driven by lager's sudden popularity, surged from 36 million to 855 million gallons. While sales of distilled spirits such as whiskey fell from 2.5 to 1.0 gallons per capita, beer drinking jumped more than tenfold, from 1.4 to 15.1 gallons. By 1900, there were 300,000 saloons nationwide. Many were important social institutions in poor communities, with ready camaraderie, a free lunch, and often the neighborhood's only public toilets. Across the country, German American immigrants became wealthy beer barons in a single generation—a success exemplified by Frederick Pabst's lakefront resort in Milwaukee with 10,000 daily visitors in 1889 and Adolphus Busch's brewery that covered 70 acres along the St. Louis riverfront by 1900.[24] The most ardent of all these beer drinkers were German Americans, numbering some 10 million by 1910, or approximately 10 percent of the country's population.[25]

In purchasing that abandoned East New York brewery, the Piel brothers were plunging into America's most competitive beer market with only a small capital and untested skills. By 1880, German immigrants had made New York City the brewing capital of America. Brooklyn had become America's third-biggest city with a population of 566,000, including 59,000 Germans.[26] The wider New York metropolitan area already had 370,000 Germans and, over the next twenty years, their numbers would more than double to nearly 900,000.[27]

As U.S. beer production climbed to 10 million barrels by 1877, the New York metropolitan region's major breweries (those making at least 12,000 barrels) produced an impressive 2.7 million barrels, compared to just 500,000 in Philadelphia, 350,000 in St. Louis, and 270,000 in Milwaukee. Indeed, the Yorkville district in Manhattan's Upper East Side was home to the country's biggest plant, George Ehret's Hell Gate Brewery, as well as its eighth largest, the Jacob Ruppert Brewery. Breaking down that total, Manhattan held forty-seven major plants producing 1.7 million barrels, Brooklyn had seventeen brewing 350,000 barrels, and northern New Jersey's fifteen breweries accounted for the balance.[28]

At the state level, New York would maintain this premier position for the rest of the century, brewing 8.4 million barrels in 1890, a third of the nation's total output, and dwarfing its nearest competitors—Pennsylvania (2.7 million barrels), Ohio (2.3 million), and Wisconsin (1.9 million). Since New York's annual per capita consumption was 124 quarts, more than double the U.S. average of 50 quarts, its producers could sell their output locally. The city's Hell Gate Brewery found "the home demand always proved so great" it could achieve "immense production . . . without any forced efforts to open new channels outside . . . New York." Similarly, the nearby Jacob Ruppert Brewery, established in 1867, reached a million barrels in 1918 by selling exclusively within New York and New England—a pattern that would persist, with few exceptions, in the metropolitan brewing industry until its end in the 1970s.[29]

The growth of Brooklyn's beer industry in the twenty years before the Piels' arrival was extraordinary. After Frederick and Maximilian Schaefer opened the first German-style lager brewery on Manhattan in 1842, "New York had gone mad for lager." Unlike the city's warm ales that were "heavy, cloudy, bitter, and completely lacking in sparkle," the new chilled lager, as Schaefer's official history later explained, was "a more palatable beer, lighter in body" with a "sparkling quality and clarity." One of Schaefer's employees, a Bavarian immigrant named Nicholas Seitz, founded Brooklyn's first lager brewery in the Williamsburg district, later adopting mechanical refrigeration and developing the massive copper vats that became the industry's standard. After starting in 1850 with just six small lager breweries, by 1867 Brooklyn, said the *Daily Eagle*, was "becoming the great brewing centre," winning awards for quality and outbidding rival regions for purchase of the nation's crop of hops, a key ingredient in brewing beer. Within five years, German lager, refreshingly cool after a hard day's labor, had become so popular there were over thirty breweries in Brooklyn, most making lager.[30]

Paralleling the rapid increase in the German population, the number of breweries in Brooklyn had grown so rapidly between 1850 and 1880 that brewing became one of the city's most important industries. By 1884 when the Piels bunged their first keg, Brooklyn already had, by one count, thirty-five breweries, with seven producing English ales, eight making a light *weiss* brew, and twenty more devoted to German-style lager. Another source, Lain's *Brooklyn Directory*, listed thirty-nine breweries and nearly 2,000 saloons. Brooklyn's annual beer production had already reached an impressive total of 981,000 barrels worth $8 million in retail sales. To brew nearly a million barrels, Brooklyn's plants employed

1,800 workers and installed new equipment, most importantly the "refrigeration machine," which increased productivity and cut costs. The city's bigger breweries—S. Liebmann's Sons, N. Seitz's Son, and Williamsburg Brewing—were each producing about 80,000 barrels annually. Reflecting the "high reputation" of Brooklyn brews, over half the city's production was reportedly shipped to "New York, Newark, Chicago, St. Louis, Milwaukee, and . . . Great Britain."[31]

Brewers' Row Bushwick

Most of Brooklyn's major breweries were concentrated around the 16th and 18th Wards in the city's Eastern Districts, where "jolly, good-natured Germans" owned eighteen breweries.[32] By 1880, Brooklyn's industry was centered in the German enclave at Bushwick where the famed "brewers' row" had eleven breweries along a twelve-block stretch from Bushwick Place to Lorimer Street.[33] Within a decade, Brewers' Row would extend for a mile-and-a-half with fourteen breweries forming a zigzag pattern within a block or two of Bushwick Avenue—from N. Seitz's Son on Meserole Street at the western end in Williamsburg all the way to Piel Bros. on Liberty Avenue in East New York.[34]

By the 1870s, several of these Bushwick breweries were growing into major firms that dominated the district's economy. In 1875, a writer from the *Brooklyn Daily Eagle* inspected one of the largest, the Boulevard Brewery on Bushwick Avenue. The reporter started his tour inside a four-story stone building where two large copper kettles, holding 50 and 140 barrels, respectively, were heated to brew a mix of water, mashed malt, and hops. That warm beer was then pumped upward into tin coolers on the third floor. Once the temperature was reduced to 70 or 80 degrees Fahrenheit, the beer was pumped down into ice-cold copper coolers that reduced the temperature to 40 degrees. Next, the cooling beer was pumped into a cold basement where giant blocks of river ice kept the raw lager at 37 or 38 degrees for twelve days of fermentation in huge tubs holding 400 to 500 kegs each. When the brewmaster was satisfied with the taste, the cooled beer was pumped through rubber hoses for 800 feet into a cold house where tons of ice blocks maintained Arctic temperatures. There, for eight months, the beer was aged in 230 enormous casks, each with a capacity of 40 barrels, filling three chilled basements that descended 54 feet beneath the ground. With a capacity of 800 kegs a day, the brewery's staff of thirty men supplied fourteen horse-wagons moving constantly to supply Brooklyn's thirst for lager beer.[35]

Apart from the German population, a major attraction for Bushwick's remarkable concentration of breweries was the "extremely soft brewing water" from Long Island's deep aquifers.[36] Manhattan's Hell Gate Brewery may have been the nation's biggest by 1890, but management freely admitted its quality was compromised by the city's water. Though "not the worst by any means," this reservoir water could not compare with those natural flows that made great beers in Bavaria or Britain.[37]

In this same period, by contrast, Brooklyn's water supply began its journey as 50 inches of annual rainfall that percolated 200 feet beneath the ground and then flowed through Long Island's geologic layers of enormously prolific aquifers for a distance of nearly 100 miles, providing billions of gallons for the deep wells that sustained the growing populations of Brooklyn, Queens, and indeed all of Long Island.[38] Starting in 1858, moreover, this groundwater also reached Brooklyn through 900 miles of underground pipes radiating from Ridgewood Reservoir in East New York.[39] Testifying to the ground water's taste, when a new brewery opened near Piels in 1901, promoters planned to use artesian wells since "the excellent quality of the output of the other two breweries in the East New York district [Piels and Schmidt] is attributed to the splendid spring water available."[40]

By then, however, Long Island was growing wary of Brooklyn's unquenchable thirst. Access to New York's massive aqueducts that carried bountiful mountain water from the Catskills forced Brooklyn to merge with Manhattan, forming the unified city of Greater New York in 1898.[41]

Through their soft water and similar brewing techniques, Bushwick brews shared a distinctive taste. All the district's beers, apart from Trommer's, which was all-malt in the Munich tradition, added rice or corn as "adjuncts." The barley used in the brewing converted the adjuncts to sugars, producing the "full-bodied, hoppy beers" popular with New York drinkers. While the average American brewer used a quarter-pound of hops per barrel of Pilsner beer, the Bushwick brewers doubled that key ingredient. Adding another element of similarity, the district's breweries, with the exception of Trommer's and Schaefer, all used the same Christian Schmidt strain of yeast, one of several hundred varieties that ferment the sugars into alcohol and lend the brew a distinctive style. The sum of these parts was a distinctive Bushwick beer with a "fuller body and mouthfeel."[42]

In sum, by the time the Piels landed at New York in the early 1880s, Brooklyn's brewing industry had all the requisites for sustained growth—skilled labor, a network of suppliers, a booming population, and, above all, a devoted clientele.[43] But major breweries already dominated the local beer market through their tied saloons, creating a closed distribution system that blocked competition from local upstarts like Piels or, in later years, Midwest shipping brewers like Milwaukee's Pabst or Anheuser-Busch of St. Louis. These brewers used the same tactic in their home markets, with Schlitz owning fifty saloons in Milwaukee and sixty in Chicago. "In this way," explained its owner, "we not only reached higher sales figures, but we also insured our clients against competition."[44] Compounding these difficulties for a newcomer like Piels, brewing was still largely a localized industry, limited in marketing range by wagon transport and keg packaging. In such a competitive, even cutthroat market, a new arrival in Brooklyn's crowded brewing industry would require both determination and innovation to survive.

Launching the Brewery

As their first step into Brooklyn's crowded beer market, the Piel brothers' decision to purchase an abandoned brewery at Brooklyn's rural fringe in East New York for $30,000 must have seemed, to contemporary observers, questionable. This ruined four-story brick building had a reputation as a haunted house that made it, said the *Brooklyn Eagle*, "one of the most famous spots in Kings County."[45]

Located at the corner of Georgia and Liberty avenues, the abandoned brewery had been one of first manufacturing firms to open when the town of East New York was founded forty years before as an ill-fated real estate venture. In 1835, a wealthy Connecticut merchant named John R. Pitkin formed the East New York Land Company, purchased four Dutch family farms in the open fields of Flatbush, and laid out an expansive urban grid for a future city meant to rival Manhattan—hence the name, East New York. Only two years later, however, Pitkin's grand plans crashed in the panic of 1837 and he was forced to return most of the land to the original owners, except for a portion between Alabama and Wyckoff avenues that retained the name East New York. In 1845, an English brewer started a profitable brewery on the future Piels' site. But within a decade, he sold out to a German immigrant named Francis Lanzer, who soon converted the plant to the production of lager beer.[46]

When a fire destroyed the original wood-frame structure in 1856, Lanzer built a four-story brick building that became the site of five suicides, earning it an eerie reputation among locals as the "haunted brewery." At the new building's opening with a picnic and brass band, tragedy struck when a German count slashed his wrists on the premises. After two more suicides by a bartender and patron, proprietor Lanzer shot himself fatally in 1871. Five years later, an employee also shot himself in a fit of despondency over a family quarrel. By the time Gottfried and Wilhelm Piel purchased the property on September 3, 1883, the brewery was derelict, its windows were smashed, and it was believed haunted by these ghosts.[47] Unfazed by this troubled history, the Piel brothers quickly transformed the dismal Lanzer premises into a working brewery.

Despite its unfortunate past, the building was surrounded by a thriving community that would prove critical to the brewery's early success. By 1880, East New York had filled many of the surrounding fields to become a town of 8,000 people with a sound infrastructure for sustained growth, including a water company, gas works, six separate rail lines, and the East New York Savings Bank. Sparked by the opening of the Brooklyn Bridge in 1883, horse trolleys were giving way to elevated, electrified lines that would later be consolidated into the Brooklyn Rapid Transit Company. Moreover, the area's German immigrants had built active community institutions—notably, the Concordia Singing Society of "prominent and wealthy German citizens" (established 1855), St. Michael's

2.5. Original Lanzer Brewery, purchased by Piel Bros., East New York, Brooklyn, circa 1883.

Roman Catholic Church (1860), the Evangelical German Church (1872), and a weekly newspaper, the *East New York Laterne* (1878).[48]

After three months' work refurbishing the old Lanzer building, the Piels installed new machinery and began brewing in early 1884, producing a quality beverage that soon won a loyal clientele in Brooklyn's competitive beer market. According to the *Brooklyn Daily Eagle*, the brothers "sprang into fame at once" as word spread that they were brewing "pure beer, made entirely of malt and hops, the latter imported from Bavaria."[49]

Three years later in 1887, the Piels purchased an adjacent orchard, giving them almost an entire city block bounded by Liberty, Georgia, and Sheffield avenues. Much of that orchard soon became the site of the new brewery's "fine summer garden." Within a year, they also built a large banquet hall with doors that opened directly into the beer garden.[50] A rare photo, circa 1905, shows a large rectangular hall filled with elegant patrons seated at round tables beneath a twenty-foot ceiling lined with domed windows and hung with wrought-iron chandeliers.[51]

Apart from the quality of the beer that Michael made as brewmaster, the excellent cooking that his wife Maria produced as kitchen manager made Piel Bros. "one of the most popular places to come because the food was so good." Not only did Maria Piel cook for hundreds of patrons daily during the brewery's first five years, but she also gave birth to five more children beyond her firstborn, William.[52]

This combination of banquet hall and beer garden provided Piel Bros. with a way to sell its beer directly to consumers, thus breaking the commercial stranglehold of Brooklyn's bigger breweries. By providing finance or bar fittings, major U.S. breweries had a controlling interest, by 1918, in over 80 percent of the country's saloons. While these tied saloons gave local breweries a protected market, their visible presence on city street corners also outraged temperance advocates.[53]

By the time the Piel brothers reached Brooklyn, the other major outlet for breweries, the beer garden, had become a favorite venue for summer outings in cities across America. Unlike the raucous all-male saloon where men lined the bar to down whiskey or beer or both, the German American beer garden, usually attached to local breweries, was a sedate, often open-air restaurant where best-dressed families would gather with children on Sundays for music, food, and a glass of cool lager.

New York's most famous, the Atlantic Garden, opened in 1858 on the Bowery just blocks from the Kleindeutschland district, and would remain a popular venue for the next half century. "On every side are family groups, father, mother, and children, all merry," *Harpers' Monthly* reported in 1871. They were gathered beneath the Garden's soaring ceiling to drink lager beer or Rhine wine without "the remotest danger of insult or disturbance or need of the presence of any policeman." But when a telegram had arrived announcing Prussia's defeat of France just a few months before, patriotic passions erupted from "this calm, stolid, Teutonic surface." Thousands of voices sang "Germans' Father-land" (*Des Deutschen Vaterland*) and "Luther's Hymn" (*Ein feste Burg ist unser Gott*) again and again "until they were hoarse." Countless glasses were raised to cheer king ("our Fritz") and commander ("Von Moltke"). "One could not help feeling," our correspondent concluded, "that a part of the 'Father-land' was here, for they had brought it with them in their hearts."[54]

Out in St. Louis, a German immigrant brewer, Joseph Maximillian Schnaider, had built what soon became the country's most famous beer garden at his Chouteau Avenue Brewery, drawing thousands of patrons for light opera, band concerts, and cold beer beneath the shade trees.[55] In Milwaukee, Schlitz Park opened in 1880 as a marvel of meandering paths surrounding an octagonal pavilion where 5,000 patrons sat sipping beer while listening to a full orchestra. By the 1880s, the venue had become so popular that the Boston "Pops" summer concert added tables to create a "German beer garden" inside symphony hall; the New York Assembly debated construction of a public beer garden at the old 42nd Street reservoir in Manhattan; and the popular Koster & Bials *biergarten* on 23rd Street moved uptown into the Manhattan Opera House. The city's, and the country's, biggest brewer, George Ehret, spent $220,000 to build a beer garden in Weehawken, New Jersey, accessed from Manhattan by express ferry—inspiring his rival Jacob Ruppert, Sr., to build his own brew spa on an island in the East River. Eager for a slice of New York's booming market, Milwaukee's Captain Fred Pabst opened beer gardens in Times Square, 58th Street, and 125th Street up in Harlem. Some survive today as beloved community institutions, notably the Scholz Garten, open in Austin, Texas, since 1866; the Bohemian Hall & Beer Garden, operating at Astoria, Queens, since 1910; and the Bevo Inn & Summer Garden in St. Louis, built by August A. Busch, Sr., in 1916 at the extraordinary cost of $250,000.[56]

Expanding the Brewery

The Piel brewery also kept pace with the industry's relentless growth and technological innovations, largely through finance provided by a new partner,

Wilhelm's younger sister Sophie Piel. Arriving from Germany in the early 1880s, Sophie married her cousin Gottfried a few years later. Starting in 1890, she came into her inheritance and invested heavily in the company, providing much-needed capital for modernization of the plant.[57]

Most importantly, the brewery installed "a huge ice machine" during an 1890 expansion and thereby joined the revolution in refrigeration that was changing America's brewing industry.[58] After centuries of cellars filled with ice blocks cut from lakes or rivers, improvements in commercial refrigeration during the 1880s, said the U.S. Brewers' Association, "practically doubled or more the capacity of the breweries, and the result was an enormous over competition." Refrigeration allowed a few national breweries such as Anheuser-Busch in St. Louis to begin shipping via rail to cities nationwide, prompting regional brewers to protect their markets by taking control of local saloons.[59]

Michael Piel's energy and innovation were central to his brewery's ability to survive the relentless competition in Brooklyn's saturated beer market. "At the outset," says his anonymous biographer, Michael was the company's "brewer, superintendent and engineer, his accumulated experience fitting him admirably for the multiplicity of his duties. In the early days of the converted [Lanzer] plant, Michael found that his hours were four o'clock in the morning till ten at night." After five years of working eighteen hours a day, "the ability of his brother as the financial head of the firm and excellence of his own products assured success and the long struggle was won."[60]

Reading between the lines of that account, by 1890 Piel Bros. had become a partnership between two married couples—Gottfried, the business manager; his wife Sophie, the main financier; Michael, the brewmaster and operations chief; and his wife Maria, chef and head of catering. By then, the other founder Wilhelm was back in Düsseldorf, managing a brickyard. Combining his traditional apprenticeship in Dortmund with a fascination for the "new science of modern refrigeration" Michael achieved that elusive combination of efficiency and quality, attracting a growing clientele of discerning drinkers.[61]

In 1890, a local reporter doing "Walks about the City" strolled into their brewery where he found the Piel brothers to be amiable hosts and formidable personalities. The firm's manager, Gottfried, was "little above the medium height, about 36 years old, . . . well built . . . sandy hair and full beard of the same hue and talks German, English and French fluently." His brother Michael, "who personally manages the brewing of the beer," was the opposite—jet black hair and moustache, "tall, of powerful frame and . . . all the movements of a trained athlete." The reporter observed that Michael "is one of the hardest working men on the premises today, and apparently he never tires." The combination of Michael's hard work and Gottfried's "business sagacity" was their "password to success" in making this brewery "one of the most valuable pieces of property in the Twenty-Sixth Ward today."[62]

Indeed, the brewery's beer garden had become what the paper called "the rendezvous of East New York's best citizens as none of the beer could be obtained in any other part of the town." In summer, the garden was "crowded with men and their families, all drinking beer and partaking of a lunch." In winter, the vast beer hall was filled with the city's elite—judges, lawyers, and Kings County politicians—dining on "Frankfurter sausages and sauerkraut or potato salad," all washed down with the brewery's superior beer.[63] "The beer garden, with tables and chairs under the trees, was a place of wonder," recalled Michael's eldest daughter Louise, who used the area as her playground. "There among the gleaming white pebbles that covered the ground, tiny sea shells in all colors could be found!"[64]

An 1895 edition of the *Brooklyn Daily Eagle* praised Piels for giving the city "the typical German beer hall" with all the features "which distinguish family resorts of this kind in the fatherland"—an amenity, said the paper, the equal of those found in Milwaukee or Manhattan.[65] By 1898, the sheer scale of this operation was enormous, with seating for 500 patrons inside the banquet hall and another 466 chairs in the adjacent beer garden, allowing Piels to serve almost a thousand patrons in a single sitting.[66]

A half-century later, Piels' in-house newsletter *Beer Facts* recalled these halcyon days back in the Gay Nineties. "Those Sunday afternoons when the Piel's 'Bier Garten,' with its cherry and maple trees, was a favorite gathering place for people who came from miles around to sit at the Viennese tables," recalled a staff writer. "There were memories, too, of Piels' famous stable of Percherons, the teams of dapple greys which won a number of ribbons in competition . . . And Piel's first bottled beer wagon, which carried the first pasteurized bottled beer package in the U.S."[67]

Although their clientele would remain local for the first decade, the triumphal inauguration of the Brooklyn Bridge in May 1883, just six months before the Piels brewed their first keg, opened an outlet to beer markets beyond the logistical cul-de-sac that was Long Island. Across the East River lay markets in Manhattan and the country beyond that would, in later years, prove critical to the company's continuing growth.[68]

Marketing

Beyond the key issues of management and quality, there appear, from reports in the local press, three factors in the Piel brewery's survival and early success—advertising, distribution, and plant expansion. Unlike many of their larger local competitors who won volume by discounting to saloons, the Piels carved a niche in Brooklyn's saturated beer market by direct sales to consumers through delivery and destination. With forty local breweries competing for market share by financing tied saloons that sold only their own beer, the number of bars in Brooklyn had nearly doubled in a decade—from some 2,000 in 1883 to 3,750 by 1892, producing a remarkable ratio of one outlet for every 200 residents.[69]

To win customers away from these omnipresent saloons, the Piel brothers had to advertise. After just eighteen months of operation, Piels placed a series of small, classified notices in the *Brooklyn Daily Eagle* throughout 1885 offering "Pure Lager Beer made of hops and malt only, at $1.25 per two dozen bottles, delivered throughout Brooklyn."[70] Unable to market their kegs to Brooklyn's tied saloons, Piels discovered, by fortuitous accident, the exceptional profitability of selling bottled beer direct to the consumer. After it began bottling beer in 1881, Milwaukee's giant Pabst brewery found its profits on bottle sales were 250 percent higher than on kegs by 1892 and 900 percent higher by 1904.[71]

Clearly the strategy proved profitable, for just five years after its founding Piel Bros. had sufficient income to expand its direct marketing by building that massive beer hall. In October 1888, the company published a series of eight-line advertisements to announce: "The Magnificent New Hall of the Piel Bro's Brewery has been opened. Built in the Italian palace style and richly decorated, it is really the finest family resort in the city. This and our well known Real German Lager Beer are a great attraction." The advertisement noted that this new beer palace was conveniently located just two blocks from the Howard House rapid transit station.[72]

Seven years later, advertising moved beyond the small-font classifieds to a twenty-six line notice that, starting in June 1895, added a new theme: "Large, Charming, Summer Garden, unrivaled in beauty, beer halls and restaurant. Brooklyn's most respectable and most popular family resort." Again, the advertisement listed all the nearby public transport that brought hundreds of patrons every weekend to their resort, including stations for the Union Line, Kings County Line, and the Long Island Rail Road.[73] Within a year, however,

Piels began to diversify its marketing, proclaiming in somewhat larger newspaper advertisements that its "real German lager" was now on tap at select bars in Rockaway Beach, Sheepshead Bay, and College Point.[74]

This marketing strategy proved successful and, for over twenty years, the Piel beer palace was a favorite destination for Brooklyn families and social groups, producing a succession of incidents reported in the local press. Wrangling over patronage appointments for police magistrates culminated in a drunken punch-up at Piels in May 1891, when a local doctor took an inebriated swing at former Republican supervisor William Watson—an incident that his friends called a "put-up job" orchestrated by Democratic rivals.[75] A divorce action heard in July 1899, mentioned that a wayward wife met her lover at Piels before repairing to a nearby hotel where her husband tracked her down.[76] In October 1890, one of the Piel brothers was "at his wit's end" when star baseball pitcher Augustus "Gus" Weyhing showed the strength of his arm by hurling bread slathered with mustard and butter upward at the ceiling portrait of brewing's patron saint Gambrinus.[77]

But baseball also brought customers to the Piels' resort. In April 1890, the Brooklyn Bridegrooms, later known as the Brooklyn Dodgers, moved to the new 12,000-seat Eastern Park stadium, built just five blocks from the Piels' brewery. For eight seasons during the 1890s, baseball spectators and players alike would pour out of the stadium and make the short walk for cool beers at Piel Bros. In later years, Michael Piel's son William recalled hosting celebratory rounds by Bridegrooms' star ballplayers—starting pitcher William "Brickyard" Kennedy, catcher Cornelius "Con" Daily, and slugger William "Wee Willie" Keeler.[78]

By century's turn, all sorts of local groups were gathering at Piels for meetings and banquets. The Brownsville Police Station hosted a dinner for their acting captain and presented him with a silver mounted revolver. The Brooklyn Engineers Club capped their visit to the Ridgewood pumping station with dinner at Piels. The Eichenkranz singers of East New York assembled for their inauguration at the brewery, toasted by Piel's manager Hermann Petersen. The venerable Concordia Singing Society met there regularly, once for a Christmas entertainment capped by gifts for 200 children, and another time for a Midsummer Night's Festival with songs by Schubert.[79] Apart from these special occasions, the beer garden also had a coterie of regulars who, judging from a list of patrons published in 1911, had Germanic surnames, modest professions, and homes within walking distance.[80]

Throughout these years of rising sales, moreover, the Piel brothers reinvested their profits in improving the physical plant—buying land, renovating structures, and building new production facilities. From city assessment records, the brewery's value enjoyed an extraordinarily rapid growth from just $8,800 in 1886 to a substantial $155,000 in 1899.[81] After adding the beer garden in 1887, the brothers concentrated on increasing plant capacity and purchasing a half-dozen neighboring lots for physical expansion.[82] In 1895, the Piels demolished the original Lanzer brew house and replaced it with a new four-story brick brewery.[83] By then, the Piels' plant had taken the shape astride Liberty Avenue that would last for another fifteen years. North of the avenue were the wagon sheds, stables, and carriage house. On the south side, the brew house ran down Georgia Avenue and the restaurant lined Sheffield Avenue, with the beer garden filling the space in between.[84]

Unions

Not only were the Piels making money, but they were loath to let any slip through their tight fists, exhibiting a fierce resistance to the social forces that threatened their business—unions and temperance. With a large labor force of skilled and semi-skilled workers toiling under harsh conditions, Brooklyn's beer industry attracted strong unions and hard-fought industrial disputes. During the century-long history of labor relations in New York's brewing industry, there were two periods of strong strikes, the 1880s and the late 1940s. In effect, the first years of the Piels' brewery coincided with a decade of determined union organizing.

Brewery work, like most industrial labor in the Gilded Age, was dangerous, demanding, and poorly paid. Though industrial accidents were commonplace, there was no workers' compensation for either injury or death. During the beer industry's peak season from June to September, the standard workweek was often ninety hours—that is, fifteen to eighteen hours Monday through Saturday, and six more on Sunday. Moving from the freezing cold ice room to the boiling hot kettles induced bronchial infections that winnowed workers above the age of 45 via disease and death. During the cold months when demand for beer dropped markedly, seasonal layoffs were common and uncompensated. No matter how long or loyal a worker's service, there was no pension.[85]

Despite such harsh conditions, tight bonds between German workers and their employers slowed unionization of the city's breweries until January 1881 when four laborers at Manhattan's Peter Doegler Brewery burned to death while doing dangerous work at the insistence of an abusive foreman. After the liberal newspaper *New York Volkszeitung* publicized the "evils existing in the breweries," the Brewery Workmen's Union of New York formed that March with 250 members in branches throughout the city. In June, the union issued demands for a twelve-hour day, no Sunday labor, and an overtime rate of fifty cents an hour. Although fourteen breweries in greater New York accepted these terms, several of the largest—Ruppert, Ringler, and Schaefer—fired the union organizers, sparking a consumer boycott that forced these brewers to concede. Emboldened by this success, the union decided on a strike that proved premature, with 1,200 workers walking out citywide. In Brooklyn, the Union Hall on Meserole Street in Bushwick coordinated a shutdown that the local press described as "successful in part only." Within two weeks, proprietors' concessions to their own workers broke the union's solidarity, and an attempted beer boycott soon fizzled. By July, the strike was broken.[86]

So confident was New York's tightly knit fraternity of German brewers that they tried to tame the union challenge with concessions. In the strike's aftermath several of the larger city breweries agreed to the strike's key demands, the twelve-hour day and diminished Sunday work. Wary of retaliation, a dozen union activists were also meeting secretly, agreeing in August 1884 to form a group that eventually grew into the United Brewery Workmen of America. After workers staged successful boycotts against the Peter Doegler Brewery and one of George Ehret's tied saloons in Manhattan, the United Brewery Workmen won a contract from the Brewers' Association in 1886 with a wage of eighteen dollars for a working week limited to sixty hours without any Sunday labor—an "extraordinary victory" that inspired the unionization of breweries from Newark to Chicago.[87]

But when labor relations again grew tense by the spring of 1888, the New York brewers, stiffened by the recent decision of the U.S. Brewers' Association to fight organized labor, canceled the union contract and imposed a citywide lockout. Their manifesto expressed "our disgust" at the union's "anarchistic tendencies," condemning it as "tyrannical in its exactions, petty in its annoyances." At noon on April 16, all seventy-eight breweries in the New York metropolitan region shut their gates, pushing 4,000 workers into the streets. Out in Brooklyn, twenty-one breweries dismissed 1,000 union members, saying they could return to work only if they agreed to be governed by their employers and "not by the rules of any union."[88]

To fill their depleted ranks, proprietors had 3,000 strikebreakers from the Brewers' Exchange, experienced kettlemen from Philadelphia, and a flood of local applicants eager to become wagon drivers. Confident that brewing required "craftsmanlike skill," the strikers were dismayed to discover that industrialization now meant "the work could be performed by anyone, even the most unpracticed." With police standing guard and pickets unable to block these new men from entering the breweries, Brooklyn's Central Labor Union retreated to a boycott of any saloon selling the proprietors' "pool beer." Even that action slowly faded from a want of "solidarity."[89]

After a full month with lost wages and lowered profits, both sides were exhausted and soon reached a settlement, with proprietors offering to take back some strikers and the unions agreeing to lift their consumer boycott. With a limited strike fund and with little support beyond the German community, the union was down to 500 members and fading fast. A year later, the local press would describe it as "smashed into smithereens."[90]

Despite these setbacks, unions remained a strong presence in Brooklyn's breweries, grounded in the city's working-class culture and German American solidarity. In September 1902, for example, the members of Brewer's Union No. 64 and Beer Drivers' Union No. 29 flooded into Ridgewood Park near East New York, banners flying, for a celebratory picnic hosted by the United Lager Beer Brewery Workers' Sick Benefit Association. With a membership of 400 men from "almost every Brooklyn brewery," the association proudly announced it had paid $4,000 in benefits during the past year, "including $1,500 to the families of members who died."[91]

Beyond Brooklyn, however, the city's brewery workers needed the support of the American Federation of Labor and long years of struggle to recover from their disastrous defeat of 1888. After fourteen years of organizing and periodic boycotts of leading brewers, in 1902 the United Brewery Workmen won a three-year contract with New York's major lager breweries that reduced the working day to just ten hours.[92] Despite these long years with many reverses, New York's brewery workers were developing a tradition of struggle that would, by the 1950s, make them the highest paid industrial workers in America, complicating the survival of their city's beer industry.

As a small, struggling brewery, Piels initially avoided any ties to either labor unions or the brewers' trade association. At the start of these labor tensions in July 1887, a delegation from the Central Labor Union visited Piels to urge employment of union men. Speaking for the firm, Gottfried Piel flatly refused since "the payment of union wages and granting of union hours would not leave him sufficient profit." If compelled to pay union scale, he would, he said, "sell out his business and go back to Germany." The delegation tried to reason, but Gottfried would not change his "ultimatum."[93]

In a later report on this meeting to the Central Labor Union, the Brewers' Union stated they had informed Mr. Piel "that his was the only brewery that was a non-union one." In his defense, Piel explained that his business was limited to "what he sold over the bar at the brewery." He was unable to expand since he "could not afford to give the saloon keepers the large percentage they get from other brewers, owing to his being a small manufacturer." Though "he made nothing but the best beer from imported German hops," he did so with a small labor force of five skilled men in the summer and three in the winter who were paid "even higher wages than the union demands." Befuddled by Gottfried Piel's mix of obstinacy and special pleading, the meeting resolved to refer the matter back to the Brewers' Union grievance committee.[94]

Two months later, the Brewers' Union No. 1 (German branch) asked the Central Labor Union for advice on ways to make their consumer boycott of Piels effective. They had advertised the action in the city's German-language newspaper *Volks Zeitung*, "but believed it had done no good." After much debate, the Central Union decided not to offer any advice until the Brewers Union gave "a plainer statement of the trouble"—a postponement that spared Piels any action while disputes with larger brewers built toward the disastrous lockout of April 1888.[95]

Temperance

Piels was equally determined in its defiance of state temperance ordinances passed to honor the Sabbath. By the time Piels brewed its first keg in 1884, some thirty years of political wrangling over licensing restrictions in New York State had drawn clear battle lines between the liquor industry and temperance advocates. During Piels' first years of operation, this struggle between "wets" and "drys" was fought with particular intensity.[96]

After several decades of agitation and lectures, the movement had gained renewed momentum in the 1870s with the founding of the Prohibition Party and the Women's Christian Temperance Union (WCTU) under the leadership of famous feminists Frances Willard and Susan B. Anthony. While the party's vote rarely broke the 1 percent barrier, the WCTU, with 73,000 registered members by the early 1880s, took a longer view by lobbying hard for compulsory temperance education in public schools, starting with Vermont in 1882, New York in 1884, and the entire nation by 1901. At the federal level, the two organizations scored their first victory, after a decade-long struggle, when President William McKinley signed legislation in 1901 banning all alcohol sales on U.S. Army bases.[97]

To fight the rising pressure for prohibition, local liquor manufacturers formed the Brooklyn Liquor Dealers' Protective Association and staged a spectacular show of force. At exactly 11:00 a.m. on August 14, 1884, the association's Grand Marshall, riding in a large wagon with a full orchestra, led a two-mile parade of 500 carts and carriages past city hall. The high point of the parade was a spectacular procession of fifty-seven brewery wagons, magnificent with their "trampling of big Percheron-Norman horses" and "rotund and rosy drivers." Riders waved colorful placards. "Down With the Temperance Law." "Equal Rights to All Men in Business." "One Flag, One Country, Two Lagers, and Three Cheers."[98]

Reflecting the rising emotions sparked by the temperance issue, a Manhattan preacher, Reverend Samuel D. Burchard, famously denounced Democrats as the party of "Rum, Romanism, and Rebellion" during the 1884 presidential campaign.[99] In Brooklyn, temperance advocates excoriated the brewing industry's system of tied saloons as the driving force behind the rapid proliferation of bars across the city. The problem, they said, was particularly acute in the German sections where "hundreds of little lager beer saloons are entirely owned by the brewers." To expand sales, the city's breweries would pick a popular local figure likely to attract a clientele, provide him a loan of at least $3,200 as down payment on a saloon mortgage, and stipulate that the establishment was obliged to sell its beer "as long as he is indebted to them." Major brewers such as Ehret and Schaefer each had $150,000 to $200,000 invested in saloon mortgages, assuring them reliable outlets for their product. With this exclusive marketing, many Brooklyn breweries could cut corners on quality, rushing their lager into the saloon without sufficient aging.[100]

Indeed, breweries made the saloon an omnipresent American institution. As new industrial methods raised beer production during the 1880s, keg prices fell by half and companies were forced to fight for market share. Since most saloons were limited to a single brand by the high cost of a keg-tapping apparatus, the big brewers could only expand by opening their own outlets. As the number of saloons nationwide swelled from 100,000 in 1870 to 300,000 by 1900, local breweries controlled up to 80 percent of these outlets in New York and Chicago. For poor working-class neighborhoods, saloons served as community centers for politics and public meetings. In New York City, the powerful Tammany machine relied upon the saloon as a "finely honed . . . political instrument." Its first native-born, Irish-American mayor, Hugh J. Grant (1889–1892), was heir to a family fortune built from "a string of successful saloons." By 1890, nearly half of New York's twenty-four aldermen were saloon owners. On election days, Tammany's ward bosses used local bars as their headquarters, mobilizing teams of "vagrants and petty criminals" for repeat voting. In effect, saloons were the engine driving the city's machine politics. Temperance advocates painted this picture in the darkest hues, depicting saloons as the sum of all corruptions—gambling, prostitution, police bribery, and political bossism.[101]

From a mix of motives, Piel Bros. did not invest in tied saloons, and instead sold direct to consumers on the premises or via home delivery. "My grandfather thought that saloons were immoral," recalled Michael's grandson William Piel, Jr. "He thought the connection between saloons and politics and corruption and crime . . . was unlike anything he ever experienced in Europe."[102]

There was, however, a selectivity to such morality. As recent arrivals in Brooklyn's crowded beer market, the Piels lacked both capital and locations had they been inclined to open their own saloons. Consequently, they sold much of their beer directly to consumers on weekends in their beer garden and banquet hall, and thus could ill afford to honor New York laws that restricted drinking on the Sabbath. In April 1889, Police Roundsman Downey slipped into the Piels' restaurant by a side door on a Sunday evening to find the "place was in full blast." The officer arrested two bartenders. The news "spread like wild fire" and soon "every saloon in the ward was closed as tight as a drum."[103]

A year later, a delegation of seven clergy called on Brooklyn's police commissioner to complain of their uphill struggle against "the evil that is overwhelming the Twenty-Sixth Ward," an area that encompassed East New York. Within the district's general moral turpitude marked by drinking and pool playing, the pastors were "especially strong in their denunciation" of three locales—Malone's saloon, the Bennett casino, and Piels brewery. At Piels, they reported, "crowds of people spend their Sundays therein beer drinking." The police commissioner explained that the "increase in wickedness" came from the "floating population that infested these resorts in the summer months." He promised to restore law and order to this "wicked ward."[104] But the Piels were not chastened. Five years later a local resident was so "very much disturbed by the spectacle" of Sunday drinking at Piels that he sought a warrant for a bartender's arrest.[105]

In March 1896, prohibition intensified markedly when New York's temperance lobby won passage of the Raines Law that restricted Sunday drinking by requiring saloons to pay $800 for liquor licenses.[106] To take advantage of the law's exemption allowing hotels with a minimum of ten rooms to serve alcohol on Sundays, Piels installed eleven furnished bedrooms inside a beer hall with seating for nearly a thousand patrons. By meeting the law's requirement for rooms, a working kitchen, and dining facilities, any establishment, Piels included, could "maintain an open bar with comparatively slight risk of punishment." Instead of shutting saloons, the new law opened thousands of small, seedy hotels. Within a decade, Manhattan and the Bronx had 1,405 of these "registered hotels," with no more than 250 of them housing real guests and the rest at best a pretext for Sunday liquor service or, at worst, "houses of prostitution and assignation."[107] In Brooklyn, the Raines Law suddenly raised the number of hotels from just thirteen to over 2,000, many of them ill-concealed fronts for prostitution.[108] From the very start of this moral crusade, prohibition had unintended consequences that true believers resolutely ignored.

In the first weeks of enforcement for the new Raines Law, Piels was singled out for special attention. The Brooklyn press stated that the brewery "was wide open all day and doing business." On the second Sunday under the law, the New York *Sun* reported the "Piels brewery resort was in full blast as usual, and at one time in the afternoon there were between 400 and 500 visitors in the mammoth drinking pavilion." Although "sandwiches, frankfurters, and other light foods were in great demand," it was understood that "a single sandwich would serve for twenty or more beers." The captain of the East New York precinct reported that his men had been watching Piels all day, and the bar was closed even though the brewery did have the right under the law to serve beer with meals. The precinct caught 285 violators of the new law on its first Sunday and 75 the second, but none from Piels, which was probably careful to combine beer with the required meal.[109]

Without their competitors' investment in tied saloons, Piels was spared the loss of revenue that the Raines Law imposed on other breweries. When the law was being deliberated, Brooklyn brewers estimated that its heavy licensing fee would drive 400 to 500 of the city's saloons out of business, precipitating the "failure of those brewers who were dependent upon the smaller class of trade." Within a year, the fees brought their first casualty when the Leibinger & Oehm Brewery on Wycoff Avenue filed for bankruptcy, dismissing over a hundred workers. Although a well-established and profitable firm, the partners had tried to save the market for their beer by advancing some $25,000 to "saloon customers who were unable to pay the big tax imposed on them."[110]

As they struggled to absorb such losses, the brewers mobilized politically to stop the temperance forces. In June 1897, Brooklyn Congressman Charles G. Bennett arrived from Washington with the welcome news for brewers that his alliance with several senators had blocked any increase in the federal excise tax.[111] A week later during a public banquet at the city's Clarendon Hotel, Brooklyn's brewers presented the state's deputy excise commissioner, Harry W. Mitchell, the man responsible for enforcing the Raines Law, with a "handsome gold badge" bearing "four magnificent diamonds" worth $500.[112] That fall, as the first mayoral elections for the newly amalgamated New York City loomed, Brooklyn's brewers met at the Claus Lipsius Brewery in Bushwick to voice their unanimous support for the Democratic candidate, Robert A. Van Wyck.[113]

Illustrating the elements that made the brewers such a potent political force, Brooklyn's Democratic Party held its closing rally for the November 1900 elections at the Trommer's Brewery on Bushwick Avenue. There the party's candidates for the House and Senate were "enthusiastically cheered" by a "large number of Germans."[114] These rallies were but opening rounds in a political struggle over temperance that would continue for decades and culminate in the complete prohibition of alcohol by 1920.

Conclusion

After fifteen years in Brooklyn's saturated beer market, Piel Bros. had survived by overcoming a succession of high hurdles. The city's entrenched breweries, with their markets protected by tied saloons, could have crushed this fledgling firm. The temperance movement was determined to shut down their industry. New unions were demanding a share of profits that a small brewer like Piels could ill afford. These two brothers had arrived in a foreign land with limited capital, small loans, and no experience in running a brewery. Launching a new business under these enormously difficult circumstances seemed a formula for certain failure.

Yet by mobilizing every possible family resource, the company had prospered. Gottfried had the business acumen to spot an opportunity and impose fiscal discipline. His wife Sophie risked her inheritance in an uncertain venture. With Michael's talent as brewmaster and plant manager, the firm had been able to produce, from the first barrel, a brew of exceptional quality that soon won loyal customers. If they came for Michael's beer, many patrons stayed for Maria's cooking. With their first profits from these direct sales to consumers, the Piels launched, after just three years in business, a clever destination marketing strategy, building a banquet hall and beer garden that sustained their steady expansion for another decade.

Through the unique capacity of a family business to inspire sacrifice, these two couples had invested this fragile enterprise with every bit of their beings— endless labor, inspired creativity, and the capital accumulated by countless generations on the land back in Germany. Without these concerted efforts from all four, their brewery would not have survived.

But, in a family, shared struggle could also produce problems. With Maria cooking while Sophie invested and Michael brewing while Gottfried managed, these uneven sacrifices fostered tensions that threatened their firm's future. In the knotty conundrum that is family business, sacrifice seemed to produce conflict. After fifteen years of maximum effort that was straining the limits of their physical and financial resources, this Piel family partnership needed a new way to do business. With an efficient brewery and the rising reputation of its beer, Piel Bros. was ready, by 1898, to expand beyond Brooklyn into regional and even national markets if, and only if, some new structure could be found. As it turned out, all these problems would be resolved through the mysteries of incorporation.

3

Incorporation

By the late 1890s, both business and family pressures pushed Piel Bros. toward incorporation. To expand beyond their beer garden and keep pace with the brewing industry's relentless growth, the company desperately needed an infusion of capital. There were also rising tensions between the two founding brothers, Gottfried and Michael, that required the mediation of a company structure less intimate than a family partnership. Thus, after sixteen years of steady growth as a small business, Piel Bros. would finally incorporate in 1898 under the laws of New York State and issue bonds to finance a major plant expansion.

The brewery might have been Piel Bros. in name, but its financial foundations lay in a series of contracts among four unequal partners. At its founding in 1883, the brewery started as a joint venture among just three principals—Gottfried, his older brother Michael, and their cousin Wilhelm Piel. While Gottfried and cousin Wilhelm had money and management skills, they depended upon Michael, a trained brewmaster, to actually produce the beer.

To purchase the old Lanzer Brewery for $30,000 back in 1883, Gottfried and cousin Wilhelm borrowed $12,000 from two Brooklyn lenders, most likely for renovations to the derelict building.[1] Three months later, Michael, just eight months off the boat from Germany, became an equal partner by paying the firm's founders $3,700 for an "undivided third part of all those two certain lot pieces or parcels of land" that comprised the brewery's site on Liberty Avenue in the East New York district.[2] After just four years in Brooklyn, Wilhelm returned to Düsseldorf in 1886, leaving the brewery's operations thereafter to the two brothers, Gottfried the manager and the Michael the brewmaster.[3]

During their first decade in business, these three Piels jointly borrowed, with Wilhelm signing before the U.S. consul in Düsseldorf, an additional $26,000 from local moneylenders to purchase property, build their banquet hall, and upgrade the original plant.[4] By the early 1890s, however, technical innovation and increased capitalization was mechanizing the U.S. brewing industry, creating enormous pressures on Piel Bros. for new investment to upgrade their antiquated equipment.

Between Piels' foundation in 1884 and its incorporation in 1898, a 50 percent jump in per capita beer consumption to 16 gallons a year doubled U.S. beer production to 37 million barrels. During these same fifteen years, moreover, bigger, better-capitalized companies raised their production by an average of 250 percent while weaker firms faded, reducing the number of breweries from 2,200 to 1,800. Driving these changes, the capitalization of the U.S. brewing industry nearly doubled to $415 million during the 1890s.[5] Clearly, Piels would have to modernize and expand if it were to survive midst such relentless competition.

As a private partnership, the company relied increasingly upon Gottfried's wife and cousin Sophie Piel for this much-needed capital, creating the tangled interpersonal tensions that can often trouble a family partnership. After marrying her first cousin Gottfried sometime in 1885–86, Wilhelm's younger sister Sophie had a child every year for the next four years, leaving her little time for any real role in the brewery.[6]

In 1890, however, Sophie's father, Maria Josephus Wilhelm Piel, died in Germany at age 72, leaving a substantial estate to his five surviving children.[7] With her new wealth, Sophie became the brewery's chief financier. In February 1890, the three male principals borrowed $48,000 from Sophie at 6 percent interest, by far their largest debt to date.[8] In a separate document signed the same day, the brothers Michael and Gottfried borrowed an additional $12,000 from Sophie, raising her total loans to the brewery to an extraordinary $60,000—over twice the firm's past borrowings and far larger than even the Bank of East New York's annual financial surplus.[9] These loans probably provided the funds four years later when the Piels spent $50,000 to replace the old Lanzer building with a substantial four-story brick brew house.[10]

This shift in control over the brewery became even more marked in September 1895 when Wilhelm Piel, Sophie's brother and one of the firm's three founding partners, died suddenly at the age of 45 from apoplexy "in Düsseldorf, Germany, where he owns a large brickyard."[11] When his will was probated three months later in Düsseldorf's district court, Wilhelm's estate, including his investment in the brewery, passed to his four surviving siblings in equal shares.[12] Since Wilhelm held German properties in addition to his Brooklyn interests, a rational division of the estate awarded his one-third share in Piel Bros. to his sister Sophie and her husband—suddenly giving Gottfried a controlling two-thirds share of the brewery.

After a decade of unceasing toil, Michael suddenly found himself a junior partner to his younger brother in a business he had built by working sixteen-hour days. These tensions were likely compounded by that unequal division of labor: Maria cooked and Michael brewed, while Gottfried managed and Sophie invested. Within just months, these conflicts culminated in a lawsuit that threatened their company's future.

Our only documentation about this conflict comes from a contract that the brothers signed on March 2, 1898, to restore amicable working relations. According to this agreement, Michael, Gottfried, and Wilhelm had originally been equal partners until the latter's death in 1895 made Gottfried, who "claims to have succeeded to his entire estate," owner of two-thirds of the business. At some point during the next three years, relations became so troubled that Michael sued brother Gottfried for an equal share. Now, through this negotiated resolution, Michael dropped his pending lawsuit that, if pursued, "would destroy the good-will of the firm, which is of great value." In turn, Gottfried agreed to sell Michael a one-sixth share in the brewery for $200,000, once again making them equal partners in a corporation that would be registered as Piel Bros. "with an authorized share capital of $1,000,000." To cover the cost of this one-sixth share, Michael promised to pay Gottfried his portion of the profits from their new company, minus living expenses of $20,000 a year, until that debt was redeemed.[13] From Michael's perspective, resolution of this sibling conflict and the solution to the brewery's chronic undercapitalization had been found within the remarkable rubric of U.S. corporation law.

Incorporating the Partnership

Indeed, just two days after the brothers signed that agreement, the *Brooklyn Daily Eagle* of March 4, 1898, reported that Piel Bros. had "filed articles of incorporation with the Secretary of State" in Albany proposing to manufacture and sell "lager beer, ales and other malt or spirituous beverages" with a capitalization of one million dollars.[14]

At its first meeting on March 29, the new company's board recorded the Certificate for Incorporation and approved the company's By-Laws.[15] The following day, two interim company officers issued Stock Certificate No. 4 for 9,970 shares to "Gottfried Piel and Michael Piel of Piel Bros."[16] The day after that, the board approved the purchase of "all the business property (real and personal) assets, effects and goodwill of the business heretofore conducted under the name of Piel Bros." from Michael and Gottfried for the sum of one million dollars, to be paid by the "delivery of one thousand Six Percent First Mortgage Gold Bonds" worth one thousand dollars each.[17] Simultaneously, the directors signed a Deed of Trust with the Kings County Trust Company acknowledging this million-dollar debt and encumbering the corporation's assets to finance these gold bonds.[18]

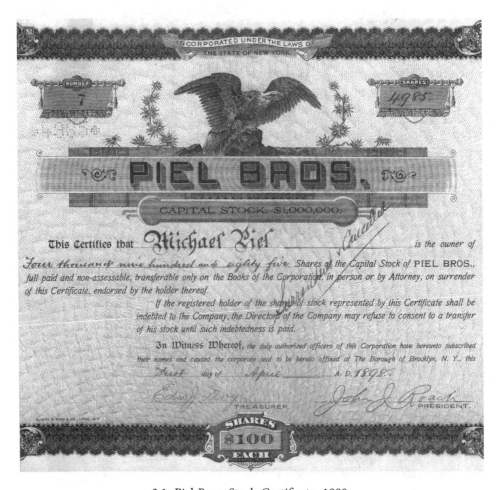

3.1. Piel Bros. Stock Certificate, 1898.

After founding the corporation and floating its bonds in the space of a month, the interim directors resigned and a new board was formed with Gottfried as president, Michael as vice-president, and the firm's trusted manager Hermann Petersen as secretary-treasurer.[19] That same day, the firm's share book showed two certificates for 4,985 shares each issued to Michael and Gottfried, who became the sole stockholders and would remain so for the next fifteen years.[20]

In retrospect, the sudden good fortune of these immigrant brothers reflects the ingenuity of the U.S. free market economy whose workings, at such times, seem almost metaphysical. After just fifteen years of doing business, the Piel brothers had, through the power of law, formed their family partnership into a public entity called a corporation—a persona with special rights to borrow working capital, but without any responsibility to repay should it fail. Then, through the alchemy of capitalism, they received a million-dollar loan that transformed their struggling local business into a rising regional brewer. In sum, the fusion of these legal and financial mysteries transmuted their slum property, tired horses, fading beer hall, and aging machinery into a corporation with capital sufficient to modernize their plant, expand their business, and make both wealthy men. That Michael Piel, a farmer's son and a newcomer to America, could have grasped the essence of U.S. corporation law so quickly indicates that his talents were not limited to matters agricultural or mechanical.

All this documentation explains how Michael gained that additional "one-sixth share" to become an equal partner in the brewery. But it does not reveal whether or when he finally paid his brother the debt of $200,000. While investigating this matter a half century later, Michael's son Paul observed: "Certainly it must have taken years for father to pay off $250,000 [sic.]"[21] Actually, with increased production from the infusion of capital, the brewery's gross sales soared to $660,000 by 1900, with a full third of that income from high-margin bottled beer. If we assume a 25 percent profit, the firm's actual figure a few years later, then Michael could have repaid his $200,000 debt to Gottfried in just three years. Confirming that inference, Michael both retired from active management and paid $10,000 cash for his Maine property in late 1900—just about three years after the brewery's incorporation.[22]

Midst the silence of yellowing papers about this payment, we must turn to the family's collective memory, in this case a story that passed from Michael to his eldest son William and then to his grandson Gerard Piel. When Gerard was young, he heard how "Michael indentured himself to Gottfried to earn out a one-sixth share to bring himself even-steven at one-half," becoming thereby an equal partner in the brewery. When that day finally came after much toil, Michael entered the brewery office, arm outstretched for a congratulatory handshake from his younger brother. At this point in the story, Gerard tucked his hands into his armpits and breathed deep for a gruff voice to deliver Gottfried's "grudging, condescending" words: "Well, I suppose you have earned your share."[23]

We have no record of Michael's reaction, but Gerard's assessment of their relationship is telling. "My grandfather," Gerard recalled, "was a man of enormous energy, physical and emotional. He was associated in business with a brother who was rather his temperamental opposite—a cold and fierce fellow." By awarding Michael that "one-sixth share," Gottfried was splitting the one-third advantage gained by his wife's inheritance to make these two very different personalities, once again, equal partners in the brewery.[24] Although tensions would persist between the two sides of the family into the next generation, the company had become Piel Bros. in name and in fact, muting the conflict between these contentious siblings.

Indeed, the impact of incorporation was nothing less than transformative, moving the family from an intimate to an impersonal business structure. When Piel Bros. operated as a family firm, the company could inspire extraordinary creativity and prodigious effort—witness Michael's sixteen-hour days, Maria's hard labor, and Sophie's willingness to risk her inheritance. As the personal tensions of family life spilled into the workplace, such success also unleashed deep sibling rivalries that brought resentment rather than reward. Once Piel Bros. incorporated, however, this legal apparatus reformed their personal relations, channeling tensions between these disputatious brothers in more productive directions. Years later when their children succeeded them at the brewery, the corporate board became an arena for both airing family conflicts and finding the means for their resolution.

As a lapsed Catholic, Michael, may have abandoned the Mass with its miracle of transubstantiation that transformed ordinary bread and wine into the savior's body and blood. But as an aspirant capitalist, he seemed to embrace the mysteries of incorporation as a secular simulacrum.

Building the Model Brewery

Midst the rapid growth of Brooklyn's brewing industry, Michael and Gottfried Piel had to modernize their aging plant if they were to survive their industry's relentless competition. Through incorporation and indebtedness, the Piels gained the capital to build a modern brewery that could produce their quality beer in sufficient volume to remain a saleable product.

Between 1870 and 1890, a synergy of technological innovations had transformed brewing from an ancient craft into a modern industry, highly mechanized and heavily capitalized. After a decade of experimentation, major brewers replaced ice cellars with mechanical refrigeration, a transition exemplified by Jacob Ruppert's installation of the Boyle ammonia compressor at his Manhattan brewery in 1879. That same year, Louis Pasteur's seminal study of beer fermentation was published in English, sparking the development of elaborate machinery for heating beer to prevent spoilage during storage in bottles. Pasteurizing, combined with the Goulding bottle-washing machine in 1884 and the introduction of the metal bottle cap eight years later, allowed Anheuser-Busch of St. Louis and Pabst of Milwaukee to begin long-distance rail shipments of their bottled beer. Starting in 1888, moreover, breweries began replacing steam power with electricity. With the introduction of the Galland-Henning pneumatic malting drum a year later, this key artisanal process also became reliably mechanized. Through a dozen major innovations—including pure culture yeast, use of unmalted grain, and a distinctive infusion process for mechanized mashing of grains—American brewing achieved an extraordinary efficiency. To fund all this innovation, the industry attracted $232 million in capital investment by 1890, with 28 percent of that total invested in New York State. The sum of these innovations raised the modern brewery from dank cellars into soaring, well-lighted factories, veritable temples of industry.[25]

By the 1890s, local and national competition was pushing Brooklyn's brewing industry toward consolidation and expansion. In an era when speculators amalgamated railroads, oil refining, and sugar processing into monopolistic trusts that quashed competition and boosted profits, New York financiers floated a succession of ill-fated schemes to form a metropolitan brewery combine. In 1899, some twenty-seven Brooklyn breweries were targeted, unsuccessfully, for takeover, including Otto Huber, Liebmann & Son, Malcolm Brewing, and Piel Bros.[26]

Although brewing was too diffuse and deeply rooted via the tied saloon for ready consolidation, expansion was still a commercial imperative for each company. Indeed, several well-capitalized new Brooklyn breweries were launched in the months surrounding Piels' incorporation in 1898, including Trommer's Evergreen Brewery with capital stock of $175,000 and the William Ulmer Brewery with $550,000 in shares.[27] In one of the city's few mergers, the recently formed Union Consumers' Brewery bought out the Conrad Eurich Company for $500,000 in 1902—a substantial price indicative of the heavy capital requirements

3.2. Federal Brewing Company of Brooklyn, circa 1902, typical of the borough's forty breweries at century's turn. (Credit: Brooklyn Public Library—Brooklyn Collection)

for a major brewery.[28] Among the many new firms formed at century's turn, the Consumers Park Brewing Company was a joint-stock company owned by a thousand saloonkeepers, featuring luxuriant grounds with a beer garden, hotel, and its own orchestra.[29] Illustrating the industry's increased scale, the Otto Huber Brewery on Bushwick Place, founded in 1866, now occupied a plant with an annual capacity of 150,000 barrels.[30]

The process of incorporation and capitalization provided Michael Piel with the funds to realize his vision for a model brewery that could meet these competitive challenges. During the ten years before he transferred the day-to-day operations to his plant manager Hermann Petersen in 1900, Michael presided over a series of industrial improvements that laid the foundations for Piels' future success. In 1887, the Sanborn Insurance Map still showed the Piel plant as a single structure, 50-by-75 feet, housing the water pump, ice machine, kettle, malting, cooling, and washing—with the bottling shop in a small wooden shed nearby.[31] Starting with demolition of the old Lanzer building in 1895, he fused "new principles" with "many ideas of his own creation" to build a plant that realized, in the words of his biographer, "Michael's constant scientific advances in the field"—notably, replacing the old cooling cellars with a ground-level building chilled by "modern refrigeration." In sum, the renovated plant represented "a new achievement in brewing construction" that attracted notice from "brewing academicians, experts, and scientists from Europe and South America."[32]

The contract with Kings County Trust at Piels' incorporation in 1898 required a detailed inventory of the brewery's expanded equipment. As the firm's major source of cash, the banquet hall had 105 tables, 500 Vienna chairs, 1,500 beer glasses, and lavish décor, while the adjacent beer garden held 466 iron chairs—allowing maximum seating for almost 1,000 patrons. Driven by three boilers and a fifty-horsepower engine, the brew house contained a malt hopper, a 250-barrel beer kettle, two vats, and eleven other assorted machines, including two Buffalo refrigeration units weighing forty tons each. The storage house had thirty-five fermenting tubs, while the stable housed forty-nine horses and twenty-seven wagons. Finally, the bottling establishment, critical for the firm's home deliveries, held eight washing machines, a corking machine, and 10,000 wooden boxes with bottles. Though the bottling plant was thus "distinct and separate" from the brew house to comply with U.S. tax law in force until the early 1890s, Piels, unlike many small brewers, cut costs by bottling its own beer.[33] In addition to these material assets, the company's workforce had grown from just five in 1887 to thirty-six men who were all, judging from a company photo circa 1900, fit and outfitted with the caps, coveralls, and boots needed for the demanding, often dangerous work inside the cavernous brewery.

Two weeks after the company's incorporation, Piels applied for a building permit to construct, at a cost of $10,000, a two-story, steel-reinforced brick boiler and engine house, 101 feet long and 75 wide, adjacent to the main brewery on Georgia Avenue.[34] To equip the new plant, the board approved, between July 1899 and October 1900, the purchase of modern equipment, including a Crown Cork capping machine, Torchiani pitching machines for packaging, a 100-barrel copper water tank, a Foster beer pump, and a new boiler.[35]

The 1908 Sanborn Insurance Map reveals the design of Michael's model plant after all this construction. With 100 feet of frontage on the south side of Liberty Avenue, the main structure was now a massive brick building that extended 300 feet down Georgia Avenue with firewalls separating five distinct units. First, the cold storage beneath a cement roof. Next, the brew house with adjacent grain hopper. Then, the washhouse. Fourth, the power plant with coal bins, condensers, dynamos, and engines. Finally, the all-important water works with a 240-ton ice machine, water filtration, and a powerful Foster pump above a deep artesian well. Facing this factory, the beer garden and its shade trees filled an open space at the center of the block. On the other side of this city block, the famed Piels resort stretched for nearly 200 feet along Sheffield Avenue with kitchen, bar, dining room, and banquet hall. Turning in the opposite direction to look across Georgia Avenue, the bottling works, linked to the brew house by a pipe beneath the pavement, extended for 300 feet with a loading dock, bottling plant, and barrel shed for resealing wooden kegs. On the north side of Liberty Avenue lay the office, wagon shed, and stables.[36]

Four years later, after declining revenues closed the beer garden and banquet facilities in 1911, the Piel complex took its final form for the next thirty years. In February 1912, the company applied for a building permit to expand the main plant, at a cost of $15,000, by demolishing the kitchen and replacing it with a two-story brick, steel-reinforced storehouse extending for 96 feet along Sheffield Avenue. In this process, the dining room and banquet hall also gave way to a reception room called the *bier stube* and the *brewmeister's* laboratory. Across Liberty Avenue, the "handsome horses from Piels' prized stable of one hundred" also disappeared after the building was converted into a truck garage.[37]

From its origins in the derelict Lanzer Brewery of 1883, the Piels' plant had thus grown, in less than twenty years, into a modern factory that was not only the equal of Brooklyn's more established breweries but set the standard for the brewing industry worldwide. The general manager later reported that, from 1910 to 1920, Michael Piel's model brewery "was visited by leading brewers and brewing experts from Canada, Cuba, Brazil, Argentina, Germany, Holland, Austria, Switzerland, France and North Africa, with praise from all for its beer and the plant, as a really progressive German-type brewery."[38]

Life and Leisure

This infusion of capital allowed Piel Bros. a decade of rising sales and strong profits. As annual beer sales surged from $660,000 in 1900 to $940,000 six years later, the company's profits, still free from federal taxation, were split between the two Piel brothers, allowing both ample wealth for a genteel lifestyle of townhouses, summer estates, and private schools for their children.[39]

In the first five years of the firm's incorporation, 1898 through 1902, the company paid Michael various credits totaling $477,000, an enormous income for a Gilded Age executive.[40] An accountant's balance sheet labeled "Michael Piel" showed disposable cash for the year 1902 of $178,000, including compensation from the brewery totaling $133,000.[41] Even in the relatively difficult year of 1910, Piel Bros. still earned a profit of $67,000, which was divided between the two stockholders. The company also paid Gottfried and Michael annual salaries of $7,500 each as president and vice-president, respectively.[42]

These were enormous sums for this era, allowing both brothers the means to launch their families into New York society. Seeming luxuries—décor, arts, leisure travel, and elite education—were part of their self-conscious strategy for assimilating into American society. Though these brothers and their wives were but a generation or two beyond the German peasantry, they were determined their children would climb to the uppermost rungs of the city's highly stratified society.

With the brewery incorporated and cash flowing, the two Piel brothers began transitions to life beyond the strenuous schedules they had maintained for so many years. The elder brother Michael, who had worked sixteen-hour days for the past fifteen years, was the first to leave. According to a posthumous biography, he "retired from active management as the technical head [brewmeister] of the corporation in 1900," devoting his last years to leisure.[43] Indeed, the board's minutes indicate Michael was largely absent for the next fifteen years, leaving the company's management first to his younger brother Gottfried and later to his eldest sons.[44]

Once incorporation assured him an income, Michael distanced himself from both his brother and the brewery, shifting his energy from endless toil to relentless recreation. Instead of the hardworking brewmaster of years past, he now became "an enthusiastic sportsman, and was particularly devoted to hunting, fishing, and yachting."[45] After purchasing hundreds of acres in the woods of northern Maine in 1900, Michael began building a sportsmen's paradise—establishing a working farm, installing new buildings, landscaping the grounds, fishing the lake, and hunting the forests. Three years later, he bought a large townhouse on Manhattan's Upper West Side, and began making annual European trips to fill its grand rooms with oil paintings, hand-woven carpets, and marble statuary.

Just months after incorporation in 1898, Michael and Maria began enjoying their affluence by returning to Germany for the first time since their migration fifteen years before, taking along eight children and a governess. After a night at the Bahnhof Hotel in downtown Düsseldorf, the family rode the tram through farmlands to Mörsenbroich, the stop closest to the old Piel farm. Then, as Louise Piel recalled, there was a joyful walk through fields of grain, meadows of wild flowers, and well-tended orchards to an "ancient little stone house with flag stone yard." There, "Grandmother awaited us in black voluminous dress and close-fitting black cap." Since Louise was then only eight, Grandmother Gertrud Piel "seemed very large to me—but how gently she patted my head. The tone of her voice is still with me as she embraced Father, saying only—'Michael.'"[46]

After so many years bound to the brewery morning to night, Michael devoted his retirement to restless pursuit of trophies to fill his showcase homes—game from Maine to Florida and artifacts from across Europe. Shipping manifests, required to list all incoming passengers after 1907, indicate he made regular trips to Germany with family in 1908, 1909, and 1911, bringing back German paintings, Italian sculpture, and vintage violins.[47]

While Michael traveled for pleasure, Maria used these trips to maintain lifelong ties to her German relatives. Even before their return, Maria took "vehement care" that her younger brother Josef should escape the family farm by studying medicine.[48] When she finally returned to the Fatherland, Maria made a lasting impression on her thrifty Heermann relatives by receiving them in a grand Düsseldorf hotel suite.[49] Even though she suspended the visits for a decade after her brother-in-law Wilhelm-Heinrich Piel tried to molest her teenaged daughter Louise, Maria still corresponded regularly with relatives and shipped them tons of relief goods during the hard years after World War I.[50]

For winter travels when the Atlantic was too rough and Maine too cold, Michael acquired the ultimate Gilded Age status symbol—a motorized yacht to cruise the Eastern Seaboard for hunting in Virginia or the Carolinas. In 1910, Michael launched the 48-foot, steam yacht *Meridrud*—home ported in Bath, Maine, and anchored at Manhattan's Upper West Side. The ship was elegance afloat. Apart from the captain, helmsman, and mechanic, Michael's crew included what Maria called "a good cook who even bakes him fine bread and serves him diligently" on a dinner service embossed with the ship's name in blue cursive print. Not only did the chef keep "everything mirror-like" in the kitchen and cabins, but he did "not allow father to take off his shoes himself." With crew running the boat, Michael could spend his time onboard listening to records on the Victrola.[51] Every winter until his death in 1915, Michael would steam south, never taking Maria but sometimes accompanied by his favorite son Rudolf, who shared his father's fascination with all things natural and mechanical.[52]

While Michael was away cruising for months on end, Maria managed their large households in Manhattan and Maine, free from his temper and capricious demands. "Father is doing well, very happy, treats Louise and me as his best and beloved ones," Maria wrote her son Paul in May 1913. "But you know how he is still demanding to the people around him. Father is so stout and he needs stimulus in the form of tobacco and strong coffee."[53] In a later letter to Paul about his plans to study in Europe after the war, Maria explained her method for handling Michael's moods. "I carefully examined the situation with Louise," Maria wrote, "and father's opposition does not strike me as very dangerous anymore. While he explodes once in a while, he is not obstinate and would not watch one of his children becoming unhappy, so he always gives in."[54]

Apart from grand homes and international travel, both Gottfried and Michael invested heavily in their children's assimilation through education. Though neither was well educated in Germany, both brothers placed their children in some of the country's most prestigious schools. By the turn of the twentieth century, as millions of immigrants crowded northeastern cities, elite universities became, along with the public schools, engines of ethnic assimilation, awarding talented emigrant children an imprimatur for social ascent. German Americans were advantaged in this process. Many faculty members had doctorates from German universities. U.S. colleges taught the German language. German American students could also find cultural support in campus clubs, usually called the *Deutscher Verein*.

In general, Gottfried picked Lawrenceville School and Princeton University for his sons, while Michael and Maria chose Phillips Andover Academy and Columbia or Harvard for theirs. Almost all of the family's second generation struggled to meet the rigorous standards of these institutions, and most benefitted enormously—learning life skills, forging friendships, and gaining social entrée beyond the German American community. In later years, the Piels would prove grateful for these gifts, with one of Gottfried's sons leaving Princeton $400,000 and one of Michael's grandsons donating a million dollars to Harvard.

Gottfried initially favored the city's private academies for his five children. In April 1902, the *New York Tribune* reported that two of his sons had excelled in the annual gymnastic competition at the prestigious Columbia Grammar School on Manhattan's Upper West Side.[55] In 1906, the eldest son, Gottfried, Jr., entered New York University and quickly joined the local chapter of Phi Gamma Delta fraternity.[56] A few years later, younger sons Robert and Walter did their secondary education at Lawrenceville School, matriculating into nearby Princeton University, with Robert graduating in 1913 and Walter dropping out after two years.[57]

Following a similar pattern, Michael and Maria first favored Brooklyn's private schools, sending William and Paul to Polytechnic Preparatory and Agnes to Packer Collegiate. After the brewery's incorporation in 1898 increased their income, the couple began paying hefty tuition for more elite schools—sending three sons to Philips Andover Academy (Henry, Paul, Rudolf), three children to Columbia University (William, Henry, Agnes), and three more to Harvard (Paul, Rudolf, Louise).

As valedictorian at Poly Prep in 1901 and an outstanding campus leader at Columbia, William's college experience was so strongly positive that three siblings would follow him to Morningside Heights, forming family ties to the university that lasted several generations. By then, Michael and Maria had moved into a new townhouse on West 72nd Street, which was just six stops from Columbia after the city opened its first subway, the IRT-7th Avenue, in October 1904.[58]

By the time Paul entered Harvard, their mother Maria was starting to fret about the cost of educating her many children, particularly the younger ones who seemed indifferent to the privilege. Writing in 1910, Maria asked that Paul devote a portion of the coming summer to tutoring his five younger siblings. "If I were to tell you that I give nine hours and $200 a day in lessons to different children," Maria wrote, "then you will understand that I am sometimes very impatient with such huge expenses." The contrast with her own childhood on the farm in Germany was almost unbearable. "I cried my eyes out because I wanted to learn so much more," Maria recalled, "but instead I had to work so hard that I strained my limbs and was waking up all stiff from work. Forgive me, child! I should not be bitter, but sometimes it is too much."[59]

Most of this heavy investment in education would, on the credit side of the ledger, pay dividends many times over. Whether they succeeded like William or led less ambitious lives, most of the second generation benefitted from their immersion in the country's elite institutions, gaining erudition, cultural skills, and friendships that made them more fully American. But in the debit column, any hopes that the Ivy League imprimatur might ease their children's entrée into New York society would soon be eclipsed, as we will see in later chapters, by two unforeseen, intertwined events—war and Prohibition.

Grand Homes

After building their business and investing its profits, the Piel brothers' next task was finding family homes commensurate with their newfound wealth and status. Not only were these houses efficient machines for American life at century's turn, but they also were dressed to project the aura of affluence necessary for good marriages and upward mobility in the Gilded Age.

During their first decade in America, both Piel brothers lived in small neighboring houses near the brewery in the struggling East New York area, a necessity born of limited income and long hours. At the birth of their eldest daughter in May 1886, Gottfried and his wife Sophie listed their residence as Sheffield Avenue, New Lots—the same street Michael and Maria gave that year for the birth of their third child, Otto.[60] On his citizenship application two years later, Michael still listed his residence as the corner of Sheffield and Liberty avenues. "Our house, just across the street from the brewery," recalled Michael's eldest daughter Louise, "was a small frame structure . . . that . . . must have been bursting at the seams by the time we moved to Lefferts Place, for by then there were six of us children."[61]

This small house near the brewery was not a home of happy memories. After the birth of healthy sons William in 1883 and Henry in 1884, Maria suffered three troubled deliveries. A daughter, born in 1886, did not reach her second birthday. Otto, born next in 1887, suffered a severe mental handicap and would live much of his short life hidden from New York society.[62] After three more healthy children (Paul, Louise, Rudolf), Albert was born in 1895 with medical problems and

3.3. Piel family, Brooklyn, 1895 (rear, left to right) Maria aged 38, Rudolf 1, William 12, Michael 46, Henry 10, Otto 9; and (front) Paul 6, Louise 4.

died in April 1898 following four days of lingering ailments.[63] Thus, East New York became the place where Maria gave birth to most of her eleven children while managing an enormous kitchen that served the beer garden's thousands of patrons every weekend—hard labor then typical of many immigrant women but, in retrospect, an extraordinary feat of physical and emotional endurance that made her the progenitor of the Piels in America.

As the brewery prospered, Gottfried bought a home in Brooklyn's upscale Prospect Heights where he remained until 1898 when he acquired a grand townhouse on Manhattan's Riverside Drive overlooking the Hudson River.[64] Two years later, the census enumerator's card showed a genteel household headed by Gottfried aged 47 and his wife Sophie aged 41, with five children ages 6 to 14 and five German-born servants aged 19 to 45—a governess, cook, laundress, housekeeper, and waitress.[65]

Michael's family moved to grandeur by slower stages. In December 1899, eighteen months after the brewery's incorporation, the family quit those cramped quarters among East New York's tenement houses for a comfortable residence on Lefferts Place in Brooklyn's Prospect Heights, just ten blocks from his brother's old place on Flatbush Avenue.[66] As eldest daughter Louise recalled, "118 Lefferts Place was a large, ivy covered, double house with Mansard roof. Set back on a sloping, trim lawn, it had . . . plenty of room for a gorgeous grape arbor, several fine old horse chestnut trees, flowers, and shrubbery. . . . Off the dining room, a small glassed-in porch was father's pride. Here he raised night blooming wonders and experimented."[67]

The Piels were the first family on the block to own a horseless carriage. During their last months there, Michael purchased a Haynes-Apperson runabout with a seven-horsepower engine that looked, recalled Louise, "like a heron set for flight." With all Lefferts Place to send them off, Michael packed several children in the car and drove off "fearlessly and definitively too," giving "full consideration of every horse." After reaching Prospect Park with surprising speed and then turning back, the car stopped at a train crossing on Atlantic Avenue. There a small boy approached and asked Michael, "Mister, is youse Mr. Vanderbilt?" With a grand wave, Michael replied, "Yes, my son" and handed him a quarter.[68]

The 1900 Census card for this address shows a large household headed by Michael Piel aged 53 and his wife Maria aged 42, with eight children from 2 months to 17 years. There were also three female German servants.[69] As the only children on this "rather dignified street" of elderly neighbors, "our world," Louise recalled, was their own yard filled "with rabbits, guinea pigs, bantams, all under

THE PALATIAL RESIDENCE

245 West 72d St.,
Size 30x95x102.2.
Four stories and basement; elegant
in all its appointments, with eleva-
tor, six baths, billiard room and mod-
ern and complete in every detail.
Price and full particulars
SLAWSON & HOBBS.

3.4. Advertisement for sale of Piel residence at 245 West 72nd Street, Manhattan, circa 1918.

Henry's dependable care. Billy [William] supervised all activities, naming critters properly and keeping detailed records of breeds, heritage, and succession"—a sibling hierarchy at play that would later be replicated at work in the brewery.[70]

Five years later in 1903, Michael again followed his brother, this time to the Upper West Side of Manhattan, where he purchased a substantial townhouse at 245 West 72nd Street, between Broadway and West End Avenue, for $140,000.[71] When Maria later put the home on the market after Michael's death in 1915, this residence, apparently too grand for its middling neighborhood, would require nearly six years before it was sold. In this same period, Gottfried and Sophie also sold their nearby townhouse and moved to the Forest Hills section of Queens, their final residence.[72]

Household Inventory

A household inventory of July 1907 reveals that Michael Piel's West 72nd Street townhouse was a showcase for success, decorated in a grand, almost grandiose, style with $60,000 in furnishings, equivalent to $1.4 million in 2014. While the bedrooms were filled with books reflecting the family's emphasis on education, the public rooms were staged to impress. Yet beneath the surface gloss, the furnishings were a surprisingly frank statement of the family's German origins, both its high culture and base prejudices.

After passing through the first floor's entry with $2,000 worth of chairs, a Japanese bronze umbrella stand, carpets, and chandeliers, the appraiser entered the parlor and music room with $14,000 in furnishings, including a five-foot marble statue titled "The Birth of Venus" by famed Italian sculptor Ferdinando

Vichi, a violin supposedly by Antonius Stradivarius with a suspiciously low evaluation of $750, and an original oil painting by Düsseldorf-school artist Eduard Schultz-Briesen. This latter painting titled "Arrest of the Gypsies" (1886) depicted disheveled, dark-skinned nomads being expelled from an archetypal medieval city by luminously pale, morally outraged German burgers—a disturbing intimation of their Fatherland's future racial purgings—that Michael and Maria gave pride of place in their sitting room. Next came the library with $4,000 worth of decor, including leather-bound volumes by German authors such as Heine, Goethe, and Schiller—an extraordinary collection for a couple whose education had not gone beyond elementary school.

Moving through the second floor, Louise's bedroom had a large library of German and English titles and Agnes's room held a somewhat smaller library.

3.5. Dining Room, home of Michael and Maria Piel, 245 West 72nd Street, New York, circa 1907. A century later, many furnishings—table, candlesticks, plates, and paintings—would be heirlooms scattered among their descendants. (Photo by H. Shobbrook Collins, 134 West 23rd Street, New York.)

Climbing the stairs to the third floor, the appraiser found eldest son William's study with over 400 volumes of German and English literature. Then came William's bedroom, with another 180 volumes, including works by Thackery, George Eliot, Kipling, Poe, Austen, and Carlyle.

The house also held Michael's fur coats ($680), Maria's seal and sable wraps ($2,900), Maria's jewelry ($10,000), household silverware ($3,000), and clothes for ten family members ($4,000).[73] Even more striking than all this luxury was the visible commitment to high culture through a collection of some 700 books of English and German classics.

Midst all the conspicuous consumption, this was a lively household with seven growing children, servants, and a chauffeur. When William lived at home during his last year at Columbia University in 1904–05, his parents were tolerant of his college carousing. "Once, quite late o' night, he stroked a jolly Kings Crown crew to victory" in drinking games, recalled his senior yearbook. "And when the spurt was o'er, the foaming draught was gone; 'twas then . . . they brought him thru paternal doors, they heard him wake the slumbering household in agonizing tones, as thus: 'Governor—O Governor—are you sure the brewery is still running?' It is? E'en so; the gods be praised; Amen!' "[74]

The Stradivarius

Freed from day-to-day demands of the brewery and his family now comfortably settled, Michael traveled incessantly—north to his summer estate in Maine, down the East Coast on his yacht, and across the Atlantic to Germany. These European trips allowed Michael to acquire the artifacts that filled his homes: six rare violins, thirty original oil paintings, large Italian sculptures, and an array of carved furniture.[75] The most valuable of these acquisitions, a genuine Stradivarius violin, is the subject of several contradictory accounts that reveal the mutability of memory and the inclination of families to weave its wisps into the legend of a larger-than-life patriarch.

According to a story that Michael's eldest son William told his youngest son David, the acquisition of the Stradivarius was an accident, a product of Grandfather Michael's extraordinary musical ear. While riding through the streets of Heidelberg in an open carriage, Michael heard the "piercing, cat-like wails of violin practice" coming from an upper window. Without hesitation, he ordered the carriage to stop, bolted up the stairs of a student rooming house, and purchased the instrument with the money in his pocket. Some fifteen minutes later, he emerged triumphantly with a battered violin case and announced to son William: "Whether one can find his mark or not, this is a masterpiece by Amati's greatest apprentice, Stradivarius." He added: "We should celebrate for I have saved this instrument for posterity." So excellent was this instrument that maestro Jascha Heifitz used to drop by their New York home to practice, later acquiring it for his legendary performances.[76]

Seeking verification for this extraordinary story of a farmer's son with an expert's ear for vintage violins, documents confirm that the family had in fact acquired an instrument now known on international registers as the "Heifitz-Piel Stradivarius." But this violin came from Stuttgart, not Heidelberg. During his 1908 trip to Germany, Michael paid 25,000 marks, then equivalent to $6,000, to purchase the so-called "Ortega Strad" from the Stuttgart dealer Hamma & Co. According to the seller's guarantee, this model was made by "Antonius Stradivarius [of] Cremona in 1711," and was "expected to be most advantageous for the beauty and tonality. . . . The varnish is orange-yellow of wonderful quality & color as you meet in the best Stradivarius violins." Another ticket attached to this document read in Spanish: "At the command of his Majesty King Carlos III, repaired by Silverio Ortega in 1799." From this inscription, the Stuttgart seller concluded "the violin belonged earlier to the instruments for the Madrid Court Church." For the past half century, the instrument had been, the dealer averred, in the possession of one "Mr. William Keller-Deffner, an art lover" and was rarely shown to anyone until the firm had purchased it.[77] From this account, Michael Piel, farmer's son and former foot soldier, had the good fortune to acquire a prime, mid-career Stradivarius from the court of King Carlos III.

Fifteen years later, when finances forced the family to sell the instrument, son Rudolf solicited an evaluation that raised questions about this violin's value. According to a 1921 report from the New York firm John Friedrich, the instrument "is a genuine example of the work of Antonius Stradivarius," but "it is evidently one of his later period." Providing a clue to the confusion over the year of manufacture, 1711 versus a more likely date of 1731, the assessor commented that, "while the ticket seems to be the original, the date has been tampered with." Significantly, "the varnish, which exists in ample quantity, is the original" with "a chippy appearance to be seen in Stradivari's later productions." With this corrected date, the instrument was worth only $12,000.[78]

Decades later in 1959, the respected violin journal *The Strad* challenged the Stuttgart seller's story, giving this instrument's manufacture as 1731—a year when the famed luthier, then 87, "made very few instruments . . . but was still capable of producing violins of outstanding merit." After a succession of sales in the late nineteenth century, Messrs. John and Arthur Beare, London violin specialists, traded it to "the well-known German dealers, Hamma of Stuttgart, who subsequently sold it to an American, a Mr. Rudolf [sic] Piel, a New York brewer." At the peak of his career from 1925 to 1950, Jascha Heifitz used this "late Stradivari alternately with his Joseph Guarneri del Gesu for all his concerts and recordings."[79]

So the Piel family did, in fact, acquire a genuine Stradivarius and sell it to the twentieth century's greatest violinist. But there were probably two violins comingled in this family fable. The first was likely an ordinary violin, perhaps bought from that hapless Heidelberg student, which was enumerated in that 1907 inventory of their West 72nd Street home at the curiously low price of $750. The other was a genuine, if overpriced, Stradivarius purchased from a sly Stuttgart dealer in 1908 and later sold to maestro Heifitz. Instead of an inspired purchase for pocket money done with all the brilliance and boldness that Piel family stories often attribute to their founder, Michael was an innocent abroad, duped by an unethical Stuttgart dealer into paying a premium for a later, less valuable Stradivarius.

Thus the third generation recast their family's past, creating an image of Michael as an extraordinary figure who combined physical strength with perfect pitch to preserve a fragment of Western culture. Such a titan cast a long shadow, not only inspiring his children to follow him into the brewery, but making them mindful of the high standard he set for brewing beer.

Nor were the Piels alone in this tendency to weave a threadbare past into the tapestry of legend. Heirlooms, a platter or a painting, tell tales. Old photos have stories. Mundane military service can become heroic in the retelling. Absent the stuff of legend, families often invent it, inspiring their young with ancestral fables of adventure, accomplishment, or heroism.

Summer Estates

With corporation launched and homes acquired, the Piel brothers became dedicated sportsmen who built summer estates that expressed both their personalities and social aspirations. In their seasonal migrations from city to country, the Piels were following the Gilded Age aristocrats who sought respite from steaming cities at summer resorts where they found friendship, courtship, and professional contacts.

For the Piels, summer leisure was serious business. Just as their Manhattan townhouses were statements of arrival, so these vacation homes were sites for social networking. If elite schools allowed the Piel children a certain social cachet, then these summer homes sank deep regional roots, accelerating their assimilation into American society. Through their play these siblings created an ad hoc hierarchy that would follow them into the brewery. And they also formed deep bonds that would unite them in shared struggle against adversity during the difficult decades of Prohibition and Depression that lay just over the horizon. In effect, the sibling partnership that assured the brewery's survival into a second generation was formed during these long months of summer leisure.

While Michael found his refuge in the remote woods of northern Maine, Gottfried seemed to prefer more genteel vacation spots on nearby Long Island. In the summer of 1899, Gottfried Piel joined the outmigration of Brooklyn's bourgeoisie, renting a seaside cottage at Shelter Island on Long Island's northern tip where he joined the local golf club and purchased a pair of motor launches.[80] Over the next decade, he also bought a substantial home on Shelter Island's waterfront and a succession of luxury touring cars, Mercedes and Stutz, to breeze along the private Motor Parkway toward Long Island's eastern tip.[81]

These summers on Long Island were a source of adventure and misadventure for Gottfried's sons. In the summer of 1910, Arthur was charged several times for reckless driving.[82] Three years later, "one of the Piel automobiles" struck a woman rider in the town of Huntington, seriously injuring her and killing the horse.[83] Next summer, Walter was motoring toward Babylon at high speed when he struck a motorcycle, destroying both machines and throwing the rider fifteen feet through the air.[84] Cruising Long Island Sound, Walter and Gottfried, Jr. harpooned a 400-pound porpoise that took their 22-foot launch on a Nantucket sleigh ride.[85] With carnage mounting to include a dead horse, mangled porpoise, wrecked motorcycle, damaged car, and two injured victims in just four summers, Gottfried's sons were showing few signs of the character needed to succeed their father at the brewery. As it turned out, with fewer siblings to divide the dividends and no offspring to worry about, Gottfried's five children would have much less motivation than Michael's to fight for their place inside the family business.

While Gottfried's family favored golf and boating on Long Island, Michael's was attracted to more rugged pursuits in the woods of northern Maine. Attending the first Sportman's Association Exhibition at Madison Square Garden in May

1895, Michael Piel, recalled his daughter Louise, "met up with Mike Marr and heard all about his 'sporting camp' at Indian Pond, Maine. Father liked Mike and he liked what he heard and decided, then and there, that it would be the ideal summer place for all of us!"[86]

By its timing, Michael's pursuit of wilderness adventure coincided with the Gilded Age's rediscovery of nature's purity as an antidote to fetid cities with their crowds and corruptions. Escaping the heat and congestion, Boston's Brahmins migrated up the Maine coast every summer. New York's elite decamped for the Adirondacks where the stone and wood-beam construction of their "great camps" became America's authentic rustic style.[87]

After several summers as an "enthusiastic sportsman" tracking "moose and deer and fishing under the most wild conditions," in 1900 Michael purchased 460 acres of farm and forest at Parlin Pond in Somerset County, Maine. Lying about fifteen miles south of the nearest railroad station at Jackman on the Canadian border, the property could only be reached by horse and wagon. Indeed, the entire region had remained inaccessible until 1889 when the Canadian Pacific Railway built a short-cut across central Maine, with a stop at Jackman, to link Montreal with an ice-free port at St. John, New Brunswick. Parlin Pond was actually a lake three-miles long and a half-mile wide, with "excellent fishing" for land-locked salmon and lake trout. While the shoreline was dotted with rustic log cabins, the property's main structure, the press reported, was "a substantial two story building used by the previous owner as a hotel," with thirty-two rooms that Michael and his large family would occupy, starting the next summer.[88]

Within two years, Michael was spending half the year at Lake Parlin, from early spring to late fall, transforming his "monster fish and game preserve" into a "beautiful and improved" property.[89] For weeks before their annual migration, Maria presided over packing a half-dozen large trunks in the billiard room at their West 72nd Street townhouse. Then, on departure day, she shepherded the party of fifteen, both help and children, downtown to Grand Central Station. After the last change of trains at Moosehead Lake, they boarded the Canadian Pacific where, as Louise put it, they were welcomed by "brakeman and conductor like a homecoming," with much chatter about ice-out and fishing conditions. At the lumber town of Jackman just before the line crossed the international border, horse teams and fringe-top carriages were waiting to take the family on the three-hour ride down the Canada Road, everyone growing excited as "rolling fields came into view; then house, barns, and all the rest of Parlin."[90]

While Michael led the children in fishing and hunting, Maria thought summer was the time, recalled daughter Louise, "to bring culture and learning into our lives." During the family's early Maine visits to Mike Marr's camp, they met an Andover Academy chemistry teacher, James C. Graham, and later retained him as resident tutor at Parlin every summer, presiding over lessons for the children in the schoolhouse. He was rewarded with special treatment by staff, starting with Melba toast in the morning. To make music a living presence, Mrs. Elinor Litt came up every summer with her family, playing the Steinway upright for "mornings of standby classics and evenings of song and dancing." For many years, "a gifted and charming young artist" spent the summer at Parlin, teaching William and the younger children to sketch. As the children grew older, Maria brought in a bookkeeper, Mr. Van Dusen, who gave them mandatory but dull classes in money management—with the children's response communicated when a dozen frogs hopped out of his suitcase during the train ride back to New York.[91]

At Home in the Wilderness

Isolated in Maine's vast north woods, Lake Parlin soon worked its magic on the Piel family. At the dawn of the twentieth century, the area was still remarkably pristine. Located far from the nearest settlement at Jackman, the Parlin farm was surrounded by forested hills teeming with natural life. The sun rose through mist on the lake and set into golden clouds. Perfect darkness carpeted the sky with stars or northern lights. Full moons soaked the woods with silver light. For nearly twenty years, Michael Piel's family enjoyed these long, leisurely summers immersed in seemingly unspoiled nature, sharing countless adventures that brought out the best in everyone and bound them all together.

During their first years in Maine, eldest son William kept journals for several of these golden summers, describing woodlands that appeared, at first glance, untouched, even timeless. His first journal for 1905 opens with a three-day odyssey from New York City to northern Maine, a daunting journey that demonstrated Parlin's isolation. After his June graduation from Columbia marked by all-night revels on the college quad and good-byes to "friends and Brothers" at Phi Kappa Sigma fraternity, William loaded an automobile and new guide aboard the steamship *Horatio Hall* for the overnight cruise up the New England coast to Portland, Maine. Driving out of that small city at 4:00 a.m. the next day at the brisk speed of 30 miles per hour, they were confident of covering the 192 miles to Lake Parlin by late afternoon. But a "malignant drizzle" soon turned the state's dirt roads into sand slides, mud holes, and slippery clay-covered hills. When darkness overtook them in the northern woods and the car's acetylene lamps would not light, William borrowed a kerosene lantern from Cushing's Hotel at The Forks for the final fifteen-mile push to Parlin. They arrived at 2:00 a.m. after a twenty-two hour slog.[92]

One afternoon, as William wrote in that 1905 "Sketch Book," a big buck slowly browsed his way within 80 yards of the house and "calmly viewed those of us who were sitting there. He was a splendid specimen . . . eight points in all, well developed." But with each passing season, William became ever more aware that the wilderness was evolving with a speed that made these summers seem both magical and fleeting. By 1916, "the frequency of touring cars coming and going between Portland and Quebec has made the deer shy," leaving a poignant memory of the family's first days in Parlin when traffic was light and deer herds were visible morning and evening.[93]

Though moose had once been "very plentiful" around Parlin, by the time the Piels arrived in 1900 their decline was already noticeable. Back in the 1880s, some specimens were awesome, such as the one their guide George McClintock shot with antlers so massive it was displayed at the 1893 Chicago World's Fair. A decade later, the Piels could still be awestruck when a young bull came within 120 yards of the main house. By then, however, the herd was already thinning. "Father's moose, killed (about 1905), on the side of [Mt.] Coburn," wrote William, "is one of the last good specimens brought down in the Parlin Basin." Its antlers were so magnificent that for years its head would adorn the dining room wall.[94]

Smaller fur-bearing animals had suffered a similar fate. Back in the 1850s, said their guide George McClintock, otter, weasel, fox, lynx, marten, sable, and beaver were thick in the Parlin Basin, sustaining local trappers. By 1905 their numbers were "insignificant," though still sufficient for sportsmen. Otter could be seen building their slides on Parlin's eastern shore. During regular tramps though the woods setting traps circa 1900, William also spotted mink, marten, and sable. Once bound for Holeb Pond on a long hike, he found the lowlands flooded for ten square miles by beaver dams, indicating healthy numbers. William himself saw a Canada lynx near Sapling Town in 1900. And twice on the Canada Road he caught sight of a golden mountain lion. One spring, William snared three bears, but still had to admit they were too scarce to sustain professional trappers.[95]

Back in 1885, recalled guide McClintock, "the woods were thick with partridge" and a hunter needed only a few hours shooting to get all he could eat. By the time the Piels arrived in 1900, the flocks had thinned, though Louise Piel once used a .22 automatic rifle to bag fifteen in an old birch on the Canada Road.[96] In sum, by the time the Piels arrived, northern Maine was in transition, on that magical cusp between untamed wilderness and accessible woodlands for summer people like themselves.

Golden Summers

By 1905, as William told his journal, "the story of Parlin is the story chiefly of fly-fishing—for to this sport the greater part of the holiday season is by law dedicated." The cold spring waters running down the slopes of nearby Mt. Coburn from its peak of 3,700 feet filled streams where trout spawned. As these waters flowed into the lake, the fry swam into Parlin Pond and there, said William, "they reach their greatest size" flourishing in clear rocky waters until they reach two to five pounds. "There are not many waters," he added, "that offer greater sport than does the beautiful three-mile lake of Parlin."[97]

That summer of 1905 was a memorable season for Michael Piel and his eldest sons, nestled in nature, far from the city and its relentless stress. One day, William and their guide George McClintock "fished with Father off the Upper Point," enjoying the dubious pleasure of casting without reward. They were about to move when Michael made a last "perfect cast" and two trout struck, a big one on his hand fly and the smaller on his tail fly. "Then ensued a superb fight," wrote William, "that called for every trick in the angler's game." For the next twenty minutes the struggle continued with "George Mac and I in silence admiring the art with which father kept his quarries busy. How the reel shrieked, laughed and cried; sometimes for a run of nearly fifty yards." After Michael played them out and his son brought the trout on board, the first was a solid three-pounder and the second somewhat smaller at two-and-a-half pounds.[98]

Just two weeks later, there was "a general day of rejoicing" when William's younger brother Henry made a lucky cast that landed a twenty-one inch, five-and-a-quarter pound "beauty"—a record-breaker, the biggest fish ever caught on Lake Parlin. Within minutes, the family's dining room became the site for "some mighty long and undignified whoops."[99]

The fishing was so good in the first years at Parlin that, as Louise later recalled, the family often took an early dinner to get back out on the lake after sunset. In the moonlight, each fisher headed across the calm waters for a favorite spot. Then, as Paul's song resonated across the water, others joined in. While the canoes drifted closer, "our four-part harmony improved," first for old tunes like "Sweet and Low," then for German favorites such as "Es war ein König in Thule." So magical were these evenings with "lake and sky now equally aglow and quiet all around, it was as though we ourselves were suspended in mid air and were a part of it all." Louise added, "How peaceful was our world, which only wild-life shared with us."[100]

Yet these woods also held adventures for those so inclined. As his daily chore, son Rudolf made the mail run to Jackman, riding the 26 miles roundtrip on Mohawk, a horse he bought wild at the New York auctions and broke up in Maine. "Once, Mohawk spooked," recalled Rudolf's daughter Margarita, "and went off into the woods with my father stuck on his back and met face-to-face with a moose. Mohawk reared up at the sight of the moose, spun around, and my father flattened himself against the horse's back because Mohawk was going through the piney woods with branches breaking. And the two of them made it back out to the road, losing the moose behind them."

A few years later, father Michael bought an Indian motorcycle for the mail run, and Rudolf started practicing stunts, becoming adept at spectacular leaps down the zigzag road on Owlshead Mountain. "One day coming back from Jackman with the mail," Margarita continued, "he saw a car approaching and thought, 'Hmm, I'll show 'em.' And so he did his great leap, and the car stopped as he took off down the mountain with a great cloud of dust quite pleased with himself. The next day he went for his motorcycle and found it had been sledge hammered, just totally destroyed. And his father Michael didn't say a word."[101]

As the summer of 1905 drew to a close, their mother's birthday was celebrated on August 20 with cook's formal dinner, the summer's supreme ritual. Gardener Ernst Droege, who by then had the grounds at their peak with lawns mowed and flower boxes full, now brought the glory inside to decorate the dining room with spruce cuttings that made the mounted moose and deer heads seem to peer from forest foliage. The family table, extended to seat twenty-four, "was covered in damask and set with gleaming silver and stemware" around Ernst's centerpiece, "a large horn-of-plenty, all created of flowers." The meal was the triumph of Big Anna, their Austrian cook, who offered a banquet celebrating their harvest from these woods—poached lake salmon, and a salad of fruit from the orchard, cress from the brook, and beefsteak tomatoes from Michael's greenhouse.

With dinner done and chairs pushed to the side, Mrs. Elinor Litt struck a chord on the upright Steinway piano to start the dancing. "Father and Mother," recalled Louise, "were the first to step out—and did they dance! Rhinelander, Schottish, Polka and more. How light were they on their feet! And proud, Father!" Everyone else joined for number after number until Mrs. Litt grew tired. Then the arrival of a three-tier birthday cake "was met with song and all was merriment." There was more dancing "until Father had had enough. With a simple, 'Kinder, ich geh zu Bett,' ('Children, I am going bed'), all gas lights were turned off, . . . the end of a perfect day." Over the next decade, Maria's August birthday would become what Louise called in a later memoir, "the high spot of Parlin summers."[102]

The Piel family's life at Lake Parlin in that summer of 1905 was filled with small pleasures—exploring the woods, fishing the lake, and working the fields. When the hay crop was cut in July and August, William joined the crew of hired hands for long days of raking, loading wagons, and unloading the dried hay into the barn. In August as blueberries ripened in surrounding fields, the whole family brought back brimming buckets. These busy days still left ample time for family activities: tennis, quoits, and foot races during the day; and piano concerts and choral singing before the help at night.

Over the next decade, Parlin's long summers would blur into an enduring memory, knitting strong family ties that would become critical for the brewery's survival. Over the next twenty years, the adversity of world war, Prohibition, and Depression would push their business to the brink of bankruptcy. It would require shared sacrifice and family solidarity to survive. Yet even when the brewery emerged from all those challenges and the second generation began fighting for control, so strong were their bonds that these Piel siblings would prefer to wrangle incessantly rather than sell out and go their separate ways.

4

Prologue to Prohibition

During the decade after incorporation in 1898, the Piel Bros. brewery quickly realized the promise of its million-dollar capitalization. By sticking to its first principles, the company achieved a steady increase in sales from $660,000 in 1900 to $940,000 by 1906. From the outset, the basic business credo at Piel Bros. was, said the founder's son William Piel, "independence and quality": that is, "independence as merchant brewers" and production of America's best beers. Writing in Germany's top brewing journal, Professor Adolph Cluss confirmed this excellence by reporting, after an inspection of U.S. breweries in 1910, that "the beers of the Piel Brewery received my highest praise" and were "America's finest pure malt beer." This quality was largely responsible for a 35 percent increase in sales from 1900 to 1906 since the brewery still refused, in these early years, to pay for salesmen or "modern advertising."[1]

To maintain its principle of independence, said William, their company "alone among American brewers, steadfastly refused to own, finance, subsidize or control saloons." Without this protected market, the company had to engage in constant innovation that made it an industry leader in marketing, packaging, and advertising. But Piel Bros. paid a price for its principles. Not only did this policy cost the company reliable outlets for increased production, but also denied it any real estate income when Prohibition later ended beer sales.[2] Although market forces would eventually impinge upon those principles, the brewery, as a closely held family business, could prioritize quality and independence over profit to produce an exceptional product.

In the first years of incorporation, these principles produced strong balance sheets. In 1905, the company had an impressive income of $870,000, divided between $530,000 in keg sales, $320,000 in bottle sales, and only $22,000 from its own beer garden and restaurant.[3] Two years later, income increased to $930,000, with 43 percent from direct sales to consumers in bottles or over the counter—an exceptionally high ratio in an industry still wedded to tapping kegs in tied

85

saloons.[4] If these upward trends had continued for another decade, Piels would have become one of biggest breweries in New York.

But at the very moment when growth seemed so promising, an unexpected blow threatened the firm's future. As the 1907 recession slashed profits, New York's brewers, mainly in Manhattan, decided to "shut out" this upstart competitor by banning its beer from their saloons.[5] This brewers' boycott was, moreover, just one of several serious challenges that would confront Piels in a decade roiled by war and Prohibition. At the very moment when troubles were mounting, the brothers who had built the company, Michael and Gottfried, retired from active management, leaving the firm's fate to an untested pair of Piel brothers, Michael's eldest sons William and Henry.

Brewers' Boycott

Just as Michael had prepared for a brewing career with an apprenticeship at Dortmund, so he had groomed his sons William and Henry to succeed him in the business. Not only was William the eldest among his seven healthy siblings, but he was also favored by his parents as their firstborn, their prince. In later conversations with his children, William would express his "frustration at having been dragooned out of his own . . . budding law practice into running the family business so that his immigrant father . . . could . . . shoot bear in Maine and take his yacht down the Intracoastal [waterway] for winter fishing in Florida."[6]

The actual story was both more and less dramatic. Not only was William the eldest, but he had blazed an impressive path from school to university, affirming his stature as the second generation's anointed leader. At Brooklyn's Polytechnic Preparatory, known as Poly Prep, he distinguished himself as a scholar and debater. Tall for that time at nearly six feet, of medium build, and handsome, William exuded confidence.[7] "Shall we then maintain our hold upon the Philippines?" William asked in a high school oration, circa 1900, that revealed the depth of his assimilation as an American. "We believe that this is the God-chosen nation for the wide-spreading of the arts of peace and the story of the Cross. Is it not for us to set an example and to teach lesser nations how they may justly govern themselves, not in license, but in liberty?"[8] After giving the valedictorian's address at Poly Prep's graduation in 1901, he placed ninth among Brooklyn's 620 applicants in the entrance exams for Columbia University.[9]

At Columbia, William not only earned consistent As in humanities classes, but was so omnipresent that his Class of 1905 voted him "the most likely man to succeed." Indeed, he headed every campus literary venture—founder of *Columbia Monthly*, editor-in-chief of the *Senior Yearbook*, editor-in-chief of *The Morningside* magazine, and elected editor-in-chief of the campus newspaper, *Columbia Spectator*. In all these ventures, William worked with young men of exceptional talent, notably his fellow editors at *Spectator*, Alfred Harcourt and Donald Brace who founded the publishing company Harcourt, Brace; and his designers at *Morningside*, Ely Jacques Kahn, the well-known architect, and Rockwell Kent, the renowned modernist painter.[10] In both his high school translations of *The Iliad*, rendering ancient Greek in fluent English pentameter, and his college thesis, reading Lessing's eighteenth-century drama *Miss Sara Sampson* in the original German, William demonstrated the acuity of a literary scholar or law professor.[11]

After graduating from Columbia in 1905, William entered its law school but dropped out after two years—denying him the credential for work in a New York corporate firm. Admitted to the bar in 1907, he built a modest practice from an apartment in Morningside Heights. His father Michael, facing difficulties in "comprehending the annual balance sheets," informed the brewery's general manager in February 1908 that he had engaged his son William as "my attorney in this particular," asking that he "be instructed in the making of these accounts" and be informed about "the regular meetings of the stockholders, etc." Judging from the $12,000 his father paid for such legal services in 1909, William's parents were his main clients.[12]

But it was passion, not parental authority, that made him trade the law for the family business. One night while still in law school, William attended a light opera by a Chicago troupe and was smitten by the contralto, Loretto Scott. He became "a Stage Door Johnny," hanging about after performances with flowers and poems. After William sent the singer's parents an offer of marriage, they told her: "He'll propose to you tonight and we want you to accept." As he approached her at the theater, "tears were streaming down her face" for a lost love and foregone career. But William thought the "tears were in response to the music." In 1908, William married Loretto, a devout Catholic and daughter of a distinguished Canadian family, at his West Side parish church. Nine months later they had a son, the first of six surviving children, creating the need for a more stable income.[13]

About this time Michael reportedly told son William: "You are the oldest. This family business is supporting your family. It is your duty to take it up. I want to step down."[14] In 1909, therefore, William joined Piel Bros. as assistant to the brewery's long-serving general manager Hermann Petersen, learning the business "under the watchful eye of the President's frequent visits to the plant."[15]

The prime mission of this new management team was beating that boycott of Piel products by Manhattan's brewers. In the decades before Prohibition, established breweries controlled tied saloons, through loans or direct ownership, that served as the main outlet for their beer and a powerful mechanism for choking off any competition. "The law-abiding Irishman and German who ran a saloon . . . was only working for the breweries," recalled a retired judge active in Brooklyn politics. "They had a chattel mortgage on his bar and everything he owned, and if he came out with $60 or $70 a week, he was doing well."[16] In 1900, brewer George Ehret was "the king of beer corners," owning forty-two saloons in Manhattan and holding mortgages on many more. By 1909, over 80 percent of all the saloons in New York City were somehow "indentured" to the major breweries—an oligopoly that made this shut-out of the upstart Piels' product devastatingly effective.[17]

Indeed, the boycott's impact was sudden and serious. "The notable falling off of keg sales in 1909," reported the board's minutes, "was due to the concerted action of local brewers, especially in Manhattan, which forbad 'proprietors' of places owned or financed by them to sell Piels' Beer." This "settled policy" of banning Piels cut the company's keg sales by a full third to 42,700 barrels by 1909, with much of that decline in Manhattan.[18] Not only were keg deliveries to

Table 4.1: Impact of 1907 Boycott by New York Brewers on Piel's Draught Sales (in Barrels), 1903–1914

Year	Manhattan	Brooklyn	Outside NY	Total
1903	31,424	11,410	15,741	58,575
1904	28,442	11,930	16,981	57,353
1905	26,505	13,789	18,964	59,258
1906	26,525	16,603	20,860	63,988
1907	23,697	16,736	20,094	60,527
1908	16,043	14,321	17,540	47,904
1909	13,575	13,149	15,929	42,653
1910	13,339	13,538	18,938	45,875
1911	12,611	12,711	20,792	46,114
1912	11,349	12,946	24,624	48,919
1913	11,538	14,707	27,233	53,478
1914	11,280	16,187	29,554	57,021

Source: Meeting of Board of Directors, May 26, 1915, Piel Bros. Minutes Book No. 1.

saloons collapsing, but by-the-glass sales at the beer garden and restaurant, long a mainstay of the balance sheet, fell from $24,000 in 1900 to just $11,000 in 1909—a decline likely caused by increased sales of bottled beer direct to consumers.[19]

At this delicate juncture, a collaboration between the veteran manager Petersen and his young assistant William forged a multifaceted survival strategy. Convinced that "the practices of the past were the sole yardstick of the future," Petersen allowed William's new ventures a trial only after a "strict and advance counting of the cost."[20]

Their first effort, launched in 1910, was to increase "family bottling sales," which had lower costs through local distribution and a higher profit margin. Between 1900 and 1910, bottle sales doubled to $400,000, prompting two expansions of the bottling plant. To stimulate further growth, Petersen sent customers an occasional "Announcement Ad" on postcards about seasonal brews, complemented by limited newspaper advertising. In July 1911, a quarter-page ad in *The Sun* newspaper trumpeted Piels' claim "that our Real German Lager Beer IS America's Finest Malt Beer." These modest promotional efforts yielded what William called "some worth-while sales compensation." Piels also did a small trade in bulk keg orders to "leading cafes, clubs, and hotels in the larger cities of the Middle Atlantic and New England states."[21]

This management team also tried to break out of the New York boycott by developing a new regional market in the South. During a Florida vacation in 1909, Petersen negotiated a distribution contract with William F. Seeba of Jacksonville as Piels' "Southern Agent for a term of ten years." The board awarded him a territory that extended from Washington, DC, down to Florida, and then around the Gulf of Mexico to Louisiana.[22]

For communications with agents and buyers beyond New York, the brewery now required a new Shipping Sales Department. In years past, the company's correspondence had been limited to succinct handwritten letters with "copies made by letter press, used scarcely more than once or twice a year." Now with distributors in Atlanta and Jacksonville, as well as retail outlets from Virginia to Texas, correspondence was imperative. At first, Petersen "sanctioned the rental of a typewriter, eventually the employment of a stenographer, and finally the designation of the combination, under his assistant [William], as the Shipping Sales Department." Through all this communication, the firm's Southern agents "remained steadfast till State Prohibition ultimately brought them to a halt."[23]

To recover market-share lost to the brewers' boycott in Brooklyn and Long Island, Petersen decided to launch new "specialty brews" that could compete with high-priced European imports. Back in the 1880s, the brewery laid claim to producing "Real German Lager Beers" with two basic brews, the "Dortmunder" and "Muenchener." In 1908, Piels introduced a Pilsner as "a light Special Brew" that it marketed successfully as "Pielsner." Four years later, Piels added "an extra dark (Holiday-type) brew" called "Kapuziner."[24]

This emphasis on special brews forced an historic shift in Piels' marketing strategy. In 1911, Petersen closed the beer garden after a quarter century of successful operation, presiding over a sentimental last session for the regulars. As William explained, "the 'café and hall'—the rendezvous of Brooklyn—[was] regretfully sacrificed to make room for greater lagering space needed for new special brews." By the time these facilities were demolished, rising sales of bottled beer for home consumption were supplanting beer gardens as a social destination, and Piels' by-the-glass sales had fallen to just $6,600.[25]

The sum of these initiatives soon reversed the dangerous slump in sales, raising bulk keg income by 7 percent to $427,000 in 1912. Reflecting this success, Petersen was promoted to treasurer and William replaced him as corporation secretary in 1911. A year later, in March 1912, William also joined his father and uncle on the board of directors.[26]

Midst this transition, William's younger brother Henry returned from schooling in Germany and joined the firm, soon rising to become Technical Director. Though hardworking, Henry lacked his older brother's scholarly mien, compiling a record of Cs and Ds at Andover Academy until he withdrew without graduating.[27] Three months later, he entered Columbia where his overall record was even worse. Fortunately for his future career as brewmaster, Henry's otherwise dismal transcript was brightened by Cs in freshman botany and a B in sophomore chemistry. By serving as assistant business manager of the campus newspaper where William had been editor-in-chief, and failing in classrooms where his brother had been so brilliant, Henry affirmed his future status as the brewery's second son.[28]

After Henry quit Columbia in his third year, Michael sent him to Europe for two years to train as a brewmaster. Following in his father's footsteps, Henry completed an apprenticeship in 1908 at the Dortmunder Union Brewery, winning commendation as an "educated, reliable, industrious and zealous young man" before moving to the Eisenberg Malt Factory in Erfurt. After a week of demanding thirteen-hour days on the factory floor, Henry sent his first wages to his father "to express my deepest gratitude for the opportunity you have granted me." Then, during two semesters at the Royal Bavarian Academy for Agriculture and Beer Brewing in Munich, Henry earned his formal certification as a brewmaster.

Finally, in September 1910, he completed his technical education with two months at the Alfred Jorgensen Laboratory in Copenhagen, there acquiring "a true understanding of the science of fermentation" through the study of yeast, complex microbes that leave an elusive imprint on every beer.[29] Upon his return to New York, Henry joined Piel Bros. and began rising fast to take "sole charge" of both research and brewing.[30]

Generational Transition

Only months after William and Henry joined the firm as trainees, the first generation that had spent thirty years building the brewery began fading from active leadership. After twenty-three years of tireless labors as general manager, Hermann Petersen began complaining of "overwork" and decided to recuperate with a month-long trip to Europe. Just a day out of New York aboard the *S.S. Cincinnati* in September 1912, he died of apoplexy at age 51. Reflecting his standing in both company and community, Petersen's funeral at his East New York home was attended by both Piel brothers, "large delegations" of company workers, and the pillars of local German American society—four German singing societies, the Bushwick *Turn Verein* athletic club, and the Manhattan Plattdeutsche cultural group, *Gehrder Freeundschafts Bund*.[31] Three months later, William succeeded Petersen as both general manager and secretary-treasurer, thereby becoming the brewery's chief operating officer.[32]

Less than three years after Petersen's passing, Michael Piel died suddenly, in June 1915, of heart disease at his Maine summer home. His death at the age of 66 was apparently unexpected. When *The Sun* newspaper telephoned his brother's Riverside Drive apartment on a Saturday night with the news, Gottfried Piel said that he "did not know before then that his brother was in a serious condition."[33]

A Maine probate court appraised Michael's estate at $334,000—including brewery stocks ($130,000), four mortgage loans ($110,400), the Lake Parlin estate ($15,200), a Stradivarius violin ($4,800), an ocean-going yacht ($4,500), a 1902 Mercedes sedan ($200), and a mounted moose head ($50).[34] In assessing the estate for New York's transfer tax, his eldest son and executor William claimed all these assets were, by virtue of Michael's Maine residence, tax free.[35] His wife Maria was sole owner of the family's West 72nd Street townhouse, so this too was exempt.[36] Since Maine had no inheritance tax and federal taxation was a year away, Michael Piel's entire estate passed tax-free to his heirs.[37] Though claiming

Maine residence to avoid New York's death duties, he was buried in Lot No. 17313 at Brooklyn's famed Green-Wood Cemetery on June 16.[38]

With Michael's estate uncontested and untaxed, his wealth passed intact to his widow Maria. Speaking in German before three witnesses, Michael had executed his will at Lake Parlin in 1908, leaving everything "unto my beloved wife, Maria Piel, all my property—real, personal, and mixed—wherever the same may be situated."[39] Three months after his death, Maria, now owner of half the brewery's stock, was elected to replace her husband as vice-president and director—positions she would use solely to support her son William as general manager.[40]

Though Gottfried continued to chair the board, he was now absorbed in other investments, leaving the brewery's management to his two nephews. In 1911, he founded the G. Piel Company for "manufacturing certain machinery and automobile accessories at No. 363 Rider Avenue in the Borough of Bronx."[41] After moving to a new factory in Long Island City, the business produced the brass "Long Horn" and an adjustable "muffler cut out" for greater speed.[42] Within a few years, however, this investment proved ill-advised, producing a sharp reversal in Gottfried's fortunes.[43] Midst accumulating difficulties and rising debts, he quit the Piel Bros. board in December 1921, following Maria who had resigned that January. With his mother's retirement, Henry now joined his older brother as a director.[44]

By the time this generational transition was done, William was managing external affairs such as marketing, while Henry was supervising internal operations, brewing and product development. Though the two brothers were, by 1914, de facto partners in shaping the firm's future, the new corporate hierarchy was set that March when the board raised William's annual salary to $10,000 while setting Henry's at $5,000.[45]

Whatever regrets William may have had about leaving the law, he prospered as heir-apparent at the brewery. With his executive salary, William and Loretto built their first home in Woodmere, Long Island, midst open fields that in those days stretched all the way to the Atlantic. Just a year after Michael's death, his widow Maria entrusted her finances to William under a broad power of attorney. In addition to hosting her regularly at their Woodmere home, wife Loretto regarded Maria "as being in her custody" and "got her back as a practicing Catholic," a faith that had lapsed during her marriage to Michael who was resolutely anti-religious.[46] By ministering to his mother's spiritual and financial needs, William was assured of her unwavering backing at the brewery.

Almost from the moment brothers William and Henry joined the firm, the brewers' boycott and a spreading prohibition would prove a harsh test of the family's second generation. Just as founding brothers Gottfried and Michael struggled to establish the brewery in Brooklyn's competitive beer market during the 1880s, so Michael's eldest sons would fight to preserve the family firm during long years of Prohibition that, starting in 1919, would soon bankrupt most of the nation's breweries.[47]

New Sales Strategies

This new generation's first task was to strengthen Southern markets and build the specialty brews that Petersen had developed in the months before his death. Between 1912 and 1914, the sum of their efforts raised the brewery's keg revenue by a solid 20 percent. Bulk sales in Manhattan, the Bronx, and New Jersey had continued to slide from $113,000 in 1910 to $97,000 by 1914. But "shipping sales," largely to new Southern markets, surged from $170,000 to $275,000, producing over half the company's income.[48] Despite all the damage from the brewers' boycott, this Southern strategy raised the value of Piels' assets from $907,000 in 1910 to $1,300,000 by 1916.[49]

In retrospect, sheer coincidence once again contributed to this success. Just as the opening of the Brooklyn Bridge in 1883 had allowed the new Piel Bros. brewery access to Manhattan, so completion of a massive engineering effort now opened rail connections for shipping to the South. In 1910, the Pennsylvania Railroad finished a monumental $160 million project that bored tunnels under the Hudson River, across midtown Manhattan to Pennsylvania Station, and then beneath the East River to Queens—allowing Brooklyn its first direct access to the nation's rail network. Within a year, the Long Island Rail Road (LIRR) had carried 6 million riders into Penn Station. To incorporate Brooklyn more directly into its network, the Pennsylvania Railroad also built a barge terminal in Greenville, New Jersey, that sent boxcars across New York harbor to a freight yard at East New York, just blocks from the Piel brewery. When the massive Hell Gate Bridge opened in 1916, linking Queens to New England's railroads, Brooklyn breweries gained ready access to yet another regional market.[50]

While developing its Southern distribution, Piels also tried to recapture some of the New York keg market by publicizing its new "special brews." Nothing could break the brewers' boycott in Manhattan, but these new brews buoyed sales in Brooklyn and Long Island. After the brewers' "shut-out" drove Piels' Brooklyn sales down from 16,700 barrels in 1907 to just 12,700 five years later, these new beers were instrumental in bringing the borough's deliveries back up to a healthy 16,200 barrels by 1914.[51]

Produced with the best European hops, the Piel specialty beers—the Dortmunder, Pielsner, and Kapuziner—were, in William's words, "of finest quality." To market these brands, the brewery found outlets in "all of the highest class of hotel, club, and restaurant trade . . . largely independent of local brewers." Looking back on this difficult period, William attributed his gains to the inauguration of "a real sales department" with agents on commission.[52]

To promote these specialty beers in the face of the Manhattan boycott, Piels also launched its first major advertising campaign in the city press. At the start of the 1913 summer season, Piels bought space in the high-circulation *Evening Telegram* announcing, in lean text and large graphics, "The Four Piel Brews" are "America's Finest Pure Malt Beer." To emphasize their exceptional quality, the

4.1. Label for Piel's Lager Beer, circa 1917: real beer at 3.9 percent alcohol, pre-Prohibition.

copy claimed that the firm used "the choicest Saazer hops and finest barley-malt purchasable."[53]

Then from January to July of 1914, Piels ran quarter-page ads in the *Evening Telegram* striking for their succinct text, modernist, sans-serif font, and stylized graphics. The first in this pioneering ad campaign celebrated the Dortmunder label as a perfect blend of "exquisite Barley Malt and Saazer Hops" that made it "an ideal brew for the family table." Physicians, said later ads, recommended Piels' Kapuziner-Braeu "as superior to the American-type lager and 'malt-extracts' . . . because of its finer digestive qualities."[54]

Advent of War

The sudden outbreak of the Great War cut Europe's beer exports to America, creating a market opportunity for quality domestic brewers. As armies were on the march across Europe in August 1914, Piels placed a quarter-page advertisement in the *Evening Telegram* headlined, "Foreign Beers Have Ceased to Be Imported and a Want Has Been Created that Only Our Brews Can Satisfy." Piels offered the "lovers of imported Pilsener, Dortmunder, Muenchener and special German dark beers, our brews of the same types, confident that our . . . Brews . . . will prove indistinguishable from the finest imported."[55] Four weeks later, Piels advertised "two new brews . . . , a *Wuerzburger* and a *Muenchener Speciell-Bräu*," which "by reason of the continental wars, are now particularly opportune."[56]

The marketing campaign was an immediate success. "The Pilsener sales have more than doubled," Henry wrote his wife that August, "and I am sure it will *treble* this present fine output." Determined to maintain quality midst the surging demand, Henry had been forced to suspend supplies to their Bottling Department for the rest of the season "so that all the Pilsener is perfect before it leaves the brewery instead of rushing it through." Using techniques learned in Germany, he was careful to preserve the current yeast in stock, and had designed a propagation apparatus to replace German imports—a process that was soon copied by a leading Canadian brewer "as a model of perfect conception and assembly."[57]

In May 1915, William won the board's support for his strategy of "campaigning for local 'imported beer trade,'" using the firm's premium Specialty Brews to fill this wartime void in the New York market.[58] Two years later when the United States entered the war, Piels' Sales Department "immediately capitalized" on the market opportunity by opening wholesale distributorships for its specialty brews in New York City, Philadelphia, Pittsburgh, Detroit, Cleveland, Baltimore, and San Francisco. Through these carload distributors, Piels beer was now being sold from Boston to San Francisco in twenty-two cities nationwide. Moreover, the company's salesmen secured "important retail house accounts" that put Piels on tap in the country's leading hotels, from the Copley-Plaza in Boston to the St. Francis in San Francisco. Although its higher price limited volume, Piels beer had thus become, for the first time, "a national product in sales."[59]

Through its distribution in the South, the heart of the temperance movement, Piels also gained a timely warning about the seriousness of the threat—allowing this small company to play a leading role in shaping the brewing industry's response. In November 1914, William Piel told his board that the firm's trusted Atlanta agent, Mr. Oppenheim, had recently visited the plant to explain his "conviction that the entire South would soon be 'dry.' " After delivering this disturbing forecast, the visitor asked whether the brewery could produce a product to "replace the splendid beer business he had been doing in Georgia."[60]

This gloomy prediction echoed William's own experience with a welter of state and local bans on alcohol. As the brewery's general manager, he had found himself "continually beset by the loss of valuable accounts in one field that required instant and vigorous efforts to recapture them in a new territory."[61] Thus "impressed with continual gains of the Prohibition Movement," William tried, in November 1914, to warn his industry's leading trade group, the U.S. Brewers' Association (USBA), about the threat of federal legislation. Other brewers actually doubted the possibility, but William felt a "presentment of a 'bone-dry nation' in five years"—a prediction realized four years and eleven months later when Congress passed the Volstead Act banning all alcohol sales in October 1919.[62]

For William and his Southern agents, Seeba and Oppenheim, the main chance of survival, circa 1914, lay in developing a "near beer" acceptable, in dry states, with an alcoholic content "under ½ of 1% by volume." Although a literature search found very few references to such a product, William told the Piel's board in November that development of such a drink might "forearm the plant against the possibility of nation-wide Prohibition." After a "prolonged discussion," the board agreed that "the Technical Director institute research work looking to the production of a Beer . . . at Prohibition's Southern standard of less than ½ of 1% of Alcohol by Volume."[63]

For the next four years, the company's laboratory, under its technical director Henry Piel, pursued development of a satisfying low-alcohol "near beer."

Since joining the firm in 1911, Henry had shown his capacity for innovation by developing the special brews, supervising manufacture of "the highest type of malt yet produced in the U.S.," and building a "model" pure yeast culture station to replace German imports. For months following their decision to develop a near beer, William recalled, "the daily luncheon-hour in the Bier-Stube was solely concerned with this topic—with theory at first, and with new ideas, suggestions and formulae to correct the errors in the samples." By mid-1916, the search for a proper head "succeeded far too well," producing a batch of "foam too thick to cap the glass" that erupted from city sewers to cover the intersection of Liberty and Georgia avenues with "a solid foot-deep blanket of white creamy snow-like layer."[64]

Testifying to its technical acumen, however, the lab soon invented a "chill proofing" technique for near beer that had eluded European researchers for a decade. To assist Henry in solving some remaining problems, the company retained a consulting chemist, Dr. Robert C. Schupphaus, and together they soon refined the process sufficiently to apply for a U.S. patent.[65]

Over a period of two years, November 1914 to March 1917, Henry Piel brewed fifty-one different beverages as he struggled to produce just one with the right mix of low alcohol, fresh taste, and a beer-like appearance. He was trying for "a potable, delightful 'near beer,' wholesome and refreshing, partaking of the character of real beer, while in fact a true 'soft drink.' " Not only were the technical problems challenging, but the temperance restrictions were daunting. Where a particular beverage, William explained, "might or might not be sold was a serious question hampered . . . by requirements as to whether made from malt or not . . . ; as to style and shape of bottles; as to connotation of name—a taboo against a beer-like name being in force in some states."[66] After two years' work, the new beverage seemed ready for a field test in Virginia. But Piels suddenly found their low-alcohol malt product violated the state's ban on "all malt products," forcing rapid development of "samples of the new beverage in its non-malt form."[67]

The relentless spread of temperance added urgency to this quest. At the company's annual meeting in March 1917, William advised stockholders that profits for the preceding year fell markedly through the "effects of Prohibition," as states and municipalities were "drying up" via local initiatives that banned alcohol. The solution, he suggested, lay in perfecting the firm's new cereals-based soft drink as a product distinct from the "fruit drinks and syrups" that were now flooding the market. Thus, he was happy to report that Henry had finally produced a "cereal drink that also had the unique characteristic of not being a Malt Beverage according to . . . the U.S. Dept. of Agriculture" and would also "contain not more than ½ of 1 percent of Alcohol"—the very attributes needed to pass muster in most dry states. After the board conducted a tasting, William won unanimous approval to test market the product in the heart of the prohibition movement: Norfolk and Richmond, Virginia. If successful there, then Piels would start sales "thruout prohibition states along the Atlantic seaboard." Indicating the severity of the situation, stockholders also agreed that, because of "the expense involved in marketing a new product," no salaries would be paid to Gottfried and Maria Piel, president and vice-president, for the year 1917.[68]

A month later, the president convened a special meeting of the board to announce that their new near beer would be sold under the trade name "Kovar." Since Virginia disapproved of anything that looked like beer and the product's market would be "chiefly confined to the South," the firm hired the J. Walter Thompson advertising agency to create a new Kovar logo for a special bottle designed by William himself. Unfortunately, just six weeks earlier the Anheuser-Busch brewery out in St. Louis had begun shipping a competing near beer called "Bevo" into Piels' regional markets. After spending $10 million to build the world's biggest bottling plant for its new label, Busch would, within a year, be shipping 5 million cases nationwide, earning $6 million in profits. But those who sampled Bevo at the Piels' Bier-Stube pronounced it "inferior in quality" to the firm's own Kovar, reviving the family's confidence in their new venture. Meanwhile, the company's consulting chemist, Dr. Schupphaus, had met with Virginia's Commissioner of Prohibition who concurred that Kovar complied with state law. Consequently, the brewery planned a first shipment to its Norfolk agent on April 20, which, the board directed, "shall be experimental."[69]

Right on schedule, Piels dispatched the first carload of Kovar to Norfolk, backed by liberal newspaper advertising. "Lo and behold!" William Piel recalled, "Kovar caught on!!" By the end of the year, Piels concluded that "it was safe to go ahead" with an aggressive launch of their near beer.[70] Writing his mother in July 1917, William proclaimed: "Henry did his work! The public has continued to applaud his product, now it is up to me to reach even further."[71]

Within months, this cautious strategy of meeting the strictest prohibitionist standards was vindicated. In May 1918, two of the firm's New Hampshire retailers were arrested "on the charge of selling a malt, brewed and fermented beverage, namely Kovar." To defend these distributors, Piels sent its expert witness Dr. Schupphaus, a PhD in chemistry from Germany's Gottingen University. After nine pages of impressively technical razzle-dazzle, Dr. Schupphaus concluded: "Kovar is, therefore, a typical soft drink." Other retailers selling root beer and sarsaparilla were convicted. But the two Kovar agents were acquitted, producing a flood of new orders from New Hampshire.[72]

That same month, the district attorney of Allegheny County, Pennsylvania, advised Piels that Kovar "was permitted only to and by licensed dealers" under the state's Brooks Law and was thus effectively prohibited. After reviewing a detailed memo from Dr. Schupphaus, the district attorney reversed himself, now "satisfied that the Kovar was not a Vinous, Spiritous, Malt or Brewed Liquor, nor an admixture thereof" and was thus exempt from local licensing requirements. "I congratulate you on this victory," said the company's Pittsburgh lawyer, "as it places your drink in a rather unique class."[73] Clearly, the prohibitionists were riding the tide of history, and only the most rigorous rebuttal would spare near beer from their crusade.

Marketing the New Product

To reap profit from its new product, Piels launched a major marketing campaign beyond anything it had ever attempted. Competition was already fierce. Anheuser-Busch had already built the world's largest bottling plant for near beer and was, by the end of 1918, shipping 5 million cases of its Bevo brand annually—a success that inspired imitation by the other big brewers, Pabst and Miller.[74] To compete, Piels expanded its office building and hired "a regular force of several stenographers" to handle the "avalanche of orders, inquiries, requests for information, advertising, etc." Simultaneously, William organized Kovar's marketing "with modern sales practice on the 'Jobber-Retailer-Consumer' system"—that is, shipping to regional brokers who then stocked their local retailers. The firm also set the new product's pricing on "a real profit calculation" that took account of inflation.[75] By the end of 1918, the success of this near beer in dry states, combined with strong wartime real beer sales elsewhere, would produce a record income of one million dollars—a 30 percent increase over the previous year and "the highest point yet reached in the company's history."[76]

Kovar was, in fact, one of just nine alternative beverages that Piels was developing to survive these difficult times. In March 1916, William Piel reported that production of a "Service Brew," with 1.75 percent alcohol for the U.S. Army and Navy, had produced surprisingly strong sales throughout 1915 "in view of the inroads of Prohibition." With its red, white, and blue label, the brew enjoyed "a good sale" at military bases along the Atlantic seaboard, in the Canal Zone, and even in the Philippines.[77]

By 1918, the brewery had developed seven soft drinks in addition to the original Kovar. That November, William won the board's support for the manufacture of a cider beverage to be sold as "Apple Kovar" in both bottles and kegs. Since the brewery was suited to the manufacture of such a product, William felt that "in 10-oz. and 12-oz. bottles, a carbonated apple juice of high quality might be marketed at popular prices to realize a good profit," while the "café, hotel and saloon trade" might accept kegs of clear or sparkling cider.[78]

To launch its new Kovar beverage into markets from Maine to the Mississippi, Piels relied upon its advertising contract with J. Walter Thompson, which handled national brands such as Yuban Coffee and Flying A Gasoline. In 1918–19, the agency placed newspaper advertisements "addressed to the average man" that would run a half-page to "start off each wholesale distributor" and then "be followed up by frequent smaller ads." One of these notices showed a doctor holding up a glass to the approving gaze of mother and child with copy promoting eight soft drinks—including, Piels' Kovar with "the delicious tang of real Salzer hops" and Piel Ale, a "temperance beer for 'wet' territories." Although Kovar's advertising costs rose from $9,400 in 1917 to $26,900 in 1919, J. Walter Thompson complained that Piels' budget was "niggardly" and proposed a "huge campaign to be paid for . . . by an issue to them of [Piels'] Preferred Stock." Since the plant could not keep up with current orders for Kovar, which surged from $49,000 in 1917 to $680,000 two years later, Piels rejected this offer.[79]

The first full year of Kovar sales in 1918 showed the brewery's shift to soft drinks was working. That November, William reported Piels' real beer sales "had suffered through general falling off of the entire industry" as localized prohibition spread from state to state, but this loss had "been practically made up by the sales of Kovar."[80] Indeed, near beer sales reached $374,000, representing 37 percent of revenue and pushing the firm's gross above that million-dollar mark. The next year, 1919, Kovar sales doubled to $777,000, accounting for 42 percent of the firm's income and compensating for the loss of real beer sales after wartime prohibition started that July. Through the "struggle of our Technical Director" Henry Piel to create this near beer, said William, the brewery had won a reprieve from the looming death sentence brought by Prohibition.[81]

Overcoming Obstacles

A sales campaign that could move a million dollars woth of Kovar had to overcome major marketing obstacles. As a soft drink, Kovar was a "short season business" with the four summer months accounting for up to 70 percent of sales. In 1919, for example, drum shipments shot upward from just 12 in January to 9,400 in June. During the frantic summer season, the plant was usually 50 to 200 carloads behind on orders, with wholesalers "using every means to assure their supply," whether by securing their own rail cars or placing standing orders. At the height of summer, there was "an almost hourly exchange of wires to explain 'Why your order has not been shipped as yet'; new applicants begging for distributorships; and the long and growing list of unfulfilled orders." Even though the brewery shipped 183 rail cars in just 26 working days, it was still over 100 cars behind for Pennsylvania alone by June 1919. Had the brewery been able to fulfill all these orders, sales for the season would have risen by 40 percent.[82]

The labor demands of this new enterprise were formidable, with reliable workers needed for the rapid-fire production, packaging, and shipping during this short season. To avoid costly labor disputes, New York's brewers now negotiated with the unions in 1914, agreeing to raise daily wages by a dollar, reduce the work day by an hour, and pay overtime—concessions that cost Piels $10,000 yearly.[83] At the start of Kovar's first full selling season in May 1918, the brewery had 188 employees, including 59 native-born Americans and the balance immigrants, largely German or Austrian.[84]

Wartime shipping shortages complicated the difficulties in satisfying this fickle market. In 1918, Piels faced hefty increases in Southern freight rates and competition from local breweries marketing low-cost near beer, cutting the number of Southern carload buyers from 48 in 1918 to 41 a year later. To compensate for this loss, Piels increased its distributors in Middle Atlantic and New England states from 42 to 105.[85]

This surge in demand also forced Piels to make some difficult decisions about packaging. To comply with state bans on the "beer bottle" and reduce the cost for special shapes, the brewery promoted, in March 1918, "Draught Kovar" in kegs tapped by a specially manufactured "Kovar Drawing Outfit" with wooden case and steel tap. Mindful of the adage "meet the demand or lose the business," Piels combined bulk keg distribution with shipment of Kovar bottles in wooden drums, thereby raising total output from 456 carloads in 1918 to 631 a year later.[86]

Advising the Brewing Industry

While Henry Piel struggled to produce a viable near beer, his brother William was warning the nation's brewing industry about the threat from temperance. With his hard-won experience of selling real beer in the dry South, William played an outsized role in the industry's struggle to forge an effective political response to prohibition. In June 1914, long before most brewers admitted a problem, Piels ran an advertisement in the *Evening Telegram* to proclaim, "One Great National Question Is the Temperance Question." Beneath the firm's Special Brew logos, its copy asserted: "Entire populations in Germany are temperate, law-abiding, prosperous, because they only drink the light, natural beer."[87]

Although at first ignored, William gained a more attentive audience among the leaders of the U.S. Brewers' Association (USBA) in 1915 as the federal government moved toward full prohibition.[88] For decades, the brewers had been able to deflect the ineffectual efforts of the Women's Christian Temperance Union (WCTU). But a new group founded in 1893, the Anti-Saloon League (ASL), was waging a determined, single-issue lobbying campaign against the saloon as social vice, winning alcohol bans from state legislatures across the South and West. With generous funding from John D. Rockefeller, 500 fulltime employees, and an unwavering focus on a single issue, the ASL was the progenitor of the modern American lobbying organization.[89] By 1910, this extraordinary group had won total prohibition in nine states and the "local option" for temperance in twenty-nine more.[90]

The brewing industry fought back. At the annual USBA meeting in October 1913, companies "on the firing line" shared war stories from battles against the Anti-Saloon League. In California, brewers had defeated a "local option" vote for temperance in major cities. But they now faced an upcoming statewide prohibition amendment backed by William Jennings Bryan and the Reverend Billy Sunday, both famed for their ability to inspire mass movements. Though the "wets" sometimes managed to slow the temperance juggernaut, many industry leaders now realized that unless they managed "to clean up the conditions in the saloons, the saloon is going."[91]

The brewers found their panacea in the person of publicist Percy Andreae. With lavish funding from a two-cent surcharge per barrel on USBA members, he mounted a massive public relations campaign through the Association of Foreign Language Newspapers and the German American Alliance. Starting in 1913, the brewing industry provided the Alliance, the country's largest ethnic association, with "heavy subsidies" for its anti-prohibition campaign. By distributing publicity to 800 newspapers with 16 million readers nationwide, Andreae's organization actually defeated a prohibition referendum in Ohio, the Saloon League's birthplace and bastion.[92]

While USBA devoted its vast corporate assets to narrow media manipulation, the ASL supported broad social reforms such as income tax (an alternative to alcohol tax) and women's suffrage (to gain temperance votes). With the start of the Great War in mid-1914, the League's long-term strategy, fueled by rising anti-German sentiment, revitalized the temperance campaign. That December, crusading congressman Richmond Hobson introduced a prohibition amendment that won a slender House majority—far from the two-thirds needed for approval but far more votes than anyone expected. A few weeks later, publicist Percy Andreae walked into a USBA meeting in Chicago to find the brewers angry over their misspent half-million dollars and walked out "stripped of his authority."[93]

At this critical juncture in the national debate, William's own research indicated that the saloon was their industry's Achilles' heel. At a meeting of brewers and distillers at Baltimore in March 1915, the USBA's secretary summarized young Piel's report delineating the saloon's derelictions: "Selling in prohibited hours, gambling, . . . brewers financing ignorant foreigners who are not citizens, . . . brewery controlled saloons, cabarets, Sunday selling." Seconding that view, John A. Cervenka of Chicago's Pilsen Brewing Company "said that his investigations had led to the same conclusions, . . . particularly the need of limitation of the number of saloons"; while Hugo A. Koehler of American Brewing Company in St. Louis "said his questionnaire led to the same results."[94]

A month later, a committee composed of Piel, Cervenka, Koehler, and two others circulated a memorandum, approved by the USBA's executive, to breweries nationwide explaining "why the saloon is so frequently and generally discredited." They argued for local laws that would bar brewers from "financial assistance to saloon-keepers." In effect, the brewers were recommending an end to their own "tied saloon." Through this skillful lobbying, William had maneuvered the brewing industry into condemning the very institution that was boycotting his own beer in the Manhattan market.[95]

Instead of their industry's quixotic efforts to stop the unstoppable prohibition crusade, Piels solicited a comprehensive review of state temperance laws by one of New York's "most prominent" law firms, Stetson, Jennings & Russell. Their study found state bans on alcohol were spreading steadily across the country—starting in 1910 (Oklahoma), gaining momentum in 1913–14 (Mississippi, Tennessee, West Virginia), and surging from 1915 to 1917 (Alabama, Indiana, Georgia, Nebraska, Oregon, South Carolina, Utah, Virginia, Washington).[96] Within a few months, moreover, the U.S. declaration of war on Germany would suddenly elevate this temperance crusade to the federal level.

4.2. Piel estate at Lake Parlin, Maine, beneath Mt. Coburn, from *Town & Country Magazine*, August 10, 1920.

Summer of 1915

Despite all the difficulties of this prewar decade, nothing could disrupt the Piels' annual migration to northern Maine, soothing the stress of city living and strengthening family ties. Even so, when William resumed his "Parlinad" journal after a ten-year hiatus, it was now a different family that gathered for the summer of 1915. William was now married with four children. Henry and wife Marie had one child. The other seven siblings were grown and, for the most part, away at college. In a jarring reminder of their fleeting time together, this was also the summer their father Michael died unexpectedly at Parlin, young for such a vigorous sportsman.

Despite all these changes, Parlin was still the place that brought out their best and bound them together. Isolated in these north woods, the siblings, now

ranging in ages from 13 to 32, were drawn from their separate city lives for two months of intense interaction—fishing, boating, evening strolls, family picnics, swimming hijinks, and contests over croquet, lawn bowls, and tennis. During the difficult years of Prohibition and Depression, the family would descend into infighting over the brewery marked by intrigues and bitterness that persisted for decades, unto death and beyond. Yet the siblings remained somehow bound together by these shared summers, preferring to fight over the family business rather than divide its assets and move on.

Though most of the Piel siblings were still in their teens and twenties, well-defined family roles begin to emerge from the pages of William's journal. As heir to his father's sporting skills and corporate authority, William presided over family affairs with quiet authority. Paul was the charming artist and aesthete. Rudolf was taciturn, among yet apart. Louise was the beloved beauty, gracing every occasion with her presence. Agnes seemed competitive and critical, coping with marginalization by obsessive attractions. Otto was becoming less capable of functioning in normal society.

In the decade since William's last journal entry in 1905, Parlin had grown into a self-sustaining summer community. At the season's close in 1915, William counted forty-two people at this clearing in the Maine woods—including, the presiding matriarch Maria, her two unmarried daughters (Agnes and Louise), five unmarried sons (Paul, Rudolf, Roland, Oswald, and Otto), Henry's wife with baby, and five guests (including Agnes's chum Margarita Schile, Louise's confidante Clara Wittemann, and family friend Bernard Schreiner).[97]

To feed, clothe, and entertain this family circle required twenty servants, with a monthly payroll of $2,000. Inside the big house, the nine female staff included chief cook Anna, Marie Exner the laundress, and Selma de Francesco, "waitress." To these we must add Dr. Armin St. George, the family physician, who, said William, "paid us a flying visit on July 13th to look over the babies, made some cuts of our help, and generally ascertain that we were in good health." Outdoor staff was composed of the family's hunting guide George McClintock, the "care-taker of the Grace Pond Camp" Robert Starke, four farm hands, and Gottfried Shutz "chauffeur, electrician and plumber and mender of all our mechanical difficulties."[98]

After fifteen seasons of improvements, the Piel estate now showed a pleasing balance of renovated wooden buildings surrounded by 80 manicured acres of field, garden, and bower, all joined by curving footpaths. In the big house, the front rooms were, through "Paul's sense of beauty," being converted into "a single large living room, with fire-place, wall book-case, colonial stairway, and generous entrance." Workmen were transforming the old toilet building into Paul's sculpture studio featuring a wide porch, an "attractive fire place," and a northern skylight. Behind the main house, younger brother Rudolf was building the new tennis courts systematically—ground excavated to a depth of three feet by horse shovel and a six-inch topping of sand-clay to "offer a perfect, quickly absorbing surface, permitting easy care, and assuring a fast game."[99]

At a "family council" that summer to manage the estate after father Michael's passing, the siblings agreed the "landscaping of the immediate grounds about the house be simplified and given unity." To finalize these plans, William drew a detailed map showing the main house surrounded by cleared grounds with tennis, lawn bowls, croquet, stables, and hayfields.[100] After spending $62,000 to build or rebuild thirty-one buildings on the property since 1900, they were on the cusp of completing these renovations by adding a windmill next season.[101]

Soon after his arrival that summer, William had toured the grounds, noting signs the estate was indeed a working farm. The milk cows, horses, and ponies in the stable were healthy. The solid new sheepfold housed a flock of twenty-five, including ram, ewes, and fifteen lambs. Inside the barn, their guide and foreman George McClintock was putting in a record crop of forty hay loads. Nearby, the poultry plant held a chicken coop, turkey house, and winter scratching yard, with 200 layers and 300 more ducks and broilers. William's rambles allowed a census of the animal population: two ponies, four plow horses, three milk cows, four pigs, twenty-five sheep, two turkeys, 500 chickens, a flock of ducks, and a gaggle of geese.[102]

Out on the lake, fishing still had its rewards. In late July, William and guide George paddled to the head of the pond. While casting from the bow into a chop without success, William and George puffed away on Havana cigars, wondering why the fish would not strike as "the last rays of the sun were gilding the white clouds . . . and brightening up the lake."[103] Midst this futile casting, they "found it a pleasure to watch Rudolf who was out in his racing shell," sculling back and forth to better his chances on the Columbia crew. As William grew drowsy, the reel suddenly shrieked and a big one made a long dash, dragging the line out another hundred feet. Arms aching, William struggled to reel him back, shifting the trout's course toward the bow where George finally netted him—nineteen inches long and nearly three pounds. After another successful strike of a three-pounder, they beached the boat at the head of the lake and "walked home under a clearing sky, in which the waxing moon grew brighter."[104]

While William and Henry fished, Paul was back home struggling with big ideas. When Jackman's parish priest, Fr. Joseph Forest, arrived at Parlin with a visitor, Monsignor Martini of Montreal's Notre Dame Cathedral, Paul, just back from studying sculpture in Italy, entertained these guests with reflections on "the individualistic tendencies of today as contrasted with the rational expression of the Greeks and the religious expression of the Renaissance."[105]

The daily routine was frequently broken by family outings. On one such adventure, all the unmarried siblings and their guests crowded into the family's Packard touring car to drive up the Canada Road for an overnight outing at a nearby lake, Heald Pond. That night, according to a journal entry by Agnes Piel, then 18 and college-bound, everyone gathered round a big stone fireplace in the main cottage while Paul "read us a villainous story by Kipling." Elder brother Henry, a passionate partisan for Germany in the Great War, "voiced his usual charitable desire that a pest sweep over England and kill man, woman, and child." As the group broke up about 10:00 p.m., Paul wound up sleeping on a couch in the girls' cottage, tossing endlessly and prompting Agnes to wonder, with transparent jealousy, "were his restless slumbers due to a certain dark haired damsel whose nose is so small that her breath whistles and growls thru it?"[106]

As usual, Agnes was holding herself apart and above. Or as her sister Louise put it, Agnes was "the non-conformist not always ready to join the general activities of the moment," often suffering "sheer boredom and rebellion at our silly pleasures." One morning a few years earlier, Agnes had appeared at breakfast dressed like Robin Hood—linen tunic boldly exposing her legs, knotted rope holding a knife at her waist—to announce she was taking a hike. She then disappeared into the woods. By evening, menfolk were scouring the trails, firing rounds into the silent forest until mother Maria cranked the telephone to the next camp fifteen miles away. "Yes, Mrs. Piel, "a voice on the line answered, "she is here and what a stir she is making among the guests in the dining room!"[107]

Two days after that outing to Heald Pond, the family marked the end of the 1915 season with a daylong picnic. With "fair South wind to ease the load," the family paddled down the lake to assemble on the slopes of a spruce-covered hill before an "open fireplace facing the pond and overlooking the last cove." As calls for lunch were shouted out, Louise and friend Edna Tompkins emerged from the lake "in swimming tights [that] made a pretty picture." While George McClintock stoked the fire, mother Maria "was the presiding genius, whose 'country stove' bounties appeased the 'inner man.' "

In the "lazy hour after lunch" ever-loquacious Paul discoursed on the "Idylls of Theocritus," translating verses from ancient Greek that described the "chatter of the women of Syracuse" and Europa riding "over the sea to Cyprus." Food digested and reflections done, "Louise summoned us to a swim." Everyone joined in and "the swim was perfect." Packing up, they returned home midst "the last glory of a sunset for this summer." Everyone hailed this as a "successful family picnic, a forerunner to many more in the future."[108]

Summer of 1916

Just a year later when the Piels again assembled at Lake Parlin, change swam just beneath the surface calm. Though none realized it at the time, this would be their generation's last summer together up in Maine.

As his auto chugged along the Canada Road after the long trip from New York, William's "mind was atingle with memory" that sharpened anticipation. "Fifteen summers spent in this retreat from care and convention flashed before me as in a dream," he told his journal, "the rod, the gun, a chain of traps, the canoe, . . . a stalk after big game: these were the objects that flashed in a kaleidoscope of treasured recollections."[109]

Entering the Parlin basin, William felt "the thrill of the flat land of green, the cozy buildings set against harmonious spruce, the hills rising round . . . [that] shut Parlin off from the work-a-day world." On the approach, William pulled over. "As a precaution, remembering the children's plague in the city," he wrote, "I had stripped at Six-Mile Spring, washed in its icy clear water, and donned knickers, long stockings, a flannel shirt, and Maine boots."[110]

The nation's first major polio outbreak was sweeping America that summer leaving 27,000 children paralyzed nationwide. New York was the epicenter of the epidemic, with 9,000 cases and 2,000 deaths. Thousands were fleeing the city to

4.3. Main house at Parlin Pond Inn, Maine, circa 1930.

nearby mountain resorts. But armed vigilantes, fearing contagion, turned back many of these urban refugees.[111]

As the deadly epidemic infected the city that summer, Henry's wife Marie arrived at Parlin with their two-year-old daughter Marie-Luise to begin, said William, "what is doubtlessly one of the most entrancing quarantines that any family ever made." Following public health guidelines, mother Maria made their cabin at nearby Grace Pond into an isolation camp for the family's ten children susceptible to this infantile paralysis. According to her plan, the youngsters would be strictly secluded at this remote pond with guide George McClintock serving as "general guardian" and the women presiding over the nursery. Every day, Rudolf and Oswald were to lead a packhorse to Four-Mile Brook "where the daily provisions will be hid in the brook for George to fetch into the camp."[112]

Not only was the Parlin estate a refuge from the city's contagions, but it was also a working farm and a work-in-progress, requiring something of everyone. "Mother," wrote William, "began her day in her vegetable garden; all morning she weeded or gathered beans and peas into a basket."[113] Paul was "the impresario of summer," overseeing the carpenters who were finishing the living room, building his sculpture studio, and expanding the henhouse "for the flock of turkeys expected next week."[114]

The youngest Oswald's "special business" was care of the two ponies, Seth and Marquis, giving rides to William's children in the basket cart. Roland, now 14, was companion to William's young children, particularly his daughter Mary. "They go off on boat trips," wrote William, "or with the other kiddies visit the hay barn to practice somersaults or other gymnastics, sometimes under Paul's tutelage."[115]

After a powerful storm soaked the surrounding fields that August, matriarch Maria summoned "all hands" to the hayfield. Paul, Rudolf, Oswald, Roland, and William answered her call. For the next hour, the Piel boys, pitchforks in hand "spread the drenched timothy to the breeze and sun." Sadly this work, William lamented, was poor tribute to their farming ancestry. "Throughout the hour, philosophy, religion and art were voiced across the field: Rudolf offering a synthesis of science and . . . Paul leading off on the Church in Italy and Greece."[116]

As always, Agnes, now 19, found ways, even in this forest fastness, to pursue the unconventional. During an outing to nearby Grace Pond with brother Rudolf, Agnes and her chum Margarita Schile sought out a secluded cove, stripped and plunged nude into the icy cold waters, swimming out to a great, grey rock and stretching "at full length in the sun with the breezes blowing and cooling your body, and the water lapping all about, and the sun a-broiling you to a lovely golden brown; then to slip off again into the cool, refreshing pond and feel your hair flow back in smooth strands like so many slippery, oily eels." As Rudolf's boat approached "ominously straight at us," the two young women beat a hasty retreat. "We leapt, we scrambled, we bounded, I don't know how to the shore—we flew into our clothes, we dashed into the canoe and were off in absolute silence—out in the middle of the pond we drift, still trembling with fright."[117]

No matter how disparate their daylight pursuits, everyone gathered each evening in Paul's new "colonial" living room. At a card table, Agnes and her friend Margarita Schile played William and Rudolf in "a desperate game of 500" that went on for twelve hands until a guest, Louise's friend Edna Tompkins, called everyone outside for a spectacular aurora borealis. With the colored northern lights filling the horizon, "the flashes appeared to rise from every quarter to meet in the circle of the zenith." The family lingered on the dew-covered lawn for a long time beneath a night sky that Agnes pronounced "thrilling."[118]

As the summer of 1916 drew to a close, William and wife Loretto joined their city friends William Cannon and wife Edith for a drive in a "comfortable Cadillac" north across the border toward Quebec City where the signs of a distant war were omnipresent. Driving through the Canadian countryside, they saw many matrons wearing black, few men of military age, and "guessed what it meant." In Quebec City, they felt the Great War "had stirred patriotism to a white heat in Canada," even capturing the hearts of French Canadians. During a trolley ride about the old city, William overheard a uniformed soldier and his wife speaking "with how much anguish—they hoped this was not the last ride together."

Checking into the famed Chateau Frontenac, they entered the Grill Room to find it "gay with laughter and dancing," as sweethearts, with chaperones, were sending-off the soldiers from a nearby encampment. At one table, comrades raised their glasses to an officer just back from Flanders; at another a toast was drowned in shouts and cheers. As the room echoed in "loud laughter, coarse jokes, an occasional oath, and much egotistical conceit," a waiter told William: "There isn't a one who knows whether he must leave tomorrow; they're going every day."[119]

After fifteen seasons on a woodland estate growing ever closer to perfection, that summer of 1916 was the last on Parlin Pond for the entire Piel family. Never again would all of Michael Piel's children assemble on this lakeshore for months of pure leisure, reveling in each other's company.

Yet these summers not only bound the Piel siblings together, they also found them companions for later lives apart. With the exception of William's stage-door romance, most who made lasting marriages did their courting on Parlin's shores—starting with Henry who married the daughter of their mother's visiting schoolmate in 1913; Louise who wed brother Rudolf's college friend in 1916; and, finally, Rudolf who married sister Agnes's "chum," the swimmer Margarita Schile, in 1919.[120] To these we should add Louise's friend Clara Wittemann who, in 1922, married that "family guest from Buffalo," Dr. Bernard Schreiner.[121] Whether it was the luminous moonlight, cool northern air, or long days stripped of pretense, Parlin became the place for Piels to find life partners.

More immediately, the martial fever that William had felt in that visit to Quebec City would soon draw America into the Great War before the next summer could come, stealing away several Parlin stalwarts—Paul and Rudolf into the U.S. Army, Louise to Turkey with her diplomat husband. To monitor the wartime loyalties of German Americans, Washington would build a pervasive security apparatus that breached the privacy of countless citizens, even those in this northern forest. The war's patriotic passions would spark government raids on the Piel homes, prompt surveillance of their sons in the service, and bring Louise and her diplomat husband home from Europe in disgrace. Moreover, the war's intense patriotism would convince Congress, in the guise of conserving resources, to enact a wartime prohibition of alcohol that soon became permanent.

Within a year of the war's end, the prohibition of alcohol would push the brewery toward bankruptcy, denying the family sufficient income to maintain this costly estate with its summer staff of twenty. These same years would also move most of Michael's children toward separate lives, increasingly prone to fighting over money, the brewery, and Parlin itself.

Lake Parlin, as the Piels had known it for so long, ended in that tender summer of 1916.

Photo Gallery: The Piel Family

Piel Hof at Mörsenbroich near Düsseldorf, Germany. (Painting by Paul Köster, 1902)

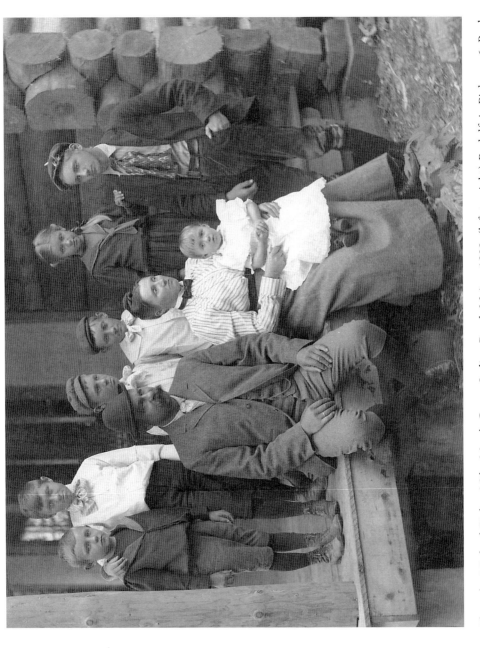

Photo by Michael Piel at Mike Marr's Camp, Indian Pond, Maine, 1899; (left to right) Rudolf A. Piel, age 6; Paul, 10; Michael, 50; Henry, 14; Otto, 13; Maria, 42; Agnes, 2; Louise, 8; and William, 16.

Michael Piel, circa 1900. (Photo by Holler)

Photo by Michael Piel, Pine Hill, Catskill Mountains, New York, 1894; (left to right) Otto Piel, age 8; Louise, nearly 4; Maria, 37; Paul, 5.

Michael Piel, New York, circa 1914.

Henry G. Piel with his firstborn son Elmar, 1918.

William Piel, Sr., probably taken when studying at Columbia University, circa 1905.

Photo by Michael Piel of children Louise and Paul, holding the book *John Halifax, Gentleman* by Dinah Marian Muloch, at 245 West 72nd Street, New York, circa 1910.

Louise G. Piel, Heald Pond, Jackman, Maine, summer of 1915.

Loretto Piel holding baby Gerard with children; (left to right) William, Mary, and Rita in haystack, Piel estate, Lake Parlin, Maine, 1915.

Agnes Piel, dressed as the fictional Indian maid Minnehaha, photographed by brother Paul at Lake Parlin, Maine, 1909.

Franz Piel, son of Wilhelm-Heinrich and Martha Piel, awarded Germany's Iron Cross for valor on the Eastern Front; killed on the Western Front, 1918.

Sergeant Paul Piel (back row, second from right) and Private Rudolf Piel (back row, far right), Laboratory, U.S. Army Base Hospital, Biltmore, North Carolina, World War I.

Walter Piel (far right) with U.S. Navy aircrew, coastal patrol, World War I.

Erwin Lange, U.S. Vice Consul at Brusa, Turkey (left); Austro-Hungarian consul (center); and Major von Villers (right), German military attaché, Turkey, 1917.

Rudolf Piel, about 18 years old, circa 1910.

Margarita Schile, cousin of Mathilde Lange and bride to Rudolf Piel, 1919. (Photo by Botto-Moscher, New York)

Loretto Piel with children; (left to right), Mary, Gerard, John, William, and Rita, circa 1916.

Margarita Piel with German shepherd "Teufel," at home, Garden City, Long Island, circa 1933.

Patsy Lyne in Austria for psychotherapy, circa 1936. (Photo by Trude Fleischmann, Ebendorferstrasse 3, Vienna)

Maria Piel, then 80, aboard the *S.S. St. Louis* with grandson Frederick Lange on her last trip to Germany, 1937.

At a June 1944 wedding in Concord, Massachusetts; (left to right) Rudolf A. Piel, bride Margarita Piel McCoy, groom Lieutenant Alfred M. McCoy, Jr., Margarita Schile Piel, and her father John J. Schile (seated).

William Piel, Sr., on a fishing expedition along the Maine-Quebec border, September 1949.

Gerard Piel and wife Mary Bird Piel with sons Jonathan, Samuel, New York City, 1945.

Margarita Piel McCoy and Alfred M. McCoy, Jr., with the author, Concord, Massachusetts, 1945.

5

The Great War

I had some really exciting news for the family. Or, at least I thought it was. As usual, the annual meeting of our family business, M&G Piel Securities, was at a fancy hotel, although off-season so we could afford it. This time our 2002 gathering was at the Cranwell Resort, a luxury spa in the Berkshires with golf course, gourmet menu, and massages. The meeting room overlooked the rolling Massachusetts hills through ceiling-to-floor windows. Perfect for my presentation. We started at 9:00 a.m., a bit early for a Saturday, particularly when people had been traveling. So there was coffee. This news, I thought, would liven things up.

When my turn came to deliver the "History Report," I announced the first, really exciting discovery after two years' research into the Piel family. Documents found in the U.S. National Archives had some surprising revelations about a relative, Dr. Mathilde Lange. The diplomatic cables and military intelligence reports were beyond amazing. She was not just the distinguished biology professor we always thought she was. During World War I, Aunt Mathilde, though still just a young graduate student, had done something extraordinary, something that shaped the fate of the family for an entire generation.

As I went on to detail these discoveries, the response was more muted than expected. Many of the forty family members present stirred uneasily. The half-dozen Lange faces in the room were stone cold.

When I sat down, a couple of these Lange cousins approached, saying their Great Aunt Mathilde was just wonderful. As children, they were awed by her— the commanding presence, resonant voice, and air of authority. They wanted to make sure that I told her full story, that I wasn't going to damage her reputation. Their words would whisper as I wrote this chapter, trying to make sense of her extraordinary life choices.

Clearly, I was treading on dangerous ground. World War I might have been almost a hundred years ago. But for some of these Piels, it might as well have been yesterday.

Dangerously Disloyal

Indeed, World War I was a time of wrenching change for the Piel family, their brewery, and German American communities across America. The war brought a jarring juxtaposition of events that quickly eliminated every manifestation of their vibrant ethnic presence from New York and other major cities. From July 1914 to April 1917, America had remained neutral as Europe's armies fought massive battles. German Americans were thus free to favor their Fatherland. Encouraged by the German embassy, community leaders raised funds for war victims and supported the Kaiser.[1] Like many of their generation, Maria and Michael Piel were passionately pro-German in these first months of war and rallied to the old country.

Then, in a rapid reversal, America declared war on Germany in April 1917, ordering its first conscription in a half-century and enacting draconian legislation to extirpate any sign of disloyalty by word or deed. Suddenly, their beloved homeland was a reviled enemy. Suddenly, fundraising for German war orphans was treasonous. Suddenly, their sons were supposed to fight against the Fatherland. No matter how quickly and sincerely German Americans made the switch, they were still subject to suspicion.

At first, many German Americans were ostracized by friends and neighbors. Then, as Washington mobilized its counterintelligence, citizen vigilantes placed them under surveillance and informed on them anonymously. From the perspective of the U.S. government, declaring war on the homeland of the nation's largest ethnic group created a serious threat, resolved by creating the country's first internal security agency. Throughout the war, this security apparatus raided German American homes, monitored their mail, and denied some of their sons the honor of commission or combat. Through this "German American ordeal during and after World War I," wrote one historian, a once vital ethnic community would be forcibly, painfully assimilated to become "100 percent American."[2]

After the declaration of war in April 1917, the Piels switched from supporting the Fatherland to backing the Allies as quickly as any German American family. Their brewery bought Liberty Bonds. Five of their sons volunteered for military service. But neighbors in both New York and Maine still thought them pro-German. Midst surveillance of German Americans nationwide, the commander of U.S. military intelligence pursued several Piels relentlessly, branding them dangerously disloyal. The family would emerge from the war stigmatized, marginalized, and demoralized, its bid for acceptance in New York society delayed for a generation. The damage they, and so many like them, suffered from secret wartime surveillance was deep and lasting.

The war also provided pretext for economic sanctions against both German aliens and German Americans. Under the Trading with the Enemy Act passed in October 1917, the Office of Alien Property custodian, headed by former congressman A. Mitchell Palmer, swelled into an all-powerful agency with hundreds of employees that confiscated nearly a half-billion dollars in "alien" German assets, managed this money through some 30,000 trusts, and later "Americanized" these properties, including Bayer pharmaceuticals and major metal firms, through closed auctions. As the sole arbiter of alien status, Palmer confiscated about $25 million from American women married to Germans. He also ruled that prominent German American brewers caught in Germany by the war were "of enemy character" and impounded their assets—notably, some $60 million from Lilly Busch, widow of St. Louis brewer Adolphus Busch, and $40 million from George Ehret, Sr., of New York, including the famed Yorkville brewery, his Park Avenue mansion, and its art collection.[3]

All this suspicion toward German Americans breached the last barrier to the full federal prohibition of alcohol. By equating the brewers' defense of their product with pro-German propaganda, the temperance movement silenced its most powerful opponent, the U.S. Brewers' Association. With their fiery patriotic rhetoric making any tolerance of alcohol tantamount to treason, the "drys" persuaded Congress to enact Prohibition as both a temporary wartime measure and a lasting constitutional amendment. Not only was the 18th Amendment prohibiting alcohol approved by Congress just months after the United States entered the war, but it sped through ratification in state after state as anti-German propaganda reached a fever pitch during the fighting's final months. In short, the war's anti-German hysteria made Prohibition possible. Clearly, for both the German American community and individual families such as the Piels, World War I was a traumatic, transformative event.

For the Fatherland

In the three years before America entered the war, both England and Germany used propaganda to court U.S. support. In this war of words, Britain had the upper hand. Eastern social elites, particularly in New York, identified with English culture and would use the war to silence the hostility of German and Irish Americans toward Great Britain.[4] Through its Reuters wire service, which distributed most world news, the British press reported Germany's "rape of Belgium" in graphic detail. These dispatches about "perverse sexual acts, lurid mutilations, and graphic accounts of child abuse of often dubious veracity" were reprinted verbatim in U.S. newspapers.[5]

To counter this portrayal of the brutal "Hun," the Kaiser's embassy tried to rouse German communities in cities across America. Throughout seventy years of continuous migration, the country's 10 million German Americans had retained their language and identity through newspapers, beer gardens, choral groups (*Liederkranz*), and gymnastic societies (*Turnvereine*).[6] Many responded strongly to appeals on behalf of suffering Germans, whether war widows or children being starved by the British naval blockade.[7]

The outbreak of war in August 1914 brought a surge of feeling for the Fatherland in the Piel household. "Every German in the country is protesting against the disfigured reports by the English press in the U.S.," Maria Piel wrote her son in the first week of war, rejecting claims in the *Brooklyn Eagle* that the Kaiser "strives to be the tsar of all Europe." After following the war for a month in twenty papers, she advised son Paul, then studying in Italy, that he should "not believe what all you see about German cruelty, etc. in the newspapers." From her experience during the Franco-Prussian War of 1870–71, when reports of French victories "were simply, frankly made up," Maria knew firsthand how the press could disseminate propaganda in the guise of real news. Coming of age in the years when Prussia was unifying Germany into a modern state, Maria would carry the imprint of that nationalism to her grave. Decades later, she still recalled her joy, as a schoolgirl of 14 in Castrop, at the news of her Fatherland's victory in the Franco-Prussian War. "When peace was declared," she recalled, "we prayed and gave thanks in that school that we were free." Her husband Michael Piel, a decorated veteran of that war, now found U.S. press reports that English ships had captured two German vessels incredible. A German crew, he said "would prefer to sink with the ship." When the German army was victorious, he hoped "to receive them in Berlin and help celebrate the heroes."[8]

In the first days of war, the saga of Germany's merchant ships enthralled Maria. The *S.S. Kronprinzessin Cecilie* was four days out of New York off the Irish coast, with $11 million in gold, when orders came to reverse course for neutral

America. With a French cruiser in pursuit, the German captain stood on the bridge for four days and nights, sailing full steam through thick fog to reach safe internment at Bar Harbor, Maine. "That man," wrote Maria, "has made himself immortal."[9] As the interned crewmen on this and other ships struggled to find work, Maria offered a half dozen German sailors refuge at her Lake Parlin estate where, she said, they were "now happy that they have shelter and something to eat for which they industriously help drag wood from the forest."[10]

Such activities soon attracted unfavorable notice. In November 1914, a front-page headline in Portland's leading newspaper, the *Evening Express*, announced: "Seek Secret Wireless at Parlin Pond. German Brewer Holds Great Estate in Wilderness. Canadian Agent on Inspection Tour of Northern Woods." After asking if there might be "a German wireless station on a mountain top on the shore of Parlin Pond," the paper reported that Maine's governor had authorized a Canadian agent to inspect the secluded area, ideal for "the operation of a secret wireless."[11] Since the only wireless on the Piel property was son Rudolf's ham radio set, it was quickly dismantled, ending the investigation.

A month later, the Piel family played a prominent role at New York's grand German Charity Bazaar. As German American veterans of the Civil War marched through city streets sounding bugles, thousands of supporters crowded into the Seventy-First Regiment Armory on Park Avenue to patronize the 200 booths. "We, whose cradle stood in Germany," Maria wrote an absent son, "are trying to forget through hard work what makes our hearts so heavy." To that end, Maria sponsored a "Hansel & Gretel" booth where her daughters Louise and Agnes sold marzipan sweets eight hours a day for two weeks. The Bazaar raised $300,000 for German war widows and orphans, with plans to reach a million dollars by February.[12] Their dedication won the Piel girls an invitation to serve as flower sellers at the upcoming German American Civic Ball at the Plaza Hotel. That effort to raise funds "for the poor of New York" showed, said Agnes, "a splendid spirit on the part of the Germans after the dirty way they have been treated by the Americans."[13]

In coming months, Maria mailed postcards celebrating Germany's wartime leaders. One showed Otto Weddigen, "commander of the German submarine boat U-9," who sank three British cruisers killing 1,400 sailors. Another featured Crown Prince Friedrich Wilhelm and his picture-perfect family.[14]

Such strident patriotism among the American Piels contrasted markedly with the more measured pride of their relations back in Germany. In December 1914, niece Maria Heermann wrote from Herne telling her aunt Maria Piel of the confidence she felt in the "competence of our army commanders, especially Field Marshal von Hindenburg." But she also mourned the heavy losses, already thirty-six dead from their small community. Two years later as hunger spread, that niece wrote: "Just as our enemy did not achieve anything with weapons, so his attempt to starve us will fail ingloriously."[15] On the other side of the family in Düsseldorf, Martha Piel wrote to Maria's son Paul, then in Italy, that she and her son Franz hoped "that you may not abandon Europe without having seen the land of your father in its greatness. You will doubtless receive a good impression of our power and unity, which you could not imagine without having seen it."[16]

German Crown Princess

5.1. Postcard from Maria Piel to son Paul in Naples, Italy, February 1915.

These German relations paid a heavy price for their patriotism, losing their most promising offspring, their hope for future generations. After heroism on the Eastern Front that won him the Iron Cross and a battlefield commission, Franz Piel, Michael's nephew, was fatally wounded on the Western Front in 1918. Two years later, Josef Heermann, Maria's nephew and heir apparent to the family farm, died in a Herne hospital from tuberculosis contracted during military service. He was buried in a war hero's grave.[17]

America Enters the War

All this support for the Fatherland during the three years of U.S. neutrality raised doubts about German American loyalty once Washington entered the war. In asking Congress to declare war on Germany in April 1917, President Woodrow Wilson issued a stern warning to German Americans, saying: "If there should be disloyalty, it will be dealt with a firm hand of stern repression."[18] And, indeed, it was. As Washington enacted strict loyalty laws and deployed a new internal security apparatus, the Piels, like other prominent German Americans, were soon caught in a web of counterintelligence that stigmatized their family as strongly, even violently pro-German.

While the Piels who served were subjected to relentless surveillance, the situation for Michael's eldest son William, though draft exempt, was even more difficult. As soon as America declared war on Germany, close hiking and drinking companions in suburban Long Island suddenly "dropped him." To demonstrate the family's loyalty, William ordered his eldest son, then eight, to "break my piggy bank and . . . buy a Liberty Bond." William himself joined the local Military Training Camp, becoming one of the 50,000 men nationwide who drilled every Sunday during the war. Despite all these patriotic displays, Long Island locals still saw these Piels as "German." When the family found "shards of glass the same color as the cereal" in their *Wheatena* breakfast food, William was angry at the "thought somebody was trying to do us in" and called FBI investigators. As his eldest son put it, "that was a tough time."[19]

Midst this vigilante surveillance, the Piel family's idyllic estate in the Maine woods now seemed suspicious. Just weeks after the United States entered the war, a civilian contractor at the Portsmouth Navy Yard informed the FBI, incorrectly, that "a party of Germans had bought property at Parlin Pond, 4th township, Somerset County, Maine, about three years ago and had ordered all but Germans away from the property." Acting on a request from the Bureau, the deputy sheriff from nearby Jackman reported "there are twelve Germans at this place, which is owned by the heirs of Michael Piel, one time brewer, now deceased, of New York City." According to the property's foreman George McClintock, at least two of these Germans had "escaped from interned [German] liners either at Boston or New York." He added that a Canadian "secret service agent . . . was at the Piel estate during the summer of 1914, investigating a report of a wireless plant," already dismantled.[20]

Suspicions aroused, the FBI agent at Portland, John C. Howard, drove north to Lake Parlin on May 25, 1917. Assisted by a special agent of the Maine Central Railroad, H. A. Russell, who had reported similar concerns, the Bureau's agent interviewed the six German workers employed on the Piel property, finding none had served in the German army. Typical was Carl Klingmuller, born in 1889 in Germany, a machinist on the German liner *S.S. Kronprinzessin Cecilie* until it was interned at Bar Harbor in 1914. Suddenly unemployed, he worked several short-term jobs until the Piels hired him as a chauffeur. After learning that "Mr. Piel had ordered all the firearms on the place locked up," the FBI agent reported "there does not appear to be anything against these men except that they are Germans and naturally subject to suspicion at this time." They cannot "do much harm where they are now," he concluded, since "they are being well watched by the natives in that section of Maine."[21]

Robert Piel, "Violently Pro-German"

As the new Selective Service system started registering all young males for conscription in June 1917, several second-generation Piels came under close surveillance, tangling the family in a web of intrigue that would mute their once-vocal opposition to prohibition. From the perspective of a nervous Washington, the conscription of German Americans to fight against Germany raised the possibility of divided loyalties and a potential security threat.

To allay this danger, the Army formed its first counterintelligence unit, the Military Intelligence Division, under the command of Colonel Ralph Van Deman, later known as the "father of U.S. military intelligence." To supplement his own staff of 1,700 soldiers, the colonel assigned 350,000 volunteer vigilantes, affiliated with the American Protective League, to surveil the country's German Americans and apprehend the supposed "200,000 and 300,000" among them "who were secret spies in this country." During its first year, the League's New

York branch was particularly active, investigating 70,000 cases of draft evasion and disloyalty. While these vigilantes handled some 3 million routine cases nationwide, Colonel Van Deman—dour, methodical, and deeply suspicious—was freed for the relentless pursuit of suspected subversives, including several Piels.[22]

Instead of waiting to be conscripted, all the draft-eligible Piels volunteered. In June 1917, Paul Piel, then 28, joined up at New York City, and rose from private to sergeant in the U.S. Army Medical Corps before honorable discharge in August 1919.[23] His younger brother Rudolf, then 24, also enlisted and served with Paul at a Medical Corps hospital in North Carolina as private first class until his honorable discharge in June 1919.[24]

Induction at first went smoothly for three of Gottfried Piel's sons—Gottfried, Jr., Robert, and Walter. After working in his father's shipyard at Greenport, Long Island, building sub-chasers for the Navy, Walter joined the Naval Reserve Flying Corps, patrolling the U.S. coast in amphibious aircraft and then serving as a blimp instructor in Canada.[25] In October 1917, both Robert and Gottfried, Jr., as college graduates, passed a board of review for commissioning in the Ordnance Officers Reserve Corps. Their commander, Major General William Crozier, quickly approved both nominations.[26]

While Gottfried, Jr.'s commission went forward, Robert soon fell under suspicion as unfavorable reports reached military authorities. On Governors Island, a colonel at the New York Arsenal received a phone call on October 21, 1917, from an acquaintance warning that Robert Piel, "the son of some prominent brewer in or near New York," who was "of well known pro-German and anti-English sentiments," was about to be commissioned.[27] His source was the wealthy New York socialite Mrs. George Trowbridge Hollister and her daughter, residents of 930 Park Avenue, who were certain that Robert and Gottfried Piel, Jr. "were pro-German in sympathy."[28]

After learning Robert's commission was blocked, Lieutenant Jack C. Rainier wrote the Army saying he knew the father Gottfried Piel as a director of his family's firm, Rainier Motor Corp., and was certain of the son's "loyalty and allegiance." After his discharge from the Naval Reserve for defective eyesight, Robert and five friends had donated a motorboat, the *Owassa*, to the war effort. Moreover, Gottfried Piel, Sr., owned the Eastern Shipyard in Greenport, Long Island, which was currently building submarine chasers for the Navy. He had also given "one or two Motor Ambulances" to the war effort.[29]

That same day, however, an agent from the American Protective League reported that "Robert Piel of Piel Bros. Brewers, East New York, before the entrance of the United States into the War, was decidedly pro-German and anti-British," expressing such "sentiments so freely in the Princeton Club he got himself generally disliked there."[30] Seizing upon that report, Colonel Van Deman ordered that "every effort be made to investigate this matter," launching an intense inquiry by the nation's entire intelligence community—the FBI, Office of Naval Intelligence, the Military Intelligence Division (MID), and its civilian adjunct, the American Protective League (APL).[31]

Consequently, the APL agent returned to the Princeton Club on East 21st Street, where one member called Robert "pro German" and another said his views were "violently anti-English." That member, R. M. Forsythe, added, however, that Robert was a boy of "the highest moral character" and was a member of "a high-class German American family" whose four sons were all "good citizens." Moreover, both members stated that "as soon as the U.S. entered the War, Piel stopped his pro-German talk."[32]

Not satisfied with these inconclusive reports, Colonel Van Deman ordered his New York office to have "a Princeton man, if possible, get all possible information about Robert."[33] Indeed, Piel had strong college ties, preparing at nearby Lawrenceville School and going on to Princeton University where he graduated in 1913 with a C– average, membership in the elite Colonial Club, and an abiding affection for his alma mater.[34]

Many of these college friends suddenly became informants, keen not only to provide information but also to smear his reputation. His Princeton advisor, Harvey W. Thayer, a professor of German, recalled him as "a careless and indifferent student," openly "pro-German" but "too obstinate and too flabby" to be "a dangerous man."[35] Moving from the negative to the nasty, Lieutenant Roger W. Straus of the Signal Corps, Robert Piel's classmate at school and college, described him as a "very likeable chap" who was "almost stupid" and "devoid of courage." He could not be involved in pro-German propaganda, Straus added, "as that requires a certain nerve which I believe is entirely lacking."[36]

On Colonel Van Deman's orders, another MID investigator interviewed three Princeton alumni, all Class of 1915, who were damningly critical. An Ordnance officer based in Hoboken, Lieutenant Thomas L. Horn, stated, incorrectly, that Robert had beat the draft with a medical certificate of defective eyesight when in fact "his eyes are not bad." A Navy intelligence officer in Brooklyn, Charles C. Hilliard, said he "refused to associate with him because of subject's pro-Germanism." An army lab technician in Manhattan, Edmund B. Jermyn, Jr., added, inaccurately, that "John North, Piel's best friend at Princeton, now refused to recognize Piel on the street, owing to the disloyalty of subject."[37]

Still not satisfied, Colonel Van Deman ordered the 78th Division's intelligence officer to interview Piel's close friend and Princeton classmate, Lieutenant Robert Sealy.[38] Describing the subject as "one of his best friends," Sealy said that both Robert and his father Gottfried believed that "Germany's cause was justifiable," adding that: "All of the Piels are very bitter against President Wilson." Although Robert "would not intentionally enter the service for the purpose of betraying this country," there was danger that he would talk about his duties "to the members of his family, who are a great deal more violent than he in his views," and thus "valuable information might get into the hands of the enemy." Coincidentally, this division intelligence officer, Captain Philip D. Hoyt (Princeton '12), noted he had known Sealy at college and considered him "thoroughly trustworthy in every respect."[39]

Despite the secrecy, Robert Piel somehow learned of these accusations and fought back. In January 1918, he unwittingly visited his Princeton classmate and accuser Roger Straus, insisting that he had only defended the German people "when they were attacked as murderers and wholesale committers of rape." Expressing his "absolute accord" with the declaration of war on Germany, Robert said he would willingly "appear before a board" to answer any accusations. He wanted a commission for combat since it was his duty, as a single man, to serve at the front. Straus reported their conversation without comment.[40]

By then, however, Robert's efforts to clear his name were in vain. After compiling nine field reports about this suspect, Colonel Van Deman concluded, in January 1918, that Robert's commission "would cause much adverse comment in New York" and he "would not be a satisfactory officer." Although MID found "no objection" to the commission for Robert's brother Lieutenant Gottfried Piel, Jr., it recommended that "his services be confined to this country."[41]

After an eight-month hiatus, Washington's renewed concerns about German subversion in 1918 prompted a reopening of this investigation. By then, after six months' service as a private with the Ordnance Department in Washington, Robert was growing desperate, telling other government workers "he thinks he should be either court martialed or commissioned."[42] That August, an FBI agent, posing as a factory inspector, visited the G. Piel Company at Long Island City and alleged the firm had no government contracts, thus rendering brother Arthur's claim to an industrial deferment "false."[43]

In October 1918, therefore, MID determined Robert Piel "is pro-German and anti-British," and his family "is very pro-German and both sons have constantly evaded any military service that would take them to France."[44] Based on this report and its own "very extensive investigation," Ordnance found Robert "unfit for further duty in Washington." He was transferred to the Eighth Cavalry in Marfa, Texas, "where he can do little or no harm." There he was honorably discharged in January 1919.[45]

Through secret investigations that collected gossip in the guise of intelligence, Robert Piel finished the war as an army private—refused a commission, denied the distinction of combat, marked a subversive, ostracized by his Princeton classmates, and outcast from New York society.

The contrast with his accusers, the Trowbridge Hollister family of Park Avenue, is instructive. In June 1917, their younger daughter, Katherine A. Hollister, married Lieutenant Truman Smith (Yale '15) in a grand society wedding at the Hollisters' Long Island estate, earning the young couple immediate inclusion in the *Social Register* and launching the groom on a distinguished military career.[46] Six months later, the family announced the union, also welcomed by the *Social Register*, of their elder daughter Dorothy T. Hollister, Robert's likely accuser, to Lieutenant Thomas L. Horn (Princeton '15)—the same officer who also made those damningly false allegations to MID about Robert's supposed draft dodging. While others with Ivy League educations were thus meeting, marrying, and amassing social capital for luminous lives, Robert would return from the war stigmatized and marginalized.[47]

Unaware of the faculty and fellow alumni who had informed on him, Robert lived out his life in Princeton's shadow. After retiring from business in his mid-40s, Robert moved back to Princeton, New Jersey, where he rented rooms in the Nassau Tavern at the edge of campus. Apart from perfect attendance at reunions, his most memorable activity was leadership of the Lawrenceville Invitational Hockey Tournament. After his death in 1952 at Princeton Hospital, friends honored his memory by establishing the tournament's Robert Piel Memorial Trophy.[48] A quarter century later, his estate donated $413,000 to establish the Gottfried & Sophie Piel Scholarship at Princeton, which, at this writing, supports about ten undergraduates annually.[49]

Surveillance of Paul and Rudolf

In contrast to the New York socialites who informed on the Gottfried Piels, Michael's family was the subject of both anonymous tips from nosy neighbors that soon proved false and seemingly accurate reports from a close relative that sparked several protracted investigations.

A year after the FBI visit to their Maine estate, the U.S. Attorney for Brooklyn received an anonymous phone call charging that "in the family of Piel, 245 West 72nd Street, Manhattan, are one or two sons . . . evading military service improperly." Consequently, a volunteer from the APL investigated, finding that the sons in question, Paul and Rudolf Piel, were already serving with the Army Base Hospital in Biltmore, North Carolina.[50] Once again, patriotic tipsters had proved unreliable.

Three months later in July 1918, however, the Piels became the subject of a serious investigation when the U.S. military attaché in Berne, Switzerland, Lieutenant Colonel W. F. H. Godson, warned MID Washington about a coterie of subversives inside the Army Medical Corps. With an almost preternatural depth of detail, the colonel stated that Dr. Armin St. George, a "German American," had shared an office at 132 East 60th Street in New York with a Dr. Norbert Stadtmuller, who was now practicing at Zietenstrasse 6, Berlin. Not only were the two still engaged in suspicious "collusion," but Dr. St. George had "brought many German Americans" into the medical corps, "among them Rudolf and Paul Piel" who are "all reported to be at the Camp at Biltmore, N.C." Hinting at a source inside the family circle for all this intelligence, the colonel stated "Dr. St. George is very pro-German and in 1916 took offence when my informant refused to drink [to] the health of the Crown Prince."[51]

In a separate report sent that same day, the colonel also advised MID Washington that Dr. Stadtmuller, though treating wounded enemy soldiers at a Berlin hospital, has "displayed great anxiety" about the valuable medical library he left behind at 132 East 60th Street, writing contacts in Switzerland repeatedly about its fate.[52] In a further report that spurred several FBI raids on this house, Colonel Godson wrote again from Berne in late August warning "it is now reported to me that Dr. St. George has taken the library belonging to Dr. Stadtmuller" from their former office.[53]

In retrospect, all this remarkable detail forces us to ask: How could a military attaché in Switzerland possibly acquire such intimate intelligence about these doings inside a Manhattan townhouse? Unconcerned about such questions, Washington was alarmed by these reports, prompting a two-pronged MID investigation. First, find Dr. Stadtmuller's medical library. Next, track down Dr. St. George's suspicious confederates, particularly those Piels already inside the army. On the surface, such suspicions about the Piels seemed plausible since they had funded Dr. St. George's medical education and he was in fact their family doctor.[54]

Locating the library proved relatively routine. Acting on orders from MID's chief to conduct "a thorough investigation and search the house at 132 East 60th Street," MID New York interviewed its owner, Mrs. Frieda Caillé, who advised the investigator that Dr. Stadtmuller had "turned over his library to Dr. A. V. St. George," who had shipped the books to his father's house at Jersey City last July. There the doctor's father showed an investigator twenty-four cases of books and paperwork from the Alien Property Custodian, all in order.[55]

A month later, the intelligence officer at Camp Upton on Long Island reported that Dr. St. George had left for overseas duty in France with the staff of Base Hospital No. 62 in late August.[56] Alarmed that a possible subversive was now serving at the front, in October 1918 the current MID commander, General Marlborough Churchill, warned the chief of U.S. intelligence in France, General Dennis Nolan, that Dr. St. George was "extremely pro-German" and had been in partnership with "one Doctor Stadtmuller, now at Zietenstrasse 6, Berlin."[57] To

5.2. Dr. Armin St. George, U.S. Army Medical Corps, World War I.

assist General Nolan's investigation, MID ordered its New York office to provide a "full account" of Dr. St. George's "previous history, antecedents and associations."[58]

Within a week, MID New York reported that interviews with the doctor's father and three colleagues confirmed he "was most certainly pro-German up to the time the United States entered the war." But one of these sources, Dr. Douglas Symmers, head of pathology at Bellevue Hospital, had added: "I never heard Dr. St. George make any disloyal remarks."[59]

Meanwhile, Military Intelligence had tracked down Dr. St. George's supposed confederates, ordering the intelligence officer at General Hospital No. 12 in North Carolina to place "Dr. [sic] Rudolph Piel, and Dr. [sic] Paul Piel . . . under discreet surveillance." After investigating, that officer reported that Paul and Rudolf Piel, enlisted men not doctors, have "pro-German tendencies." But, he added: "At no time have I had evidence that either made disloyal statements," though "both will be kept under further observation."[60]

That investigation revived in October when the MID chief, General Churchill, ordered the hospital's intelligence officer to conduct "a very discreet effort . . . to extract from Rudolf and Paul Piel all the information they have concerning Doctor St. George." To that end, he should examine "the effects of the Piels, with a view to locating letters and documents which may be of interest in this case."[61] A secret search of Private Rudolf Piel's possessions found two letters from his mother in German that were forwarded to Washington. There translation revealed much discussion of knitting socks and sweaters for cold nights on guard duty. In one letter, Maria Piel expressed sadness at America's casualties, remarking: "Maine especially has done its part. Each place has losses."[62] Though Maria would remain patriotically pro-German for the rest of her life, the wartime surveillance was apparently effective in silencing such loyalties.

A month later, the hospital's intelligence officer wrote Washington that he had "nothing further to report on subjects Rudolf and Paul Piel, and am of opinion that their cases can be dropped."[63] In January 1919, therefore, the MID chief wrote his counterpart in France that investigations confirmed Dr. St. George's "pro-Germanism" prior to U.S. entry into the war, but "no definite evidence of pro-Germanism after that date has been discovered."[64]

Throughout this investigation, Dr. St. George was in fact rendering exemplary wartime service. During twenty months at a U.S. Army field hospital in Dijon, France, treating soldiers with horrific war wounds, he was promoted to captain and won two citations "for distinguished service." After the war, moreover, he achieved eminence as president of the American Society of Clinical Pathologists.

For his pioneering investigation of lethal radium poisoning among watch dial workers, he was honored with the Silver Medal Award from the American Medical Association.[65]

In MID's final case summary in June 1919, the entry for Dr. St. George read "no evidence of disloyalty since our entry into the war." The entry for Rudolf and Paul Piel stated, "Pro-German tendencies—anti-English. No evidence of disloyalties."[66] In other words, case closed.

Family Spy

Unbeknownst to the Piels, the source of these suspicions was a close relative then working as a spy for the U.S. government in Switzerland—Mathilde Lange. In retrospect, the web of seemingly impeccable intelligence in Colonel Godson's reports about Dr. St. George and his Piel confederates was woven entirely from Mathilde's family ties. She knew about Paul and Rudolf Piel's military assignments since her brother had married their sister. Moreover, her cousin Margarita Schile was also Rudolf's fiancée. She was also well aware that Dr. St. George shared an office with the suspicious Dr. Stadtmuller on East 60th Street because her mother lived there and her mother's sister Mrs. Caillé owned that house. The colonel's story that Dr. St. George was offended, sometime in 1916, "when my informant refused to drink [to] the health of the Crown Prince," probably occurred between the doctor and Mathilde herself at her brother Erwin's marriage to Louise Piel just before America went to war.[67] Ignoring the risks of informing on relatives, Mathilde had dressed up the intimacies of her family life in the guise of real intelligence, thereby winning the military's trust and an entrée into wartime espionage.

With a fiery patriotism that trumped personal loyalties, Mathilde proved a formidable counterintelligence operative, ferreting out suspected enemy agents, whether in foreign embassies or her own family. Educated in Germany and America, Mathilde spoke both flawless high German and erudite English that allowed her to move fluidly within both societies. Through her American patriotism, Prussian hauteur, supreme self-confidence, and razor-sharp intellect, Mathilde Lange became a secret agent of exceptional ability—resourceful, relentless, and, at times, ruthless. Despite all her brilliance and cunning, Mathilde was nonetheless caught between cultures, resolving the ambiguity of her own German American identity with a blindly zealous Americanism she would live to regret.

Her unique binational biography made her one of the most extraordinary spies who served on either side during the Great War. Through her parents, Mathilde was both an assimilated German American and a member of Prussia's landed aristocracy. Her mother Julia's parents had arrived with the wave of German "48ers," the defeated liberals who fled the Fatherland after their failed democratic revolution of 1848. During the Civil War, her grandfather also served with the Eleventh New York Regiment and then returned to Manhattan where he ran a business and raised a family. All this made Mathilde a third-generation German American on her mother's side.[68]

Mathilde's father, by contrast, was a recent German immigrant who belonged to an aristocratic family with a large estate in East Prussia. Arriving in New York during the 1880s, her father Conrad Lange and his older brother Friedrich established separate medical practices. Friedrich practiced at a prime midtown location where he soon became wealthy as the "pioneer of German surgery in America." Conrad, by contrast, practiced in a declining middle-class area of Harlem.[69] In this uptown neighborhood, Conrad himself delivered three children by his wife Julia—Conrad, Jr., in 1887, Mathilde in 1888, and Erwin, the future husband of Louise Piel, in 1890.[70]

In June 1894, Mathilde's family suffered a severe blow when their father died suddenly during a visit to Berlin and was buried at the family estate in East Prussia. Returning to New York with her three children that October, Julia had no income and moved into her father's home in Washington Heights.[71]

After several years of this penurious life, Julia's position in New York became even less tenable, circa 1900, when her wealthy brother-in-law retired to his estate in East Prussia and her father died of stomach cancer. Since, as she later wrote, "I did not have much money," and hearing that "I could give the children a better education in Germany with much less money than in New York City . . . I . . . took the children to Weimar," thinking it "the Athens of Germany." Dissatisfied, Julia moved on to Leipzig where the schools were more to her liking. There, daughter Mathilde entered Leipzig's rigorous *Realgymnasium* for girls founded by Dr. Catherine Windscheid, the first woman to earn a doctorate from Heidelberg University. After graduation in 1910, Mathilde sampled classes at several universities before settling on Leipzig where, over the next five years, she studied for her doctorate by taking courses in biology and zoology.[72]

While she was enriched by these Atlantic crossings, Mathilde's two brothers suffered the strains of this life between cultures, particularly the eldest Conrad, Jr. From 1904 to 1914, Conrad lived in Berlin where his uncle Dr. Friedrich

Lange had him institutionalized for manic depression under the care of Dr. Julius Hallervorden, a neuroscientist later notorious as a Nazi doctor. Instead of allowing him any recuperation at his estate in East Prussia, Dr. Lange had Conrad apprenticed at Berlin's immense Siemens-Schuckert factory where the stress may have aggravated his depression. After returning to the United States in 1914, Conrad's periodic institutionalization continued for the next three years at sanitariums in New York, New Jersey, and Washington, DC.[73] To cover the cost of this treatment, which his mother Julia could ill afford, Dr. Lange paid for his nephew's care and then established a trust fund for him at a New York bank.[74]

In a later declaration when he was quite lucid, Conrad stated that Dr. Friedrich Lange was, in fact, his real father and his mother Julia's marriage to the brother Conrad, Sr. was arranged "to save the family reputation." If so, that would account for the money that allowed Julia, without property or employment, to live in Germany for a decade while her children studied at elite institutions. And it would explain why Dr. Lange paid such great sums to keep Conrad far from the country estate where he and his proper German wife were model Prussian aristocrats.[75]

5.3. Mathilde, Erwin, and Julia Lange, East Prussia, circa 1904. (Photo by A. Gems, Guttstadterstrasse 18-19, Allenstein, Germany)

During these same years, Mathilde's younger brother Erwin survived tuberculosis and an abusive guardian to finish high school near Frankfurt with top grades. He started a course in political economy at Leipzig University before transferring to Harvard where he graduated in 1913.[76] In his senior year, Erwin befriended freshman Rudolf Piel, who invited him to vacation at his family's Lake Parlin estate. There Erwin met the Piels' marriageable beauty, Louise, then 23 and, as a niece recalled, small and slender, blond and beautiful, with "a lovely voice." As a probationary student at Radcliffe a few years earlier, Louise had starred in several light operas but skipped final exams, an oversight that soon sent her back home to New York City.[77] There she practiced Beethoven sonatas and singing "for the sake of the songs," while waiting for a beau to take her on life's journey.[78]

By the time Erwin arrived at Lake Parlin, Louise knew that brother Paul's Harvard chum Cabot Daniels "cared for me," but was far away with Paul on an extended European tour. Midst this uncertainty, Erwin pressed his suit and within a year the two were engaged secretly to avoid her father Michael's fiery temper.[79]

After passing the Foreign Service exam, Erwin was hired as a probationary interpreter and arrived at the U.S. Embassy in Istanbul in July 1914. Assigned as consular agent at the coastal city of Brusa, he was "constantly watched by spies who dogged every step I took." But he soon reduced such suspicion by explaining that America did not necessarily support Britain in its war against Germany, Turkey's ally. This stance led Ambassador Henry Morgenthau, Sr., himself German-born, to caution the young consul about his "pro German attitude"—concerns compounded by rumors about Erwin's loyalties. Harvard's alumni bulletin for 1914 reported "it is probable that he is fighting for the Kaiser." An informer later warned the FBI that Erwin's Harvard roommate said he "showed strong pro-German sentiments." Nonetheless, he passed his first Foreign Service review after the embassy decided he should eventually be able to correct "the impression that he is . . . more German than American," thus making him "a useful consular official." By the time Erwin returned to New York on home leave in October 1916, his life had taken a positive turn—promotion to vice consul approved, diplomatic career launched, and marriage proposal to a wealthy brewer's daughter, Louise Piel, accepted.[80]

While Erwin was adapting to diplomatic life, sister Mathilde was making steady progress toward her doctorate at Leipzig University until the war intervened. En route back to Germany in 1915 from a summer scholarship at the famed Stazione Zoologica in Naples, she was interrogated by French authorities who suspected her of espionage. Upon reaching Leipzig, Mathilde was approached by

German agents who offered her $25,000 and the doctorate if she would return to France as a spy. But she managed to convince the agents she was just "a harmless and rather senseless" young student.[81]

In 1916, as Germany's wartime austerity deepened, Mathilde escorted her mother back to New York and became a bridesmaid at brother Erwin's wedding to Louise Piel. The bridal party included sister Agnes Piel, Mathilde herself, and her own cousin Margarita Schile, fiancée of the bride's brother Rudolf, thus providing her with much of that intelligence on the Piels she later gave Colonel Godson.[82]

Now in her mid-20s, Mathilde was a striking presence, "a handsome woman," wrote one reporter a few years later, who radiated an aura of "vitality" with dark, piercing eyes, waves of jet black hair that framed her "firm, well cut features," a rich, resonant voice, and an aristocratic aura of supreme self-confidence.[83]

5.4. Mathilde Lange, circa 1918.

After the wedding, her brother Erwin returned to Turkey with his bride and, in January 1917, Mathilde resumed her studies in Germany. "Leipzig was a different city from that which I had left a few months earlier," she later told a Boston reporter. "Foodstuffs were so scarce that they were rationed in such small lots as one egg every three weeks! I lost 40 pounds in less than a year."[84] Realizing the strategic significance of such privation, Mathilde began reporting to the U.S. vice consul at Leipzig, William P. Kent, thus serving, during the months before America entered the war, in "an unofficial capacity for the United States intelligence department."[85]

Advent of War

Once America declared war on Germany in April 1917, Mathilde was, as a U.S. citizen, expelled from Leipzig University and required to report daily to city police. For the next five months she was caught in legal limbo—denied her degree, under police surveillance, and working desperately though a local lawyer to win an exit visa.[86]

Meanwhile, America's entry into the war brought her brother Erwin and his bride Louise Piel unexpectedly to Berne, Switzerland. The young couple had enjoyed just two months of languid consular life in the diplomatic backwater that was Brusa, Turkey, before America declared war on Germany in April.[87] Almost immediately, the Ottoman Empire severed relations with Washington, forcing the entire U.S. delegation, including the Langes, to take the train from Istanbul to neutral Switzerland, reaching Berne on May 23. There, waiting at the U.S. embassy, was a welcome telegram from Washington promoting Erwin to consul at Vigo in northern Spain, a strategic port astride Atlantic sea-lanes.[88]

But the situation in Switzerland soon took an unfortunate turn. Just days after arrival, Erwin had a revealing conversation with the U.S. consul at Berne, William P. Kent, who had befriended his mother and sister Mathilde during a previous posting at Leipzig. "Consul Kent informs me," the U.S. ambassador, Pleasant A. Stovall, cabled the Secretary of State on June 1, 1917, "that in conversation with Vice-Consul Erwin Lange and Mrs. Lange, who are now in Berne, Lange scoffed at the participation of the United States in the war saying we could not raise an army and if we did the Germans would sink all the ships." Referring to Louise Piel Lange, he added: "Mrs. Lange was violently pro-German in conversation and stated emphatically that she was *Deutsch-Freundlich*

[German Friendly]." In reference to Erwin's new post in Spain, the ambassador stated: "It is most dangerous to have such a man in our Consular service at this time." Three days later on June 4, Secretary of State Robert Lansing replied via telegram: "Instruct Lange proceed America. Immediately."[89] After Erwin reached Washington in mid-July, the State Department granted him a month's leave while his loyalty was under review.[90]

Midst this hiatus, Erwin's sister Mathilde finally secured an exit visa and, in early August, crossed the German border into Switzerland. Almost immediately, she called on William Kent, her former Leipzig contact who was now U.S. consul in Berne. Impressed by her insights into Germany's war economy, Kent interrupted his transmission of a cable to Washington with "confidential information regarding the state of affairs in Germany" to include additional information obtained "through the unexpected arrival from Germany of an American young lady . . . of unusual intelligence and rare powers of observation." Now, in a rapid-fire recitation for this cable dated August 7, Mathilde enumerated the signs of Germany's economic crisis—strikes at Leipzig's munitions plants, a spreading sense of defeatism, and press propaganda that any army the United States might raise will "be destroyed on the voyage to Europe."[91]

While debriefing Mathilde, Consul Kent was also compiling a five-page "Confidential Report" for the Secretary of State about her brother, vice consul Erwin Lange, repeating all that negative information he had already given to the ambassador. But now he added some disturbing new details. The consul's wife, Louise Piel Lange, "expressed to me in the presence of Lange, and without disclaimer from him, such pro German sentiments that I observed to her: 'The jails in America are full of lesser traitors than you.' "[92]

All this was damaging enough, but the last two pages of Consul Kent's report were full of damning new details that could only have come from Mathilde, Erwin's own sister. Since his return to New York, Kent continued, Erwin Lange "has failed to hold any relations with his mother because of her lack of sympathy with the position he has taken." And for similar reasons, the consul added, "he is at variance with his sister in Switzerland." Moreover, Erwin "has married the daughter of a German American brewer in New York of pronounced German sympathies. The name of the family is Piel." Since Erwin's return to live with his Piel mother-in-law, her home "in New York as well as her summer home in Maine have been searched by the secret agents of our government." With his "fires of patriotism . . . blazing high," Kent insisted that he "will omit nothing, however disagreeable," to place the full facts before the Department.[93]

A month later, State replied that "the statements in your dispatch" concerning Consul Lange "have been carefully noted," adding "the Department requested and accepted his resignation."[94] Through these reports, Erwin was also blacklisted as an "alien-suspect" in the confidential *List A* of subversives that the Office of Naval Intelligence (ONI) circulated among U.S. security agencies. Moreover, Military Intelligence now listed him as "former US consul; pro-German."[95]

While Consul Kent's summary of his conversation with Erwin seems accurate, he misconstrued this family feud whose causes sprang, not from politics, but from the outlandish personality of Erwin's mother, Julia Lange. When Louise was hospitalized shortly after the marriage, Julia accused Maria Piel of fobbing off an ailing bride on her brilliant son. Maria replied that the accusation "astonished me," insisting "my daughter was in possession of complete healthfulness."[96]

Refusing to be placated, Julia Lange sharpened her attacks on the Piels. Just weeks after Erwin's forced resignation, she walked uninvited into the Albany office of FBI agent Roland Ford to demand the name of the person who had informed on her son. When the agent refused, Julia, unaware that the informer was her own daughter Mathilde, blamed her daughter-in-law Louise Piel, insisting "her son's wife was Pro-German in every way and that she had caused him a great deal of trouble and annoyance because of his Diplomatic Office." Though mystified, the agent duly recommended an investigation of Louise Piel Lange.[97]

After his dismissal and return to New York in August 1917, Erwin was soon embroiled in a desperate appeal to win his brother Conrad a draft exemption on psychological grounds. Although Conrad himself told his draft board near Albany that he was eager to serve, Erwin appealed for an exemption by submitting doctors' depositions documenting fifty-one months of institutional treatment from 1904 to 1917. The doctors warned that military service would "almost surely bring on a new attack of his psychosis, of indefinite duration."[98]

Despite all the detailed medical evidence, Agent Ford advised his FBI supervisor that, in light of Erwin Lange's "pronounced pro-German sentiments," it was very likely that he was "simply endeavoring to keep his brother out of the American Army." So tainted was Erwin's name that the local draft board found his brother Conrad "normal except when excited by the efforts of his mother and others who are apparently pro-German in their sympathies." After shipping him off to Massachusetts for basic training, the board did, however, advise the camp commander he should "be placed under strict observation."[99] A few years after the war, Conrad Lange died, reportedly by suicide, in his mother's home at the age of 38 and was interred in the mausoleum of his mother's family, the Schiles, at Woodlawn Cemetery.[100]

Agent "Adolph"

While Erwin's disloyalty sealed brother Conrad's fate before a New York draft board, their sister Mathilde was becoming a trusted U.S. secret agent in Switzerland. In the weeks after she reported brother Erwin's disloyalty, Mathilde impressed staff at the U.S. embassy with her valuable information about Germany's economy. After a briefing by Mathilde, whom he described as "a woman of unusual intelligence," Ambassador Stovall cabled State that his "informant does not believe German army can be broken down." Instead of a purely military solution, she advised that "Germans can be most easily attacked on the political side," with propaganda emphasizing "German diplomatic blunders such as Mexican note . . . and . . . cruelties on part of Government regarding submarine warfare." Attesting to the value of this intelligence, the ambassador's cable concluded, with reference to the U.S. military commander in France: "Pershing informed."[101]

Not long after she filed this report, the U.S. consul at Berne, William Kent, advised Mathilde that "a certain Mr. X would call on me within a few days." Indeed, an embassy staffer soon "came offering me the position with American Intelligence," initially with the Office of Naval Intelligence (ONI) and later with the army's Military Intelligence Division (MID). As a neutral buffer between France and Germany, wartime Switzerland was a nest of spies with eleven U.S. military attachés, all assigned to intelligence, in an embassy staff of just nineteen personnel. Though she refused to return to Germany as a spy, a suicide mission, Mathilde agreed to use "my fluency with three languages" to aid U.S. intelligence in Zurich, then the epicenter of wartime espionage. As cover, she entered the Zoology doctoral program at Zurich University and MID assigned her the code name "Adolph."[102] For the next two years, she would work on her doctoral dissertation under a leading Swiss biologist, while operating undercover in both U.S. intelligence and counterintelligence—that is, both espionage to penetrate enemy networks and counterespionage to expose potential subversives inside Allied ranks.[103]

To block Germany from using Swiss neutrality to procure strategic war materiel, Mathilde moved into a Zurich boarding house. There, as she later told a reporter, "several German buying agents were living . . . successfully smuggling materials they needed to carry on the war, such as oils, cotton, fats, and sugar." Using her fluency in German to monitor their conversations and her laboratory forceps to extract "letters from the mail boxes of her German fellow boarders," she sent the U.S. embassy coded messages identifying suspect shipments.[104]

Mathilde's work in counterintelligence was by no means limited to her own family. When the U.S. vice consul at Berne, Charles L. Chandler, advised ONI that the Argentine consul-general at Paris, George de Frias, was a German agent, Mathilde intercepted a postcard addressed to him in Switzerland "which conclusively proved his guilt." In October 1918, she spotted the Argentine at Zurich and kept him under observation until he left for Lausanne.[105]

Though usually careful to conceal her work with codes and "cut-outs," in January 1918 Mathilde adopted the public guise of a loyal American expatriate to accuse the U.S. consul at Zurich, James C. McNally, of espionage on behalf of Germany. The State Department, she said, believed "he is procuring valuable information for them through his son-in-law [Lieutenant Fritz] Menzing, an officer in the German navy." But Berlin, she warned, was well aware of the contact and still allowed this officer "to repeatedly cross the German frontier and visit his father-in-law in Zurich." She suggested "the German Government may be using him . . . to send communications to German spies and secret agents in America." Consequently, she denounced McNally as "utterly unfit to hold a consular office."[106] Since the military attaché Colonel Godson was one of her covert contacts, Mathilde's efforts were likely part of his attack on Consul McNally who was in Zurich on a special intelligence mission for the State Department.[107]

All these tensions erupted just a week after receipt of Mathilde's letter when State gave Consul McNally permission to travel to Spain with Lilly Anheuser Busch, widow of famed St. Louis brewer Adolphus Busch. Caught by the war at the family's Rhineland estate, Mrs. Busch, ailing and escorted by her legal counsel Harry Hawes, was homeward bound to avoid confiscation of her fortune by the U.S. Alien Property Custodian—an entourage that offered apt cover for "intelligence work." Nonetheless, Ambassador Stovall cabled Washington from Berne expressing "considerable uneasiness" about this consul and his German son-in-law. In reply, Secretary Lansing instructed the ambassador to monitor Consul McNally's activities "discretely."[108]

When McNally passed through Paris en route back to Switzerland, French authorities, suspicious of his German son-in-law, refused him an exit visa. With the consul thus locked in diplomatic limbo during March and April of 1918, the U.S. delegation at Berne maneuvered desperately to block his return. At this sensitive juncture, Mathilde again wrote the Secretary of State reporting that while socializing with the consul's daughter, the wife of that German navy lieutenant, "it was quite obvious . . . that her father was trying to promote the German peace intrigues."[109]

But Consul McNally used a mix of bluff and bluster to best his critics, Mathilde included. In mid-April, he bluffed the U.S. ambassador in Paris with claims that "the actual plans for the German offensive await me in Zurich."[110] Consequently, Secretary Lansing consulted President Wilson and then cabled the ambassador to "request French Government to permit McNally to return to Zurich."[111]

Next, came the bluster. After six weeks back in Zurich, Secretary Lansing cabled the consul asking about that "pertinent military information." Blaming his enemies, McNally replied that "while I was unjustly detained in Paris to gratify the petty jealousy of . . . the Military Attaché [Godson], valuable . . . military information concerning German second offensive" was lost when his informant left Zurich.[112] To resolve this conflict, Secretary Lansing dispatched Colonel Van Deman, the former MID chief now in Paris. He met McNally at Zurich, found his accusations against colleagues baseless, and ordered him to forward any future intelligence via his erstwhile enemy, Colonel Godson.[113]

After the Armistice in November 1918, Mathilde undertook a final mission for Military Intelligence. Ordered to "investigate Bolshevik activities in Zurich," Mathilde joined the local communist party as a student member. Volunteering as a courier, she "carried messages to their comrades in Paris," which were "first read by the intelligence department." After several months of this dangerous undercover assignment, Mathilde was discharged from the service in April 1919. She was finally free to finish her laboratory research.[114]

Within three months, Mathilde completed her doctoral dissertation "On the Regeneration and Finer Structure of the Arms of the Cephalopods," using octopus specimens gathered at Naples and Monaco that she examined at Professor Karl Hescheler's Zurich laboratory. In approving her dissertation, the professor found her dissections "technically flawless" and her conclusions reached with "the necessary caution." Demonstrating the quality of this work, Dr. Lange published her dissertation in a 1920 issue of the *Journal of Experimental Zoology*.[115]

Before leaving Zurich, Dr. Lange performed a private ritual to mark the end of her undercover career as agent Adolph. "Over a flame a piece of paper was held," she later told a Boston reporter. "On that paper was written the name Adolph. When that paper lay black and charred my whole official record as a spy was destroyed. That is the best way. A spy dies when the war dies."[116]

Adrenaline Addiction

Not really. Mathilde was so addicted to the adrenaline of this double life that she would make repeated attempts to resume her covert career, again informing on her family circle to establish credibility with the intelligence community. Leaving Zurich in late October 1918, she traveled by train 500 kilometers beyond Berlin to the old Lange estate deep in East Prussia at Lonkorrek (now Lakorek, Poland), collecting intelligence at every stop. As soon as she landed at New York in January 1920, Mathilde briefed the former vice consul at Berne, Charles Chandler, now working for a Philadelphia bank. He forwarded the intelligence to ONI, reminding them "she did a great deal of work . . . to the satisfaction of Colonel Van Deman," and was "highly commended by the General Staff." During that recent visit to East Prussia, she had learned, through her relations in the "old German nobility," about "a vast conspiracy . . . by members of the old national nobility to place the little boy William, the son of the Crown Prince . . . on the throne of Germany." To this end, East Prussia's aristocrats "have given all their silverware, spoons, and plates to be melted for a fund." At the end of his letter, Chandler suggested Mathilde deserved some "recognition" for wartime service, adding that she "is very anxious to secure a position in the Bureau of Animal Research in the Department of Agriculture."[117]

In a later letter, Chandler reported that Mathilde was now living in New York with her aunt at 132 East 60th Street, the same house "that was raided for the library of Dr. St. George, and where machinations of various German agents were carried on during the war." Since Mathilde reported that Dr. St. George had "destroyed a large number of papers" after the wartime FBI raids and was now colluding with a suspicious German spy, Chandler recommended the doctor should be watched. At this volatile cusp between the war's anti-German hysteria when "alien" assets were seized and the postwar "red scare" when thousands of resident aliens were deported, Mathilde's betrayal of family confidences was potentially quite dangerous. Fortunately for the Piel family, Washington was, with the war over, now more concerned about Bolsheviks than German brewers.[118]

In March 1920, ONI replied, calling Mathilde's report "very interesting" and adding they would assist her with employment so "she will feel that whatever information she may gain will rightly belong first to the Office of Naval Intelligence." Within a week, its director, Admiral Albert P. Niblack, wrote a friend in the Department of Agriculture on her behalf and Mathilde was soon hired as a researcher in their New York office. Continuing her investigation of the royalist restoration, Mathilde advised ONI in July that "large sums of money are being raised in New York among certain Germans and German Americans for the purpose of . . . restoring the Kaiser to the throne." Through the leadership of the city's avowed monarchists, she said, "funds are being collected under the guise of money for feeding starving German children." In response, ONI said it was "much interested" and encouraged her further investigation.[119]

After a year with Agriculture, Mathilde chafed at the restraints on her own research and began applying for academic jobs. Finding her "one of the best equipped . . . teachers in the country," Wheaton College, a small women's school near Boston, hired her to chair its Biology Department in the fall of 1921. For the next thirty years, Mathilde built a reputation as a dedicated teacher who nurtured women scientists. Throughout this long academic career, she also stayed close to her brother Erwin's family, spending holidays at Lake Parlin, Maine, with Piel in-laws who remained utterly oblivious about her wartime work.[120]

5.5. Dr. Mathilde Lange, Wheaton College, Massachusetts, circa 1930. (Credit: Smithsonian Institution Archives. Image SIA2008-5063)

Yet the war's shadow lingered. When she was awarded a year's sabbatical in 1927–28 at the Stazione Zoologica in Naples, Italy, her thoughts again turned to espionage. Through her wartime comrade Chandler, Mathilde contacted Naval Intelligence asking "if there would be any opportunity for me to serve the government" as she had during the war since the college was too poor to pay her sabbatical salary. ONI inserted this letter in her file. But there is no record of any reply.[121] Cut free from government service, Mathilde would spend the next forty years reflecting on the meaning of her wartime work, caught between countries and cultures, burning with a blinding patriotism.

At the end of this sabbatical in 1928, the death of her uncle Dr. Friedrich Lange brought Mathilde back to the family estate at Lonkorrek, East Prussia—a ten-bedroom manor house surrounded by 2,000 acres of orchards and pastures. Since her brother Erwin had spurned this inheritance, several of the local gentry and tenant farmers had called "begging me to take it." But she refused to become a Prussian landlord, calling this "an entirely new mode of life in surroundings which are quite foreign to me." Instead, she packed the estate's library, with books dating back to the eighteenth century, for shipment to Wheaton College, and caught a trans-Atlantic liner to start stumping her Hudson Valley county for the Democratic presidential candidate, Alfred E. Smith.[122]

A decade later at the start of World War II, Washington asked Mathilde to resume her espionage work, but she "decided she'd had enough," even though she considered any Nazi victory "a calamity."[123] Instead, she decided to warn Wheaton College students about the dangers of war.[124]

In November 1941, just weeks before Pearl Harbor, Professor Lange stood before the student body in the campus chapel and read a letter from an American lieutenant stationed on the coast of Iceland.[125] "For me," wrote Frederick Lange, her brother Erwin's son, "it has been ages of feverish activity, nights spent in open motor boats on storm-swept seas with the sea water drenching through to the skin." He closed saying: "The feeling you have of being one of several thousand men, each giving more than he thought he could give, for a common purpose. If only we could carry over that spirit in our later civilian life."

"Twenty-three years ago," Mathilde continued, "I too was at an outpost. I too was conscious of being one of many giving what they could to a common cause. But I was not as wise as this young man is today. I did not see the let down that would follow." During the Great War, she and others felt they were serving "a common ideal" of spreading "democracy and freedom" through a "greater amount of international cooperation." For her the real euphoria came, not at Germany's defeat in November 1918, but six months later. Hiking the hills above Zurich, she heard church bells "joyously proclaiming" formation of the League of Nations and the expectation of "a saner world."

When she came home to New York in 1920, "then came the let-down." Everyone was dismissing the League of Nations as "a gang of crooked diplomats" and retreating from the world with the cry of "Back to Normalcy." Today, with the advent of a new war, "we are being presented with a staggering bill for the lunacy of 'back to normalcy.'" If, at the end of this war, we again "make the same fatal mistake and allow history to be turned back," then in another twenty-five years, Mathilde warned these college students, "history will be grimly repeating itself for your generation, as it is grimly repeating itself for my generation today."[126]

Indeed, twenty-five years later in the mid-1960s, America became mired in the Vietnam War and the generations were divided as never before. By then Mathilde had long since retired to her home in Central Valley, New York, that she called "Little Lonkorrek" after her foregone Prussian estate. At the peak of the anti-Vietnam War protests, she joined the nearby Monroe Peace Council.

Young and old for peace

5.6. Dr. Mathilde Lange protesting the Vietnam War, Monroe, New York, 1971. (Credit: Chris Farlekas, *Sunday Record*, Middletown, NY)

A photograph in the local paper of their monthly vigil in April 1971 showed a white-haired lady standing beneath a flower-power banner, raising her hand in a peace sign. The caption identified her as Dr. Mathilde Lange, attending the rally to celebrate her 83rd birthday, which, it turned out, would be her last.[127]

This dramatic change in Mathilde's response to America's wars, from secret agent to antiwar activist, seemed almost an act of penance. Yet we can only wonder whether she ever felt any remorse for all the damage she had done, and tried to do, to both her brothers and Piel relations by informing on her family circle.

Legacy of Surveillance

Looking back a century later, World War I left scars on the Piel family and many German Americans that seem deep and lasting. By war's end, the Piel name was tarred with the brush of subversion, delaying the family's acceptance into New York society for another generation. The five Piel cousins who served were generally denied the distinction of commission or combat, instead relegated to demeaning stateside duties.

The Piel experience makes them exemplars of the war's wrenching, coerced assimilation. From the bitter aftermath of Germany's Revolution of 1848 through the start of World War I in 1914, Germans had migrated freely to America— becoming the country's largest ethnic group, enjoying unprecedented prosperity, and forming urban enclaves where they reveled in their language and culture. But at the start of war with Germany in 1917, Washington dealt with the threat of disaffection from these millions of immigrants, many still loyal to their Fatherland, by a forced-draft assimilation that soon obliterated every public sign of Germanic identity. Washington also contained any possible threat of German American espionage by creating the country's first internal security apparatus and conducting surveillance of their communities unprecedented in scale and scope.

None of the Piels ever learned the source of the pervasive hostility they encountered during the war. They never knew they were victims of a vast security apparatus, with countless informers that included neighbors, college classmates, and their own relative. So strong was the wartime prejudice against German Americans that even the most assimilated like Mathilde Lange, granddaughter of a U.S. Civil War veteran, felt compelled to prove her Americanism unequivocally, perhaps even to herself, by loyal, even blindly loyal service that superseded all personal ties, whether to friends or family. In retrospect, we cannot calculate the intangible cost that her espionage and the wider wartime surveillance inflicted upon the Piel family circle, which was broken in spirit by war's end. Many family members would hide their humiliation by quitting the city after the war and scattering to remote rural locations where they retreated into private lives.

For those caught in the maw of state security and stigmatized as disloyal, as were several of these second-generation Piels, the experience was both demoralizing and damaging. For German Americans as a whole, the forced Americanization was painful—their language outlawed, orderly lives terrorized by mob violence, community organizations banned, and their signature beverage prohibited. During the war, half of the forty-eight states restricted the teaching of German language in schools and several banned speaking the language in public. By war's end, half the country's 500 German-language newspapers had folded. Countless German American families were, like the Piels, subjected to intrusive investigations by the 350,000 vigilantes of the American Protective League, even though, as a U.S. commission later reported, "no actual spy was ever apprehended by this semi-official network." Conscription of German Americans was relentless, with draft raids to ferret out "slackers" and no exemptions for pacifist German sects, the Mennonites and Hutterites, many of whom fled to Canada "under a barrage of patriotic oppression."[128] Confronted with such formidable pressures, the once vibrant German American identity was largely extirpated by the time Armistice came, even though it had been just twenty months since the United States had declared war on Germany.

Yet if we compare this treatment of German Americans to the wartime experience of other ethnic groups, all this surveillance and suppression seems comparatively benign. From its founding through the present, the United States has often dealt harshly with groups whose alien loyalties were deemed threatening in times of war.

During the American Revolution, many loyalists, the despised "Tories," remained steadfast for Great Britain, with 19,000 volunteers serving in forty-two crown militia. Stripped of property and fearing retribution at war's end, some 80,000 Loyalists left the country, with half settling in Canada where they established that country's English-speaking community. The Treaty of Paris ending hostilities in 1783 provided that Congress would "earnestly recommend" the states restore the Loyalists' lost property. But the states all refused. To provide some compensation, the British Parliament paid £3 million to just 2,291 Loyalist claimants—but a tiny fraction of the many thousands more who had lost everything. Under the Jay Treaty of 1795 that restored commerce between the two nations, Britain paid $10 million for wartime damages to American ship-owners. But there was no compensation for Loyalists.[129]

Just a generation after World War I, the United States went to war with Japan and dealt with the imagined threat of Japanese-American espionage by incarcerating some 120,000 West Coast Nisei and confiscating their property—houses, farms, stores, and fishing boats. In 1948, Congress passed the Japanese-American Claims Act that paid just $38 million for property losses the Federal Reserve estimated at $400 million. Some thirty years after the war in 1987, Congress approved payments of $20,000 to each of the 82,219 Japanese-American survivors who had suffered internment—too little, too late to compensate for all the lost life opportunities brought by the wartime confiscation of accrued family assets.[130]

Unable to incarcerate 10 million residents of German descent during World War I, Washington opted instead for systematic surveillance. Although a transgression of civil liberties that came with heavy emotional costs, this policy spared most German Americans any loss of assets, preserving the capital they would need to adapt, survive, and prosper. Instead of incarceration or confiscation, they were forced, often by the threat of mob violence, to invest in Liberty Bonds that were redeemed, with interest, after the war—a striking contrast to the treatment of both the Tories and Nisei.

If sheer numbers protected German Americans from punishment or property losses, the wealthiest members of their communities, the brewers, became surrogates, veritable scapegoats for all that virulent wartime hostility. By branding the brewers as subversive and punishing two of the biggest by impounding their fortunes, the resurgent temperance forces won a succession of wartime prohibition measures that would, just a year after the war's end, destroy over a thousand German American breweries.

Wartime Rationing

Apart from the covert surveillance, the war also brought a cascading repression of German language, culture, and identity that culminated in the prohibition of beer, the German American community's iconic beverage. Midst the general "anti-German panic," Beethoven was banned from symphonies. German language was purged from schools. Mobs attacked suspect Germans, beating hundreds, killing dozens, and, most notoriously, even lynching an innocent immigrant miner in

Illinois. There was also a surge of xenophobia toward distinctive German American products—sauerkraut, hamburger, and beer. Sauerkraut was quickly renamed "liberty cabbage." Hamburger became "Salisbury steak." But beer was beer. The convergence of patriotism with temperance would bedevil its brewing throughout the war.[131] Sensing trouble, Piels jettisoned their slogan "Real German Beer" and accelerated the search for new beverages that would pass the test of temperance.

Just as the family's young men volunteered for military service, so their brewery enlisted in the war effort. By the third Liberty Loan bond campaign in April 1918, Piel Bros. went "over the top" with 100 percent participation by all 188 employees for an impressive total of $10,200. To achieve this distinction, the company donated ten bonds for a company lottery and underwrote subscriptions for all "worthy men of good standing in the company's service," even those likely to default on their payments. To support the country's "Americanization Program," the company reported that two-thirds of its employees, 124 out of 188, were native German speakers, although everyone spoke English and all but three were naturalized U.S. citizens.[132]

Despite these gestures toward Americanism, neither the Piels' brewery nor its industry could escape the consequences of their Germanic identity. Before the United States entered the war, the pressure for prohibition of all alcohol had increased slowly but steadily from 1915 onward, with a growing number of states going dry and Eastern towns enforcing temperance through "local option elections." Once Washington declared war on Germany in April 1917, however, the taint attached to all things German allowed an intensification of the prohibition movement, dressing its nativism in nationalist guise.[133]

Playing upon the rising wartime hysteria, the Anti-Saloon League (ASL) cranked out pamphlets asking, "How can any loyal citizen, be he wet or dry, help or vote for a trade that is aiding the pro-German Alliance?" Such patriotic pressure effectively silenced the brewing industry's opposition to prohibition.[134] Congress quickly banned alcohol inside a five-mile "dry zone" around all military installations and imposed total abstinence upon the armed forces, on base and off. Just four months after America entered the war, Congress passed the Lever Food Act in August 1917, authorizing the president to limit grains for alcohol manufacture.[135]

With intimations of a national prohibition, that December President Wilson issued an executive order cutting grain allocation for brewing by 30 percent and limiting beer to 2.75 percent alcohol. Unlike many brewers, Piel Bros. reacted positively to the news. At its board meeting that month, Henry Piel said that, since they used 25 to 50 percent more ingredients, hops and malt, than competitors, "a beer, made from 70% of raw materials, brewed so as to reach full attenuation with Alcoholic Content of 2.75% by weight would be an excellent brew."[136]

Just three days later, on December 18, 1917, Congress, which had rejected a similar bill just three years earlier, now passed enabling legislation for the 18th Amendment to the Constitution stipulating that, a year after ratification, "the manufacture, sale, or transportation of intoxicating liquors . . . for beverage purposes is hereby prohibited." Although the amendment still required ratification by thirty-six of the forty-eight state legislatures, Prohibition was now a palpable threat to the brewing industry.[137]

A month later, William Piel made an unsuccessful attempt to persuade the board of the U.S. Brewers' Association (USBA) of the need to fight the amendment's ratification. Unable to speak publicly midst the war's rising hysteria, William worked quietly behind the closed doors of industry associations. Though temperance advocates were "growing continuously stronger every year," they could still be checked, he advised the USBA, by a "major campaign" funded from a "running assessment on the monthly barrelage of the members to create a huge annual fund."[138]

Although it rejected his recommendation, the USBA invited William "to formulate ways and means of fighting the Prohibition Movement"—allowing him an entrée to turn the industry toward defense of his own company's new product, near beer. The Midwest "shipping breweries" Pabst and Anheuser-Busch agreed, William said, "there was a real danger that Prohibition might some day become a national law." The big northeastern brewers were, by contrast, "most emphatic that this danger would never overtake the industry." In this discussion, William was the only dissenting voice among these Eastern brewers since his experience with temperance in the South was, he felt, the "straw that shows which way the wind blows." Even though the momentum for ratification was accelerating, this USBA meeting ended with a delusional consensus that "the Prohibition Amendment would lack the necessary state ratifications to carry." Reporting on this meeting to the Piel's board in January 1918, William warned that wartime grain restrictions "indicated a prohibition trend" and recommended "every effort be made to build up the near-beer business of the company."[139] As a small family business, Piels was far more attuned to the public mood than its big regional competitors who seemed dangerously detached from political reality.

After failing to persuade the nation's beer barons that Prohibition was imminent, William invested his energies in more realistic advocacy groups. While the USBA wallowed in denial, dissident Western brewers met at Chicago that January to form an alternative association, the National Association of Cereal Beverage Manufacturers, on a shared belief that "the possibility of country-wide Prohibition had to be reckoned with." Reflecting his growing reputation in industry circles, William was the only Eastern executive invited to join a board of prominent Midwest brewers.[140]

A month later, William was also elected president of a statewide organization formed to fight Prohibition, the Bottling Brewers Protective Association of Greater New York.[141] With the unanimous backing of his fellow directors, William arranged the printing of aggressive anti-Prohibition neck labels for pasting on every bottle of beer:

—"The more the Legislators hear from you, the less you will hear of Prohibition. Protest!"

—"Agitators want a Prohibition Amendment to the United States Constitution to take away your liberty. Protest!"

To support this campaign, the Piel's board authorized William's use of these labels on the company's bottles "for such length of time as he may determine."[142]

In an attempt to draw the Western and Eastern brewers into a united anti-prohibition campaign, William Piel drafted a thirteen-page memo urging the formation of "an Eastern auxiliary" to the Chicago-based National Association of Cereal Beverage Manufacturers. Balancing the industry's needs with his own firm's interests, William argued that the temperance movement's tolerance of near beer "having ½ of 1% alcohol" represented a viable pathway to their industry's survival.[143]

Without the united efforts of the nation's brewers, this infant near beer industry will, William warned, "be murdered in its cradle." In the event of national prohibition, this association should defend near beer by promoting "attractive soft drink stores" free from "the objectionable features of the brewer's saloon." With the full backing of the National Association's Chicago headquarters, William convened five of New York's leading brewers in July 1918 to form an Eastern Auxiliary of low-alcohol producers that would protect their new product.[144]

Subversive Brewers

After decades of a losing fight against temperance laws at state and local levels, the U.S. Brewers' Association (USBA) was finally silenced during the war by accusations that their anti-prohibition publicity was akin to pro-German propaganda. Once ratification of the 18th Amendment shifted to the state legislatures, the Anti-Saloon League arranged for Congressional hearings into German American subversion, using secret funding to procure key witnesses. In February 1918, the Senate Judiciary Committee began investigating the National German American Alliance's attempts to promote German language instruction— the first in a succession of hearings that became increasingly accusatory.[145]

In its report, the Senate committee condemned the German American Alliance as disloyal. "Instead of summoning those of German descent to join with all other citizens in the defense of those things which we hold dear," the Senate concluded, "it urged them to 'hold together closely and intimately' with the . . . enemies of our country."[146] The committee's principal witness charged, without evidence, that the Alliance "was operating in favor of the German general staff." By interrogating the USBA's publicist, Percy Andreae, the committee found breweries had provided 80 percent of the funding for the Alliance's anti-prohibition activities.[147] Broadcasting this revelation in a mass-circulation pamphlet, the ASL's leader Wayne Wheeler insisted the Alliance must be prohibited, as should the "pro-German, crime-producing, food-wasting, youth-corrupting, home-wrecking, treasonable liquor traffic." After a unanimous vote by Congress in July 1918, President Wilson signed legislation revoking the federal charter for the German American Alliance.[148]

Three months later, as the 18th Amendment's ratification continued its march through state legislatures, the Alien Property custodian, A. Mitchell Palmer condemned the USBA as "a vicious interest because it has been unpatriotic" by "spreading German propaganda and sentiments in this country." Specifically, Palmer charged that four prominent brewers—Jacob Ruppert, George Ehret, Gustav Pabst, and Joseph Uihlein—had funded Arthur Brisbane's acquisition of the *Washington Times*. Palmer, later notorious for leading the postwar "red scare," actually had the owner of the *New York Evening Mail* arrested for purchasing the paper with funds from the Busch family, owners of the Anheuser-Busch brewery.[149]

Within days, Senator Lee S. Overman (Democrat, North Carolina) convened his Special Subcommittee that concluded, after nine months of hearings, the

USBA had made "contributions to political campaigns without precedent in the political history of the country" and influenced electoral results by "manipulation of the foreign-language press." Yet testimony quickly discredited Palmer's specific charges that the brewers had tried to control the media.[150] To tar them with guilt by association, inspector Thomas J. Tunney of New York's Bomb Squad testified about the real German agents, directed by their embassy's military attachés, who had set off nearly a hundred bombs in U.S. factories and ships. The 1916 explosion at Jersey City's Black Tom munitions depot was so powerful that it actually shattered windows in Manhattan and damaged the Statue of Liberty.[151]

In its final report of June 1919, the Overman committee charged that the German government drew upon the "powerful German influence in America," particularly the "brewing interests . . . controlled by citizens of German extraction," to accomplish three key aims: (1) block arms shipments to the allies, (2) propagate propaganda to prevent the U.S. from entering the war on England's side, and (3) use the German American Alliance to bring "all citizens . . . of German extraction together and to work publicly and privately for the aims of Germany."[152] In support of this latter charge, the report reproduced the Seminary Endowment Association's expression of gratitude to brewers Gustave Pabst and Gottfried Piel for championing "the cause of German instruction in America."[153] The Senate report concluded that "the political activities of the liquor interests" were, along with Russian Bolshevism, the most serious threats facing the nation.[154]

This malign equation between brewing, Bolshevism, and German propaganda blocked the brewers from any further opposition to the temperance forces. With the once-formidable USBA now silenced, there was no political force left in America that could slow the momentum for a federal prohibition of alcoholic beverages.

Intimations of Prohibition

The war's last months brought a flurry of legislative victories for the "drys" that moved the nation, step-by-step, toward the complete prohibition of all alcoholic beverages. In state after state, legislatures were speeding ratification of the 18th Amendment, bringing the constitutional ban on intoxicating beverages ever closer.[155] Not even the end of hostilities on November 11, 1918, could stop the use of the war as pretext to prohibit alcohol. Just ten days later, President Wilson reluctantly signed the Emergency Agricultural Appropriation Bill, with a rider called the Wartime Prohibition Act, banning alcoholic beverage production after May 1919 and any sale of intoxicating drink after July 1. Since the act did not specify what constituted "intoxicating," the Justice Department accepted the ASL's metric of no more than a half percent alcohol.[156]

On November 23, 1918, just two days after passage of this Wartime Prohibition Act, the Piel's board reached a consensus that this measure was "the first step toward a permanent national prohibition enactment." Consequently, the company resolved to expand output of Piel's low-alcohol Kovar beverage "to the fullest extent."[157]

Showing the prescience of Piel Bros., just eight weeks later, on January 16, 1919, Nebraska became the thirty-sixth state to approve the 18th Amendment, thus ratifying Prohibition, which would start one year from that date. At Piels' annual meeting in March, William reported the plant was preparing for the ban by producing, in addition to its near beer Kovar, a line of bubbly low-alcohol beverages including Apple Ale, Birch Beer, and Ginger Ale as a "new and favorable branch of business."[158]

Two months later, the Piel's board convened a special meeting to consider the impact of the Wartime Prohibition Act's interim ban on real beer sales, effective July 1, 1919. Although President Wilson had asked Congress to rescind this emergency prohibition in light of the rapid military demobilization, the Piel's directors were pessimistic and felt compelled to plan for the law's start. Adding to their conviction, the company's legal counsel advised that a temporary injunction won by the Jacob Hoffman Brewery would not be upheld by higher courts. Piels' sale of real beer with 4 percent alcohol should thus end before July 1.[159]

In light of this advice, William announced that the company's preparations for Prohibition were underway. In recent months, the brewery had produced 11,500 barrels of near beer and soft drinks, an output that was approaching the level of their real beer sales for the first half of the year. There was every reason, William confidently predicted, to expect that the volume of low-alcohol beverages would soon double their earlier beer sales. Consequently, the board granted him "full discretion and power to organize the sales policy of this company to overcome the indicated loss of $300,000 in lager beer sales in 1919."[160]

As the emergency ban on alcohol approached in mid-1919, Piels could look back on these tumultuous war years with some satisfaction. Starting from a base of $680,000 for beer sales alone in 1916, the firm added a line of soft drinks in 1917. Within just two years, the company broke the million-dollar mark for all products, with soft drinks accounting for over 70 percent of these record revenues. By the time Piels ended all real beer production on July 1, 1919, its near beer and soft drink lines were well-established, positioning the firm to maintain sales at this million-dollar mark when permanent Prohibition started in January 1920.[161]

Unlike many of the bigger breweries, Piel Bros. had no doubt been agile in its response to the sweeping changes brought by the war. But even its prescient leaders could not have foreseen the surprising market response that soon would make Prohibition far more difficult for the brewing industry than they could ever have imagined.

6

Prohibition

We were sitting around a room at the Waldorf-Astoria Hotel in midtown Manhattan. It was one of those deep black December afternoons, just before Christmas in 1997, a full year before this book was even an idea. Everyone was exhausted by endless hours of stock trends and tax matters at the quarterly meeting of the family business, M&G Piel Securities, Inc.

To relax, I was deep into William Kennedy's novel *Legs*, the fictionalized biography of New York's notorious bootlegger Jack "Legs" Diamond, who was gunned down at Albany back in 1931. Seeing that big print title on the cover from across the room, Mother, who was then 75, interrupted my reading.

"That was one of my first memories," she said.

"What, you mean you actually knew Legs Diamond?" I asked, somewhat skeptical.

"I was about four and was playing in the large area inside the brewery where the beer wagons used to turn when some cars pulled in," she replied. "My father called me over and I stood next to him, holding his leg as some men got out of the cars. While he spoke to the men, my father's leg started shaking against my hand. It was an unforgettable memory because that was the first time I experienced my father feeling fear. When we got home, I heard my father say to Mommy, 'Legs came today.' Later, when I was older, my mother told me that the bootlegger Legs Diamond had come to the brewery to demand the real beer before it became near beer. The family sent my father out to meet Legs and tell him 'no.' The family often gave him those sorts of difficult jobs."[1]

My mother is a retired professor who delivers her statements lecture-like, to be written down and remembered for the final exam. So I opened my laptop computer, created a document called "Piel Interviews," and wrote a first, short paragraph, pretty much as it appears above. Today that document runs to 300 pages of interview notes from dozens of relatives.

So Mother had started me thinking. Maybe, in all these family stories she had been telling us for the past fifty years, there was something more than a bankrupt brewery and bitter family feuds. A year later when I decided to start this book, I realized that her family had a front-row seat for one of the most disastrous chapters in American history—that "noble experiment," the Prohibition of alcohol.

Prohibition at Piel Bros.

Indeed, the advent of Prohibition in 1919 plunged the Piel family and their brewery into a dismal decade of economic hardship, capricious law enforcement, and gangland death threats. Despite years of planning to survive the absolute ban on the sale of alcoholic beverages, the Piels found the law's actual implementation was full of unpleasant, unexpected twists that brought their company close to bankruptcy.

Their brewery's original destination marketing strategy from the 1880s, with its own beer garden but without any of those "tied saloons," now placed Piel Bros. in a uniquely difficult situation. Many New York brewers survived by either becoming silent partners with bootleggers or selling the prime corner lots once occupied by their own saloons. "When this Constitutionally sanctioned destruction of everybody's living in the business came along," recalled William Piel, Jr., "all those poor saloon keepers were put out of business . . . with no recompense from anybody. So the brewers foreclosed on their mortgages and acquired property at a time when New York real estate was beginning to boom." Seconding this view, his brother Gerard added: "The Piel family did not find itself in possession of the best drugstore sites in New York City, which is what the saloons became. We had nothing but the brewery." These other brewers, explained William, Jr., were hurt by Prohibition, "but they weren't crippled, made poor the way we were."[2]

To survive Prohibition, the Piels would have to market their legal "near beer," with less than a half percent alcohol by volume, while both complying with strict federal regulations and fending off gangsters who demanded either "protection money" or illegal production of real beer. In these challenging times, Piels' second generation needed, and somehow achieved, that absolute solidarity difficult for any family firm. Yet their company's size and structure also had advantages. Just as their agility had allowed them to compete effectively against the big Manhattan brewers before Prohibition, so it would again serve them well when mobsters formed a bootleg combine that favored volume over quality.

By the time an interim wartime prohibition finally came into force on July 1, 1919, Piels at first seemed set, said William, for "the magnificent sweep of a real victory, chiefly due to the growth of Kovar [near beer] Sales." Fulfilling these rosy expectations, the first month's sales of their Kovar near beer that July were "magnificent," shipping 16,000 barrels of beverage—the highest one-month total in the brewery's history. In twenty-six working days that month, the firm loaded 183 carloads of Kovar, an average of seven per day.[3]

Like most of the nation, William Piel would soon be surprised, even stunned, by the events that followed. His predictions of a coming national prohibition had been prescient. But his estimation of its impact was wide of the mark. Only days after those July 1919 sales figures promised such a bright future, an unforeseen market response to Prohibition would soon subvert the firm's survival strategy.

The second month of this temporary wartime prohibition, August 1919, brought Piels a rude awakening from Pennsylvania, until then the firm's "banner state" for Kovar near beer sales. Several customers canceled unshipped orders

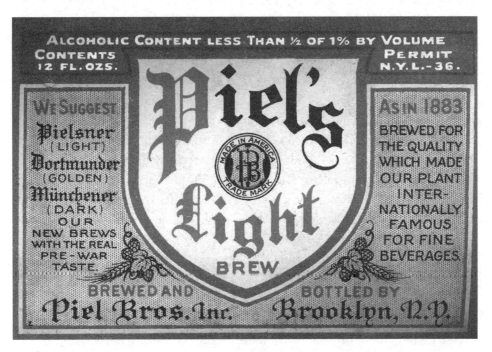

6.1. Label for Piel's near beer with less than 0.5 percent alcohol during Prohibition.

without explanation, mystifying staff at the Piel plant. After William wired the firm's salesman instructions to investigate, the man then visited each of these customers and phoned New York to report, time and again, "Our distributor can't sell near-beer in competition with real beer!" The firm's local distributors subsequently complained about the bootlegging of real beer to local courts, district attorneys, and the federal collectors then enforcing this prohibition. But the illegal sales of real beer kept on proliferating with surprising speed. In the coming weeks, more and more customers canceled orders, extending "this epidemic . . . to New Jersey, New York, Massachusetts and Connecticut." Sadly, William Piel was forced to conclude, "Prohibition had failed to prohibit."[4]

Just four months later in November 1919, the Piel's board called a special meeting "to consider a report by the General Manager on the probable effect of the final passage of [the] Volstead Act upon the future of this corporation." Formally titled the National Prohibition Act, this legislation provided regulations for implementation of the 18th Amendment's ban on intoxicating beverages. Most importantly for the brewers, this law interpreted the vaguely defined constitutional prohibition of "intoxicating liquors" to mean any beverage with alcohol above half of one percent by volume. As one writer put it, this absurdly low level of permissible alcohol "proscribed the lightest of wines, the most diluted forms of beer." While Congress was drafting this law that September, former President William Howard Taft, then a professor at Yale Law School, predicted the manufacture of alcohol "will go out of the hands of law-abiding members of the community, and will be transferred to the quasi-criminal class," making this federal law "a subject of contempt and ridicule in some parts of the nation."[5]

At first, the Volstead Act's impending passage had prompted a flood of orders for the firm's Kovar near beer. Anticipating a surge in demand, the Piel's brewery had hired additional trucks and made plans for accelerated production. When the news of the law's approval reached New York on October 27, 1919, Piels made rush shipments of its near beer late into the night, delivering "the greatest day's draught sales for the winter season in the plant's history." Soft drink production for 1919 surged to nearly 70,000 barrels, far exceeding the 51,000 barrels of real beer sold the previous year. William boldly predicted that "enforcement of the Prohibition Act would prove a boost to the business and . . . the plant would enter a new era of prosperity."[6] Indeed, he noted, "for the first time in our history, we actually prayed for the success of prohibition."[7] Sadly for Piel Bros., former President Taft would prove a better judge of the law's likely impact.

Failure of Prohibition

The federal government simply failed to enforce the legislation's ban on alcohol. Although the Volstead Act's regulations were strict, Congress funded just fifty-five revenue cutters to patrol 5,000 miles of coastline. Washington had only 1,500 underpaid Prohibition agents to cover the whole country. An agent's annual salary of $1,800 was not a living wage. But even so, said the U.S. attorney for the Southern District of New York, "men clamor for the jobs"—a disparity hinting at the corruption to come.[8]

In April 1920, after only three months of full Prohibition, William reported that bootlegging had led to the "general sale in Pennsylvania, New Jersey, upper New York State, Massachusetts, Connecticut, and Rhode Island of real beer." The ready availability of illegal alcohol meant the loss of "almost the entire carload trade" for the firm's Kovar near beer would likely continue indefinitely. To compensate for lost sales, William proposed dealing with chain grocery stores such as Atlantic & Pacific Tea Company (A&P), Bohack Stores, and Gristede Bros., whose 8,000 retail outlets would more than compensate for the loss of about 10 percent of the 800 independent grocers currently customers.[9] Despite this setback from flawed enforcement, William was still optimistic that the brewery was "well equipped to face the future: a splendid product, a deserved reputation for quality, . . . and a well-equipped Sales Force."[10]

Compounding the firm's difficulties, the Cuban government suspended debt payments in October 1920, suddenly curtailing Kovar's exports. For the previous six months, Piels had shipped $280,000 worth of its near beer to Havana as *Extracto de Malta* and had orders worth another $142,000. Now, the firm was stuck with 20,000 gross of ten-ounce Kovar bottles, and had to write off 14,655 barrels of near beer as "cancelled orders."[11]

As financial pressures mounted in early 1921, Piels' directors—Gottfried, Henry, and William—struggled for a survival strategy. Through close analysis of the firm's sales, William reported that, since August 1920, the market for near beer "had slumped badly due to the sale of real beer throughout the Middle Atlantic and Eastern states." Soft drink sales had tumbled from $145,000 in July 1920 to just $29,000 in November. To "combat the loss of business" from bootlegging, the company's best strategy, said William, was marketing its near beer and soft drinks through chain grocery stores such as A&P with demand for "not less than ten thousand cases per week."[12]

But at the start of the next season in early 1921, Piels was forced to fight for this business. Competing near beers, both national and local, were crowding a shrinking market. Desperate for income, Anheuser-Busch was pushing its "Bevo" label, national rival Schlitz had "Famo," and regional breweries were churning out dozens of new brands. As bootleggers captured most of the market and new near beer brands fought for the crumbs remaining, even Busch's Bevo, launched with such success in 1917–18, was now "in serious trouble." Within two years, Bevo sales would fall to "virtually nothing." Nationally, the brewing industry's output plummeted from 60 million barrels of beer in 1917 to just 9 million barrels of near beer in 1921 and only 5 million two years later.[13]

Midst this cut-throat, price-slashing competition, two of the largest chain stores, A&P and National Grocery, advised Piels in mid-1921 "they could no longer afford to pay our price." To counter this threat, William met National Grocery's buyer in Jersey City; he opened bottles of Piels' near beer and its cut-price competitor Ringler. As the two sampled these brews, William winced at "the terrible grain and cooked taste" of Ringler's before asking his host, "What is your verdict?" The buyer conceded saying, "there is absolutely no comparing them— you've got the goods." He added, "Your price is alright, but do not sell [to] any other chain store cheaper than you are [selling to] us." After a similar taste test with Ehret's near beer, A&P's buyer agreed to give Piels an exclusive order of 14,000 cases weekly for their New York stores. Brother Henry, the brewmaster, was optimistic that Piels' quality would soon squeeze Ballantine's low alcohol product out of A&P's New Jersey stores, giving Piels 3,000 exclusive retail outlets in the metropolitan area. With William's win in this "uphill fight," said Henry, "our prospects are good and we hope only to have these sales large enough until real beer comes back."[14]

Struggle to Survive

Without new financing, the company pared every possible expense to the bone, selling off 22,000 surplus kegs and seeking expert advice for plant efficiencies to survive in these hard times.[15] In April 1921, the firm's consulting engineers Ford, Bacon & Davis delivered an efficiency report that William decided to implement almost in its entirety. The sudden decline in the company's business had created costly redundancies—75 percent of plant capacity idle, excess containers accumulating in the yards, bloated labor force, high refrigeration costs, and

Table 6.1: Piel's Sales By-the-Glass at Plant, Bottled Beer, and Soft Drinks, 1900–1932

Year	Beer Barrels	Beer By Glass	Bottled Beer	Beer Total	Soft Drink	Total	Operating Profit (Loss)
1900	n.d.	$23,898	$210,620	$664,185	$ -0-	$664,185	$ n.d.
1901	n.d.	27,570	221,110	722,351	-0-	722,351	n.d.
1902	n.d.	17,972	238,597	776,777	-0-	776,777	n.d.
1903	58,575	28,766	258,572	810,419	-0-	810,419	n.d.
1904	57,353	16,809	276,323	794,514	-0-	794,514	n.d.
1905	59,258	22,328	317,601	868,303	-0-	868,303	n.d.
1906	63,988	17,846	362,808	938,612	-0-	938,612	n.d.
1907	60,527	17,169	383,491	927,417	-0-	927,417	n.d.
1908	47,904	15,145	396,770	830,968	-0-	830,968	n.d.
1909	42,653	11,363	398,598	780,879	-0-	780,879	n.d.
1910	45,875	7,249	415,720	823,258	-0-	823,258	n.d.
1911	46,114	6,603	427,346	834,523	-0-	834,523	n.d.
1912	48,919	-0-	375,697	803,259	-0-	803,529	n.d.
1913	53,478	-0-	376,660	838,289	-0-	839,893	n.d.
1914	57,021	-0-	371,902	881,590	-0-	882,134	n.d.
1915	n.d.	-0-	316,749	789,269	-0-	789,169	n.d.
1916	92,299	-0-	325,579	792,173	-0-	792,172	n.d.
1917	n.d.	-0-	358,927	776,003	48,736	824,741	n.d.
1918	n.d.	-0-	n.d.	784,370	384,689	1,169,059	n.d.
1919	n.d.	-0-	n.d.	610,465	682,915	1,293,381	n.d.
1920	77,085	-0-	-0-	-0-	1,132,759	1,132,759	28,690
1921	40,071	-0-	-0-	-0-	573,612	573,612	12,106
1922	38,735	-0-	-0-	-0-	498,752	498,752	5,185
1923	32,974	-0-	-0-	-0-	358,798	358,798	23,347
1924	30,106	-0-	-0-	-0-	359,016	359,016	(661)
1925	50,517	-0-	-0-	-0-	563,183	563,183	102,731
1926	47,940	-0-	-0-	-0-	541,025	541,025	84,039
1927	55,246	-0-	-0-	-0-	656,909	656,909	102,109
1928	73,884	-0-	-0-	-0-	762,276	762,276	181,380
1929	75,315	-0-	-0-	-0-	856,431	856,431	242,231
1930	70,320	-0-	-0-	-0-	n.d.	n.d.	n.d.
1931	51,590	-0-	-0-	-0-	n.d.	n.d	n.d.
1932	28,821	-0-	-0-	-0-	n.d.	n.d.	n.d.

Source: Board of Directors, May 26, 1915; Memorandum on Beer Business, February 24, 1920, Piel Bros. Minutes Book No. 1. Board of Directors, March 11, 1930, January 29, 1932, December 20, 1933, Piel Bros. Minutes Book No. 2. Board of Directors, February 1, 1934, Piel Bros. Minutes Book No. 3.

excessive inventory of malt and hops. Within just ten days, William proposed economies "effected by a better layout in plant and through a redistribution of labor," as well as the introduction of "effective cost accounting systems" for both sales and operations. To this end, he had "a heated conference with the Labor Unions" that resulted in the dismissal of many fulltime workers, reducing labor costs to $2,000 weekly. With these projected savings, William planned to work with J. Walter Thompson of Madison Avenue to raise summer sales by 125 percent through "local newspaper advertising." Some of this optimism was based on William's hopes for approval of medicinal sales of real beer, though his consulting engineers had noted, pessimistically, that this "is predicated entirely on the ruling of a government official and not on a court decision."[16]

Disappointing sales in the 1921 summer season confirmed the wisdom of these economies. After excellent returns in 1919 when "the Plant had sold Sparkling Apple Juice to the leading N.Y. hotels at a price of $19.50 per Half-Barrel," sales began dropping. Competitors, William reported, "were now selling clarified, sparkling ciders at such low prices that the market had been ruined."[17] By August 1921, the situation was so dire that the company's bondholders, Gottfried and Maria, wrote the board jointly suggesting sale of redundant properties and equipment to generate operating capital.[18] By the end of the year, the brewery's annual sales had fallen by over half to $570,000, with an operating loss of $37,000 after interest on outstanding bonds. Between 1900 and 1919 revenues had climbed steadily from $660,000 to $1.3 million, but now the company's income plunged under Prohibition to a nadir of $360,000 in 1923 before starting a slow, painful climb to recovery.[19] By mid-1923, the brewery's arrears in bond interest due to Gottfried and Maria reached $420,000, though both agreed to waive repayment.[20]

Midst all the restructuring of 1921, the Piel Bros. brewery completed a major generational transition. In January, Maria resigned as vice-president and director, posts she had held since her husband's death in 1915, and was replaced by her second son, Henry Piel.[21] That December, Gottfried Piel gave up his posts as president and director midst the bankruptcy of his auto parts factory. He disappeared from the brewery, prompting a major management shake-up. At their next meeting, the directors elected William Piel president, Henry Piel treasurer, and Gottfried's middle son Arthur as secretary and director. For the next decade, this second generation, operating as a three-man board, would be sorely tested as they struggled to survive pressures that would bankrupt most of their competitors.[22]

Within a few years, moreover, this generational transition was accompanied by a decisive shift in the power balance between the two families who owned the brewery. Though dominant in both the finance and management for nearly thirty years, Gottfried's bankruptcy was soon followed by the death of his wife Sophie, which, combined with their children's diffidence toward the business, soon reduced their side of the family to a secondary role. Anticipating high sales for his automobile "muffler cutout," Gottfried had borrowed $250,000 to build a new factory in the Long Island City section of Queens. With surprising speed, however, that product died from a lethal cocktail of problems—disinterest from motorists, rejection by major manufacturers, "increasing State and Municipal legislation against its use," and loss of product patent through litigation. Although the bulk of his company's debt of $407,000 was eventually covered by the sale of this factory, the Corn Exchange Bank decided to encumber his half of the Piel Bros. bonds worth $250,000, which Gottfried had deposited as collateral for these loans.[23]

Determined to protect Piels' bonds from an outside sale, William undertook what he called the "very delicate job" of persuading the bank, in September 1923, that sale of Gottfried's factory was pending and they could safely release his bonds. They were then stamped with a five-year renewal, preventing any buyer from bankrupting the brewery by demanding immediate repayment.[24]

Adding to his difficulties, Gottfried's wife Sophie—exercising her rights under New York's Married Woman's Property Act of 1848—had left a will placing her assets in a trust that denied him any access to her capital. In a testament signed nine months before her death in March 1924, Sophie assigned her "beloved husband Gottfried Piel" a nugatory stipend of $5,000 per annum for life. She vested the balance of her estate worth $1.2 million, four times the value of Michael Piel's legacy, in a trust whose income, largely from Piel Bros. shares, was divided equally among her five children. By appointing a local lawyer, along with sons Arthur and Walter, as executors and trustees, Sophie's will denied Gottfried any access to the capital that had been the basis for his business career. Significantly, Sophie's trust also became a template for transferring brewery ownership to the next generation—a format Maria would follow six years later by giving her half of the Piel shares to her own children through the Michael Piel Trust.[25]

Family Survival Strategy

As the financial pressures from Prohibition mounted, the Piel family struggled to provide livelihoods for the dozen children of its second generation. Although Maria owned half the brewery, those stocks and bonds were no longer paying any income. With cash flow curtailed by Prohibition after 1920, the business could only employ two of her seven healthy children. During the Roaring Twenties when their peers enjoyed unprecedented prosperity, the Piels suffered sudden penury, prompting them to remark, "for us the Depression came early."[26]

Though Maria received few dividends during Prohibition, she had inherited sufficient wealth from her husband to invest in their children's futures. The ledger that son William used for her finances showed assets, in 1922, totaling $1.4 million (worth $20 million in 2014). Her $172,000 in debentures and mortgages was, of course, highly negotiable. But she also owned thirty-two German paintings worth $53,000, such as the horridly racist "Arrest of the Gypsies," that had limited appeal in America. Apart from generous loans to launch their lives, Maria also gave her children smaller cash gifts after Michael's death that seemed scaled to reflect her affections—ranging from $18,500 to her favorite Paul, $11,600 to handicapped Otto, and $8,500 to lovely Louise down to just $5,300 for unloved Agnes, $2,500 to cantankerous Rudolf, and $1,100 for farm-bound Oswald.[27]

Despite his privileged position as company president, William also found that the combination of familial and financial pressures made these Prohibition years most difficult. Some months after the birth of their twins in 1916, Loretto went into the nursery one morning to discover that her little girl had suffocated. "Billy, Billy, Billy, come back here," she cried out to William who was leaving for the commuter train. "You see what I've done," she wailed, thinking she had somehow killed the baby. Realizing his traumatized wife was overwhelmed with five young children and no help in their isolated Long Island suburb, William moved back to his mother's home in Manhattan.[28] After a year or so under her roof, in 1917 Maria gave William a $22,000 loan to build a second home on Long Island. As war and Prohibition squeezed the brewery's profits, however, William was "just squeaking through" and Loretto went from "a house full of servants" to cooking and cleaning on her own.[29]

As Prohibition's hardships increased, William's younger brother Henry began looking beyond the brewery, using his technical skills to seek outside offers. At the end of the 1921 season, Henry headed south for Havana to consult with Luis Bacardi about adding a brewery to their famed rum distillery. At Bacardi's home in Santiago de Cuba, Henry found a "gigantic problem" in the dirty, sediment-laden water that required excessive filtration. Although the technical issues defied immediate resolution, four years later Henry was back in Santiago de Cuba to prepare the Bacardi brewery for its "solemn grand opening." With payments of

$5,000 for consultancies in Chicago and Cuba, Henry's outside fees were fast approaching his salary from the brewery.[30]

While William and Henry could get by at the brewery, their five younger siblings, all coming of age during this Prohibition decade, had to find opportunities outside the family business. After growing up in a luxurious Manhattan townhouse with travels to Europe, summers in Maine, and education at the finest schools, most of Maria's younger children now returned to their farming roots, starting with a cider scheme that brought a surprising number of second-generation Piels to rural Ohio.

Between army discharge in June 1919 and marriage that November, Rudolf Piel, accompanied by his brother-in-law Erwin Lange, searched central Ohio for apple concentrate to supply the Piel brewery's new line of non-alcoholic beverages. For some unexplained reason, they found the remote town of Killbuck, lying midst steep hills with poor soil, a frontier of opportunity that would, for several years, sustain a Piel colony of nine family members. As their first venture, Rudolf and Erwin purchased, with a loan from mother Maria, the Killbuck Cider & Vinegar Co. for $15,000, conveniently located opposite the town's C.A. & C. Railway depot.[31] Somewhat later, Rudolf founded the Seven Valleys Hatchery at Killbuck, producing 10,000 chicks weekly with the assistance of his brother Oswald as culling expert and brother-in-law George Schile as secretary-treasurer.[32]

Eighty years later, I drove down Killbuck's Main Street on a Saturday afternoon, past an abandoned movie theater, shuttered shops, fading mobile homes, and dilapidated frame houses. Along Main Street itself, most storefronts, like the movie theater, were boarded up. There were no patrons or pedestrians, lending the town a desolate air. On Railroad Street where the Piels once lived, the rails had been torn up, but the homes were tidy, a few flying Confederate flags, and the old Piel place was still neat and occupied. The horse buggies carrying Amish farmers, who know the good soil, disappeared about five miles north. Compared to the prosperous towns just thirty minutes in any direction, Killbuck seemed an economic miasma. With poor soil, limited transport, and listless commerce, how, I asked myself, could my grandfather Rudolf have imagined that this was the very place to make his fortune?

Within two years, the cider business proved unprofitable. The combination of tax payments and unpaid deliveries soon cut the cash flow needed to purchase apples for the brewery's juice production. "Rudolf and Erwin were in N.Y. today," said Maria in a letter dated January 1922, "to dissolve the partnership of the Cider

& Vinegar business" following "the friendliest conversation and compatibility between the two married couples, Rudolf & Margarita and Louise & Erwin." Looking forward, Rudolf "will try to rescue what is possible from the business," and "has gone to great trouble to sell the Stradivarius."[33] After trying to raise the violin's value by loaning it to Jascha Heifitz for concerts, Rudolf finally sold it to this cantankerous maestro for $9,000 that May.[34] He spent another three years trying to save the Killbuck business, but finally sold the cider factory in 1925 for $5,000, just a third of its original purchase price.[35]

After the young couples returned to New York, Maria deployed her assets to subsidize their transition to a more conventional lifestyle, starting with the family's now problematic summer property in Maine. As Prohibition pushed the brewery toward bankruptcy, an advertisement appeared in the August 1920 issue of *Town & Country* magazine reading: "Beautiful 'Lake Parlin' for Sale. Beneath Mt. Coburn in the Heart of the Maine Woods." Under an enticing sketch of a settlement nestled in the sweep of a mountain slope, buyers were offered "Two Hundred and fifty acres . . . comprising Residence, 15 bedrooms; 20 Buildings, 80 Acres of farm land under cultivation; Vegetable and Flower Gardens; Lawns, Bowling Green, etc. Splendid hunting and fishing, . . . a sportsman's paradise. Price $126,000."[36]

But even in the Roaring Twenties when money flowed like bootleg beer, there were few takers for a remote estate requiring a staff of twenty. Complicating any sale, Maria still had strong emotional attachments to her summer place and responded to offers by raising the price.[37]

To salvage something from this estate, Maria leased the farmlands to daughter Louise in 1922. But she failed to make any payments and Maria suffered additional losses of $9,000. In early 1924, therefore, Maria and Louise telephoned William, voiding that debt and telling him Louise would "take over the Farm Property as Mother's manager at $50.00 per month; that she & Mother share in profits on a percentage basis yet to be determined" from the property "being worked as a hotel."[38]

At first, with husband and helpmate Erwin at her side, Louise's attempts at hotel management got off to a rocky start. When brother Paul tried to bring along his brother-in-law Clarence Dettmers, a skilled chef who could improve Parlin's kitchen, Erwin staged "jealous scenes" like a "silly child," forcing Maria to rescind the invitation. Writing from Parlin, Maria's youngest son Roland reported, "everyone in The Forks and Jackman and at the hotel that know Erwin have a great distrust of him and a *violent* dislike." By ruining automobiles and inspiring "hatred" among Waterville dealers, he had "permanently injured our reputation for honesty and cost the farm about $1,400." Through his "near-pathologic egomania," Erwin fought with the only farm worker who could maintain the tractor, forcing a good man to quit and causing additional costs.[39]

In a skillful bit of domestic diplomacy, Maria soon found a way to save Louise from her husband's help. In January 1924, Maria invested $3,500 in a stock-trading partnership with her son-in-law whose financial prowess quickly earned her $510 and doubled their portfolio's valuation to $7,000. Within a year, Erwin parlayed this investment into a desk at Harley, Stuart & Co. on Wall Street where he earned a solid annual salary of $3,000 and later, during the 1930s, attempted venture capital loans to Turkey.[40]

Spared the help of husband and mother, Louise quickly learned the hotel business and began to turn a profit. With Maria summering at Oswald's Pennsylvania farm and Erwin working in the city, Louise supervised the start of the 1927 season on her own—greenhouse planted with vegetables, lawns readied, flower beds blooming, boats painted, and guests arriving. Her efforts turned a small profit of $1,000 and, with William's assistance, allowed plans for a more professional operation. With a bank loan of $5,500 for renovations and wages for a staff of fourteen, the hotel could, by hosting twenty-seven guests daily at eight dollars each, gross $17,500 each season.[41]

For the next twenty years, Louise offered her "home in the Maine woods," for "paid hospitality" at eight dollars per day, to tourists traveling the Canada Road to Quebec City. Every summer, Maria worked her extensive vegetable gardens to provision the hotel kitchen and feed the growing number of Piel grandchildren who visited as part of Parlin's now secondary role as the family's summer retreat.[42]

After six years in Ohio, Rudolf and Margarita Piel returned to New York in 1925 and moved in with her parents out in Hempstead, Long Island. Once again, Maria used her assets to alleviate adversity—forgiving his Killbuck debts, giving him a $2,000 commission on the sale of the Stradivarius to Jascha Heifitz, and loaning money for a house.[43] After two years with his in-laws in Hempstead, Rudolf built a pleasant home of his own design at nearby Garden City, while Erwin and Louise Lange bought a small tract house just three miles away. During the next decade as the brewery struggled through Prohibition and repeal, Rudolf and sister Louise remained close allies despite the financial fall-out from their ill-fated Killbuck commune.[44]

In sharp contrast with the failed Ohio venture, Oswald's dairy farm on 360 acres in Downingtown, Pennsylvania, was a success. As he entered his twenties with no direction, Maria insisted Oswald "must finally have the courage and self-confidence to find himself," ordering son Roland to shun him since "he relies on you and remains dependent." After Oswald opted for a career in agriculture, Maria bought him this farm for $19,500 in 1925. Then she had son William vet the contract, filled the household with furniture, and forced Oswald "to plant vegetables." Sensing something missing, Maria imported a young German woman from her native village "as a possible wife." At an opportune moment, she "got undressed and stood stark naked at the head of the stairs," prompting Oswald's flight and her rapid repatriation. For some twenty years, Maria would spend part of each year on Oswald's farm where, as a farmer's daughter, she "kept his house and cooked for him." With an initial budget of $4,500, he plunged into acquiring a dairy herd, tending the hundred acres of neglected apple orchards, and planting crops of clover, timothy, and winter wheat.[45]

This wonderful farm was also the site of a tragedy that cost the family the most promising member of its second generation. Admitted to Princeton with the class of 1925, Roland made steady academic progress through his first three years, excelling in math, majoring in politics, and selected for the eating club, Dial Lodge. In his last semester, however, a serious illness forced him to withdraw. Returning for a repeat senior year with the class of 1926, Roland scored grades of A+ in advanced philosophy and osteology until illness again forced him to take leave.[46]

Midst his recuperations, Roland worked up in Maine on the Piel family farm, out in Montana with the U.S. Geological Survey, and in Pennsylvania on his brother's dairy farm. There, he suffered a small scratch that soon resulted in serious blood poisoning. According to the coroner's report, Roland Piel, aged 24, occupation "tree sprayer, Brandywine Orchard," had died of "streptococcus following infected finger."[47]

"Roly was of a reserved and unaffected nature, and was possessed of profound and keen intellect," wrote five Princeton classmates who mourned his passing.[48] His grieving mother Maria gave up her burial plot at Brooklyn's Green-Wood Cemetery. There, three days after his death in July 1926, he was buried next to his father Michael.[49]

About the same time, another family member made a sad voyage into oblivion. Once a promising violinist, Otto began to suffer from schizophrenia, which recurred in Maria's family, and was removed from her household for care by a fulltime aide. In 1920–21, Paul was charged, wrote his future wife Edith Dettmers, with "going to look for a cottage 'on the island' for the insane brother & attendant & himself," prompting her to pause their courtship. Three years later, Otto left with his caregiver, a Dane named Mr. Paulsen, for lifelong exile at a coastal town in Denmark where Maria built them a house after selling some securities. Though a few family members made visits during their European travels, Otto lived there in obscurity until his death in 1932.[50]

Midst the family's rural misadventures, only Paul, the aspirant artist, chose the city, adopting a comfortable Bohemian lifestyle thanks to a mother's generosity for a favorite son. According to family stories, Paul "was a very sickly little baby," making Maria "carry him around with her on a pillow for the first months of his life," forming deep bonds.[51] Following his brothers to Andover Academy, Paul earned good grades and became close to classmate Charles Cabot Daniels, a fellow artist and lifelong friend. After failing the entrance exam and keen to join chum Cabot at Harvard, Paul sought the help of Andover's principal, Alfred E. Sterns. "I can most heartily endorse his application," the principal wrote Harvard's secretary. "The son of a German brewer, he is about as conspicuous example as I have ever known of what American institutions will do for the second generation of our incoming foreigners." Graduating from Harvard in 1911 with an unquenchable thirst for pure knowledge, in all its beauty and impracticality, Paul spent two years on a grand European tour, accompanied by Cabot Daniels, to prepare for their careers as artists.[52]

Once the Armistice ended his military service in 1918, Paul rented an apartment on Patchin Place, an artists' cul-de-sac in Greenwich Village. There he tried and failed to reinvent himself as an inventor. His patented Piel System of Roof Construction found no market. His Transposition Piano sold just one unit, the prototype, to composer Irving Berlin.[53] A Patchin Place neighbor, English novelist John Cowper Powys, recalled Paul bounding up the stairs each morning, pausing to drum irreverently on the door of poet E. E. Cummings, and then "present himself before me with shining face, shining eyes . . . and some torrential outburst of real, noble Goethean, Germanic culture!"[54]

In the Village's moveable feast of artists and writers, Paul became interested in an aspirant piano accompanist, Edith Dettmers, whom he had met during the heady Armistice Day celebrations in North Carolina. After she and her brother opened a Greenwich Village restaurant, Ye Waverly Inn, the relationship slowly grew into courtship.[55] To encourage their union, in 1923 Maria Piel loaned Edith $3,500 for the restaurant and financed Paul's $30,000 purchase of a small apartment building on nearby West 11th Street that he renovated with great gusto to entice more affluent tenants.[56] Four years into the marriage when their firstborn arrived, Maria accepted Paul's payment of "love and affection and one dollar" to forgive his debt on the townhouse. That endowed her son with an asset that freed him from work for the rest of his life.[57] With a townhouse in lower Manhattan, a small artist's studio inside the brewery, and his mother's favor, Paul was now primed to play a determinative role in the internecine struggle that would soon start among his siblings for control of the brewery.

An unexpected arrival soon joined this family circle in the West Village. Agnes was her mother's unloved ugly duckling—tall, dark, brilliant, sharp-tongued, and relentlessly iconoclastic. Indeed, her 1920 Barnard College yearbook, *The Mortarboard*, proclaimed her belief "that all is doomed which is conventional."[58]

Our most vivid account of Agnes and her college years comes from anthropologist Margaret Mead, who graduated from Barnard in a later class. Since the sole dormitory was full, Agnes had roomed with "unusual girls . . . well known in later life" who were "permitted to live in an apartment and do cooperative housekeeping" right across from campus. Though that co-op had dissolved by the time Mead arrived in 1920, the tight ties among this group, called the "Ash Can Cats," carried over to her group apartment in the same building. "We knew about Freud. Agnes Piel was being analyzed and occasionally spent the night with us," wrote Mead, recalling words so strange they remained etched in memory. "The first time she came, I made up the bed for her . . . Ag looked at me and said 'Well, the man you will marry will certainly have an Oedipus fixation on you, which will be all right if it isn't joined to an incest complex.'"[59]

Another member of that group, Léonie Adams, later the U.S. Poet Laureate, recalled that Agnes sometimes prompted them to play Freud by categorizing their friends' sexuality. "Agnes was the Grande Amoreuse," recalled Adams, "and I was something of a masochist—timid, likely to fall for the wrong sort. Margaret did something bad to men, something with a Freudian name—castration."[60]

Upon graduation from Barnard in 1920, Agnes dallied in the city for graduate study before heading west to teach disabled children in Lawrence, Kansas, for a year.[61] Uprooted from family and college friends, Agnes found the isolation emotionally draining. On weekends in this town of just 12,000 people, she could "nearly die of miserable isolation" as she sat before a solitary campfire, roasting a wiener and feeling despair at the prospect of "long, long years of work & perhaps modest achievement with no love in them." Midst these weeks of isolation, she came to a realization that she confessed in a letter to brother Roland: "I love Paul and I must root him out because he is a substitute for a lover and he is taboo—anyhow he only half reciprocates my feeling." This attachment to her older brother was so strong that "I carry Paul's image with me everywhere—the measure of all men, and they don't measure."[62] Within six months, Agnes had grown "weary of the celibate life" and was dating a civil engineering student at the University of Kansas, Elmer W. Lyne, whom she described as "husky physique, naively honest, and emotionally simple."[63]

After marriage to Mr. Lyne in 1922 and the birth of their daughter Patsy two years later, Agnes soon was back in New York, separated and settled in Greenwich Village. There her unwitting mother bought her a small apartment building at 259 West 11th Street for $20,000, just 200 feet down the block from Paul's place at number 276. By 1928, Agnes, now divorced, had changed careers and began writing a nationally syndicated column for the Associated Press on "child guidance." These columns were "based on family happenings" with fictitious names and several, said sister Louise, "refer to Paul." While purporting to advise America on child rearing, Agnes, the amateur Freudian, began psychologizing her daughter into years of therapy.[64] In effect, circumstances had brought Agnes back into Paul's orbit just in time to make her his reliable ally in the bitter infighting over the brewery that was soon to come.

Midst her children's many moves, Maria finally left the city where she had lived for the past thirty years, opting for the life of an itinerant grandmother among her children's many homes.[65] By default, Lake Parlin became Maria's only permanent residence. With the big house no longer affordable as a private home on her reduced income, Maria purchased another twelve acres on the lakeshore for $1,450. In 1921–22, she spent nearly $8,000 to construct a classic Maine lake camp she dubbed *Waldfrieden* (Forest Peace) that would become, nearly a century later, the only part of Parlin that remained in the Piel family.[66]

In these same years after World War I, Maria was absorbed in sending a flood of food parcels across the Atlantic, sustaining her relatives midst Germany's terrible postwar shortages. Between 1919 and 1921, she mailed 230 packages to friends and relatives, largely in her ancestral region of Westphalia. Always attentive to a favorite younger brother, she sent twenty-five shipments, with over 830 pounds of food and textiles, to Dr. Josef Heermann at his clinic in Essen. Overall, she provisioned eleven Heermann kin, three Piel in-laws, and a dozen more distant relatives with steady supplies that kept them fed and clothed through these difficult postwar years.[67]

But Maria's generosity could not save her younger brother Heinrich from his own folly. After inheriting the family farm in 1880, Heinrich, forgetting their grandfather's stern dictum above the barn door ("If the head of the house does not work, then the workers' labors are useless"), leased the land to a tenant in 1906. He then retired, at age 47, to the town of Herne, living from the rent and working as a minor civil servant. From a trip to Paris he brought back syphilis as present for his wife, who was "particularly pious and attended church daily." During the postwar recession, Heinrich first tried to "to make a lot of money unjustly" by selling the property to Maria at a grossly inflated price that she rejected. Ignoring warnings about Weimar's volatile inflation, he then sold the ancient Heermann homestead, 60 prime acres and a solid Westphalian house-barn, to the city of Bochum in 1923 for "millions" of *Papiermarks*, the country's new currency. They were soon worth no more than a box of cigars. A year later, he was dead, possibly of syphilis, leaving his family economically disenfranchised. Of his six surviving children, Maria brought the three more capable ones (Maria, Hedwig, and Wilhelm) to America during the 1920s, at first finding them work on her children's farms. But she left the others to live out modest lives in Herne, all dying childless. Indeed, her nephew Heinrich, Jr. tried to please and got good grades during his decade in Maria's New York household. But she disapproved of his teen-aged romance and sent him back to Germany midst the postwar

6.2. German *Papiermark* currency for two million marks, issued in 1923.

privation—where he was unemployed, grew "strangely passive and inhibited," and never married. When Heinrich, Sr.'s wife followed him in death twenty years later, her "coffin fell into the grave and shattered into pieces," a dismal end to four centuries of Heermanns on that land.[68]

By the late-1920s, the Piels' rural adventures were largely over and most were again arrayed around the brewery in a pattern that would last another decade. While Paul and Agnes lived in Manhattan, their uncle Gottfried was in Forest Hills, Queens, ten minutes from the Piels' plant. The two brothers managing the business, Henry and William, owned suburban homes in Woodmere, Long Island, only twenty minutes from work by express highway. Nine miles north, Rudolf and Louise were buying homes in the new suburb of Garden City, just thirty minutes by car. Gottfried's son Arthur lived further out on the island at Locust Valley, but that was still only an hour's commute. As the brewery's income slowly increased, first from near beer sales and then from repeal of Prohibition, family members would use this proximity to play an active role in Piel Bros. Under the pressures of Prohibition they were allied in a shared struggle, but would later split into warring factions to fight for the rewards that came with its repeal.

Challenging the Federal Government

While his siblings adapted to the family's reduced circumstances during those first hard years of Prohibition, William was left alone to develop the brewery's strategy for survival. Reflecting his leadership in the national beer industry, Piels fought Prohibition at the federal level but generally remained aloof from the wrangling over alcohol regulation in New York state politics.

When Governor Al Smith signed a bill in May 1920 allowing 2.75 percent alcohol for beer brewed in New York State, William Piel was generally supportive, saying such a limit would "make a very good quality of beer" and help the beverage become "a regular part of the daily meal, rather than as means of intoxication."[69] Within a year, however, the U.S. Supreme Court affirmed the .05 percent alcohol limit as the national standard. At the end of his two-year term in 1920, Governor Smith was defeated for re-election by a strong Prohibition advocate, Nathan L. Miller, who soon won passage of an aggressive anti-alcohol bill, the Mullan-Gage Act. Then, after defeating Governor Miller in 1922 over the Prohibition issue, Al Smith came back into office to overturn the Mullan-Gage Act, effectively eliminating any local law enforcement that might disrupt

Manhattan's 5,000 speakeasies. Starting in 1925, however, the U.S. attorney for the Southern District of New York, Emory Bruckner, sparked a renewed federal effort, padlocking speakeasies and inventing the "plea bargain," which swapped light fines for guilty pleas to clear the court's backlog at the rate of 500 Prohibition cases per session. Even so, during Bruckner's term from 1925 to 1927, the city's speakeasies soared to an estimated 32,000.[70] Once New York City voted overwhelmingly (seven to one) against the Volstead Act in the statewide referendum of November 1926, Bruckner realized the futility of his crusade and resigned. His successor refused to issue indictments for violations, effectively ending any meaningful Prohibition enforcement inside the city.[71]

In contrast to its passive role in state politics, Piels' management decided to challenge the federal government's Prohibition authority. In mid-1921, a trade group advised Piels that Washington would soon promulgate regulations for medicinal beer and issue the company a permit to brew this product. But William Piel was pessimistic, noting that the Anti-Saloon League had threatened to "pass legislation to prohibit medicinally prepared beer."[72] On October 24, 1921, the Treasury Department promulgated these promised regulations. Ten days later, just two breweries, Piels and Joseph Schlitz of Milwaukee, received permits for the "sale of lager beer for medicinal purposes." But in late November, Congress preempted those sales by passing the Willis-Campbell Act prohibiting doctors from prescribing beer, effectively killing any legal market for medicinal alcohol. Acting on some senators' statements that this act was unconstitutional, William Piel decided to test the legislation's legality in the courts. He retained a Wall Street law firm, promising a contingency fee should the litigation succeed.[73]

Accordingly, Piels sued New York's federal prohibition director, Ralph A. Day, in December 1921, arguing that the Willis-Campbell Act violated the right of physicians to prescribe medications, thus exceeding Congressional authority under the 18th Amendment. Passage of the Willis-Campbell Act, Piels claimed, had done serious harm to its business—ruining its $60,000 investment in production facilities after receiving a medicinal permit and destroying a trade that earned $65,000 in just twelve days.[74]

In deciding *Piel Bros. v. Day* for the government, federal district judge Edwin L. Garvin noted that Congress had found, after a thorough investigation, "little or no value in beer . . . as a therapeutic agent," and thus "did not abuse its power . . . by enacting the Willis-Campbell Act."[75] The Circuit Court of Appeals soon affirmed the district court's decision, allowing Piels a hearing before the U.S. Supreme Court.[76]

Thus, Piel Bros. petitioned the Supreme Court in June 1922, challenging the idea that "Congress conducted a careful investigation into the medicinal properties of beer." In his initial brief, the U.S. solicitor general, James M. Beck, asked that he be allowed to enter similar responses to "The Beer Cases"—*Piel v. Day*, *James Everard's Breweries v. Day*, and *Edward and John Burke v. Blair*. In his supplemental brief defending Prohibition as "a noble experiment in moral reform," the solicitor general argued, with words of unintended wisdom, that "no scheme of legislation can long endure if hostile to the political capacities and moral convictions of the people."[77]

On the same day that the Supreme Court heard arguments in the Everard case, the Piel matter was separated from the other two appellants. Then, with assistant attorney general Mrs. Mabel Walker Willibrandt representing the government, the Piel case was dismissed with costs to the appellant.[78] In a June 1924 decision, *James Everard's Breweries v. Day*, the U.S. Supreme Court ruled that "neither beer nor any other intoxicating malt liquor is listed as a medicinal remedy in the United States Pharmacopeia," and the decisions of the federal district courts were thus affirmed.[79] Anticipating an unfavorable outcome after the district court decision, Piels had already abandoned its planned line of malted medical supplements.[80]

Simultaneously, however, William Piel was lobbying the U.S. Brewers' Association (USBA) to adopt a more agile political response to Prohibition. "The Volstead Act has failed," William wrote in a twenty-page memo, so badly that it threatens the one solid accomplishment of Prohibition—assuring that the "curse upon the country" called the saloon "shall never again, in any guise or form, have a legalized existence." Yet the failure to enforce Prohibition has bred "a multiplying spawn of greedy speak-easies" that replaced every padlocked saloon with two or three of these "blind tigers." To check the "bootlegging fraternity," William argued that allowing 2.75 percent alcoholic content for near beer would provide most workingmen with a satisfactory substitute for bootleg beer and bathtub gin.[81]

Enforcement Pressure

Piels' challenge to the government's prohibition powers brought immediate retaliation in the form of zealous law enforcement. In May 1922, federal agents accused Piels of manufacturing, during the past five months, "large quantities of beer above the legal alcoholic content," transporting liquor in violation of the Volstead Act, and maintaining a public nuisance. The U.S. attorney asked federal judge Thomas I. Chatfield to consider an injunction that would close the Piel brewery. But both realized they would need a conviction before taking such a drastic step.[82] In late June, therefore, the U.S. district attorney obtained a temporary injunction to restrain the brewery's operations as a "public nuisance." When William Piel's counsel offered a $10,000 bond as "security that there would be no violation of the law," Judge Chatfield agreed to vacate the order, effectively granting Piels a reprieve from a corporate death sentence.[83]

While ignoring thousands of speakeasies, city police targeted Piels for Prohibition violations. Within weeks of the federal charges, two Manhattan police detectives stopped a Piel's truck near the brewery and confiscated sample bottles, which reportedly tested at 1.93 percent alcohol, well above the legal limit of 0.5 percent for near beer. Thus armed with a warrant, the detectives then raided the brewery with fourteen police, seizing 2,018 boxes of beer stored in the "medicinal beer" room. On June 1, police arrested brewmaster Henry Piel and the firm's truck driver, charging both with violations of New York's Mullan-Gage Act. In his defense, Henry contended he had brewed this beer under a Justice Department ruling that had briefly legalized medicinal beer and then stored it pending refund of federal sales taxes. Nonetheless, the two accused were still bound over for trial on $1,000 bail.[84] In the aftermath of these arrests, police raided the brewery again to confiscate another 3,523 cases of "real old-fashioned beer" valued at $30,000.[85]

At a subsequent hearing in mid-June, Henry's defense attorney insisted that the truck had been carrying soft drinks but "the beer was placed on the truck by some unknown person with the intent to reflect discredit on the brewing concern."[86] Ten days later, Piels' counsel was back in court to petition, unsuccessfully, for return of the seized beer, which, he claimed, had been legally brewed under a medicinal permit.[87] When the case finally came before the Kings County Grand Jury in September 1922, Henry waived his immunity and appeared with documentation showing that the beer in question had been brewed under the government's "medicinal" license. In a surprise victory for the family, a Brooklyn grand jury refused to indict Piel Bros.[88]

While bootleggers operated illegal breweries with impunity, Piels' legal near beer production was subjected to close, continuous scrutiny. Five years after these police raids, Prohibition agents again inspected the Piel plant, finding 450 barrels of cider had fermented to one percent alcohol—just half a percent above the legal limit. At a meeting with the Prohibition administrator and five federal agents,

William admitted to seven technical violations and agreed "to destroy 450 Bbls of Sweet Cider, . . . of excess alcoholic content in the presence of two agents." In the aftermath of this punishment, the Piel's board, with regrets, "unanimously agreed to discontinue . . . the Apple Juice business." In making this decision, the directors noted that three of their apple products were "regarded as the best in the market" and, with proper advertising support, "might have been developed into popular . . . all-year-beverages."[89]

When Henry's Technical Department produced a new near beer in 1926 with a deceptively real taste, the police arrested a truck driver with the load. The sample tasted "so close to the real 4% that the driver was taken to the Federal Building" until actual chemical testing found the near beer was just 0.42 percent alcohol, well within the legal limit. Instead of recoiling in fear, Henry hoped for press coverage of the arrest to promote the product.[90]

To avoid further arrests, the brewery had to court federal Prohibition agents with what one family member, Marie-Luise Kemp, called "courtesies." To make its near beer, Piels first had to allow the yeast to reach full fermentation, thereby producing a full-bodied real beer with 4.0 percent alcohol. Then, in compliance with the Volstead Act's limit of 0.5 percent, the brewery put the "real beer" through a de-alcoholization process that made "near beer," producing surplus alcohol discharged into a metered sewer under the watchful gaze of a federal agent. "One of the revenue men used to come," recalled Marie-Luise, "and he would drink and drink and drink so much beer, they'd have to put him in the car and send him home. Because he could drink real beer before . . . the alcohol was separated from the beer and run into the metered sewer."[91]

Bootleggers

Apart from capricious law enforcement, Prohibition also brought the Piels constant threats from predatory gangsters. Through urbanization, migration, and Prohibition, the bucolic East New York neighborhood of the 1880s had become, by the 1920s, a violent slum, a spawning ground for the city's most murderous criminal syndicates. In an oral history, former city mayor William O'Dwyer recalled observing this rapid change firsthand, from 1917 to 1941, in his roles as policeman, magistrate, and district attorney.[92] When he started walking a beat back in 1917, "Brooklyn was a small town," or a series of small towns separated by grasslands, dairy farms, and cornfields. But then as "transportation got going—subways, elevated, trolley cars, . . . the automobile," O'Dwyer recalled, "these things showed me the growth of villages . . . into township." Then, "all of a sudden in the twenties they merged, without keeping too many of their own local characteristics, . . . into the great borough of Brooklyn."[93]

Through this improved transport, Jews "left [the] DeLancey Street section [of lower Manhattan] and went out into Brownsville just to improve their living conditions," said O'Dwyer, with the result that "the Jewish district was definitely East New York and Brownsville sections."[94] The nearby district of Ocean Hill just west of the Piel's brewery, recalled veteran Democratic leader John J. Lynch, "became an Italian immigration area." In nearby Brownsville during the 1920s, Lynch added, "some of the worst elements of Hebrews and Italians moved into that neighborhood. The neighborhood deteriorated."[95]

Indeed, during Prohibition the Brooklyn neighborhoods adjacent to Bushwick's "brewers' row"—Ocean Hill, Brownsville, and East New York—produced the city's toughest gangsters. Why so many mobsters from such a small section of the city? Absent any other explanation, simple proximity to a dozen under-utilized breweries as a source for bootlegged beer may have helped make the area's petty criminals into major racketeers. As the epicenter of the city's brewing industry on the eve of Prohibition, Brooklyn became the bailiwick of leading Irish bootleggers such as Charles "Vannie" Higgins, who "built a profitable rum-running and bootlegging business in Bay Ridge;" powerful Italian *Mafiosi*, Frankie Uale, Joe Adonis, and Albert Anastasia; and a coterie of tough Jewish mobsters, Benjamin "Bugsy" Siegel, Louis "Lepke" Buchalter, Joseph Amberg, and Irving Shapiro.[96]

Throughout the city and across the country, reports mafia historian Selwyn Raab, Prohibition "had been the catalyst for transforming the neighborhood gangs of the 1920s into smoothly run regional and national criminal corporations. Men like Luciano, Bonnano, and Lucchese began as small-time hoodlums and graduated as underworld leviathans. Bootlegging gave them on-the-job executive training in a dangerous environment."[97]

Beer was a bulky, low-cost commodity that had to be "bootlegged" locally, ideally by diverting real beer from a legal brewery before it was de-alcoholized to make near beer. By contrast, hard liquor commanded a premium price that sustained "rum-running" from Canada or Europe. By the early 1920s, the city's crime kingpin, Arnold "The Brain" Rothstein, had an armada of six speedboats to meet freighters at "rum row" off Long Island, a fleet of fast cars guarded by armed mobsters like Meyer Lansky, and distribution warehouses in Queens.[98]

Even though bootlegging beer was more mundane, the profits were enormous. A barrel of beer that cost just $5 to brew could be sold to speakeasies for $36. Years later, Charles "Lucky" Luciano told a Hollywood movie producer that, in 1925 alone, he earned $12 million in gross revenues from bootlegging while spending $8 million in payroll for truck drivers, guards, and corrupt law enforcement, leaving him a hefty $4 million profit.[99]

One study of the New York area found that Prohibition transformed some seventeen young street thugs into the metropolitan area's major bootleggers, including Jack "Legs" Diamond, Lucky Luciano, Meyer Lansky, and Bugsy Siegel.[100] During the 1920s, Legs Diamond built his bootlegging racket by diverting fully fermented real beer from legitimate breweries before de-alcoholization. In August 1930, city police raided an ordinary parking garage at 876 De Kalb Avenue, Brooklyn, and seized eight trucks loaded with 1,080 barrels of real beer. They also found a racking machine connected to an elaborate underground piping system—running from a drain in the garage floor, across the block to another garage, and from there under the street to the Excelsior Brewery, licensed to produce near beer. After the firm's vice-president, Milton Mandel, admitted his company owned that second garage, federal agents impounded the plant. According to one press report, "the regular beer which it produced was sold through the Jack 'Legs' Diamond organization, which sold the beer to speakeasies."[101]

Similarly, in June 1931 a federal flying squad raided the old Barmann Brewery in Kingston, 90 miles north of the city, finding the plant "in full operation" with 4,000 barrels of real beer in the vats and more loaded on ten trucks "for the holiday trade." A gunman pulled a .38 caliber pistol and "commanded the driver to proceed." But he balked. Armed agents then arrested the gunman, who turned out to be one John Sheehan, "a New York character identified with the Legs Diamond gang."[102]

The most successful bootlegger of them all was Irving "Waxey Gordon" Wexler who started as rum runner for the city's kingpin Arnold Rothstein and graduated to bootlegging beer from New Jersey breweries licensed to produce near beer. He also bribed police and politicians, notably Jersey City Mayor Frank Hague, to overlook his bootleg shipments into eastern Pennsylvania—the same area where bootlegged beer had suffocated Piels' near beer sales at the start of Prohibition.[103] In 1928–29, Waxey Gordon and his associates formed the biggest bootleg syndicate in the East to impose criminal control over some thirteen legal breweries, including the Peter Hauck Brewery in Harrison, New Jersey; the Peter Heidt Brewery in Elizabeth, New Jersey; and the Kings (Excelsior)

Brewery in Brooklyn. With an illicit income of $2 million a year, Gordon lived large with suites at the Waldorf and a mansion in the Palisades. But just weeks after Prohibition ended in 1933, he was jailed for $380,000 in back taxes and died years later, broke, in Alcatraz.[104]

Indicative of the scale of this illicit industry, Prohibition agents raided the Heidt Brewery in September 1930, seizing vats filled with 200,000 gallons of the syndicate's real beer. While four federal agents were dumping the illegal beer, twenty-five gangsters arrived with pistols drawn and the agents only escaped when forty armed officers arrived as reinforcements.[105]

Although these bootleggers were making a "lush living," they still faced the constant "danger of hijacking by another bootlegger," observed ex-mayor O'Dwyer who was a police officer during Prohibition. So they "organized armed gangs to protect their trucks."[106] Indeed, recalled Solomon Klein, an assistant district attorney who prosecuted these criminals, "there was a great deal of competition among different groups in the bootlegging field, in fact to a point where they kept killing each other off."[107] Systematic bootlegging also required what O'Dwyer called "corruption in the Police Department," bringing "the era of fabulous fortunes in many sections of the Police."[108]

As Prohibition drew to a close, an alliance of younger Italian and Jewish gangsters from Brownsville and East New York, led by Abraham "Kid Twist" Reles, began killing rivals for control of Brooklyn's remaining rackets, winning the borough's "slot machine war" in 1930–31 and taking over "book making, pinball machines, crap games, labor unions, . . . and 'shylocking.'" Simultaneously, a new national "commission" reorganized the city's top criminals into the famous "five families" and turned to Albert Anastasia, underboss in Brooklyn's Mangano family, to enforce the new order. Anastasia was a formidable figure, running the borough's rackets from his social club in Ocean Hill and ruling the Brooklyn docks through his brother, Anthony "Tough Tony" Anastasio, head of the longshoremen's union. Out in East New York, their ally Louis Capone, operating from the counter of his Italian *pasticerria* on Pacific Street, a half-dozen blocks from the Piel's plant, recruited younger hoodlums for a Mafia-connected crew that did some 400 to 500 contract killings for the commission during the decade. For this service, Capone's thugs were paid $250 a week, awarded control of Brooklyn's crap games, and "given a free hand in Brownsville and East New York" for "extorting merchants, bullying bullies, running scams."[109]

By 1940, Brooklyn's incoming district attorney, William O'Dwyer, found "there were so many murders through Brooklyn, out in East New York, and down on the waterfront" that he launched an investigation, which soon exposed the existence of "Murder, Inc." His assistant district attorney Burton B. Turkus mapped 200 unsolved murders "in Brownsville, East New York and Ocean Hill," which he called "a blighted area—a pesthole."[110] In effect, Italian gangsters under the leadership of Louis Capone and his deputy Harry "Happy" Maioni, whom one district attorney called, "a ruthless little killer, absolutely ruthless," controlled the mean streets around the Piel's brewery.[111]

Three of the Piels who were children during Prohibition have strong memories of living with the threat of death from these criminals. At the height of Prohibition in 1924 or 1925, Henry Piel, the brewery's plant manager, faced strong pressure to cooperate with the bootleggers. "My father was abducted once by . . . one of the well-known racketeers," Marie-Luise Kemp recalled, "and taken to New Jersey. They wanted him to either sidetrack the unfiltered beer or start a brewery for them, so they could have real beer. But he wouldn't do that, and they threatened him by saying that they would abduct his children." During the mid-1920s when she was about ten, Marie-Luise continued, "I saw kids thumbing their way [home] for a ride, and I thought that would be pretty neat. So . . . my aunt saw me out on the street thumbing, and she thought 'Oh, my goodness, that child will be picked up and abducted and taken to God knows where!' So I was given a long lecture, and then I was told why I couldn't do that."[112]

About three years later, Henry Piel's younger brother Rudolf, who worked as technical consultant to the brewery, had a similar experience with famed bootlegger Legs Diamond, his own legs trembling in fear as he stood outside the brewery, facing down gangland's reigning psychopath. Rudolf was cantankerous, even aggressive. But he was still small, only five-foot-six, and slender at 140 pounds. Legs had come with an entourage of armed bodyguards. Rudolf only had his four-year-old daughter, Margarita. Yet Rudolf still told Legs that he could not have the real beer, challenging this gangster's business model. Legs often erupted in a murderous rage when anybody crossed him. Why he just drove away and never came back, we'll never know. Maybe, just maybe that ruthless killer had a soft spot. Maybe, a four-year-old girl was the best defense against armed mobsters.[113]

Even so, Rudolf had good reason to be afraid. After a few arrests for petty crimes, Prohibition had elevated Legs Diamond to the peak of the city's bootlegging racket, operating the Hotsy-Totsy Club on Broadway and battling Arthur "Dutch Schultz" Flegenheimer to supply Manhattan's speakeasies. Legs also became a feared enforcer, first with labor racketeer Jacob "Little Augie" Orgen and then with famed gambler and bootlegger Arnold Rothstein. Throughout the Roaring Twenties, Legs built a reputation as a killer who was shot fourteen times, faced five homicide charges, and killed many more, both rival gangsters and ordinary businessmen who defied his demands. Feared as a psychopath who "lost control of himself," he once tortured a trucker "by applying burning matches to the soles of his feet." Another time, he murdered eight bystanders at his own club (bartender, hat-check girl, and customers) who happened to be looking on as he pulled a pistol and shot a gangland rival point-blank, execution style.[114]

Piels' aversion to accommodating these gangsters prompted a murder attempt on its president William Piel. According to his youngest son David, William's steadfast refusal to pay protection "insurance" to three Brooklyn gangsters led to a near fatal automobile accident. On a winter's night around 1930, three years before the end of Prohibition, William got into his Ford coupe at the brewery, found the windows jammed, but decided to head home along the new Sunrise Highway. "The invading carbon monoxide fumes were so dense," recalled son David, "they made him drowsy and he passed out, careening off the highway and into mud and brambles along the side of the road." On that pitch-black night, with little traffic, William might have suffocated had not a couple parked nearby pulled him from the car and flagged down a police patrol. "On examining the wreck," said son David, "the police discovered that the . . . windows were . . . jammed with wedges, between the glass and door . . . A cardboard cone of some sort had been taped to the exhaust and forced up into the floor of the cabin."[115]

When the police visited him in hospital where he was being treated for extensive injuries, William recalled that some "insurance salesmen" had come to his office several times "to assure him that the under-utilized, almost vacant brewery would not be vandalized if he did himself the favor of paying his visitors for protection. The alternative, they suggested, would be one he would find unacceptable—even risky." Instead of paying "protection" to people whom his son David described as "Mafia," several German-speaking brewery employees guarded the family's Woodmere home with "large pipes," showing they "weren't afraid and . . . they didn't want to buckle under." Federal agents joined "local police in keeping the brewery . . . safe from unwanted solicitation" by local gangsters who were probably allied with Louis Capone, an underboss in Albert Anastasia's organization later electrocuted at Sing Sing. By the time William came home from hospital, his full lower-body cast had been signed by sympathetic anti-Prohibition politicians, including Al Smith, James Farley, and Franklin Delano Roosevelt.[116]

Declining Revenues

From these many pressures, the Piels brewery suffered a steady drop in revenue. After strong sales of its near beer in the first year of Prohibition, revenue fell sharply from $1.1 million in 1920 to just $500,000 in 1922, with an adjusted operating loss of nearly $10,000. Plant "efficiencies" helped the bottom line, but Piels still ran at a deficit during the first five years of Prohibition. By lowering the labor cost for filling each case from twenty-seven cents in 1920 to just thirteen cents four years later, Piels reduced its unsecured debt from a dangerous $475,000 in 1921 to a manageable $90,000.[117]

Midst this decline in sales and profits, Piels pursued a long-running appeal to the U.S. Treasury Department for relief from some $32,000 in unpaid federal beverage taxes for the years 1920–21. William went to Washington three years later, and negotiated "an offer in compromise" that reduced Piels' payment to $10,000—a figure the firm gratefully accepted.[118] Simultaneously, Piels appealed to the city's Department of Taxes and Assessments in October 1923, arguing that Prohibition had reduced its real estate's worth from $390,000 to just $200,000. Under Prohibition, Piels' once-model brewery was quickly losing its value.[119]

Compounding the pressures of high taxes and low sales, the brewery also faced major costs to maintain "the battery of five boilers," now increasingly inefficient from both age and the extra energy needed for near beer production. In effect, the boilers were under strain from the additional step, not anticipated when the brewery was built circa 1900, of extracting alcohol from real beer to produce the legal near beer. To cut coal costs, the board agreed on the immediate purchase of two large water tube boilers to replace the present battery of five.[120]

As total beverage sales plunged by over half to just 33,000 barrels in 1923, chairman William Piel was certain that "the illegal competition of real beer bootlegging" was still the chief culprit.[121] This dismal trend continued into 1924, as competition from gangsters pushed sales down to 30,000 barrels and cut near beer revenues to $359,000, a 28 percent drop in two years.[122]

This slow, seemingly inexorable slide into bankruptcy was suddenly halted in 1925 as the company's combination of efficiency and marketing began to yield results. At the annual stockholders' meeting, president William reported a "remarkable sales increase of over 60%," turning a net loss of $14,300 in 1924 into an operating profit of $102,700 for 1925. He attributed this turnaround to "the enthusiasm of the Sales Directors of several Grocery Chain-Store Accounts"—

A&P, Bohack, and others—that the company had been cultivating so assiduously for the past five years. Even so, competition from bootleggers meant that profits sufficient for dividends were, said William, "still some five or six years away"— another of his predictions that would prove prescient.[123]

Yet such success would produce other sorts of problems, not from these outside pressures but from inside the Piel family with its volatile mix of personalities. As their brewery absorbed blow after blow from federal courts, city police, and predatory gangsters, tensions were building inside the family. Underlying conflicts from the generational succession within their business could be delayed by Prohibition but could not be denied. Sadly for the Piels, the hard-won solidarity that allowed them to survive Prohibition would end once its repeal restored profits and they could, at long last, afford to indulge their suppressed sibling rivalries.

7
_____

Repeal

After the 18th Amendment had swept to ratification by forty-six of the forty-eight states in little more than a year back in 1918–19, reversal of this constitutional ban on alcoholic beverages seemed almost unimaginable. Yet with surprising speed, Prohibition's dismal spectacle of bootlegging, gang violence, and wide-open speakeasies sparked a call for change. Challenged by the moral argument that Prohibition led to defiance of the law, temperance advocates first tried redoubling their repression. After the defeat of the "wet" Democratic candidate Al Smith in the 1928 presidential election, the "drys" enacted the Jones Law that turned the Volstead Act's misdemeanors into felonies. Anyone who sold even small amounts of alcohol, say a farmer offering guests a glass of hard cider, now faced the absurdly harsh penalty of five years' imprisonment.[1]

As public criticism of Prohibition intensified after 1928, the movement for repeal drew male millionaires and female activists into a potent coalition. The wealthy males were clearly motivated by self-interest. Before Prohibition, the temperance movement had advocated the income tax to replace federal alcohol revenues. So now America's first families of industry—du Pont, Firestone, Goodrich, and the once-dry Rockefellers—backed repeal in hopes of undoing that tax and protecting their assets. One of America's richest men, Pierre du Pont, the former president of General Motors, provided leadership and lavish funding for the Association Against the Prohibition Amendment.[2]

Their wives and daughters were, by contrast, exercising hard-won political rights. For decades before Prohibition, the Women's Christian Temperance Union (WCTU) had fought for female suffrage as a way to advance prohibition. But now ratification of the 19th Amendment in 1920, giving women the vote, freed many to break with the dour matrons of "dry." Indeed, New York socialite Pauline Sabin used her wealth and contacts to launch the Women's Organization for National Prohibition Reform, the most prominent among the half-dozen groups that challenged the dowdy WCTU's claim to speak for America's women.[3]

"I was fooled," Mrs. Sabin announced angrily after Herbert Hoover, at his inauguration in 1929, backed away from campaign promises to do something about Prohibition. Though she had been New York's first woman to serve on the Republican National Committee, Sabin now resigned from the party in a blaze of publicity and turned her formidable energies to repealing Prohibition. Republican stalwarts like William Ward, the party boss of Westchester County whose grandson later married into the Piel family, called her a "loser." She soon defied such expectations. With the city's social elite lending cachet to her crusade, Sabin soon recruited 166,000 members in New York. She organized motorcades to sweep through dry counties upstate, motorcycle police in the vanguard of chauffeured limousines with fluttering "Repeal" banners. She appeared on the cover of *Time* magazine, hair fashionably bobbed, string of perfect pearls about the neck. Within two years, her "dynamic leadership" and "charismatic personality" attracted over 600,000 members nationwide and, a year later, 1,325,000. Her once-cosseted society ladies plunged into gritty campaigns for "wet" candidates, battling city ward bosses and state political machines. By mobilizing middle- and upper-class women to break with the Republican Party's embrace of Prohibition, Mrs. Sabin created a political opening that made its repeal possible. As she told Congress in 1930: "I am here to refute the contention by dry organizations that all the women of America favor prohibition."[4]

Within the family, Marie Muessen Piel, wife of the brewery's technical director, was active in the Women's Organization. In her frequent public forays with leaflets and buttons, Marie was often joined by her teenaged daughter Marie-Luise and sister-in-law Louise Piel Lange. Marie-Luise recalls wearing her best blue silk dress while "standing in front of Grand Central Station . . . giving out papers for the repeal of the 18th Amendment." In recognition of her role as a "mover and a shaker" in the movement, the Women's Organization later presented Marie Piel with a silver trophy.[5]

With the sordid spectacle of bootlegging and gangsterism in cities across America, the Anti-Saloon League's donations were drying up, cutting its budget from $2.5 million in 1920 to just $120,000 by 1933, eviscerating this once-powerful organization. With the Saloon League in retreat, and Mrs. Sabin's organization, her membership swelling to 1.5 million, on the attack, the 1932 presidential election became a referendum on repeal. "Prohibition," Franklin Roosevelt proclaimed in an August campaign speech, has been a "complete and tragic failure . . . Corruption, hypocrisy, crime and disorder have emerged . . . All the time a steady flow of profits . . . was running into the pockets of racketeers . . . This was the business that was the direct product of the 18th Amendment and the Volstead Law—a business which is lucrative, vicious and corrupting." Only three months after Roosevelt's election, Congress passed the 21st Amendment, which stated succinctly: "The eighteenth article of amendment to the Constitution of the United States is hereby repealed." In the interim while the states were voting to ratify, Congress raised the permissible alcohol content, in March 1933, from 0.5 percent to 3.2 percent—an event celebrated by boisterous, beer-drinking crowds in cities across America. With women's organizations campaigning vigorously, states began approving the 21st Amendment so fast that, by December 1933, repeal was ratified and Prohibition was over.[6]

Nonetheless, fourteen years of Prohibition had left their mark upon the brewing industry. By 1933 just thirty-one breweries out of the 1,345 operating in 1915 had survived. In the New York metropolitan area, Prohibition had winnowed breweries from forty-four to just fourteen, with seven of those survivors in Brooklyn, including Liebmann, Piels, Schaefer, and Trommers.[7]

As the industry revived after repeal, some 750 breweries were operating nationwide by 1934. By the end of that year, the brewing industry produced 38 million barrels, an impressive recovery but still far from its pre-Prohibition peak of 66 million barrels. Concentration and modernization were also accelerating at a torrid pace, sparking a relentless growth by the big shipping brewers— Budweiser, Miller, Schlitz, and Pabst—that would soon squeeze smaller family firms like Piels. Prohibition had forced regional breweries to sell off their tied saloons, eliminating the main bulwark that once slowed the spread of national brands. Now, freed from that restraint and fueled by network radio advertising, the big Midwest breweries started their unchecked ascent. Within five years after repeal, the average nationwide output per brewery had jumped by 70 percent. The industry's total sales had grown by 26 percent, but Anheuser-Busch's were up by 173 percent to a record 2 million barrels. Investment of $84 million in the company's St. Louis plant between 1932 and 1951 would raise sales of its Budweiser brand nearly fivefold to nearly 5 million barrels. Adding to these difficulties for regional brewers, America had lost its taste for alcohol. Per capita consumption of beer plunged from twenty-one gallons in 1914 to just ten gallons in 1935. It would take another twenty years to reach even sixteen gallons.[8]

These years leading to repeal were a time of major change for the Piel family and their brewery. During the Prohibition decade of the 1920s, the family, siblings and cousins alike, had been united in their struggle for survival by forgoing dividends, selling company property, and suppressing personal resentments. The two brothers leading the brewery, William and Henry, were relentless in their pursuit of efficiency by cutting costs, slashing salaries, and investing in new equipment. Their strategy was successful. They overcame enormously adverse conditions to bring the brewery back into the black well before the end of Prohibition—not only surviving, but preparing for future profitability.

If adversity had produced solidarity, then affluence fostered spite. Once repeal seemed imminent with President Roosevelt's election in 1932, suppressed resentments over past sacrifices sparked bitter personality clashes that soon spilled into the boardroom. Three of the younger Piel siblings allied for an emotional challenge to their elder brother's privileged position—reflecting the sibling rivalries that can roil generational succession inside a family business as "these new owners inherit . . . all of the other feelings, hurts, dreams, and conflicts that are part of any family."[9] Backed by his mother Maria and her control over the family's wealth, William would eventually win these corporate battles, purge his relatives from the firm, and build a new, more professional management with outside directors.

In retrospect, William's win would launch the third distinct phase in the company's history: first, a private partnership between brothers Gottfried and Michael (1883–1898); next, an incorporated family firm (1898–1937); and finally a professionally managed corporation with external directors and family stockholders (1938–1962). In the brewing industry nationwide, the era of the legendary "beer barons" was coming to an end, symbolized by management changes at New York City's biggest breweries. In January 1939, industry titan Jacob Ruppert, Jr., died, leaving an estate of $100 million, much of it in city real estate. Apart from the Knickerbocker brand inherited from his father, he owned the New York Yankees, had bought Ehret's famed Hell Gate Brewery, and ruled the U.S. Brewers' Association. He was much mourned, with 15,000 people attending his funeral at St. Patrick's Cathedral. But his outsized presence had left no successor and his firm's future was uncertain. Just a year before, Brooklyn's historic Schaefer Brewery had reached a million barrels, ranking among the country's top ten after the young heir Rudolph Schaefer, Jr., an advocate of modern methods, had hired a cadre of professional managers to improve efficiency.[10]

Though William's modernization strategy would shed many of the handicaps that often troubled family firms and brought his corporation two decades of steady growth, such progress would come with a heavy cost. In trying to catch up with the country's management revolution, useful reforms became entangled in the personal conflicts that often trouble a family business. The seven Piel siblings who once summered together on the shores of Lake Parlin would now split into factions for feuds exacerbated by their strong personalities. With the end of Prohibition, the corporation would prosper and the family would suffer, almost in equal measure.

Survival Strategy

In a retrospective for the annual stockholders' meeting of March 1930, company president William Piel reviewed the strategy he had deployed for the past ten years to survive Prohibition and its competition from "a new, powerful, eminently successful . . . industry: *illicit booze.*" While most breweries were bankrupt, the Piel "plant emerges, at the end of the decade, in fine condition, ready for the . . . *relief from Prohibition* . . . to increase its sales and profit." In explaining how the brewery's dangerous net loss of $106,000 in 1920 became a profit of $26,000 by 1929, William emphasized four factors—innovative marketing, product quality, plant efficiency, and, above all, close cooperation within the Piel family.[11]

Realizing the old marketing model of delivering kegs to saloons was fading, the company had contracted with chain stores such as A&P to sell bottled near beer direct to shoppers. Instead of the common industry practice of selling bottles at a loss "to promote the brewery bulk business," Piels' bottled beer was "priced to produce a profit." By 1929, 94 percent of the brewery's output was sold in bottles, raising production from just 30,100 barrels in 1924 to 75,300 by 1929.[12]

With so many low-alcohol near beers on the market by the mid-1920s, Piels needed a quality product to keep its chain-store customers. Concerned about a new Budweiser near beer label about to hit the market for the 1926 season, William instructed brother Henry to proceed with "the special experimental brew [he] already had in mind."[13] By August, Henry reported that, "our new special brew is remarkably fine," and the bottleshop was "running full blast over 4,500 cases every day." Since there was "no pure real beer on the market," Henry felt confident "the brewery should soon come back to life!"[14] As the brewery readied for the 1927 season, William told mother Maria proudly that "we have really obtained the 'real-beer' flavor in our new brews."[15]

The subsequent surge in sales strained the capacity of their now aging brewery, still operating largely on improvements father Michael had made at century's turn. As chain-store sales rose to 500,000 cases for 1926, William reported that the "depleted condition of the Bottling Department's equipment" had caused an unwelcome 20 percent increase in production costs.[16] After Michael's son Henry and Gottfried's son Arthur conducted a close analysis of the plant's operations, documented with data-dense tables, William persuaded the board that an investment of $42,000 in machinery, particularly a conveyor belt, could cut bottling expenses by 50 percent while raising "output capacity" by 25 percent.[17]

Close collaboration by the Piels made these changes with minimal cost and maximum efficiency. Among the troika of second-generation directors, Arthur Piel alone had the mechanical skills, honed by a decade as manager of his father Gottfried's auto parts factory, to supervise construction of the new bottling plant, designing the production line and directing installation of new machinery.[18] As sales doubled and doubled again in the first months of the 1929 selling season, William assigned Arthur to install a third bottling unit, at a cost of $55,000, in time for the next season.[19] By such investments in efficiency, Piels cut the cost of filling each case of bottled beer from twenty-seven cents in 1920 to just eight cents by 1929.[20]

Cooperation among the family was essential for the firm's survival during this challenging Prohibition decade. Through rigorous analysis that juxtaposed statistical trends against more fluid human factors, this young corporate board from the family's second generation—William (45-years-old), Henry (42), and Arthur (39)—made tough decisions that, in case after case, maximized opportunity in a difficult market.

Financial Decisions

After eight years of sustained losses during Prohibition, the Piels and their brewery faced, by late 1927, three intersecting financial problems. Most urgently, the earlier failure of Gottfried Piel's auto parts factory, along with his children's borrowings against the estate of their mother Sophie Piel, had left bad bank loans totaling $81,000 secured by brewery bonds. With the Corn Exchange Bank now threatening a public sale of the $250,000 in Piel Bros. bonds that Gottfried had encumbered as collateral for these debts, the family faced, said William, "a grave danger" that these bonds would pass "into the hands of strangers." To eliminate this threat, the brewery agreed to pay his loans, and Gottfried's side of the family promised to reimburse the firm within a year. Moreover, the brewery had to service an $82,000 debt from the Kings County Trust Company dating back to its original incorporation in 1898. And it needed $40,000 in capital for modernization of the bottling plant.[21]

To meet the brewery's need for operational funds, its primary stockholder, Maria Piel, loaned the company $30,000 and led shareholders in accepting a mortgage of $150,000 on the plant that provided much-needed operating capital. As the brewery climbed back to profitability by 1929, the turnaround reduced the risk of these financial pressures.[22]

Through all these measures, financial and industrial, the corporation was, William assured the 1930 annual meeting, emerging from this difficult decade with a "proven ability to make a profit, whether or not the Volstead Act be modified or retained."[23] The key factor in raising profits sixfold from 1928 to 1929 was, he said, the success of technical director Henry Piel in simultaneously cutting costs and improving quality.[24]

As Henry himself told stockholders, his department had responded, during the past two years, to "very keen competition in bottle beers" with a "finer bottle product," achieved by mixing twenty barrels of an experimental de-alcoholized beer with 100 barrels of their old near beer Kovar to produce a new "special" brew. Sufficient production of this new beverage for the upcoming summer season had required improvements in the Zahm Dealcoholizing Plant. Thus, in November 1929 the board had agreed that Rudolf Piel "be engaged by the President to make such . . . amplifications and/or alterations in the Corporation's present Dealcoholization Machinery . . . for the enhancement of the flavor of this Company's Near-Beer."[25]

Among the half-dozen members of his generation who joined the brewery, Rudolf would prove the most creative and contentious. Unlike his siblings, Rudolf's talents were inwardly directed toward music and engineering, making him something of an outsider in this voluble, literary family. Although he graduated from Andover Academy in 1912, he had failed several courses—a harbinger of worse to come at Harvard College.[26] He later told his daughter that he quit Harvard to protest the unfair tryouts for the freshman crew, walking out of the boathouse, packing his bags, and catching the next train to New York. But, in fact, he had cut almost all classes and was expelled for earning Ds and Fs.[27]

To give him a taste of life's harsh alternatives, older brother William arranged an engineering apprenticeship at Phoenixville, Pennsylvania. "These iron mills are an immense affair," Rudolf wrote his mother upon arrival, with "tall, black, iron chimneys which manage to keep the whole place covered with a low-hanging, yellow-black pall." Inside, hundreds of men work to the light of "an angry yellow glare across acres of red painted girders" while the air "seems filled to bursting with a ceaseless overpowering crash and roar."[28]

Faced with repeating freshman year at Harvard, Rudolf instead enrolled as a sophomore at Columbia where he enjoyed three productive years, learning some science and studying with Franz Boas—the brilliant anthropologist whose repudiation of his field's scientific racialism left a lasting impression.[29] Apart from the chastening taste of factory work, another factor in his newfound academic interest was the failure of his musical aspirations. Practicing with his father's Stradivarius, Rudolf, his daughter recalled, "worked very hard at trying to become a violinist and knew, after a while, that he didn't have what it took," leading him to "close down that dream" and loan the Stradivarius to rising star Jascha Heifitz.[30] By June 1917 when most of his Columbia class graduated, Rudolf, though still shy some credits, volunteered for military service, ending his education without a career or credential.[31]

Nonetheless, Rudolf's mix of formal education and restless tinkering gave him the uncommon skills to accomplish the brewery's challenging assignment. Instead of the usual, unsatisfactory methods of making near beer by either stopping fermentation prematurely or heating real beer to evaporate alcohol above the legal limit of 0.5 percent, Rudolf, said William's son Bill, developed a radical new technique that preserved the brew's full flavor. "What we do," Rudolf suggested, "is cart it up to the top of the brewery and drop it into a long vertical tunnel." When others objected that the drop would damage the beer, he replied: "Well it won't if we keep it cool and drop it through a vacuum." By testing, Rudolf developed the correct drop distance that evaporated the excess alcohol by the time the beer reached the bottom of the tube with flavor undiminished. Not only did Henry use this innovation successfully, but, said nephew Bill Piel, "none of his competitors had it."[32]

These important technical innovations were supplemented by systematic renovations to the plant, including an upgrade of the fermenting vats, a new wooden brine tank, repair of existing chip casks to increase storage by 4,000 barrels, and a 10,000-gallon water tank atop the brewery.[33] Such efficiencies were timely, since the market conditions that produced Piels' recent profits were attracting some aggressive competition.

Through an invisible interaction with bootlegged beer, the brewing industry was experiencing a sudden surge in demand for its legal, low-alcohol brand. In a 1930 column for the Baltimore *Evening Sun*, writer H. L. Mencken complained long and loud that the supply of bootleg beer "is apparently endless, but the quality runs from indifferent to atrocious." Before Prohibition, he said, very few brewers, apart from "such superior American beer as Michelob or Piel's," made a decent drink. Otherwise, "the common suds of the saloon . . . was often harsh and metallic" because the hops were actually picric acid. By contrast, from 1922 to 1928 the bootleggers of northern New Jersey brewed excellent beer "that might have been drunk with respect in Munich itself." But in recent months, Mencken noted sadly, "good beer is becoming hard to find." Significantly, this sudden decline in quality coincided with mobster Waxey Gordon's syndication of New Jersey bootlegging in 1928–29, taking control of at least thirteen breweries and their illicit distribution across the Northeast.[34]

Like most conglomerates, the mob had apparently sacrificed quality for volume and profit—a foreshadowing of what legal corporations would do in later decades after they achieved a similar market share. The sharp decline in the flavor of the illegal product naturally raised public demand for fine tasting near beer and drew Piels' competitors into the market.

By October 1929, a "competitive price-challenge" from rival near beer brands, particularly the Jacob Ruppert Brewery of Manhattan, forced Piels to cut its wholesale price from ninety-five cents to seventy cents a case for chain-store customers.[35] To survive a "war" with small-scale, peddler-brewers who invaded the near beer market, their company, William said, had "to meet Competition by . . . giving the Consumer still finer quality" and by pursuing every possible efficiency. To this end, the firm agreed to fund "constant research toward improvement of the quality of the Corporation's brews," with Henry's Technical Department developing better-tasting special brews. Piels would, moreover, cut costs by reducing the volume in each bottle by a half an ounce—an almost invisible change that would add up to major savings across an annual production of 850,000 cases.[36]

Significantly, all this success had been achieved through the efforts of many Piel family members—William, his brothers Henry and Rudolf, their mother Maria, and from the other side of the family, Gottfried Piel and his son Arthur. Moreover, the Piel Bros. board was still very much a family affair, with Arthur, Maria, William, and Henry serving as directors while Rudolf was secretary pro tem.[37] Prohibition may have cut profits and pushed the brewery to the brink of bankruptcy, but adversity also brought the Piels together in a shared struggle for survival, fostering a fragile solidarity critical to the success of any family business, particularly a brewery in the midst of Prohibition.

Michael Piel Trust

With the firm stable and family relations amicable, Maria Piel, now 73, decided to transfer all her Piel Bros. shares to a trust for her children and live from its income. Since the agreement would shape generational succession within the family business, Maria's seven children, evidently rather wary of each other, sought independent legal advice. In February 1930, William's counsel, William C. Cannon, senior partner at the powerful law firm Davis Polk, submitted a memo recommending the trust's entire block of Piel Bros. stock be voted "in accordance with the direction of a majority of the directors." Henry's lawyer agreed, suggesting the trust directors convene before each Piel Bros. annual meeting to allow for "proper instructions" about the voting of these shares. These arrangements, counsel advised Henry, would "accomplish the result of relieving your mother of the responsibility of the brewery business & place it upon the 7 children," while giving her "an iron clad agreement . . . to pay her the net income from the stock and bonds of Piel Bros. for the rest of her natural life."[38]

Under the final agreement of September 1930 drafted by attorney J. Julian Tashof, Paul's old army buddy, Maria transferred Piel Bros. gold bonds worth $375,000 to a trust managed by her seven children. In turn, the children agreed to pay their mother a fixed income for life. To avoid anything akin to the bitter litigation amongst Gottfried's children over their mother's trust, Maria barred her seven trustees from filing "any suit, action or proceeding in law or equity."[39] On that same day the trust took effect, Maria also divided her fifty shares of Piel's common stock among her seven children as a simple gift, without codicils or conditions. Thanks to what Paul later called "a veritable interregnum on property transfers," both gifts were free from any tax.[40]

At a formal meeting four weeks later, the seven siblings agreed to transfer "all of their right, title, and interest" in these Piel Bros. stocks and bonds to the Michael Piel Holding Corporation, which would manage this investment by a majority vote of shareholders. They also elected Paul Piel president of this trust—a position he would hold for the next thirty years, slowly accumulating an informal influence over the brewery's affairs.[41]

Within a few months, William found that the $277,000 in deferred interest that the brewery owed Maria after eight years of Prohibition made the company's balance sheet "unbankable" for future financing. In exchange for waiving this bond interest, Maria's children promised to pay her the dividends from the brewery's common stock for the rest of her life.[42]

In ways they could not have foreseen, all these terms would shape family dynamics for decades to come. Maria could have divided the shares evenly among her children, establishing each one as an independent stockholder, free to vote, buy, or sell as they saw fit. Instead, this trust would bind these seven siblings together as a body corporate while simultaneously splitting them into factions, majority versus minority, for winner-take-all fights over their mother's half of the Piel Bros. voting stock and its power over the brewery.

Boardroom Battles

After ten years of failed Prohibition, it was clear, by early 1931, that reform or repeal was just over the horizon. As one of only thirty surviving breweries nationwide, Piels was well positioned for rapid expansion and extraordinary profits. In anticipation of repeal, management redoubled renovations to its aging, thirty-year-old plant and struggled to find sufficient capital for needed expansion. Midst this sudden turn for the better, the Piel family's solidarity began to fracture as the second generation split into feuding factions to battle for control of the company. Determined to transform his family firm into a modern corporation, William maneuvered slowly and successfully for control—playing upon sibling rivalries, attacking his brother Henry, and marginalizing his other relations. In effect, the tensions that often accompany generational succession in a family business, long postponed by Prohibition and its financial pressures, now roiled the Piel Bros. board as these sibling partners schemed.

Buoyed by a sense of optimism about the possibility of repeal, the family at first cooperated throughout 1931 on refinancing and renovation. Starting that September, the second generation's company officers—William, Henry, Arthur, and Gottfried, Jr.—surveyed the plant's operations to determine its potential for expansion, finding that, unlike competitors, they had maintained their facilities with updated equipment.[43]

Looking forward, management agreed they needed financing that would "put the Plant in such shape as will best favor the highest possible valuation for purposes of recapitalization or of sale to a successor 'Piel Bros. company.'" They further agreed on the need for low-cost renovations "so as to approximately double the Plant's maximum capacity" to 369,000 barrels.[44]

Consequently, as William told the stockholders in September 1931, "preliminary figures indicated that, for the sum of $200,000, the plant's capacity could be increased, depending on the brews to be made, from 50% to 100%."[45] At first, the family was united in the search for this much-needed capital. In 1931, both sides of the family waived any payment of the $553,300 in accrued interest that the company owed them as bondholders, and also approved a bank loan of $200,000 to improve its parlous cash position.[46]

While seeking the family's approval for these modest loans, William began searching privately for major finance to remake Piels into a national brand like Budweiser or Miller once Prohibition was repealed. Whether driven by his own ambitions or pressed by his wife's quest for acceptance into New York's *Social Register*, William's maneuvers slowly moved beyond the ambitious to the reckless.[47]

Though many details have been lost, surviving documents in William's private papers indicate he was negotiating, sometimes secretly, to transform Piels from a closely held family firm into a publicly traded corporation. In September 1931, William corresponded with the vice-president of a Wall Street firm, the Commercial National Bank and Trust, about preparing a prospectus for investors.[48] An undated "Private Memorandum" laid out plans for a "$3,500,000 Capitalization Set-up" by an initial public offering of 103,750 shares of common stock and 27,500 preferred shares, with 51 percent held by "Piel Central" and the balance available to investors "by sale thru Bankers."[49] A similar document titled "Expansion Budget: Piel Bros., 1931," listed precise estimates for increasing the plant "from 150,000 to 500,000 Bbls. annual capacity" by expending exactly $1,715,168.49—far more than any of the figures William was then sharing with family stockholders.[50]

William's maneuvers sparked infighting among his siblings so bitter that it remained, even a half century later, imprinted in their children's memories. "When Prohibition was repealed," recalled William's son Gerard Piel, who was then about 17, "my father said we're not going to survive as a small local brewery, we've got to go national. To go national, we've got to get big capital into this business and he went to Wall Street and he lined up a big float of Piel's stock." After his father began negotiating with major bankers such as Bear Sterns, Gerard added, "the family went through the roof at the thought of surrendering its control and ownership. They would become minority shareholders."[51] In retrospect, sibling rivalries among the second-generation partners coincided with market pressures for corporate reforms to produce a dispute of exceptional intensity.

While William was negotiating with Wall Street to take the firm public, his younger siblings, led by Louise and Rudolf, maneuvered, in anticipation of the 1930 annual meeting, to curb their elder brother's ambitions and privileged position. While there was a surface rationality to their criticisms, the vehemence of their attack seemed to spring from deeper family scripts. Rudolf had been their father's favorite, while William was their mother's. Louise was marginalized by the patriarchy embodied in brother William. Henry was chafing in his ascribed role as the lesser second son.

Following a "protracted argument" at a trust meeting when William refused to consider a salary cut to cover company losses, Henry and Louise invited attorney Elmer Wigg to become the first non-family member on the board, replacing cousin Arthur whom they found problematic. Within a week, Louise had formed a consensus among the family's rebels: Arthur would step down as director in favor of Wigg; William and Henry would share management responsibilities; and, as Henry put it, there would be an end to the policy of "paying William a premium and forgetting my services." Henry was relieved to be freed from dealing with cousin Arthur, whom he called "a loud mouth know-it-all." Confronted by their unanimous demand for a salary cut, William insisted he "has an offer elsewhere and does not have to accept whatever the directors give"—a claim that most considered a "barefaced bluff." Cousin Walter told William he was "on probation." All agreed he would have to "give an accounting of his time." Accordingly, at its next meeting that September, the board voted a 20 percent pay cut for all company officers, William included.[52] Inside this cauldron of family business, the stew of personal resentments was boiling over.

After a premature attempt to expand the Piel Bros. board from three to five directors at the 1930 annual meeting collapsed, the rebel siblings returned two years later fully prepared to achieve that end. After William and Henry Piel, and Elmer Wigg, attorney for the Sophie Piel estate, were elected unopposed, Louise moved that "the Board of Directors be increased to five members." That motion was approved, along with Rudolf's amendments to the by-laws strengthening stockholders' control.[53]

Once Albany approved the board's expansion, a stockholders' meeting in September 1932 elected Rudolf and Gottfried Piel, Sr. as the fourth and fifth directors.[54] Within a week, director Wigg nominated Rudolf as "assistant to the President," who then signaled his approach to such assistance by moving that the president's salary be slashed by almost half to just $6,500—effective yesterday. Though William and his uncle Gottfried voted no, a majority of Rudolf, Henry, and Wigg carried the motion.[55]

For the next six months, Rudolf and his allies continued their close scrutiny of William's executive privileges large and small. At the next meeting in November

1932, Wigg informed the board that William had taken overdrafts from company funds "in excess of $8,000." In his own defense, William claimed that $5,000 had been covered by "a bonus payment" approved by his mother Maria Piel. Another $2,500 was "written off as an additional bonus payment" upon recommendation of his uncle Gottfried Piel, Sr. After Wigg pointed out that Gottfried was "not a stockholder at that time" and thus lacked any authority to authorize anything, the directors approved a motion, over William's objections, that "any and all overdrafts of any officer or employee of the company" shall be a documented loan charged 6 percent interest. Upon advice from Rudolf that the executive lunchroom "took practically the entire time of one man," Wigg won approval for a ban of this privilege. The board also voted that the fueling and servicing of private cars in the company garage for "any member of the Piel Family be discontinued," another slap at William who drove to work.[56]

All this infighting was accompanied by wrangling over the best way to reap the rewards that would surely follow the end of Prohibition. The first step toward repeal came on March 22, 1933, when President Roosevelt signed the Cullen–Harrison Act authorizing the sale of beer with 3.2 percent alcohol—still lower than the 4.0 percent natural fermentation but far above the 0.5 percent allowed under the old Volstead Act. To meet this demand, Piels was planning, Henry said, to increase its brewing capacity by 50 percent to 1,200 barrels daily.[57] Just four days before the law took effect on April 7, a Piel's board meeting confirmed this expansion of the brewery—authorizing $100,000 in new finance and approving the purchase of 3.6 million new bottles.[58]

Midst all this change, William was still determined to win finance for a major nationwide expansion and was willing to split the family if necessary. Acting on "the consent given by a majority of those present at an informal meeting" back in December 1930, he had approached the brewery's Wall Street banker, the Commercial National Bank and Trust. But they found the Piel's balance sheet "unbankable." Still needing $25,000 to replenish the plant's operational cash, William began "negotiations with the Forest Hills National Bank . . . through a friendly introduction."[59] After this bank made its loan contingent upon a pledge of brewery bonds, William declined that offer and instead secured the same finance from two reputable Brooklyn banks.[60]

Nonetheless, William continued to discuss a possibile stock float with the president of the Forest Hills Bank, Louis C. Gosdorfer, whom he described as "a leading realtor of Queens County." Generously donating his expertise without any charge, Gosdorfer, William reported, had "made an official appraisal of the plant real estate," which the Piels agreed to print as a prospectus for future investors.[61] The hook was in.

Two years later, with repeal on the horizon and several siblings opposing his plans for a major stock float, William, acting for a bare majority of the Michael Piel Trust (which represented only half the shareholders), drafted a memo to Louis Gosdorfer at the Forest Hills Bank proposing to merge Piel Bros. into a new, well-capitalized corporation. For reasons that elude the written record, his siblings, at a meeting of the Michael Piel Trust in January 1933, unanimously approved William's proposal to sell Gosdorfer "all the stock of Piel Bros. for the sum of $1,500,000 in cash and $1,500,000 in preferred stock to be issued by . . . a successor corporation," contingent upon the buyer first providing a good-faith credit of $25,000.[62]

Within weeks, however, Paul Piel, as president of the Michael Piel Trust, was slapped with a summons in an unexpected civil suit, *Gosdorfer vs. Piel Bros. et al.*[63] How had a multi-million-dollar partnership to create a national corporation collapsed into costly litigation at such breathtaking speed?

As it turned out, the family's vote of confidence in William's judgment of character was ill-advised. Finding Wall Street bankers still unwilling to back a brewery, William had moved down the financial chain to find a bottom-feeder. Gosdorfer was not the "leading realtor" William had imagined. He was a wheeler-dealer with a checkered past. In May 1930, a strike force of twenty Prohibition agents had raided a Queens speakeasy, the Forest Hills Inn, and arrested its proprietor, the same Louis C. Gosdorfer. The local WCTU chapter called him "unfit for a federal position," and insisted he be removed from his patronage post as a supervisor for the 1930 census. In his defense, political allies said the raid had been an ill-disguised attack on the boss of the Queens County Republican Party by arresting his "business partner and loyal leader," this same Gosdorfer.[64]

Consonant with his reputation as a bootlegger and machine politician, Gosdorfer now used the ongoing negotiations with Piels as pretext to sue the entire family for damages, first $250,000, later $500,000, by filing a civil suit before Queens County judges—cronies who had reached the bench through politics and patronage. Admitting his failure to deliver the initial $25,000 loan, Gosdorfer nonetheless insisted, in his civil complaint, that William had asked him to seek "further financing." He had therefore located "one Siegel [who] was interested in the proposition and was introduced by the plaintiff to the defendants William and Arthur Piel."[65]

The legal grounds of Gosdorfer's claim for damages were remarkably weak. Ruling on Piels' motion to dismiss in May 1933, Judge Mitchell May found it "difficult to determine the theory upon which the plaintiff can proceed," noting that Gosdorfer's "action is founded upon a contract which . . . is unenforceable." His "claim for services can barely be made out," the judge said, ordering a trial to resolve the issue.[66]

Nonetheless, another Queens judge, elected by machine politics, ruled in favor of Gosdorfer's claim based on this same "unenforceable" contract. Although the plaintiff did not even offer Siegel's first name much less his financial bona fides, New York's Appellate Division affirmed the lower court's judgment against the Piels.[67] According to the *Brooklyn Daily Eagle*, Gosdorfer then doubled his claim for damages to $500,000 in May 1935, alleging he was promised this amount in Piels stock as compensation for finding an investor.[68]

Desperate to transform his small family firm into a national brand and inept at finding Wall Street finance, William imagined that a suburban lender, who could not even deliver a small-business loan, could somehow arrange $3 million in corporate finance. Chasing the chimera of wealth and social status, William had led his family into legal entrapment by a local hustler.

Corporate Coup

Underlying all these family disputes were competing visions of the company's future—a script oft replayed inside family firms on the cusp of change. Seeing expansion as salvation, William would remake his regional brewery into a national corporation with network advertising, mass marketing, and professional management. His brother Rudolf, by contrast, saw the firm's strength in its traditions. "At the time of repeal," Rudolf later wrote, "I did my utmost to induce the brewery to continue its old time policy of keeping its quality and sales price . . . in direct competition with none except the imported beers." He negotiated contracts with Pullman Sleeping Car Company and top hotel chains "on an exclusive basis if we would maintain our price position." Sadly, he concluded: "This is one fight I lost. At that time I foresaw that if we sold at competitive prices it would force us into endless and accelerating expansion."[69] A full half-century before craft beers became a marketing phenomenon, Rudolf had a quite similar vision of Piels surviving as a regional brewer by producing small lots of high-quality beer in competition solely with costly imports.

Niche market versus mass marketing. Quality brewing versus national brand. Family firm versus modern management. With such stark, irreconcilable visions, one brother would win and the others would have to lose.

After months of pointed criticism, William fought back. With his salary slashed, privileges curtailed, and authority circumscribed, he evidently colluded with Elmer Wigg, attorney for the Gottfried side of the family, against his own siblings. Acting on information from inside the Michael Piel Trust that likely came from William, Wigg told the brewery's board in April 1933 that Rudolf and Louise had held "an invalid proxy" from their family trust at the last stockholders' meeting—thus, voiding the board's expansion to five members and effectively expelling Rudolf and Gottfried. With the directors once more under his control, William then issued a scathing denunciation of Henry, his company treasurer and partner for the past twenty years, charging that he "had absented himself from the plant beginning Tuesday morning, April 4th . . . , greatly embarrassing the company . . . in procuring the necessary excise stamps." And he left the firm "similarly embarrassed" by his failure to pay both real estate taxes and city beer licenses.[70]

Just three weeks later in May 1933, William chaired two special stockholders' meetings, the first mustering proxies for a duly constituted election that raised the size of the board to five directors, and the next choosing a new board that, for the first time, was composed largely of non-family members.[71] Upon nomination by loyal brother Paul Piel, who as head of the Michael Piel Trust held the proxies for half the stockholders, William was unanimously elected chairman along with four non-Piel directors—Elmer Wigg, lawyer for the Gottfried Piel family; Julian Tashof, attorney for Michael's heirs; former IBM president Frank N. Kondolf; and the brewery's financial officer. Confirming this change in the company's character, Henry moved and stockholders approved a motion that the "restriction of directors to shareholders be eliminated."[72]

Once elected, the new board convened, first, to elect William company president and, then, to raise his salary to $15,000 per annum, more than doubling the reduced figure of $6,500 that Rudolf had imposed a few months earlier.[73] At its next meeting in May 1933, the board affirmed William's right to "exercise clear and firm authority in every respect over the Technical Director"—effectively bringing his dissident brother Henry to heel. Reversing Rudolf's short-lived attempt to restrain William's use of employees as servants, the board endorsed the "President's actions in the matter of 'Officer's Mess.' " Looking forward, William agreed to share, at some point in the future, his plans for "increased productive capacity," delivering "copies of such reports . . . on certain financial overtures, as had not yet been placed before all the individual board members."[74] Clearly, the company was aware that William had been negotiating in secret.

William's maneuvers ignited the tinder-dry sibling rivalries inside this family business and soon stoked them into bitter feuds. Four days after this May meeting, Rudolf telephoned Wigg about a report from external director Frank Kondolf that "the liability of Gottfried Piel had been wiped off the company's books [in] an effort to conceal such liability," a reference to the ongoing dispute over Gottfried's company bonds. Rudolf added that, according to William, this had been done on Wigg's instructions to the firm's accountants Block & Zirkle.[75]

Wigg shot back that the firm could not "hold Mr. [Gottfried] Piel for any deficiency" over his "right of ownership in the bonds," and denied the accountants had changed the company books. Rudolf then responded that "this meant a fight." Wigg replied that "the sooner it went to a fight the better it would be for all of us because then . . . we would know where we stood." With tempers rising, Rudolf retorted all this did not make much difference anyway since "there were rumors all over town that the A. & P. had us by the throat and were going to take us over." To this Wigg asked mockingly "had he heard the rumor which reached me the other day that Al Capone was financing us?" When Rudolf answered "no," Wigg added, "if you want to go insane, that's your privilege and you probably will with your propensities of giving serious regard to everything you hear." After Rudolf threatened "to raise hell about the whole situation," Wigg hung up while "he was still talking."[76]

In the battle over Elmer Wigg and his accountants, the Piel family, as it often did, split down the middle. Paul Piel sided with Wigg and William. But Rudolf, Louise, and Henry agreed that Wigg had to go.[77] To preempt any such move, Wigg won the board's approval, after his argument with Rudolf, to renew their contract with Block & Zirkle as company accountants.[78]

Underlying these boardroom battles of 1933 was a deep factional split in the second generation, revealed in an angry letter that their mother Maria, now 76, wrote son William complaining about his failure to repay some personal debts. Evidently, he and his sibling allies had persuaded Maria to provide them a line a credit through a substantial cash advance. "When you, Agnes, and Paul came to me and induced me," Maria wrote, "to send a large part of my money for you all, you convinced me that I would regularly receive payments." They had already spent $5,000 from this advance, but now Maria said bluntly, "I forbid you to make any more of these payments." She asked pointedly, "What would be left over for me if I, as would be right and justifiable, had given the same amount to Louise, Henry, and Rudolf? Until now, I have not been able to give these three anything."[79]

Travels to Germany

To manage her contentious children during these difficult years, Maria began sending them on extended European sojourns, first Agnes and then those three disadvantaged siblings: Rudolf, Henry, and Louise. With the brewery slowly recovering, Agnes became the first to enjoy the family's new affluence, leaving Greenwich Village for a two-year stay in Vienna where she sought treatment for her troubled seven-year-old daughter Patsy.

After her arrival in Austria, Agnes contacted Anna Freud. But the famed therapist demurred in favor of another specialist, Editha Sterba, who in turn placed Patsy in the school and home of a teacher named Gina Bettelheim, wife of Bruno Bettelheim who later became a famed psychologist. With her daughter under treatment, Agnes was free to travel—Budapest for New Year's 1932, Germany's historic cities that summer, and the Balkans as a freelance reporter for the Associated Press in early 1933. During her periodic visits to Vienna, she also did psychoanalysis with another member of the tight Freud circle, Editha's husband Dr. Richard Sterba, and sometimes stayed with the Bettelheims. After returning to New York in December 1933, Agnes left her daughter Patsy under their care for the next five years—a seemingly pragmatic decision that would produce complications once Nazi Germany occupied Austria.[80]

Rudolf was the next sibling sent off on the grand tour. Just a month after his expulsion from the brewery's board in May 1933, Maria, drawing funds from her Düsseldorf properties, gave his family a trans-Atlantic trip so luxurious they thought it a "bribe" to ease him out of the business. With the end of Prohibition approaching and Piel Bros. lagging in brewing technology, study of recent German innovations provided a pretext for the trip. So that June, the whole family sailed for Europe on the *S.S. Stuttgart*—father Rudolf, mother Margarita, German shepherd Teufel, and their 10-year-old daughter Margarita, then called Peggy.[81]

After landing at Cherbourg and touring Paris, they drove south toward Switzerland in their big Pierce Arrow sedan, Peggy in back next to Teufel who sat bolt upright. They spent the summer in Berne where Rudolf worked at a brewery operated by Albert Hess, Henry's classmate at brewing school, while the family enjoyed visits to his "magnificent" estate for tennis and swimming.[82]

In late August, the family left Berne and drove north across the German border, unaware that they were heading into a political maelstrom. Germany's economy was reeling from the accumulated effect of war reparations, spiraling inflation, and the Depression. Unemployment was dangerously high. Hunger was widespread. Youth gangs roamed city streets engaging in vandalism and violence. Promising order and a path forward, Hitler had won dictatorial powers just a few months earlier in March 1933. The Nazi Party was tightening its authoritarian grip. The Gestapo was already rounding up trade unionists and communists for the concentration camps.[83] Instead of another family vacation in the Fatherland, they were on a voyage into the underside of Fascism.

"We would go from brewery to brewery and my father would get recommendations from one brewmaster to go talk to so-and-so," their daughter Peggy recalled. "We didn't skip a single brewery. That's how we made our way to Berlin." At one such stop outside the Dortmund brewery, Peggy and her mother were seated in the car with Teufel waiting for Rudolf. Suddenly, a gang of teenaged boys started pounding on the windows, shouting and flashing knives. Teufel leapt about the car, barking frantically. As the car started rocking side-to-side, mother and daughter grew frightened "They would probably have succeeded in tipping it," Peggy recalled, "when my father appeared with a group of men from the brewery, bidding farewell. The boys vanished. There was much consternation and apologizing. It was explained there was no purpose in calling the police, because vandalism with unruly youth was so common."[84]

By such stages they reached Düsseldorf where Peggy, still an ungainly girl in heavy boots to correct childhood polio, was paired with cousin Erika Piel, a vivacious young woman of 30 who took her everywhere, making sure everyone paid attention. Her parents also made a duty call on the few remaining Heermann relations at Herne, but Peggy was left behind in Düsseldorf because they might prove unpleasant. Indeed, her mother returned from that visit "shuddering at the narrow, dour, quite awful people she had met."[85]

After Düsseldorf, they drove on to Berlin where life was more than difficult. Dining at the fashionable Kempinski's restaurant when Hitler's voice came over the radio, the entire establishment froze for the duration of his speech—waiters would not serve, patrons fell silent. Once, as Hitler passed by in a car, their fellow pedestrians were suddenly awe-struck, erupting in Nazi salutes and shouts of *"Sieg Hiel!"* In restaurants, cafés, and beer halls, the Hitler Youth would march in, start a patriotic song, and everyone would join, the music carrying them in unison to an emotional crescendo.

"We got to see a lot of Berlin in looking for places to rent," their daughter Peggy recalled. "And over and over, we would go to an apartment and it would be marvelously luxurious, beautiful things around, paintings and furniture, and rents that were incredibly cheap. And my father would always say, '*Danke sehr, aber nein*.' And I finally said to my mother, 'why aren't we going to rent any of these places, they're so nice.' And my mother said, 'They belong to Jews and the Jews are leaving and we can't do that, can't take advantage of people like that.' "

In the building where they finally rented near Tiergarten Park, the affluent residents, doctors and lawyers, openly disdained the concierge's shiftless son until he came home one day in the long pants of the Hitler Youth. Suddenly, the tenants started using terms of deference. As the Nazis swept teenaged boys off the streets and into the Hitler Youth, that boy began bringing his uniformed friends to ransack apartments in search of subversive materials. By the end of their six months in Berlin, the entire building was living in terror.

While her father studied brewing at the University of Berlin, Peggy rode the U-Bahn, or underground, out to Podbielski Allee in the city's southwest suburbs where she attended the American School. Walking to the subway at the end of her last day in the distinctive school uniform, with heavy blue coat and wide-brimmed cap, she was followed by a group of boys. She walked faster. They walked faster. Stones started hitting her back. She ran. They ran. Then they surrounded her and knocked her down, pelting her with stones and mud while screaming, apparently thinking American and Jewish were synonymous, "*Amerikanischer Jude! Amerikanischer Jude!*" Suddenly, two strapping older boys from the school appeared, scattering the mob. They told Peggy the principal had sent them to escort her to the subway, surprised to learn that she had been walking by herself every day. When she reached home, her mother's face fell to see her little girl covered in mud, face bruised and bloodied.

Two days later, the family, repulsed by the surveillance and spreading fear in Hitler's Reich, cut short their stay. In February 1934, they drove to Hamburg, loaded the Pierce Arrow into the hold, and boarded a liner for the crossing to America, never to return. By the time they reached New York after eight months abroad, William had tightened his control over the brewery and Rudolf was effectively marginalized.

Over the long term, this bitter experience of Nazi Germany alienated Rudolf from his mother and much of the family. As Hitler consolidated power and prepared for the conquest of Europe, Maria and her children, Henry and Louise in particular, would remain oblivious, still sentimental about the Fatherland. By contrast, Rudolf turned his back on Germany. Whether it was listening to Professor Franz Boas critique scientific racism as a student at Columbia or just working in New York, Rudolf was repulsed by the Reich's anti-Semitism. His daughter Peggy grew up an ardent American—married to a U.S. military officer and deeply committed to Hitler's defeat.

Thirty years later when I was starting high school, I decided to take German, the language of my ancestors. "A bad decision," said my mother Margarita, formerly known as Peggy, in a tone that did not invite discussion. "The German language carries the seeds of Fascism. Study French, it's the language of liberty." Clearly, these were sentiments most of her cousins did not share.

Gottfried's Bonds

Midst all these European travels, Gottfried's ongoing negotiations with the brewery over recovery of his bonds, the subject of Rudolf's earlier complaint, produced litigation that divided the family. After two banks threatened to sell the $250,000 in brewery bonds that Gottfried had encumbered for personal debts, he reached "an oral agreement" with his nephew William that the brewery would pay the banks the $66,000 due and "hold the bonds as collateral" until he could repay within two years.[86] As that due date approached in March 1931, Arthur Piel asked the Michael Piel Trust to grant his father Gottfried additional time to repay from his residual brewery income. Henry opposed the settlement, calculating it would take Gottfried ten years to liquidate the debt. But brother Rudolf, understanding the dynamics of a family business, persuaded his siblings to accept the offer, saying "the interests of Piel Bros. Inc. required harmony among all of its stockholders."[87]

When the new due date arrived that July, Gottfried could not make the prescribed payment. So, in exchange for forgiveness of debts now totaling nearly $68,000, he transferred bonds worth $250,000 to the brewery.[88] But then, in September 1932, Gottfried deemed the deal unfair and sued the company to recover $182,000, the difference between his actual debt to the brewery and the original face value of his bonds.[89]

For the next four years, Gottfried, now virtually bankrupt and living on a modest stipend from his wife's estate, wrangled endlessly—pleading, cajoling, and demanding to recover brewery bonds that, by all rights, he had lost. Just as his brother Michael had once sued Gottfried to claim a half interest in the company, so Gottfried now filed suit against Michael's children to reclaim his share of the brewery, his last bit of wealth. Eventually, Gottfried relented and both branches of the family reached a negotiated settlement, with the brewery paying him $159,000 in bonds and cash just weeks before his death in May 1935.[90]

Gottfried's death completed the firm's generational transition. An obituary in the *Brewers Journal* hailed him as the one of the Piel Bros. founders responsible "for the rapid and successful growth of the business," most importantly the policy of "not to control, directly or indirectly, or to finance any of its [retail] outlets," thus avoiding the notorious tied saloon.[91] Another obituary in the *Brooklyn Daily Eagle* celebrated him as "a leader in German charitable and social work in this city."[92] Although Maria was now the sole survivor among the brewery's five founders, she had transferred her shares to the children and only intervened intermittently to defend William against his siblings. The second generation was now in charge.

Transition to Repeal

As America moved toward full repeal of Prohibition throughout 1933, Piel Bros. experienced a surge in sales and profits. The first step came that March when President Roosevelt kept his campaign promise by signing legislation legalizing beer with 3.2 percent alcohol starting on April 7, sparking a celebration that exceeded even Armistice Day revelries at the end of the Great War. When the clock atop the Budweiser Brewery in St. Louis struck midnight, 25,000 people cheered and 1,500 trucks lined up to take deliveries of legal beer. Just after midnight in Milwaukee, a special Midwest Airways flight took off for Washington, DC, loaded with seven cases of beer from the city's breweries—each one labeled "To President Franklin D. Roosevelt. Beer 3.2 Percent. From The Nation's Beer Capital, Milwaukee. In Gratitude."[93]

Around New York City, trucks rolled out of the region's breweries at dawn to slake thirst at the city's 32,000 speakeasies and countless legal venues, many crowded to "standing room only." From Flushing to Coney Island and all across Manhattan, there was a "Mardi Gras" jollity at crowded sidewalk beer stands. Demand was so heavy the Piel's plant warned there might be shortages. The nearby Trommer's Brewery announced it had to ration sales. Midst all the carousing, Anheuser-Busch's team of six Clydesdale horses, trucked all the way from St. Louis, made their first-ever appearance, prancing spectacularly down Fifth Avenue to the Empire State Building. There Al Smith, the "wet" 1928 presidential candidate, was delighted to receive a case of legal Budweiser—an ominous harbinger for the future of the city's brewing industry. To meet the surging demand for 3.2 percent beer, Piels would produce 1.1 million cases from April to December, which William called "the largest bottling sale in our history." The legalization of 3.2 beer raised the firm's sales fivefold, from just 28,800 barrels the year before to 147,200 barrels by the end of 1933.[94]

With the company back under his control by May 1933, William and the board made plans to profit from the full repeal of Prohibition, now imminent as the 21st Amendment was being ratified in state after state. That interim law legalizing 3.2 beer had boosted demand, but Piels' plant improvements were still incomplete and the brewery could not fulfill all its orders. Once renovations solved refrigeration problems and a new artesian well cut expenditures for costly city water, bulk draught beer sales began breaking company records. At long last, Piels could curtail its discounted bottle sales to chain stores. In just four months

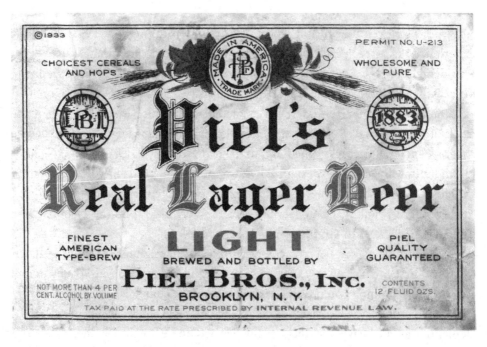

7.1. Label for Piel's Light Lager Beer, with 4 percent alcohol, after Prohibition, circa 1934.

following the legalization of 3.2 percent beer, the brewery's sales reached $1.8 million, double the figure for all of 1929.[95]

Still desperately short of funds, the directors recommended to stockholders that they raise "sufficient working capital" by selling "a minority portion of the stock" to outsiders.[96] In defense of this proposal, somewhat similar to William's earlier ill-fated finance scheme, directors calculated that an outlay of $325,000 for new equipment could earn an additional $5 million in annual sales of 3.2 percent beer. Currently, however, the firm had only a pathetic $3,700 in working capital. Expansion was critical since competition, the board predicted, "will be considerably more acute in the not distant future."[97]

With Prohibition's end just weeks away, William called a board meeting in October 1933 to consider "the effect of the Repeal of the 18th Amendment on the business of this Corporation."[98] To compete with national brands such as Schlitz, Piels needed an immediate price cut in its East Coast shipping territory and accelerated preparations to brew real beer with "natural alcoholic content."[99] Within a month, the plant had slowed production of low-alcohol beer and expanded fermenting capacities "for the full strength beer." To promote its real beer, the president planned to supplement the traditional "point of sale advertising," such as bar signs, with a tentative first step into radio by sponsoring college football games, particularly those of his alma mater Columbia.[100]

Midst this modernization of the brewery, William continued to stoke the family feud, rewarding brother Paul's loyalty with nomination as supervisor of the yeast culture station, a technically demanding position for which he had no training. All the directors approved the appointment except Frank Kondolf, who was allied with dissident siblings Rudolf and Louise.[101]

A few months later, another of William's loyalists, sister Agnes Piel Lyne, joined the firm as advertising manager, even though her work experience was limited to teaching elementary school and writing a child-care column.[102] Louise's husband, Erwin Lange, had already left the brewery and was now supervising the reopening the Harvard Brewing Company near Boston in time for repeal.[103]

With Erwin gone, Rudolf ousted, and Arthur and Henry to soon follow, William was slowly purging his family critics from the firm, leaving his loyal acolytes Agnes and Paul in comfortable sinecures. William, ironically, was still playing primordial family politics in his bid to modernize the company, a contradiction that would continue to bedevil the brewery.

On December 5, 1933, the day Utah became the final state needed to ratify the repeal of Prohibition, William gave the board an optimistic assessment of the firm's prospects. The number of independent retailers stocking Piels in the metropolitan region had jumped from 100 to 1,000 since legalization of 3.2 percent beer. In the wider Maine-to-Florida market, the signing of ninety-nine new shipping accounts was, William said, "auspicious." Indeed, just hours after he spoke those words, news of Utah's vote swept the nation and a somewhat muted celebration of "Repeal Day" started spontaneously at 5:32 p.m. As heavily loaded trucks flew out of the brewery's gates over the next twenty-four hours, Piels shipped 2,175 kegs of beer—an output, the president said, that far "exceeded our expectations."[104] Two weeks later, William reported the brewery had sold 129,000 barrels in the past eight months, shattering its old record of 92,000 barrels set before Prohibition back in 1916.[105]

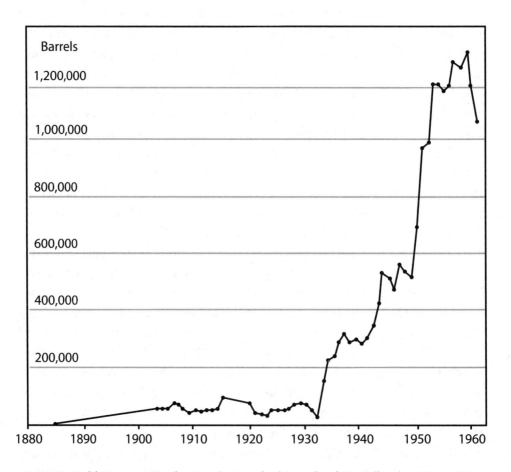

Figure 2. Piels' Beverage Production (in Standard Barrels of 31 Gallons), 1884 to 1961.

Sales Surge After Repeal

In March 1934, the start of the first full season after repeal, sales were so strong William became concerned that rising demand for real beer might exceed the plant's limited capacity of 30,000 barrels monthly, forcing a "curtailment of our Shipping Areas." These projections proved prescient, since Piels' sales would soon double to 320,000 barrels by 1937 and double again to 710,000 barrels by 1950.[106]

Although Prohibition's end brought prosperity to the brewing industry, a surprising number of firms were failing as repeal's euphoria collided with the Great Depression's reality. In the nine months after Prohibition, ten breweries in the New York area would fold, with six more slated for closure by year's end.[107]

To survive, Piels required a delicate balance of expansion, quality, and marketing. Repeal and its promise of prosperity momentarily stilled the family feud. As the plant "stepped up to full capacity" in preparation for the first year of unrestricted sales in 1934, technical director Henry Piel reduced his projected output from 28,750 barrels monthly to just 25,500 "due to an increased fermentation period, now required by him for enhancement of quality." With production so constrained, William pursued a conservative marketing strategy of matching, but not exceeding, price cuts by competitors. Thus, as the big Midwest brewers prepared to flood his Southern shipping territory with "cheap beer to retail at 10¢ a bottle," William expanded the number of distributors and cut their commissions by 40 percent.[108]

As part of these cost controls, Piels also recalibrated its advertising strategy, slashing the newspaper subsidy for regional distributors, cutting radio spots, and trimming the overall budget. While Piels' promotional outlay of $161,000 for nine months in 1933 seemed substantial, advertising manager Agnes Piel Lyne reported it was no more than the industry average of $1.09 per barrel. Nonetheless, Piels now planned an economy-minded campaign of just $90,000 for all of 1934, with 17 percent allocated for newspapers and the bulk, some 60 percent, for so-called "point-of-sale advertising" such as "illuminated signs and road signs."[109] Significantly, this Piel's budget had no allocation for radio in an era when the CBS network, with a hundred affiliates nationwide by 1937, sold $30 million of advertising that made brand names into household words.[110]

While major consumer corporations were hiring slick Madison Avenue agencies, Agnes had no advertising strategy, nor any plans for the radio spots that big brewers such as Pabst were using so effectively. Reflecting their lingering love of the Fatherland, Piels' newspaper and point-of-sale advertising featured kitschy

Germanophile drawings unlikely to appeal to American beer drinkers who then thought of Germans as pillaging Huns or goose-stepping Nazis. Without any market research, Paul Piel developed a coterie of Germanic gnomes for the Piels point-of-sale products such as beer trays, coasters, and bottle openers. Newspaper advertising featured an alien slogan, "Why go to Westphalia for Yeast?" Beneath a line drawing of an overweight couple in German peasant attire, she in *dirndl* dress and he in Alpine hat, the convoluted text read: "Seems a long way, doesn't it? And equally far to the little district of Saaz, in old Bohemia, and the neighboring 'gardens' of Bavaria where Piels' beer gets all its hops."[111]

Despite tone-deaf advertising and inadequate plant capacity, Piels' sales shot up by 60 percent during the first full year of repeal—from 147,000 barrels in 1933 to 240,000 barrels in 1934. Looking forward, the president proposed, at year's end, a "low cost" expansion to an actual production of 350,000 barrels in a plant with a rated annual capacity of 500,000.[112]

7.2. Piel Bros. beer coaster with Germanic elf theme, 1934.

Expanded Board of Directors

As Piels' production soared with Prohibition's end, it became clear to directors and stockholders alike that their antiquated management required reform. By 1934, Piel Bros. had grown far beyond the five laborers employed in 1887 or the thirty-six in 1900 to become a medium-sized firm of 270 employees, including 180 plant workers and drivers, 51 head-office employees, and 8 regional sales representatives from New England to Texas.[113]

Yet with a half-dozen family members in management and a paternalist personnel policy, this mid-sized company still operated like a small family firm. When brewmaster Henry Jakoby died unexpectedly in 1934 after thirty-six years on the job, the Piel's board, lacking any death and disability insurance, voted his widow a modest monthly pension of $100 and posted a plaque in his honor at the plant.[114]

Following the national trend toward professional management, in mid-1934 stockholders agreed to balance family interests with external expertise by expanding the board to seven directors. At a meeting of the Michael Piel Trust in June 1934, the siblings voted unanimously to nominate four family representatives and three outside directors, including a lumber executive, a Wall Street financier, and aviation pioneer La Motte Cohu.[115] When Wigg objected, on behalf of the Sophie Piel Estate, to "two Wall Street men," the Michael Piel Trust agreed to retain La Motte Cohu and—over the objections of Louise, Henry, and Rudolf—to nominate attorney Julian Tashof, Paul's good friend.[116] Yet even at this moment of reform, the family influence remained strong with William continuing as company president and both Piel trusts nominating three members each—producing a new board of seven including three Piels, their two family counsel, and two external directors.[117]After their unanimous election at the annual meeting two weeks later, William welcomed these directors warmly, saying: "I think I can say that you now have a harmonious group of stockholders behind you and that our business prospects appear bright."[118]

At its September meeting, this expanded board adopted a streamlined organization table for the firm, with president William Piel at the apex, five departments, and separate sales divisions whose supervisors were divided evenly between family members and professional managers. Yet family politics still slowed progress. When William proposed that orders of 1,200 packages should be loaded as early as 9:00 a.m., cousin Arthur, as head of packaging delivery, agreed; but brother Henry, insisting that racking belonged to his brewery department, objected saying he needed a one-day notice.[119]

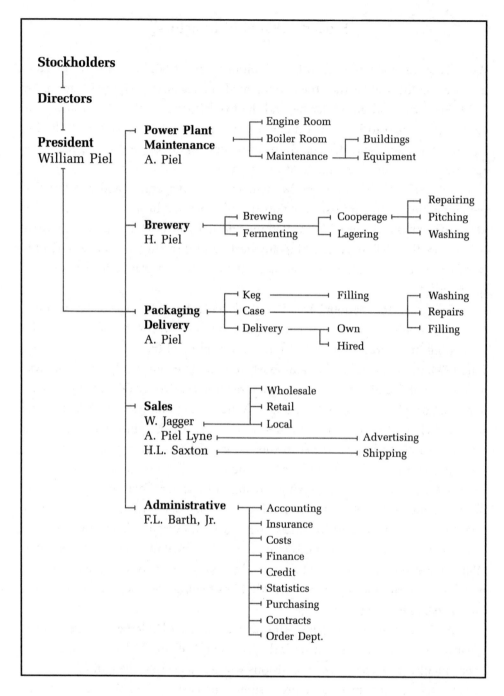

Figure 3. Organization of Piel Bros. Brewery as Family Business, 1934.

In the search for efficiency, the shipping department was a barrier to increased profits. In May 1934, William told the board that a detective agency had found "all our drivers are taking dishonest advantage of the Company in the time claimed for them for their deliveries . . . in order to accumulate their 'overtime' charges." William ordered a staff study that found potential savings of $62,000 by outsourcing to hired carters—something rival Schaefer and Lion breweries were already doing.[120]

As Piels transferred deliveries to its contractor, Snediker Transportation, William convened talks with his union locals, which started "belligerently" since they were caught in a nationwide "jurisdictional issue" between the Teamsters, representing the truck drivers, and a rival union for the helper on each truck.[121] After a six-month trial of the new arrangement, the company's comptroller settled the issue by reporting contract cartage saved $15,000 a year, prompting the board to shut down a shipping department that dated back to the days of beer wagons.[122]

Seeking a balance between cost and quality, the board also searched for savings in the purchase of hops, their product's most essential ingredient. In October 1934, the board interviewed their long-time supplier, Samuel Simon Steiner, New York's leading hops broker and an in-law of the German-Jewish Liebmann family that brewed Rheingold Beer. When the Piel's board asked why "prices of hops abroad [were] higher than the basic price of hops in this country," Steiner, showing his command of this complex global market, explained that Germany's new National Socialist government, regarding beer as "food for the workman," had limited exports of hops to raise domestic beer production by 30 percent. By waiting until Berlin had "a large quantity of hops left over and had been compelled to make concessions for export," Steiner "was quite proud that, as a non-Arayan, of whom Mr. Hitler disapproved, he had been able to import 91% of all German hops which came to the U.S."[123] After Steiner left, Wigg suggested they "should get competitive bids." But Henry replied the hops purchased earlier from another firm "had been picked about two weeks too soon"—an experience that affirmed the need to deal with an expert like Steiner.[124]

Strong sales also raised the contentious issue of compensation. At the new board's first meeting in July 1934, William suggested forming a committee to review executive salaries—a motion that the directors, over brother Henry's objections, approved.[125] Three months later, that committee, chaired by director La Motte Cohu, reported that "the earning power of the corporation has improved tremendously during the last few months," and the president's salary should be increased from $15,000 to $20,000 per annum. With William abstaining and Henry opposed, the board approved.[126]

The question of dividends proved even more critical for the company's future. At that July 1934 board meeting, William suggested payment of $14,000 in dividends to stockholders, with Tashof supporting the idea since "this was a family-owned corporation." One of the new external directors, lumber executive Arthur Curry, was opposed since the firm "owed creditors so much money." His colleague La Motte Cohu disagreed, saying he would not support a dividend for a publicly traded corporation. But Piels was, he said, "a two-family-owned business, quasi partnership . . . entitled to the enjoyment of a modest share" of profits—a view that carried the board.[127]

That modest $14,000 dividend soon grew into a hefty slice of profits that reached $400,000 for 1934. Clearly, the family's stockholders were tired of Prohibition's enforced austerity. During the nine years before World War II, the brewery would pay dividends totaling nearly $1.2 million—almost equal to the $1.5 million loan that William had once sought so desperately to finance the firm's expansion.[128]

A quarter-century later, as Piels' profits withered, Paul Piel, the firm's close, constant observer, would find the seeds of the brewery's decline in those dividends. "At the end of prohibition in 1932," he told his sister Louise, citing the example of Brooklyn's biggest brewery, "Schaefer could hardly have been 100,000 barrels larger than Piel—if that much. By 1942 Schaefer was 1,650,000 barrels larger than Piel! Why? No doubt partly because Rudi Schaefer, having fewer famished stockholders snatching at dividends, was able to plow back more earnings, but mainly because Rudi was an energetic and imaginative executive who sensed the new type business set-up which America had evolved . . . under prohibition." With a "free hand to show what he could do," Schaefer "surrounded himself with vigorous junior executives able to exploit his then consistently good advertising. No switching from agency to agency; no false economies in the advertising budget. Remember his shiny aluminum kegs while we were reconditioning 'perfectly good' oak ones? . . . And when, finally, [Piels' manager Henry] Muessen stood his ground and completely abandoned oak, remember the howls, lest 'that extravagance' curtail dividends."[129]

This board meeting of July 1934 thus proved a precursor for the company's directions over the next decade. With the restraint of Prohibition now removed, the new professional board would allow the firm to realize its potential as a mid-sized brewery in a growing but competitive metropolitan market. For a time, the new external directors would mute the emotional rivalries among the Piel family's second generation, restraining William's misguided financial schemes and curtailing the family's amateurish administration, thereby creating a clear separation between management and shareholders.

That increase in dividends also proved a palliative for the family's strong passions, allowing them to move away from the brewery and, in due course, each other. Simultaneously, however, the family's demand for dividends diverted profits from needed investments in plant efficiency and product quality.

In the conundrum that is family business, every gain thus came with a loss. By embracing the corporate ethos, William gained the authority to push aside family rivals and modernize their company's management. Yet his capacity to impose this seeming rationality was grounded, ultimately, in irrational family intimacies. William and his loyalist Paul gained much of their authority as their mother's favorites. And as the embodiment of the family's control over the company, their very presence compromised the modern management they purported to promote. Dismissal of family rivals for reasons of efficiency simply increased William's primordial power and removed any real restraint on his decisions—whether Rudolf's efforts to curtail his costly executive prerogatives or Henry's insistence on slowing output to insure quality.

With the family's shareholders mollified and increasingly marginalized by these high dividends, management was free to make mistakes. And in later years, as we will see, William's corporate team would make mistakes. Major mistakes. Fatal mistakes.

8

Purging Piels from Piel Bros.

The repeal of Prohibition in 1933 brought New York's breweries both the promise of expansion and the threat of competition. During their industry's forced holiday from 1919 to 1933, brewing had missed the modernization and consolidation that had swept other consumer industries. Those pressures now arrived with undeniable intensity, threatening regional brewers nationwide, Piels included. In the decade following Prohibition, metropolitan brewers would also face the more immediate challenges of Depression, global war, and postwar demobilization.

Pressed by the synergistic growth of national brands and network radio during the 1930s, company president William Piel tried to remake his mid-sized family firm into a major corporation, with mass production and professional management. Within just five years, 1932 to 1937, William transformed the closed board of three family members into a corporate body with only one Piel (himself) and six external directors, including some prominent businessmen.

With the guidance of this external board, Piel Bros. moved beyond the family management that had marked the past half century: first, by Gottfried and his brother Michael from 1883 to 1912; then by Michael's two sons, William and Henry, for the next twenty years. While both sets of Piel brothers combined the essential skills of brewing and management, intense competition from national brands after repeal now required specialists in advertising, finance, production, law, and marketing. With surprising speed, this new board led the brewery in hiring professional executives to address these critical areas. Simultaneously, William pushed five family members out of the firm, removing them from key areas such as advertising, brewing, and transportation. The sum of these changes lifted the firm from the stagnant sales of prewar years to sustained growth by the end of World War II.

In pressing for these reforms, William was, at one level, bringing modern management into his family business. With over a hundred universities offering business courses by 1916, specialists in accounting, finance, and marketing contributed to "the growing professionalization of the managers of large industrial enterprises." As leading companies such as General Electric and General Motors innovated during the 1920s, "new accounting, budgeting, and forecasting methods were becoming normal." But not in brewing. This "managerial revolution" coincided with Prohibition, slowing change in these family enterprises for a full fourteen years. Even Pabst, one of the most dynamic of pre-Prohibition brewers, had to adapt, said an authorized history, to "the change that had taken place in methods of business policy," adopting, during the 1930s, "modern functional divisions and specialized jobs."[1] In a parallel effort, William Piel was introducing modern business practices into his small corner of the tradition-bound brewing industry.

William's reforms also produced a clear separation between management and stockholders, a solution common for family firms going through a generational transition. As rising profits allowed the Piels to build homes, buy farms, and pursue private interests, siblings who had once fought bitterly over the brewery were now concerned almost solely about the size of their dividends.

This change brought gains and losses. In pushing his relations out of the brewery, William would achieve corporate success at the price of family solidarity—illustrating that, in the commingling of the personal and professional inside a family business, attempts to reconcile these irreconcilable forces often yield an ambiguous outcome.

Admittedly, Piels' new professional management proved skilled in marketing and cost accounting. But William's reform agenda also became mired in a bitter generational battle for control of the company, producing a tempestuous transition that left a hybridized management, neither familial nor fully modern. Above all, the purge of family members weakened the Piels' commitment to quality that had been their hallmark for two generations, leading to the firm's later demise. In terms of current theory about the "succession transition" within family businesses, this "sibling partnership" among the Piels' second generation was denied "sufficient time, space, and help to explore their choices," making it most unlikely the resulting "operational structure . . . will be feasible . . . in the long run."[2]

New Management

In the five years following repeal in 1933, William pursued corporate growth guided by two overriding tenets: expanding brewing capacity and building a management team. In pursuit of the first goal, William worked to modernize his aging plant, increasing efficiency and finding low-cost ways to raise production. After a fourfold increase in sales strained the brewery's limited capacity, William announced construction of a two-story building in May 1937 with over 16,000 square feet for lagering and fermenting. This temple of industry was designed by his old college friend Ely Jacques Kahn—famed for his "modern classicist" skyscraper at 120 Wall Street and immortalized as the character Guy Francon in Ayn Rand's novel *The Fountainhead*.[3]

When Piels' new building was completed that December, a correspondent from the *Brewers Journal* was smitten, describing its design in rapturous prose as "thoroughly modern and efficient in its equipment." The artesian well pumped "1,800 gallons of crystal-clear water per minute." The power plant, recently converted from coal to fuel oil, "showed one of the highest efficiencies in . . . the New York metropolitan area." The brew house had "the newest type of 6-roller Malt Mill." Reflecting the bias of a business journal, the firm's 400 employees, many sons and grandsons of earlier workers, reportedly preserved "the Piel atmosphere of management-worker loyalty" and enjoyed their breaks in "two beautiful bowling alleys." Significantly, Piels' executives, "masters of brewing, distribution, and merchandising," maintained "unwavering insistence on spotless sanitary conditions." Every day, this management team met for lunch in the "famous Piel Bier-Stube" for "superb food" from the brewery's kitchen.[4]

To build that management team, William had been forcing family members out of the firm while recruiting executives with the expertise demanded by a fast-changing consumer economy. Rudolf had been eased out several years earlier, but now, in 1936–37, William removed four more family employees. Through harsh, even ruthless moves against his antagonists, he ousted brother Henry as technical director and cousin Arthur as mechanical director. His loyalist Paul disappeared from the post of yeast station supervisor he had held, without any qualification, after repeal. In early 1936, another ally, the family's amateur advertising director Agnes Piel Lyne, was replaced by a professional, the former assistant advertising manager at J. P. Morgan's Standard Brands.[5]

A few months later, William rolled a bowling ball down the alley in the Bier Stube to trigger the lighting for a spectacular neon sign on the brewery's roof—reportedly "the largest electrically animated brewery sign in the world." Weighing fourteen tons and measuring one hundred feet across, the sign used 2,000 feet of neon tubing to show a massive Piel's gnome raising a glass of beer. Years later, one local resident recalled it as "very effective advertising," visible from nearly a mile away by evening commuters at the Eastern Parkway elevated rail platform. That illumination marked the start of Piels' billboard advertising along state highways from Maine to Florida, from Boston to Pittsburgh.[6]

A year later, a new marketing staff launched the firm's first full-spectrum advertising campaign. Under a contract with the Kenyon & Eckhardt agency, Piels doubled its advertising budget in 1937 for heavy coverage in newspapers, magazines, neon signs, and, at long last, radio.[7] That August, William announced the company's first major radio campaign, focused initially on its Southern shipping territory surrounding WMBG Richmond, WBT Charlotte, and four Alabama stations.[8] After changing agencies to Sherman K. Ellis, Piels' newspaper copy showed celebrities taking the blindfold test to assure consumers that, "Piel's Flavor Wins Over Imported Beers."[9]

All this advertising was part of the company's struggle to cope with the relentless press of technological change, unleashed upon their industry by Prohibition's repeal. While network radio advertising helped big brewers build brand recognition nationwide, the introduction of the beer can, lighter and stronger than bottles, cut their shipping costs by over 60 percent and eliminated the expense of returns—the shipping, washing, and handling of glass bottles. Earlier attempts to can beer before Prohibition had failed. Ordinary tins could not contain the 80 p.s.i. pressure of pasteurized beer, and the brew reacted to untreated metal by producing precipitated salts, making it utterly undrinkable.[10]

After repeal, major can companies quickly solved these problems with stronger, coated containers. In 1935, Krueger Brewing of Newark did a marketing test in Virginia that found the beer can, with no deposit and better taste, was popular with consumers. Canned beer soon swept the South, slashing Piels' sales and sparking a burst of "for-God's-sake-do-something" messages from its distributors. Skeptical about the can's new vinyl coating, William instead adopted the non-returnable "stubby" bottle as an alternative that revived those Southern sales. After two years of "extensive research and careful experimentation," in 1938 Piels finally launched its "Special Light Dortmunder Type" in a distinctive cone-top can, manufactured by Continental Can of New York. Not only did drinkers prefer this shape, but it could be filled on the current bottling line, sparing Piels the cost of new flat-top canning machinery. While Piels dithered, Miller Brewing of Milwaukee made their beer can the new centerpiece in a half-million-dollar newspaper and radio marketing campaign, transforming themselves, in the late 1930s, from a regional Wisconsin beer into a national brand sold in forty states.[11]

Family Feud

Despite all these innovations, Piels' sales and profits slowed while competition sharpened during the Depression—clear signs of the need for more fundamental change inside the company. The strong demand for real beer right after Prohibition's repeal in 1933 had brought Piels an initial surge of production and profits. But both soon sagged as their plant's capacity and management's abilities reached their limits. Such stagnation inside the company stood in stark contrast to the rapid growth of Brooklyn's brewing industry. Only five years after repeal, the borough's ten breweries were producing 3.4 million barrels, up from the pre-Prohibition peak of 2.4 million. The biggest of them, Schaefer, was fast becoming the nation's fourth-largest brewery.[12]

That partial repeal of 1933, permitting beer with 3.2 percent alcohol, had boosted Piels' production by nearly 500 percent to 147,000 barrels. The full repeal ratified that December raised next year's output by another 60 percent, prompting plans for a future "low cost" increase of brewing capacity to 500,000 barrels.[13] But absent finance for a major plant expansion or sufficient advertising to compete in New York's crowded market, Piels' production plateaued at 238,000 barrels in 1935, and thereafter crawled upward to only 347,000 barrels by 1942.[14]

Profits proved even more elusive. After a full year of selling real beer, Piels' net profits for 1934 soared to $380,000, allowing the first substantial dividends for family stockholders in fourteen years.[15] As sales slowed in the late 1930s, however, profits declined and total dividends, which were divided among twelve family members, dropped to just $77,000 in 1939.[16]

Not only were dividends declining, but there was also a conflict between management's need to reinvest in plant and the stockholders' demands for a bigger slice of profits. After Piel Bros. made a hefty $400,000 profit and awarded shareholders modest dividends in December 1936, four of Gottfried's children wrote the directors complaining about their "very unreasonable and illiberal attitude toward the declaration of fair dividends to the stockholders." With only one stockholder on the board (William Piel), the directors, they complained, "have insisted upon putting the profits into new machinery, plant expansion, and the creation . . . of a very large working capital." To provide just compensation for shareholders, who had been denied any return throughout Prohibition, Gottfried's heirs insisted that the portion of profits for dividends be raised from the current 32.5 percent to 35 percent. Joined by their cousins in the Michael Piel Trust, the Piel shareholders finally won higher dividends from the board after a "bitter fight."[17]

This tension over growth versus dividends exacerbated conflicts within the Piel family during the late 1930s, producing another round of shareholder criticism, sibling rivalry, and management reforms. By the end of the decade, summers together on Lake Parlin were a fading memory. Indeed, the second generation was now scattered and growing apart—Louise in Maine running the Parlin resort, Rudolf on a poultry farm in Massachusetts, Oswald on his Pennsylvania dairy farm, and William commuting to the brewery from his Connecticut estate. Among the Gottfried Piels, Walter was in Florida, Robert in Princeton, and Arthur out on Long Island, while Sophia traveled incessantly.

William's aspirations for status complicated matters further, intensifying the bitter infighting among his siblings. With singular determination, his wife Loretto recast their lives to win social acceptance from New York's Anglo aristocracy, despite their demerits of German descent, Catholic religion, and modest means. Instead of vacationing at Lake Parlin in the rough Maine woods, Loretto preferred summers at fashionable resorts near New York and, after 1929, life as country squires on their Connecticut estate evocatively named "Salmon Kill."

Instead of familial visits to Piel relatives, most of whom she disdained or despised, Loretto cultivated New York families who could facilitate her social ascent. "Mother wanted us," recalled her son Gerard, "to reject our Germanicism. She wanted to dissociate her branch of the Piel family from the rest of the family." In Loretto's view, he explained, assimilation was a social imperative: "My mother always regarded the Piels as being backward on this business of becoming American. They talked German at home and she thought that Henry's household, in particular, the one closest to us, was 'too German!'" Indeed, said his younger brother David, their mother "squashed any contact with the Piel clan—only Paul and Agnes were exempt." In her catalogue of disregard, Loretto treated Henry with a "sort of contempt," and thought Paul "an amiable silly fellow." Rudolf "got under her skin and bothered her." She "detested Louise," and "thought Ozzie was a silly person." Some of the Piels responded in kind, notably Rudolf who railed against her "social climbing."[18]

William's strained finances as president of a struggling brewery forced Loretto to create the illusion of affluence since Piel Bros., unlike other brewers enriched by sale of their saloon properties during Prohibition, had no real estate and was skirting bankruptcy. "But people just mistakenly assumed that the Piels had tons of money, because they were brewers," said William's grandson Anthony, adding that: "Loretto played her cards close, using this misunderstanding to stretch what little they had, which helped significantly to get them through those tough years."

Through these maneuvers, William and Loretto climbed ever higher into New York society—building a grand $35,000 residence on Long Island, paying $25,000 for a 365-acre Connecticut country estate, and getting listed in the city's exclusive *Social Register* by 1938.[19]

As William won acceptance in New York society, he began to distance himself from both business and family. "Mother," recalled their son Gerard, "had the sense that the rest of the family were his dependents and they just didn't appreciate him and he had sacrificed everything for them." In moving from Long Island to northern Connecticut in the mid-1930s, William had traded a ten-mile commute for a hundred-mile journey. By 1940, New York's *Social Register* listed "Piel, Mr & Mrs Wm (Loretto Scott)" as residing at "Phone No. 312 Lake, 'Salmon Kill Farm,' Salisbury, Ct." For stays of two or three days in the city, William rented an apartment on Fifth Avenue, which was little used since he was increasingly absent from the brewery "for a period of one or two or three weeks at a time."[20]

As William maneuvered to consolidate this social success by remaking Piel Bros. into a national brand, he would prove ruthless in forcing his relations out of the business—buying off one brother, firing another, and ruining the reputation of a cousin. While William no doubt felt these firings were essential for his management reforms, they were complicated by the convoluted emotions of a family firm undergoing a generational transition.

Henry's Ouster

Midst this wrenching shift from family business to modern corporation, travels to Germany again helped ease dissidents out of the brewery. Apart from serving as a bonus to soften the blow of termination, these trips also revealed the growing complications of the family's German identity, particularly the dissonance between their idealized Fatherland and Hitler's Reich.

In 1936, just two years after Rudolf's return from Berlin, Piel Bros. sent Henry and his family on an extended European trip that proved a precursor to dismissal. That April, Henry's eldest child Marie-Luise, then 22 and searching for a career, sailed for Europe with a girlfriend, meeting some "really lovely people" on the boat, including Walter Hövel, the Nazi police chief of Cologne, and a young SS officer named Rolf von Getzsen. When they reached Germany, the SS man took Marie-Luise and her friend on a trip down the Rhine, staying at historic hotels and seeing sights along the river. She also visited her great aunt who lived in a five-story mansion on Graf Reckestrasse in Düsseldorf. Moving on to Paris, Marie-Luise interned at fashion ateliers and studied sketching. By August, she was back in Germany for the 1936 Berlin Olympics. "All the Hitler youth were marching up and down singing," she recalled, adding drama to the grandiose stadium capped by giant swastikas and filled with 100,000 Germans flashing fascist salutes at their Führer, visible to all from his raised podium.[21]

That fall Henry, accompanied by his wife Marie, arrived on a buying expedition for the brewery, first malt from Brussels, then hops from Munich. At that latter city, they visited Helmut Steiner, brother of the brewery's long-standing hops supplier, who was preparing to leave Germany for Switzerland. Since Steiner was Jewish, he spoke frankly of the ugly reality behind the Reich's grand façade. But Henry's family, like his mother Maria, shrouded the country in a romance that made them oblivious to this underside. Continuing their travels, Henry's family made a Christmas visit to Düsseldorf, enjoying the mansions of Martha, Michael's widowed sister-in-law, and her daughter Marga, now married to the owner of a chemical factory. En route back to Paris, the family accompanied Martha Piel on her first visit to the military cemetery near Verdun where her only son Franz was buried, a casualty of the Great War. While Marie-Luise stayed on in Paris for another six months to enjoy parties, attend concerts, and continue her fashion studies, father Henry was back at the brewery by early 1937 where, after twenty-five years, his employment was ending.[22]

Henry's actual dismissal was particularly bitter. Just months after his return from Europe, he was demoted from technical director to technical assistant to the president. Then, at the end of that year, William terminated him. "Oh, it was terrible," recalled Henry's daughter Marie-Luise. "You can't imagine! I was visiting *Tante* Lou . . . in Garden City and I was upstairs in the bedroom over the living room doing my homework, and they were having a meeting downstairs in the living room. And they were cutting my father up into ribbons, just ribbons! Because he'd always say the wrong thing at the wrong time, you know. He was his own worst enemy. He was a great brewer, I tell you, he made wonderful, wonderful beer and it never was the same after he left."[23] Indeed, little more than a decade after Henry's ouster, Piels began producing an unpalatable beer that would become the prime cause of the firm's failure. As for Henry, his career as a brewmaster was over. He retired on the income from his Piels shares, living quietly in Long Island and later in Maine.

With Henry gone, sister Louise lost her last independent source of information inside the brewery, effectively ending her role as an activist stockholder.

Whether by accident or design, Maria took daughter Louise and her eldest son Fred Lange on a last grand European tour in the summer of 1937, crossing the Atlantic on the *S.S. St. Louis* and sweeping across Germany. After a loop down the Rhine for sights in Cologne, Bonn, and Munich, they were back in Herne for Maria's birthday celebration on August 20. In a meadow near the house-barn of her birth eighty years before, ten relations, four from America and six from Germany, gathered to present Maria with "an honest farmer's bouquet," eat cake, and sing German songs. As she said in a letter to son Henry, "it really could not have been more beautiful."[24]

8.1. Maria Piel's ticket on the Hamburg-America Line, New York to Hamburg, 1937.

The visit also featured a flying tour of Berlin, the bustling capital of the Third Reich. There grandson Fred Lange, an engineering student at MIT, sent a postcard from "the busiest airport in the world" at Templehof, describing "the exciting experience" of watching "planes coming in from all over," a Douglas from Java and Junkers landing every four minutes.[25]

All that aeronautic energy was just months away from being unleashed for the conquest of Europe. But Louise's family, like Henry's, was oblivious to the threat implicit in these enticing displays of German power. Like many immigrant families, the second-generation Piels experienced assimilation as a ragged, uneven process, leaving an attachment to the Fatherland that blurred the distinction between Hitler and the Kaiser. The striking disparity between their apparent admiration of the Third Reich and Rudolf's earlier revulsion may well have contributed to his coming expulsion from both the brewery and the family.

Rudolf's Departure

Rudolf's removal from any oversight of the firm involved more of William's deft maneuvers. After years of criticizing his brother's management, in mid-1940 Rudolf assigned his shares in the Michael Piel Holding Corporation to a permanent trust under William's control, appointed their mother as guardian of his interests, and turned his back on the company.[26] Why had Rudolf suddenly conceded control to William after fighting him so hard, for so long?

Convinced his brother's ambitious plans were leading Piel Bros. "into endless and continually accelerating expansion" whose dismal end was "inevitable," Rudolf decided to diversify his investments, moving "first into the hatchery business" and later "into the ranching business."[27] While living on Long Island during the 1930s, Rudolf had continued his interest in poultry genetics, breeding gamecocks and tracking their lineages in elaborate ledgers. To test his theories, he entered his birds in New York's premier illegal arena, the Albany Main, keeping a clinical distance from this gritty underworld of cockfighting by reputedly refusing to bet even when his bird was a sure winner. Asked about Rudolf's decision to place his Piel shares in trust, daughter Margarita (once known as Peggy) replied: "They must have loaned my father money to start a poultry business, that's the only explanation. My father was terrible with money, always buying things he could not afford, like expensive cattle in later years." Indeed, just three months after consigning his Piel bonds to William's care, Rudolf obtained a $35,000 loan from the brewery's banker,

Grace Bank, sold his Garden City home, and moved to Concord, Massachusetts, where he started the Piel Poultry Farm to breed improved birds.[28] With his shares in trust and his energies devoted to building a business in another state, Rudolf would no longer play any real role in the brewery.

Apart from ending his involvement in the company, Rudolf's career move also sparked a bitter fight at the family's emotional center, Lake Parlin. Throughout the lean years of Prohibition and Depression, the family had cut staff by half but retained their land, about 200 acres. While Louise kept the big house open as a hotel, several family members owned smaller, adjacent parcels—including Maria's lakeshore lodge, Henry's nearby fishing camp, and Rudolf's hilltop lot overlooking the big house. During the 1930s, the second generation, except for William, sent their many children to summer at the old estate, which Louise now managed as a travelers' inn she called Lake Parlin Farm. Her son Rollo Lange said "it was supposed to be kind of a ritzy place," with a small, select clientele that Louise coddled with home-cooked meals, fishing guides, and elaborate outings. Rudolf's daughter Margarita recalled wonderful times there as a child, helping in the kitchen, waiting tables, and pitching hay onto the horse wagons.[29]

As a first step in building his poultry business, Rudolf shuttled his breeder hens and their eggs between rented barns in Smithtown, Long Island, and a custom-built hatchery on his hilltop above Lake Parlin, where isolation protected his chicks from disease in the years before antibiotics. According to Rollo, Rudolf had perfected the genetics to breed a "fast fleshing bird" and thereby feed the Depression-era demand for affordable protein. Nonetheless, the noise and smell from 3,000 chickens atop that nearby hill complicated sister Louise's efforts at gentility for paying guests in the main house. During one of his visits in the summer of 1940, these tensions sparked words with Rudolf that led him to a serious breach with Louise, their mother, and Lake Parlin.[30]

In a July 1940 sworn statement, right after that unfortunate visit to Parlin, Rudolf transferred his twenty hilltop acres, with an assessed value of $500, to his mother Maria for one dollar. And in two related documents, Rudolf released his mother, Louise, and her husband Erwin Lange from any claims for damages dating back to "the beginning of the world." But Rudolf retained "all my rights in . . . ten poultry range shelters, each with three poultry mash hoppers . . . , and one oil painting by Kröner depicting a group of deer which are now on said Lake Parlin Farm, and which are my property and are to be returned to me."[31] For the past twenty years, Louise and Rudolf had been allies in the brewery, business partners, and near neighbors, first in Ohio and later on Long Island.

These tensions produced a long hiatus in an important alliance that had, in years past, checked William's dominance over the family firm.

Through these events, Rudolf had been bought out of the brewery, forced off the Parlin estate, and evicted from the family circle. His mother Maria played a central role in this rupture, serving as guardian of the trust for Rudolf's shares and the recipient of his land at Lake Parlin. "Grandmother seemed to play divide and rule with her own children," observed Rudolf's daughter Margarita, "playing them off against each other to push them to succeed." In earlier years, Maria had used her corporate bonds as collateral for loans to subsidize Rudolf's life changes, first farming in Ohio and then suburban life on Long Island.[32] But such maternal generosity had apparently reached its limits. Henceforth, Rudolf would distance himself from his brother, mother, and their brewery, devoting himself entirely to his farming ventures, first chickens and later cattle. He would never speak to his mother again.

In retrospect, it seems this breach between mother and son was caused by something more than some chickens. With the Battle of Britain starting in that same summer of 1940, issues of loyalty, Anglo versus German, had revived with passionate intensity. Even as a child visiting Lake Parlin, Anthony Piel felt this cultural clash. In the summer of 1941, Anthony's father Bill Piel, a workaholic Wall Street attorney, decided to revive his failing marriage with a family vacation at Lake Parlin, the site of pleasant boyhood memories. But wife Mary was a New York socialite who volunteered to host British Navy officers in port for Lend-Lease shipments. She was appalled by this German-speaking household headed by grandmother Maria, and returned to New York alienated from her husband's immigrant family—a contributing factor in their impending divorce.[33] With the Nazi regime bent on conquest and Parlin a nest of Germanic sympathies, Rudolf, whose American assimilation was complete, apparently dealt with this conflict by breaking with his mother, their summer home, and the family business.

Arthur's Dismissal

The dismissal of cousin Arthur Piel, the brewery's mechanical director, was both protracted and painful. In January 1936, the chief of the brewery's engine room, Ralph Watts, came to William with a confession that he had been using company labor and materials for electrical work on Arthur's home in Glen Cove, Long Island. Several days later, Watts attempted suicide, creating what William called "quite a stir in our organization." The next day, William summoned Arthur, who denied any intention to defraud and immediately wrote a personal check for $835.35 to cover these costs. Within weeks, however, William, twisting a minor "courtesy" into a major crime, accused Arthur of fraud before the board, which was meeting in the law offices of director Elmer Wigg. After a unanimous vote, the directors "demanded the resignation of Arthur Piel as an employee of Piel Bros. and also as a member of its Board of Directors." Humiliated before the family and angry at "the company which had treated me so shamefully," Arthur could not even muster a protest when Piel Bros. failed to deliver its promised severance pay.[34]

Almost immediately, however, Robert Piel came to his brother's defense, recalling, quite accurately, that "for years various members of the family of my father and uncle have had some items of work done at their homes and to their automobiles by workmen of the brewery without reimbursing the company." These allegations against Arthur were, charged Robert and two of his siblings, of a "trifling nature"—a mere pretext by Elmer Wigg, their mother's executor, to gain "more complete domination and control" over her estate and its considerable assets.[35]

Since William himself had long used complimentary company labor to cook his lunch, service his automobile, and guard his home, it seems likely that he had once again colluded with Wigg to remove another family member from the Piel's board, freeing himself from oversight by querulous relatives.

To block any retaliation by Arthur and his angry siblings, who still held half the company's shares, William helped twist their mother's estate into a legal tangle that distracted the Gottfried Piels from the brewery's affairs. After Wigg helped him fire Arthur, William reciprocated by providing Wigg, the joint executor of Sophie Piel's $1.2 million trust, with evidence that Arthur had "conspired . . . to wrong, cheat, and defraud Piel Bros."—first, by approving $35,000 in inflated trucking charges and then by accepting $13,500 in kickbacks from that same trucker disguised as personal loans.[36] With documentation of this dereliction provided from William's files, Wigg petitioned the surrogate court for Arthur's removal as his co-executor, charging he was unfit to administer his own mother's estate. After four years of relentless litigation, Arthur finally resigned as executor of the Sophie Piel Trust in February 1940, effectively ending his role in the brewery.[37]

In firing his relatives, William was driven by mixed motives. During the difficult years of Prohibition when most breweries had failed, their teamwork—William's management, Henry's successful near beer, Rudolf's clever de-alcoholization, and Arthur's bottling innovations—had saved the brewery from bankruptcy. Whether casting off embarrassing Germanic relatives, purging troublesome directors, or simply doing his wife's bidding, William had betrayed his partners. He would carry a burden of guilt for years to come.

Yet even so, workplace interactions among these kinfolk were becoming so fraught that Piels' productivity was lagging and reforms were necessary. Cousin Arthur and brother Rudolf were undeniably divisive. But Henry's dismissal denied the company a master brewer not easily replaced. Inside the conundrum that is family business, every gain came with a cost.

By the outbreak of World War II, only two among the second-generation Piels were still active in the family business: William, the New York socialite and president of Piel Bros.; and his younger brother Paul, Greenwich Village artist and long-serving president of the Michael Piel Trust. For the better part of fifteen years, from Henry's expulsion in 1937 to William's death in 1953, these two brothers, William and Paul, would collaborate in the modernization of their family firm, recruiting experienced external directors and keeping all the Piels, save William himself, remote from any role in management.

Modern Management

Whatever William's motives were, these changes had profound implications for the brewery's future. Like his father before him, Henry, through his rigorous German training, had maintained Piels' tradition of quality beer against formidable odds. Although an ancient craft, brewing remained a subtle organic process requiring real skill to avoid the risk of spoilage that, in fact, grew as modern companies raised volume, increased shipping distance, and extended shelf life. With Henry's ouster and William's later incapacity through illness, the company would become vulnerable to such production problems.[38] More broadly, these tensions within the Piel brewery exemplified major transitions within American business—from family firm to modern corporation, from craftsman quality to mass marketing, from local loans to finance capital.

With his relatives out of the way, William was finally free to transform his family business into a modern corporation that mass-produced beverages and moved product by brand-name advertising. In lieu of family members, William relied on a board of prominent executives and a staff of professional managers. After several years of a diffident board, Piels elected two new directors in 1939 with extensive corporate experience: Graham B. Grosvenor, the founding president of American Airlines;[39] and, after aggressive recruitment by Paul Piel, Kenneth S. Baxter, a senior executive at the distiller Seagram, best known as father of famed actress Anne Baxter.[40]

To find Piel's a new sales manager, board member Baxter personally interviewed the candidates and made an unconventional choice—Bruce Berckmans, a former assistant bureau director in the U.S. Commerce Department with a "keen, dynamic, tactless" personality that was, said Paul, "badly needed to break encrusted inertia and apathy" inside the brewery's marketing arm. As he rose to vice-president and then general manager over the next two years, Berckmans identified his salesman Henry Muessen as executive material, promoting him to sales manager and then grooming him as his successor by the time Berckmans left for a better job at Brooklyn's Schaefer Brewery.[41]

In presenting his marketing strategy to Piels' finance committee in January 1941, Berckmans explained their prime objective should be "a higher ratio of profits to net sales rather than primarily sales volume." Since the highest profit potential still lay in the metropolitan market, he recommended "more intensive cultivation of the four major New York City boroughs" and a corresponding cut in sales staff for Long Island where "delivery costs are abnormally high." More broadly, Piels had to move beyond its "apparent belief that merchandising . . . can be . . . regarded . . . as a necessary evil." To survive, Piels would have to adapt to what Berckmans called New York's "unique" consumer environment. Alone among major U.S. markets, the city was "no longer dominated by quality considerations," requiring that "an unusually high percentage of revenue [be] devoted to creating consumer demand."[42] In effect, Berckmans was the voice of modern management, pronouncing quality passé and proclaiming marketing paramount.

After displaying eighteen data-dense graphs to show "the necessity for Radio Advertising . . . over newspaper advertising," Berckmans took the directors on a chart-by-chart tour of Piels' patchy retail coverage, ranging from a healthy 72 percent of independent retailers in midtown Manhattan to a dismal 18 percent in the Bronx.[43] To correct these deficiencies, Piels' agency, Sherman K. Ellis, planned to move away from the old mix of newspaper advertising and bar paraphernalia toward an aggressive radio campaign backed by billboards. While the "newspaper reader's attention is diverted by many advertisements," explained Berckmans, "the radio listener is more apt to absorb what is said"—prompting him to propose full-blast coverage from station WCAE Pittsburgh to WOL Washington.[44]

Upon assurances from William that the company could maintain its profit margin by cost savings at the plant, the finance committee approved Berckmans' proposed $600,000 outlay for the 1941 marketing campaign. Not only was this expenditure nearly seven times the radio-averse budget that advertising director Agnes Piel Lyne had drafted just six years before, but the new themes were strikingly different.[45] Instead of her quaint newspaper copy about *lederhosen*, *dirndl* dress, and mittel-European geography, the Piels' "All Sports Quiz" on Radio WOR now featured boxing champion Jack Dempsey's all-American argot. "It's three strikes on thirst when you ask for Piel's Extra-Premium Pielsner," the champ told his listeners. "Piel's is aged extra long . . . So Piel's slides past your throat silkier than [Dodger pitcher] Whit Wyatt's outcurve."[46]

Stockholder's Critique

Whatever their long-term yield might be, all these management reforms had mingled short-term results, raising sales slowly while letting profits slide from $210,000 in 1938 to $180,000 in 1941.[47] Midst this decline, Henry Piel wrote a long letter, dated December 1940, with a withering critique of brother William's new corporate management. From his intimate knowledge of company operations, Henry cited four key deficiencies "as contributing in large measure to the unfavorable balance sheet": (1) excessive expenditure for advertising and sales; (2) increasing maintenance costs; (3) costly equipment purchases; and (4) rising executive salaries. For the next six months, Henry's letter made him Banquo's ghost at multiple meetings of the Piel's board, its marketing committee, and an investigative subcommittee—sending William's new management team on an urgent quest for profits.[48]

But, above all, it was Henry's allegations about unwise equipment purchases, with their implicit critique of his successor in the post of technical director, which seemed to sting. Rejecting his criticism of the firm's weak commitment to quality, William's subcommittee insisted that the plant's new Test Brew House would produce research leading to "the reduction of production costs and/or the enhancement of the quality of the company's beer." Reviewing operations of the Technical Division since May 1, 1937, the date of Henry's demotion, this committee exonerated his successor for any role in two industrial accidents. After weeks of vibrations so deafening they caused complaints from local residents, Air Compressor No. 2 crashed through the factory floor that December, doing

$7,000 in damage. Instead of faulting the current technical director for ignoring this thunderously obvious problem, the committee blamed the equipment's improper installation back in 1934—when Henry was still in charge. After a diesel engine burned up from want of oil in May 1939 causing $11,000 in damages, the committee found the technical director bore only a "general responsibility." William's subcommittee also agreed with this director's decision to blame a subordinate, the watch engineer, thus ignoring clear signs of incompetence by the key employee responsible for their beer's quality.[49] Effectively taking sides in this sibling rivalry, the board imperiously waved away Henry's well-considered concerns about cost, efficiency, and, most importantly, quality.

In their vigorous defense of these equipment purchases, the board provided inadvertent information that cost-cutting may have changed, and diminished, the flavor of Piels' most important brews. The Laeuter Tub, used to separate mash from the liquid wort, that Henry had installed in 1936, his last full year as brewmaster, produced, by 1940, annual savings of $16,000 in materials (malt, rice, and hops). In a close financial analysis, the board noted that main saving came from a 27 percent reduction in the pounds of hops per barrel for both its Dortmunder and Pielsner brews. Since Piels purchased a costly variety of "noble hop" from Saaz, Czechoslovakia, famous for lending an aromatic flavor to the brew, this significant reduction in such a key ingredient may well have diminished the beer's quality.[50] With war about to cut the supply of these rich Saaz hops from Nazi-occupied Czechoslovakia and force a shift to less robust domestic varieties, cutting back on this key ingredient did not bode well for the company's commitment to quality.

At year's end, however, the board could not ignore the core of Henry's complaint, shared by all the stockholders, about the allocation of profits. By October 1941 management's new marketing strategy produced "a decidedly better sales performance," yielding profits of $76,500 available for either working capital, executive bonuses, or special stockholder dividends. During a luncheon meeting at the New York Athletic Club, the board's finance committee comprising William and the family lawyers, Julian Tashof and Elmer Wigg, quickly approved $11,600 in raises and $13,000 in bonuses, including $2,500 for sales manager Bruce Berckmans. But they hesitated over that extra dividend for family shareholders, mindful of the $95,000 in working capital needed for the upcoming summer season. Like a patriarch providing for spendthrift children, William admitted his relations "were entirely dependent upon dividends from the Company." Gottfried's children divided both dividends and bond interest among just five of them, but

Michael's heirs paid all their bond income to mother Maria and then had to split their half of the stock dividends seven ways, not five. Since an individual dividend "less than $2,000.00 would very definitely work a hardship on them," the finance committee, at William's suggestion, unanimously approved a special dividend totaling $28,000.[51]

On the eve of World War II, the division within the family was now complete. William was the executive who ran the brewery with unchecked authority; while his siblings and cousins were beneficiaries, mere dependents living genteel lives from the generous dividends their inheritance provided.

Brewing Goes to War

As the nation mobilized for war in early 1942, New York's brewing industry, Piel Bros. included, found this second world war far less traumatic than the first. Indeed, just a generation after the pervasive suspicions of World War I, Washington was no longer concerned about German American loyalties. In 1939, the *Deutsch-amerikanische Volksbund*, known as the Bund, had massed 20,000 supporters for a pro-Hitler rally at Madison Square Garden. During the first six months of war in 1942, German submarines sank over 200 U.S. ships off the East Coast, raising public fears of possible espionage. But the federal government was still confident that the millions of German Americans were, in the words of a U.S. commission, "so fully assimilated that there was no doubt of their undivided loyalty."[52]

Even so, the brewing industry was nervous about a revival of the anti-German, anti-alcohol hysteria that had marked the First World War. To preempt possible sanctions, the big shipping brewers sponsored victory bond drives and launched patriotic advertising campaigns. Anheuser-Busch employees bought nearly a million dollars of war bonds, enough to fund two bombers dubbed *Miss Budweiser* and *Busch-whacker*. At the war's start, the head of the U.S. Brewers' Association, Rudolph Schaefer, Jr., assured the nation that every one of his industry's 60,000 employees would buy war bonds. The workers at his Brooklyn brewery gave 128 pints of blood to the Red Cross, a national record for a single day's donation. The association also ran sentimental magazine ads on the theme "Beer Belongs." So successful was this effort that brewing was spared the grain rationing that had hampered production during World War I. Per capita consumption of beer grew by 50 percent during World War II, as did Budweiser's sales, reaching a new peak of 3.7 million barrels.[53]

With a half-dozen of the younger Piels on active duty, and several serving in combat against Germany, the family no longer harbored divided loyalties. "The Germans leave mankind no other choice—they only learn the hard way—perhaps not even then!" wrote Paul Piel as allied bombers razed German cities in late 1944. "Such regressive degeneration as German youth has recently gone through is not easily outgrown," he continued in a letter to his brother-in-law Erwin Lange, who had been dismissed from the U.S. Foreign Service as pro-German during World War I. "Sooner or later the Germans too will have to come round to see that humanity is far more precious than any *Deutschtum* [German race]."[54]

Absent accusations of pro-German treason or threats of prohibition, mobilization for total war against the Axis became a mixed blessing for New York's breweries, bringing both shortages of raw materials and an unquenchable demand for every bottle they could brew. On balance, said Piels' general manager Henry Muessen, "the Brewing Industry flourished" during World War II and the immediate postwar years. Piels certainly shared in that prosperity.[55]

With wartime shipping restrictions keeping the national brands at bay, all New York area breweries grew, but the biggest grew ever bigger. At the start of the war in 1942, Ballantine's large plant in Newark, a trade journal reported, "sold beer and ale throughout most of the nation;" while Piels, by contrast, "conducted a scattered shipping business in a score of seaboard and southern states in addition to a moderate local business." Although Piels ranked at number sixty in sales among the nation's 600 brewers, its production was still near the bottom among the metropolitan area's nine major breweries—ranging from Ballantine (1.85 million barrels), to Schaefer (1.7 million), Rupert (1.35 million), and Liebmann (975,000), all the way down to Piels and Rubsam & Horrmann (340,000 each). Driven by surging wartime demand, Piels' output suddenly jumped by 36 percent to 424,000 barrels for 1943. But Ballantine's increased by 30 percent to reach a hefty 2.4 million, nearly six times larger than Piels.[56]

Wartime economic controls created serious constraints for all New York brewers. After the fall of Singapore, tin was suddenly in short supply and cities sponsored can drives to collect this scarce metal. With strict metal rationing, the larger breweries relied on scrap collection to manufacture their bottle caps. Malt deliveries were cut by 7 percent. There were also serious shortages of corn, which many brewers, including Piels, used as an adjuvant. To conserve fuel, the Northeast states restricted bottled beer deliveries to once a week and kegs to twice. As empties stacked up in cellars and garages, brewers joined with the milk and soft drink distributors in a patriotic bottle campaign, prompting millions of returns that met their needs. Limitations on railroad mileage and gasoline rationing forced Brooklyn's top brewers, Schaefer and Liebmann, to close their remote distribution depots. Piels too pulled back from far-flung markets—circumscribing their sales to an arc around Boston, Buffalo, Pittsburgh, and Richmond, as "the most distant points which would receive any sales-advertising support." To conserve gasoline, the sounds of horse hooves were once again heard on city streets as Schaefer, Trommer, and Liebmann used beer wagons for deliveries. By war's end, Schaefer alone had a stable with a hundred draft horses. Federal beer taxes rose to eight dollars a barrel, a heavy burden that contributed to the decline of the nation's breweries from 714 in 1934 to only 523 at war's end.[57]

In marked contrast to the total abstinence imposed on military personnel during the First World War, the government now ordered, in November 1943, that many brewers allocate 15 percent of production for military use. Piels was one among eighty breweries nationwide enrolled in this defense effort, with its deliveries to the army peaking at 110,000 cases in August 1944.[58] Military procurements denied Piels sufficient bottles to satisfy growing civilian demand, but the government contract also allowed the company access to scarce resources for plant improvements needed to sustain its increased output. After months of running the plant's ice machines beyond capacity round-the-clock, the installation of "two, new compact ice-machines" in late 1944 averted what could have been "a complete tie-up of the brewery" had either of the old engines broken down.[59]

Adding to these wartime constraints, the Internal Revenue Service (IRS) also limited advertising to control consumer demand. After the IRS set the firm's expenditure at $450,000 for 1944, Piel's board considered sponsorship of news coverage to inform the public about the war, but opted instead for more escapist copy.[60]

Piels did its patriotic duty with bond drives and beer production for soldiers. But its advertising avoided the war and instead basked in the bright lights of Broadway. Starting in 1944, the firm ran regular quarter-page spreads in New York newspapers hailing Piel's Light Beer as "A leading 'Light' on the Great White Way." One of the first in this series showed the stars of the Broadway show *Ziegfeld Follies*, ventriloquist Señor Wences and songstress Sara Ann McCabe, raising foamy glasses to proclaim, "We like Piel's clean, tangy flavor." At the bottom of this crowded frame, the Piel's gnome waved a magic wand at the slogan, "De-licious. De-lightful. De-mand It!"[61]

As the company's campaign expanded, this Broadway theme became Piels' leitmotif on city airwaves. Listening to the classical station WQXR-FM while working at *Life* magazine during and after the war, Gerard Piel recalled hearing the jingle "Piel's Light Beer of Broadway Fame" so often he could still sing it a half-century later.[62] In the postwar period, the brewery, recalled Margarita Piel McCoy, lent substance to that slogan when the Hotel Astor, at Broadway and 44th Street, agreed to serve its beer exclusively, making Piels, quite literally, "the beer of Broadway fame."[63]

For the next four years, the company's newspaper advertising would continue with the same elements—stars of the latest hit show raising a glass of appealing Piels, a female dancer showing shapely legs or deep cleavage, and, starting in mid-1948, the impish gnome sparking the snappy slogan—"Piel's Light Beer of Broadway Fame." Every week, New York newspaper readers saw a succession of Broadway stars celebrating with a cold glass of Piels—notably, "mock strip tease" dancer Joan McCracken from *Bloomer Girl* (September 1945), "light on her toes" Sono Osato in *On the Town* (October 1945), and comedian Phil Silvers in *High Button Shoes* (March 1948).[64]

8.2. Piel Bros. beer coaster with Broadway star Ethel Merman, circa 1948.

Transition to Peacetime

Despite the restraints of wartime rationing, Piels' production, spurred by appealing advertising and sales to thirsty soldiers, grew steadily during the last two years of World War II. By the end of 1944, output rose by 25 percent over the previous year to hit 532,000 barrels—funding bonuses for non-union employees and comfortable dividends for family stockholders.[65] At war's end, the brewery's auditors reported "a steady improvement in operating results" over the past six years, with sufficient working capital, "close control of inventories," and annual sales doubling to $5.5 million by 1945.[66]

To maintain these strong sales in the competitive postwar market, Piels needed a major infusion of capital to expand its overtaxed plant capacity.[67] After seventy years of family finance and mortgage loans from local banks, Piels found that Wall Street financiers, long wary of brewing, were finally warming to their industry. Starting in March 1944, general manager Henry Muessen retained the engineers H. A. Kuljian & Co. of Philadelphia to survey the Piel's plant for "a possible postwar expansion" to a million-barrel capacity.[68] With the approval of the two family trusts, the directors signed celebrity architect Ely Jacques Kahn, designer of their 1937 addition, to schedule the structural steel for a new stock house. To persuade stockholders of the need for major finance, management printed a brochure titled *The Future of Piel Bros.* Now all the company needed was capital.[69]

After many years of bitter failure, Piels' hunt for finance now found an expert guide in their director Julian Tashof. From his law office at 80 Broad Street in Manhattan's financial district, Tashof used his extensive contacts to conduct a cautious, year-long reconnaissance of Wall Street that led, by sure-footed steps through corporate offices and private clubs, to an optimum offer. After spurning overtures from Smith Barney, Mutual Life, and Sir Ellice Victor Sassoon, Tashof met a partner from the firm of financier Ferdinand Eberstadt who had an enticing proposal from Equitable Life Assurance—specifically, an $800,000 loan at 3.5 percent interest secured by thirty-year bonds.[70] Unlike William's earlier entrapment by that shady Queens banker Louis Gosdorfer, Tashof's impeccable Wall Street contacts had produced eight solid offers and a viable proposal from a reputable financier. The contrast may have accounted for William's uncharacteristic silence throughout these negotiations.

But when Equitable's offer reached stockholders, several siblings were far from silent, reflecting deep divisions within the Piel family. After reading the board's case for finance in that printed brochure, Henry responded from his Long

Island home with a counter-proposal to control executive salaries and protect dividends. Rudolf, writing from his poultry farm in Massachusetts, expressed prescient reservations about taking on a million dollar debt for expansion when "shrunken markets" midst a likely postwar recession would make "the same increased capacity stand idle."[71]

The board's reply to this criticism came hard and fast. The directors dismissed Henry's suggestion for stockholder supervision of executive salaries as a "serious embarrassment to the company." And they waved away Rudolf's pessimistic predictions by citing the company's recent record of success—a metric that would later prove irrelevant. Most importantly, the board warned that "prospective competition by local brewers and by two national brewers [Schlitz and Pabst] now locating plants in the metropolitan area" made Piels' plant expansion imperative. Without increased capacity, the company could not meet peak summer demand, threatening the firm with the loss of 130,000 barrels in sales and a corresponding reduction in dividends.[72]

While these formal memos circulated openly, the family's dissident stockholders exchanged a hurried round of private letters, seeking to use the financing as leverage for redress of long-standing grievances. Still stung by their ouster from the firm years before, Henry, Rudolf, and Louise shared reservations about the proposed expansion, anger at years of sparse information, and a desire for representation on the brewery's board. In letters to Rudolf and Louise, Henry, the firm's former brewmaster, insisted that they should have "access to all the papers" about the expansion, and complained that Piel's board was disbursing generous management bonuses while denying the stockholders reasonable dividends. In a lengthy memo, Louise's husband Erwin Lange, the former president of Harvard Brewing, highlighted the problems of expanding the brewery's East New York plant, which was "distant, involving expensive handling even to N.J." and had a "natural territory more limited to Brooklyn."[73]

After years of sending proxies, consideration of this financing in March 1946 brought all seven siblings to the Brooklyn Heights home of Agnes Piel Lyne for a meeting of the Michael Piel Trust. Anticipating opposition, William had circulated a memo urging immediate approval of Equitable's $800,000 financing "in view of the impatience already expressed by their negotiators." Any alternative to this "private placement" would, he warned, mean a "public underwriting"—that is, an open sale of company bonds with higher interest and unwelcome ownership by non-family members. After discussion of William's document, the siblings split along entrenched factional lines. Henry, Louise, and Rudolf were firmly opposed; while

Agnes, Paul, Oswald, and William himself were strongly supportive. With the loan approved by this narrow margin, the siblings all agreed to set aside company by-laws, allowing Agnes to transfer her shares to handicapped daughter Patricia Lyne.[74]

Even with this approval, the Piel's board still needed the stockholders' consent to subordinate their existing Piel gold bonds to new debentures for Equitable's financing. Seeking family unity at this critical juncture, Gottfried's five children, heirs to the Sophie Piel Estate, wrote their seven cousins embodied in the Michael Piel Trust, urging them to approve this final step for Equitable's investment. They argued persuasively that "the plant facilities must be . . . enlarged if Piel Bros. is to maintain its competitive position" and continue to pay adequate dividends, which "is most important to us since so many of the members of both our families depend upon dividends for practically their entire income."[75]

At this sensitive juncture, the three dissident siblings tried to use the bond issue as leverage to win a seat on the brewery's board and end their years of marginalization. The by-laws of the Michael Piel Trust required near unanimity (75 percent of shares) for such major financial transactions, giving this minority faction clout for the first time since William had captured the board a decade before. Insisting "we do not wish Paul and William to push us around," Henry advised his fellow rebels that "we are now in the position to protect ourselves for the future" by demanding the right to nominate a director "before consenting to the [bond] subordination." To that end, Henry met with a prospective director, attorney Eugene A. Sherpick, who had represented the family during the disastrous Gosdorfer litigation. But by early April, the brewery, discouraged by continuing government economic restrictions, was backing away from rapid expansion and wavering about the Equitable financing. After what he called "a long-winded telephone call from Paul," Henry told his fellow rebels they were no longer "holding a gun" and Paul would not "consider our desire to choose a director."[76]

By June, the brief stockholders' revolt was fading. Midst all this maneuvering, Rudolf, the most assertive of the dissidents, succumbed to tuberculosis, contracted as an infant from his German nanny, straining their tenuous solidarity. Unable to work, he had been forced to put his Massachusetts poultry farm on the market, selling his breeding stock for meat at a loss and offering his house for sale at a reduced price. Even if the sale were successful, liquidation of loans from Grace Bank used to buy the place and the Farm Bureau for hurricane damage would leave so little money that his wife Margarita had "already approached three stores for a part time job." Faced with possible death and bankruptcy that would leave his wife penniless, a desperate Rudolf phoned Louise up in Maine, venting non-stop for thirty minutes. He dismissed brother Paul as a do-nothing. He insisted on his independence even "if it costs my life." He pleaded with her to pressure their mother Maria for permission to sell his share of the Piel Bros. bonds. While listening to him rage, ignoring any counsel she tried to offer, Louise, her throat going dry, felt "heartsick, haunted by the specter of Rudolf losing his mind." Finding him so "utterly unbalanced" that he "can ruin his family and himself," she refused his request and asked brother Henry to support her in this stressful decision, which he did. Within weeks, Rudolf had entered a sanatorium near Boston and was once again dependent upon his mother's generosity to pay for what would become several years of costly treatment.[77]

At the next meeting of the Michael Piel Trust, Henry turned up alone to nominate a minority representative for the Piel Bros. board and was decisively crushed by a vote of one-to-four. As usual, the slate of directors put forward by the long-dominant majority (William, Agnes, Paul, and Oswald) won handily. The dissident stockholders were again shut out and their revolt was over.[78]

In the end, Piel Bros. decided that the uncertain postwar conditions made both rapid expansion and major financing premature. Instead of proceeding with Equitable's bond issue, in September 1946 the company negotiated a line of credit with Grace Bank, backed by Massachusetts Mutual Life, which allowed the brewery to draw up to $800,000, as needed, at a reasonable 4 percent interest.[79] Throughout this contentious, protracted process—lasting twenty-one months from Tashof's first meetings to the Grace Bank contract—the Piel brewery had finally secured sufficient capital for postwar expansion.

By war's end, Piel Bros. had emerged from four years of rationing and restrictions in surprisingly good shape. Driven by that unquenchable wartime thirst, there had been marked increases in sales, profits, and dividends. The company's board now included skilled executives who presided over a modernized management. To fight the national brands for New York's market, Piels had a top Madison Avenue agency churning out copy for newspapers, radio, and billboards. But most importantly, Piels had finally secured, after decades of failure, the capital to expand its plant capacity.

All this progress notwithstanding, the brewery was still a mid-sized family firm facing pressures from aggressive national brands and resurgent trade unions that would, within a few decades, prove fatal for New York's brewing industry. By his continuing presence, moreover, William himself embodied an atavistic family influence inside Piels, compromising his company's management reforms and crippling its response to these relentless market pressures.

Photo Gallery: Brooklyn's Breweries

Home of Michael and Maria Piel with Piel Bros. East New York Brewery wagon, 1880s.

Workers at Piel Bros. Brewery, Liberty Avenue, East New York, 1900, with sign reading "Piel Bros. Real German Lager Beer." (Credit: Brooklynpix.com; B. Merlis and R. Gomes, *Brooklyn's East New York and Cypress Hill Communities*)

Worker at Piel Bros. Brewery, Brooklyn, opening valve on tank, circa 1916.

Piel Bros. Brewery, looking southeast at the corner of Liberty and Georgia avenues, East New York, Brooklyn, circa 1938.

Horse-drawn beer wagon, a familiar sight, circa 1900, brought back into service to conserve gasoline during World War II, Trommer's Brewery, Bushwick, Brooklyn, 1942. (Credit: Brooklyn Public Library—Brooklyn Collection)

Schaefer Brewery, built on the East River at Kent Avenue, Williamsburg, Brooklyn, 1915–16. (Credit: Brooklyn Public Library—Brooklyn Collection)

Policeman with Anthony Anastasio, crime boss and head of Brooklyn Longshoremen's union, during violent union elections, Brooklyn waterfront, December 24, 1953. (Credit: Brooklyn Public Library—Brooklyn Collection)

Louis Capone (center), mafia boss of East New York, being sentenced to death for murder with gangster Louis "Lepke" Buchalter, King's County Court, Brooklyn, November 30, 1941. (Credit: Brooklyn Public Library—Brooklyn Collection)

As president George Trommer (right) breaks a bottle of beer with 3.2 percent alcohol to mark Prohibition's end on April 6, 1933, delivery trucks pour out of Trommer's Brewery, Bushwick Avenue, Brooklyn. (Credit: Brooklyn Public Library—Brooklyn Collection)

William Piel (right) and employee examining beer's clarity, Piel Bros. Brewery, Brooklyn, circa 1936.

William Piel (left) and worker, Piel Bros. Brewery, Brooklyn, circa 1936.

From left at rear, Henry J. Muessen, general manager; Ralph Sherwood, vice president; and William Piel, president, watch as Fred Riedel, brewmaster, pumps beer into storage tanks in Piel's new seven-story cooling facility, 1948. (Photo by the Howe Service, 154 Nassau Street, New York)

Board of Directors, Piel Bros. Corporation, 1941, including, Rear (left to right) Kenneth S. Baxter, Graham B. Grosvenor, Donald B. Tansill; Front (left to right) Julian J. Tashof, Gottfried Piel, Jr., William Piel (president), Elmer Wigg.

Bottling plant, production line, Piel Bros. Brewery, Brooklyn, circa 1936. (Photo by Sickles Photo-Reporting Service, 31 Fulton Street, Newark, New Jersey)

Driver Fred Schmidt posts pro-union sign ready to work after George Ehret Brewery agreed to drop delivery speed-up clause, Montgomery Street, Crown Heights, Brooklyn, 1948. (Credit: Brooklyn Public Library—Brooklyn Collection)

Beer rolls off assembly line at the F. & M. Schaefer Brewing Company, 430 Kent Avenue, Williamsburg, Brooklyn, as deliveries resume after three-month strike, 1949. (Credit: Brooklyn Public Library—Brooklyn Collection)

Driver waving from Schaefer Brewing Company truck, 1949. (Credit: Brooklyn Public Library—Brooklyn Collection)

Piel Brothers special stockholders' meeting, Hotel Astor, Broadway, New York City, January 1960. *Above, Top* (left to right): William "Bill" Piel, Jr., Fred Lange, Alfred M. McCoy, Jr. *Above* (left to right): Henry Piel, Jack Tashof, Paul Piel. *Right, Top* (left to right): Carleton Healy, Eleanor Green Piel, Eleanor Jackson Piel, Gerard Piel. *Right, Center*: Rudolf Piel and William Piel, Jr. *Right, Bottom*: Oswald Piel and Agnes Piel Mueller.

Piel Bros. brewery's new cooling facility, East New York, Brooklyn, 1948. (Photo by Wurts Brothers, Huntington, Long Island. Credit: Brooklyn Public Library—Brooklyn Collection)

9

Corporate Expansion

After securing major finance for its plant expansion, Piel Bros. reached an historic benchmark in 1951 by producing a million barrels of beer—far, far beyond those 850 barrels first brewed back in 1884. That million-barrel figure, which came near the end of William Piel's forty-year tenure as chief executive, made his company the seventeenth-biggest brewery in the United States. Though far behind the nation's leader Jos. Schlitz with 5.7 million barrels and the New York area's top producer P. Ballantine & Sons at 4.0 million, Piels was still ahead of prominent brands such as Adolf Coors at 660,000 barrels.[1] Yet this milestone of progress soon became a road sign to decline.

The decade following this signal achievement was a challenging one for the brewing industry. The 1950s were, of course, a time of unprecedented prosperity. But this was also the decade when a small Depression-era generation came of age, cutting potential buyers in beer's prime 20-to-40 age cohort by a full third. As tailored, close-fitting clothes became fashionable, a nation of calorie counters disdained beer as fattening. In their embrace of the modern, consumers also favored processed foods, canned soups, and TV dinners, with a bland, sugary taste. Full-bodied, malted, hoppy beers had strong flavors that grated on this new national palate. During this decade, annual per capita consumption of beer consequently slid from 18.4 gallons to just 15 gallons and national sales were stubbornly stagnant at 84 million barrels.[2]

The 1950s were particularly difficult for regional brewers like Piels. When the company started back in the 1880s, brewing was a localized industry, limited in range by wagon transport and in volume by the heavy kegs tapped at every saloon. Over the next thirty years, however, refrigeration and railroads allowed the rise of the national "shipping brewers" like Anheuser-Busch that threatened regional breweries such as Piels. As keg deliveries to saloons gave way to canned beer sold directly to consumers, accounting for half of all beer sales in the early

43

1940s, brand name recognition became critical—part of the burgeoning U.S. consumer culture that advantaged major corporations and disadvantaged their smaller competitors, whether in appliances, automobiles, food, or beverages. To capture this consumer market, by 1950 the national beer brands had already raised their advertising to $1.36 per barrel, a full 25 percent over prewar levels, with about 10 percent of that outlay for air time on a new medium, television.[3] As these costs soared throughout the decade, the big national brewers, with bulk production and network advertising, would slowly squeeze regional companies across the country. And no regional market was rougher than New York's, with its combative unions, expensive media, and gridlocked streets.

After World War II, the tough New York beer market suddenly got much tougher. Local labor unions, quiescent during the decades of Prohibition and Depression, now gained real leverage midst full employment and Democratic Party dominance of city politics. As workers fought for their slice of the American dream, endless strikes would shut down the city's brewers for weeks and even months, opening their lucrative market to the national brands. And when television replaced radio as the arbiter of consumer tastes and advertising costs rose, these big brewers gained another advantage over local companies like Piels. To better compete in this metropolitan market, the national brands, armed with seemingly limitless capital, began acquiring plants in and around New York City.

In this postwar struggle for market share, Piels scored some victories that soon proved Pyrrhic. By adopting the national brewers' methods—heavy finance, relentless expansion, and aggressive advertising—Piel Bros. at first seemed to defy trends that were pushing other regional brewers into liquidation. The sudden infusion of finance for plant expansion raised Piels' sales and profits. After a succession of mediocre campaigns, the firm finally scored big in New York's advertising wars with its brilliant "Bert and Harry" television spots.

Yet, in retrospect, the "managerial revolution" at Piel Bros. was half-baked, leaving a stew of executive failings that made this advertising success an ingredient for decline. Caught on the cusp of a transition from family business to modern corporation, Piels had abandoned their elders' commitment to quality without achieving the efficiency of professional management. Masked by the glow of that television triumph, the company's endemic problems—antiquated plants, problematic management, and, above all, weak quality control—would send the firm on a slow slide toward stagnant sales, falling profits, and eventual liquidation. The company's emphasis on volume over quality would ultimately exact a heavy price.

Expansion as Watchword

With national brands encroaching on its home market, Piels made expansion its first principle. Advantaged by economies of scale in production and advertising, the big national brands started squeezing regional companies, cutting the number of U.S. breweries from 725 after repeal in 1934 to just 225 by 1962.[4]

To avoid this fate, William devoted his final decade as chief executive, 1943 to 1953, to expansion—seeking adequate finance, increasing plant capacity, and, during his last years, acquiring a nearby brewery that made Piels the seventeenth-, then the sixteenth-biggest brewer in America.[5] If William hoped to save Piels by climbing a few notches higher, then his strategy underestimated the relentless consolidation that would eventually crush family firms and concentrate the U.S. beer industry into just two global conglomerates.

At first, William's strategy allowed steady growth in production, profits, and dividends. After World War II, Piels' output rose steadily from 520,000 barrels in 1945 to 640,000 by 1948. Simultaneously, the company's gross sales were up from $10 million to $14 million. "With strikes out of the way & volume greater than 1946," an excited Henry Piel wrote sister Louise, "the net profit for 1947 will be very handsome!" Indeed those net profits, freed from wartime rationing, soared from a solid $273,000 in 1945 to a surprising $948,000 by 1948.[6]

These profits made the Piels wealthy for the first time in thirty years. Between 1945 and 1950, annual dividends averaged $28,000 a year for Gottfried's five children and $24,000 for each of Michael's seven heirs, putting all of them in the top one percent of U.S. incomes.[7] Such prosperity placated the once contentious Piel stockholders, focusing their complaints almost solely on the size of the dividend. "I learned that March sales equaled 44,000 barrels," Henry Piel wrote sister Louise in 1947, "and I see no reason why a protest on our part cannot be justly made. We should receive nice extra dividends, at least $35,000 extra each quarter, and still leave *plenty* with which to pay a handsome year-end dividend."[8] Such single-minded concerns allowed William's executives the freedom to manage the brewery as they saw fit.

At the start of this prosperity in 1948, William Piel noted with satisfaction that production had increased 15 percent while ongoing expansion of the stock house and brew house would soon provide new capacity. There were, however, signs of trouble. Postwar "recessionary tendencies," compounded by "a slight decline" in total beer sales nationwide, raised the specter of long-term problems. Of even greater import, William noted, "more and more centralization of volume

Table 9.1: Top Thirty U.S. Breweries, Including Five in New York, 1953
            (In Barrels of 31 Gallons Each)

Anheuser-Busch, Inc. (2 plants)	St. Louis, MO	6,711,222
Jos. Schlitz Brewing (2 plants)	Milwaukee, WI	5,255,000
Pabst Brewing (4 plants)	Milwaukee, WI	4,250,000
P. Ballantine & Sons	Newark, NJ	3,882,000
Liebmann Breweries (3 plants)	Brooklyn, NY	3,100,000
Falstaff Brewing (4 plants)	St. Louis, MO	2,911,393
F. & M. Schaefer Brewing (2 plants)	Brooklyn, NY	2,600,000
Miller Brewing	Milwaukee, WI	2,083,418
Jacob Ruppert (2 plants)	New York, NY	2,004,975
Lucky Lager Brewing (3 plants)	San Francisco, CA	1,739,930
Theo. Hamm Brewing	St. Paul, MN	1,685,795
Geobel Brewing (4 plants)	Detroit, MI	1,579,826
Griesedieck-Western Brewing (2 plants)	Belleville, IL	1,483,631
Pfeiffer Brewing (2 plants)	Detroit, MI	1,441,600
Drewrys Ltd. U.S.A. (3 plants)	South Bend, IN	1,420,230
Piel Bros. (2 plants)	**Brooklyn, NY**	**1,375,000**
C. Schmidt & Sons	Philadelphia, PA	1,373,839
Stroh Brewing	Detroit, MI	1,145,044
Carling Brewing	Cleveland, OH	1,096,025
San Francisco Brewing	San Francisco, CA	1,017,997
Blatz Brewing	Milwaukee, WI	998,965
Jackson Brewing	New Orleans, LA	934,000
Duquesne Brewing	Pittsburgh, PA	923,320
Griesedieck Bros. Brewing	St. Louis, MO	840,000
National Brewing	Baltimore, MD	840,000
Genesee Brewing	Rochester, NY	815,000
Adolph Coors	Golden, CO	812,000
Gunther Brewing	Baltimore, MD	800,000
Geo. Wiedemann Brewing	Newport, KY	780,000
Pearl Brewing	San Antonio, TX	770,121

Source: Modern Brewery Age 51, no. 3 (March 1954), 26.

in the hands of the nation's largest brewers" meant "competition has become keener" for regional brewers like Piels. But the real wild card in their corporate deck was labor. With the current contract due to expire on March 31, 1949, Piel's management was concerned that "the growth of radicalism in Brewery Workers' unions" had left "the labor situation far from satisfactory."[9]

Devastating Strikes

Indeed, back-to-back strikes in 1948 and 1949, totaling 117 days in a nine-month period, would prove devastating for New York's brewing industry. After thirty years of industrial peace dating back to 1917, the Union of United Brewery Workers was now, said Piels' management, dominated by "extremely left-wing leadership" since its recent affiliation with the Congress of Industrial Organizations (CIO).[10]

Emerging from the long years of Depression and global war, American workers were now claiming their share of the country's unprecedented prosperity. As economic growth topped 10 percent in 1950 and U.S. unemployment tumbled to a record low of 2.9 percent by 1953, labor unions, with membership reaching a full third of the nation's workers, demanded living wages and better benefits. While industrial disputes roiled the economy, the centers of U.S. brewing faced a surge of major strikes—in Minneapolis, Milwaukee, and New York.[11] Midst all this labor militancy, nobody was tougher than truckers. And New York's truckers were some of the toughest of them all.

As the city's gridlocked traffic drove the metropolitan beer industry's delivery costs toward the $15 million mark by 1948, management attributed these soaring expenses to their malingering drivers. In rebuttal, truckers complained about heavy traffic and "a back-breaking job" manhandling heavy kegs with frequent injuries. In his attempted mediation, the city's respected arbitrator, Theodore W. Kheel, found there was, in fact, "an enormous problem of absenteeism and an undue amount of overtime." But employers, he said pointedly, also "shared much of the blame" for allowing workers to build such "presumptive rights"—a mutual culpability that made both sides blindly stubborn.[12]

On October 13, 1948, after Ruppert's management punished some drivers, workers at their Manhattan plant walked out, sparking a month-long wildcat strike that soon spread to 3,000 truckers at all eleven New York City breweries, Piels included. At first, pickets blocked trucks carrying beer from New Jersey's breweries at the Hudson River bridges, warning them "to turn back." But the strikers soon relented, wary of sparking a reprise of their violent "Pittsburgh Beer War," marked by bombings and beatings, with the Teamsters union that also represented these Jersey drivers. Within a week, outside beer was flowing into the city. Though five smaller breweries soon settled, the larger firms, including Piels, fought back through the courts.[13]

Indeed, on November 6 the Brewers Board of Trade filed a "double barreled action" against the United Brewery Workers, seeking an injunction to stop the strike and $8.3 million in damages. The next day, the strikers authorized the union to act on their behalf, pushing aside the rebels and their activist attorney Paul O'Dwyer, whom the breweries refused to recognize even though he was the mayor's younger brother. After five days of round-the-clock meetings, the brewers and union reached a settlement. That night, some 5,000 angry drivers crowded into a Manhattan arena, shouting down the CIO officials until O'Dwyer persuaded members to approve the deal. Beneath the surface, however, the truckers were still seething over wages, benefits, and, above all, management's strict supervision. The city's breweries estimated their combined losses from the four-week strike at $2 million. In its aftermath, they continued to lose about 22 percent of their sales to out-of-town brands.[14]

After a brief hiatus of four months, the United Brewery Workers-CIO declared a second, epochal strike that became a lasting blow to the city's brewing industry. At 2:00 a.m. on April 1, 1949, some 7,000 workers walked out midst contract negotiations, shutting all eleven of the city's breweries. After picketing bridges and tunnels to block beer shipments into the city, the United Brewery Workers, again fearing the jurisdictional violence with the Teamsters, allowed New Jersey's breweries to supply the city's 12,000 taverns and 15,000 retail outlets.[15] On April 14, a "solid line of Jersey beer trucks" rolled across the Hudson River carrying an estimated 10,000 barrels of beer, over three times the usual shipment.[16]

As the walkout entered its second week, the labor lawyer Paul O'Dwyer, now representing the Brewery Workers, appeared on Radio WMCA to defend the strike, citing the "6,400 brewery workers . . . killed or injured in this state over the last four years." In rebuttal, the Brewers Board of Trade took out full-page newspaper advertisements claiming their offer of a $74 weekly wage was the highest for any brewery worker in America.[17] Meanwhile, New York's beer production had dropped by 67 percent, while shipments into the strike-bound city boosted production in New Jersey.[18]

After eighty-two consecutive days, the strike was settled on June 21 when the union and the city's seven major brewers finally reached an agreement. A thirty-four hour, non-stop bargaining session ended with the brewers conceding a 37.5-hour week, two men on every truck, an industry-funded pension plan, a base weekly wage of $73, and an end to strict supervision of the drivers. Meeting in secrecy, 90 percent of the union membership approved the new contract.[19]

This long strike did lasting damage to the city's brewing industry. Apart from the immediate loss of $75 million in gross sales, the protracted closure, in the words of the *New York Times*, "set the stage for an unprecedented battle for markets." Not only had Milwaukee's Blatz and New Jersey's Ballantine entered the city "with a vengeance," but New York breweries had lost "lucrative markets" outside the city.[20] To recapture these wayward customers, Piels placed large advertisements for its "Light Beer of Broadway Fame" in upstate newspapers, letting drinkers know, "We've been out of town a while—we're mighty glad to be back!"[21]

In retrospect, these two strikes brought a basic shift in labor relations within the city's brewing industry. With each successive labor contract over the next fifteen years, wages and benefits would rise from generous to unsustainable, making New York City the most expensive place in America to brew beer. When management tried to resist, as they would in June 1958, the city's 7,000 brewery workers, now represented by the Teamsters, walked out, shutting the city's five surviving breweries—Rheingold, Ruppert, Schaefer, Schlitz, and Piels. Though their numbers were much reduced from the glory days before Prohibition, these brewers still produced 10 million barrels annually, making New York "the country's largest beer-producing center."[22]

To settle an eight-day shutdown during the 1958 summer season, owners had to increase their weekly wages, already the nation's highest, by $5.00 effective June 1 and another $4.75 within a year. Moreover, the contract required "two men on all trucks and trailers for deliveries" within the eight metropolitan counties. So onerous was this agreement for Piels, now the city's smallest brewer, that two Teamster locals agreed to grant the company "some relief" by allowing up to fifteen "solo" deliveries daily.[23] Despite all these union troubles, Piels remained a relatively equitable employer. With a union pension plan after 1949 and another for "executives, office, and sales employees" three years later, most Piel workers were loyal and long serving.[24]

Looking back on this decade of labor troubles in 1960, Piels' management would conclude that "serious mistakes in . . . handling of negotiations were made by New York City brewers," allowing their labor costs to become "the highest in the nation." Indeed, the nation's brewers were paying $104 per week by 1957, far above the country's top manufacturing wage of $75. Even so, increases in New York's brewing wages outpaced the rest of their industry for the next four years to reach a new peak of $130—a trend that would eventually prove unsustainable.[25]

Raising Production

The 1949 strike was a heavy blow to Piels' postwar progress, depressing the firm's output by 20 percent to 520,000 barrels for 1949.[26] Net profits fell even more sharply from $950,000 to $500,000, a 47 percent decline.[27]

Even before the strike, Piels' management had realized the need for increased production to defray the per barrel cost of their growing advertising. In 1947–48, the firm spent $1.5 million in plant expansion, building a seven-story, ziggurat-style cooling facility that would, said William, increase production by 50 percent.[28] With the once-open spaces for beer garden and horse wagons now entirely covered by a massive, multi-story plant, further expansion must come elsewhere, either by high-cost construction or acquisition of an existing brewery.

In the aftermath of the 1949 strike, William and his general manager Henry Muessen decided expansion was imperative to fight the national brands. In January 1950, industry titan Anheuser-Busch became the first brewer to sponsor a prime-time television show, broadcast nationwide by fifty-one stations on the CBS network. A year later, Busch followed Pabst and Schlitz into the New York market by opening a massive new plant in Newark, New Jersey, signaling its arrival with a spectacular hundred-foot neon sign in Times Square, animated by a giant Budweiser eagle taking flight. These national shipping brewers were targeting the combined 12 million barrels made by the metropolitan region's big four—Ballantine, Liebmann (Rheingold), Ruppert (Knickerbocker), and Schaefer—that

9.1. Label for Trommer's Malt Beer, Brooklyn, New York, circa 1934.

continued to sell the bulk of their beer in New York and the Northeast. With the exception of Ballantine's slick national marketing, New York's brewers had remained resolutely regional and thus vulnerable. Rheingold lost heavily on its short-lived California expansion in the mid-1950s, as did Schaefer in Ohio during the early 1960s. Meanwhile, Ruppert kept its Knickerbocker brand proudly local. But smaller regional brewers like Piels also had good reason to be concerned. To counter the "continuing centralization of volume in the hands of larger brewers," Piels decided "the acquisition of additional capacity . . . and a continuation of aggressiveness in sales and advertising policies are . . . essential."[29]

Between 1948 and 1951, therefore, Piels' promotional expenditures more than doubled from $770,000 to $1.7 million, raising the price of advertising per barrel from $1.21 to $1.69. The only way to cut that unit cost was to produce more barrels of beer. But concerned about the "prohibitive cost of new construction," Piels decided "the most practical solution to the problem would be to acquire an existing plant." After considering breweries in New England, upstate New York, and Pennsylvania, the directors paid $1.4 million in 1951 to purchase Trommers, just four blocks away on Bushwick Avenue.[30]

At first, the acquisition met management's expectations. With Trommer's additional capacity of 200,000 barrels, Piels raised its production by 40 percent—joining the elite echelon of U.S. breweries making over a million barrels a year.[31] In 1953, moreover, output grew rapidly to 1.2 million barrels, raising Piels to its peak ranking as the sixteenth-biggest brewery in America.[32] While plant capacity was one essential for growth, America's burgeoning consumer culture of the 1950s required effective advertising if the company hoped to sustain those sales.

Advertising Wars

Indeed, selling beer in the nation's media capital demanded clever, costly advertising. In 1948, seven New York brewers accounted for a full third of the nation's newspaper advertising for beer. Brooklyn's Schaefer spent $553,000 on newspaper ads—far more than even the national brands Budweiser ($376,000), Pabst ($91,000), and Miller ($41,000). Close behind Schaefer came New York's other big brewers, including Rheingold at $507,000, Ruppert at $434,000, and Piels at $234,000.[33]

At the dawn of Madison Avenue's golden age, Piels' postwar promotions muddled through a few years of mediocrity before the company began producing some of the most creative advertising in America. The first success was a low-calorie lifestyle campaign that sparked opposition, and imitation, within the brewing industry. Several years later, the company scored big with its humorous "Bert and Harry" television spots that virtually invented "soft sell" advertising.

Starting in 1948, the fifth year of its tired Broadway theme, the company's copy adopted a more modern aesthetic that was less obsessed with the female form and more focused on the company's first successful slogan, "Piel's Light Beer of Broadway Fame." In its last years, this campaign moved upscale in its choice of shows, featuring actress Yvonne Adair raising "a glass of golden brew" backstage at the hit *Gentlemen Prefer Blondes* and Janet Medlin smacking her lips over a frothy glass between scenes of *Kiss Me Kate*.[34]

After seven years with the Broadway theme, Piels dropped that campaign in 1951 and switched decisively from print to broadcast media. As its newspaper expenditures dropped sharply from $634,000 in 1951 to just $194,000 two years later, Piels invested heavily in television, everything from sporting events to stage plays.[35] In 1952, the company sponsored the "Broadway TV Theater" on New York's WOR-TV, featuring full-length dramas every evening, Monday to Friday.[36] During a Ranger–Bruins hockey game at the start of the 1952–53 season, Piels launched its sponsorship of ninety-three events broadcast from Madison Square Garden by WPIX-TV, everything from basketball games to dog shows.[37] While Piels was now a strong presence on city channels, its advertising budget was still dwarfed by Pabst, which spent a hefty $3 million in 1953 (double Piels' entire annual income), including $2.3 million on network television.[38]

Piels' programming may have tuned in to popular taste, but it still needed creative copy to reap the reward of its heavy investment in television. After seven years of Broadway showgirls, its advertising now turned soberly scientific to reflect the postwar obsession with dieting, grooming, and body image.[39] By emphasizing its low-calorie brewing, the company's "Less N.F.S. (Non-Fermented Sugar)" campaign was one of the first into the fight for a low-calorie beer. In the space of a few months, Fort Pitt introduced its "pale, dry, less filling" pilsner and Ruppert proclaimed its Knickerbocker beer "extra light," but Piels alone was explicit in its questionable claim of less sugar and thus fewer calories.[40] Not only was the theme widely imitated by competitors, it soon attracted unwelcome attention from federal regulators.

In early 1951, Piels' new agency Kenyon & Eckhardt launched the "Less N.F.S." campaign with dense newspaper copy that read like a chemistry textbook.[41] By summer, the campaign had lightened up with graphics of trim

American couples fishing or yachting with a glass of Piels beneath the slogan, "More Satisfying because it's More Dry! Yes—Less N.F.S. (Non-Fermented Sugar)."[42]

This low sugar campaign resonated so strongly with calorie-counting Americans that the company's copy sparked opposition from both competitors and regulators. Indeed, Piels' claims may or may not have violated federal regulations for alcohol advertising, by then so recondite they required twenty pages of explanation from the Internal Revenue Service (IRS).[43] As it had done at the start of Prohibition, Piels soon found itself challenging Washington, pushing beyond the bounds of accepted practice and suffering the consequences.

When Piels intensified its low-cal campaign for the 1951 summer season, the IRS pushed back with a three-year effort to curb these claims. "At one point in the television presentation," said the first IRS complaint, "a diner is shown sprinkling sugar on a steak in such a manner as to imply . . . unfermented sugar in beer results in an offensive taste similar to that created by adding sugar to steak." Such advertising, said the IRS, contravened its ban on "any statement that is disparaging of a competitor's products."[44]

After debating the IRS over the actual sugar content in rival beers, Piels made only minor modifications to its copy. Indeed, it persisted in these claims, releasing new ads with the picture of a pinhead to illustrate how little sugar there was in its quart bottle.[45] Competitors continued to complain and government regulators renewed their pressure on Piels to desist.[46] Nonetheless, the N.F.S. advertising became even bolder, asserting "Piel's is the only beer that actually measures dryness for you!" Below that headline, a large teaspoon brimming with sugar from a competitor's bottle was juxtaposed against a tweezers holding a single grain from Piels. Then came the big, bold slogan: "Piel's Light Beer—Driest of the Dry Beers Because it has Less N.F.S."[47]

The Brooklyn brewer Philip Liebmann, maker of Rheingold Extra Dry, filed a formal complaint, and the IRS advised Piels that its graphic comparison was "misleading and should not be continued."[48] Since its current advertising agency, Young & Rubicam, assured Piels the "Less N.F.S. theme is very effective copy," Piels' manager Muessen wrote the IRS in January 1953 insisting these claims of superior dryness contained "no inference of disparagement" of competitors. He also complained that such federal enforcement will "stack the cards against smaller brewers like Piel Bros."[49]

Aware his authority was limited since New York had loose state regulations, deputy IRS commissioner Dwight Avis turned to the court of public opinion, advising the U.S. Brewers Foundation that all claims of less sugar were "misleading."[50] Seizing upon that letter, Philadelphia's Ortlieb Brewing took out full-page advertisements in *The Evening Bulletin* and *Philadelphia Inquirer* under the banner headline, "U.S. Treasury Department States the Facts about SUGAR IN BEER."[51]

The issue simmered until the start of the 1954 selling season when Brooklyn's leading brewer, Rudolph J. Schaefer, Jr., unleashed advertisements mocking the low-cal/low-sugar claims of Ballantine, Krueger, Knickerbocker, and Piels.

> Pity Miss Martha Marrow
> Who drank only the thinnest thin brew
> Till her waist got so small
> It was no waist at all
> And poor Miss Marrow snapped in two.[52]

Clearly, lifestyle advertising had proliferated far beyond Piels. Inspired by the success of lo-cal soft drinks, the U.S. Brewers Foundation was advising its members to fight the idea of beer as fattening by "showing slender, attractive people in beer advertisements." Consequently, Krueger Brewing of Newark papered New Jersey with a pamphlet claiming an eight-ounce glass of its beer had fewer calories than orange juice. Midst this cacophony of competing claims, the IRS forced Krueger to change its advertising, and was ready, reported *Advertising Age*, "to toss the Piel case back to the Federal Trade Commission."[53]

Within weeks, the IRS wrote Piels that Connecticut's recent ban on deceptive alcohol advertising now gave it jurisdiction over all broadcasts in nearby New York, lending, for the first time, legal force to its complaints about Piel's N.F.S. campaign.[54] After confirming that its broadcasts indeed reached Connecticut, Piels conceded. Its new television ads admitted that the calories in "all the leading brands are about the same (around 150)."[55] A few weeks later, its nemesis Dwight Avis notified Piels that its "calorie treatment" now conformed to federal regulations. The IRS, he said, would be "closing our files with respect to your earlier advertisements."[56]

After more than two years of wrangling with Washington, Piels had finally been forced to abandon any claim to lower calories, a retreat that reduced its sales during the 1954 summer season.[57] With its lifestyle theme now eviscerated, it was time for Piels to try something different, maybe even something funny.

Path to Penance

At this sensitive juncture in their marketing, the Piels experienced a confluence of major changes that would shape their company's character during its last decade. By the late 1940s, the second generation's stockholders, now in their 60s and ready to retire, were absorbed in their private lives. Most had entrusted the company to their eldest, William. But now, after suffering both the loss of his wife and health problems, William began delegating major decisions to his underlings. Simultaneously, the factional alliances among his siblings were breaking apart over personal disputes, crippling any collective response to their company's troubles. Midst challenges from both national brands and tough unions, Piels was adrift for nearly five years, without effective leadership or a viable corporate strategy.

In these same years, personal disputes among the Piels stymied any stockholder response. Only two years after the breach between Rudolf and Louise over Lake Parlin in 1940, another pair of close sibling allies, Paul and Agnes, long William's loyal supporters, also had a bitter falling out. Not long after Paul settled in Greenwich Village during the 1920s, recalled son Mark, "lo and behold, Aunt Agnes rented an apartment on the same block, opposite." As they went on weekend outings and worked together at the brewery during the 1930s, Agnes grew possessive of Paul, prompting her to reprimand his wife Edith, after dining at her neighborhood restaurant, for "the extreme rudeness of your conduct" and "your well known unfriendliness." So when Agnes started eyeing a house just seven miles from their summer place in Vermont, Paul, at his wife's prompting, wrote his sister saying: "It's not such a good idea for you to come up here to be in the next town over, you know, we should sort of lead our own lives."[58] By then, of course, the family fight over the brewery's future was largely resolved, and Paul no longer needed her vote in the company's boardroom battles.

Spurned, Agnes married again to Piels' salesman Percy H. Crane in 1937 and moved to Greenwich, Connecticut. They were soon joined by Agnes's teenaged-daughter Patsy, who arrived unexpectedly from Vienna where she had been undergoing psychotherapy for the past six years. On March 12, 1938, the day German troops marched into Austria, the U.S. Consulate at Vienna issued Patsy's caregiver, Gina Bettelheim, a U.S. entry visa that Agnes had arranged through Secretary of State Cordell Hull. After Gina and Patsy landed safely in New York, Agnes brought her daughter home and installed Gina in a nearby hotel.[59]

Tensions soon troubled this accidental household. To protect Patsy, Gina Bettelheim had fled Vienna hurriedly, leaving behind her husband Bruno, a Jewish businessman who was sent to concentration camps at Dachau, then Buchenwald. To win his freedom, Agnes pressured the State Department relentlessly—filing an affidavit of financial support in May 1938, pressing the Berlin consulate to intercede with the Gestapo chief in November, and finally effecting an order for his release in February 1939. By the time Bruno Bettelheim reached New York, his wife Gina had already left Connecticut from fear of her patron's "lesbian tendencies," helped by Agnes's brother Paul who offered his city apartment as a rent-free refuge. Angry at Gina and "very jealous of her brother," Agnes severed relations with the Bettelheims.[60] Separation from her second husband soon followed, and Agnes wound up back in New York as a single mother to her daughter Patsy.[61]

Some months later when Paul presumed to discuss Patsy's problems with a teacher at their local school, all of Agnes's pent-up feelings for her brother erupted. In view of his implication that "Patsy, among her other handicaps, has a depraved nature," Agnes now demanded that Paul, if he possessed "even a shred of the decency I used to attribute to you," should desist from disturbing "the corpse of a past relationship." After this break, Agnes eventually moved to an isolated corner of Connecticut where she was much less involved in the brewery's business, further reducing stockholder oversight.[62]

A few years later, Oswald and his sister Louise also suffered a bitter falling out over the Lake Parlin property. At the end of World War II, their mother Maria, then nearing 90, was again obsessed with shipping relief goods to surviving German relatives, reducing the funds available to support her children's farms. After months of retrenching her many expenses, such as a costly Long Island residence she now unloaded at a loss, Maria ended her subsidies for Parlin's upkeep in 1948 by signing over the property to Louise and Erwin Lange. With their son Rollo, they were struggling to keep the old place afloat as a travelers' resort. This was a doomed effort driven by family attachments to the place so deep, so strong that a half century later Rollo's granddaughter would be named Parlin. After Maria wrote to announce these changes, Oswald, whose Pennsylvania dairy farm had long benefitted from her support, was outraged. This "unpleasant, cold, inhuman and calculating letter," Oswald told counselor Jack Tashof, "was prepared by *Louise & Erwin* and only written by Mother and not the product of her noble thoughts and affection."[63]

In this postwar period, William too distanced himself from the brewery. In 1948, his wife of forty years died of cancer, leaving him bereft. He set a place for her at dinner every night, hiked alone in the woods of his Salmon Kill estate, and fished almost daily on his property's trout stream. Midst this grieving, William cut his Brooklyn commute to just a few days every month, staying overnight at son Bill's walk-up apartment in Greenwich Village.[64]

Noticing that William "was having a hard time in every way," Bill advised his father to cash in his life insurance and start traveling. And William did just that, spending his last years fishing his way across America.[65] Instead of the outgoing executive of years past, William now turned inward—for quiet reflection on his trout stream and the introspection of journal writing, which he resumed after a forty-year hiatus. But, above all, he sought reconciliation with those he had slighted during his long quest for success.

In a journal titled "Salmon Kill Commentary: Part I," William documented both his devotion to fly casting and his disinterest in the family business. While William was fishing in Connecticut for 86 of the 180 days surrounding that disastrous 1949 beer strike, his journal's 354 pages made just two brief mentions of the brewery—the first, on June 5, has William leaving Piels' staff "standing by" at strike headquarters in Manhattan while he "went a-angling" for two weeks; and the last, on June 24, when he writes: "Well, I'm back in town. The strike is over after 82 days of idleness." Absorbed in his grief and focused on fly casting, he was oblivious to the strike's implications for his brewery.[66] Not only was the company denied his skilled leadership of years past, but as a mid-sized family business it lacked a successor who could chart a future course, threatening its survival.

During these years of semi-retirement on full pay, William combined fishing and reconciliation. "Distance was stretched between them," said son Gerard, "between my father and the rest of his family, by my mother's sentiments, with their reciprocal in the rest of the family. After my mother's death in 1948 that barrier came down." Through a mix of pilgrimage and penance, William devoted his last years to renewing frayed family ties.[67]

William used his own trout stream to effect a reconciliation with brother Henry, healing a breach that had opened a dozen years before when William fired him from the brewery. At the start of the 1949 fishing season, Henry came up from his home on Long Island and "did himself justice" by catching ten trout. At day's end, Henry expressed the hope that "I may, with good conscience, be able to have my Salmon Kill host renew his fishing at my Camp on the very shore of old Parlin Pond." When Henry returned for fall fishing, William noted, hinting at the depth of their breach, "Marie, Henry's wife came with him (at last!) to Salmon Kill on September 24th. Verily, marvelous lady that she is, she did have a lovely day of it and strongly rejoiced in her husband's triumphs here," with Henry catching twelve trout to William's strategic eleven.[68]

To document his fishing forays across America, William ordered a new embossed journal titled "Salmon Kill Commentary: Part II," which would be, he explained, "an account of 'Anglers Away' from Salmon Kill's brook land," tying the present to past outings dating back to "the 'Parlinad'—my accounts of the great fishing, forty years ago, at Parlin . . . under the brow of magnificent Mt. Coburn."[69]

After his first foray away from his own stream, fishing the Adirondacks with son Bill and grandsons Michael and Anthony in August 1949, William drove south to St. Joseph's convent in Pennsylvania, where he joined his brother Henry in celebrating their mother's 92nd birthday. William was delighted to see that Maria, now living among these loving Catholic nuns, "rejoices hourly in her rewon faith, for which daily she remembers my blessed Loretto who helped her to regain this felicity."[70]

Then, with no time for business, William drove to northernmost Maine with several friends for two weeks' fishing along the Canadian border. En route he saw, on the horizon, "the high mass of Mt. Coburn, that looks down upon my youth's haven: Lake Parlin. It aroused fond memories of . . . a wildwood world of waters, hills and mountains, my home-hills along the international boundary!" But the old family estate was now managed by sister Louise, whom his beloved Loretto had long detested. So that short drive north to Parlin was one road he dared not travel.[71]

His penance pilgrimage continued in April 1950 when William went West to fish for trout and son John, the one who got away midst the family's relentless social climb.[72] After transcontinental trains to San Francisco, William checked into the Fairmont Hotel to address the Brewers Foundation, fish the High Sierra, and spend several days with his son. Between dinners and drives, they inspected John's new medical clinic with "the last word in equipment and appointments." Reflecting on the visit in his journal, William was finally reconciled to his son's decision to live so far from family, proud that "John is truly progressing in his chosen branch of pediatrics." To close this chapter in his journal and his life, William finished the entry with a Latin quotation, "*Ave atque vale!*" The full line from the famous eulogy by Roman poet Catullus was, as William well knew, "Atque in perpetuum frater ave atque vale," meaning: "And forever, Brother, hail and farewell."[73]

After a serious heart attack kept him homebound for much of 1951, William resumed his travels, this time in pursuit of his most elusive quarry, younger brother Rudolf. After skipping out of the Brewers Foundation meeting at New Orleans in January 1952, William caught an overnight train to Florida. These brothers had not spoken since Rudolf's last attempt to reform the brewery back in 1946 and his subsequent move to Florida to recuperate from tuberculosis. So when William wrote him about taking a Florida fishing vacation, Rudolf had agonized with his wife Margarita before agreeing, most reluctantly, to play host.[74]

Riding the "Gulf Wind" express from New Orleans to Florida, William was nervous about visiting a brother he had not seen for nearly a decade, and even then relations were rocky from fights over the brewery. But he soon relaxed when Rudolf met him at the West Palm Beach station in his Buick Roadmaster. The two brothers swapped "family inquiries" non-stop as they sped along the two-lane highway at eighty-five miles per hour, crossing Florida through "a heavily farmed belt . . . flourishing in garden produce, in sugar cane, and in beef cattle."[75] Welcomed with a dinner at Rudolf's Fort Myers home, William was impressed with the small garden his brother had grown on the four-acre lot—citrus, mango, and bee hives, all showing that "Rudi has our father Michael's keen interest in nature."[76]

While William rode that train nervously through the night, Rudolf was evidently concocting an elaborate practical joke, with a pointed message for the brother who had expelled him from the family business. Whether driving about the countryside or fishing on the Caloosahatchee River, Rudolf somehow felt compelled to wax rapturously about Florida's cattle industry. Florida's cowboys were "abler than the Texan." Florida would soon beat Texas to become the nation's top beef producer. As Rudolf stacked one outrageous claim upon another, almost as if trying to bait his brother, William struggled to silence his skepticism. Through all these chats, Rudolf gave no hint of what he was really doing in Florida.[77]

One morning while reading his mail at a beachfront lodge, William was delighted at the news that Belgium's Institut International d'Alimentation had awarded Piel's Light Beer its Cross of Honour for "overall quality, taste, bouquet and quality"—one of the highest awards in a competition for American and Canadian brands. "For the standard we set at our Company's founding," he told his diary in a paean of family pride, "I feel that 'Piel' is itself an honor to these titles, for we have steadfastly sought to lead in quality of the product."[78]

During his fourth week in Fort Myers, the reason for this health holiday made an unwelcome appearance. After William felt a shortness of breath at 11:00 p.m., the hotel summoned Rudolf who arrived with a doctor and oxygen to get his brother safely through the night until transfer to Lee Memorial Hospital in Fort Myers. During two weeks of enforced bedrest, William had visits from Rudolf, his own daughter Mary, and Rudolf's daughter, his niece Margarita McCoy—all helping "to shorten and brighten my confinement: the blessings family bestows." Not entirely. "William was a bit dismissive, even condescending," recalled Margarita about her visit, discerning William's still lingering disdain for her father beneath all the current friendliness. She added: "I really wondered why I had bothered to come."[79]

On the very last day of this vacation, waiting at the lodge for his ride to the train, William was surprised when he picked up the local *News Press* newspaper. On the front page was a photo of brother Rudolf feeding a breeding bull above a three-column headline, "Clover Proves Success Here: Prize Cattle Enjoy Lush Pastureland on Piel Ranch." Apart from the clover, Rudolf had also propagated a native Bermuda grass growing wild in the woods to cover 400 acres of pasture. With that feed for his herd, he was cross-breeding purebred Santa Gertrudis cattle from Texas with thirty Brahma for commercial beef. "It's not only a science based on the Mendelian laws of heredity," Rudolf told the paper, "it's hard patient work plus the luck and chance of having one in a thousand you can use to breed for better characteristics." After a month in Florida, William still had no idea, no idea at all, that his brother had a ranch, much less cattle and clover.[80]

9.2. Rudolf Piel feeding his bull clover at Piel Ranch, Fort Myers, Florida, 1952.

During their drive to the train later that day, Rudolf told William about "his ownership of 1,440 acres of land; the start of a new business based on his . . . magnificent achievement by his growth of clover, which, hitherto, had defied the efforts of farmers and the State's agricultural experts." Rudolf added that the King Ranch was shipping him fifty head of prime Santa Gertrudis breeding cattle from Texas. His share of the costs would be covered by a 50–50 split—half the calves sold to repay the King Ranch and the other half kept to build his own herd.[81] William's diary did not record their parting. But it would be their last.

When the train reached New York, friends met William at the station and took him directly to St. Vincent's Hospital for coronary tests, which proved satisfactory.[82] Within months, however, he was back at St. Vincent's, this time for an advanced bladder cancer so debilitating he was unable to read and was often delirious. In April 1953, William finally expired after months of pain, bringing a sudden, unplanned end to his forty years as the brewery's chief executive.[83]

His passing was much remarked upon within both New York business circles and the nation's brewing industry. Obituaries in the *Brooklyn Daily Eagle* and the *New York Times* remembered him as an industry leader and an executive who expanded his brewery "from 90,000 to more than a 1,000,000 barrels a year."[84] Privately, his death was much mourned. Apart from the sheer number and diversity of condolences, many of these letters conveyed a sense that William Piel had somehow touched lives.[85]

In marked contrast to the infighting among the Gottfried Piels, William's will passed through probate smoothly. His assets, valued at $271,000, were surprisingly modest for a man who had spent forty years as chief executive of a mid-sized corporation. All those decades of service to the brewing industry and socializing in the city had evidently come at a price. Apart from $10,000 in bank accounts, $14,000 in insurance, and the Connecticut property, William's sole significant asset was a one-seventh share of the Michael Piel Holding Company.[86] His father Michael had left an estate worth $875,000 in 1915 (when adjusted for inflation), and aunt Sophie Piel had assets of $1.8 million in 1924 (also adjusted). But now William, the wealthiest member of the second generation, had an estate assessed at just $206,000 after taxes in 1953.[87] Clearly, the family's fortunes were fading.

Juxtaposing William's moderate liquid assets against his lavish Connecticut estate—360 acres, private trout stream, and historic homestead—he had lived the life of a successful executive without commensurate means. The family was in the *Social Register*, all four sons were Ivy League educated, and his two daughters had grand society weddings. Yet William clung to his Piel's salary through disease and debility. His estate's inventory showed an entry of $277.77 as "accrued salary due from Piel Bros. for period from 4/1/53 through 4/6/53"—the day of his death. Once his children had picked over the chipped crockery, held a yard sale for the household goods, sold the country estate, and divided his assets, each inherited a modest $34,000, largely in non-negotiable shares in the Michael Piel Trust. This bequest could supplement but certainly not replace whatever they earned from their middle-class professions—law, medicine, publishing, and advertising.[88] None of his six children had followed their father into the family firm. So, for the first time in seventy years, a Piel would no longer manage Piel Bros.[89]

Just as William had given his family status beyond assets, so he left the brewery with profits beyond market fundamentals. In late 1953, Dr. Hermann K. Scheyhing, the chief economist at the firm's financier Grace Bank, explained the reasons "the investing public is not very optimistic over the long-term outlook for the small and medium sized breweries" like Piels. Beer sales had doubled in the seventeen years since 1935. But market share for the nation's seven biggest brewers jumped from 20 percent in 1946 to 35 percent in 1952, cutting the number of breweries by half from 766 to 357. Adding to the pressure on Piels, the "Big Three national giants" had acquired plants near New York—with Pabst purchasing a Newark company in 1945, Schlitz buying a venerable Brooklyn brewery four years later, and, most recently, Anheuser-Busch building a new $34 million factory in Newark with a crushing capacity of 1.6 million barrels.[90]

With their vast volume, these big brands could, said Dr. Scheyhing, "afford national advertising programs . . . which many small and medium sized breweries can not." As sales in cans or bottles soared and keg deliveries to saloons slumped, consumers, not barkeeps, were making the choice by brand name recognition. In short, advertising was more important than ever. With higher administrative and advertising costs per unit, Piels' earnings had dropped dramatically from $1.90 per barrel in 1946 to just $0.73 in 1952. Meanwhile, Anheuser-Busch's earnings remained robust at $1.80.[91] In short, the prospect for family-owned breweries like Piels was not promising.

Three months after William's death, the board picked general manager Henry J. Muessen, who had worked his way up from salesman, to become the third president of Piel Bros.[92] As the first non-Piel to head the family firm, Muessen's promotion seemed, at first blush, the culmination of the modern corporate culture that William Piel had fought so hard to instill. Yet as the youngest in a large farming family, Muessen's education went no further than vocational high school. And he had climbed the corporate ladder through family connections not professional qualifications—getting his first job as a janitor at Western Electric through his brother, a talented engineer; starting as a salesman at Piel Bros. through his brother-in-law Henry Piel; promoted as the protégé of former general manager Bruce Berckmans; and positioning himself for the top job as dutiful amanuensis for an ailing William Piel.[93] In retrospect, it seems unlikely Muessen, with his limited qualifications, would have been promoted outside this family firm, say at Pabst or Schaefer.

Similarly, Bruce Berckmans, a trained and talented executive, found any advance at Piels beyond general manager blocked by William's endless tenure. So he moved on and up to become executive vice-president at Schaefer, Brooklyn's biggest brewery, and then president of International Breweries, Inc., a mid-sized national firm.[94] It seems likely that Piel Bros. would have fared far better under a competent professional such as Berckmans or a committed family member such as Henry or Rudolf. Reflecting the power of family business as a social formation, William, by his very presence, embodied the family's atavistic authority, unwittingly blocking his own managerial revolution and stalling, even crippling the company's modernization.

With William's death and Muessen's promotion there were no longer any Piels at Piel Bros. Nor was there anyone on the board who knew anything about brewing beer. Indeed, the directors were all presidents of companies that had little to do with brewing—Hoffman-LaRoche, pharmaceuticals; American Home Products, also pharmaceuticals; National Selected Products, food producer; P.J. Ritter, catsup maker; and M. Lowenstein & Sons, textile manufacturers.[95] All could read balance sheets and manage men. But none of them, Muessen included, understood the delicate organic process of brewing beer—a failing that would soon prove problematic. After only five years on Muessen's watch, Piel's prize-winning brews, awarded Belgium's Cross of Honour in 1952, would become known as a "bum beer."

Rubsam & Horrmann Fiasco

As a ten-year veteran of William's management team, Piels' new president Henry Muessen shared his mentor's faith in expansion. By July 1953, rising sales exceeded the rated capacity of 1.1 million barrels at Piels' two Brooklyn plants—forcing the company to ration deliveries and quit some secondary markets such as Virginia. Consequently, that October, just months after his promotion, Muessen began negotiating the purchase of a second New York brewery, the venerable

Rubsam & Horrmann Brewing Company on Staten Island.[96] Rather than taking a year or more to build a new plant, Piels' sales staff calculated this acquisition could provide instant access, in the upcoming 1954 season, to Rubsam's sales of 711,000 barrels in Delaware, New Jersey, and Pennsylvania. Simultaneously, the acquisition could cut Piels' own delivery costs in the same territory.[97]

With such optimism driving negotiations, Muessen's management team planned a disciplined takeover of Rubsam & Horrmann—with a complete plant "shut-down," removal of remaining liquids, dismissal of all 200 employees, and a publicity blackout until just "one day prior to Piel personnel appearing at the plant."[98] As scheduled, the principals—Henry Muessen and August Horrmann— signed the sales contract on November 16, 1953, and Piels paid a 10 percent deposit against a final price of $1,850,000. In a tribute to Piels' current credit worthiness, Massachusetts Mutual Life Insurance readily provided $3.1 million at 4.3 percent interest to finance both the purchase and retirement of $1.3 million in existing debt.[99] Since Piels paid about fifty cents on the dollar for a brewery with $3.4 million in working assets, the acquisition seemed, at the outset, a real boon for the company's expansion plans.[100]

9.3. Label for Rubsam & Horrmann Bock Beer, Staten Island, post-Prohibition.

From there, however, things started to go wrong, badly wrong. "Having risen in the organization through the Sales Department," Muessen later explained, "and because of the importance of constantly increasing sales had demanded priority of attention from me, I was almost wholly unaware of the ramifications"—of both the invisible red ink in Rubsam's balance sheet and the mechanical deficiencies hidden throughout its plant.[101]

Despite Piels' careful plans for controlled publicity, an enterprising reporter from the *Staten Island Advance* scooped the impending sale with banner headlines on December 3, 1953, inferring that Muessen's tight-lipped evasions were "a virtual admission that the transaction . . . was about to take place." Although Rubsam & Horrmann had produced 700,000 barrels back in 1946 to rank fourth in the state, it had never recovered "a host of draft beer outlets" lost to New Jersey breweries during that disastrous 1949 strike. It was now slated, the paper claimed, to become the fourteenth metropolitan brewery to fail in the last eight years.[102]

On December 10 as planned, Muessen announced the acquisition, saying it "gives us a capacity in excess of 2,000,000 barrels a year." Within hours, however, the U.S. Food and Drug Administration (FDA) ordered the Rubsam & Horrmann plant to destroy over 1,000 barrels of "unsanitary" beer. More seriously, FDA inspectors had found an "unsanitary condition consisting of live beetles, ants, moths, cockroaches and pigeon feathers" in the brewery's storage area. Publicly, Muessen waved it all away as "mildly embarrassing," assuring the press that "the whole place will be cleaned out from stem to stern." Nonetheless, news of this contamination, appearing prominently on page three of the *New York Times* business section, was a heavy blow to Piels' reputation for brewing a pristine product.[103] For a family firm reputation is everything—cultivated for generations, lost in an instant.

The complications arising from the FDA's condemnation were considerable. During an on-site examination, the agency's inspector discovered serious insect infestations throughout the Rubsam plant, including the grain bins, malt mill, conveyor belts, and brew house. The original court order, issued at the FDA's behest on December 9, restrained Rubsam & Horrmann from "directly or indirectly . . . delivering or causing to be delivered . . . into interstate commerce" any of the brewery's current stock of beer.[104] Five days later, Piels reached an agreement with the FDA that they would "dump all beer on hand at the plant" and federal prosecutors would, in turn, extend the time for their reply to the preliminary injunction until January 1954.[105] Even so, another FDA inspection in mid-February found eleven instances of infestation, including dead beetles in the malt conveyor, pigeon droppings on the hoisting platform, and mouse pellets on the malt screen floor.[106]

Instead of Muessen's instant increase in capacity, the Rubsam purchase embroiled Piels in costly renovations to an antiquated, unsanitary plant. After six months of cleansing, Muessen advised the board that resolution of charges before the federal courts was imminent.[107] But when brewing finally began at Rubsam & Horrmann in April 1954, Piels' management still encountered "serious difficulties . . . in maintaining proper sanitary conditions" and ordered a rush expenditure of nearly $50,000 to repair the malt mill.[108]

Over the next year, this outlay proved a mere down payment on urgent repairs that soon climbed far beyond Muessen's optimistic estimate of $400,000 toward $700,000 for a roster of renovations beyond his ken—everything from additional lager tanks ($350,000) to retubing the compressors ($10,900).[109] Even after repairs added up to half the original purchase price, the Rubsam plant still harbored serious, ultimately fatal deficiencies. Within a few years, this brewery would produce the "bum beer" that ruined Piels' hard-won reputation for quality.

There were, moreover, other reasons to question this entire expansion strategy. Just a year after acquisition of the Trommer's Brewery back in 1952, Piels' management noted a "faster than expected decline of the Trommer brands." Within two years, they decided to demolish the brand's Bushwick plant. Despite

9.4. Label for Piel's Light Beer from the Staten Island plant that brewed "bum beer," mid-1950s.

Muessen's original optimism about reaching 1,380,000 barrels by 1954 en route to a production of 2 million barrels, Piels' sales actually dropped to 1,182,000 barrels in 1955. In his annual report that year, however, Muessen assured stockholders there were already some "encouraging" signs for future growth.[110]

Bert and Harry

This optimism midst stagnant sales came from the surprising success of the brewery's new "Bert and Harry Piel" television commercials. Not only did they break decisively with the family's fondness for German kitsch, all those gnomes and costumed peasants, but these humorous spots also captured the country's craving for whimsy midst Cold War tensions over thermonuclear war. These cartoon Piel brothers soon became nothing less than a "landmark campaign" in the history of American advertising.[111]

In an era of "hard sell" advertising that hammered the product's name into the brain with relentless repetition, a junior copywriter at Young & Rubicam named Ed Graham, then in his 20s, came up with the idea for something radically different—a humorous "soft sell" approach. Finding his agency's "Less N.F.S." commercials for Piels "full of stupefyingly solemn numbers" and "pretty horrible," he worked with staff artist Jack Sidebotham to create two cartoon characters, Bert and Harry Piel. To animate his creations, Graham sketched out fictional biographies. Born in Brooklyn and educated at P.S. 3 and Samuel J. Tilden High School in Flatbush, the brothers started out in separate careers—short, bombastic Bert in auto sales and tall, studious Harry in chemistry. But then Harry's discovery of "colloidal suspension" became "the priceless formula for the brewing of a dry beer." For their voices and scripts, Graham turned to his friends Bob Elliott and Ray Goulding. As the improv comedy duo "Bob and Ray," they were already livening New York's morning radio with their madcap characters.[112]

Not only did Bert and Harry "revolutionize" advertising, but the fictional brothers debated this change in almost every television spot with a subtle, self-referential irony. In a hundred ads over the next five years, the gruff, stout Bert would plunge headlong into a hard-sell push for Piels until the taller, soft-spoken Harry suggested more modest claims.[113]

There was no precedent for this soft-sell approach. Agency executives were skeptical, even suspicious. First, they insisted on dozens of auditions before agreeing that Bob and Ray had the best voices. Then Young & Rubicam demanded extended, out-of-town trials at Harrisburg and Binghamton in the summer of 1955. Piels' sales soared in both cities. By December, agency executives were sold, and Bert and Harry spots were broadcast in all of Piels' markets.[114] Rather than the usual twenty seconds for a brief burst of image and jingle, Young & Rubicam bought sixty-second television slots that gave Bob and Ray sufficient time to develop the comedic interplay between the fictive brothers.[115]

By the spring of 1956, Bert and Harry were a hit. A big hit. As New York's *Daily News* later put it, they were "the most astonishingly successful salesmen TV advertising had ever known." In an unprecedented move, newspapers began listing broadcast times for the ads in their television programs. People stayed home to watch. Viewers formed Bert and Harry fan clubs. People, believing them somehow real, wrote letters. Even now, decades later, viewers who access these ads via *YouTube* on the Internet still laugh as Bert Piel, on ice at Madison Square Garden, brashly mistranslates for French-Canadian hockey player Philippe

9.5. Bert and Harry Piel beer coaster, 1956.

Duprès to make the pitch for Piels, while soft-spoken Harry tries hopelessly to intercede. By the end of 1956, Piels' package sales for the year had jumped by nearly 10 percent to the highest level in the company's history.[116] In this golden age of Madison Avenue advertising, Piels had discovered the power of humor to push product.

The advertising industry celebrated this success. "One of the most effective hucksters on eastern TV," *Time* magazine reported in May 1956. "Since January, when Harry and Brother Bert made their debut . . . , they have won such fame that even the most blurb-worn viewers are changing their ways: instead of ducking out when the commercial goes on, Easterners are now turning on their sets to catch the Piel cartoons."[117] Famed columnist Walter Winchell proclaimed "the Harry & Bert commercials are more entertaining than most entertainers."[118] In a survey that December by industry authority *Advertising Age*, television viewers ranked Piel's beer number one for "best liked commercials." Two months later, over a thousand advertising and public relations executives polled by the trade's *Tide* magazine voted Bert and Harry "the best ad campaign in any medium for 1956."[119]

As the series swept major media awards, Madison Avenue took notice. "Encouraged by the success of the entertaining Piel skits," *Daily News* editor Worth Gatewood wrote in January 1957, "more and more ad men who once believed solely in the hard sell are venturing into a field where only Bert and Harry dared tread a year ago." In its annual report, Piel Bros. stated that the campaign's "very great amount of favorable publicity" had been catalytic in reversing the "downward trend in profit" by raising company income to $740,000.[120] Within the Piel family, there was much ribbing about who was which, with some saying Harry was based on "tall, quiet, sensible" Henry and Bert was modeled on "short, loud, exuberant" Paul.[121]

But after five years and over a hundred Bert and Harry television spots, there were signs of trouble. Piels still ranked a lowly fifth in sales for its viewing area during 1957–58.[122] Despite the campaign's phenomenal popularity, annual sales had remained stubbornly stagnant—climbing slowly by just 3 percent to 1,321,000 barrels in 1959 before sliding downward to 1,202,000 barrels in 1960.[123] Close analysis of Piels' market share in twenty-nine cities across its Northeast advertising region indicated that national brands were not the problem. In its top market Princeton, New Jersey, where a college crowd probably liked the ads, Piels captured 16 percent of sales (with five regional brands holding 75 percent of market). But its overall share fell to an average of 7 percent in the other twenty-eight cities. More typical was Schenectady, New York, where Piels won just 7.9

Map 1. Piel Bros. Sales Territory Showing Percentage of Local Markets, 1960.

percent of the market and placed last among that city's five top-selling brands—Utica Club, Schaefer, Dobler, and Ballantine, all regional beers—that together still held 65 percent of local sales. In short, Piels was losing out to purely local rivals.[124] How could America's best ads fail to make the sale? If good advertising could sell ice to Eskimos, then something was seriously wrong at Piels.

As an experienced salesman, Muessen had clearly mastered the art of promoting the product. But his management team, ignoring the delicate art of brewing, had failed to maintain the Piel family's tradition of quality. In effect, William's attempt to bring the U.S. "managerial revolution" into his family firm was half-done, locking Piels in an incomplete transition from family business to professional management. By firing his brother, a skilled brewmaster, while positioning a loyal acolyte to succeed himself as president, William, the ultimate familial atavism, had formed a management team that could compromise even the most brilliant advertising.

"The big mistake with that campaign was that it got people to taste Piel's Beer," reported Jerry Della Femina in his classic study of American advertising. "A guy would take a sip of it and say, 'Screw Bert and Harry, like they were a lot of fun and I like to look at them on the late news but they're not going to make me drink this stuff.'"[125]

A definitive article in *Sports Illustrated* on beer and sport was even more damning. "Unfortunately, the beer itself was not very good," explained Jerry Steinman, publisher of *Beer Marketer's Insights*. "Because of the great ads, all kinds of people bought it for the first time, hated it, and spread the news everywhere about how awful it was. It was a case of terrible word of mouth caused by a wonderful ad campaign."[126] Once famed for making one of America's best beers under founder Michael Piel and his son William, the brewery was now making one of its worst.

Sadly for the company, Rudolf Piel's prediction, sent from his poultry farm in Massachusetts back in 1946, that this "increased capacity [might] stand idle," had proven prescient. In effect, management had spent $3 million, equivalent to ten years' dividends, to acquire two breweries for increased capacity that far exceeded the firm's actual sales during the succeeding decade.[127] Even more sadly for their brand's reputation, Henry's concerns, mailed from his Long Island estate back in 1940, about the competence of his successors in the Technical Division, guardians of the beer's quality, had proven accurate.[128]

All these negative trends culminated in the uncommonly cool summer of 1960 when the temperature rarely rose to ninety degrees Fahrenheit and beer sales sank nationwide. On a Wednesday night in October, as Piels sales tumbled by 100,000 barrels toward a dismal total of 1,200,000 for the year, Bert and Harry failed to appear during the eleven o'clock news on WCBS-TV. In their place was an inane jingle that hammered the Piel name six times in the sort of hard sell that Bert and Harry had supposedly superseded.

> Piels, Piels, Glorious Piels
> The beer with the long lasting head,
> With a smooth lager flavor and glorious crown
> It holds the flavor all the way down
> Oh, it's Piels, Piels, Glorious Piels
> Oh, what a wonderful beer.[129]

Perplexed, a reporter for the *New York Times* contacted Bert and Harry's creator Ed Graham, now a partner in Goulding-Elliott-Graham Productions. He said that Young & Rubicam had spurned a bid to test-market his cartoon creations against the jingle. Evidently the agency, the paper reported, "hoped that the public can gradually be weaned away from their affection for the Bert and Harry characters." As rumors of their demise spread, respected *New York Times* theater critic Brooks Atkinson hailed them as American cultural icons that "rank with Mickey Mouse." But now they will "take second place to mass stupidity" in the form of "photographed commercials of happy imbibers with good teeth living it up out of doors, playing jolly games together, and escaping loneliness by simulating ecstasy in a mob."[130]

Such high-brow loyalty seemed to confirm the critical view of William's son Gerard Piel who, as publisher of *Scientific American* magazine, knew about advertising. "Harry and Bert sold one can of Piels beer to every gin and tonic drinker who ever saw their commercial or heard it," he explained. "And never sold it to anyone who drank beer. It was right over the heads of the sweaty guys who really make the market for beer. So it was the most mis-placed, mis-calculated advertising campaign in the world."[131]

In December 1960, a headline on page three in the *New York Times* business section announced, "Curtains for Bert and Harry." Concluding that the clever cartoon characters were not selling beer, Young & Rubicam had canceled its $80,000 per year contract with Goulding-Elliott-Graham Productions and persuaded a most reluctant Piel Bros. that it was time for a change. Avoiding any formal announcement about the fate of Bert and Harry, the agency had been cutting back on their appearances slowly "to avoid a public storm of protest."[132]

That strategy failed. As actors with anodyne good looks seemingly plucked from daytime television cavorted in the Piels' time slot, some 1,500,000 viewers wrote "irate letters" mourning the passing of Bert and Harry. The *Daily News* called the decision to terminate the campaign "one of the biggest blunders in the history of advertising."[133] As it turned out, this was just one of several such blunders that would, in just eighteen months, lead to the sale of Piel Bros.

10

Demise

By the late 1950s it seemed no strategy, whether bigger plants or better advertising, would allow a regional brewer like Piel Bros. to compete with the big national brands in metropolitan markets. And whatever chance Piels might have had to survive as a quality local beer was scotched by a series of dubious, even disastrous decisions by its own management. Cosseted inside their corporate offices, Piel's executives compounded the firm's losses by persisting in a losing strategy with two slender tenets: first, expand plant capacity to make more beer and, then, advertise heavily to push the product.

Even though the siblings of the second generation owned substantial shares in this closely held firm, their interpersonal dynamics blocked any intervention that might have slowed the brand's slide to becoming a "bum beer." With the family's pressure for high dividends and the lingering influence of a few siblings over company executives, the modernization of Piel Bros. had stalled—no longer a family firm committed to quality, but not yet a corporation capable of real efficiency.

The central figure in shaping the family's response, or non-response, to their company's malaise was Paul Piel, the third among Maria's surviving children—sometime inventor, part-time artist, and full-time family manager. After graduating from Harvard, touring Italy, and serving as a sergeant during World War I, Paul settled into a four-story townhouse in Greenwich Village, a gift from his doting mother, living off the rents and dabbling in his nominal career, sculpture. When eldest brother William died in 1953 after nearly forty years as chief executive, Paul was his self-anointed successor as family patriarch. With his siblings now scattered from Maine to Florida, Paul, as the last one living in New York, served as the sole representative of the Michael Piel Trust, which held half the company's shares, from William's death in 1953 to the brewery's sale in 1962.

Through his sedulous courtship of external directors and constant intrusion in company affairs, Paul both personified and perpetuated the company's ambiguous character, stymied in transition from family business to modern corporation. Like William before him, Paul, by his very presence, embodied a residual family influence that compromised the very modernization they both advocated so relentlessly.

From his townhouse in Manhattan and artist's studio inside the Brooklyn brewery, Paul was well placed to observe the growing problems at Piel Bros. But driven by strong loyalties and fixed opinions, he could not see the seriousness of the situation. His long-established role as the family's favorite, pleasing authority figures, whether parents or executives, with his quick mind and exceptional erudition, led him into an almost sycophantic relationship with the company's management. Instead of questioning their executive decisions, Paul seemed to revel in proximity to the powerful, offering personal loyalty in exchange for insider information to sate his insatiable intellectual curiosity. Once these authorities honored him with their confidences, Paul then used his persuasive powers to still any criticism from his siblings, whom he often treated as lesser minds needing a firm hand to limit the influence of their ill-considered views.

Family Manager

With no formal employment and little work as an artist, Paul was "a man of leisure" who dabbled in sculpture but devoted himself to managing the family's affairs.[1] As part of these many self-designated duties, Paul used his fluency in German for trans-Atlantic negotiations to liquidate their father's properties in Düsseldorf—another selfless service that added to his informal influence within the family. Before his death in 1915, Michael had told son William that his brother Wilhelm-Heinrich could be trusted to manage their share of the old family farm in Mörsenbroich, just outside Düsseldorf. But that same brother ignored William's repeated requests for an accounting until he died and his heirs finally forwarded a statement in 1924 with a first payment of $798.[2] Then, starting in 1936, William and sister Louise struggled in vain to secure compensation for the German army's expropriation of the Piel farm.[3]

After World War II, Paul worked with redoubled determination through a distant maternal cousin to sell the remaining Piel parcels in Mörsenbroich, now engulfed by the city of Düsseldorf. Through years of patient correspondence,

Paul distributed nearly $34,000 from these sales to each of the seven siblings between 1960 and 1964. Ten years later when a first cousin, Marga Piel Müller of Düsseldorf, died childless, Paul engaged in "seven years of embittered litigation" to contest her will, winning another $20,000 for each of his grateful siblings.[4] Since Marga was the last surviving descendant of father Michael's seven siblings, this litigation thus liquidated the trans-Atlantic family ties that had survived for a century after Michael's migration in 1883. These welcome windfalls won Paul a certain authority inside the Piel family circle.

As president of the Michael Piel Trust throughout its thirty-year history, 1930 to 1962, Paul acquired insider information about the brewery and translated that knowledge into influence. Through incessant maneuvering, he used his control over half the company's stock to shape selections for the Piel Bros. board.[5] Writing relatives, Paul could prattle on for pages about the board—recounting in 1944 how director Kenneth Baxter hoped "to reunite his family broken ever since [his daughter] Anne chose a movie career" in Hollywood, and reciting, in 1959, the qualifications of eight directors over the past twenty years, with vivid character portraits for those he had personally recruited.[6]

"How come I ever accepted the role of President of the Michael Piel Holding Company?" Paul wrote a relative in 1959 after nearly thirty years in office. "For one thing the family were clever enough to flee the city, where all the time-consuming chores had to be done, and left me holding the bag! Then again, I must admit that I have, over the years, acquired a sneaking admiration for the sometimes extraordinary administrative skills of your true businessman, who, respecting the free personalities of each of his employees, can yet make the most divergent talents and temperaments work in perfect harmony toward a common goal. I have watched [Piels' president] Henry Muessen do just that."[7]

As his influence grew during the 1950s, Paul came to play the patriarch, setting the pecking order for the next generation by deciding who should join the family's corporate boards. After William died in 1953 and his brother Henry resigned from the Michael Piel Trust in grief, Paul found worthy successors in brother William's son Gerard Piel, publisher of *Scientific American* magazine, and sister Louise's eldest Frederick Lange, a New Jersey utility executive. To fill another vacancy the following year, Rudolf's son-in-law Alfred M. McCoy, Jr., an electronic engineer who had impressed Paul with "his quick mind and quiet demeanor," also joined the board. When the Michael Piel Trust met at the Astor Hotel in 1958, Paul's patriarchal handiwork was self-evident. Seven male directors, including three from the family's third generation (Frederick Lange, Gerard Piel, and Alfred M. McCoy, Jr.), were seated at the table. Four of the family's women, all quite competent, sat in silence as mere "guests" (Louise Piel Lange, Eleanor Jackson Piel, Margarita Piel McCoy, and Marie-Luise Kemp).[8]

After William's death in 1953, Paul also became the main liaison to their elderly mother Maria, acquiring all the moral and fiscal authority of this important office. At the approach of her 98th birthday in April 1955, Maria asked that her share of the family trust be partially liquidated so she could distribute $55,000 while still living. To that end, Paul convened eight hours of family meetings until his siblings' many questions were "one by one painstakingly disposed of before we dared to vote."[9] As their attorney Julian Tashof later explained, the Michael Piel Trust was purchasing "the life interest of Maria Piel for a substantial consideration," freeing them from paying her the interest earned on the Piel Bros. bonds.[10]

Once the directors approved that modified trust, Paul and nephew William "Bill" Piel, Jr., drove down to St. Joseph's Manor, a Catholic convent outside Philadelphia where Maria had been living for the last decade. While Bill Piel read the trust document and Paul translated the legalese into German, Maria "seemed alert, asked sensible questions, and, being satisfied, requested to speak personally to the Mother Superior," saying she "would soon be able to surprise her with something helpful." Several days later, after the $55,000 check had been deposited in Maria's account, Paul returned to St. Joseph's with brother Henry. "It was," wrote Paul, "a moving scene when our very old, but still eager mother . . . actually signed and gave Mother Hiltrudis the check for $15,000." As Maria announced "it is for your new hospital program," the two women "embraced one another spontaneously while Henry and I were touched by the genuine, the tender, human warmth between them."[11]

But Maria's health was fading slowly, almost imperceptibly. During her long years in the convent, she had grown frail and partially blind. She rejoiced in visits from her grandchildren, though "morose," as she often said, that so few of them were baptized Catholics. A few months before her death, my mother took me to meet my great-grandmother. Her once-round face was thin and her body bent. But she delighted in showing us her simple life, the shared bath and communal dining room. When she was in grade school like me, Abraham Lincoln was president—a realization that made her seem a living monument, carved in pale alabaster.

A few months later, Maria told her grandson David, as he kneeled for her blessing: "I have lived long enough. Next year, I would be one hundred years old. When you reach one hundred years, they make too much of a fuss." So in February 1956, she asked a priest for the last rites while seemingly in good health, kissed her caretaker nuns goodbye, and was gone by nightfall. Maria had died just six months shy of her 100th birthday. On the death certificate, her attending physician attributed the cause of death to "myocordosis," or degenerative heart disease.[12]

With the funeral just days away, her scattered children and grandchildren quickly assembled at the convent. Though he had not spoken to his mother for fifteen years, Rudolf flew up from Florida and then, while suffering stomach spasms from the tension, drove to Pennsylvania with his daughter Margarita McCoy. "After the service," she recalled, "we left as soon as we could." Apart from her father's awkward position, Margarita had her own reasons for not lingering. "My grandmother lived in fear. She was a very rigid person, never smiled, and was very strict with her grandchildren," particularly in matters of sexuality. One summer at Parlin when Margarita was just four or five, her grandmother sewed a modesty panel over her bathing suit's scooped neck, and then, at the end of the visit, sent her home on the train covered in long sleeves and winter knee socks, sweating in the middle of summer. Looking back on Maria's obsession with sexuality, Margarita observed: "Grandmother seemed troubled by something, something she had done wrong."[13]

Another of Maria's grandchildren, Gerard Piel, achieved an unexpected epiphany during the eulogy about the reason for her fears. "The priest at the convent," who was likely her confessor, recalled Gerard, "was saying that we didn't understand the problems that Maria had had. And so it all fit Paul's story that Maria was burdened with the sin of never having been married." Uncle Paul had told Gerard that his father William "was born in Verviers, Belgium and Verviers was the place, apparently, where anonymous deliveries were made of illegitimate children." If correct, that story would explain why Maria, midst Michael's departure for America in 1883, traveled nearly 200 kilometers from home to give birth in this city where the Sisters of Notre Dame de Namur ministered to unwed mothers. That story might only mean that Maria's firstborn William was conceived out of wedlock. Or perhaps Maria had never married. Either way, these were mortal sins punishable by hell fires.[14]

As was customary among Michael's children, the probate of Maria's will was uncontested. In her original testament dated 1925, Maria had divided her estate among nine surviving children after assigning $35,000 to Paul in trust for her schizophrenic son Otto, then living in Denmark; $8,000 to Agnes for her handicapped daughter Patsy; and $8,000 for her youngest Roland, then just 24 and still finishing college. She also assigned each child a piece from their father's art collection. In an apparent attempt at reconciliation, she gave Rudolf a pair of paintings by Düsseldorf school artist Johann Christian Kröner, "Deer at Edge of Forest" and "Wild Boar Hunt," and "the antique Amati violin formerly belonging to his father, which he also has in his possession."[15]

The intervening thirty years had simplified Maria's estate. Roland had died accidentally a year after she signed this will. Otto passed away in 1932. Since Maria had already transferred her Piel shares to a trust and the Lake Parlin estate to daughter Louise, Paul, the sole executor, simply divided the remaining cash and jewelry evenly among the seven surviving heirs. In keeping with the family's sense of shared guardianship, three siblings—Louise, Paul, and Oswald—assigned their shares ($2,751 each) to Agnes's handicapped daughter Patsy.[16] Whether Paul was remiss in his duties or Rudolf was not to be reconciled, the second painting of the boar never reached him.

Those two Kröner paintings, with their matching frames, would not be paired for another fifty years. I inherited the deer canvas when I went off to Columbia University in New York City, perfect Mother thought for my room on fraternity row along 114th Street, just a few doors from where her father Rudolf had lived during his college days. With its ornate gilded frame and ten-point stag, the quarry of kings, that canvas somehow gave me a sense of my great-grandfather's aspirations.[17] But its companion went missing for decades until a distant cousin in Maine put it on the market to pay for graduate school. After reading Maria's will and realizing her intention, I bought something I couldn't afford. Today deer and boar are reunited, making me curator, like so many of my cousins, for some of those floridly Germanic artifacts that Michael and Maria once collected to grace their grand homes.

Through letters, luncheons, and such financial duties, Paul placed himself at the epicenter of the Piel family, becoming almost omniscient about its affairs. When Rudolf called the brewery in 1959 to register some shares in his daughter's name, he was surprised to find Paul shadowing his transaction. "How and why Paul knew that I had phoned and why he butted in I have no idea," wrote Rudolf. "I do think it is worth to note that no matter who one talks to they report to Paul."[18] Within the fractious Piel family, the sum of such knowledge was power— albeit problematic power Paul used to quash criticism of executive decisions that, in retrospect, could have benefited from either stockholders' oversight, management independence, or both.

Mismanagement

Even midst the success of the Bert and Harry commercials, there was ample reason to question the company's management. Although this advertising was wildly popular, the beer's quality was slipping and sales actually fell fractionally during the campaign's first full year in 1956. But management attributed the stagnant sales to demographics, telling stockholders that the nation's "per capita consumption of beer decreased again in 1956 making the struggle to maintain volume very real."[19] None of the Piel stockholders challenged that excuse.

By the late 1950s, the relentless growth of the national brands, fueled by finance capital, was transforming the beer industry, creating structural problems for regional brewers like Piels. As the president of Falstaff Brewing Corp. of St. Louis explained: "The trend in the brewing industry today is no different than the consolidations that took place in the auto, cigarette and appliance industries years ago." In the twenty years following repeal in 1934, the number of breweries had dropped from 714 to just 281, with an accelerating decline in recent years. Since the nation's beer consumption remained flat at about 84 million barrels annually, the big five brewers, accounting for 30 percent of the nation's production, were invading local markets across the country, building new plants and increasing advertising. "We can't afford to match advertising with the national brands," said the chairman of Metz Brewing Co. of St. Louis. "We're not going to spend our profits on advertising and can't expect to get the cost per listener on radio or television that the big breweries get."[20] Clearly, Piels management would need innovation, efficiency, and fiscal discipline to survive these adverse trends.

Sadly, all these attributes were absent. After a half-century of working in modest offices, Muessen's management team built themselves a costly administration building in 1958 with the hefty price tag of $730,000—far more than their recent investments in plant efficiency. To justify the expense, management circulated a memo claiming the new facility would consolidate employees from five different offices, two rented and three antiquated, cutting costs and raising morale in ways that might, they argued, prevent unionization of white-collar workers. Meanwhile, a confluence of negatives—a short strike before the July Fourth weekend, a continuing decline in America's per capita beer consumption, and competition that cut retail prices—reduced Piels' income for 1958 by another 2 percent.[21]

A few months later in May 1959, Paul wrote family stockholders approvingly about a proposal from star architect Ely Jacques Kahn to construct a new

45,000-square-foot bottling plant at a cost of $2.2 million.[22] After chief executive Muessen announced the company was proceeding with this ambitious project, director Julian Tashof also wrote to explain that the new facility would eliminate the double handling now required by lack of "proper storage facilities," producing an annual labor savings of $320,000.[23] To preempt any criticism of management priorities, Paul praised the two projects, office building and bottling plant, as "another positive step in the never-ending campaign to equip Piel Bros. to carry on the competitive battle for growth and survival."[24]

Not everyone in the family shared his Panglossian perspective. That same month, May 1959, Louise wrote her brother Rudolf at his Florida ranch about her "general misgivings" over the decision to spend $730,000 "on a new office building ahead of the new bottleshop, which all agree seems to be badly needed." While the company's marketing was "outstanding," she noted that the "physical condition[s] of portions of the plant are poor," raising the possibility that "marketing has been emphasized at the expense of efficiency in production." To correct this situation, Louise felt the need for "a closer family contact with the business direction." She suggested Rudolf's son-in-law, Alfred M. McCoy, Jr., who, as an engineer with "an unusual talent for figures, seems most urgently needed to assist the Board in arriving at constructive decisions." Apart from the director's salary, such an appointment carried a certain prestige, Louise said, that might advance Alfred's career within his own company, Raytheon electronics.[25] Though Louise showed far more insight than company executives, she was doubly disadvantaged in gaining a hearing—a stockholder denied inside information and a woman marginalized by patriarchy.

Since Louise had sent copies to brothers Henry and Oswald, this letter soon reached Paul. Just two weeks later, he replied with a ten-page blast that mixed rage with ridicule. "Frankly," Paul wrote, "this charging the Board with gross error in approving the building sequence has been exaggerated and ballooned out of all proportion . . . in a self-deceiving effort to justify an impossible demand for special representation and a private window on the Board." Under the long-standing agreement that the Gottfried and Michael Piel heirs nominate three non-family directors each, Paul did not "on principle oppose a member of the Piel clan on the Board provided we all give up the lolly-pop theory of office as a reward for good little boys or the view that the Board becomes a training school for young hopefuls who need a feather in their cap." Like a corporate chairman fending off activist stockholders, Paul condemned Louise for suggesting that they break with their "tradition," over the past sixteen years, of "delegating full responsibility and complete authority to . . . men of *wide* and *seasoned* business experience, men of standing in the business world" who can work closely with president Henry Muessen, himself an executive with a "rare gift for leadership and . . . capacity for far-sighted decisions."[26]

When Louise wrote back that June presuming to defend her position, Paul delivered suppressing fire in the form of two chiding letters that ran to thirteen single-spaced typed pages. After a pro forma apology for "the vigor of my rhetoric," Paul explained that Louise's suggestion for a family member on the board threatened "the principle of professional management with delegated powers . . . which . . . had rescued Piel Bros. from the crowded graveyard of family-owned businesses." From his artist's studio inside the brewery, Paul had enjoyed "the opportunity of observing during years of almost daily contact— without ever butting in or spying about—the tremendous transformation of Piel Bros. from an intensely personal, old fashioned, captain-of-industry type of business . . . into the thoroughly modern, dynamic organization we enjoy today."[27]

In his second letter to Louise, Paul quashed his sister's suggestion that the brewery's president might welcome a family member on the board, saying "it would distress Muessen no end to see one of his team-mates, Don, Jack or Larry—for so he calls them—cashiered to make way for Al, Gerard, Fred, or any other member of our family."[28] Then, Paul extended his counterattack to brother Henry's wife, Marie Muessen Piel, rejecting her "wholly unexpected charge that I am inconsistent in opposing the younger generation's taking turns in filling seats upon the Board in order to learn the business."[29]

To allay any hurt this rejection might have caused, Paul forwarded the latter letter to one of the spurned nominees, nephew Gerard Piel, by now a successful publisher, with a soothing note portraying himself as the Piels' wise patriarch. "Educating the family," he explained, "to what stands around in the business world is, I am sure, chiefly a matter of gradually bringing into the open all the affective blocks of apprehension." His detailed description of the directors' virtues for sister Louise was, Paul explained, "aimed at overcoming the sense of alienation, the feeling that the company which father and uncle once built and loved, is now being run by a lot of strangers." To drive home his criticism of sister Louise and sister-in-law Marie, Paul added: "The crude Italian saying, 'Le donne pensano col utero'—women think with their wombs—has, I fear, much application in our situation."[30]

A week later in October 1959, Paul tried to repair relations with the other rejected member of the younger generation, Rudolf's son-in-law Alfred M.

McCoy, Jr., writing him that: "The proposal made by Louise that you go upon the Board of Piel Bros. to replace one of our old directors put me into the painful position of appearing less friendly to you than the rest of the family." As an artist and amateur mathematician dedicated to the pursuit of knowledge, Paul now found himself in the ironic position of defending the businessmen who, he felt, had served Piels so well. In his closing remarks, Paul pulled out the emotional stops: "Believe me, Al, there was never any personal animus against you. I have no difficulty imagining how proud it must make Rudolf to be able to call you son."[31]

Through such relentless slapping and stroking, Paul managed to stifle any criticism of management from his sibling shareholders for the better part of a decade, preventing any deviation from the company's ill-fated course. Throughout this formidable display of insider information, Paul seemed oblivious to the irony that he represented, by his constant interventions, a residual element of that "intensely personal, old fashioned, captain-of-industry" influence that was restraining their company's transformation into a "thoroughly modern" corporation.

In these weeks when Paul was assuring relatives near and far of management's firm hand and steady course, Rudolf also wrote his son-in-law about the brewery's prospects, revealing a prescience that contrasts sharply with such myopia. Driving back to Florida after visiting his daughter Margarita Piel McCoy in Massachusetts, and his grandson, the author, at boarding school in Connecticut, Rudolf called on Piels' director Jack Tashof at his offices in lower Manhattan. With dividends constant while net earnings were dropping, with prices stagnant while costs "are continuously rising," Rudolf concluded the brewery's trajectory "points to a basically unhealthy condition." Although "our business has done amazingly well in the face of the invasion of our market by the new Busch plant," Rudolf, mindful of the economic pressures on family firms, felt that "the brewing industry is becoming national in character and a local brewery is at a terrible disadvantage due to its limited advertising budget against such competition." Since "the position of the brewery could easily start to deteriorate at an accelerated rate," the firm needed new finance for diversification. When the time came to move in that direction, Rudolf advised, "we don't want to be at the start of a long-winded family feud. The principal difficulty has always been distrust within our own group."[32]

Within a month, Paul attempted to contain such concerns by convening a meeting between family stockholders and company directors "of whom they had heard so much but few of whom, if any, they had ever met."[33] During this meeting at the Hotel Astor in January 1960, Muessen attributed the company's decline to the "predatory practices" of the national brands, particularly their cut-price labels backed by "large scale ad campaigns." Midst this "battle of the giants," small brewers such as Piels faced "higher advertising budgets, sales spending, new and costly packaging, softening of prices and so-called dumping of beer at distress prices."[34]

With New York's unions raising wages and the industry's over-production driving down prices, the city's breweries, Muessen continued, were caught in an economic squeeze. Nor were labor costs likely to stabilize. As management was fully aware, the tough Teamsters had supplanted their industry's longtime labor contractor, the Union of United Brewery Workers (CIO). At a recent mass meeting in the city, Teamster boss Jimmy Hoffa had promised to fight for an even better contract from New York's brewers. On a more optimistic note, Muessen was confident that their company's "young, aggressive and enthusiastic organization" could produce solutions that would raise sales and restore dividends.[35]

"Bum Beer"

Yet all Muessen's reassuring words could not save the company from its own mismanagement. By the summer of 1960, Louise's concerns about plant efficiency proved prescient as Piel's beer began showing impurities called "haze" that can cloud clarity and produce "undesirable flavors." Ironically, Gerard Piel's *Scientific American* magazine had recently published an article on beer's complex microbiology, which he illustrated with a flow chart "based upon the brewing cycle at Piel's . . . prepared with the help of their technicians." Every brewmaster, the essay explained, has to manipulate "some of the subtlest processes of life" through a succession of sensitive stages. After some 6,000 years of practicing this "remarkable art," brewmasters now faced the additional challenge of producing a beer that, though shipped long-distance, must still be "crystal clear" when finally poured into a glass. To allow this longer shelf life, the brew must be precisely pasteurized to kill "most of the microorganisms capable of growing in beer." Unfortunately, some organisms can continue growing after fermentation, precipitating small particles during storage that form a "pronounced haze." These problems were usually prevented by "strict attention to cleanliness in the brew house"—the very problem that Piels' new Staten Island plant had neglected.[36]

After several years of declining quality, Piels' beer began exhibiting contagions that could no longer be ignored. When Henry Piel, the brewery's former technical director, telephoned in September 1960 to express concern, company president Muessen admitted there were some "product problems," possibly from "yeast contamination or infection" but probably from "refrigeration problems in some of our cellars resulting in some unsatisfactory fermentations at both plants." During trips upstate that summer, three wholesalers had told Muessen that the foam on beer from his Staten Island brewery—the same plant cited for unsanitary conditions just a few years earlier—"was not as good." Customers were complaining that this beer was "different." Nonetheless, Muessen was confident the company had "well-qualified master brewers," Fred Riedel and Fred Draeger, who were "well equipped" to fix any problems.[37]

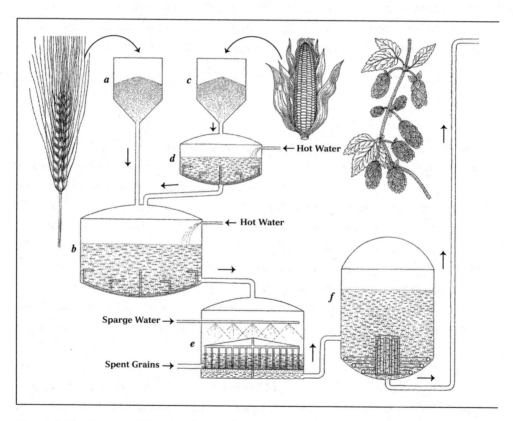

Figure 4. The Process of Brewing Beer at Piel Bros., Brooklyn, as shown in the June 1959 edition of *Scientific American* magazine. The barley corns are ground and placed in the mash hopper (*a*); from thence they go to the mash tub (*b*). Corn (or other adjunct) is placed in the adjunct hopper (*c*), boiled in the adjunct cooker (*d*) and added to the mash. The malt wort is then filtered in the lauter tub (*e*). The clear wort goes to the brew kettle (*f*), where hops are added.

Muessen's Maneuver

Belying his outward confidence, these problems were evidently so serious that, the very next day, Muessen wrote the directors offering a way out of this crisis. He would accept the suggestion at a recent ad hoc meeting with company principals—Julian Tashof, Leonard Lazarus, Gerard Piel, Frederick Lange, and, of course, Paul Piel—by delegating daily operations and devoting himself henceforth "to visiting other brewers in an effort to seek opportunities for favorable sale or merger of Piel Bros." If he failed to either improve earnings or effect a "favorable sale" within six months, then he asked that his resignation be accepted.[38]

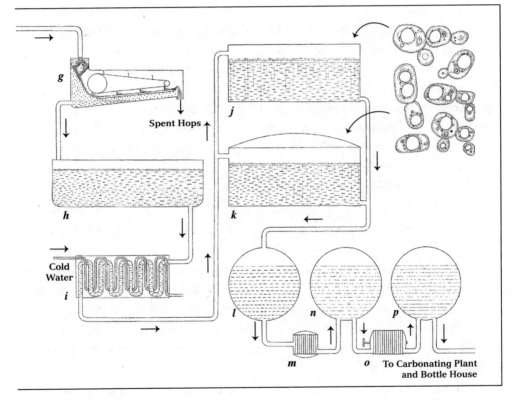

The hops are removed by the hop strainer (g); other substances, by a settling tank (h). The wort is now cooled (i) and sent to open (j) and closed (k) fermenting tanks. In the closed tank carbon dioxide is collected and later used to carbonate the beer. After fermentation, the green beer goes to the lagering tanks (l, n and p). As it passes from one tank to the next, it is filtered (m and o). (Credit: Eric Mose, Jr.)

News of his decision stunned the Piel family. Within days, Henry wrote brother Paul demanding to know why stockholders had not been advised about the brewery's "precarious position." After that "impromptu meeting," Henry now demanded Paul call "an official meeting of the Michael Piel Holding Corp., in order that we may *all* be informed about the affairs of the business."[39] But Paul ignored this request, avoiding any formal gathering that would constrain the room for maneuvers in small groups that were his forte.

In November 1960, Henry's son Mike Piel, now a director of the holding company, met with Muessen at the plant for an unfiltered view of Piel's prospects. Afterward, Mike reported, "competition with large breweries will be overwhelming" and the "future of the brewery is very dark." Moreover, the firm's long-standing "product superiority" had, Mike said, been lost from the current "product difficulty." Muessen now admitted "his failure to recognize the fact that [the brewmaster] Mr. [Fred J.] Draeger was not doing a good job," but was reluctant to remove him since doing so "would have been an admission to other brewers that we did, in fact, have product difficulties." Skillfully shifting the blame, Muessen said that had the family "refrained from taking dividends the first few years after repeal [back in 1933] . . . Piels could now be as big as Busch." Looking forward, Muessen felt the only salvation lay in the brewery's sale at a minimal price of $7.5 million. Reiterating Paul's constant message, Muessen advised that the Piel family "should not panic and start taking up the strings of remote control." Mulling all this over, young Mike agreed with his father Henry and aunt Louise that a "trial in the quality market," with a new brewmaster who could make "a really fine beer," a craftsman's brew, was still an alternative to sale or merger.[40]

While this painful family conversation continued, profits plunged from a peak of $1.2 million in 1955 to just $86,000 in 1960.[41] That November, Louise wrote nephew Gerard Piel faulting Muessen's decision to sell just at the moment when "the industry is on the threshold of a substantial expansion of its market." Instead of selling out, she advocated merger with the dynamic Western brewer Falstaff.[42]

Simultaneously, her son Fred Lange wrote his uncle Paul expressing strong reservations about Muessen's management. Fred remarked wryly that construction of the new office building proved Parkinson's law that "plant efficiency is inversely proportional to front office grandeur"—that is, the bigger the executive offices the poorer the product. Until a new director with technical expertise was found, an inspection by Henry Piel could, Fred said, provide an objective assessment of plant conditions.[43]

Through all these difficulties, however, Paul remained Muessen's ardent, adamant defender. Responding to nephew Fred Lange in late November, Paul suppressed the derision he had directed at his own siblings. The brewmasters, Fred Draeger and Fred Riedel, seemed to Paul "very much on the ball" and were doing their best under trying circumstances. With Piels' current break-even point climbing to 81 percent of retail price, only "a slight reduction in volume spells TROUBLE." Once the brewery was sold, said Paul with genuine insight, investing the proceeds in a new mutual fund offered a way to both minimize the capital gains tax and gain the "expert guidance" needed for reliable returns. He dismissed the idea of putting some "chemical handyman" on the board. But he agreed that an inspection by brother Henry, their former technical director, could offer Muessen a valuable "appraisal of brew house operations."[44]

Fired by one brother (William) and derided by another (Paul), Henry was not about to play white knight, riding in to find fault with the work of successors whose damage was already done. Instead, Henry and son Mike tested sample brews up in Maine and mailed Muessen their results. Writing from his sheep farm that December, Mike found two cans of Piels stamped 0266 "distinctly off-flavored" with "a very fine suspension of particles" when studied in strong light. In reply, Muessen excused those cans as some of "the spotty brews with which we experienced some difficulties" in late summer. When Henry reported bad beer in his "blindfold tests" of more recent Piel's batches, Muessen still insisted "we have at least recovered substantially from our position of last summer insofar as quality of product is concerned."[45]

Throughout this crisis over quality, Muessen responded to every Piel complaint by saying small problem, problem solved, anything to keep the stockholders at bay. But millions of beer drinkers thought otherwise. The beer's quality had been sliding for at least five years throughout the famed Bert and Harry campaign until it hit rock bottom with that distasteful haze in the summer of 1960. With Muessen stonewalling and Paul manning the battlements to repel stockholders, the company, caught in a transition from familial to corporate management, could continue unchecked on its downward plunge.

Instead of addressing the critical issue of beer quality, Muessen, ever the salesman, ordered "changes in label design and advertising," while launching a million-dollar media campaign to promote the company's new low-calorie beer sold under their Trommer's label. In his press release of August 1961, Muessen announced "a truly new and different beer product . . . the first truly low calorie beer ever made!" He hailed this diet drink as an innovation comparable to "Coca Cola in the beverage field, Ford in automobiles, and Jello in dessert products."[46]

Table 10.1: Piel's Production, Income, Profit (Loss), and Dividends, 1933–1961

Year	Barrels	Income	Profit (Loss)	Dividends
1933	147,229	$256,075	$220,865	$ -0-
1934	230,279	432,777	373,270	400,800
1935	238,263	263,506	237,544	118,400
1936	287,582	451,225	343,637	140,000
1937	319,309	285,516	220,516	91,000
1938	287,368	254,409	212,409	84,000
1939	296,038	272,828	225,397	112,000
1940	292,194	184,767	142,249	98,000
1941	299,946	258,943	181,869	119,000
1942	346,593	454,019	122,574	112,000
1943	423,515	700,327	164,142	126,000
1944	532,225	960,872	270,000	126,000
1945	518,636	882,573	273,008	126,000
1946	468,094	1,432, 915	888,914	238,000
1947	554,615	1,588,613	986,236	301,000
1948	539,159	1,545,546	958,239	315,000
1949	516,917	827,384	502,384	315,000
1950	706,393	1,678,397	918,397	315,000
1951	985,339	1,646,222	751,222	351,400
1952	1,041,604	1,562,604	757,104	348,600
1953	1,204,800	1,965,260	815,260	390,600
1954	1,210,127	1,519,113	1,108,113	390,600
1955	1,182,615	836,185	1,161,185	390,600
1956	1,208,434	1,576,408	929,408	390,600
1957	1,283,695	1,903,939	923,939	390,600
1958	1,264,448	1,372,001	664,001	390,600
1959	1,321,293	1,542,365	740,365	390,600
1960	1,202,196	245,409	(107,409)	229,600
1961	1,077,367	927,279	(494,279)	37,800

Source: Meeting of Board of Directors, February 1, 1934, Piel Bros. Minutes Book No. 3; Piel Bros. 1933–1960, enclosure in H. O. Diesl, letter to Alfred M. McCoy, Jr., November 9, 1960, Margarita Piel McCoy Papers; M. & G. Piel Securities, Inc., Condensed Statements of Profit and Loss, Years 1943 Through 1961, Gerard Piel Papers; Piel Bros., *Annual Report 1961* (March 14, 1962).

The industry's reaction was less than celebratory. Brooklyn's most successful brewer, Rudolph J. Schaefer, Jr. thundered his disapproval, calling the new product, "damaging to the brewing industry." Schaefer derided these low-cal brews by Piels and Ballantine as "more like the near beer we used to sell during prohibition days." Muessen struggled to counter this withering blast from an industry titan, insisting that his new low-cal beer was "a naturally brewed product made without artificial flavoring." After less than a year, however, the new brew had proved so unpopular with consumers that Piels' management was wondering "whether the product should be taken off the market."[47] By the end of the dismal year that was 1961, sales, stuck at 1.2 million barrels for the past seven years, suddenly took a 10 percent plunge.[48]

Sales and profits for the first half of 1962 continued their downward course, forcing Muessen into makeshift measures until the brewery could be merged or sold. That March, management found the sales figures for 1961 so grim they marked the company's annual report "Confidential" and restricted its distribution to a handful of company officers. After climbing steadily from 520,000 barrels in 1945 to a peak of 1.3 million in 1959, Piels' sales had started a precipitous, two-year plunge downward to a bare million barrels by 1961.[49]

Sale of Piel Bros.

Midst this succession of setbacks, company president Henry Muessen began selling the only thing he had left to sell—the Piel Bros. brewery. By April 1962, Muessen advised counsel Sullivan & Cromwell that negotiations with Drewrys, a mid-sized Indiana brewer, had reached thirteen basic points of agreement, with a signed sales contract expected by June.[50] When June came, Muessen reported talks had overcome "all major obstacles" except for renewal of Piels' labor contract, which would soon be resolved.[51]

Within a month, however, these negotiations encountered "financial snags." Unable to secure sufficient funds in Chicago to complete the purchase, Drewrys' chair Carleton S. Smith "has come east to see what he could land in the Big City" where bankers were suddenly "jittery" after the recent stock market slump. Consequently, Drewrys was now downgrading their offer by proposing to pay just $3 million in cash and the other $3 million in "a subordinate, less secure financial position."[52]

As Drewrys' financing from a consortium of five insurance companies firmed in coming weeks, Piels' counsel Sullivan & Cromwell reviewed the details of their downgraded offer. Instead of paying the full $6 million purchase price up front, Drewrys now proposed to give Piels half in cash and the balance in its own unsecured Class B notes, payable over the next fifteen years at 5.5 percent interest. Even though this commercial paper was not readily negotiable, Sullivan & Cromwell strengthened Piels' position with a clever contract clause stating that Drewrys could not sell any "substantial part of its property without the consent of the noteholders."[53]

On August 22, 1962, eleven members of the Gottfried and Michael Piel families gathered for an "historic" stockholders' meeting at The 60 East Club, a richly appointed establishment on the 26th floor of the Lincoln Building. In a room that seemed to float among midtown Manhattan's skyscrapers, the meeting opened with a review of the contract's main points. Most importantly, the Piels were selling their brewery's $16 million in assets—real estate, machinery, inventory, contracts, trademarks, patents, name, and goodwill—for $6 million, half in cash and half in the buyer's subordinated fifteen-year notes. Then Muessen took the floor, explaining that if the Piel family wished to reject this purchase offer and continue to brew beer on their own, they would have to inject new capital and "forego dividends for several years."[54]

After waiters served "an excellent meal" beneath glass chandeliers, the meeting reached a consensus that "the proposed contract contained the best price and terms available." As the two family trusts withdrew for deliberations at separate tables, Gerard Piel, seconded by uncle Henry Piel, moved "that the Michael Piel Holding Company hereby . . . authorizes the sale by Piel Bros., to Drewrys Limited." As Henry then moved to adjourn, "thus ended an historic occasion in the life of this Corporation." The minutes showed the time as 2:10 p.m.[55]

At the closing on October 1, Drewrys Limited completed the purchase with the payment of $2,658,000 in cash and $3,000,000 in those Class B subordinated notes.[56] A month later, Drewrys, through its new subsidiary Piel Bros., Inc., satisfied the million-dollar mortgage that Gottfried and Michael Piel had signed with the Kings County Trust Company back in 1898.[57] After nearly eighty years of operations spanning three generations, Piel Bros. became another of the hundreds of family-owned breweries bought out by larger firms. Within a year, a real estate developer bought the Ruppert's Manhattan brewery, and a year after that the Liebmann family sold Rheingold and its Brooklyn plant to Pepsi-Cola United Bottlers.[58]

The silence over these hush-hush negotiations was soon broken when the *New York Times* reported, in early September, that Drewrys Ltd. had purchased

Piels for an estimated price "between $8,000,000 and $10,000,000," creating America's ninth-biggest brewery with combined production of 3 million barrels—smaller than Schaefer at 3.5 million barrels but larger than Rheingold at 2.9 million. While the actual sale price of just $6 million made the deal far less lucrative for shareholders than the *Times* imagined, Muessen himself did very nicely—winning a seat on the Drewrys board, serving as president of their new Piel's subsidiary, and becoming manager of their Hampden-Harvard division in Massachusetts.[59]

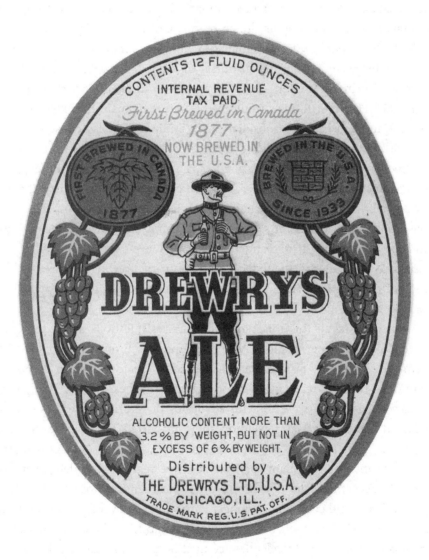

10.1 Label for Drewrys Ale, Chicago, Illinois, post-Prohibition.

Within weeks, however, the new owners made decisions that raised serious questions about Muessen's past management. Just two weeks after Drewrys took control, the Young & Rubicam offices on Madison Avenue announced that cartoon characters Bert and Harry Piel were back, albeit with a twist to address the campaign's key problem. "Last time some of you . . . were laughing at our commercials and not buying our beer," a chastened Bert told television viewers. "Not this time. The free ride is over. All hitch hikers off. This time we have a new theme, 'I'm laughing with a Piels in my hand.'" That campaign would run, with moderate success, for another eighteen months before the company dropped the duo in favor of humorous spots drawn by cartoonist Walt Kelly of *Pogo* fame.[60]

That November, Piels' new management also announced closure of the troubled Staten Island plant and dismissal of all 300 workers, shutting the old Rubsam & Horrmann brewery that had proven so ill-fated since its acquisition back in 1953. Henceforth, Piels would be brewed at its main Brooklyn plant and Drewrys' Hampden-Harvard subsidiary in Willimansett, Massachusetts.[61]

With that sale, Piels had disposed of both breweries purchased in management's earlier rush to raise plant capacity. In effect, the entire expansion strategy, launched by William Piel and sustained by acolyte Henry Muessen, had spent almost $6 million, including $3 million for those two breweries, to double production capacity for sales that never came. Not only was the expansion redundant, but it was also distracting, perhaps even damaging. After these acquisitions, Piels' management faced the strain of brewing at three different plants, two of them badly antiquated, possibly contributing to that fatal slide in the beer's quality.

More broadly, all this mismanagement raises questions about the quality of the company's modernization. After the repeal of Prohibition in the 1930s, William Piel, backed by brother Paul, had tried to create a modern corporation by purging his kin and replacing them with professional executives. Though these latter-day Piel brothers were forceful advocates of reform, their very presence constrained the managerial revolution they purported to promote. Since the family's stockholders were by then remote from the company's management, there was no restraint when William spent his last five years as president in de facto retirement, delegating daily operations to an amanuensis whose chief asset was loyalty. In this hybrid company, no longer familial but not yet fully corporate, that loyal acolyte Henry Muessen was promoted beyond his skill set to preside over the company's demise midst relentless competition. And as sad as all that might seem, the Piel family's own fault-finding over their brewery's fate was even sadder.

Recriminations

Reflecting the family dynamics that blocked an effective response to their firm's decline, the brewery's sale sparked a new round of recriminations. Only days after the deal with Drewrys was finalized on October 1, 1962, Paul began lobbying the directors of the family's new M&G Piel Securities Corporation to award Henry Muessen a hefty finder's fee of $60,000 for his "splendid achievement" of selling the brewery.[62]

Disagreeing sharply, Paul's older brother Henry expressed surprise "that you consider inviting Henry Muessen to serve with the new company, which is strictly a Piel family affair," adding he did not think a bonus appropriate since the man had already been paid "to do the best job he could for Piel Bros. in every respect." During the brewery's last months when stockholders received no dividends, the president had not suffered any salary reduction. Now the brewery was sold, Henry added pointedly, "our personal incomes are reduced by about 40% when compared with our last dividend years."[63]

Louise wrote Paul a personal note agreeing with Henry's letter "100%." In her view, the "Piel Bros. Board failed in their job. They served for compensation—what did they do for it?" Answering her own question, she returned to the tainted brew, saying: "The quality of our beer, the pride of our parents and family was allowed to deteriorate and our unique and wonderful advertising—the talk of the town where ever it appeared, became identified with a 'bum' beer . . . resulting in complete cessation of dividends to stockholders. The officers and Board, however, I understand, continued to draw their full compensation. After 1½ years of no dividends their solution was—Sale of Piel Bros." Continuing her withering critique, she added: "It was the responsibility of the Board to watch, above all, over the quality of the product and to keep in close touch. In this they failed. Piels should be where Schlitz, Pabst, Schaefer are today."[64]

In reply, Paul minimized the spoilage of their beer, both its duration and impact, in a bid to exculpate management, particularly his friend Muessen. "I too believe that 'bum beer' played a part in our downward slide," he seemingly agreed before subverting that same point. "But I do not believe that it was a major part. The slide began *before* we had the bad beer!" Insisting that tainted brew was a common problem, Paul recalled "the sight of the foam on the East River, visible from the Manhattan Bridge, where it passes close to the brewery, when Schaefer dumped . . . over 40,000 barrels of bad beer." In Muessen's defense, Paul reminded Louise that their brother Henry, when technical director, "had his occasional product problems." Even their father Michael had once returned from a hunting trip to find the beer had "a disgusting, musty aftertaste. [Conrad] Boss, whom father had himself trained and installed as brewmaster, had put out the stuff during the several weeks of father's absence." Paul then added, inaccurately: "What corrections were made, I do not know, but they did *not* include firing Boss." And in a sad commentary on their generation, he added: "We must face the fact that only a few of the M. Piels and *none* of the G. Piels—all in their sixties and seventies—had either the resources or the reckless pride to stick it out."[65]

Renewing his case for that $60,000 finder's fee, Paul told his sister that Henry Muessen "did a magnificent job of negotiation during one of the worst stockmarket periods in years . . . A finder's fee, which I hear has already won G. Piel approval . . . is something we all ought to be able to fork up with a smile!"[66]

M&G Piel Securities

Slowly, however, Paul's move to reward Muessen was pushed aside as the family made a wrenching shift from brewing beer to managing money. To invest their $6 million from the sale of the brewery, the dozen Piels heirs agreed to form a new company, M&G Piel Securities, that would operate like a closed-end mutual fund, managing both the Drewrys debentures and a new portfolio of common stocks purchased with the $3 million in cash from the brewery's sale. Again, the Piel family's experience mirrored a major trend in the country's social history.

Once the exclusive domain of the wealthy, the stock market, starting in the 1950s, gained millions of middle-class investors who moved their savings into so-called mutual funds that allowed affordable access to expert management and diversified portfolios. From just 161 mutual funds with assets worth $17 billion in 1960, this sector would swell a thousandfold by 2013 to 17,000 funds managing $17 *trillion*, representing 22 percent of all U.S. household financial assets. By the start of the twenty-first century, nearly a hundred million Americans had—through pensions, 401(k) accounts, and mutual funds—entrusted their financial future to the stock market.[67] Throughout all this change, M&G Piel Securities, as a small family fund with skilled management, would generally outperform the market.

As the euphoria from their brewery's successful sale faded, the Piel heirs began to confront the complexities of money management. Their first problem was finding an expert financial adviser. Keen to manage the Piel millions, Grace

Bank's chief economist, Dr. Hermann K. Scheyhing, gave Paul and Bill Piel a tour of his unit in October 1962, showing off his "economic charts that covered Europe, Canada, and South America, as well as the U.S.A." Impressed by the "immense amount of work done with Germanic thoroughness," Paul was rapturous at the way Scheyhing's tables "focus not on the bare statistics but on its derivative, that is on the shifting *rates* at which growth or decline deviates from the waxing or waning of Dow Jones"—and doing so not by "using the logarithmic chart paper, as one might expect," but by plotting "the log of his data upon paper ruled in elongated rectangles at equal intervals, the color of the graph line, red or blue, indicating negative or positive acceleration."[68]

Reviewing the first balance sheet of M&G Piel Securities that month, Michael Piel's heirs found these assets of $6.8 million produced a severe reduction in their dividends since half the brewery's sale price had been paid in those Drewrys low-yield debentures.[69] More broadly, the Piels would struggle, over the next four years, 1962 to 1966, for solutions to three overlapping problems: building a portfolio of profitable investments; liquidating the $3 million in those Drewrys Class B debentures; and merging three redundant family holding companies into a single, viable corporation.

At the first meeting of M&G Piel Securities in December 1962, the directors agreed, after comparing offers from four New York banks, that Grace Bank should manage its stock trades.[70] With his supple econometric methods, Dr. Scheyhing soon solved their first problem with purchase of common stocks that produced impressive returns. At the close of their first full year in March 1964, chairman Muessen announced that, by following Scheyhing's counterintuitive stock trades, the firm had made a gross profit of $281,000 for 1963 that, combined with a tax credit for the brewery's earlier losses, allowed "the largest dividends ever in the history of Piel Bros." In so doing, the board met the insistent demand of director Leonard Lazarus that his clients, the aging, childless Gottfried Piels, should "at long last, be able to maintain that standard of living to which they felt entitled." The ever-cautious counselor Tashof, representing the Michael Piels who had heirs to consider, still grumbled about this dividend being "no small invasion of surplus" that would diminish their assets' long-term appreciation.[71] Over the next two years, however, these tensions dissipated as the value of the firm's common stocks grew by 40 percent and the overall Piel portfolio swelled to an impressive $7.6 million despite payment of these generous dividends.[72]

Yet all this success could not correct the new company's underlying structural weakness. With $3 million tied up in those second-class Drewrys bonds, the

M&G Piel board faced the immediate problem of low yield and the longer-term risk of a complete, crippling loss. Consequently, chairman Muessen had "a casual chat" with Drewrys' current president, "who smilingly proposed buying back our . . . Class B debentures at a 25% discount, only to be told laughingly, that 3% would be a more likely figure."[73]

After the Piel's board voted in June 1965 to sell the Drewrys' paper, even at a heavy discount if necessary, chairman Muessen, ever the skilled salesman, rose to the challenge. Spurning an offer from Drewrys to repurchase their $3 million debt at a punitive 22 percent discount, Muessen learned that its chairman "was pinning his hopes of arresting the company's decline in profits . . . on a merger with the . . . successful and growing Associated Brewing of Detroit"—a merger that M&G Piel could block by a "judicious use of our veto power" written into the terms of their brewery's sale. To bait this trap, Piels solicited an offer to purchase their Drewrys notes from Banker's Life Insurance Co. of Miami. Suddenly, there was a barrage of panicky phone calls from Drewrys, now determined "to be rid of the hampering veto powers" of these Piels' debentures by buying back its debt. Instead of a 25 or even 22 percent discount, Drewrys accepted a modest markdown of just 6 percent—thereby increasing Piels' income from this sale by a solid $530,000.[74]

But the M&G Piel board found it far more difficult to resolve the last of their problems by untangling the family's three interlocking holding companies. After some thirty years of managing their brewery shares through two trusts, the Michael Piel and Sophie Piel corporations, the family had been forced to add a third such company, M&G Piel Securities, to serve as legal successor for the Piel Bros. brewery, thereby attracting double taxation.[75] When the M&G Piel board decided, in June 1966, to proceed with consolidation, Sullivan & Cromwell's top tax expert, Robert J. McDonald, persuaded the IRS that this merger of the three Piel firms "constitutes a 're-organization' exempt from Federal Income Tax."[76]

With the tax matter resolved, directors of both the Michael Piel and Sophie Piel trusts met that December at the Bankers Club in lower Manhattan to effect the merger of their three corporations into a single, unified firm—M&G Piel Securities, Inc. By this time, the family was at the cusp of a major generational transition. On the Gottfried Piel side, four of his five heirs were now deceased, sole survivor Sophia was 80, and none had biological children. On the Michael Piel side, five of the seven siblings were still alive, but all had begun assigning shares to their heirs, most of whom already had children of their own. In striking contrast to the wrangling that had roiled the family business for the past eighty years, this complex merger was accomplished with absolute unanimity, setting the family's mutual fund in its final form for the next half-century.[77]

Corporate Afterlife

For decades after the brewery's sale in 1962, Piels' beer lived on in a spectral corporate afterlife—a brand without a brewery, a brew without a brewmaster, and the Piel name without the Piel family. Under the terms of the buyout, the Piels had sold their history, persona, and images along with the physical plant.

"It all started over 80 years ago, when the Brooklyn Bridge was brand new," read a Piel's beer advertisement of February 1964. "Gottfried Piel had recently come over from Germany . . . the tiny Landser Brewery [sic] in the section of Brooklyn known as East New York was for sale . . . He wrote his brother Michael, a young brewmaster still living in Germany. 'Don't buy any brewery,' Michael wrote back, 'until I check the water.' Michael Piel sailed the ocean and . . . was delighted with sparkling artesian well water."[78] A month later, this family saga continued in a second advertisement: "Michael . . . was fanatical about the beer he was making . . . and the word soon spread of the terrific lager beer."[79]

In its final chapter, this commercial fable added a domestic dimension. "Maria Piel was Michael's wife, and a terrific cook," read the newspaper copy. "Her marinated herring was the best. On weekends farmers used to come from miles around on bicycles, to . . . eat and drink the good lager beer. Michael once asked her, 'Are they coming here for my beer or your herring?' 'Both dear,' was Maria's strategic reply."[80]

With Germany now a close Cold War ally, this fictional celebration of the family's ethnic roots apparently worked. In October, the president of the newly formed Piel Bros., Inc., Thomas Hawkes, announced that sales for 1964 were already up by nearly 20 percent.[81] The romanticized real Piels could evidently sell indifferent beer better than their cartoon facsimiles, Bert and Harry.

But not even the cleverest advertising could save New York's brewing industry from the relentless pressure of consolidation. In 1960, the New York metropolitan region was still the country's brewing capital, producing 18 million barrels, more than a fifth of the nation's output. And half of those 18 million barrels were brewed in Brooklyn.[82]

Change came with almost stunning speed. The U.S. brewing industry sold a record 122 million barrels in 1970 and per capita consumption was up to

18.7 gallons, close to the pre-Prohibition peak of 21 gallons. But the big five brands now controlled over 50 percent of U.S. production. Of the 700 breweries that opened after Prohibition's repeal in 1933, only 65 remained by 1972. Midst this ceaseless concentration, Drewrys was acquired by the Associated Brewing Co. of Detroit not long after its purchase of Piels. By buying up well-known regional beers such as Jacob Schmidt of St. Paul, Hampden-Harvard Brewing of Massachusetts, and Piels, Associated became the country's tenth biggest brewer in 1970 with sales of 3.7 million barrels. After five years of successful operations, however, Associated's profits slumped and management began selling off its brands, offering the Piels label, unsuccessfully, to Rheingold. Finally, on September 20, 1973, Associated's successor firm closed the Piels' East New York plant and dismissed all 350 employees. They also sold the corporate name to Brooklyn's Schaefer Brewing, which announced that Piels would henceforth be brewed, under its original formula, at its new plant in Allentown, Pennsylvania.[83]

During the collapse of Brooklyn's brewing industry in the 1970s, Piels' original Liberty Avenue plant was demolished, reducing Michael Piel's model factory to what beer historian Will Anderson called "a square block of nothing but rubble." At this writing, those ruins have been paved over to become a parking lot for yellow school buses.[84]

From a peak of forty-eight breweries in 1898, there were now just two breweries left in Brooklyn, indeed in all of New York City. In January 1976, these last two, Rheingold and Schaefer, both closed, leaving the city without a brewery for the first time in over 300 years. Management shuttered Rheingold's Bushwick brewery after 122 years of operations, saying they could save $1.6 million in utilities by shifting production to Orange, New Jersey. City Council president Paul O'Dwyer, the labor lawyer who once led the 1948–49 beer strikes, now said using the Rheingold plant for deliveries was the best that could be expected.[85]

A week later, Schaefer came to similar conclusions about the prohibitive costs of brewing in New York City, firing all 850 Brooklyn workers and moving production to its Pennsylvania plant. The president of the United Brewery Workers blamed Schaefer's management, saying: "Of the top five officers . . . all but one came directly from the financial community with a background only in bottom lines."[86]

Ignored amid all this finger pointing was the logistics underlying the end of brewing in New York City. As breweries started shipping nationwide via roads not rails, Brooklyn had become a logistical dead-end in the age of long-distance trucking.[87] Once trucks replaced rail after World War II, New York breweries had to fight Manhattan's gridlocked traffic to approach the Holland Tunnel en route to the Mid-Atlantic states. Or they crawled across Queens to the Whitestone Bridge for New England. By contrast, plants in nearby New Jersey had ready access to national railheads at Newark Bay and on-ramps for the New Jersey Turnpike, which opened in 1951. Thus, a brewery like Ballantines in northern New Jersey, the nation's third largest during the 1950s, could ship quickly and cheaply via tunnel to Manhattan or rail and road to markets nationwide.[88]

The nadir for Brooklyn's famed Brewers' Row was not far off. East New York, home to the Piel brewery, was one of the first areas to plunge deep into poverty. As African Americans quit Southern agriculture and Puerto Ricans fled their island's fading sugar industry, these great waves of migration washed across upper Manhattan and the South Bronx, pushing this human tide out into Brooklyn, particularly into poorer areas such as East New York. After predatory "blockbuster" realtors panicked white homeowners into selling cheap, the area shifted, during the mid-1960s, from 80 percent white to 80 percent African American and Puerto Rican, with 40 percent of all households living in poverty. In this rapid transition, hundreds of small businesses closed, "while churches and synagogues were abandoned, then vandalized and burned." As East New York smoldered from 1,400 fires in 1965 alone and riots broke out between African Americans and Italians in the summers of 1966 and 1967, "shootings, knifings, and gang terror were common." Parallel trends produced similar conditions in Bedford-Stuyvesant, Bushwick, and Brownsville, which, recalled a community planner, became "a completely devastated black ghetto."[89]

On July 13, 1977, a defective transformer knocked out the city's power at 9:40 p.m. Midst the blackout, Bushwick, with 80 percent of its 100,000 residents unemployed, erupted in a devastating night of looting that ended with the biggest mass arrest in the city's history. About a hundred stores and buildings burned, doing $300 million in damage. Four days later, three teenagers set fire to an abandoned factory, incinerating twenty-three buildings along Knickerbocker Avenue, the city's worst single blaze in fifteen years. In the decade that followed, an urban cocktail of entrenched poverty, unemployment, and crack cocaine made much of Bushwick a "wasteland" of abandoned buildings infested with rats and stray dogs.[90]

Reflecting trends in older cities across America, the entire Borough of Brooklyn was rapidly deindustrializing—half the manufacturing jobs lost, the once-great Navy Yard closed, and much of the waterfront abandoned as container shipping shifted to New Jersey. The loading of the world's first containership at

Port Newark in April 1956 marked the start of a revolution in "international waterborne commerce" that slowly emptied much of the Brooklyn waterfront. Across the borough, block after block looked like the "bombed-out communities of wartime."[91]

Along with the South Bronx, Bushwick became what one local legislator called a "virtual sideshow . . . of urban ruin." By the late 1980s, over 1,500 buildings had been burned or abandoned, with the city clearing rubble from entire blocks. During the next twenty years, however, Bushwick began to rebound as the city sponsored construction of 2,386 new residential units, starting with the low-density Hope Gardens where tenants developed "a true sense of community." During the 1990s, the 83rd Precinct, which covered much of Bushwick, reported a steady drop in major crimes, with robberies falling from 2,242 to 700. After clearing the detritus of decades from the Rheingold Brewery's seven acres, the city opened hundreds of apartments and a daycare center on the site by 2003. The director of development for New York's Housing Department, John Liebmann, great-grandson of Rheingold's founder, said this site had once been a refuge for his immigrant family and would be so again "for the residents and owners who move in."[92]

Meanwhile, starting in the 1990s, "urban pioneers in the arts and cultural communities" were moving into Brooklyn from lower Manhattan, first into the Dumbo or Williamsburg areas and then into Greenpoint and Bushwick—raising the latter's population by 8 percent between 2000 and 2010. Brooklyn's ongoing gentrification was reviving Bushwick's businesses and attracting new residents to the district's still affordable housing. By 2015, the transformation was nothing less than remarkable. Apartments in Bushwick were renting for more than somewhat smaller units in the Yorkville section of Manhattan's fashionable Upper East Side.[93] Simultaneously, small- and medium-scale manufacturing, characteristic of Brooklyn from 1850 to 1950, was again flourishing in both Williamsburg and Greenpoint. As these neighborhoods became "hip" and "hot," the consequent gentrification created "demand for custom furniture, high-end food products, fashion and any other number of products"—including beer.[94]

As blocks burned, the rubble cleared, and gentrification followed, the Piel name lived on, sold by Schaefer to Stroh and Stroh to Pabst. At this writing in 2015, Pabst, which no longer owns a brewery and operates solely by marketing heritage brands, still uses the old Piel family name for indifferent low-cost brews, popular with college students and budget shoppers in its former marketing area from Maine to Maryland.[95]

Craft Brewing

While other U.S. breweries and their labels were sold and resold like Piels, the beer industry's consolidation juggernaut continued unchecked. Between 2002 and 2013, two transnational conglomerates invested nearly $200 billion to dominate brewing worldwide. Starting in 2004, the biggest of these multinationals began growing when Belgium's Interbrew merged with Brazil's Ambev to form InBev. Four years later, this multinational spent $52 billion to purchase America's biggest brewer, Anheuser-Busch, which had just acquired one of China's biggest brewers, Harbin. The sum of these mergers was a global brewing giant, now called AB InBev, with $36 billion in annual sales. After a $20 billion merger with the Mexican brewer Grupo Modelo in 2013, AB InBev captured nearly half of the U.S. beer market—surpassing the nation's number one brewer, the London-based SAB Miller. Founded in 2002 when South African Brewery purchased the U.S. brand Miller for $5.6 billion, SAB Miller began buying up breweries around the globe. By 2013, SAB Miller was marketing 200 brands through 70,000 employees in 75 countries with $35 billion in total sales. Together these two conglomerates, AB InBev and SAB Miller, controlled nearly 80 percent of all U.S. beer sales. Two years later, the Brazilian financiers behind AB InBev negotiated a $104 billion merger with SAB Miller to create a corporate giant with 224,000 employees, 400 beer brands worldwide, and up to 49 percent of global beer sales.[96]

But whatever label they might use, the two transnational conglomerates that dominated the U.S. market were brewing beer rated as "awful" by connoisseurs in an era when middle-class Americans were rediscovering food and flavor.[97] So bland did these corporate beers become that craft brewers, known for their commitment to taste, grew from just a dozen in 1980 to over 2,600 by 2014, with 1,500 more in planning stages. While sales of the big brands Budweiser and Miller began slipping, craft breweries achieved double-digit growth to reach a solid 14 percent of U.S. beer production. Driving this sea change in consumer choice, the large "baby boom" generation, born between 1946 and 1964, rejected their parents' preference for processed foods and bland beverages as they came of age during the 1970s and 1980s. Instead, they embraced the artisan ethos of craft brewing in countless ways—making the *Whole Earth Catalog* and *Diet for a Small Planet* iconic texts; forming food co-ops to promote local produce; embracing the "slow food" movement that resisted the globalization of fast food chains; and favoring small craft or regional breweries for their aura of authenticity.[98]

From the brewer's perspective, the ascent of craft brewing was a triumph of individual dreams over harsh market realities. When Piels was sold back in the early 1960s, there was exactly one craft brewer in the entire United States— Anchor Brewery in San Francisco—and it survived near death only because an investor, Fritz Maytag III, realized its "all malt, hoppy brew" could compete with costly imports. Not only did he devote decades to building Anchor into a profitable company producing 100,000 barrels, but Maytag was a tireless advocate for the trade, sharing his skills with neophyte brewers and giving "spellbinding speeches" about brewing's venerable traditions. But craft brewing did not spread much beyond California until the late 1970s when Congress cut the excise tax for brewers making less than 60,000 barrels and legalized home brewing. By 1984, there were eighteen microbreweries nationwide, including two short-lived New York pioneers, Wm. S. Newman Brewing in Albany and New Amsterdam in Manhattan.[99]

During the next decade, as traditional brewers dropped to just thirty-seven nationwide, craft breweries grew steadily to 537 by 1994. Even the failure of several industry pioneers was somehow an inspiration. Visiting the short-lived New Amsterdam Brewery in Manhattan, two Brooklyn buddies, would-be brewers Steve Hindy and Tom Potter, were awestruck by the "shining copper brewkettles" that gleamed behind a towering wall of glass. Just about the time New Amsterdam was going bankrupt in 1988, Hindy, a journalist who learned home brewing while reporting in the alcohol-free Arab world, persuaded his friend Potter, a banker, to partner in launching their own craft brand, the Brooklyn Brewery. Inspiration came from an accidental meeting with beer historian Will Anderson while jogging in Brooklyn's Prospect Park; $300,000 in capital from friends, family, and a local bank; the formula from notebooks of a long-dead brewer who had worked in Brooklyn circa 1900; the logo from design genius Milton Glaser, creator of the "I Love New York" campaign; the beer from one of the few surviving regional firms, F. X. Matt Brewing upstate in Utica; and a distribution warehouse at the historic Huber-Hittleman Brewery on Meserole Street, once the heart of Brooklyn's Brewers' Row. In this fledgling venture, the past was much more than prologue.[100]

After eight years in business as the "Brooklyn Brewery," Hindy and Potter were selling 11,000 barrels of beer, still brewed under contract by F. X. Matt up in Utica. Sensing their historic borough was on the cusp of a real renaissance, they decided to take a chance by bringing brewing back to Brooklyn. Finally in 1996, twenty years after Piels, Rheingold, and Schaefer had quit the city, these two entrepreneurs risked $2 million to open the actual Brooklyn Brewery inside an abandoned Williamsburg factory, with city Mayor Rudolph Guiliani serving as honorary brewmaster. After a $12 million expansion in 2009, the company increased its production to 216,000 barrels over the next four years, becoming one of the country's top twenty breweries. "But their success story is about more than the birth of a brewery," said Mayor Michael Bloomberg in 2005, "it's about the rebirth of a borough." Brooklyn Brewery, he explained, "helped make Williamsburg hip—sponsoring block parties and music festivals and opening the brewery to tours," thereby helping to transform the area "from a decaying industrial center to a vibrant residential neighborhood."[101]

Such success inspired imitation. Utica's F. X. Matt Brewing, a traditional third-generation brewery founded in 1888, decided to join the craft movement. After losing a million dollars a year producing conventional brews like Utica Club in competition with the big national brands, F. X. Matt, one of the country's few surviving regionals, got back in the black after 1991 by promoting a craft-style "all-malt lager" called Saranac. Over the next twenty years, Matt Brewing grew into the country's fifteenth-biggest brewer, with annual sales of 200,000 barrels. By 2014, New York City was home to a dozen craft breweries, including five in Brooklyn and the small Flagship Brewery on Staten Island, the borough's first brewer since the Piel's plant closed there in the 1960s. Statewide, New York had 165 craft brewers, producing a combined 860,000 barrels with an economic impact worth $2.2 billion.[102]

By brewing and selling in the same city, these craft firms have restored beer's all-important aura of authenticity—that elusive combination of local craftsmanship and the fruits of the land blended into a single glass whose taste evokes a particular place. "The consumer palate has evolved," observed one industry expert, "and is more interested in the flavor nuances and complexities in craft beer styles."[103] In the industry's "125-Year Brewery Count," the history of American brewing thus follows a parabolic curve, with the number of breweries dropping from 2,011 in 1887 to just 89 by 1980, and then rising to 2,403, mostly small craft brewers, by 2012.[104]

In retrospect, the idea that Piel Bros. could survive relentless corporate consolidation by remaining a craft brewer famous for flavor—a vision those dissident siblings Henry, Louise, and Rudolf shared back in the 1950s—was, sadly for the Piel family, a half-century ahead of its time.

11

Third Generation

For my sister, myself, and many of our cousins, the Piel family really starts with our parents, the family's third generation here in America. Great-grandfather Michael and his Brooklyn brewery are only legends, someone and something we only know about from stories told and re-told countless times in the hundred years since his death.

Our grandparents, Michael's children, who were outlandish characters when alive, are also starting to become legends. Even if we met them in childhood, their memory is fading. Now, writing this, I search my memory for some strong sense of my grandfather Rudolf Piel.

Here it is. When I was six, sitting in the passenger seat of his big Buick Roadmaster, Rudolf's right hand reached past my face for the gun in the glove box, flicked open the chamber with the bullets' brass casings inches from my eyes, and steadied the pistol on his wrist, covering his hired man who was warning off poachers, visible through the front window, stealing melons from a field on his Florida ranch. That's not a lot for a man I met many times and admired.

Even his brother Paul, who lived twenty years longer and was omnipresent at family meetings, is starting to fade. Yet you really couldn't forget Paul. When I attended my first meeting of the family business in the late 1970s, Paul told a joke over lunch at Le Chateau Richelieu, one of those fancy Manhattan restaurants he favored. The punch line was in German.

"Uncle Paul," I said, "please translate for the younger generation. We don't speak German."

Suddenly he got serious. He really spoke to me for the first and only time. "Don't you forget," he said, referencing my first book about Asian drug lords, "you couldn't have written that book, figuring out all those details, if you weren't German." And he added, with a back handed slap at my father, "The Irish have humor, they have vitality, but not that sort of mental discipline."

I suddenly felt like the product of a mixed marriage, saved only by a drop of the right blood. Unreal, I thought, two world wars with how many millions dead and here is Paul still proudly German. Everybody in his world is defined by their ethnicity—Irish, German, Chinese—like characters in a Joseph Conrad novel about the British Empire. Even with Uncle Paul right there next to me, he seemed a stranger from another century.

For Piels as actual people, feet on the ground, living in this world, it is my mother and her cousins. They seem to bridge the family's past and present. If Michael died too young, they certainly knew his wife, the matriarch Maria. They summered at the family place on Lake Parlin. They all spoke at least some German. And they lived through all the family fights over the brewery for years, decades even. Yet they moved beyond being German or half-German to live in the here-and-now as fully American.

Somehow, they had unknotted the family's tangled past. They moved beyond their parents' nasty fights. They held dinners and reunions to bring the family back together. Instead of cashing out to live high, they cleaned up the family company and made it an actual business. And they did it all for us, their children and grandchildren, who will never really understand what they did, why they did it, or how difficult it was.

We can never really feel that passionate family pride that made them work so hard to carry some fragment of their past into our present as their gift, their legacy for us, their children and grandchildren. While recording their interviews for this history, I realized, with both sadness and a sense of relief, that these third-generation Piels were the last of the real Piels. They may not have migrated across oceans or built a big business, but their accomplishments were still considerable.

The Cousins

Viewed in purely economic terms, the Piel family's third generation was on a downward slide. The brewery, pride of their parents, was sold. Lavish dividends that had made their elders wealthy were now greatly diminished. Whether working in the family firm or just enjoying its profits, their parents had incomes that placed them comfortably in the country's top one percent. Most of the third generation, by contrast, would spend long working lives building assets for retirement.

Yet in a larger sense, this third generation built upon their elders' most important legacy: not the money, but more lasting attributes of aspiration and ability. If we adopt sterner standards of social benefit rather than monetary reward, the Piel family's third generation seems comparable to its first. Just as Michael and Maria Piel ventured across the Atlantic to build a successful business, so most of their grandchildren aspired to acceptance in America's rigorous middle-class professions. Indeed, several of them did much more, not only entering the professions, but doing so with the family's contrarian spirit that challenged—and changed—these important social institutions.

Among Maria and Michael's fifteen grandchildren, four of these cousins seem to embody their generation's achievement. While his father and uncles were stigmatized as disloyal during World War I, Bill Piel, eldest son of the brewery's president William, parlayed his Harvard law degree into a sensitive War Department post during World War II, preparing top-secret briefings for the president. He then went on to a long, successful career as a corporate litigator.

With little more than a history degree from Harvard and social contacts inherited from his parents, Bill's younger brother Gerard launched a new magazine, *Scientific American*, that both created modern science journalism and challenged the U.S. national security state at the peak of its Cold War powers. Now thoroughly assimilated like most German Americans of his generation, Gerard maneuvered confidently for the capital to sustain his controversial publishing venture. For nearly forty years, his monthly journal offered a sustained critique of U.S. nuclear policy and encouraged scientific dialogue across the Iron Curtain.

Not only was Gerard a prominent publisher, but he also collaborated closely with cousins Margarita Piel McCoy and Frederick Lange in transforming their family's mutual fund, M&G Piel Securities, from a transitory tax haven into a stable foundation for middle-class life. After several decades as a suburban housewife, Margarita earned a graduate degree in her mid-40s. She then rose fast in the male-dominated profession of urban planning, shattering gender stereotypes at every step and becoming the first woman to chair an academic planning department in the United States.[1] In reforming this family mutual fund, Margarita forged a close alliance with her cousin Fred Lange, an MIT-trained engineer who had the skills, fiscal and personal, to manage both family dynamics and market forces. Through their long years of service, these two would move the mutual fund beyond its roots in the old brewery, and beyond its patriarchal ethos, toward a more open, shared management.

Freed from the demands of pursuing careers inside a family business, these four cousins healed the deep divisions from their parents' battles over the brewery, restoring the amity necessary for the survival of their family's mutual fund. In effect, they completed that three-generational cycle common to many family businesses: first, the founders whose long shadow complicates succession; next, an uneasy "sibling partnership" among their children; and, finally, a "cousins' consortium" that struggles to resolve residual tensions.[2]

Individually and collectively, these Piel cousins reveal the demanding requisites for entry into the American middle-class: educational achievement, professional credential, social contribution, and capital accumulation. In its broad outlines, they shared this life experience with millions of immigrant descendants who turned their founders' business—whether brewery, retail shop, or family farm—into credentials, careers, and capital that lodged them securely in the country's middle class. These Piel cousins thus exemplify a major strand in the American tapestry.

But aspects of their achievements also resonate with more particular family traits. Although Gerard embraced the very American aspiration to be a "self-made man," his publishing career was built upon family foundations— grandfather Michael's economic legacy and his parents' social capital. Gerard's emphasis on integrity in his magazine parallels his forebears' quest for quality at their brewery. Like grandfather Michael who came to brewing comparatively late, Gerard and cousin Margarita also demonstrated a parallel pursuit of lifelong learning. And like other Piels, they advanced through an innate confidence in their intellect, resistance to received knowledge, and, above all, an inclination to question authority. There were also some negatives to this family legacy, sometimes manifest in contentious personalities, an ingrained impracticality, and a patrician sense of entitlement. Just as his father William had been the brewery's guiding patriarch, demanding loyalty from siblings and subordinates, so Gerard would show a similar inclination in his later years at the magazine, operating in a patrician manner that fostered conflict inside an impersonal corporation.

City Careers

Since William had been his father Michael's chosen successor at the brewery, and thus invested with the lion's share of its rewards, his children started life advantaged by affluence and social status. While William headed the brewery for forty years, 1912 to 1953, his wife Loretto Scott, daughter of a distinguished Canadian family, labored tirelessly for an entrée into New York high society, winning inclusion in the city's exclusive *Social Register* by 1938.[3] The combination of William's comfortable income and Loretto's social capital gave their six children a wide range of life choices not open to their less affluent cousins.

Acceptance by New York's Anglo aristocracy was a considerable accomplishment for these two outsiders, a German American and a Canadian. But it was, in fact, doubly impressive. Not only were their finances strained, but Loretto was assertive about the family's Catholicism, then disdained by New York's established Anglo-Protestant elite.[4]

From this social promontory, Loretto launched the lives of her six children, all born between 1909 and 1923, by arranging Ivy League educations for her four sons and society marriages for her two daughters. Absent any college or vocational training, marriage became her daughters' default career, making it imperative, from Loretto's perspective, to manage their choices with care.[5] In

11.1. William Piel at the wedding of his daughter Mary to William Ward, Salisbury, Connecticut, 1937. (Photo by David Berns, New York)

April 1937, the *New York Times* published an elegant Bachrach Studio portrait of Miss Mary Scott Piel above the news of her "betrothal" to William E. Ward, scion of a prominent Westchester County family. The groom was grandson of the long-serving Republican Party boss, William Lukens Ward, famed for ruling the county as "a benevolent despot" from an estate called Ward Castle. In due course, the groom would become the fourth-generation president of the family firm, Russell, Burdsall & Ward Bolt & Nut Company.[6]

A year later, Loretto arranged a marriage for her younger daughter Rita to Hobson Brown, heir to a fifth-generation banking fortune, at St. Patrick's Cathedral in New York. For denizens of the *Social Register*, the groom's pedigree was impeccable. Several generations had built Brown Brothers into one of the nation's premier investment banks, from its founding at Philadelphia in 1818 to its merger into Brown Brothers Harriman in 1931. The groom's grandfather had been a lifelong "gentleman of leisure." His father was similarly renowned in Philadelphia society as a big-game hunter, captain of the Bryn Mawr Polo Club, and an early aviation enthusiast who died in 1916 when his biplane crashed into the Delaware River.[7]

Though they were more independent, Loretto also managed proper society unions for three of her four sons, with each bride's distinguished Anglo lineage duly reported in the society pages of the *New York Times*—starting with Bill in 1934, next Gerard following his graduation from Harvard in 1937, and, after wartime service with the Marines, their youngest son David while a student at Yale.[8]

These society weddings into wealthy families secured their sisters' futures. But this conventional path did not work for Loretto's sons, whose marriages, once the bedrock of New York society, soon ended in divorce. With a small inheritance and no interest in a career at the brewery, all would have to make their way in competitive, middle-class professions—law, medicine, journalism, and advertising.

Although they winced at their mother's relentless social climbing, these connections were still useful for the three sons who pursued careers in and around New York. As a first step up the social ladder, William and Loretto took care to provide their sons with educations that combined intellectual rigor and social cachet, starting with their eldest William, Jr., known as Bill. Admitted to Princeton with the class of 1932, he raised his grades from C to A– over the next four years, allowing him to graduate with honors and a rank of 182 in a class of 460—sufficient for admission to Harvard Law School. Although he had to work selling student laundry contracts to pay his tuition, Bill Piel still graduated from

Harvard in 1935 in the top 10 percent of his law class, winning the distinction of *cum laude*.[9]

During Thanksgiving break in his last year at law school, Bill Piel, already married with a child on the way, came to New York in search of badly needed employment. Through personal contacts, he interviewed at Sullivan & Cromwell, was hired on the spot, and worked there for the next forty-five years, becoming partner in 1946 and the firm's senior litigator for many years before his retirement in 1980. During World War II, he was appointed, through his contacts to Colonel Alfred McCormack, senior partner in another top New York law firm, as chief of the order of battle section in the Special Branch of the Military Intelligence Service. Bill's duties included preparing the daily briefings for the president and secretary of war. He also led analysts in exploiting the super-secret Anglo-American code breaking, the Ultra and Magic programs, for intelligence coups such as pinpointing Japan's main aviation gasoline plant for bombardment. These duties required the "highest security classification" and won him the War Department's Medal for Exceptional Civilian Service—a striking contrast with the second-generation Piels who had been blacklisted as subversives during World War I.[10]

Returning to Sullivan & Cromwell after the war, Bill Piel became a formidable anti-trust litigator, defending top corporations such as Ford Motor Company and General Electric. This service won him a seat on the boards of several Fortune 500 corporations, Campbell Soup, Phillips Petroleum, and others.[11] In sum, Bill Piel—with social standing, strong education, and incisive intellect—rose fast within that nexus of corporations, state security, and New York society that defined, in mid-century America, the nation's power elite.

William and Loretto's fourth child Gerard also found the family's social connections critical in launching his career as a science writer and publisher. Ironically, Gerard avoided science in both high school and college, instead devoting himself to language and history. At the start of his last term at Andover Academy in February 1933, the headmaster advised Gerard's father about his possible "failures in German, Physics, and French—three very serious courses." Within a week, William wrote his son that this performance was "absolutely unpardonable." Though insisting that Gerard cut back on extracurriculars, William made an exception for wrestling, understanding its importance to his son's identity. Gerard soon raised those midterm Fs to final Bs. But he still failed to graduate because he refused to take algebra, instead adding French to his mastery of Latin and German.[12]

After Princeton rejected him, Gerard was admitted to Harvard on the strength of his Scholastic Aptitude Test scores (709 out of 800 in the Verbal Section), an endorsement from Andover's headmaster ("good brain . . . curious about many things"), and a glowing reference from the Piels' family doctor Armin St. George ("intelligent, alert, loyal, generous almost to a fault, strictly honest").[13]

At Harvard, Gerard continued to avoid all math and hard science. Instead, he studied the sociology of science with his tutor Robert K. Merton, a pioneer in this nascent field, also gaining an informed introduction to Durkheim, Weber, and Marx—readings that left him "completely immunized to the infantile attraction to the Communist Party that attracted so many of my contemporaries." During his last two years, he focused on history to the exclusion of almost all else, graduating Phi Beta Kappa and *magna cum laude* with a 130-page honor's thesis on "The Formation of the Parti Socialiste."[14] In a sweep through French history from the Paris Commune to World War I, Gerard explored how the socialists, exemplified by Jean Jaurès, used Marxian dialectics as "a method of understanding the historical evolution and a spring for action to hasten its course," thereby negotiating an age made dangerous by industry, imperialism, and militarism.[15]

Through this study, Gerard would later draw parallels with his own age made even more dangerous by the clash of nuclear-armed superpowers. He was determined that he too could somehow mitigate the chance of conflict, but without the bullet that found Jaurès. By studying the career of this famed reformer who resisted France's entry into World War I, Gerard learned how he might insert himself into his own historical present, locate an Archimedean lever for change, and then lift the orb, by degrees, in that promising direction. Outside the classroom, he was on the college wrestling team for all four years, learning that sport's close-in competitiveness. During his college days as well, he worked summers at the *Brooklyn Daily Eagle* and *The Herald* in North Dakota, gaining both tuition money and the skills needed for his future career as an editor and publisher. He was later self-deprecating about the limits of this liberal education, calling his History B.A. "a certificate, *magna cum laude*, of illiteracy in science." Yet this historical training gave him both an understanding of science's role in society and an ability to discern issues of long-term import for analysis or activism.[16]

Upon graduation from Harvard in 1937, Gerard failed the test for an editorial post at *Fortune* magazine. Instead, he found work as an office boy in the J. Stirling Getchell advertising agency because "Mr. Getchell had great ambitions to get the Piel brewery account." Fortuitously, Getchell soon launched his short-lived *Picture Magazine*, giving Gerard both his first experience as a reporter and a pretext for asking Connecticut neighbor Ralph Ingersoll, then vice-president of Time-Life publications, to get him a job at *Life* as an office boy.[17] There he was soon plucked from the pool of proofreaders to become the magazine's science editor for the next six years "because they wanted someone who knew nothing about science." Through this collaboration with scientists, Gerard sensed their interest in a popular medium that could educate the public about science.[18]

This experience also introduced him to the political issue that became his life's work. Reporting for *Life* in 1943–44, Gerard heard whispers about a top-secret weapons project. His search for the truth behind this secrecy was prompted, ironically, by a telegram from the wartime Office of Censorship warning the magazine that certain topics, such as "atomic energy," "critical mass," and "uranium," were now classified. "I took that telegram as a reading list," Gerard recalled. His next insight came when censors terminated his interview with physicist Albert O. C. Nier at the University of Minnesota. On assignment from *Life*, Gerard was in the midst of "photographing an elegant demonstration of the mass spectrometer" when the professor abruptly terminated their collaboration "for reasons he could not discuss." This incident told Gerard the censors "were taking mass spectrometry seriously as a method of distinguishing the U238 from the U235"—the form of uranium used for nuclear fission. For his next clue, Gerard first heard the name "Manhattan Project" whispered one night "in the middle of a deserted . . . street" by a procurement agent for the Canadian embassy, his future partner Donald H. Miller, Jr. Even Canada could not compete with this mysterious project for certain strategic war materials.[19]

But the real epiphany came in 1944 during an interview with physicist Robert W. Wood at Johns Hopkins University. Gerard was doing a story about the German discovery of the conical "shaped-charge" that had punctured the armor of Allied tanks during the battle for North Africa. Coincidentally, Wood was quietly fuming that this mysterious Manhattan Project was placing heavy orders for his replica diffraction gratings, needed for spectroscopic research, but refused him any information about their actual use. "He tells me," Gerard recalled, " 'By golly, I figured out what it is for. They're engaged in making the most frightful weapon.' " Wood had also intuited a key principle being used to build the atomic bomb. Using the same physics that propelled the German armor-piercing shell, a nuclear shaped-charge, Wood explained, "offered the surest way, by implosion, to assemble and hold the critical mass of fissionable material in place for the split instant of its explosion." Hoping that the press might stop this "reckless and criminal" project, the physicist added: "These fools don't know what they're doing. They're going to destroy mankind, they're going to destroy all life on earth. They can make a fine explosive. But they're forgetting about the aftermath of it, and the poisoning of the ground . . . with radioactive elements."[20]

Launching *Scientific American*

Realizing the "Age of the Atom" was dawning, Gerard spoke with several close colleagues at *Life* about his idea for a new publication that could somehow tame these weapons. "I was just then in the process of retiring from the employ of Henry R. Luce," whose hard-right political turn Gerard found troubling, "and about to go out in the big world to learn how to start a business working for Henry J. Kaiser." Joining this industrialist as an aide in January 1945, Gerard saw how his fusion of capital and state power had raised whole shipyards on the shores of San Francisco Bay. After the atomic bombing of Hiroshima and Nagasaki that August, Gerard felt an acute need for an independent medium to restrain the capacity of science and government, once joined, for unchecked destruction. "I am forever grateful to Henry Kaiser," said Gerard, "for learning how to read a balance sheet, learning how to run a cash flow statement, and also being a close eyewitness to . . . seeing a man raise 20 million dollars in 24 hours."[21]

Not long after Gerard quit Kaiser in early 1946 to search for start-up capital, his plans for a new magazine hit what seemed an insurmountable barrier. Sensing the atomic bomb had whetted the public's appetite for science, McGraw-Hill, the world's largest publisher of trade magazines, launched *Science Illustrated*. Hearing that news, Gerard and his partners realized they could not compete and shelved their own plans. But when the first issue of *Science Illustrated* appeared in April 1946 with seemingly solid sales of 150,000 copies, they greeted its arrival "with glee." To their discerning eyes, the new journal had a populist "gee whiz" approach that would soon alienate any serious scientific readership. After the inevitable swimsuit cover appeared that July with a "buxom young lady reclining provocatively on the beach," Gerard resumed his search for funding "with gusto."[22]

In the view of Gerard and his partners, their new magazine's real market would be found among expert laymen, scientists, and engineers, who needed to read outside their own narrow fields. And if nuclear weapons were too dangerous to be left in the hands of government, then perhaps these scientists could, if they had a collective voice, check the threat of thermonuclear holocaust. To become a vehicle for informed communication, first in America and then on both sides of the Iron Curtain, this new magazine would have to be financially independent—free from the pressures and inducements that government could bring to bear upon large, diversified publishers such as Henry Luce at Time-Life. A more focused publication, grounded in the scientific community, could, Gerard felt, have genuine editorial independence.[23]

His partners in launching this risky venture were two men who would remain close colleagues for the next forty years, *Life* buddy Dennis Flanagan and an old New York friend, Donald H. Miller, Jr., a seasoned business manager. An older mentor, lawyer Leo Gottlieb, drew up a prospectus and then took the three young partners to lunch with Lessing Rosenwald, the former chair of Sears Roebuck, at the Harmonie Club in midtown Manhattan. After Rosenwald perused the prospectus and committed $250,000, the three partners were "walking down Fifth Avenue about three feet off the ground, saying . . . we were actually going to carry this dream off." Under the terms of their incorporation, 60 percent of shares were reserved for investors and the balance was divided among the principals—15 percent for Gerard as publisher, 7.5 percent each for Miller as general manager and Flanagan as editor, and the last 10 percent for future employees.[24]

Through his New York social connections, Gerard raised an initial $450,000 by 1947 from leading venture capitalists: John Hay Whitney, publisher of the *New York Herald Tribune*; publishing tycoon Marshall Field III; industrialist Henry Kaiser; presidential adviser Bernard Baruch; and former General Electric president Gerard Swope. These funds were just enough to relaunch the venerable but now moribund *Scientific American* magazine as the vessel for Gerard's vision, just as Henry Luce had once bought the old *Life* to start his new photo magazine. Although Gerard paid just $40,000 for a famous name that had first appeared in 1845, he would need another million dollars to bring his new magazine into the black—funds he secured slowly through social and corporate contacts. Explaining why he eschewed any finance from the Piel's brewery, Gerard said, "I don't like to lose my claim on the title of being a self-made man."[25]

The new magazine's editorial approach was elegantly simple. Leading scientists would explain developments in their fields to intelligent readers. To translate their convoluted texts into literate prose, Gerard recruited *Time* magazine's science editor Leon Svirsky, who had "a marvelous intelligence and a beautiful style, rigorous and clean" with an unerring gift for the right metaphor. The new magazine also allocated fully half its space for evocative graphics, photos, tables, and schematics. Within the expanding universe of modern science, the editors "staked out five major regions: the physical sciences, the biological sciences, the social sciences, medicine, and engineering." Each issue would carry eight major essays by senior scientists, leavened by editorial columns titled "The Amateur Astronomer" and "Science and the Citizen," with the latter an outlet for Gerard's own views. Every fall, *Scientific American* published a special issue, starting in 1950 with a sweeping review of scientific progress over the past half-century—J. Robert Oppenheimer on nuclear physics, Linus Pauling on chemistry, Sir Edmund Whittaker on mathematics, and A. L. Kroeber on anthropology. This editorial formula captivated its educated audience, attracting essays by over seventy Nobel Prize winners, including Albert Einstein, Niels Bohr, and Francis Crick.[26]

While Gerard and his young coterie were launching their landmark venture, the FBI was watching, worried about the loyalty of these men who knew too much. After Gerard recruited colleagues from *Life* to staff his new magazine, famed informer Whitaker Chambers, then senior editor at *Time*, told the FBI "that a group of three or four people left *Time* and became editors of *Scientific American*. 'Jerry' Piel was the leader of this group, which included Dennis Flanagan," whom the Bureau identified as the "son of Nan Brayman, well-known CP [Communist Party] member." Chambers also reported "the group members were probably Communist sympathizers," adding scurrilously that "a mysterious subsidy became available for the purchase of *Scientific American*."[27]

In these dangerous early days of the Cold War, the new magazine faced surveillance and blacklisting that threatened its survival. Anyone less informed by history or less protected by social connections who tried to challenge America's military might with a science journal would have become little more than a latter-day Don Quixote, tilting at nuclear reactors with a rolled-up magazine. Indeed, *Scientific American*'s first issue in May 1948 coincided with events that fostered a spreading climate of fear across America—the successful Soviet nuclear test in September 1949, atomic scientist Klaus Fuchs's confession to spying for the Russians, President Truman's decision to build the hydrogen super-bomb in January 1950, Senator Joseph McCarthy's charges about communists inside the U.S. government in February, and, a month later, legislation requiring loyalty tests for nuclear scientists. Famed physicist Albert Einstein warned that this new super-bomb was capable of "radioactive poisoning of the atmosphere and, hence, annihilation of all life on earth." To silence such criticism of his decision to build the H-bomb, Truman issued a "gag order" that stilled official dissent.[28]

Throughout 1949 and 1950, *Scientific American* punctured this suffocating silence with short, critical commentaries about excessive fear of nuclear spies ("The Insecurity of Security") and government restraints on scientific discussion ("Scientific Intelligence"). After FBI director J. Edgar Hoover branded physicist Edward Condon an "espionage agent in disguise," and then used the press and House Un-American Activities Committee (HUAC) to sully his reputation without proof, Gerard asked his former Harvard tutor Robert K. Merton, now head of Columbia University's Bureau of Applied Social Research, to conduct a computerized "content analysis" of this media coverage. The results, published in the magazine's February 1949 issue, showed Condon was a victim of "trial by press" that repeated these slanders without confirmation—providing grounds for some self-reflection among the media.[29]

In March 1950, *Scientific American* continued this critical coverage with a four-part inquiry into the hydrogen bomb. In the first installment, scientist Louis Ridenour criticized "the fully authoritarian way" that Truman made the decision to build this destructive weapon. He condemned the "bankruptcy of our secrecy policy" that stifled public debate.[30]

Cold War Witch-Hunt

The real test of Gerard's political skills came just a month later when he published the next in this series critiquing the hydrogen bomb. Writing in the April 1950 issue of *Scientific American*, Dr. Hans A. Bethe, famed physicist and future Nobel Prize winner, argued passionately that "we must save humanity from this ultimate disaster" by reconsidering the president's decision to build the super bomb. "I believe the most important question is the moral one," Bethe wrote with words weighted by his role as a senior scientist in the Manhattan Project. "Can we who have always insisted on morality and human decency between nations as well as inside our own country, introduce this weapon of total annihilation into the world?" Since he had circulated his draft essay among colleagues, the Atomic Energy Commission (AEC) soon saw the text and telegrammed the magazine barring publication of Bethe's article, already in press. When Gerard demanded specific objections, arguing all the technical data in Bethe's text was already published elsewhere, the AEC bristled saying any details could compromise national security. In this closed-door confrontation, Gerard refused to back down. The AEC finally agreed to permit publication of the issue with some "ritual deletions" that still required the destruction of copies that had already come off the press.[31]

Once that agreement was reached, Gerard's partner Donald Miller asked the AEC security officers: "Well, what do we do with the 3,000 copies already printed of the magazine?" Setting a trap for these media-challenged security people, Miller suggested ever so helpfully: "Well, there are good shredders up there. But then, you know, someone could take the shredded pieces and put them back together again. Maybe it's better to burn it, don't you think?" Oblivious to the symbolism of a book burning in the aftermath of a world war against the Nazis, the tone-deaf AEC security men agreed. All of those 3,000 printed copies were incinerated—an act almost without precedent in America. Adding to the gravity of this action, the issue featured an essay by Albert Einstein, commissioned by Gerard during a visit to the scientist's Princeton home, which propounded a "comprehensive field theory that would hold physics together."[32]

Although the matter had been quietly resolved, Gerard was still worried. His magazine was "a very fragile little institution," with just over 100,000 circulation and regular losses from insufficient advertising. "The Atomic Energy Commission or somebody in it at any time can leak this to the House Un-American Activities Committee or Joe McCarthy," he thought, "and we'll be cooked. So I called up the New York Times and said I have a story."[33]

On April 1, 1950, the New York Times appeared with front-page coverage under the provocative double-column headline, "U.S. Censors H-Bomb Data; 3,000 Magazine Copies Burnt." The story's lead sentence read: "Gerard Piel, editor of the Scientific American, attacked the censorship policies of the Atomic Energy Commission yesterday when he disclosed. . . ." The article went on to report that the AEC had also destroyed every trace of Dr. Bethe's original text by melting down the "objectionable linotype slugs" at the printing plant and then incinerating the "complete file of proofs" along with those 3,000 printed copies.[34]

Suddenly, the incident became what Gerard called "a nationwide overnight sensation" that protected him from accusations of breaching national security. "Strict compliance with the commission's policies," Gerard told the Times, "would mean that we could not teach physics." Three weeks later, he addressed the American Society of Newspaper Editors, saying, "we have tolerated too much secrecy and neglected too long this phase of the Government's relation to the press." In an editorial, the Times seconded his critique, warning that "censors . . . run the risk of doing great harm."[35]

Gerard's bold speech on nuclear issues won him both admiration from the press and closer surveillance by the FBI. In the aftermath of this incident, agents reported that Gerard and his wife Mary Bird Piel, then living in Greenwich Village, "were active in the '12th Street Neighbors for Peace,' which was connected with the Stockholm Peace Petition," a movement advocating an absolute ban on nuclear weapons. At one of their meetings, Gerard reportedly "spoke on the hydrogen bomb." To indicate their subversive import, the Bureau reported that one meeting, on July 19, 1950, was held at the 12th Street home of Mark Shulman, whose wife Pearl Mullen "was identified as an active Communist from 1930 to 1945." In this same period, the Bureau noted, the Communist Party "had increased its pressure on the 'peace offensive' ranging from national headquarters down to neighborhood groups." In October, the FBI interviewed Gerard "concerning his association with . . . Abraham BROTHMAN and Miriam MOSKOWITZ [who] were convicted in the Federal Court . . . on [the] charge of obstructing justice in connection with the trial of Julius ROSENBERG." Gerard replied that he knew Brothman as "a chemist of distinction" whom he had once tried to recruit for Henry J. Kaiser. He had only spoken to the co-accused Miriam Moskowitz when she "had called him after her arrest asking for financial help," a request he had refused.[36]

Right after the Rosenbergs were sentenced to death for espionage in March 1951, Gerard's "Science and the Citizen" column opened with a confrontational sentence: "History's most elaborately guarded secret—how to make an atomic bomb—was casually let out of the bag in a courtroom last month." Provocatively, he added, "Or was it?" The simple sketch of the bomb that Julius Rosenberg stole, Gerard insisted, "was not much of a secret . . . without quantitative data and other accompanying technical information." Recalling his wartime interview with physicist Robert Wood, Gerard argued that the "principle of 'implosion' by means of a shaped-charge has often been suggested in speculation on a possible mechanism for detonation of the atomic bomb." As soon as that issue of *Scientific American* hit the newsstands, said Gerard, the AEC's suspicious "intelligence agents came to visit . . . and we showed them our sources," sending them away satisfied there was no security breach.[37] Midst the FBI manhunt for Soviet spies that culminated in the Rosenbergs' execution, Gerard's daring combination of criticism in his columns and anti-nuclear activism in his community risked both arrest and black listing.

Indeed, state scrutiny of *Scientific American* was just beginning. At the peak of the McCarthy-era's witch-hunt for communists in May 1953, the Senate

Internal Security Subcommittee summoned Leon Svirsky, now the magazine's managing editor. He had once been a member of the secret communist cell at *Time* magazine that circulated an anonymous newssheet entitled "High Time" loaded with "the most vicious kinds of office gossip"—something Gerard called "a typical communist way of subverting an organization by clawing at its vitals." With skilled counsel provided courtesy of *Scientific American*, Svirsky, with Gerard's tacit consent, "simply lied under oath" by denying his Communist Party membership during a closed Senate executive hearing. "And he did it so well," said Gerard, "that they dropped the examination of him and we got away with it." Since this testimony was nothing less than perjury, Gerard kept it "an absolute secret" from both his editor Dennis Flanagan and company counsel Leo Gottlieb.[38]

While investigating alleged communists inside the U.S. Army in July 1954, the Senate's Internal Security Subcommittee subpoenaed the magazine's promotions director, Stephen M. Fischer. He had been both a party member and press secretary for Henry Wallace's 1948 presidential campaign. With the adept lawyer Gerard provided, Fischer evaded prosecution by confessing, in a closed-door executive session, his party membership while refusing to name names. "I feel that at any time, sir, that I know of anyone who, to my knowledge, has performed any treasonous, subversive action against the United States, I would," he testified at a public hearing, "personally and immediately get in touch with the FBI." But, he added, "I know of no one, sir, who, to my knowledge, has done anything wrong." Without the usual threat of perjury charges to break this silence, the committee's red-baiting chair, Senator William E. Jenner (Republican, Indiana), excused Fischer. Even so, the magazine's rather conservative board, led by Leo Gottlieb, demanded that Fischer, as a confessed communist, be dismissed. Gerard adamantly refused. With the backing of his brother Bill, an influential Wall Street attorney, he arranged the financing to buy out disgruntled directors if necessary, forcing them to back down and Gottlieb to resign.[39]

Loyalty Board

But the most challenging security case was Gerard's own. When the Surgeon General asked him to become a zero-dollar adviser for a journal published by the U.S. Public Health Service, Gerard's acceptance subjected him, under President Truman's Federal Employee Loyalty Program, to an FBI security check. The

Bureau determined, said Gerard, "I was a subversive and disloyal to the United States." Rather than leave this dangerous stain on his name, he decided to fight the FBI. Brother Bill drafted Gerard's affidavit with "solid craftsmanship," and "also proceeded to round up supporting affidavits" from "a whole succession of people, who knew different aspects of my life over different periods"—thereby producing "quite a presentation a couple of inches thick."[40]

At the subsequent Loyalty Board hearing, the FBI disclosed some of its adverse information, which Gerard dismissed as "preposterous." In its most serious charge, the FBI reported that *Scientific American* had "derided" the evidence in the Rosenberg atomic espionage case, which, said Gerard, "it certainly had." Another demerit was his friendship with Harvard astronomer Harlow Shapley, a contributor to the magazine and a peace activist who had blasted HUAC's "Gestapo methods," dismissing Senator McCarthy's accusations of his disloyalty as "untrue and vague." The FBI dossier also reported that Gerard's brother David was married to Hedwig Seligsohn, who had reportedly said, during World War II, that "when V.E. Day comes she would wrap herself in the Red Flag and make a speech on Times Square." As the daughter of Dr. Julius L. Seligsohn, who had headed the Aid Association of German Jews and died in a Nazi concentration camp, his sister-in-law, Gerard said, was "a fierce young woman and had reason to be." Finally, the FBI report accused him of membership in the American Labor Party, a progressive group allied with Mayor Fiorello LaGuardia, which, said Gerard, "I certainly was." Since this was "the sum total of that nonsense," his name was cleared from the stigma of disloyalty.[41]

Exoneration came with a cost. Indicating the tenor of these dangerous times, brother Bill was reportedly stripped of the "highest security classification," hard-won during World War II, as punishment for counseling Gerard during this loyalty review.[42] Though a powerful establishment figure, Bill Piel still paid a high price for preventing their family name from being tarred by the brush of disloyalty—the same charge that had so damaged their uncles during World War I. To this roster of assets that saved his reputation, we must add Gerard's own exceptional social network reflected in that thick file of affidavits. Twenty years later, he could dictate, from memory, a 700-page oral history populated by over 500 personal names, with biographical details that placed each one in a mental matrix of mid-century American power elites.[43]

Despite three executives investigated for disloyalty, an editor branded a communist by the FBI, a book review editor (James R. Newman) denied employment with AEC after an "adverse report" about his loyalty, and an editorial policy sharply critical of U.S. nuclear weapons, *Scientific American* survived.[44] By deftly manipulating the historical forces at play—press freedom versus national security, social connections versus security agencies—Gerard had created an open forum for criticism of U.S. science policy during the coldest years of the Cold War.

Instead of being stigmatized, such dissent elevated his own status from neophyte editor to public intellectual. Indeed, Gerard was showered with an amazing array of public honors. Director of the American Museum of Natural History (1955). Director of the American Civil Liberties Union (1957). Recipient of the George Polk Award (1961). President of the Salk Institute (1962). Chairmanship of the commission to reform New York City's hospitals (1966). Trustee of Harvard University (1966). Honorary degrees from Brandeis, Colby, Columbia, and Rutgers.[45]

Family Matters

Midst all this success, Gerard still found time for family. No matter how busy, he welcomed visits from even the most distant cousin. In the fall of 1963 when I was a high school senior, my mother sent me to talk to her cousin Gerard about attending Harvard, his alma mater. I was disheveled and dirty after a four-day, non-stop drive from California. But Gerard received me in the Madison Avenue offices of *Scientific American* like a visiting luminary, telling his secretary to hold calls while he focused on teen-aged me with the same close attention he gave famous scientists. And I was by no means unique. In private meetings, social gatherings, and family life, Gerard gave generously of his time. For nearly twenty years he served on the boards of the Piel holding companies, first the Michael Piel Trust during the 1950s and then M&G Piel Securities after the brewery's sale in 1962.

Although Gerard's society wedding had ended in divorce, the marriage produced two sons who followed him to Harvard. In a confidential reference for the younger son, his school principal called Samuel Piel "talented, thoughtful and passionate," closing with a telling comment: "This is a fascinating family."[46] Gerard's second marriage to attorney Eleanor Jackson in 1955 also produced a daughter who became the last of the ten Piels to attend Andover Academy en route to Harvard for both B.A. and medical degree.[47]

Through publishing and family ties, Gerard also became enmeshed in the care of a handicapped cousin, Patsy Lyne, the daughter of his Aunt Agnes.

The first strand in this tangled web was Gerard's own relationship with famed psychologist Bruno Bettelheim, Patsy's "foster father" for seven years while she was undergoing therapy in prewar Vienna. After Agnes facilitated Bettelheim's release from a Nazi concentration camp in 1939, he landed at New York with three dollars in his pocket and a doctorate in art history. By claiming, falsely, that he had used his expertise "in all fields of human and social psychology" to successfully treat a patient suffering from a syndrome only recently identified as "autism," he became director, in 1944, of a residential treatment facility, the Orthogenic School at the University of Chicago.[48]

That patient was, of course, Agnes Piel's daughter Patsy. In the fanciful treatment fable that Dr. Bettelheim told and retold famously for the next forty years, the mother of his first autism patient supposedly "got drunk and had intercourse with someone she did not know." After several botched abortions, she had a child who remained "virtually mute all her life" until she came under his care at age seven in Vienna. For months he drew her out carefully by playing peek-a-boo games. Finally, the patient "uttered this her first sentence . . . in perfect English, 'Give me the skeleton of George Washington.'" Then, in a bit of pseudo-Freudian babble that wowed audiences worldwide, Bettelheim would explain that "as an American girl with no known father she could only think of the father of her country as a solution to her problem. Since the unknown father was 'the skeleton in the closet' of her life, she asked for his skeleton."[49]

His story was pure fabrication from start to finish. Agnes had, of course, married Patsy's father after a formal courtship. Patsy's cousins Margarita McCoy and Marie-Luise Kemp recall her playing, and speaking, quite normally during their pre-Vienna playdates. His ex-wife Gina Bettelheim, who cared for Patsy throughout those seven years in Vienna, said he was "lying" about the silence. Since he was a lumber merchant and an art historian, not a psychotherapist, Bettelheim never treated Patsy. There were no peek-a-boo games. There were no words about George Washington. There was no therapy. Nonetheless, Bettelheim parlayed this purported treatment of Patsy into a reputation as a leading international expert on autism and child psychology.[50]

As publisher of an influential journal, Gerard Piel helped build Bettelheim's reputation as "a gentle sage who . . . spearheaded a revolution in child psychology." At the start of his career, *Scientific American* featured three articles by Bettelheim: "Prejudice: An Account of a Significant Statistical Study of Racial Discrimination" (1950), "Schizophrenic Art: The Drawings and Painting of a Child . . . Show How She Changed over Three Years of Successful Treatment"

(1952), and "Joey: A 'Mechanical Boy': How a Child who Thought He was Run by a Machine was Brought Back to Reality" (1959).[51] During this decade of Bettelheim's professional ascent, those celebratory subtitles constituted nothing less than unpaid advertisements for his brilliance.

The other strand in this family entanglement was Gerard's relationship with his Aunt Agnes, a near neighbor in northwest Connecticut. After moving to the town of Sharon around 1951, Agnes remarried for a third time, briefly and disastrously, to an in-law of the German Piels, a Mr. Fritz Mueller. He soon ran off with the cook, leaving Agnes on this isolated property with daughter Patsy, now a troubled young woman. A few years later, Gerard and Eleanor bought a summer place in nearby Lakeville, renewing his relationship with an aunt whom he regarded, along with his Uncle Paul, as "the most romantic figures in the family."[52]

Yet Gerard was also concerned that Agnes and Patsy were becoming an unhealthy pair, suffering from what he called "folié a deux" or shared psychotic disorder. Consequently, he sought out Bettelheim in Chicago circa 1960. Spurning Agnes's repeated promises to leave her money to his institute, Bettelheim instead insisted she pay for Patsy's placement in an independent living facility that he had found, one that could provide quality care. Upon return, Gerard broached the matter with Agnes who, enraged, fired him as executor of her will and appointed his wife Eleanor. For the next quarter century, Agnes kept Patsy isolated from outside contact, much like her schizophrenic brother Otto who had died hidden away in a Danish village. After Agnes passed away in 1983, Eleanor would serve as Patsy's guardian for the next thirty years, keeping her in the home she loved by selling most of its surrounding sixty acres to a wealthy neighbor, the artist Jasper Johns, and redeeming the Piel shares inherited from her mother.[53]

Publishing Success

Family matters did nothing to slow Gerard's professional ascent. In January 1951, just nine months after the AEC burned the H-bomb issue, *Scientific American* "went into the black" for the first time, and he was well on his way to publishing the world's premier science journal. By making the complex comprehensible to thinking citizens, Gerard, in the words of one analyst, "virtually invented modern science journalism."[54] Despite its "uncompromisingly cerebral" style, the magazine built a circulation that reached 335,000 by 1963 with an enviable $4.6 million in annual advertising revenues.[55]

Commercial progress did not mute *Scientific American*'s critique of the U.S. atomic arsenal. Right after the Soviet Union broke America's nuclear monopoly with a successful atomic test in 1949, Chester I. Barnard, one of the authors of the Acheson-Lilienthal report recommending international control of atomic power, reviewed that document to again urge diplomacy in lieu of an arms race. When the national press responded with "reverence and solemnity" to Herman Kahn's 1961 book arguing that nuclear war was winnable despite the millions who would die, *Scientific American*'s James Newman mocked it as "a moral tract on mass murder: how to plan it, how to commit it, how to get away with it." To counter such amoral advocacy, British physicist and Nobel laureate P. M. S. Blackett argued, a year later, that both superpowers had nuclear weapons "so overpowering" that only a mutual reduction to "a very low and purely retaliatory role" could make much difference.[56]

Such coverage also made Gerard an important dissident in Cold War America. When Washington launched a crash program to build fallout shelters for every American in 1961, Gerard called this "a sinister development because it . . . gives sanction of action to the delusion that a thermonuclear war can be fought and survived. It encourages statesmen to take larger risks predicated upon first-strike credibility and post-attack recuperative capacity."[57] Gerard's pointed condemnation of this "hoax and illusion" joined a chorus of criticism from the scientific community that soon stopped the $6 billion shelter program.[58]

After America renewed the arms race in the late 1970s with the neutron bomb and multiple-warhead missiles, *Scientific American* featured sharp critiques of this swelling nuclear arsenal. The most salient analysis came from Herbert Scoville, Jr., the CIA's former deputy director for technology and Gerard's Andover classmate. His writing, said Gerard, "put *Scientific American* in the forefront blowing the whistle . . . on, for example, the second generation of nuclear subs . . . as first-strike weapons." For over thirty years, the magazine's message was clear and consistent: scientific rationality demanded nuclear disarmament.[59]

This activism prompted persistent state surveillance. In September 1960, Gerard's FBI file showed that "he attempted to contact Raul ROA, Foreign Minister of Cuba, at the Cuban Mission to the United Nations, to invite Roa to dinner." According to the Bureau's report, "Mrs. ROA said that PIEL was a friend of theirs." Gerard and his second wife, Eleanor Jackson Piel, were, moreover, "invited to a reception on 24 September 1960 sponsored by the Fair Play for Cuba Committee in honor of Fidel Castro in New York City"—that famous reception at Harlem's Hotel Teresa attended by 250 of America's liberal illuminati. For the next three years, moreover, the FBI found a number of Gerard's associations similarly suspicious, including his "contribution of $100.00 on 5 February 1960 to the Citizens Committee to Preserve American Freedoms;" his service "on the Board of Trustees of the Institute of Policy Studies" in 1963; and his wife's presence on the board of the new-left magazine *Ramparts* from July 1966 to June 1967.[60]

But the FBI dossier failed to note that, in April 1962, Gerard and his wife Eleanor were also associating with President John F. Kennedy at a White House reception to honor the nation's Nobel Prize winners. During the dinner, Eleanor, a well-known civil liberties lawyer, bantered with Attorney General Robert Kennedy "about the provenance of a cigar." Afterwards, as the elegantly attired guests walked from West Wing dining to East Wing ceremonies, Eleanor and Gerard were swept away by violinists playing Viennese waltzes. They broke protocol and led a half-dozen of the Nobel laureates, including Eva and Linus Pauling, in spontaneous dancing, eliciting approving smiles from the first couple.[61]

Such social agility, moving between a reception for Fidel Castro in Harlem and dinner with President Kennedy at the White House, allowed Gerard to survive the Cold War repression of dissidents unscathed. While the earlier generation of Piels was stigmatized by their German identity during World War I, Gerard, now thoroughly assimilated, had wide social contacts and boundless confidence that allowed him to challenge the U.S. security state in ways that would have amazed his elders.

Commercial Benchmarks

Just as Gerard danced through the dangers of Cold War America, so he promoted his magazine with exceptional agility. Although *Scientific American* never advertised, several of his promotions resonated powerfully with America's affluent elites—what he called "the professional-technical element in our society." After Wassily Leontief published an article on "input-output economics" in a 1951 issue, Gerard turned that representation of the U.S. economy into "a marvelous graphic display table [that] became a status symbol for business economists to have . . . on their walls." Then, in a masterstroke of marketing, *Scientific American* took a full-page ad in the *New York Times* to announce, in December 1966, the "1st International Paper Airplane Competition." The copy asked overgrown boys in executive suites across America: "Can it be there's a paper plane which makes the SST [Super Sonic Transport] 30 years obsolete?"[62]

Interviewed by the *Times* at the Harvard Club in midtown Manhattan, Gerard said his staff would award the titanium "Leonardo" trophy after flying entries around their offices. He punctuated this announcement by lofting a dart-shaped exemplar that "floated gracefully across the room." The contest was enormously popular, attracting 12,000 entries, each one tested by a team of aeronautic engineers. A book of the winning designs soon won an avid readership. By 1968, *Scientific American*'s circulation was soaring to 400,000 on its way to a peak of 700,000 ten years later.[63]

With domestic sales stable, Gerard moved to internationalize the magazine, embracing local languages as his media for global communication. He launched the first foreign edition in 1968, collaborating with Italy's premier publishing house, Mondadori, for a print run of 15,000 that soon sold out.[64] After starting translated editions in Japan (1973), Spain (1976), France (1977), and Germany (1978), Gerard negotiated successfully with China's Deputy Prime Minister Feng Yi (1979) and the Soviet Academy of Sciences (1984) for editions to serve their markets—an initiative he called "our contribution to the healing of this division of the world." At its peak in 1986, the magazine had over a million well-educated readers worldwide, some 700,000 in the U.S. and another 400,000 for its nine foreign-language versions, making *Scientific American* one of the first truly global publications.[65]

As Gerard's long tenure at the company came to a close, corporate pressures brought welcome and unwelcome changes. By the 1980s, *Scientific American*'s long success inspired imitation, with Hearst redesigning *Science Digest* as a look-alike publication and Time, Inc., launching its simulacrum *Discover*. With massive promotional budgets, both magazines began cutting into *Scientific American*'s circulation and advertising. At the very moment when competition was intensifying, the magazine's articles, under Dennis Flanagan's fading editorial skills, became less comprehensible, prompting what Gerard called "complaints from devoted scientists who loved the magazine."[66]

The solution Gerard decided, all on his own, was dissolution of the partnership that had managed the magazine for nearly forty years. Just as grandfather Michael had picked eldest son William to run the brewery, so Gerard now selected son Jonathan, an editor at the magazine for the past eight years, as his successor. And just as his father William had, a half-century before, dismissed the Piel family partners who blocked his plans for their brewery's future, so Gerard, who had observed these maneuvers close-up, now ousted his magazine's founding partners to facilitate a familial succession. During a sealed oral history interview in 1982, Gerard confided that "my son, who began in our company as an editor, has demonstrated his capacity as a manager and entrepreneur," winning the respect of directors who would hopefully support his appointment as chief executive. "It would be wonderful," Gerard added, "if I could see that happen."[67]

His father William's maneuvers at the brewery had been successful because he could, as the eldest sibling, persuade family shareholders that those management reforms would assure their financial future—important advantages his son did not have. In a corporation with outside investors and an independent board of directors, Gerard was nonetheless operating in an unconscious family-business mode, unleashing a tempest of complications.

Among the magazine's original troika of partners, the first to retire was Donald Miller, stepping down as general manager at Gerard's behest. The next to leave was the long-serving editor Dennis Flanagan, then turning 65. "My friend Dennis," recalled Gerard, "has lost his bearings with respect to how the magazine ought to be put out and I say to Dennis, this is 1984, . . . that 'we're going to retire, and the next generation has got to take this enterprise over.'" Without really consulting his old partners, Gerard then "advanced Jonathan Piel to the directors as the man to whom I would entrust the management." So, in 1984 at the age of 68 Gerard moved up to chairman of the board while his son succeeded both Gerard as president and Dennis Flanagan as editor-in-chief. By easing his old friends Donald and Dennis into retirement on full salary, Gerard assumed this change was welcomed by all.[68]

But their retribution came quickly.

White Knights/White Sharks

A few months later in January 1985, Gerard was traveling in China when he got an urgent call from son Jonathan, warning about a hostile takeover from the Canadian publisher Macleans. "'Oh, well, we can handle that,'" Gerard replied. "'We've got Dennis and Don and my shares.' That was 40 percent of the stock between us. Jonathan says 'I'm not so sure about those guys. You'd better get home.'" After an overnight flight from China to New York, Gerard was shocked to find that these two close colleagues, working through the magazine's former managing editor Stephen Fischer, were the ones soliciting the takeover bid from Macleans. "They do this behind my back," Gerard recalled, momentarily forgetting his own stealth in arranging their retirements. "They violate the trust of their fellow directors and the offer was for $100 per share, and the board rejected it. And then I have two guys who are ready to sell their shares at $100 . . . I've got to get them bought out. So I got Arthur Sackler"—the fabulously wealthy entrepreneur who had endowed a dozen museums and medical schools in cities worldwide. By acquiring his partners' shares representing 15 percent of the company, Sackler, said Gerard, "comes in as my white knight. Then I discover he's really a white shark."[69]

Indeed, just two years later Gerard faced a hostile takeover by Dr. Sackler, who had acquired "a dangerously large holding" and was now unhappy with the magazine's falling advertising revenues. Sackler's drive to acquire 85 percent of the company made Gerard fear for the future of his own 15 percent equity. These concerns redoubled after Sackler rejected a million-dollar investment by Warren Buffet that Gerard had solicited, dismissing this beneficent billionaire as " 'a big take-over artist.' " So in March 1986, Gerard persuaded the board, over Sackler's objections, to put the magazine on the open market. Midst a bidding war among *Time*, Thompson Company, *The Economist*, and the ruthless British press lord Robert Maxwell, Gerard found his second white knight in Germany's von Holtzbrinck Group, already sales representative for his German edition. After "getting back-channel talk from Sackler," robber baron Maxwell made the top bid of $52.5 million. So Gerard countered by breaking "every rule in the book to see to it that the von Holtzbrincks came in with the proper bid" of $52.6 million—a razor-thin winning margin of just $100,000 or 0.02 percent. Though Maxwell then made higher bids, Gerard persuaded his board to accept the von Holtzbrinck offer since they promised to respect what son Jonathan called "our commitment to quality and integrity in publishing."[70]

In the end, Gerard felt vindicated by this sale "at $253 per share instead of $100 that my stupid partners sold for." Although son Jonathan stayed on as editor, Gerard's position as chairman ended after a year's grace and he cashed out for a comfortable retirement.[71] With some $8 million for his shares after thirty years at the magazine, Gerard placed a million dollars in trusts for his two surviving children and made a million-dollar donation to Harvard in memory of deceased son Samuel. All that left him a net worth of $5 million—far beyond that inheritance of $34,000 from his father's forty years at the brewery.[72] In 1986 dollars corrected for inflation, this line of the Piel family had gone downward from grandfather Michael's $3.6 million estate (1915) to father William's assets of $850,000 (1953), and then sharply upward to grandson Gerard's $8 million fortune (1986).

Within months of his retirement, Gerard was elected president of the American Association for the Advancement of Science (AAAS), the first journalist so honored, and was soon immersed in these new duties. In his presidential address at the 1986 annual meeting, Gerard lambasted the Reagan administration's manipulation of research funding to silence criticism of its "Star Wars" missile-defense program. It was now imperative, Gerard concluded, to "reconstruct the relation between our universities and the federal government" so that once more Washington can respond "to the will of the people and to the dictates of reason and sanity."[73]

For his retirement home, Gerard converted the former ballroom of brewer Jacob Ruppert, Jr., into a penthouse apartment. From this aerie at Fifth Avenue and 93rd Street overlooking Central Park, Gerard kept an eagle eye on a changing world—continuing his role as a public intellectual, and encouraging science to work for society. As a delegate to the UN's historic Earth Summit at Rio de Janeiro in June 1992, Gerard, at age 77, was one of the "architects" of Agenda 21, an initiative for balancing economic growth with environmental protection through civil society activism. Although later attacked by the Republican Party's 2012 platform "as erosive of American sovereignty," Agenda 21 would inspire a worldwide movement by over a thousand local governments to promote sustainable development and green energy.[74]

Ten years after the Rio conference, Gerard, at age 86, published *The Age of Science,* a 500-page survey of scientific progress throughout the twentieth century. This ambitious analysis of five major fields was infused with what one laudatory reviewer called "an optimistic vision of the fate of the world if we can all only learn to think and act like natural scientists."[75]

But even the most successful life has its reverses. After editing *Scientific American* for eight years, Gerard's son Jonathan was forced to tender his resignation in 1994. Operating in patriarchal mode akin to his father's management of the brewery, Gerard had arranged a familial succession as if the company were still his own, apparently unmindful that the new German owners might have their own preferences—producing a collision of irrational intimacies between these two families, German and American. The von Holtzbrincks had appointed the manager of the magazine's German edition as the new company's president. According to Gerard, this executive "was certainly jealous of Jonathan," maneuvered "underhandedly" against him with staff, and "started to undermine the Piels to the von Holtzbrincks." A year later, when this president's successor fired Gerard's protégé as head of the magazine's book subsidiary, that young woman sued for gender discrimination and Gerard backed her—unmindful of complications now the company was no longer his own. That German executive then "lowered the boom on Jonathan." The company coolly explained that "science is . . . becoming more and more difficult to convey to the general public, and we decided that we will let someone else take a look at it."[76]

The feeling was mutual. "I can't even look at an issue of *Scientific American*," Gerard wrote a relative a few years later. "And because I bought the old name to put on my *Scientific American*, not many people know I invented the magazine they have known under that name. They see me now as the former publisher of the dumbed-down, vulgar magazine called *Scientific American*."[77]

Steps to Success

Looking back on Gerard's remarkable career, creating a global scientific publishing empire with a history degree and no capital, raises intriguing, yet ultimately unanswerable questions about the ingredients for such success. There are, however, several noteworthy aspects of his achievement that merit comment.

The New York social connections hard-won by their parents gave Gerard and brother Bill an intangible yet invaluable career advantage. Though Gerard became a prominent public intellectual, he was by no means the best scholar among the Piels. In 1936, a chemistry teacher at Andover Academy compiled a two-generation comparison of Piel grade averages, with Paul at the top (75 percent), Gerard in the middle (70 percent), and Henry's younger son Mike at the bottom (33 percent). But all these Piels were overshadowed by cousin Margarita's future husband, Alfred M. McCoy, Jr., whose average (84 percent) was the second highest in his Andover class of 200 boys.[78]

Yet Al McCoy with his tip-top 84 percent average, like Mike Piel with his rock-bottom 33 percent, later served with the U.S. Army's 89th division—Mike as a rifleman and McCoy as an artillery forward observer—engaging in heavy combat across Germany, liberating a Nazi death camp, and suffering trauma and alcoholism that led to their early deaths, Mike at 55, McCoy at 45.[79] Despite their truncated careers, both were men of some achievement. Mike Piel developed the new smooth-haired Katadhin breed on his Maine sheep farm and worked with Heifer International to disseminate breeding stock among the poor of Central America as low-cost protein.[80] Al McCoy became the systems engineering director for the U.S. Defense Satellite Communications Program, supervising, during the space race of the 1960s, the design and launch of twenty-six satellites that became the first global telecommunications satellite system.[81]

By contrast, both Gerard and his brother Bill had the social connections for non-combat posts, war production and War Department, respectively. After World War II, they could pursue their long, rewarding careers free from the psychological trauma that afflicted millions of returning U.S. veterans. And they had an additional thirty years in their working lives denied their cousins who saw combat.

In addition to this social advantage, Gerard's study of history, though he minimized its import with wry self-deprecation, nonetheless taught him how to adjust his career deftly to society's larger trajectory—first science journalism in the age of science, then anti-nuclear activism in the atomic age, and finally environmentalism in the post-industrial period. Of equal import, his mix of aggression and discipline, acquired on the wrestling mats of Andover and Harvard, primed him to seize every opportunity and dominate every situation. His colleagues at *Scientific American* recalled this attribute, saying "he carried that fitness and determination with him throughout his life."[82]

Cousins' Consortium

While Gerard added new luster to the Piel name, neither he nor any of his ambitious siblings had time to devote to the family firm, M&G Piel Securities. Though Gerard served dutifully on its board and later bonded with his many Piel cousins, he was the only one among William's descendants to do so. It was the Piels' less prominent lines that assured the survival of the family's mutual fund, M&G Piel Securities, along with the personal ties the company sustained. At the old brewery, their parents had experienced an unplanned succession from founding patriarchs to a "sibling partnership" fraught with personal conflict. At the mutual fund, by contrast, the third generation would handle their transition to a "cousins' consortium" through a careful, consultative process.[83] In managing their investment portfolio collectively, these cousins would follow what is now considered best practice by serving as "active stewards and responsible owners in making key decisions and overseeing their assets."[84]

Foremost among the third-generation's leaders was Louise Piel's eldest son, Frederick Lange, who, along with cousins Gerard and Margarita, had the combination of analytic ability and tolerance for quirky elders needed to guide the new family company through its first critical decades. Graduating from Andover in 1936 with good grades, Fred majored in electrical engineering at MIT, completing a thesis on electricity generation in Maine—appropriate training for his later career, following wartime service, as an executive for a New Jersey power company.[85]

After serving as director for the old Michael Piel Trust during the 1950s, Fred transitioned to the board of its successor firm, M&G Piel Securities, as a deferential representative of the family's younger generation. In the first years after its founding in 1962, this investment firm operated as an ad hoc extension of the old brewery, with former president Henry Muessen as chairman, the perennial Paul Piel as secretary, and his nephews Gerard Piel as "honorific president" and Fred Lange as treasurer. With the shares evenly divided between the two sides of the family, the Gottfried and Michael Piel heirs chose three directors each and a seventh by mutual consent.[86]

There was a striking continuity from the old brewery to the new mutual fund, both in personnel and patriarchal management. Like the brewery's board in its later years, the new firm's directors formed a chummy all-male club that allowed Fred's Uncle Paul, first as secretary and later as omnipresent guest, to operate in his preferred mode of indirect influence. Usually, Paul's friend Muessen opened the meetings with a business report and the brewery's former accountant Harry Diesl noted expenses. Then Paul's hand-picked adviser Dr. Herman Scheyhing recommended investments, and the family's trusted counselors from brewing days, Julian Tashof or Leonard Lazarus, considered the tax angle. Throughout these proceedings, the younger generation, Gerard and cousin Fred Lange, maintained a respectful silence as Uncle Paul and friend Muessen dominated proceedings, much as they had in the brewery's last years. The stockholders were, once again, largely absent.[87]

Dissident Stockholder

For nearly a decade, this board kept its shareholders at a distance, favoring the small, clubby meetings that were Paul's forte. As tumultuous international events roiled markets in the 1970s, however, Margarita Piel McCoy, Fred Lange's cousin and childhood friend, became a critical voice at company meetings. Though not a director, an unexpected reversal of fortune forced her to start attending as a "guest" in 1972, monitoring shares inherited from her father, Rudolf Piel.

After twenty years as a postwar housewife, Margarita's marriage had collapsed, leaving her without income or means to make a living. So, in her mid-40s, she entered graduate school in urban planning, which like architecture was an almost exclusively male profession. While Gerard with his history degree had reinvented himself as an interpreter of science, so Margarita with her English B.A. showed a similar mix of curiosity and confidence that allowed her to master this technical field. Over the next thirty years she would chair the urban planning program at a large California university, advocate for women's place in the profession, and, at the age of 82, win a national award as a distinguished woman planner.[88] Just as she challenged the male dominance of her chosen profession, so she would, with her family's contrarian streak, disrupt the cozy, all-male ambience of M&G Piel Securities.

In the four years before her husband's death in 1968, his carousing had burned though most of Margarita's assets. He withdrew $103,000 in cash from joint checking in just one year. He failed to repay his personal loans from Grace Bank, secured by her Piel stock certificates, pushing her toward bankruptcy. Then he moved out, asked for a divorce, and died in an alcohol-fueled accident. When the bank sent a threatening letter, Margarita flew to New York to meet a skeptical vice-president. But mindful of his firm's special relationship with the Piels, the banker soon softened, apologized for the "rough handling in the demand letters," and gave her additional time to repay. To make the first payments before she could start work as an urban planner, Margarita held a yard sale of family heirlooms and sold some of her Piel shares to the company's disapproving directors. Simultaneously, she sued Aetna to collect her husband's life insurance and used that money to liquidate the Grace Bank loan, thereby recovering control of her M&G Piel shares, "the only legacy I had for my children."[89]

Actually, Margarita wasn't just fighting for her children. She was fighting for her life. Take those cash withdrawals of $103,000, three times her husband's annual salary or about $750,000 today. I came home during spring break from Columbia to find my father moved out and my mother devastated. She couldn't understand why or what was happening. So I broke into my father's desk, found his checkbook, and added up the cash withdrawals. In just a year, he had somehow spent $103,000 in petty cash at a time when my college tuition was just $2,000. When I told her, Mother realized he wasn't just divorcing her. He was destroying her. That night when he came by the house in his new Avanti sports car, Mother ran down the drive. On that warm California night, in front of our million-dollar house, she started screaming "a hundred and three thousand dollars!" over and over into a street filled with movie star homes. Standing on the curb, just making sure things didn't get physical, I watched my parents play out that sad drama like I was at the movies. But things soon got real enough. When I came back that summer, Mother had moved to a small apartment, affordable only because the building was slipping into the sea. That fall I got a city hack license and drove a taxi nights through the lightless, lawless streets of Harlem and South Bronx to finish my Ivy League degree. Reminded of that confrontation, which she had pushed from memory, a half-century later when I was writing these pages, Margarita could recall, with satisfaction, being well dressed for the occasion in an elegant knit dress with long sleeves and golden buttons.[90]

Concerned about the company's direction, Margarita, though just an ordinary stockholder, rearranged her life for a transcontinental grind to the quarterly board meetings of M&G Piel Securities. Rush-hour drive to Los Angeles Airport after teaching her class. Cheap overnight "red-eye" flight to Kennedy Airport. Bus into Manhattan's airline terminal. A dawn march up Park Avenue to the Waldorf-Astoria. Quick cleanup at the Ladies Lounge. Short walk to a mid-morning board meeting in Midtown. Overnight flight back to Los Angeles. "At first, I knew nothing about investments," Margarita recalled. "I didn't even know what an equity was. But I knew that if the older generation kept going the way they were, the company would be bankrupt in ten years."[91]

In those days, M&G Piel existed largely for tax minimization, to avoid any onerous capital gains penalties from the sale of the brewery. "Back in the early 1970s," recalled Margarita, "the directors were trying to liquidate the company as fast as possible by paying out maximum dividends and enjoying long, expensive lunches, which were all business expenses. There was no thought for the future." In contrast to Uncle Paul who seemed uncomfortable with her presence, chairman Henry Muessen patiently explained the business of investing, giving meaning to the arcane terms she read in the financial press.[92] When teaching forced Margarita to miss a meeting, Muessen sent summaries with helpful explanations, saying in a June 1975 letter that "your cogent, intelligent questions and suggestions are what our meetings need more of." After signing himself "Henry," he added affectionately "or Heinz as your mother, father, and other Piels have always called me."[93]

For five years Margarita attended quarterly meetings regularly, usually the only guest along with her Uncle Paul, who made no move to ease her transcontinental grind with a seat on the board or a bed at his Manhattan home.[94] After sitting in silence for a few years, Margarita started questioning the quality of investment advice from Marine Midland Bank and suggesting solutions to the rash of redemptions draining their company's capital.[95] By then, even Uncle

Paul was taking notice, sending her occasional notes to explain the company's peculiar history. After one meeting, he escorted her on a walking tour of Fifth Avenue, paying "absolutely no attention to traffic lights, wandering across streets as it suited him, like Moses parting the Red Sea."[96]

During all those years flying in from Los Angeles for quarterly meetings as a guest, none of the directors made any move to nominate Margarita to their all-male board. Some months after Henry Muessen suffered a severe stroke in 1979, Louise Piel Lange complained openly that "it has been several years since a stockholders meeting was held," prompting the new chairman, her son Fred Lange, to correct that oversight. Meeting at Marine Midland Bank on Park Avenue in June 1980, the eight Piel stockholders present chose Paul to chair the session "by acclamation." When nominations for the board opened, the lawyer for the Gottfried Piels, Leonard Lazarus, told Margarita quietly: "You should be on the board, but Paul will not allow it. So I will appoint you as a representative of the Gottfried Piels." When Paul called on them to nominate their quota of three directors, their proxy Lazarus announced that Margarita would represent the other side of the family, an unexpected, unprecedented move Paul was powerless to block. Then, on behalf of the Michael Piel shareholders, Paul announced his three all-male nominations of Gerard Piel, Fred Lange, and family lawyer Martin Rothenberg. All shareholders then jointly nominated Henry Muessen, now recovering from his stroke, for the seventh seat.[97]

After fifty years of leading the Piel holding companies, Paul, for the first time since 1930, would no longer exercise remote control over the family business. In an ironic twist, he marked his half-century of service by chairing a meeting that not only overturned his exclusion of women from the board, but also elected one who would soon transform the closed, clubby corporation he had long cherished. This change had come just in time. M&G Piel was now facing an uncertain future. After the deaths of all five of Gottfried's children without heirs, their shares were passing to institutional beneficiaries that were selling out. When Princeton University redeemed Robert Piel's shares for $330,000 in 1980, total capital withdrawals since incorporation in 1962 reached an unsustainable total of $1.7 million.[98]

New Broom

After her election, Margarita McCoy and her Uncle Paul continued to ignore each other politely at the quarterly meetings, much as they had for the past seven years as guests. "It didn't take long for Fred and I, who were the only two of our generation on the board, to start changing M&G Piel from a tax dodge into an investment company," she recalled. "Fred and I thought we could build something to last—something that would bring the family together and provide a financial foundation for future generations. So we started coming up with suggestions, and gradually the other board members began to agree with us and accept our ideas. It was then that Paul just quietly gave up and stopped attending."[99]

With their elders fading from the company, the cousins of the third generation, long separated by their parents' feuds, began to knit close personal ties at these board meetings. As cousins not siblings, and as mutual fund members not company employees, they could create a more functional dynamic for their family business. Margarita recalled with delight, "that wonderful moment when Gerard discovers you, as his very own invention," like one of those Nobel Prize winners he recruited for his magazine. Gerard then wrote his beloved brother John Piel and wife Carolyn out in San Francisco, giving Margarita's address. After their meeting, the first of several that followed, John wrote her a short note from his prescription pad saying, "I had a glorious time recovering a cousin, but especially discovering a totally enchanting lady—you!" Margarita also formed a friendship with her generation's other Californian, Paul's son Daniel, who had quit New York advertising to teach art in San Luis Obispo.[100]

Among these cousins, Margarita's alliance with Fred Lange would become central to the firm's survival. By 1979, these two were exchanging long, complex letters about advisers, strategies, and macroeconomic trends. In family terms, these renewed ties brought her back to northern Maine for the first time in nearly thirty years, visiting Fred at his lakeshore cabin, inherited from grandmother Maria and mother Louise Piel Lange. There Margarita found Lake Parlin and its woods "as beautiful as I remembered them from long ago."[101]

Within two years, the new board—led by Margarita's strategy as an urban planner and Fred's acumen as an engineer—took the family company in new directions that Paul might have seen as unprecedented, even unwelcome. After decades with attendance limited to a half-dozen directors, the 1983 annual meeting was a major departure, with eighteen family stockholders present and frank discussions about the firm's future.[102]

In these tumultuous economic times, the Piels decided to make their transitory, tax-avoidance scheme into a lasting institution. At the December 1984 meeting, Robert McDonald of Sullivan & Cromwell, the tax expert who had helped create the company, returned after a twenty-year absence. Back in 1962, he said, nobody had expected that M&G Piel "would endure for a long period of time." But now "with a long and reasonably successful history," it seemed advisable to "retain the status quo." He warned, moreover, that any major change would have "serious tax consequences for some stockholders."[103] Confirming the wisdom of his advice, the Piel portfolio enjoyed good growth of 6 percent in the next quarter, climbing back to an $8 million valuation for the first time in many years.[104]

The 1980s also saw the fading of the family's second generation. Apart from reliable financial management, the family was also a source of emotional support for these seniors in their last years. After the death of her husband Erwin, Louise Piel Lange moved to a retirement community in Jamesburg, New Jersey, where she became, said niece Margarita, "terribly depressed, wondering why she was still alive." Her brother Paul, riding the bus from New York several times a week, "took her on long walks, advised her on books to read, stimulated her interest in pursuing hobbies, and made it possible for her to open this new chapter of her life with a more positive outlook."[105]

11.2. Louise Piel Lange (rear) visiting (left to right) Mrs. Weismann, Elisabeth Weismann, and Maria Weismann, at the Heermann Hof, Herne, Germany, in 1953, seventy years after her mother Maria Heermann Piel migrated to New York.

Louise tried to reciprocate, inviting her youngest brother Oswald, childless and recently divorced, to share her retirement home. But he proved a difficult housemate, so Louise encouraged his move to Maine under the care of their niece, Marie-Luise Kemp.[106] With income from his Piel shares, Oswald also began traveling, circling the globe on a Pan Am ticket, with stops at Hawaii, Sri Lanka, and points west. In 1987, just two years before his death, he took three younger Piel relations on a trip to Europe, performing the family's ritual visit to the Heermann farm in Herne, Germany, where the family's Westphalian house-barn still stood a full century after Maria had left for America. "The legend," wrote one of those family members, Bjorn Lange, "is that the young Maria looked out of the large window and first saw the strapping Michael sowing seeds in an adjacent field. Another variant is that Michael had come to . . . break horses. Either way, a lot of us stemmed from that encounter."[107]

These were also years when a quick succession of deaths took the family's second generation: Henry, Louise, Agnes, Paul, and Oswald. Nine months after attending his last board meeting in December 1983, Paul's passing and his half-century of service were marked by president Fred Lange's tribute at the annual meeting. In a private letter, Fred hailed Paul as "a man of so many talents . . . art, music, math and his Greek translations [that] he was born in the wrong century," a sentiment that cousin Margarita certainly shared.[108] In June 1985, Henry Muessen retired from the board after fifty-two years' service to the Piel family—loyalty they honored with an elegant dinner at the Harvard Club and an appointment as "director emeritus" until his death six years later. Along with the passing of the second generation, the deaths of these long-serving associates—Muessen, Julian Tashof's law partner Martin Rothenberg, and accountant Harry Diesl—severed the last ties between the mutual fund and the old brewery.[109]

With women starting to join corporate boards across America, stockholders at the 1984 meeting elected Margarita Piel McCoy as their president, the first woman to head the family business in 101 years.[110] At her initiative, women, once excluded from the board, soon became the majority—including Margarita herself, by then a distinguished urban planner; Eleanor Jackson Piel, a celebrated civil liberties lawyer married to Gerard; Ruth H. Lange, Rollo Lange's wife and a successful retailer; and Marie-Luise Kemp, Henry's daughter and board secretary.[111] Under their leadership, the portfolio's valuation soared from $7.9 million in November 1986 to $8.5 million five months later, a new record. As Margarita wrote cousin Marie-Luise, "we can afford to feel pretty good about our history," though she still feared the possibility of "rockier times" in the near future, which the company would in fact weather, even the market's chilling plunge in October 1987.[112]

After thirty-five years' service to the family firm, president Fred Lange, now seriously ill, delivered his valedictory at the 1987 annual meeting, celebrating the portfolio's recent appreciation yet expressing concern about the unresolved generational divide over income versus growth.[113] In anticipation of his resignation, Fred wrote cousin Margarita in March 1988, effectively entrusting her with stewardship of the family's affairs. Reflecting their shared concern about "the direction of our country," Fred worried that costly military procurements were eroding the nation's economic foundations. But, he added, eventual reconstruction of crumbling infrastructure, both roads and rails, would give M&G Piel Securities a role to play in any future recovery. With a hint of finality in early 1989, Fred wrote about the foreign purchases of real estate that seemed to be sustaining the U.S. economy, saying: "The sweet fruits of folly might be our diet for another ten years and then—well, not on our watch."[114]

At decade's end, the 1989 annual meeting seemed the sum of continuity and change within the family. As corporate secretary, Marie-Luise Kemp delivered a valedictory for her uncle Oswald Piel, the last survivor of the family's second generation. As president, Margarita Piel McCoy eulogized cousin Fred Lange, who had been her generation's first member to join the board. Though she spoke with confidence from the chair, Margarita later called "making that transition without Fred the hardest thing I have ever done." Significantly, nearly half the thirty-two stockholders and guests present were from the family's fourth generation, now represented on the board by Fred's son Bjorn Lange.[115]

In this spirit of change, the family finally cut their century-long ties to Grace Bank. As finance capital consolidated banking just as it had brewing, the Piels weathered Grace's takeover by the New York regional bank Marine Midland. But they could not tolerate their shabby treatment following its acquisition, in 1987, by the global giant Hong Kong & Shanghai Bank. After agreeing on the need for new advisers, a vetting committee headed by Gerard Piel, now back on the Piel board after selling *Scientific American*, announced "a very solid personal commitment" from their preferred candidate, Harvey Ross of Fahnstock Corporation. When Leonard Lazarus expressed a strong preference for the big banks, Gerard praised Fahnstock as a solid German American company with a long tradition of reliable service. Harvey Ross was, Gerard added, a chess grandmaster with "a long-term strategy to move the company's assets strongly into equities for future growth . . . of particular interest to our younger shareholders." With his quiet authority in the family, Gerard settled the question.[116]

Over the next twenty years, Harvey Ross would realize the promise of those words. From 1994 to 2014, his skillful stock trades nearly doubled the value of the Piel portfolio from $7.8 to $14 million while simultaneously paying family stockholders an additional $14 million in dividends and share redemptions. From the 1990s technology boom through the 2008 recession and beyond, the company averaged a solid 7 percent return, meeting the younger generation's demand for growth while also paying seniors fixed dividends for retirement income. By 2014, the company's 175,000 shares were divided among 120 members of the extended Piel family. The few survivors of the third generation held substantial blocks of several thousand, while the young adults of the fifth generation owned just a few shares each.[117]

Looking back on the half-century history of M&G Piel Securities, Inc., 1963 to 2014, the extended Piel family had realized multiple benefits from their mutual fund. Through their fortunate choice of financial advisers, first Dr. Herman Scheyhing and then Harvey Ross, their company achieved a deft balance of steady growth and reliable quarterly dividends totaling $20 million during these fifty years. Although the dispersal of shares among the younger generations meant nobody could live on that income alone, those dividends were still sufficient to underwrite the essentials of middle-class life—education, business ventures, home purchases, travel, and retirements.[118] The company has also provided family members with training in financial management, a process exemplified in late 2014 when the third generation's last director, Margarita Piel McCoy, who had learned the business at these quarterly meetings, retired at the age of 91. She was replaced by Josephine Cutts, 27 and a member of the family's fifth generation, who was now positioned to reprise that experience.[119]

As a bonus of intangible value, the company's annual meetings have served, every summer since 1989, as reunions that brought the Piels back to New England from across the country and around the world, knitting ties that otherwise would have frayed as siblings gave way to cousins and then second cousins. Through their decades of service, this consortium of third-generation cousins had moved the family beyond their parents' acrimony and forged bonds that strengthened the family firm.

Gerard's Passing

Gerard Piel played a central role in this reconciliation. After his retirement from *Scientific American* in 1986, he and wife Eleanor hosted an annual Christmas dinner for the entire Piel family at their Manhattan penthouse. Seated at the head of a long banquet table, graced by his grandfather Michael's marble statuary and grandmother Maria's heirloom silver, Gerard presided over memorable evenings of reunion and reminiscence for thirty to forty family members. At the 2002 dinner, he raised a glass to wryly toast the ghost of their old rival Colonel Jacob Ruppert, surely spinning in his grave at the presence so many Piels in his former ballroom.[120]

When he finished that toast, Gerard motioned for me to sit beside him. By now warming to his second martini, he wanted to clear up some things he had told me in our oral history interviews about his older brother. Bill Piel was a peerless litigator, genteel and articulate, admired by his peers. But in his personal life Bill could be capricious, even harsh. Back in the late 1930s when they were both starting out, Gerard at *Life* and Bill at Sullivan & Cromwell, they had dinner at his brother's apartment, nearby on Fifth Avenue at 93rd Street. Suddenly, Bill gave his four-year-old son Mike what Gerard called a "vicious spanking." It seemed that Bill was punishing the boy to get back at his wife Mary Loomis who was aristocratic and aloof. Gerard was horrified. But he said nothing. "You have [to] understand," he explained, "Bill was ten years older. He was my role model, my hero. He was an Eagle Scout and Pack Leader, but I was just an Eagle Scout and never a Pack Leader. He was always that much better at everything than I." Looking back, Gerard said, he could understand why that boy Mike grew up rebellious, kicked out of boarding schools, becoming a business failure who, literally, ran away with the circus, traveling the country for years as ringmaster with Ringling Bros. and the Lipizzaner Stallions. What could he have done to stop that train wreck?[121]

I sat silent, dumbfounded. Gerard and Bill were family titans. They rose to the top of their professions on sheer talent. For the first time in my life, Gerard had invited me inside my mother's family, something I knew as an abstraction, a story, but never a lived reality. Now I was there, closer than I could have imagined, maybe too close. It seemed that every member of my mother's generation, the family's third, wanted to confess their darkest failings, their deepest secrets, to me the family historian. How to tell their story and somehow respect their privacy was becoming impossible. I was paralyzed. I wouldn't be able to write a word for another decade, until their passing somehow freed me.

Just months after the last of these Christmas celebrations, Gerard suffered a serious stroke and, following a long hospitalization, died in September 2004 at age 89. In an extended obituary, the *New York Times* credited him with building

Scientific American into an "authoritative monthly" that published over a hundred Nobel Prize winners, with fifteen foreign editions and a million-plus circulation. The magazine hailed him as a "landmark figure in journalistic letters . . . who helped to redefine the modern era of science journalism."[122] The Piels mourned the passing of a relative who was the founding president of their family firm, M&G Piel Securities, and still held the post of vice-chair at the time of his death.[123] All that public service and generous social life had exhausted most of the $5 million saved from his magazine's sale, leaving an estate with little more than an apartment and country home that his widow would soon have to sell.[124]

While Gerard lay dying in hospital, his son Jonathan, long since fired from *Scientific American*, began lobbying the M&G Piel board to transform their corporation into a "limited liability partnership" under his direction. In emails and private meetings with directors, he cited potential tax savings from this radical change. So in October 2004, right after his father's death, Jonathan made his pitch to the board, then meeting at the Banker's Trust Building, a cube of curtain glass on Park Avenue. To clarify their choices, president Margarita Piel McCoy opened the discussion with documents showing that, over the past ten years, the company had "an excellent record of managing tax" by paying a modest 12 percent to the IRS. Their portfolio also showed strong gains averaging 9.4 percent overall and 11.4 percent on equities. Almost immediately, director Diantha Pack, heir to Walter Piel's shares, demanded, "Why should we disrupt this smooth-running machine?" When director Margarita Candace Ground asked about the tax implications of the proposed change, treasurer Jerry Salomone estimated the cost at $1.5 million—a punitive 20 percent of the portfolio's value. After she asked about the governance implications, Jonathan assured them "we could have a board just as we have now." That statement provoked an undercurrent of unease. Several directors knew well that limited partnerships usually empowered a single partner. When the president called the question, nine hands, including that of Jonathan's stepmother Eleanor Jackson Piel, shot up, producing a unanimous, 9-0-0 rejection of his proposal.[125]

A few minutes later, the firm's financial adviser Harvey Ross joined the meeting to review his recent stock trades. One of the directors broke in, asking how long would it take to eliminate the portfolio's long-held stocks subject to heavy capital gains tax, a requisite for Jonathan's proposal. In an unwitting serve at his single-partner idea, Harvey estimated at least seven years, unless we wanted to pay some really nasty taxes. Thinking all this might be making Jonathan uncomfortable, I attempted some small talk at our far end of the room's enormous conference table, carved from a block of money-green marble. Wasn't Harvey's 11.4 percent return pretty good? "Not really," Jonathan replied, "I am doing much better." Just chatting, I asked, "Do you have a private portfolio?" Archly he answered, "I'm not giving out free financial advice." A few minutes later, Jonathan looked at his watch and quick-stepped out the door.[126]

After following Gerard first into science journalism and then into *Scientific American*, Jonathan had failed in his bid to succeed his father and grandfather as head of the family firm and, by extension, the Piel family. Like Gerard in his last years at the magazine, Jonathan had tried to play patriarch inside a company with formal corporate governance. And, like his father, he had felt the consequences. For the first time in nearly a century, the Piels had moved beyond the leadership of this single dominant lineage.

In retrospect, Gerard's last years and his celebratory memorial service marked a florescence for the Piel family—a flowering that carried the seeds of decline. Nobody in the family, before or since, had a memorial like Gerard's. Crowded into the Century Association's grand space in midtown Manhattan were 300 mourners, distinguished scientists and relatives from every branch of the spreading family tree—Gerard's dozen grandchildren, his many nieces and nephews, and distant cousins from all the surviving Piel lineages. There were thoughtful tributes from well-known scientists such as the late Oliver Sacks. Yet all the words could not compensate for a loss that left the family feeling diminished. Walking up Fifth Avenue after the service, Bia Piel, a social worker from New Hampshire, remarked, "For Gerard all family members were special." Years ago just out of college and passing through New York, she was pleasantly surprised when he took her out to lunch, making her feel important even though she was a distant cousin, still unemployed. Gerard had shared his success with the family.[127]

Nobody in the family's succeeding generations seemed likely to achieve anything approaching Gerard's mix of professional achievement and intellectual influence. Among the forty-six members of the next generation, most were middle-class professionals, three had continued the family tradition at Andover, and nine had attended Ivy League schools, including five at his alma mater Harvard. Many in this fourth generation of the Piel family were accomplished in their respective fields.

But none has approached Gerard' global influence and historic impact. It took three generations of the family's striving in America to produce a public figure like Gerard. It seems unlikely there will be another like him in the next three generations. But should one appear further down the generational line, he or she will probably not feel that same strong sense of self as a Piel, with all the familial and ethnic resonances, as Gerard and others of his third generation certainly did. That unknown, unwitting descendant will likely self-identify with another of the many strong families whose sum is nothing less than American society and, ultimately, the human community.

Ave Atque Vale

After fifteen years' work on this history, let me close by dropping the historian's guise of critical distance that I have tried to maintain throughout this research and writing. Let me offer some personal reflections, first, on family business and, then, on the writing of family history.

As we have seen in almost every chapter above, conjoining the words "family" and "business" has created an oxymoron in that common term "family business" whose contradictory attributes are generally unappreciated. Both are dynamic institutions with deeply embedded characteristics—most importantly, the irrational intimacies of any family versus the market rationality of corporate management. Both are social formations with the power to impose their peculiar demands upon individual will and condition collective behavior.

By their missteps, Piel family members have revealed the social discipline embedded in the corporation. Just as William's presence was an unwitting familial barrier to the brewery's full modernization, so his son Gerard, operating as patriarch midst a modern corporation, alienated his business partners in ways that cost him the company he had founded. Though there are still many family firms, large and small, the corporate ethos has been ascendant in the past half century, either eclipsing or affecting the character of family business.

On balance, this change has registered gains and losses on both sides of America's social ledger. Major corporations offer economies of scale, research, and marketing that make new products available to countless consumers. Their fusion of scientific invention and finance capital has created important innovations in fields such as communication, transportation, manufacturing, and energy. Their supple structure can incorporate diverse individuals into a productive team. The introduction of their management techniques into a family firm can thus become a catalyst for major change, often producing efficiency and increased profitability.

Even admitting all that, the long decline of family businesses in more artisanal fields, such as brewing and publishing, may well have diminished the quality of American life. Bitter infighting might be endemic, but family businesses are also infused with a fierce pride that can inspire innovation and a commitment to quality. If your name is on the label or the masthead, it has to be good. "Doing things right seems to be more of a cultural obsession in these companies," observed a specialist at Harvard Business School.[128] While family firms like Piel Bros. might stifle individual creativity by denying heirs the chance to discover other talents, they also offered a secure income and a certain imprimatur for those who ventured into other fields.

In sum, these small- and medium-scale family firms like the Piel Bros. brewery, with their tangled histories across the span of generations, have made us who we are. In my own view, we have been enriched by their enterprise, are diminished by their passing, and will be renewed by their reappearance at the fringes of cities, cyberspace, and corporate conglomerates, much as the Piels' mutual fund has done since their brewery's sale.

Working on this project for so long has left me with some final thoughts, about both the process of writing family history and this particular family. For those who might read this book in search of ideas for their own family history, let me offer the most important lesson I have learned from these years of work: Every family, no matter how ordinary it might seem, has a hidden history whose discovery, though sometimes troubling, is not only meaningful for members but also revealing of wider social trends.[129]

Unless family members achieved some fame or social prominence, there is a natural tendency, I suspect, to assume that their story is purely personal. But if we shift our focus from narrow political history to a broader social context, then even the most ordinary of lives can reveal significant societal or cultural trends. That lesson, repeated in every chapter of this book, is the most important insight this Piel family history might have for those countless millions of American genealogists searching graveyards, county courthouses, or Internet sites for the details of their personal pasts.[130]

So, when we consider this broader context, what lessons does the history of the Piel family offer? Two. Survival is less common than we might think. And social context is the wild card in any family's success. Within the Piel family circle, extinction was surprisingly common. Among Michael and Maria's ten siblings who lived to adulthood, only two lineages would both survive and prosper. Within Michael's own birth family of six surviving siblings, his were the only Piel descendants to reach the third generation. With the death of Gottfried's daughter Sophia in 1973 and their brother Wilhelm-Henrich's child Marga a year later, the other branches of the Piel family became extinct. Gone. Ashes. Dust.

Among Maria's four Heermann siblings, three had offspring. Her younger brother Heinrich consigned his five children to penury by selling the family farm for a pittance midst Weimar Germany's inflation, swapping centuries of sweat equity for currency worth a box of cigars. By contrast, Maria raised seven healthy children and helped found a family business in 1883 that has lasted 130 years and is, at this writing, passing to the fourth and fifth generation of her descendants. With similar resilience, her younger brother, Dr. Josef Heermann, opened his ear-nose-throat (ENT) clinic at Essen in 1888. Among his eighteen descendants over the next four generations, most were accomplished professionals, including six ENT specialists who have sustained this medical practice for 125 years.[131]

More broadly, the survival of these two lineages over five generations—on top of the Heermanns' 400 years as successful Ruhr farmers—confirms recent findings, from a study of surnames in eight nations, that familial ascent/descent "can take 10 to 15 generations (300 to 450 years), much longer than most social scientists have estimated."[132] The surprising persistence of these family names for so many centuries has, in all likelihood, been accompanied by an equally relentless winnowing over the span of generations, akin to that experienced by the Piels and Heermanns.

Someday through cognitive science, we will better understand how those attributes shared by Josef and sister Maria contributed to the success and survival of their lineages. Whatever elusive, unknowable personal traits they might have shared, a determinative factor may well have been something so simple as a willingness to venture beyond the safe, known world of the family farm and try their luck in large, competitive cities, Essen for Josef and Brooklyn for Maria. Once there, both had the drive and discipline, demanded by their grandfather's call for endless toil carved above that barn door back in the Ruhr Valley, to take advantage of opportunities created by larger social forces—the rise of medicine as a modern profession for Josef, and the unquenchable U.S. demand for German-style lager beer for Maria and husband Michael. For the time being, we can probably attribute much of their achievement to some intangible mix of shared personal traits and the separate opportunities presented at certain historical junctures in their respective cities, Essen and Brooklyn.

While the Piels' fortunes have varied over time, their assimilation into America, along with millions of European immigrants, is complete. As ties to Germany faded after the second generation, the Piels formed deep, lasting attachments to New York and New England, city and country. For 130 years, the family's firms have found trusted advisers in New York City, from the brewery's early managers through their current investment counselors. For over a century, the family has carried on a romance with the New England woodlands, first those long summers in northern Maine and, in later generations, outdoor life in Connecticut, New Hampshire, and Maine. Little more than a century after Michael and Maria Piel had put aside their love of Fatherland to venture across the Atlantic to America, their grandchildren had become, after much struggle and many setbacks, firmly rooted in this country's great middle class.

In thinking about the Piels for all these years, I have also discovered, rather late in life, the importance of family as a fragile yet essential vehicle for sustaining humanity across centuries and cultures. Bound together by the wisps of custom and emotion, these ephemeral groupings are essential in nurturing the young and sustaining the old. We might be so much dust beneath the relentless press of humanity's progress, but inside a family each person is essential for passing on a cultural, material, and physical inheritance from forebears to future generations. The untimely loss of just one member can, as we have seen, extinguish an entire lineage. As the lives of these Piel and Heermann families have amply shown, our life decisions do make a difference for descendants whose names we will never know and whose lives we cannot imagine. We might be dust. But, in a family, individuals do matter.

Over the years, I have met many of the family members who became actors in this historical narrative. Their lives have enriched my own. Their character traits, good and ill, are part of my persona. The money they made and the wealth they passed on helped pay for my education and are now paying for my children's education. If I did not express my affection and my gratitude more openly at the time, then that is a cause for regret. That, of course, would have been out of character for this contentious family. But now, in closing, let me admit that I loved them all, miss those who have passed, and will treasure their memory.

Ave atque vale. Hail and farewell.

Abbreviations

AA-PAA	Academy Archive, Phillips Academy Andover
AB	*American Brewer*
ABR	*American Brewers' Review*
AWMP	Alfred W. McCoy Papers, Madison, WI
BCA	Barnard College Archives
BC-NY	Book of Conveyances, City Registers Office, Borough Hall, 210 Joralemon St., Brooklyn, NY
BC-NYCo	Books of Conveyances for New York County, City Registers Office, New York County, 66 John St., 13th Fl., New York, NY 10038
BDE	*Brooklyn Daily Eagle*
BDE-A	*Brooklyn Daily Eagle Almanac*
BF	*Beer Facts*
BJ	*Brewers Journal*
BLI	U.S. Senate, 66th Congress, 1st Session, Subcommittee on the Judiciary. *Brewing and Liquor Interests and German and Bolshevik Propaganda. Report and Hearings, Vol. 1.* Washington, DC, 1919.
BT	*Brooklyn Times*
CUA	Columbia University Archives
DB-NY	Department of Buildings, 210 Joralemon St., 8th Fl., Brooklyn, NY
DJP	David J. Piel
DN	*Daily News* (New York)

ENY-SB	East New York Savings Bank
ET	*Evening Telegram* (New York)
FF-WCA	Faculty Files, Wheaton College Archives, Norton, Massachusetts
FIT-SC	File: Federal Income Taxes, 1954–56 (Piel Bros.), Sullivan & Cromwell
FTC	Federal Trade Commission
GC-SC	File: General Correspondence (Piel Bros.), Sullivan & Cromwell
GP	Gerard Piel
GPP	Gerard Piel Papers, New York, NY
HPP	Henry Piel Papers, Dover-Foxcroft, ME
HT	*Herald Tribune*
HUA	Harvard University Archives
In Sophie Piel	*In the Matter of the Petition for the revocation of Letters Testamentory granted to Arthur Piel, as one of the Executors under the Last Will and Testament of Sophie Piel, deceased*
IRS	Internal Revenue Service
LP	Lange Papers, Lake Parlin, ME
MA	Municipal Archives, 31 Chambers Street, New York, NY
MBA	*Modern Brewery Age*
MBD-MGPS	Meeting of the Board of Directors of M&G Piel Securities, Inc.
MBD-MPHC	Meeting of the Board of Directors of Michael Piel Holding Corporation
MBD-PB	Meeting of the Board of Directors of Piel Bros.
MGPS-AM	M&G Piel Securities, Inc. Annual Meeting
MP	Mark Piel
MPHC	Michael Piel Holding Corporation
MPP	Mildred Piel Papers, Madison, WI
MaPTF	Maria Piel Trust Fund

MaPP	Maria Piel Papers, Dover-Foxcroft, ME
MGP-BSU	M&G Piel Brooklyn Storage Unit Papers
MID	Military Intelligence Division
MLPK	Marie-Luise Piel Kemp
MLKP	Marie-Luise Kemp Papers, Dover-Foxcroft, ME
MMPP	Marie Muessen Piel Papers, Dover-Foxcroft, ME
MPM	Margarita Piel McCoy
MPMP	Margarita Piel McCoy Papers, La Habra Heights, CA, and Madison, WI
MT	*Morning Telegraph* (New York)
NARA	National Archives and Records Administration
NY-CRO	New York Country Registers Office, Room 205, 31 Chambers Street, New York, NY
NYC-RIS	New York City Department of Records and Information Services
NYDT	*New York Daily Tribune, New York Tribune*
NYSA	New York State Archives, Albany, NY
NYT	*New York Times*
OHRO-CU	Oral History Research Office, Columbia University
PB-AMS	Piel Bros. (Annual) Meeting of Stockholders
PB-AR	Piel Bros. Annual Report to Stockholders
PB-CM	Piel Bros. Committee Meeting
PBM#1	Piel Bros. Minutes, Book No. 1
PBM#2	Piel Bros. Minutes, Book No. 2
PBM#3	Piel Bros. Minutes, Book No. 3
PBM#15	Piel Bros. Minutes, Book No. 15
PB-SC	File: Piel Bros., Sullivan & Cromwell
PBR-SC	File: Piel Bros. Reorganization, Sullivan & Cromwell

PF-SP	Probate File of Sophie Piel, File #260-1937, Queens County Surrogate's Court
PPP	Paul Piel Papers, Grafton, VT
RAP	Rudolf A. Piel
RPP	Roland Piel Papers, Dover-Foxcroft, ME
TNY	*The New Yorker*
TS	*The Sun* (New York)
TSG	*The Spy Glass*
TWN	*The Wheaton News*
SA	*Scientific American*
SGM-PU	Seeley G. Mudd Manuscript Library, Princeton University
SLPD	*St. Louis Post Dispatch*
SPHC	Sophie Piel Holding Corporation
S&C	Sullivan & Cromwell, New York City
USBC	U.S. Bureau of Census
USNA	U.S. National Archives
WD-GSS	War Department General and Special Staffs
WP	*Washington Post*
WP-SC	File: W. Piel—Personal File, Sullivan & Cromwell
WPJ	William Piel, Jr.
WPSP	William Piel, Sr. Papers, New York, NY

Notes

Chapter 1

1. In 1960, "Louise Piel Lange et al." were owners of 218 acres on Parlin Pond, but by 1968 she had sold to Parlin Farms, Inc. See *Annual Report of the Board of State Assessors of the State of Maine 1960* (1961), 246; and *Annual Report of the Board of State Assessors of the State of Maine 1968* (1969), Somerset County—Townships.

2. Interview, MLPK, Dover-Foxcroft, Maine, 3/31/2001; email from Olga Lange to author, 2/27/2015.

3. My mother's cousin, William Piel, Jr., told a less dramatic version of this story, quoted in chapter 2. (Interview, WPJ, Sherman, Connecticut, 1/20/1997.)

4. Interview, MPM, La Habra Heights, California, 3/13–14/2000.

5. Sworn Statement, RAP, 7/1940, MGP-BSU.

6. Sworn Statement, RAP, 9/5/1940, MGP-BSU.

7. Interview, MPM, 10/20/2004, 8/31/2013.

8. Ibid.

9. Although my meaning is different, this sentence is close to a novel's famous opening: "The past is a foreign country: they do things differently there." (See L. P. Hartley, *The Go-Between* [London, 1953], 1.)

10. Andrew Carnegie, *Triumphant Democracy or Fifty Years' March of the Republic* (New York, 1886), 365–66.

11. Ibn Khaldun, *An Arab Philosophy of History* (Princeton, 1987), 116–18; Richard M. Segal, "Shirt Sleeves to Shirt Sleeves in Three Generations," *Corp!* 7/1/2008, http://www.corpmagazine.com/special-interests/family-business/itemid/28/shirt-sleeves-to-shirt-sleeves-in-three-generations, accessed 4/26/2013.

12. Sonya Nance Rodriguez, Gladys J. Hildreth, and Joseph Mancuso, "The Dynamics of Families in Business," *Contemporary Family Therapy* 21, no. 4 (December 1999), 454; Barbara Murray, "The Succession Transition Process," *Family Business Review* 16, no. 1 (2003), 18, 24–30.

13. One writer claimed that Internet genealogy had allowed him to identify 80,000 distantly related cousins. (See A. J. Jacobs, "Are You My Cousin?" *NYT*, 2/2/2014.)

14. David Leon Chandler, *The Binghams of Louisville* (New York, 1989); Marie Brenner, *House of Dreams* (New York, 1988); William Manchester, *The Arms of Krupp* (New

York, 2003). Shane Tritsch, "Tremors in the Empire," *Chicago Magazine*, December 2002, http://www.chicagomag.com/Chicago-Magazine/December-2002/Tremors-in-the-Empire/, accessed 4/28/2014. In 2002 alone, the business press reported serious familial tensions among the Angellis of Fiat (*NYT*, 7/7/2002), the Bronfmans of Seagram (*NYT*, 7/3/2002), the Mohns of Bertlesmann Publishing (*NYT*, 8/12/2002), and the Pritzkers of Hyatt Hotels (*NYT*, 12/11/2002).

15. Alfred D. Chandler, Jr., *The Visible Hand* (Cambridge, 1977), 9–11, 464–68, 498–500.

16. John Kenneth Galbraith, *The Affluent Society* (New York, 1998), 71–74.

17. Chandler, *The Visible Hand*, 492–93; Robert J. Larner, "Ownership and Control in the 200 Largest Nonfinancial Corporations, 1929 and 1963," *The American Economic Review* 56, no. 4 (1966), 777–87.

18. Robert J. Bennett, *Entrepreneurship, Small Business, and Public Policy* (London, 2014), 8–9, 46, 59, 63, 74–83, 94–104.

19. Rodriguez et al., "The Dynamics of Families in Business," 453–54; *NYT*, 4/25/2015, 4/27/2015; Joann Muller, "VW is Already the World's Leading Automaker," *Forbes*, 4/18/2013, http://www.forbes.com/sites/joannmuller/2013/04/18/vw-is-already-the-worlds-leading-automaker/, accessed 4/29/2015.

20. Rodriguez et al., "The Dynamics of Families in Business," 453–55; *NYT*, 5/16/2015. One of the most important of these journals is the *Family Business Review*. Families in Business: From Generation to Generation, Harvard Business School, http://www.exed.hbs.edu/programs/fib/Pages/default.aspx, accessed 5/17/2015; and the Center for Family Business at Northeastern University, http://www.damore-mckim.northeastern.edu/en/faculty-and-research/research-centers-and-institutes/the-center-for-family-business/, accessed 9/27/2014.

21. Rodriguez et al., "The Dynamics of Families in Business," 455–68.

22. Giovanni Arrighi, *The Long Twentieth Century* (London, 1994), ix–x, 2–7, 58–74, 220–22, 269–300; Chandler, *The Visible Hand*, 240–58, 301, 503–12; Thomas C. Cochran, *The Pabst Brewing Company* (New York, 1948), 54, 73, 74.

23. David S. Landes, *The Unbound Prometheus* (Cambridge, 1969), 1–12, 222–26; Chandler, *The Visible Hand*, 9–10, 75–78, 81–94, 122–44, 237–38, 240–72, 280, 411–14, 426–29.

24. Rudolf Hilferding, *Finance Capital* (London, 1981), 301.

25. Anthony H. Rose, "Beer," *Scientific American* 200, no. 6 (1959), 90–100.

26. George Ehret, *Twenty-Five Years of Brewing* (New York, 1891), 7–43; "Beer into Cans," *Fortune*, 13, no. 1 (January 1936), 75–84.

27. Cochran, *The Pabst Brewing Company*, 392–94.

28. Arrighi, *The Long Twentieth Century*, 274–75, 280–81, 295–98; Chandler, *The Visible Hand*, 480–83, 492–93.

29. Arrighi, *The Long Twentieth Century,* 72–73; Greta R. Krippner, *Capitalizing on Crisis* (Cambridge, 2012), 2–3, 28–29, 30–33.

30. *One Hundred Years of Brewing* (Chicago, 1903), 611; Martin Heidegger Stack, "Liquid Bread: An Examination of the American Brewing Industry, 1865–1940" (PhD diss., Notre Dame University, 1998), 79; *NYT,* 7/14/2008.

31. Caitlin Kenney, "Beer Map: Two Giant Brewers, 210 Brands," *Planet Money,* National Public Radio, 2/19/2013, http://www.npr.org/blogs/money/2013/02/19/172323211/beer-map-two-giant-brewers-210-brands, accessed 4/29/2013; *NYT,* 7/14/2008, 12/19/2013; Steve Pearlstein, "Beer Merger Would Worsen Existing Duopoly by AB InBev, SABMiller," *WP,* 2/2/2013.

32. John Higham, *Hanging Together* (New Haven, 2001), 87; Russell A. Kazal, *Becoming Old Stock* (Princeton, 2004), 1–4, 292–93; Frank Bass, "U.S. Ethnic Mix Boasts German Accent Amid Surge of Hispanics," *Bloomberg,* 3/5/2012, http://www.bloomberg.com/news/2012-03-06/u-s-ethnic-mix-boasts-german-accent-amid-surge-of-hispanics.html, accessed 5/11/2014.

33. Kazal, *Becoming Old Stock,* 4–13.

34. *NYT,* 11/27/2013; New England Historic Genealogical Society, "Applying for Membership in the Mayflower Society," http://www.americanancestors.org/applying-for-membership-in-the-mayflower-society/; Daughters of the American Revolution, "How to Join," http://www.dar.org/national-society/become-member/how-join; United Daughters of the Confederacy, "Membership Eligibility," http://www.hqudc.org/membership/; The Holland Society of New York, "Surnames," http://www.hollandsociety.com/surnames.html, all accessed 7/21/2014; John Seabrook, "The Tree of Me," *TNY,* 3/26/2001, 58.

35. Seabrook, "The Tree of Me," 58.

36. There are some exemplary U.S. histories of African-American, Latino, religious, and presidential families, including, Edward Ball, *The Sweet Hell Inside* (New York, 2001); Ana Carolina Castillo Crimm, *De León* (Austin, 2003); Phyllis Cole, *Mary Moody Emerson and the Origins of Transcendentalism* (New York, 1998); and William R. Polk, *Polk's Folly* (New York, 2001). There are also broader social histories of family, including, Elizabeth Foyster, *Marital Violence* (Cambridge, 2005); and Steven Mintz and Susan Kellogg, *Domestic Revolutions* (New York, 1988).

37. Alfred W. McCoy, "Rent Seeking Families and the Philippine State," in Alfred W. McCoy, ed., *An Anarchy of Families* (Madison, 2009), 429–536.

38. Jeremy D. Popkin, "Historians on the Autobigraphical Frontier," *The American Historical Review* 104, no. 3 (1999), 727, 731–32.

39. David F. Musto, "The Youth of John Quincy Adams," *Proceedings of the American Philosophical Society* 113, no. 4 (1969), 269–82; David F. Musto, "The Adams Family," *Proceedings of the Massachusetts Historical Society* 93 (1981), 40–58.

40. Interview, GP, Lakeville, Connecticut, 12/26/1999.

Chapter 2

1. *BDE*, 12/23/1883.

2. Arnold Markoe, "Brooklyn Navy Yard"; Margaret Latimer, "Brooklyn," in Kenneth T. Jackson, ed., *The Encyclopedia of New York City* (New Haven, 2010), 170, 180–81.

3. Belgenland, Port of Embarkation: Antwerp, Arrival: 9/22/1882, No. 1367, Passenger Lists of Vessels Arriving at NY 1820–1897, Roll 457, USNA Microfilm Publications; N.R.P. Bonsor, *North Atlantic Seaway, Vol. 2* (Jersey, Channel Islands, 1978), 851.

4. USBC, 1900 Soundex, New York, Piel, Gottfried, Vol. 150, E.D. 483, Sheet 13, Line 22; "Piel, Michael," *The Cyclopedia of American Biography, Vol. VIII* (New York, 1918), 403.

5. "Piel, Michael," *Cyclopedia*, 403.

6. Andrés Solimano and Nathalie Watts, *International Migration, Capital Flows and the Global Economy* (Santiago, 2005), 11–21, www.cepal.org/publicaciones/xml/7/22007/lcl2259i.pdf; Michael A. Clemens and James G. Williamson, "Where Did British Foreign Capital Go?" *NBER Working Paper 8028* (2000), 1–29, http://www.nber.org/papers/w8028.pdf, both accessed 9/14/2014; Farley Grubb, *German Immigration and Servitude in America, 1709–1914* (London, 2011), 400–19.

7. Tom Goyens, *Beer and Revolution* (Urbana, 2007), 19–20; Eric Homberger, *The Historical Atlas of New York City* (New York, 1994), 98–99; Edwin G. Burrows and Mike Wallace, *Gotham* (New York, 1999), 745–46.

8. *The Brooklyn Directory* (Brooklyn, 1884), 1302; Henry R. Stiles, ed., *The Civil, Political, Professional and Ecclesiatical History and Commercial and Industrial Record of the County of Kings and the City of Brooklyn, N.Y. from 1688 to 1884, Vol. II* (New York, 1884), 771–73; Dorothee Schneider, *Trade Unions and Community* (Urbana, 1994), 132–33, 155.

9. Schneider, *Trade Unions and Community*, 155, 170–71.

10. "Piel, Michael," *Cyclopedia*, 403. Schedule of Distribution in Accordance with Adjudication of Alfred L. Taxis, Jr., President Judge filed 11/17/1959, In the Estate of Maria Piel, Deceased of the Township of Abington, No. 6068, Orphans Court of Montgomery County, Pennsylvania.

11. "Piel, Michael," *Cyclopedia*, 403.

12. Louise Piel Lange, "Legacy to the Piel Clan," 1978, LP; Christian Heermann, "Der Heermann-Hof in Östrich unter der adligen Familie der Freiherren von Romberg" (Jesteburg, 3/20/2009), 3–6, 11–16, 19; Christian Heermann, "Aus der Geschichte des Heermanns Hofes" (n.d.), 2–11; Christian Heermann, "Zur Geschichte des Heermanns Hofes" (Jesteburg, 6/26/2000), 5; Christian Heermann, "Familie Heermann Östrich" (Jesteburg, 9/4/2005), 17, MLKP.

13. "Hof Waning," http://www.hof-waning.de/der-hof/veranstaltungen/, accessed 1/17/2015.

14. Lange, "Legacy to the Piel Clan"; Heermann, "Familie Heermann Östrich," 16–17.

15. "Piel, Michael," *Cyclopedia*, 403.

16. Heermann, "Familie Heermann Östrich," 17.

17. Marriage of Michael Piel and Maria Heermann, 3/29/1883, Bochum, HPP and MLKP.

18. SS Belgenland, From Antwerp, Arrival: 8/24/1883, No. 1077, Passenger Lists of Vessels Arriving at NY 1820–1890, USNA; Michael Piel, 4/11/1898, Passport Applications, 1795–1905, Collection Number: ARC Identifier 566612/MLR Number A1 508, NARA Series: M1372, Roll #504, NARA. Wiliam F. J. Piel was born at Vervieres, Belgium, on 5/10/1883. (See *HT*, 5/29/1951.)

19. Elmer E. Wigg, letter to Sophia Piel Pinkney et al., 4/20/1937, MPP; Leonard Lazarus, "Piel Property in Düsseldorf," enclosed in Leonard Lazarus, letter to Dr. Liessem, Notary, Düsseldorf, Germany, 7/28/1959, GPP.

20. Heermann, "Zur Geschichte des Heermanns Hofes," 1.

21. Interview, MLPK, Dover-Foxcroft, Maine, 3/29/2001; interview, WPJ, 1/20/1997.

22. Dr. John E. Siebel and Anton Schwarz, *History of the Brewing Industry and Brewing Science in America* (Chicago, 1933), 56–57; Tom Acitelli, *The Audacity of Hops* (Chicago, 2013), 5.

23. Maureen Ogle, *Ambitious Brew* (Orlando, 2006), 71–78, 84–84; Amy Mittelman, *Brewing Battles* (New York, 2008), 54–55.

24. K. Austin Kerr, *Organized for Prohibition* (New Haven, 1985), 15; Daniel Okrent, *Last Call* (New York, 2010), 26–33.

25. Carl Frederick Wittke, *Refugees of Revolution* (Philadelphia, 1952), 43–55; *BLI*, vi; Burrows and Wallace, *Gotham*, 1162.

26. USBC, *Statistics of the Population of the United States at the Tenth Census* (Washington, DC, 1883), 460, 464, 468 472, 521; USBC, "Table 11: Population of the 100 Largest Urban Places: 1880," http://www.census.gov/population/www/documentation/twps0027/tab11.txt, accessed 11/2/2013.

27. Stanley Nadel, "Germans," in, Jackson, ed., *The Encyclopedia of New York City*, 505–06.

28. Absent other sources, I derived city totals by adding the output of "major" breweries (more than 12,000 barrels) in *One Hundred Years of Brewing*, producing figures lower than the likely total for all breweries. This method indicated that Milwaukee's major breweries produced 271,942 barrels for the year ending 5/1/1877, proximate to that city's Chamber of Commerce totals for all breweries of 279,286 barrels for 1875 and 321,611 for 1876. (See *One Hundred Years of Brewing* [Chicago, 1903], 374–75, 609–12;

Wm. J. Langson, *Trade and Commerce of Milwaukee* [Milwaukee, 1902], 182.) George Ehret, *Twenty-Five Years of Brewing* (New York, 1891), 48, 51; Nadel, "Germans," in *The Encyclopedia of New York City*, 506.

29. Ehret, *Twenty-Five Years of Brewing*, 51, 104, 107; Mittelman, *Brewing Battles*, 91.

30. Will Anderson, *The Breweries of Brooklyn* (Croton Falls, NY, 1976), 14, 21; *BDE*, 8/16/1867, 6/23/1873; *The Brookyn City and Business Directory* (Brooklyn, 1870), 742; *One Hundred Years of Brewing*, 213, 230; Burrows and Wallace, *Gotham*, 741; F.&M. Schaefer Brewing Co., *To Commemorate Our Hundredth Year* (New York, 1942).

31. Stiles, *Civil History of Brooklyn, Vol. II*, 771–73; Anderson, *The Breweries of Brooklyn*, 20–21; *The Brooklyn Directory (1883)*, 1302, 1407–24.

32. *BDE*, 8/14/1873.

33. Anderson, *The Breweries of Brooklyn*, 18.

34. This conclusion was reached by locating fourteen breweries in Volumes Eight and Nine, Sanborn Map Company, *Insurance Maps, Borough of Brooklyn, City of New York* (New York, 1904).

35. *BDE*, 8/12/1875.

36. Ben Jankowski, "The Bushwick Pilsners," *Brewing Techniques* 2, no. 1 (1994), 38–39.

37. Ehret, *Twenty-Five Years of Brewing*, 83–84.

38. Paul E. Misut and Jack Monti, Jr., *Simulation of Ground-Water Flow and Pumpage in Kings and Queens Counties, Long Island New York* (Coram, NY, 1999), 1, 4; R. Busciolano, *Water-Table and Potentiometric-Surface Altitudes of the Upper Glacial, Magothy, and Lloyd Aquifers on Long Island, New York, in March–April 2000, with a Summary of Hydrogeologic Conditions* (New York, 2002), 1–14.

39. *BDE-A 1910* (Brooklyn, 1910), 471; Brian Merlis and Riccardo Gomes, *Brooklyn's East New York and Cypress Hill Communities* (New York, 2010), 33–37.

40. *BDE*, 12/15/1901.

41. Burrows and Wallace, *Gotham*, 1226–36.

42. Jankowski, "The Bushwick Pilsners"; *NYT*, 5/27/2014.

43. *BDE*, 12/4/1891.

44. Ogle, *Ambitious Brew*, 93.

45. *BDE*, 10/26/1890.

46. *BDE*, 4/10/1871, 12/23/1883, 7/29/1888, 10/26/1890, 10/9/1895; Stiles, *Civil History of Brooklyn, Vol. I*, 306–07; Merlis and Gomes, *Brooklyn's East New York*, 21, 77; Burrows and Wallace, *Gotham*, 583; Schedule 1, Page 44, Free Inhabitants in the Town of New Lots, Kings County, NY, Enumerated: 6/11/1860, Post Office: East New York, USBC.

47. *BDE*, 4/10/1871, 12/23/1883, 7/29/1888, 10/26/1890, 10/9/1895; Indenture between Gottfried Piel and Wilhelm Piel to Sebastian H. Appel, 8/29/1883, MGP-BSU; 129 Georgia Avenue, Block 3702, BC-NY.

48. Stiles, *Civil History of Brooklyn, Vol. I*, 307–09, 314, 316–18; Merlis and Gomes, *Brooklyn's East New York*, 77–97.

49. *BDE*, 10/26/1890.

50. Ibid.

51. Merlis and Gomes, *Brooklyn's East New York*, 234.

52. Interview, MLPK, 3/29/2001.

53. Christine Sismondo, *America Walks into a Bar* (New York, 2011), 128–29, 133, 195.

54. *NYT*, 10/4/1910; "Bowery Saturday Night," *Harpers' Monthly*, April 1871, 673–80; Homberger, *The Historical Atlas of New York City*, 98–99.

55. Henry Herbst and Don Roussin, *St. Louis Brews* (St. Louis, 2009), 63–64.

56. Ogle, *Ambitious Brew*, 87–89; Mittelman, *Brewing Battles*, 53; Jim Farber and Gina Salamone, "As Astoria's Bohemian Hall Turns 100, a Look at New York's Best New Beer Gardens," *DN*, 5/22/2010, http://www.nydailynews.com/life-style/eats/astoria-bohemian-hall-turns-100-new-york-best-new-beer-gardens-article-1.178158; "Scholz Garten, Politics and History," August Scholz, http://www.scholzgarten.net/politics.htm; "History Now and Then," The Historic Bevo Mill, http://thebevomill.com/history-and-now/, all accessed 2/3/2014; *NYT*, 6/27/1886, 3/12/1891, 8/29/1893; "Ground Plans of the Proposed Delmar Gardens and Theater," *SLPD*, 2/14/1900.

57. Creating some confusion, a Sophie Piel appears on a ship's manifest in November 1882, described as 21, single, and from Mecklenberg (this family's Sophie was 23 and from Prussia). The 1920 census gave 1882 as the year of Sophie's arrival; but her 1924 death certificate gave her U.S. residency at forty years, for an arrival in 1884. In June 1900, Sophie and Gottfried told a U.S. census enumerator they had been married fourteen years. See Ira A. Glazier and P. William Filby, *Germans to America. Volume 44: August 1882–November 1882* (Wilmington, 1995), 393, 398; Twelfth Census of the United States, Schedule No. 1—Population, Borough of Manhattan, 34 E.D., Block D, New York City, Enumerator: Melville E. Hale, June 7, 1900; Department of Commerce, Bureau of the Census, Fourteenth Census of the United States: 1920—Population, Borough of Manhattan, New York City, E.D. 577, Sheet 7A, Enumerator: Agnes M. McClure, January 18, 1920; Department of Health, City of New York, Standard Certificate of Death 7928, Sophie Piel, March 18, 1924.

58. *BDE*, 10/26/1890.

59. *BLI*, 82–84.

60. "Piel, Michael," *Cyclopedia*, 403.

61. Ibid.

62. *BDE*, 10/26/1890.

63. Ibid. A 1905 insurance map shows the brewery occupying frontage on Georgia Avenue and a "casino" on Liberty Avenue, leaving an open space for the beer garden. See

Hugo Ullitz, *Atlas of the Borough of Brooklyn, City of New York, Vol. 4* (Brooklyn, 1905), plate 7, Part of Ward 26, Sect. 12.

64. Lange, "Legacy to the Piel Clan."

65. *BDE*, 11/3/1895.

66. Schedule B, Deed of Trust from Piel Bros. to Kings County Trust Company as Trustee, 3/30/1898, MGP-BSU.

67. *BF*, no. 114 (8/12/1948), 1, Piel Bros., S&C.

68. *NYT*, 5/24/1883.

69. *The Brooklyn Directory (1883)*, 1302, 1407–24; *Lain's Brooklyn and Long Island Business Directory 1892* (Brooklyn, 1892), 34, 124–41; Martin Heidegger Stack, "Liquid Bread: An Examination of the American Brewing Industry, 1865–1940" (PhD diss., Notre Dame University, 1998), 132–33.

70. *BDE*, 7/27, 8/1, 8/10, 8/27, 9/4, 9/7/1885.

71. Stack, "Liquid Bread," 140–45.

72. *BDE*, 10/31, 11/11, 11/21, 12/2/1888.

73. *BDE*, 6/9/1895.

74. *BDE*, 7/19/1896.

75. *BDE*, 5/17/1891; *BDE-A 1890, Vol. V* (Brooklyn, 1890), 222.

76. *BDE*, 7/6/1899.

77. *BDE*, 10/24/1890, 4/23/1891.

78. *BDE*, 7/17/1937; Merlis and Gomes, *Brooklyn's East New York*, 145.

79. *BDE*, 3/24/1899; 7/11/1900; 12/28/1901; 6/19, 8/23, 11/12, 12/3, 12/8, 12/24/1902.

80. The addresses for the sixteen attendees in the *Brooklyn Daily Eagle* were found in the *City Directory*. See *BDE*, 12/15/1911; *The Brooklyn City Directory, Vol. LXXXVIII* (Brooklyn, 1912), 452, 733, 829, 1092, 1452, 1462.

81. Annual Record of the Assessed Valuation of Real Estate in the Borough of Brooklyn, Ward 26, Vol. 3, 1886 to 1887; Annual Record of the Assessed Valuation of Real Estate 26th Ward Vol. 5, Blocks 284 to 361, 1891 to 1894; Annual Record of the Assessed Valuation of Real Estate Brooklyn County 26th Ward Blocks 284 to 361, 1894 to 1898; MA.

82. *BDE*, 1/10/1891, 9/17/1892. 40 Georgia Avenue, Block 3701; 303/313 Liberty Avenue, Block 3684, and 104–116 Georgia Avenue, Block 3685, BC-NY.

83. *BDE*, 9/21/1895.

84. Sanborn Map Company, *Insurance Maps of Brooklyn, New York, Vol. Eight* (New York, 1887); George W. & Walter S. Bromley, *Atlas of the City of Brooklyn* (Philadelphia, 1893), plate 38; Ullitz, *Atlas of the Borough of Brooklyn, Vol. 4*, plate 7, Part of Ward 26, Sect. 12; Sanborn Map Company, *Insurance Maps, Borough of Brooklyn, Vol. Eight* (New York, 1908).

85. Joseph G. Rayback, *A History of American Labor* (New York, 1966), 181–84, 264–66; Schneider, *Trade Unions and Community*, 137, 145.

86. *BDE*, 6/6, 6/7/1881; Schneider, *Trade Unions and Community*, 141–52; Hermann Schlüter, *The Brewing Industry and the Brewing Workers' Movement in America* (Cincinnati, 1910), 100–07.

87. Mittelman, *Brewing Battles*, 56–57; Schneider, *Trade Unions and Community*, 156–67; Michael A. Gordon, "The Labor Boycott in New York City, 1880–1886," *Labor History* 16, no. 2 (1975), 221–23; Schlüter, *The Brewing Industry and the Brewing Workers' Movement in America*, 106–41.

88. *BDE*, 10/13/1887; 3/27, 4/16, 4/17, 4/18/1888; Schneider, *Trade Unions and Community*, 156–67; Schlüter, *The Brewing Industry and the Brewing Workers' Movement in America*, 142–46, 148–58.

89. *BDE*, 4/19, 4/20, 4/21/1888; Schlüter, *The Brewing Industry and the Brewing Workers' Movement in America*, 156–59.

90. *BDE*, 5/9, 5/18, 6/4, 7/9, 11/30/1888; 1/7/1890; Schneider, *Trade Unions and Community*, 169–73; Schlüter, *The Brewing Industry and the Brewing Workers' Movement in America*, 157–59.

91. *BDE*, 9/22/1902.

92. Schneider, *Trade Unions and Community*, 172–76; Schlüter, *The Brewing Industry and the Brewing Workers' Movement in America*, 188–205.

93. *BDE*, 7/1/1887.

94. *BDE*, 7/5/1887.

95. *BDE*, 8/29/1887.

96. Roscoe C. E. Brown and Ray B. Smith, *Political and Governmental History of the State of New York, Vol. III* (Syracuse, 1922), 416–17.

97. Okrent, *Last Call*, 16–23; Ogle, *Ambitious Brew*, 140–41; Mittelman, *Brewing Battles*, 68–69.

98. *BDE*, 8/14/1884.

99. *NYT*, 6/25/1908.

100. *BDE*, 2/10/1889.

101. Kerr, *Organized for Prohibition*, 11, 23–24; Okrent, *Last Call*, 27, 30; Michael A. Lerner, *Dry Manhattan* (Cambridge, 2007), 22–23, 104–05; Burrows and Wallace, *Gotham*, 1100, 1108.

102. Interview, WPJ, 1/20/1997.

103. *BDE*, 4/22/1889.

104. *BDE*, 9/17/1890.

105. *BDE*, 11/26/1895.

106. Brown and Smith, *Political History of New York, Vol. III*, 415–16.

107. Schedule B, Deed of Trust from Piel Bros. to Kings County Trust Company as Trustee, 3/30/1898, MGP-BSU; John P. Peters, "Suppression of the 'Raines Law Hotels,'" *Annals of the American Academy of Political and Social Science* 32 (1908), 86–88.

108. Okrent, *Last Call*, 50.

109. *BDE*, 4/6/1896; "Brooklyn Not So Very Dry," *TS*, n.d.

110. *BDE*, 5/29, 10/4/1897; *NYT*, 6/16/1895.

111. *BDE*, 6/24/1897.

112. *BDE*, 7/2/1897.

113. *BDE*, 10/22/1897.

114. *BDE*, 11/4/1900.

Chapter 3

1. *BDE*, 12/23/1883; Gottfried Piel and Wilhelm Piel, Bond to Caspar Spiess, 9/18/1883; Indenture between Gottfried Piel and Wilhelm Piel to Caspar Spiess, 9/18/1883; Gottfried Piel and Wilhelm Piel, Bond to Sebastian H. Appel, 8/29, 9/18/1883; Indenture between Gottfried Piel and Wilhelm Piel to Sebastian H. Appel, 8/29/1883, MGP-BSU.

2. Indenture between Gottfried Piel and Wilhelm Piel parties of the first part, and Michael Piel party of the second part, Kings County Register's Office, 2/18/1884, Liber 1542, 327–28. While this legal document showed a payment of just $700, records of Michael's payment of $700 and $3,000 were published in *BDE*, 2/22/1884.

3. Gottfried Piel and others, Bond to ENY-SB, 12/30/1886 (Wilhelm Piel, signature before U.S. Consulate Düsseldorf, 1/13/1887); Gottfried Piel, Michael Piel, Wilhelm Piel, Bond to Sophie Piel, 2/3/1890 (Wilhelm Piel, signature before U.S. Consulate Düsseldorf, 2/21/1890), MGP-BSU.

4. Gottfried Piel, Michael Piel, Wilhelm Piel, Bond to ENY-SB, 1/31/1887; Gottfried Piel and Michael Piel, Bond to Caspar Spiess, 4/2/1887; Gottfried Piel, Michael Piel, Wilhelm Piel, Bond to ENY-SB, 12/5/1888; Indenture of mortgage by Gottfried and Sophie Piel, Michael and Maria Piel, Wilhelm Piel (unmarried), to ENY-SB, 12/5/1888, MGP-BSU.

5. Morris Weeks, Jr., *Beer and Brewing in America* (New York, 1953), 77; Martin Heidegger Stack, "Liquid Bread: An Examination of the American Brewing Industry, 1865–1940" (PhD diss., Notre Dame University, 1998), 79; *One Hundred Years of Brewing* (Chicago, 1903), 611; *NYT*, 7/14/2008.

6. Twelfth Census of the United States, Schedule No. 1—Population, Borough of Manhattan, 34 E.D., Block D, New York City, Enumerator: Melville E. Hale, June 7, 1900.

7. Church of Latter Day Saints, Microfilm Reel No. 0186029, Bilk, Düsseldorf, Germany; Paul Piel, Tentative Genealogical Chart of the Descendants of Jacob Piel, NYC, 6/4/1957. According to the LDS microfilm records, Maria Josephus Wilhelm Piel (born in Derendof, Düsseldorf, 4/15/1808) was married in Düsseldorf on 5/24/1849 to Elisabeth Rosendahl (born in Oberbilk, Düsseldorf, 8/25/1824) and she gave birth to seven children in "Düsseldorf" or the city's district of "Oberbilk," including Sophie on 2/17/1858. When the estate of Wilhelm's widow Elisabeth Piel nee Rosendahl (or Rosenthal) was probated

at Düsseldorf in March 1892, two children were deceased. (See Anton Greiss, Düsseldorf notary, letter to Elmer Wigg, NY attorney, 7/7/1936, MPP.)

8. Gottfried Piel, Michael Piel, Wilhelm Piel, Bond to Sophie Piel, 2/3/1890, MGP-BSU.

9. Ibid. On 7/1/1890, the Bank of East New York had a surplus of $47,726 above the $543,091 due depositors. (See *BDE-A 1890, Vol. V*, 162.)

10. *BDE*, 9/21, 10/9/1895.

11. *ABR* 9 (7/1895–6/1896), 134.

12. Anton Greiss, letter to Elmer Wigg, 7/7/1936, MPP.

13. An Agreement made this second day of March in the year one thousand eight hundred and ninety-eight, between Gottfried Piel, Michael Piel, and Hermann Petersen, HPP.

14. *BDE*, 3/4/1898.

15. Meeting of the Incorporators and Directors of Piel Bros. held at the office of Messrs. Guggenheimer, Untermeyer & Marshall, 30 Broad Street, NYC, 3/29/1898, PBM#1.

16. Piel Bros. Stock Certificates No. 4, 3/30/1898.

17. MBD-PB, 3/30/1898, PBM#1.

18. Deed of Trust from Piel Bros. to Kings County Trust Company as Trustee, 3/30/1898, MGP-BSU; *BDE-A 1897*, 337.

19. MBD-PB, 1/1/1898, PBM#1.

20. Piel Bros. Stock Certificates Nos. 1–14, 3/29–4/1/1898; PB-AMS, 4/27/1904, PBM#1, MGP-BSU.

21. Paul Piel, letter to Henry Piel, 3/19/1957, GPP.

22. William Piel, "Memorandum on a Decade of the Beer Business (1910 to incl. 1919 in Piel Bros' Career)," 2/24/1920, 7, PBM#1; Messrs. Piel Brothers, East New York Brewery, Brooklyn, NY, Profit and Loss A/c for 12 Months Ending 12/31/1905, William Waddell, Public Accountant, 71 Wall St., NYC, WPSP.

23. Interviews, GP, Lakeville, Connecticut, 12/26/1999, NYC, 12/6/2002; Gerard Piel, letter to Margarita McCoy, 7/29/2000, MPMP. In the Lakeville interview and this letter to cousin Margarita McCoy, Gerard attributed the story to his uncle Paul Piel and in the NYC interview he credited his father William Piel, Sr.

24. "The Reminiscences of Gerard Piel" (OHRO-CU, 1984), 2.

25. Stack, "Liquid Bread," 89–97; *One Hundred Years of Brewing*, 62–75, 108–11, 122–47, 611; Louis Pasteur, *Studies on Fermentation* (London, 1879); Dr. John E. Siebel and Anton Schwarz, *History of the Brewing Industry and Brewing Science in America* (Chicago, 1933), 845–101, 113–14.

26. *BDE*, 1/28/1899.

27. *BDE*, 8/2/1897, 1/18, 6/30/1898.

28. *BDE*, 9/25/1902.

29. *BDE*, 1/13/1898; Will Anderson, *The Breweries of Brooklyn* (Croton Falls, NY, 1976), 36–38.

30. *BDE*, 12/20/1896.

31. Sanborn Map Company, *Insurance Maps of Brooklyn, New York, Vol. Eight* (New York, 1887).

32. "Piel, Michael," *The Cyclopedia of American Biography, Vol. VIII* (New York, 1918), 403; MBD-PB, 12/15/1898, PBM#1.

33. Schedule B, Deed of Trust from Piel Bros. to Kings County Trust Company as Trustee, 3/30/1898, MGP-BSU); David G. Moyer, *American Breweries of the Past* (Bloomington, 2009), 5; Philip Van Munching, *Beer Blast* (New York, 1997), 17; *BDE*, 7/5/1887.

34. Permit No. 187, Plan No. 682, Detailed Statement of Specifications for Brick Buildings, Submitted: 4/14/1898, DB-NY.

35. MBD-PB, 7/17/1899, 1/29, 3/13, 4/2, 10/15/1900, PBM#1; *Pure Products, Vol. III* (New York, 1907), 36.

36. Sanborn Map Company, *Insurance Maps, Borough of Brooklyn, Vol. Eight* (New York, 1908).

37. Permit No. 1044, Inspector's Memorandum of Application for Brick Buildings, Approved: 3/13/1912, DB-NY; Sanborn Map Company, *Insurance Maps of Brooklyn, City of New York, Vol. 16* (New York, 1928); *BF*, no. 114 (1948), 2, PB-SC.

38. Piel, "Memorandum on a Decade," 46.

39. Ibid., 7.

40. Michael Piel Account Current—1/1/1898 to 12/31/1902, Haskins & Sells, Certified Public Accountants, 30 Broad Street, NY, WPSP.

41. Michael Piel, Accounting Work Sheets for 1902, WPSP.

42. MBD-PB, 6/25/1910, MBD-PB, 12/31/1910, PBM#1.

43. "Piel, Michael," *Cyclopedia*, 403–04.

44. Between 1898 and 1914, the Board's minutes show Gottfried Piel as almost always present and Michael Piel absent twenty-three times. (See PBM#1.)

45. "Piel, Michael," *Cyclopedia*, 403–04.

46. Louise Piel Lange, "Legacy to the Piel Clan," 1978, LP; Michael Piel, 4/11/1898, Passport Applications, 1795–1905, NARA.

47. List or Manifest of Alien Passengers for the United States, *S.S. Kronprinzessin Cecilie*, from Bremen, 6/23/1908; same ship, from Bremen, 4/6/1909; and *S.S. Kaiser Wilhelm*, from Cherbourg, 7/20/1911, http://ancestry.com/Browse/print_u. aspx?dbid=7 488&iid=NYT715_1716-0061, accessed 8/16/2011.

48. Christian Heermann, "Zur Geschichte des Heermanns Hofes," (Jesteburg, 6/26/2000), 5.

49. Christian Heermann, "Aus der Geschichte des Heermanns Hofes" (n.d.).

50. Interview, MLPK, 3/31/2001; Maria Piel, letter to Roland Piel, 11/5/1925, RPP.

51. U.S. Bureau of Navigation, Department of the Treasury, *Forty-Fifth Annual List of the Merchant Vessels of the United States* (Washington, DC, 1913), 244. Michael Piel's granddaughter, Margarita Piel McCoy, had such a plate in her kitchen for many years. Letter from Maria Piel, 12/29/1913, PPP; interview, MP, NYC, 12/9/2000.

52. Maria Piel, postcards to Paul Piel, 4/29/1913, 1/25/1914, 1/27/1915, PPP; Margarita Piel McCoy, letter to author, 9/2001.

53. Maria Piel, letters to Paul Piel, 2/2/1910; ca.1913–14; 5/14, 11/30/1913, PPP.

54. Ibid., 3/5/1915, PPP.

55. *NYDT*, 4/13/1902.

56. *New York University Bulletin* VII, no. 1 (1907), 41; *The Phi Gamma Delta* (Indianapolis, 1907), 757.

57. C. B. Newton, ed., *General Catalogue of Graduates and Former Students Lawrenceville School* (Lawrenceville, NJ, 1910), 134–35; *The Nassau Herald* (Princeton, 1913), 6, 68; Walter Piel, Class of 1917, Candidate for B. Litt. Degree, Transcript; Walter Piel, Biographical and Class Record Information Blank, Class of 1916, 4/1930, SGM-PU.

58. *NYT*, 10/28/1904.

59. Maria Piel, letter to Paul Piel, 2/2/1910, PPP.

60. Andrew Otto Piel, Record of Birth, 2545, Brooklyn (New Lots); Sophia Piel, Record of Birth, 2742, Birth Records 1886, MA.

61. Michael Piel's Petition for Naturalization, City Court, Brooklyn, NY, 10/5/1888, Vol. 56, Rec. 197, USNA, 201 Varick Street, NY; In the Matter of the Application of Michael Piel to become a Citizen of the United States, 10/5/1888, Hon. Wm. J. Osborn, WPSP; Lange, "Legacy to the Piel Clan."

62. Piel, Tentative Genealogical Chart, NYC, 6/4/1957; Lange, "Legacy to the Piel Clan."

63. Albert Richard Piel, Certificate of Death, No. 5932, Department of Health, City of Brooklyn, MA.

64. Indenture between William W. Hall and Emily Parker Hall and Gottfried Piel, Liber 60, 259, 3/4/1898, NY-CRO; *BDE*, 4/23/1898.

65. Volume 158, Sheet 13, Line 22, 1900 Census Index; Twelfth Census of the United States, Borough of Manhattan, 34 E.D., Supervisor's District No. 1, Enumeration District 483, Block D, Sheet No. 13, 7/7/1900, USBC.

66. Grantor Williams Bellew, Grantee Michael Piel, Liber 15, 494, 12/1/1899, BC-NY.

67. Lange, "Legacy to the Piel Clan."

68. Ibid.

69. Volume 67, Sheet 14, Line 68, 1900 Census Index; Twelfth Census of the United States, Kings County, Borough of Brooklyn, 88 E.D., Supervisor's District No. 2, Enumeration District 88, Block D, Sheet No. 14, 6/12/1900, USBC.

70. Lange, "Legacy to the Piel Clan."

71. Indenture between Frank Tilford and Maria Piel, 5/5/1903, Liber 93, 266–67, NY-CRO.

72. Statement, 7/10/1930, 245 W. 72nd Street, Block 1164, Lot B, Record, Office of Housing Preservations and Development, Division of Housing, Department of Buildings, 3280 Broadway, NY, NY. 245 West 72nd Street, Grantor: Maria Piel, Grantee: Max Carnot, Alfred Timen, 5/14/1921, Liber 3209, 471; 148 Riverside Drive, Grantor: Gottfried & Sophie Piel, Grantee: Eva Bennett, 12/16/1919, Liber 3116, 397, BY-NYCo; William Piel, Ledger for Maria Piel, 236, GPP; *Polk's New York City Directory (Boroughs of Queens and Richmond 1933–1934)* (New York, 1934), 774.

73. Appraisal and Inventory of Household Furnishings Including Furs and Linens Excluding Wearing Apparel, Jewelry Belonging to Mr. M. Piel, 245 West 72nd Street, NYC, Appraised and Inventoried 1/17/1907, by the Fidelity Appraising Company, Incorporated, 60 Wall Street, NY, PPP.

74. *The Senior Year Book of the Class of Nineteen Hundred and Five: A Record of the Senior Class of Columbia College* (New York, 1905), 63.

75. Piel, Ledger for Maria Piel, 158–66.

76. David J. Piel, *Piel Bros & the Piels* (Carson City, NV, 2001). Other Piel relations told a similar story to the children of the family's fourth generation. (Interview with Dr. Ernie Lange, M&G Piel Annual Meeting, Portsmouth, NH, 6/25–26/2004).

77. Piel, Ledger for Maria Piel, 182; "Historic Guitar Makers of the Madrid School," Zavaleta's, La Casa de Guitarras, Tuscon, AZ, http://zavaletas-guitarras.com/content/index.cfm?action=view&ContentID=65, accessed 3/3/2012; Garantieschein, Die Firma Hamma & Co. in Stuttgart, dass die durch Herrn Michael Piel, aus America, Violine Antonius Stradivarius Cremona anno 1711, Stuttgart, 3/24/1908, PPP.

78. Friedrich & Bro., letter to Mr. Wm. F. J. Piel, 12/23/1921, PPP.

79. "The ex-Heifitz Stradivari, 1731," *The Strad* 69, no. 828 (1959), 430.

80. *BDE*, 3/31, 7/21, 8/10/1899; *NYDT*, 7/1/1906.

81. Thomas M. Burns, Sworn Statement, 2/10/1925; Premises owned by Sophie Piel at Deering Harbor, Shelter Island, List of Furniture and an appraisal of the separate articles, *In the Matter of the Appraisal Under the Transfer Tax Law of the Estate of Sophie Piel, Deceased*, 3/19/1924, PF-SP; interview, MLPK, 3/29/2001.

82. *BDE*, 8/29/1910.

83. *BDE*, 2/12/1914.

84. *NYDT*, 8/12/1914.

85. *NYDT*, 8/7/1914.

86. *NYT*, 4/7/1895; Lange, "Legacy to the Piel Clan."

87. David L. Richards, *Poland Spring* (Lebanon, NH, 2005); Richard S. Jackson, *Houses of the Berkshires* (New York, 2011); Carole Owens, *The Berkshire Cottages* (Stockbridge, MA, 1984); Harvey H. Kaiser, *Great Camps of the Adirondacks* (Boston, 2003).

88. *BDE*, 9/27/1900; *NYDT*, 9/28/1900.

89. *BDE*, 7/20/1902.

90. Lange, "Legacy to the Piel Clan."

91. Ibid.

92. William Piel, "An Impromptu Sketch Book of the Summer of 1905" (original pencil manuscript), 6/17–18/1905, 6/19/1905.

93. William Piel, "Game at Parlin: From the 1905 Sketch Book."

94. Ibid.

95. Ibid.

96. Ibid.

97. Ibid.

98. William Piel, "Reminiscence: From My 'Impromptu Sketch Book of the Summer of 1905,'" 6/24/1905.

99. Ibid., 7/6/1905.

100. Lange, "Legacy to the Piel Clan."

101. Interview, MPM, 3/14/2000.

102. Piel, "An Impromptu Sketch Book of the Summer of 1905," 9/7/1905; Lange, "Legacy to the Piel Clan"; Louise Piel Lange, letter to Henry Piel, 3/9/1979, LP.

Chapter 4

1. Piel Bros., "An Open Letter To the Medical Profession," *American Journal of Surgery* 29, no. 12 (1915), 472, citing an article by Professor Adolf Cuss in the *Zeitschrift für das gesamte Brauwesen* (May 20, 1911); William Piel, "Memorandum on a Decade of the Beer Business (1910 to incl. 1919 in Piel Bros' Career)," 2/24/1920, 1–4, PBM#1; MBD-PB, 3/13/1900, PBM#1.

2. Piel, "Memorandum on a Decade," February 24, 1920, 1–2.

3. Messrs. Piel Brothers, Profit and Loss A/c for 12 Months Ending 12/31/1905, WPSP.

4. Ibid., December 31, 1907.

5. MBD-PB, 5/26/1915, PBM#1.

6. William Piel, Jr. and Martha Moore, *Lamplighters* (New York, 1981), 184–85.

7. *BDE*, 11/12/1899.

8. William F. J. Piel, "Territorial Expansion. Shall We Maintain Our Hold on the Philippines?" 4/6/1900, WPSP.

9. *BDE*, 12/2/1900, 1/20, 2/17, 6/4, 6/8, 7/6/1901; *Polyglot 1901* (Poly Prep, Brooklyn); W. F. J. Piel, "Valedictory for Class of 1901," 6/7/1901, WPSP.

10. Columbia College Transcript, William F. J. Piel, A.B. Degree Conferred 6/1905, CUA; G.A. Younger, "Class History," *The Senior Year Book of the Class of Nineteen Hundred and Five*, (New York, 1905), 63, 110–11; *The Columbian Nineteen Hundred and Five* (New York, 1905), 60, 65; *Columbia Spectator* XLVII, no. 173 (1904), CUA.

11. William F. J. Piel, "Dozen or Sixteen Lines," translation from *Iliad*, Book A, 192–218, 12/24/1900, WPSP; William F. J. Piel, "The Introduction of the Middle Class Tragedy into German Literature" (A.B., Columbia, 4/1/1905), 11, 46, 48–49, No. Co/F05, Master Negative # 20000-2051, Columbia University Libraries.

12. Michael Piel, letter to Hermann Petersen, 2/17/1909; Capitulation of Expenditures by William F. J. Piel for M. Piel, From 1/2/1909, to and including 1/10/1909, WPSP.

13. *The Columbian* (New York, 12/1906), 62, 170; Columbia University, *Catalogue of Officers and Graduates of Columbia University, XVI Edition* (New York, 1916), 656–57, 1324; "Business and Finance Leaders. William Piel Sr.," *HT*, 5/29/1951; interview, DJP, Lenox, Massachusetts, 5/11/2002; Certificate and Record of Marriage, No. 1476, William F.J. Piel and Loretto B. Scott, 1/8/1908; Certificate and Record of Birth, No. 59327, William F.J. Piel, Jr., 11/28/1909, City of New York, Department of Health; interview, WPJ, Sherman, Connecticut, 1/20/1997.

14. Interview, WPJ, 1/20/1997.

15. Piel, "Memorandum on a Decade," 9.

16. "The Reminiscences of George J. Joyce" (OHRO-CU, 1962), 40.

17. Daniel Okrent, *Last Call* (New York, 2010), 30; *NYT*, 3/22/2012.

18. MBD-PB, 5/26/1915, PBM#1.

19. Piel, "Memorandum on a Decade," 7–8.

20. Ibid., 9.

21. *TS*, 7/14/1911; Piel, "Memorandum on a Decade," 5, 9–10; MBD-PB, 10/15/1900, PBM#1.

22. Piel, "Memorandum on a Decade," 10; MBD-PB, 6/25/1909, PBM#1.

23. Piel, "Memorandum on a Decade," 10–11, 17; MBD-PB, 2/23/1912, PBM#1.

24. Piel, "Memorandum on a Decade," 12, 15.

25. *BDE*, 12/15/1911; Piel, "Memorandum on a Decade," 7, 11, 13.

26. MBD-PB, 5/22/1911; PB-AMS, 3/12/1912; Piel, "Memorandum on a Decade," 13.

27. *Pot Pourri 1905* (Phillips Academy Andover), 53; Henry Gottfried Piel, College Examinations, 6/1905, AA-PAA.

28. Columbia College Transcript, Henry Gottfried Piel, Date of Entrance: 9/18/1905; *The Columbian* (New York, 1909), 54, 187, 234, 256, 295; *The Columbian* (New York, 1906), 81, CUA.

29. Dortmunder Union Brauerie, 12/31/1908; Eisenberg Maltzfabriken, Certificate, 4/1/1909; Henry Piel, letter to Michael Piel, 1/27/1909; Henry Piel, Absolutorium der Brauerabteilung, Royal Bavarian Academy for Agriculture and Beer Brewing at Weihenstephan, 7/31/1910; Alfred Jorgensen, Gargungsphysiologisches Laboratorium, 9/30/1910, MLKP; "Ein Familienfest in Lake Parlin," *Sonntagsblatt Staats-Zeitung und Herold* (NY), 8/17/1947, MMPP; Henry Piel, letter to Paul Piel, 1/17/1910, PPP; *NYT*, 5/27/2014.

30. MBD-PB, 3/11/1914, 1/15/1921; Piel, "Memorandum on a Decade," 14.

31. *NYDT*, 10/5/1912; *BDE*, 10/23/1912.

32. MBD-PB, 12/23/1912, PBM#1.

33. *NYT*, 6/14/1915; *TS*, 6/14/1915; Certified Abstract of a Certificate of Death, Department of Human Services, State of Maine, Michael Piel, Date of Death: 6/12/1915.

34. Schedule of Goods and Chattels, Michael Piel, 8/10/1915, Probate Court, Somerset County, Maine.

35. *NYT*, 2/4/1916; Wilhelm Carl Heinrich Jacob Josef Ferdinand Piel, Deposition, Schedule A, 1/6/1916, In the Matter of the Appraisal under the Transfer Tax Law of the Estate of Michael Piel, Surrogate's Court, County of New York.

36. Maria Piel, Deposition, 1/24/1916, In the Matter of the Appraisal under the Transfer Tax Law of the Estate of Michael Piel, Surrogate's Court, County of New York.

37. Julian Tashof, Re: Michael Piel Holding Corporation Memo, 2/25/1957, GPP.

38. Burial Search, Green-Wood Cemetery, Michael Piel, Burial Date: 1915-06-16, Lot: 17313, Section: 152; Roland O.P. Piel, Burial Date: 1926-07-08, Lot: 17313, Section: 152, http://www.green-wood.com/burial_results/index.php, accessed 1/2/2013.

39. Last Will and Testament of Michael Piel, 8/2/1908, In the Matter of the Appraisal under the Transfer Tax Law of the Estate of Michael Piel, Report of Appraiser, 2/3/1916, Surrogate's Court, County of New York; Matthias Litt in answer to questions by Hon. Edward P. Danforth, counsel for the executrix, Transcript of Testimony, Estate of Michael Piel, Probate Court, Somerset County, State of Maine, 7/13/1915.

40. *BT*, 7/15/1915; *BDE*, 3/2/1916; MBD-PB, 9/15/1915, PBM#1.

41. G. Piel Co., Business Incorporation Certificate, File No. 02401, Filed: 1/4/1911, Supreme Court, New York, 60 Centre Street, NY; "Long Standing Limits on Volume Removed—Entire Field Expanded," *Printers' Ink* (6/10/1920), 8–9.

42. *G-P Muffler Cut-Out* (Long Island City, 1913); *The LongHorn* (Long Island City, 1919), Benson Ford Research Center, Dearborn, Michigan.

43. Appraisal of the Investors Agency, Inc., *In Re: Estate of Sophie Piel, Deceased 3/19/1924*, PF-SP.

44. Gottfried Piel, letter to the Secretary of Piel Bros. Inc., 12/24/1921; MBD-PB, 1/15/1921, PBM#1.

45. MBD-PB, 3/11/1914, PBM#1.

46. Maria Piel to William Piel, Power of Attorney, 2/8/1916, New York, NY, MGP-BSU; interview, GP, 12/26/1999; interview, WPJ, 1/20/1997.

47. Gottfried Piel, letter to Secretary of Piel Bros. Inc., 12/24/1921; MBD-PB, 1/15/1921, PBM#1.

48. Piel, "Memorandum on a Decade," 13.

49. Piel Bros., City of New York, Department of Taxes and Assessments, 3/13/1908, 1/10/1910, 10/2/1916.

50. William Couper, *History of the Engineering, Construction and Equipment of the Pennsylvania Railroad Company's New York Terminal and Approaches* (New York, 1912), 7–16, 32; *NYT*, 9/9/1906; Brian Merlis and Riccardo Gomes, *Brooklyn's East New York and Cypress Hill Communities* (New York, 2010), 105–06.

51. Piel, "Memorandum on a Decade," 12; MBD-PB, 5/26/1915; Contract, Louis Deutz of 430 First St. Brooklyn, N.Y., 11/5/1913, PBM#1.

52. Piel, "Memorandum on a Decade," 12, 15, 17; Contract, Louis Deutz, 11/5/1913; MBD-PB, 5/26/1915, PBM#1.

53. *ET*, 7/1/1913.

54. *ET*, 1/18, 1/25, 3/23, 6/7, 7/26/1914.

55. *ET*, 8/18/1914.

56. *ET*, 9/18/1914.

57. Henry Piel, letter to Marie Muessen Piel, 8/12/1914, HPP; Maria Piel, letter to Paul Piel, 9/1/1914, PPP; MBD-PB, 10/13/1914; Piel, "Memorandum on a Decade," 15.

58. MBD-PB, 5/26/1915, PBM#1.

59. Piel, "Memorandum on a Decade," 45–46.

60. Ibid., 17; "'One Man Tells Another' About Piel," *BJ* 78, no. 1 (1938), 34.

61. Piel, "Memorandum on a Decade," 16.

62. MBD-PB, 11/25/1914, PBM#1.

63. Ibid.; Piel, "Memorandum on a Decade," 17.

64. Piel, "Memorandum on a Decade," 15–18.

65. Henry Piel, letter to Paul Piel, 7/15/1914, PPP; PB-AMS, 3/14/1916, PBM#1.

66. Piel, "Memorandum on a Decade," 18, 20; Henry G. Piel, "What 'Kovar' Is," MBD-PB, 4/10/1917, PBM#1.

67. William Piel, "Kovar Experiences Under Prohibition Laws of the States of Virginia, New Hampshire, and Under the Brooks High License of Pennsylvania," 1/21/1920, 4–5, PBM#1.

68. Piel, "Memorandum on a Decade," 17; PB-AMS, 3/13/1917, PBM#1.

69. MBD-PB, 4/10/1917, PBM#1; Peter Hernon and Terry Ganey, *Under the Influence* (New York, 1991), 105–06; Roland Krebs and Percy J. Orthwein, *Making Friends is Our Business* (Chicago, 1953), 96–98.

70. Piel, "Memorandum on a Decade," 23.

71. William Piel, letter to Maria Piel, 7/7/1917, MaPP.

72. MBD-PB, 6/28/1918; Dr. Robert C. Schupphaus, Affidavit, NY, 5/18/1918; Dr. Robert C. Schupphaus, "Detail Analysis of Kovar," 5/18/1918, PBM#1.

73. Piel, "Kovar Experiences Under Prohibition Laws," 6–7.

74. Okrent, *Last Call*, 249–50.

75. Piel, "Memorandum on a Decade," 22–23.

76. MBD-PB, 9/28/1918, PBM#1.

77. PB-AMS, 3/14/1916; Piel, "Memorandum on a Decade," 45.

78. MBD-PB, 11/5/1918, PBM#1.

79. Piel, "Memorandum on a Decade," 42–44; *BDE*, 6/30/1919.

80. PB-AMS, 3/12/1918, PBM#1.

81. PB-AMS, 5/24/1919; MBD-PB, 9/28/1918; Piel, "Memorandum on a Decade," 21–22, 23–24.

82. Piel, "Memorandum on a Decade," 34–37, 40–41.

83. Marie Piel, letter to Paul Piel, ca. 7/16/1914, PPP.

84. MBD-PB, 5/8/1918, PBM#1.

85. MBD-PB, 4/10/1917; Piel, "Memorandum on a Decade," 24–35.

86. Piel, "Memorandum on a Decade," 38–39; E.F. Lange, "Backing Up the Jobber in a New Business: Kovar," in Piel, "Memorandum on a Decade of the Beer Business."

87. *ET*, 6/7/1914.

88. MBD-PB, 5/21/1917, PBM#1.

89. Okrent, *Last Call*, 35–43.

90. Count Skarzynski, "The Influence of Prohibitory Laws Upon the Manufacture and Consumption of Alcoholic Liquors in the United States," in *BLI*, 1091–93.

91. *BLI*, 1142–55.

92. Ibid., 1182–99.

93. Okrent, *Last Call*, 56–57, 64–65, 84–86; Ogle, *Ambitious Brew*, 162–67; Russell A. Kazal, *Becoming Old Stock* (Princeton, 2004), 132–33.

94. *BLI*, 1065–68.

95. Ibid., 1068–71.

96. *NYT*, 12/6/1920; Stetson, Jennings & Russell, letter to Messrs. Piel Brothers, 11/17/1917, PBM#1.

97. William Piel, "The Parlinad," 9/7/1915.

98. The Final Account of Maria Piel and William Piel, Executrix and Executor of the Estate of Michael Piel, Schedule B, 11/16/1915, Probate Court, Somerset County, Maine; Piel, "The Parlinad," 7/21/1915.

99. Piel, "The Parlinad," 7/21/1915.

100. Ibid., 7/22/1915.

101. Ibid., 8/3/1916; William Piel, Ledger for Maria Piel, 268.

102. Piel, "The Parlinad," 8/3/1916.

103. Ibid., 7/23/1915.

104. Ibid., 7/23, 7/27/1915.

105. Ibid., 7/27/1915.

106. Ibid., 9/4/1915.

107. Lange, "Legacy to the Piel Clan."

108. Piel, "The Parlinad," 9/6/1915.

109. Ibid., 8/3/1916; "Beautiful 'Lake Parlin' for Sale," *Town & Country* 77, no. 3782 (1920), 4.

110. Piel, "The Parlinad," 8/3/1916.

111. Joseph L. Melnick, "Current Status of Poliovirus Infections," *Clinical Microbiology Reviews* 9, no. 3 (1996), 293.

112. Piel, "The Parlinad," 8/25/1916.

113. Ibid., 8/11/1916.

114. Ibid.

115. Ibid., 8/10/1916

116. Ibid.

117. Ibid., 8/19/1916.

118. Ibid., 8/27/1916.

119. Ibid., 8/16–17/1916.

120. "Romantic Wooing of Henry G. Piel," *MT*, 1/19/1913; Henry Piel, letters to Marie Muessen, 7/6, 12/25/1912, HPP; Maria Piel, postcard to Marie Muessen, 2/13/1908, MLKP; Maria Piel, letters to Paul Piel, 7/19, 8/6/1913, PPP; *NYT*, 11/27/1919.

121. "Jacob Frederick Wittemann," *American Bottler* 35, no. 10 (10/15/1915), 60; "Schreiner, Bernard Francis," in Georgina Pell Curtis and Benedict Elder, eds., *The American Catholic Who's Who 1946 and 1947 (Two Years) Vol. 7* (Grosse Pointe, MI, 1948), 396; "Schreiner, Bernard F., Jr., M.D. Obituary," *Rochester Democrat and Chronicle*, 9/28/2009, http://www.legacy.com/obituaries/democratandchronicle/obituary.aspx?n=bernard-f-schreiner&pid=133603201, accessed 5/21/2012.

Chapter 5

1. Russell A. Kazal, *Becoming Old Stock* (Princeton, 2004), 151–70; "The Rape of Belgium," *NYDT*, 11/5/1917, 14.

2. Kazal, *Becoming Old Stock*, 8–13, 171–86.

3. Daniel A. Gross, "The U.S. Confiscated Half a Billion Dollars in Private Property During WWI," *Smithsonian*, 7/28/2014, http://www.smithsonianmag.com/history/us-confiscated-half-billion-dollars-private-property-during-wwi-180952144/?no-ist, accessed 5/8/2015; Amy Mittelman, *Brewing Battles* (New York, 2008), 83–84; Maureen Ogle, *Ambitious Brew* (Orlando, 2006), 174–78; *NYT*, 4/8/1919.

4. Courtney Johnson, "'Alliance Imperialism' and Anglo-American Power after 1898," in Alfred W. McCoy et al., eds., *Endless Empire* (Madison, 2012), 112–35.

5. Nicoletta Gullace, *The Blood of Our Sons* (London, 2002), 17–20.

6. La Verne Rippley, *The German Americans* (Lanham, MD, 1984), 164.

7. German University League, Henderson Contributions, Food Fund Nos. 1, 2, and 3, Office of Naval Intelligence, General Subject "CAP" Files, 1901–1927, Box 2, Folder CAP 41, 21003-110, E-79 ONI-General Files, RG 38 (Chief Naval Operations), NARA.

8. Maria Piel, letters to Paul Piel, 8/8, 8/22, 9/1/1914, PPP; Maria Piel, letter to Marie M. Piel, 1/26/1950, MMPP.

9. Maria Piel, letter to Paul Piel, 8/8/1914, PPP.

10. Maria Piel, letter to Paul Piel, 1/29/1915, PPP; Report made by John C. Howard, Portland, In re. Heirs of Michael Piel and Others European Neutrality Matters, 5/25/1917, E-31 OG (Old German) Files 1915–1920, M-1085, Reel 347, RG 65 (FBI), NARA.

11. *Portland Evening Express*, 11/10/1914, LP.

12. *NYT*, 12/6, 12/21/1914; Maria Piel, letter to Paul Piel, 12/2/1914, PPP.

13. Letter from Agnes Piel to Paul Piel, 1/20/1915, PPP.

14. Maria Piel, postcards to Paul Piel, n.d., 1/21, 2/5, 3/25/1915, PPP.

15. Maria Heermann, letters to Maria Piel, 12/6/1914, 1/6/1916, MaPP.

16. Martha Piel, letter to Paul Piel, 4/22/1915, PPP.

17. Memorial card for Franz Heinz Piel, LP; Heinrich Heermann, letter to Maria Piel, 12/7/1912, MaPP; Christian Heermann, "Familie Heermann Östrich" (Jesteberg, 9/4/2005), 30.

18. Woodrow Wilson, "Address to Congress Requesting a Declaration of War Against Germany," 4/2/1917, Miller Center, University of Virginia, http://millercenter.org/president/wilson/speeches/speech-4722, accessed 1/25/2015.

19. Interview, WPJ, 1/20/1997; Ralph Barton Perry, *The Plattsburgh Movement* (New York, 1921), 219–21.

20. Report made by Bailey V. Emery, Ports. Navy Yard, In re. Heirs of Michael Piel and Others European Neutrality Matters, 5/14/1917, NARA.

21. Report made by John C. Howard, Portland, E-31 OG (Old German) Files 1915–1920, M-1085, Reel 347, RG 65 (FBI), NARA.

22. Emerson Hough, *The Web* (Chicago, 1919), 13, 24, 34, 88; Alfred W. McCoy, *Policing America's Empire* (Madison, 2009), 296–308; Kenneth Campbell, "Major General Ralph H. Van Deman," *American Intelligence Journal* 8 (Summer 1987); "Definite Plan First Need in 'Slacker Drive,'" *TSG* 1, no. 7 (1918); "Round Up These Delinquent Enemy Aliens," *TSG* 1, no. 8, (1918); "Wide Scope of New York Division's Work, *TSG* 1, no. 9 (1918), APL Newsletter, Box 1, Folder: Spyglass, E-16 APL, RG 65 (FBI), NARA.

23. Paul Piel, Army Serial No. 2,593,924, Form 724-1, A.G.O., Records of World War I Veterans, NYSA.

24. Rudolf A. Piel, Army Serial No. 2,593,793, Form 724-1, A.G.O., Records of World War I Veterans, NYSA.

25. Walter Piel, letter to Princeton University, 1/2/18; Walter Piel, Biographical and Class Record Information, SGM-PU; William Piel, letter to Rudolf A. Piel, 8/22/1918, MaPP; Eastern Shipyard of Greenport, NY, *The Trow Copartnership and Corporation Directory of the Boroughs of Manhattan and the Bronx* (New York, 1910), 235.

26. Memorandum for the Personnel Section, Officers' Section, Room 131, Applicant: Gottfried Piel, Jr. 10/1/1917; Form O.O.R.C.-EE, Piel, Gottfried, Jr., 10/2/1917; Form O.O.R.C.Y-2, Record of Examination for Ordnance Officer Reserve Corps, Gottfried Piel, Jr., 10/2/1917; O.O.R.C.Y-2, Record of Examination for Ordnance Officer Reserve Corps, Robert Piel, 10/3/1917; Major General William Crozier, 326.11-Piel, Gottfried, Jr., 10/11/1917; Major General William Crozier, 326.11-Piel, Robert, 10/12/1917; Folder 10402-26/1-26/59, Box 3122, MID, 1917–1941, E-65, RG 675 (WFGS), NARA.

27. Colonel O. B. Mitcham, Subject: Appointment of Robert Piel as officer in Reserve Corps, 10/22/1917, Folder: PF 41161, Box 632, E-67 (MID-PF Files), RG 165 (WD-GSS), NARA.

28. Intelligence Office, Eastern Department, Informant: Col. Mitcham, Ordnance Officer, Governors Island, Suspect: Gottfried Piel, Jr. and Robt. Piel, 12/11/1917, Folder 10402-26/1-26/59, Box 3122, MID, 1917–1941, E-65, RG 165 (WD-GSS), NARA; *NYT*, 5/30/1917; Henry G. Gole, *Exposing the Third Reich* (Lexington, 2013), 17–19; *Social Register, New York, 1917, Vol. XXXI*, no. 1 (New York, 1916), 320.

29. Lieutenant Jack C. Rainier, Carriage Division, Office of the Chief of Ordnance, Washington, DC, Memorandum to the Personnel Division, 10/24/1917, Folder 10402-26/1-26/59, Box 3122, E-65, MID, 1917–1941, RG 165 (WD-GSS), NARA.

30. R.L. Benson, A.P.L., American Protective League, NY, In re: Robert Piel, Brooklyn, 10/24/1917, OG (Old German) Files, 1915–1920, M-1085, Reel 459, E-31, RG 65 (FBI), NARA.

31. Lt. Col. R.H. Van Deman, Memorandum to the Adjutant General, 11/5/1917; Colonel R. H. Van Deman, Military Intelligence Section, letter to A. Bruce Bielaski, Chief Bureau of Investigation, 11/23/1917; R. H. Van Deman, Memorandum for the Adjutant General of the Army: Subject: Robert Piel, 11/28/1917; Colonel R. H. Van Deman, letter to Commanding Officer, Rock Island Arsenal, 11/23/1917, Folder: 10402-26/1-26/59, Box 3122, MID, 1916–1941, RG 165 (WD-GSS), NARA; Chief, letter to W.M. Offley, 12/1/1917, M-1085, Reel 459, OG (Old German) Files, 1915–1920, E-31, RG 65 (FBI), NARA.

32. R. L. Benson, American Protective League, NY, In re: Robert Piel, 12/5/1917, Folder: 10402-26/1-26/59, Box 3122, MID, 1916–1941, RG 165 (WD-GSS), NARA.

33. Colonel R. H. Van Deman, letter to Major Nicholas Biddle, 302 Broadway, NY, 12/10/1917, Folder: 10402-26/1-26/59, Box 3122, MID, 1916–1941, RG 165 (WD-GSS), NARA.

34. C.B. Newton, ed., *General Catalogue of Graduates and Former Students Lawrenceville School 1810–1910* (Lawrenceville, NJ, 1910), 134–35; *The Nassau Herald*, 6, 68; Robert Piel, Class of 1913, Transcript, SGM-PU; *NYT*, 6/27/1952.

35. Harvey W. Thayer, 12/12/1917. Folder: 10402-26/1-26/59, Box 3122, MID, 1916–1941, RG 165 (WD-GSS), NARA; *Columbia Alumni News* 2, no. 3, (1910), 60.

36. R. W. Straus, File Memorandum, 12/12/1917, Folder: 10402-26/1-26/59, Box 3122, MID, 1916–1941, RG 165 (WD-GSS), NARA; Newton, ed., *Catalogue of Lawrenceville School,* 134–35.

37. Investigated By: Mr. H. J. Smith, Case of: Robert Piel, 12/15/1917, Folder: 10402-26/1-26/59, Box 3122, MID, 1916–1941, RG 165 (WD-GSS), NARA; *Directory of Living Alumni of Princeton University* (Princeton, 1917), 207–08.

38. Colonel R.H. Van Deman, letter to Intelligence Officer, 78th Division, 12/14/1917, Folder: 10402-26/1-26/59, Box 3122, MID, 1916–1941, RG 165 (WD-GSS), NARA.

39. From: Intelligence Officer, To: Chief, Military Intelligence Section, War College Division, Subject: Robert Piel (at request of C.M.I.S.), 12/17/1917, Folder: 10402-26/1-26/59, Box 3122, MID, 1916–1941, RG 165 (WD-GSS), NARA; *Directory of Living Alumni of Princeton University,* 184.

40. Lieutenant Roger W. Strauss, Memorandum Re: Private Robert Piel of the Ordnance, 1/7/1918, Folder: 10402-26/1-26/59, Box 3122, MID, 1916–1941, RG 165 (WD-GSS), NARA.

41. From: Colonel R.H. Van Deman, Chief, Military Intelligence Section, To: Chief of Ordnance, War Department, Subject: Robert Piel, Gottfried Piel, Folder: 10402-26/1-26/59, Box 3122, MID, 1916–1941, RG 165 (WD-GSS), NARA.

42. Carl W. Jones, War Services Exchange, letter to Robert Piel, 6/18/1918, Folder: 10402-26/1-26/59, Box 3122, MID, 1916–1941, RG 165 (WD-GSS), NARA.

43. D. Davidson, Bureau of Investigation, NY, In Re: Piel Brothers, Draft Evaders, 8/26/1918, M-1085, Reel 459, OG (Old German) Files, 1915–1920, E-31, RG 65 (FBI), NARA.

44. Subject: Brewery Interests, Piel Brothers, Military Intelligence Branch, Office of the Chief of Staff, War Department, 10/14/1917, Folder: PF 41161, Box 632, E-67 (MID-PF Files), RG 165 (WD-GSS), NARA.

45. From: H. M. Raymond, To: Captain Henry G. Pratt, Subject: Robert Piel, 11/12/1918, Folder: 10402-26/1-26/59, Box 3122, MID, 1916–1941, RG 165 (WD-GSS), NARA; Robert Piel, War Records, Final Notice, Princeton University, 12/10/1924.

46. *NYT,* 12/3/1916, 5/30, 7/11/1917; *Social Register New York (1917),* 337; Gole, *Exposing the Third Reich,* 17–19.

47. *NYT,* 12/15, 12/16/1917; *Social Register New York (1917),* 341.

48. *In the Matter of the Petition of Sophia Piel Pinkney, Gottfried Piel and Arthur Piel to obtain an order construing the Last Will and Testament of Sophie Piel, deceased,* 12/12/1940; Statement by Robert Piel, 9/10/1951, *In the Matter of the Petition of Sophia Piel Pinkney, Gottfried Piel and Arthur Piel for issuance of Supplementary Letters of Trusteeship under the Last Will and Testament of Sophie Piel, deceased, to Robert Piel in the Place and stead of A. Paul Loshen,* In Re: Estate of Sophie Piel, Deceased 3/19/1924, PF-SP; *Polk's New York City Directory (Boroughs of Queens and Richmond 1933–1934)*

(New York, 1934), 774; *Town Topics* (Princeton), 12/19/1954; *1913—15th Reunion Book* (Princeton, 1928), 35–36; *Princeton Alumni Weekly*, 9/26/1941; *1913—25th Year Record* (Princeton, 1938); Robert Piel '13, *Princeton Alumni Weekly*, 10/3/1952, SGM-PU.

49. Chris Hill, Office of Stewardship, Princeton University, email to author, 11/12/2013; Endowed Undergraduate Scholarships, Princeton University, http://giving. princeton.edu/scholarships-fellowships/scholarships/endowed4, accessed 7/29/2013.

50. American Protective League, NYC, In RE: Paul and Rudolf Piel, 245 West 72nd St. (Alleged Draft Evaders), 4/16/1918, E-31 OG (Old German Files), 1915–1920, Reel 575, RG 65 (FBI), NARA.

51. From: Military Attaché, Berne, Switzerland, Lieutenant Colonel W. F. H. Godson, To: Chief, Military Intelligence Branch, Executive Division, Subject: Dr. St. George, 7/10/1918, Folder: PF 24262, Box 357, Entry 67 (MID, PF Files), RG 165 (WD-GSS), NARA.

52. Ibid.; *NYT*, 11/19/1916.

53. From: Military Attaché, Berne, Switzerland, Lieutenant Colonel W. F. H. Godson, To: Chief, Military Intelligence Branch, Executive Division, Subject: Dr. St. George, 8/27/1918, Folder: PF 24262, Box 357, Entry 67 (MID, PF Files), RG 165 (WD-GSS), NARA; Charles Lyon Chandler, letters to Lieutenant Commander Fred F. Rogers, Navy Department, 2/21, 3/5/1920, Folder 21000-498, Box 554, Entry 78A, Confidential Correspondence, 1913–1924, RG 38 (Chief of Naval Operations), NARA.

54. Maria Piel, letter to Roland Piel, 2/23/1925, RPP; interview, MLPK, 3/29/2001.

55. From: Chief, Military Intelligence Branch, Executive Division, Colonel M. Churchill, To: Major Nicholas Biddle, 302 Broadway, NYC, Subject: Dr. Stadtmuller, 8/12/1918; From: Cantonment Intelligence Officer, Captain Emery L. Bryan, To: Major Nicholas Biddle, Subject: Norbert Stadtmuller, 8/22/1918; From Office of M.I.B., Lieut.-Colonel Nicholas Biddle, To: Captain Emery L. Bryan, Camp Upton, Subject: Robert [sic] Stadtmuller (PF 16613, MI4-34); From: Office of M.I.B., Lt.-Colonel Nicholas Biddle, To: Director of Military Intelligence, Washington, DC, Subject: Dr. Norbert Stadtmuller, 9/13/1918; From: Office of M.I.D., To: Alien Property Custodian, 110 W. 42nd Street, NYC, Attention of Mr. Walter Measbay, Subject: Dr. Norbert Stadtmuller, 12/7/1918, Folder: PF 16613, Box 235, Entry 67 (MID, PF Files), RG 165 (WD-GSS), NARA.

56. From: Camp Intelligence Officer, Captain Emery L. Bryan, Camp Upton, NY, To: Director Military Intelligence B, 1330 F Street, NW, Washington, DC, Subject: Dr. A.V. St. George (Norbert Stadtmuller), 9/5/1918, Folder: PF 24262, Box 357, Entry 67 (MID, PF Files), RG 165 (WD-GSS), NARA.

57. From: Director of Military Intelligence, Brig. General M. Churchill, To: Ass't. Chief of Staff (G-2), G.H.Q., A.E.F. France, Subject: Dr. A.V. St. George (Lt.), 10/28/1918, Folder: PF 24262, Box 357, Entry 67 (MID, PF Files), RG 165 (WD-GSS), NARA.

58. From: Director of Military Intelligence, Brig. General M. Churchill, To: Lt. Col. Nicholas Biddle, Subject: Dr. Ammon [sic] V. St. George, M.C., 10/28/1918, Folder: PF 24262, Box 357, Entry 67 (MID, PF Files), RG 165 (WD-GSS), NARA.

59. From: Office of M.I.B., Lt.-Colonel Nicholas Biddle, To Director of Miltiary Intelligence, Washington, DC, Subject: Doctor Ammon [sic] V. St. George, M. C., 11/5/1918, Folder: PF 24262, Box 357, Entry 67 (MID, PF Files), RG 165 (WD-GSS), NARA.

60. From: Chief, Military Intelligence Branch, To: Intelligence Officer, U.S. General Hospital No. 12, Biltmore, N.C., Captain Jens Christensen, Subject: Dr. St. George, Dr. Rudolph Piel, and Dr. Paul Piel, 8/23/1918, Folder: PF 24262, Box 357, Entry 67 (MID, PF Files), RG 165 (WD-GSS), NARA.

61. From: Director of Military Intelligence, Brig. General M. Churchill, To: Intelligence Officer, U.S. General Hospital #12, Biltmore, N.C., Subject: Doctor St. George, Rudolf Piel, Paul Piel, 10/28/1918, Folder: PF 24262, Box 357, Entry 67 (MID, PF Files), RG 165 (WD-GSS), NARA.

62. Letter from Captain Jens Christensen, 11/4/1918; From: Director of Military Intelligence, Brig. General M. Churchill, To: Intelligence Officer, General Hospital No. 12, Biltmore, N.C., Subject: Dr. St. George, Rudolf Piel and Paul Piel, 11/13/1918; Translation from the German, Frau Maria Piel to Cabot, 9/12/1918; Translation from the German, Mother to Rudolf, 8/9/1918, Folder: PF 24262, Box 357, Entry 67 (MID, PF Files), RG 165 (WD-GSS), NARA.

63. From: Director of Military Intelligence, Captain E.M. L'Engle, To: Intelligence Officer, Gen. Hospital #12, Subject: Dr. St. George, Rudolf Piel and Paul Piel, 12/11/1918, Folder: PF 24262, Box 357, Entry 67 (MID, PF Files), RG 165 (WD-GSS), NARA.

64. From: Director of Military Intelligence, Captain E. M. L'Engle, To: Assistant Chief of Staff G-2, G.H.Q., A.E.F., Subject: Lieutenant A.V. St. George, M.C., 1/3/1919, Folder: PF 24262, Box 357, Entry 67 (MID, PF Files), RG 165 (WD-GSS), NARA.

65. Letter from W. B. Simpson, Clerk, College of Pharmacy, Columbia University, 9/19/1910; *Catalogue of Officers and Graduates of Columbia University* (New York, 1910), 884; Columbia University, *One Hundred and Sixtieth Annual Commencement* (New York, 1914), 9; M. L. Fleming, letter to Dr. William Darrach, 9/17/1920; "Dr. St. George Dies," *HT*, 11/21/1943, CUA; *NYT*, 11/21/1943.

66. File No. P.F. 24262, Section No. M.I. 3-D, Summary, Subject: Ammon [sic] St. George, 6/20/1919; File No. P.F. 24262, Section No. M.I. 3-D, Summary, Subject: Rudolf Piel and Paul Piel, 6/20/1919, Folder: PF 24262, Box 357, Entry 67 (MID, PF Files), RG 165 (WD-GSS), NARA.

67. From: Military Attaché, Berne, Switzerland, Lieutenant Colonel W. F. H. Godson, To: Chief, Military Intelligence Branch, Executive Division, Subject: Dr. St. George, 7/10/1918, NARA.

68. Ira A. Glazier and P. William Filby, eds., *Germans to America, Vol. 3* (Wilmington, DE, 1988), 182; Schedule 1, Inhabitants in New York, in the County of New York, enumerated by Frederick W. Schmidt, *United States Census for 1880*, Film 875, 350A, NARA; *NYT*, 10/13/1901; *NYDT*, 1/15/1895; *New-Yorker Staats-Zeitung*, 1/12/1895; *Trow's New York City Directory Vol. CVII* (New York, 1894); *Sonntagsblatt der New-Yorker Staats-Zeitung*, 10/13/1901; "Champion Rower of 1883 Celebrates 80th Birthday," 9/23/1938, LP.

69. *NYT*, 2/27/1882; "Dr. Friedrich Lange," *Zentralblatt für Chirurgie* 52 (1927); "Dr. Friedrich Lange (Chirug)," http://de.wikipedia.org/wiki/Friedrich_Lange_(Chirurg), accessed 8/7/2013; Rudolf Steege, "XXXV. Bekannte Personlichkeiten aus dem Kreise Neumark. 1. Dr. ju. h.c. Regimontanus et Dr. med. Friedrich Lange—Lonkorrek," in *Heimatbuch für den Kreis Neumark in Westpreußen bis 1941 Kreis Löbau* (Selbstverlag des Heimatkreises Neumark, 1979), 311–15; *Trow's New York City Directory Vol. XCVIII* (New York, 1885), 991; George F. Shrady, ed., *Medical Record, Vol. 45* (1894), 408; *Annals of Anatomy and Surgery* 9, no. 1 (1884), 5; Gilbert Osofsky, *Harlem* (Chicago, 1996), 69–92.

70. Birth Return, Conrad Edward Lange, No. 485657, 3/28/1887; Certificate of Birth, Mathilde Margarette Lange, No. 10663, 4/14/1888; Certificate of Birth, Erwin Frederick Lange, No. 10663, 9/18/1890, NYC.

71. *The Chicago Medical Recorder, Vol. VII* (Chicago, 1984), 150; *Trow's New York City Directory Vol. CVIII* (New York, 1895), 93; *Trow's New York City Directory Vol. CIX* (New York, 1896), 814; *NYT*, 10/26/1894, 10/17/1895; Schedule No. 1—Inhabitants in New York, in the County of New York, *Tenth Census of the United States*, 350A; Schedule No. 1—Population, Borough of Manhattan, Supervisor's District No. 1, Enumeration District No. 637, Sheet No. 12, New York, enumerated by Henry Wittenmeyer, *Twelfth Census of the United States; Harvard Class of 1913* (Cambridge, 1963), 378–80.

72. Julia Lange, letter to Dr. John Edgar Park, 4/8/1944, FF-WCA; Faculty Appointment, Mathilde M. Lange, Associate Professor of Biology, 5/1921; "Interviews Show Wheaton Professors Received Education in All Parts of World," *TWN*, 6/20/1938; Marion Harney Hutchinson, "Wheaton Professor of Zoology Once American War Spy" (Boston, 1930), FF-WCA; "Käthe Windscheid," Frauenpersönlichkeiten in Leipzig, Arbeitsgruppe Senioren und Internet Universität Leipzig, http://www.uni-leipzig.de/~agintern/frauen/index.htm, accessed 8/7/2013; Mathilde Lange, No. 280, Verzeich nis der als gehort bescheinigten Vorlesungen, W.S. 1912/13-W.S. 1916–17, Universitatsarchiv Leipzig; Certificate and Record of Death, No. 31012, Henry J. Schile, State of New York, 10/12/1901; Steege, "XXXV. Bekannte Personlichkeiten aus dem Kreise Neumark," 311–15; Mathilde M. Lange, "On the Regeneration and Finer Structure of the Arms of the Cephalopods" (Inaugural-Dissertation zur Erlangung der Philosphischen Doktorwürde, Universitat Zürich, 1920), Curriculum Vitae.

73. Statement made by Conrad Lange, 10/5/1917 at the office of John C. Tracy, 520 Warren St., Hudson, N.Y., in Roland Ford, Albany, NY, Matter of Conrad E. Lange—Draft

Matter, 11/30/1917, Reel 432, E-31, OG (Old German) Files 1915–1920, M1085, RG 65 (FBI); statement by Conrad Lange, 10/8/1917, in Report by Roland Ford, Albany, NY, Matter of Conrad E. Lange—European Neutrality, 10/8/1917, Folder 9140-4196, Box 2101, E-65 (MID Correspondence, 1917–41), RG 165 (WD-GSS), NARA; William E. Seidelman, "Medicine and Murder in the Third Reich," *Dimensions* 13, no. 1 (1999), http://archive.adl.org/braun/dim_medicine_murder.asp, accessed 8/14/2013.

74. Statements by Conrad Lange, 10/5, 10/8/1917, NARA; Dr. Friedrich Lange, letter to Erwin Lange, 9/11/1916, LP.

75. Statement by Conrad Lange, 10/8/1917, NARA; Steege, "XXXV. Bekannte Personlichkeiten aus dem Kreise Neumark," 311–15.

76. Interview, Olga Lange, Dover-Foxcroft, Maine, 3/30/2001. Erwin Frederick Lange, Committee on Admission, 10/27/1911; Julia Lange, letter to J. G. Hart, 8/23/1911; Wir Rektor und Senat de Universitat Leipzig, beurkunden durch dieses Abgangszeugnis, dass Herr Erwin Lange, 8/8/1911; *Harvard Class Album Volume* XXIV (Cambridge, 1913), 160, HUA. Erwin Lange, Auszug aus den Zeugnisprotokollen vom 8/8/1911, Universitat Leipzig. Hugo Münsterberg, "The Germans at School," *Popular Science Monthly* 79 (1911).

77. Maria Piel, letters to Paul Piel, 7/19, 8/6/1913, PPP. *Radcliffe College Register of Students* (Cambridge, 1916), 120; *The Book of the Class of 1914* (Cambridge, 1914), 97, HUA. Record of Louise Gertrud Piel, Call No. RGXXI, Ser. 1, Schlesinger Library, Harvard University; interview, MLPK, NYC, 12/10/1999.

78. Louise Piel, letter to Paul Piel, 7/27/1914, PPP.

79. Louise Piel, letter to Paul Piel, 5/17/1915, PPP.

80. Maria Piel, postcard to Paul Piel, 1/27/1914, PPP; *Register of the Department of State* (Washington, DC, 1917), 108; *Secretary's First Report* (Cambridge, 1914), 183, HUA. Morgenthau, Constantinople, telegram to Secretary of State, 7/10/1914; Louise G. Piel, letter to Wm. Carr, 11/27/1914; Erwin F. Lange, letter to Gabriel Bie Ravandal, American Consul General Constantinople, 1/6/1916; Director of Consular Services, US State Department, letter to Mr. Phillips, 2/29/1916; E. W. Dunning, letter to William M. Offley, Bureau of Investigation NY, 1/28/1916; A. Bruce Bielaski, Bureau of Investigation, letter to Lester H. Woolsey, Department of State, 1/31/1916; George Montgomery, letter to Hoffman Philip, Chargé d'Affaires, American Embassy Constantinople, 6/3/1916; American Embassy Constantinople, letter to the Secretary of State, 6/3/1916; Wilbur J. Carr, letters to Gabriel Bie Ravandal, 8/22, 9/9/1916; Philip, telegram to Secretary of State, 8/22/1916; letter from Erwin F. Lange, 10/18/1916, Folder 2, Box 1488 (From: 123L251/64 To: 123L325/12), Decimal File (1910–1929), RG 59 (Department of State), NARA.

81. Mathilde M. Lange, letter to S. V. Cole, 4/11/1921; Faculty Appointment, Lange, 5/1921; Hutchinson, "Wheaton Professor," FF-WCA.

82. Louise G. Piel, letter to Wm. Carr, Secretary of State, 11/27/1914; Wilbur J. Carr, letter to Louise G. Piel, 12/1/1914, Folder 2, Box #1488 (From: 123L251/64 To:

123L325/12), Decimal File 1910–1929, RG 59, NARA; *NYT*, 11/5/1916; Hutchinson, "Wheaton Professor."

83. Hutchinson, "Wheaton Professor."

84. Polizeidepartment: Akten: Einwohnerkontrolle: Registerkarten der Einwohnerkontrolle, Mathilde M. Lange, Stadtarchiv Zürich. Hutchinson, "Wheaton Professor"; "Woman Spy, Adventure Was Thrust Upon Her," *The Providence Sunday Journal*, 5/29/1927, LP.

85. Ibid.; "Dr. Lange Speaks to Large Audience," *TWN*, 4/29/1934, FF-WCA.

86. Ibid.; Statement made by Conrad Lange, 10/5/1917, NARA.

87. Erwin F. Lange, letter to G. Bie Ravandal, 2/7/1917, Folder 2, Box #1488 (From: 123L251/64 To: 123L325/12), Decimal File 1910–1929, RG 59 (Department of State), NARA; Erwin F. Lange, letter to Maria Piel, 4/2/1917; Louise Piel Lange, letter to Maria Piel, 3/1917, MaPP.

88. Wilbur J. Carr, letter to William F. J. Piel, 6/7/1917, 123L261/22; Note ED, 5/12/1917, Folder 2, Box #1488 (From: 123L251/64 To: 123L325/12), Decimal File 1910–1929, RG 59, NARA; Louise Piel Lange, letter to Maria Piel, 1/7/1917, MaPP.

89. Stovall to Secretary of State, From Pontarlier (Berne), 6/1/1917, 123L261/23; Lansing to AmLegation, Berne, 6/4/1917, 123L261/21a, Folder 2, Box #1488 (From: 123L251/64 To: 123L325/12), Decimal File 1910–1929, RG 59, NARA. Indicating Mathilde Lange knew William P. Kent in Leipzig before 4/1917, Julia Lange wrote State inquiring after Mathilde, saying she: "Left New York City Dec. 5, 1916 for Leipzig Germany to complete her studies in Biology at the Leipzig University. Mr. W. P. Kent was U.S. Consul at Leipzig until the Break of diplomatic relations." (Julia Lange, letter to U.S. State Department, 2/21/1917, Folder 3, Box 4370, Decimal File, 1910–1929, RG 59 [Department of State], NARA.)

90. Wilbur J. Carr, letter to Erwin F. Lange, 7/19/1917, 123L261/27, Folder 2, Box #1488 (From: 123L251/64 To: 123L325/12), Decimal File 1910–1929, RG 59, NARA.

91. Associated Press, "United States Consuls Finally Reach Zurich," *Cornell Daily Sun*, 2/22/1917; William P. Kent, Consul, Berne, To the Honorable Secretary of State, Confidential Report, 8/7/1917, Department of State, 862.50/171, Decimal File 1910–1929, RG 59, NARA; Julia Lange, letter to Maria Piel, 3/15/1917, MaPP.

92. William P. Kent, American Consulate Berne, The Secretary of State, Confidential Report, 8/25/1917, 123L261/30, Folder 2, Box #1488 (From: 123L251/64 To: 123L325/12), Decimal File 1910–1929, RG 59, NARA.

93. Ibid.

94. Wilbur J. Carr, letter to William P. Kent, 9/20/1917, 123L261/30, Folder 2, Box #1488 (From: 123L251/64 To: 123L325/12), Decimal File 1910–1929, RG 59, NARA.

95. Office of Naval Intelligence, Navy Department, *List A* (Washington, DC, 1918), 1201, Box 1, E-118: Confidential List of Aliens-Suspects ("List A"), 1918, RG 38 (CNO-ONI), NARA; Lange, Erwin F., Great Neck Station, Long Island, N.Y., File Number 9140-4026,

DJ-Oct. 8, 1917, Cross-Reference Card, Military Intelligence Branch, Microfilm #0336, RG 165 (WD-GSS), NARA.

96. Julia Lange, letter to Maria Piel, 3/15/1917; Maria Piel, letter to Julia Lange, 3/16/1917; William Piel, letter to Maria Piel, 7/7/1917, MaPP.

97. Roland Ford, Albany, NY, Matter of Julia Lange—European Neutrality, 9/7/1917, Folder 9140/4196-9140/4206, E-65 MID, 1917–1941, RG 165 (WD-GSS), NARA.

98. Erwin Lange, letter to Conrad Lange, 10/3/1917; Dr. B. Onuf, letter to Exemption Board for Columbia County, 10/22/1917; From: Local Board for the County of Columbia, To: The Commander of Camp Devane, Ayer, Mass., Subject: Conrad Edward Lange. O.N. 739, S.N. 357, 11/7/1917, in Roland Ford, Albany, NY, Matter of Conrad E. Lange—Draft Matter, 11/30/1917, Reel 432, E-31, OG (Old German) Files 1915–1920, M1085, RG 65 (FBI), NARA.

99. Roland Ford, Albany, NY, letter to William M. Offley, NYC, 10/16/1917; From: Local Board for the County of Columbia, To: The Commander of Camp Devane, Ayer, Mass., Subject: Conrad Edward Lange. O.N. 739, S.N. 357, 11/7/1917, NARA.

100. *NYT*, 10/10/1925; interview, MLPK, 3/31/2001; Conrad E. Lange, 38 years, 118951, 10/7/25, Lot No. 8652-8656, Plot Highland, Sec. 43/55/56, Area 1,449', Deed No. 9880, Aff. No. 1,647, Henry J. Schile, Woodlawn Cemetery, Bronx, NY.

101. P. A. Stovall, E. E. & M. P., To Secretary of State, Berne, 8/24/1917, Department of State, 862.50/152; Pleasant A. Stovall, E. E. & M. P., To Secretary of State, Berne, 8/27/1917, Department of State, 862.50/182; P. A. Stovall, E. E. & M. P., To The Secretary of State, Berne, 9/14/1917, Department of State, 862.50/173, Decimal File 1910–1929, RG 59, NARA.

102. Hutchinson, "Wheaton Professor"; *Register of the Department of State* (Washington, DC, 1919), 44; Lieutenant Commander Fred F. Rogers, Navy Department, letter to Comdr. C.L. Arnold, 1/24/1923, Folder 21000-498, Box 554, Entry 78A, Confidential Correspondence, 1913–1924, RG 38 (Chief of Naval Operations), NARA.

103. "Festscrift Karl Heescheler zur Vollendung seines siebzigsten Alterjares," *Beiblatt zur Vierteljarsschrift der Naturforschenden Gesellschaft in Zürich* 83, no. 30 (1938).

104. Hutchinson, "Wheaton Professor"; Registerkarten der Einwohnerkontrolle, Mathilde M. Lange, Stadtarchiv Zürich.

105. Charles Lyon Chandler, letter to the Secretary of State, 11/14/1918, 125.1973/74, Folder 1, Box 2057, Decimal File, 1910–1929, RG 59 (Department of State), NARA; Charles Lyon Chandler, letter to Commander Fred F. Rogers, U.S.N., Navy Department, 3/5/1920, Folder 21000-498, Box 54, E-78A Confidential Correspondence, 1913–1924, RG 38 (Chief of Naval Operations), NARA.

106. Mathilde Lange, letter to Secretary of State, 1/4/1918, Folder 3, Box 1517, Decimal File 1912–1929, RG 59 (Department of State), NARA.

107. *NYT*, 4/9/1914; Woodrow Wilson, letter to Robert Lansing, 9/1/1917; Office of the Counselor, Department of State, letter to the President, 9/7/1917, Folder 3, Box 1517 (123M23/91-123M23-304), Decimal File 1912–1929, RG 59, NARA.

108. Wilson, Berne, telegram to Secretary of State, 2/28/1918; Stovall, Berne, telegram to Secretary of State, 3/5/1918, 3/10/1918; Lansing, telegram to Amlegation Berne, 3/15/1918; Folder 3, Box 1517 (123M23/91-123M23-304), Decimal File 1912–1929, RG 59, NARA; Roland Krebs and Percy J. Orthwein, *Making Friends is Our Business* (Chicago, 1953), 93–94; Peter Hernon and Terry Ganey, *Under the Influence* (New York: 1991), 94–101.

109. Mathilde Lange, letter to Secretary of State, 3/27/1918, Folder 3, Box 1517, Decimal File 1912–1929 (123M23/91-123M23/304), RG 59, NARA.

110. Sharp Paris, telegrams to Secretary of State, 4/13, 4/18, 4/29/1918, Folder 3, Box 1517 (123M23/91-123M23-304), Decimal File 1912–1929, RG 59, NARA.

111. Robert Lansing, letter to the President, 4/19/1918; Polk Acting, telegram to AmEmbassy Paris, 4/20/1918, Folder 3, Box 1517 (123M23/91-123M23-304), Decimal File 1912–1929, RG 59, NARA.

112. Lansing, telegrams to AmLegation Berne, 6/17, 6/26/1918; Stovall, telegrams to Secretary of State, 6/22, 7/2/1918, Folder 4, Box 1517 (123M23/91-123M23-304), Decimal File 1912–1929, RG 59, NARA.

113. Lansing, telegrams to AmLegation Berne, 6/29, 8/22/1918; Polk Acting, telegram to AmEmbassy Paris, Very Secret, From Harrison for Colonel Ralph H. Van Deman, General Headquarters, 7/12/1918; Stovall, telegrams to Secretary of State, 7/4, 8/2, 8/6, 8/8, 8/15/1918, Folder 4, Box 1517 (123M23/91-123M23-304), Decimal File 1912–1929, RG 59, NARA.

114. Godson Berne, telegram to MID, Office of the Chief of Staff, War Department, 1/16/1919; Dunn, War Department, telegram to US Military attaché, Berne, 2/4/1919, Folder 9140-4196, Box 2101, E-65 (MID Correspondence, 1917–41), RG 165 (WD-GSS), NARA; Hutchinson, "Wheaton Professor."

115. Lange, "On the Regeneration and Finer Structure of the Arms of the Cephalopods," 3–5 (diss.); Karl Hescheler, Gutachten zu der dissertation, 6/19/1919; Mathilde Lange, Decanat der Philosoph. Facultat, Universitat Zurich, 6/19/1919, Zentralbibliothek, Universitat Zurich; Mathilde M. Lange, "On the Regeneration and Finer Structure of the Arms of Cephalopods," *Journal of Experimental Zoology* 31, no. 1 (1920), 1–57.

116. Hutchinson, "Wheaton Professor."

117. Registerkarten der Einwohnerkontrolle, Mathilde M. Lange, Stadtarchiv Zürich; Charles Lyon Chandler, letter to Lieutenant Commander Fred F. Rogers, Navy Department, 2/21/1920, Folder 21000-498, Box 554, Entry 78A, Confidential Correspondence, 1913–1924, RG 38 (Chief of Naval Operations), NARA.

118. Letter from Charles Lyon Chandler to Lieutenant Commander Fred F. Rogers, Navy Department, 2/21/1920, 3/5/1920, Folder 21000-498, Box 554, Entry 78A, Confidential Correspondence, 1913-1924, RG 38 (Chief of Naval Operations), NARA.

119. Lieutenant Commander Fred F. Rogers, Navy Department, letters to Charles Lyon Chandler, 2/28, 3/4, 7/8/1920; Charles Lyon Chandler, letters to Lieutenant Commander Fred F. Rogers, 3/5, 7/1/1920, Folder 21000-498, Box 554, Entry 78A, Confidential Correspondence, 1913–1924, RG 38 (Chief of Naval Operations), NARA.

120. Letter from M. J. Young-Fulton, American & Foreign Teachers Agency, NY, 4/9/1921; Mathilde Lange, letter to S. V. Cole, 4/13/1921; Mathilde Lange, letters to Dr. Park, 4/23/1928, ca.1929, ca.1934, 9/11/1936, 5/19/1937, 8/20/1938, 8/6/1940; Mathilde M. Lange, Curriculum Vitae, ca.1928; Mathilde Lange, "Report for the College Year 1929–30, Department of Zoology," 6/12/1930; "Dr. Lange Reports Her Delightful Western Tour," *TWN*, 9/28/1935; "Interviews Show Wheaton Professors Received Education in All Parts of World"; Mathilde Lange, "Vocational Opportunities for Students who take Advanced Work in Biology, Botany or Zoology at Wheaton," ca.1943; Mathilde Lange, letter to Dr. Meneeley, 5/26/1945, FF-WCA. Mathilde wrote Wheaton's president in 1938 that she would spend a week "c/o Mrs. Piel, Lake Parlin, P.O. Jackman, Maine"; and in 1945, she asked permission to attend a nephew's wedding in "northern Maine." (See Mathilde Lange, letter to Dr. Park, 8/20/1938; Mathilde Lange, letter to Dr. Meneeley, 5/26/1945, FF-WCA.)

121. Mathilde M. Lange, letter to Mr. Chandler, 9/25/1927, Folder 21000-498, Box 554, Entry 78A, Confidential Correspondence, 1913–1924, RG 38 (Chief of Naval Operations), NARA.

122. Mathilde Lange, letters to Dr. Park, 7/19, 8/23/1928, FF-WCA; *Harvard Class of 1913: Fiftieth Anniversary Report* (Cambridge, 1963), 378–80; "Łąkorek: Secesyjny dwór Friedricha Lange," *Moje Mazury,* http://mojemazury.pl/164777, Lakorek-Secesyjny-dwor-Friedricha-Lange.html#axzz3G2EeqG6i, accessed 10/12/2014.

123. "Norton Woman Through Spying for Government" (newspaper title deleted), 10/6/1939, LP.

124. Mathilde Lange, letter to Miss Remick, 11/22/1942, FF-WCA.

125. "Cole Memorial Chapel," Wheaton College History, http://wheatoncollege.edu/college-history/1910s/cole-memorial-chapel-1917/, accessed 3/18/2014.

126. "Miss Lange Gives Talk in Chapel," *TWN*, 11/8/1941, FF-WCA.

127. Julia Lange, letter to Dr. Park, 9/24/1938; "Dr. Lange Dies; Headed Biology Dept. at Wheaton," *The Evening News* (Newburgh, NY), 6/19/1972; "Obituary," *Wheaton College Newsletter* 59, no. 10 (1972), FF-WCA; "Mrs. Lange Dies at 101," *County Courier* (Central Valley, NY), 4/11/1959, Woodbury Historical Society, Highland Mills, NY; Probate Proceeding, Will of Mathilde M. Lange, 7/8/1965; Donald C. Anderson, Vice President, Wheaton College, 12/2/1974, Receipt in Satisfaction of Decree, In the Matter of the Final Judicial Settlement of the Account of Proceedings . . . of the Estate of Mathilde M. Lange, Deceased, Surrogate's Court, County of Orange, State of New York; "Young and Old for Peace," *Sunday Record* (Middletown, NY), 4/18/1971, LP; Bjorn Lange, conversation, NYC, 12/7/2001.

128. Report of the Commission on Wartime Relocation and Internment of Civilians, *Personal Justice Denied* (Washington, DC, 1983), chapter 12, http://www.nps.gov/history/history/online_books/personal_justice_denied/index.htm, accessed 7/31/2014.

129. Thomas B. Allen, *Tories* (New York, 2010), 323–33; Robert M. Calhoon, *The Loyalists in Revolutionary America* (New York, 1973), 500–06; Wayne S. Cole, *An Interpretive History of American Foreign Relations* (Belmont, CA, 1974), 54–55; Maya Jasanoff, *Liberty's Exiles* (New York, 2011), 324–34.

130. Library of Congress, *Thomas*, "Bill Summary & Status, 100th Congress (1987–1988), H.R. 442, C.R.S. Summary," http://thomas.loc.gov/cgi bin/bdquery/z?d100:HR00442:@@@D&summ2=m&; Democracy Now, "WWII Reparations: Japanese-American Internees," 2/18/1999, http://www.democracynow.org/1999/2/18/wwii_reparations_japanese_american_internees, all accessed 7/31/2014; Report of the Commission on Wartime Relocation and Internment of Civilians, *Personal Justice Denied*, chapters 4, 12.

131. Kazal, *Becoming Old Stock*, 176–77; *NYT*, 9/23/2015.

132. MBD-PB, 5/8/1918, PBM#1.

133. William Piel, "Memorandum on a Decade of the Beer Business (1910 to incl. 1919 in Piel Bros' Career)," 2/24/1920, 18–20, PBM#1.

134. Michael A. Lerner, *Dry Manhattan* (Cambridge, 2008), 30–32.

135. Daniel Okrent, *Last Call* (New York, 2010), 99–100; Maureen Ogle, *Ambitious Brew* (Orlando, 2006), 168–69.

136. Woodrow Wilson, "Executive Order 2681: Authority to Organize Food Administration Grain Corporation," 8/14/1917, http://www.presidency.ucsb.edu/ws/index.php?pid=75432#axzz1xhUHteRB; "Executive Order 2736: Providing for Requisitioning of Foods and Feeds," 10/23/1917, http://www.presidency.ucsb.edu/ws/index.php?pid=75449#axzz1xhY2J4Sh, all accessed 6/13/2012; MBD-PB, 12/15/1917; PB-AMS, 3/12/1918, PBM#1.

137. "House Adopts Prohibition Amendment by 282 to 128," *NYDT*, 12/18/1917.

138. MBD-PB, 1/22/1918, PBM#1.

139. Ibid.

140. MBD-PB, 2/9/1918; William Piel, "Memorandum on the Cereal Beverage Industry of the Eastern States," 7/18/1918, 3, PBM#1.

141. MBD-PB, 2/9/1918, PBM#1.

142. MBD-PB, 10/18/1918, PBM#1.

143. Piel, "Memorandum on the Cereal Beverage Industry," 2, 14.

144. Ibid., 3–14.

145. Okrent, *Last Call*, 94–95, 100–03.

146. U.S. Senate, 65th Congress, 2d Session, Subcommittee on the Judiciary, *National German American Alliance* (Washington, DC, 1918), 697–98.

147. Ibid., 205–23.

148. Anti-Saloon League, *The National German American Alliance and its Allies* (Westerville, OH, 1918), 18–19; Kazal, *Becoming Old Stock*, 182.

149. *BLI*, iii–iv, 5–12; Ogle, *Ambitious Brew*, 178–79.

150. *BLI*, iii–iv, 5–12; Ogle, *Ambitious Brew*, 179–80.

151. *BLI, Vol. 2*, 1788–94, 1804–06, 1847–48, 1907, 1941, 2024–25, 2292–93, 2671–90, 2692–721; Michael Warner, "The Kaiser Sows Destruction: Protecting the Homeland the First Time Around," Library, Central Intelligence Agency, https://www.cia.gov/library/center-for-the-study-of-intelligence/csi-publications/csi-studies/studies/vol46no1/article02.html, accessed 10/28/2013; John P. Jones and Paul M. Hollister, *The German Secret Service in America, 1914–1918* (Boston, 1918), 5–27, 73–81, 100–38, 154–70.

152. *BLI*, vi–ix.

153. Ibid., 1097–98.

154. Ibid., xlv, xlix.

155. Lerner, *Dry Manhattan*, 44-45; Okrent, *Last Call*, 104-08; MBD-PB, 11/23/1918, PBM#1.

156. Walter Thompson, *Federal Centralization* (New York, 1923), 182–86; Lerner, *Dry Manhattan*, 42–44.

157. MBD-PB, 11/23/1918, PBM#1.

158. PB-AMS, 3/11/1919, PBM#1.

159. MBD-PB, 5/24/1919, PBM#1.

160. Ibid.

161. MBD-PB, 2/9/1921, PBM#1.

Chapter 6

1. Interview, MPM, 12/20/1997.

2. Interview, WPJ, 1/20/1997; "The Reminiscences of Gerard Piel" (OHRO-CU, 1984), 3.

3. William Piel, "Memorandum on the Cereal Beverage Industry of the Eastern States," 7/18/1918, 33, 47–48, PBM#1.

4. Ibid., 47–48.

5. Michael A. Lerner, *Dry Manhattan* (Cambridge, 2008), 44–45; Daniel Okrent, *Last Call* (New York, 2010), 107–11; *The 1918 Yearbook of the United States Brewers Association* (New York, 1919), 23–27.

6. MBD-PB, 11/30/1919, PBM#1.

7. Piel, "Memorandum on the Cereal Beverage Industry of the Eastern States," 49.

8. Okrent, *Last Call*, 136–37, 144–45.

9. MBD-PB, 4/3/1920, PBM#1.

10. Piel, "Memorandum on the Cereal Beverage Industry," 50.

11. MBD-PB, 10/8/1920, PBM#1.

12. MBD-PB, 1/15, 2/9/1921, PBM#1.

13. Philip Van Munching, *Beer Blast* (New York, 1997), 20; Peter Hernon and Terry Ganey, *Under the Influence* (New York, 1991), 105–06; Roland Krebs and Percy J. Orthwein, *Making Friends is Our Business* (Chicago, 1953), 100; Dr. John E. Siebel and Anton Schwarz, *History of the Brewing Industry and Brewing Science in America* (Chicago, 1933), 74–75.

14. Henry Piel, letter to Marie Muessen Piel, 7/26/1921, HPP.

15. MBD-PB 2/15, 5/10/1921, PBM#1.

16. MBD-PB, 5/10/1921, PBM#1.

17. MBD-PB, 9/16/1921, PBM#1.

18. Maria and Gottfried Piel, letter to Piel Bros., 8/15/1921, PBM#1.

19. William Piel, "Memorandum on a Decade of the Beer Business (1910 to incl. 1919 in Piel Bros' Career)," 2/24/1920, PBM#1.

20. MBD-PB, 7/20, 10/26/1923; Minutes of Adjourned Meeting of Bondholders, 8/2/1923, PBM#1.

21. MBD-PB, 9/15/1915, 1/15/1921, PBM#1.

22. Gottfried Piel, letter to Secretary of Piel Bros. Inc., 12/21/1921, MBD-PB, 12/31/1921, PBM#1. Gottfried Piel, letter to Arthur Piel, 2/14/1922; Maria Piel, letter to William Piel, 1/16/1922; PB-AMS, 3/14/1922, PBM#1; William Piel, letter to Maria Piel, 9/19/1923, MaPP; Appraisal of the Investors Agency, Inc., *In Re: Estate of Sophie Piel, Deceased, 3/19/1924*, PF-SP.

23. Deposition of Elmer E. Wigg, 3/16/1925, *In the Matter of the Appraisal Under the Transfer Tax Law of the Estate of Sophie Piel, Deceased*; Appraisal of the Investors Agency, Inc.; A. Paul Loshen, Brief for Petitioners, 3/25/1941, *In Re: Estate of Sophie Piel*.

24. William Piel, letter to Maria Piel, 9/19/1923, MaPP.

25. Sophie Piel, Last Will and Testament, 7/19, 1923, *In Re: Estate of Sophie Piel*; William F. Hagarty, Acting Presiding Justice, Order on Appeal from Order, Appellate Division of the Supreme Court of the State of New York, 10/22/1937, PF-SP; "Married Women's Property Laws," *Law Library of Congress*, http://memory.loc.gov/ammem/awhhtml/awlaw3/property_law.html, accessed 4/30/2014.

26. Margarita Piel McCoy, daughter of Rudolf Piel, often finished the stories she told the author about her childhood during the 1920s and 1930s with that memorable phrase.

27. William Piel, Ledger for Maria Piel, 98–99, 161–62, 170–71, 174–75; Estate of Maria Piel, 9/30/1922, MaPP.

28. Interview, WPJ, 1/20/1997.

29. Indenture from William F.J. Piel and Wife to Maria Piel, County of Kings, 2/9/1917, PPP; interview, WPJ, 1/20/1997; Piel, Ledger for Maria Piel, 98–99, 246–47.

30. Henry Piel, letters to Marie Muessen Piel, 10/26, 10/30/1921, 6/26, 8/5/1926, HPP; Henry Piel, letter to Maria Piel, 8/1925; Marie M. Piel, letter to Maria Piel, 8/9/1925, MaPP.

31. Sale by Isaac F. Kirkendall and Meda Kirkendall, to Rudolf A. Piel and Erwin F. Lange, Vol. 87, 442, 10/6/1919, Holmes County Clerk's Office, Millersburg, Ohio; USBC, *Fourteenth Census of the United States: 1920—Population*, Supervisor's District No. 15, Enumeration District No. 6, Sheet No. 13-A, 1/8, 1920, Killbuck Village, Killbuck Township, Holmes County, Ohio; Piel, Ledger for Maria Piel, 110–11; J. E. Seaholm and T. E. Graham, *Soil Survey of Holmes Country, Ohio* (U.S. Department of Agriculture, 1998), 1–4, 15–17.

32. Rudolf Piel, letter to Maria Piel, 1/13/1925, MaPP.

33. Louise Piel Lange, letter to Roland Piel, n.d.; Maria Piel, letter to Roland Piel 1/21/1922, RPP.

34. Piel, Ledger for Maria Piel, 165, 182; interview, MPM, 1/14/2001; "Jascha Heifetz [*sic*]," *The Straits Times* (Singapore), 3/15/1927, http://newspapers.nl.sg/Digitised/Article/straitstimes19270315-1.2.65.aspx, accessed 11/29/2013.

35. Sale by R. Piel to W.J. Brown Co., 6/9/1925, Vol. 100, p. 11, Holmes County Clerk.

36. "Beautiful 'Lake Parlin' for Sale," *Town & Country* 77, no. 3782 (1920), 4; Piel, Ledger for Maria Piel, 268.

37. J. M. Estes, Maine Central Railroad, letter to William Piel, 7/2/1925; William Piel, letter to J. M. Estes, 7/8/1925; William Piel, letter to Maria Piel, 7/8/1925, MaPP.

38. Piel, Ledger for Maria Piel, 70–71, 112–15, 134–35.

39. Paul Piel, letter to Maria Piel, 7/26/1925; Roland Piel, letter to Maria Piel, n.d., MaPP.

40. Agreement between Maria Piel and Erwin Lange, 1/11/1924; Piel, Ledger for Maria Piel, 70–71, 112–15, 134–35; Maria Piel, letters to Roland Piel, 8/5, 8/11/1925, RPP; Mehmet Namik, letter to Erwin Lange, 4/19/1930, LP; Erwin Lange, letter to Maria Piel, n.d. [ca.1924], MaPP.

41. Maria Piel, Individual Income Tax Return for Calendar Year 1926, Form 1040, U.S. Internal Revenue Service, PBM#1; Lake Parlin Farm, Employment Schedule and Budget, n.d.; Louise Piel Lange, letter to Maria Piel, 6/25/1927, MaPP.

42. Piel, Ledger for Maria Piel, 112–13, 269.

43. Interviews, MPM, 11/28/2004, MLPK, 12/10/1999; Piel, Ledger for Maria Piel, 128–29, 133, 182; Contents of Box No. 94 under names of William Piel and Henry G. Piel, Manufacturers Safe Deposit Co., NY, opened 1/20/1954, WP-SC; Mrs. Lange Hostess, P.O. Jackman Station, LP.

44. Interview, MPM, 11/28/2004.

45. Interviews, WPJ, 1/20/1997, MLPK, 12/8/2000; Maria Piel, letters to Roland Piel, 4/30/1922, 5/4, 5/12, 8/5/1925, RPP; Henry Piel, letter to Maria Piel, 8/31/1925,

MaPP; Christian Heermann, "Der Heermann-Hof in Östrich unter der adligen Familie der Freiherren von Romberg" (Jesteburg, 3/20/2009), 19; Margarita Piel McCoy, letter to author, 9/2001.

46. Roland Parlin Piel, Class of 1926, Candidate for B.S. Degree, Transcript, Princeton University; *The Nassau Herald* (1925), SGM-PU; Rudolf Piel, letter to Roland Piel, n.d.; Roland Piel, letter to Maria Piel, 3/23/1923, RPP.

47. Interview, MPM, 11/9/2013; interview WPJ, 1/20/1997; Roland Piel, letters to Maria Piel, 6/7, 6/13, 8/3/1925, MaPP; Roland O.P. Piel, File No. 75502, Certificate of Death, 7/8/1926, Chester Country, Commonwealth of Pennsylvania.

48. Roland Parlin Piel '25, *Princeton Alumni Weekly*, 9/24/1926, SGM-PU.

49. Piel, Roland, O.P., Burial Date: 1926-07-08, Lot 17313, Section 152, Green-Wood Cemetery, http://www.green-wood.com/burial_results/index.php, accessed November 10, 2013.

50. Edith Dettmers, letter to Clarence Dettmers, n.d., PPP; Maria Piel, letters to Roland Piel, 7/16/1924, 9/16/1925, RPP; William Piel, letter to Maria Piel, 10/13/1926, MaPP; interview, MLPK, 3/30/2001.

51. Interview, MLPK, New York City, 12/10/1999. Margarita Piel McCoy, letter to author, 9/2001, with commentary on MLPK, interview.

52. Transcript, P. M. Piel, Year '03–'04 to '05–'06, Phillips Academy Andover; *Pot Pourri 1906* (Phillips Andover Academy), 58; Paul Michael Piel, College Examinations, 6/1906, AA-PAA. Name: Paul M. Piel, Committee on Admission, Harvard University, n.d.; Alfred E. Sterns, principal Phillips Academy, letter to Prof. J. G. Hart, secretary Harvard University, 9/27/1906; Paul Piel, Official Student Folder (UAIII 15.88.10); *Harvard College Class of 1911: Decennial Report June, 1921* (Boston, 1921), 104; *Harvard College Class of 1911* (Cambridge, 1936), 543–44, HUA.

53. D. B. Steinman, "Report on the Piel System of Roof Construction," 3/1923; Letters Patent, Paul Piel For His Roof and Wall Contructions, No. 1458498, 6/12/1923; Williams & Pritchard, letter to Sergeant Paul Piel, 7/14/1918; Paul Piel, letter to Strauch Bros., 2/26/1920; Paul Piel, letter to Williams & Pritchard, 3/10/1920; Letters Patent, Paul M. Piel of New York, Transposition Keyboards, No. 1507423, 9/2/1924, PPP; interview, MP, 12/9/2000.

54. John Cowper Powys, *Autobiography* (New York, 1934), 518–19; Bernard Oldsey, ed., *British Novelists, 1930–1959, Vol. Fifteen* (Detroit, 1983), 448–64.

55. Paul Piel, letters to Edith Dettmers, 10/24/1919, 8/13/1920, 6/1/1923; Paul Piel, letter to Clarence Dettmers, 10/27/1921; Edith Dettmers, letters to Clarence Dettmers, Wednesday, Sunday night, Wednesday, PPP; interview, MP, 12/9/2000; LindaAnn Loschiavo, "Lancelot the ocelot and the story of Ye Waverly Inn," *The Villager*, 3/1/2006, http://thevillager.com/villager_148/lancelottheocelotand.html, accessed 1/29/15.

56. Indenture between Williams-Dexter Co. and H.C.O. Realty Co., 6/10/1924, PPP; interviews, WPJ, 1/20/1997, MP, 12/9/2000; Piel, Ledger for Maria Piel, 35, 40–41, 98,

146–47; Edith Dettmers, letter to Clarence Dettmers, Wednesday; Invitations to Church and Reception, n.d.; Wedding Invitation, 11/14/1924, PPP.

57. General Release, Maria Piel to Paul Piel, 3/12/1929, NYC, PPP; interview, MP, 12/9/2000.

58. Interview, MLPK, 12/10/1999; Confidential Information for the Use of the Committee on Admissions of Barnard College, Agnes H. Piel, n.d.; Assistant to the dean in charge of employment, Barnard College, letter to Miss Alicia A. Knox, The Greenwich Academy, Connecticut, 5/28/1924; Agnes Helene Piel, Transcript, AB '20, Office of the Registrar, Barnard College; *The Mortarboard. Vol. 26* (New York, 1920), 158, BCA.

59. *The Mortarboard. Vol. 26*, 169–71, BCA; Margaret Mead, *Blackberry Winter* (New York, 1972), 102–03.

60. Jane Howard, *Margaret Mead* (New York, 1984), 42–45, 49–50; *The Mortarboard. Vol. 26*, 171, BCA; Assistant to the Secretary, Barnard College, letter to New York School of Social Work, 9/15/1920, Office of the Registrar, Barnard College.

61. Barnard College, letter to Mrs. McNeil, n.d.; Barnard College, letter to Alicia A. Knox, 5/28/1924; New York School of Social Work, letter to the Secretary, Barnard College, 1/6/1921; Confidential Recommendations for Mrs. Agnes Piel Lyne, n.d., Occupation Bureau, Barnard College; Agnes Piel, Barnard College—Alumna Record, #2918, ca. 1940, Office of the Registrar, Barnard College.

62. Agnes Piel, letters to Roland Piel, 10/18, 10/20/1921, RPP.

63. Agnes Piel, letter to Roland Piel, 4/4/1922, RPP; *The Jayhawker Yearbook* (Lawrence, KS, 1922), 302.

64. Barnard College, *Directory of the Associate Alumni 1893–1934*, 1920 Piel, Agnes, BCA; Louise Piel, letter to Henry Piel, Saturday, LP; William Piel, letter to Martha Piel, 6/29/1926; Henry Piel, letter to Maria Piel, 6/15/1926, MaPP; Maria Piel, letter to Roland Piel, 4/27/1925, RPP; Affidavit attached to letter from Agnes Piel Crane to R. B. Shipley, 7/17/1939, Chief Passport Division, Department of State, 362.1143, Crane, Agnes P., Richard Pollak Papers, University of Chicago; interview, MLPK, 3/30/2001; Certificate of Incorporation of Michael Piel Holding Corporation, 8/13/1930, MPHC Minutes, 1930–1931.

65. H. Goldschmidt Real Estate Headquarters, Cedarhurst, Long Island, letter to Chas. Douglis, NYC, 9/23/1923; Piel, Ledger for Maria Piel, 144–45, 234–38, 246–49.

66. Piel, Ledger for Maria Piel, 112–13, 269.

67. Maria Heermann Piel, Memoranda, Shipments to Germany 1919–1920, Oswald Piel Trunk, Thomas Kemp Farm, Dover-Foxcroft, Maine.

68. Christian Heermann, "Zur Geschichte des Heermanns Hofes" (Jesteburg, 6/26/2000), 6; Christian Heermann, "Familie Heermann Östrich" (Jesteberg, 9/42005), 17–18, 30-33; Heinrich Heermann, letters to Maria Piel, n.d., 6/28/1915, 6/24, 7/6/1919, 4/25, 5/1, 5/3, 7/5, 7/12/1920; Franz Busch, letter to Maria Piel, 4/23/1920; Louise Piel, letters to Maria Piel, 5/30/1926, 6/25/1927; Employment Schedule and Budget, n.d., MaPP; Heinrich Heermann, Jr., letter to Paul Piel, 6/8/1913, PPP.

69. *BDE*, 5/25/1920.

70. *NYT*, 10/15/1921, 12/30/1922; Okrent, *Last Call*, 242–43, 263–65, 316–17; David E. Kyvig, *Repealing National Prohibition* (Kent, 2000), 56–58.

71. Ellen McKenzie Lawson, *Smugglers, Bootleggers, and Scofflaws* (Albany, 2013), 96–97; *NYT*, 11/3/1926.

72. MBD-PB, 6/14/1921, PBM#1.

73. PB-AMS, 3/14/1922; William Piel, letter to Olcott, Bonynge, McManus & Ernst, 12/3/1921, PBM#1; T.D. 3239, Medicinal Use of Malt Liquors and Wines—Labeling of Liquor of All Kinds Sold on Prescription, Regulations No. 60, Office of Commissioner of Internal Revenue, 10/24/1921; Form No. 1404, Application for Permit under the National Prohibition Act, Serial No. of Permit, N.Y.-A-82, 10/25/1921; Form No. 1405, Permit Issued under the National Prohibition Act and Regulations Issued Thereafter, Serial No. N.Y.-A-82, 11/3/1921, in, *Piel v. Day U.S. Supreme Court Transcript of Record with Supporting Pleadings* (*Making of Modern Law: U.S. Supreme Court Records and Briefs, 1832–1978,* (Farmington Hills, MI, 2011), 16–26; "First Permits for Medicinal Beer," *Syracuse Journal*, 11/4/1921.

74. Piel Bros., Complainant, against Ralph A. Day, Federal Prohibition Director for the State of New York, Bill of Complaint, United States District Court, Eastern District of New York, 3/8/1922, in, *Piel v. Day U.S. Supreme Court Transcript*, 2–16.

75. "Piel Bros. v. Day," *The Federal Reporter, Vol. 278* (St. Paul, 1922), 223; *NYT*, 2/9/1922.

76. *NYT*, 2/9/1922; *Piel Bros. v. Day et al.* (Circuit Court of Appeals, Second Circuit, 5/15/1922), No. 313. Appeal from the District Court of the United States for the Eastern District of New York. Circuit Court of Appeals, 281 Fed. 1022, http://www.archive.org/stream/gov.uscourts.f1.281/281.f1_djvu.txt, accessed 6/19/2012.

77. Assignments of Error. United States Circuit Court of Appeals from the Second Circuit, Piel Bros., Complainant-Appellant against Ralph A. Day, 6/30/1922; Petition, *Piel Bros. Appellant, against, Ralph A. Day, Appellees*, Supreme Court of the United States, 10/9/1922; Brief for the Appellees, 1/1924, *Piel Bros., Appellant, v. Ralph A. Day*, In the Supreme Court of the United States, 10/Term 1923; Supplemental Brief for Appellees, The Beer Cases Nos. 95, 200, 245, *Piel Bros., Appellant, v. Ralph A. Day, No. 95, James Everard's Breweries, Appellant, v. Ralph A. Day, No. 200, Edward and John Burke (Limited), Appellant, v. David H. Blair, No. 245*, 3/1924, in, *Piel v. Day U.S. Supreme Court Transcript.*

78. *Supreme Court of the United States*, 3/4/1924, Mr. Walter E. Ernst and Mr. Nathan Ballin for *appellant*. Mrs. Mabel Walker Willebrandt, Assistant Attorney General, and Mr. Mahlon D. Kiefer for appellee, *PIEL BROTHERS v.* Ralph A. Day, http://wy.findacase.com/research/wfrmDocViewer.aspx/xq/fac.19240304_0040176.SCT.htm/qx, accessed 6/25/2012.

79. U.S. Supreme Court, *James Everard's Breweries v. Day*, 265 U.S. 545 (1924), *FindLaw*, http://caselaw.lp.findlaw.com/scripts/getcase.pl?court=us&vol=265&invol=545, accessed 6/20/2012.

80. PB-AMS, 3/14/1922, PBM#1.

81. William Piel, Sr., "To Win the People's Cooperation with the 18th Amendment (3/10/1924)," WPSP.

82. *NYT*, 5/10/1922; *BDE*, 6/2/1922.

83. *NYT*, 6/27/1922.

84. *BDE*, 6/2/1922.

85. *BDE*, 7/7, 9/16/1922.

86. *BDE*, 6/19/1922.

87. *BDE*, 6/29/1922.

88. *NYT*, 9/17/1922; *BDE*, 9/16/1922.

89. MBD-PB, 4/8/1927, PBM#2.

90. Henry Piel, letter to Marie Muessen Piel, 8/18/1926, HPP.

91. Interview, MLPK, 12/10/1999.

92. "The Reminiscences of William O'Dwyer," (OHRO-CU, 1965), 77.

93. Ibid., 76, 790–91, 793.

94. Ibid., 420, 798–99.

95. "The Reminiscences of John J. Lynch" (OHRO-CU, 1962), 1–3, 12–13, 66.

96. Alan May, "Vannie Higgins: Brooklyn's Last Irish Boss," *Crime Magazine*, http:// crimemagazine.com/vannie-higgins-brooklyns-last-irish-boss; "Frankie Yale," *Encyclope-dia Britannica*, http://www.britannica.com/EBchecked/topic/651367/Frankie-Yale, both accessed 12/16/2012; *BDE*, 12/12/1949; *NYT*, 6/20/1932; Rich Cohen, *Tough Jews* (New York, 1999), 28–29, 67–75, 77–78.

97. Selwyn Raab, *Five Families* (New York, 2005), 36.

98. Cohen, *Tough Jews*, 53–57; Lawson, *Smugglers, Bootleggers, and Scofflaws*, 1–6, 59–63.

99. Raab, *Five Families*, 25, 37.

100. Alan Block, *East Side–West Side* (New Brunswick, 1983), 131–33.

101. *United States v. Two Soaking Units and Various Other Articles, Claim of Excelsior Brewery, Inc. et al. No. 2554*, District Court, E. D. New York, *44 F.2d 650 (1930)*, 10/20/1930, http://www.leagle.com/xmlResult.aspx?xmldoc=193069444F2d650_1489.xml&docbase=CSLWAR1-1950-1985, accessed 12/10/2012; "Even with Prohibition, The 1920s Roared in the Old Neighborhood," *Ridgewood Times* (Ridgewood, NY), 2/27/2003.

102. "Agents Claim Diamond Gang Handled Barman Beer," *The Kingston Daily Freeman* (Kingston, NY), 6/2/1931.

103. Alan May, "Waxey Goldon's Half Century of Crime," *Crime Magazine*, http:// crimemagazine.com/waxey-gordon's-half-century-crime, accessed 12/5/2012; Cohen, *Tough Jews*, 52–54.

104. Block, *East Side–West Side*, 133–41; *NYT*, 5/23/1933; Cohen, *Tough Jews*, 141, 161.

105. "Hunt Gunmen in Beer Raid," *The Pittsburg Press* (Pittsburg, PA), 9/18/1930.

106. "Mayor William O'Dwyer—4/1961—by John Kelly," excerpts from the Kefauver Committee hearings, commented upon by O'Dwyer (OHRO-CU, 1965), 5–6.

107. "The Reminiscences of Solomon A. Klein" (OHRO-CU, 1962), 72–73.

108. "The Reminiscences of William O'Dwyer," 98–99.

109. *NYT*, 11/30/1941, 3/2/1963, 10/16/1976, 8/31/2012; Robert J. Kelly, *Encyclopedia of Organized Crime in the United States* (Westport, CT, 2000), 11–13, 223; Patrick Downey, *Gangster City* (Fort Lee, NJ, 2004), 235–42; Burton B. Turkus and Sid Feder, *Murder, Inc.* (New York, 1951), 13, 29–30, 462–64; Block, *East Side–West Side*, 84–86, 97–109, 185–95; Records, Office of District Attorney, Kings County, New York, dictated by John Kelly, 8/3/1961; "The Reminiscences of William O'Dwyer," 27–29; excerpts from the Respondent's brief, the statement of the District Attorney, argued by Solomon A. Klein, 94–95, testimony of Abraham Reles, 121–30, (OHRO-CU); Brian Merlis and Riccardo Gomes, *Brooklyn's East New York and Cypress Hill Communities* (New York, 2010), 198–99; Cohen, *Tough Jews*, 23–32, 62–63, 66–77, 89–93, 122–23, 163, 176–78.

110. "The Reminiscences of William O'Dwyer," 402; Turkus and Feder, *Murder, Inc.*, 23.

111. "The Reminiscences of Solomon A. Klein," 86, 88, 90, 91; Carl Sifakis, *The Mafia Encyclopedia* (New York, 2005), 359–61.

112. Interview, MLPK, 12/10/1999.

113. Interview, MPM, 12/20/1997.

114. *NYT*, 12/19/1931; Kelly, *Encyclopedia of Organized Crime in the United States*, 96.

115. David J. Piel, *Piel Bros & the Piels* (Carson City, NV, 2001), "Mafia—The Insurance Salesmen"; interview, DJP, 5/11/2002.

116. Ibid.; MBD-PB, 2/5/1929, PBM#2; *NYT*, 3/5/1944.

117. PB-AMS, 3/13/1923, PB-AMS, 3/11/1924, PBM#1; William Piel, letter to Maria Piel, 7/17/1923, MaPP.

118. MBD-PB, 7/27/1926; Eugene McGovern, Office of Internal Revenue, letter to Piel Bros. Inc., 10/16/1926, PBM#1.

119. MBD-PB, 11/13/1923, PBM#1.

120. Report on Boiler Test, Boiler No 5, 5/22/1916; MBD-PB, 12/15/1926, PBM#1.

121. PB-AMS, 3/11/1924, PBM#1.

122. PB-AMS, 3/10/1925, PBM#1.

123. PB-AMS, 3/9/1926, PBM#1.

Chapter 7

1. Daniel Okrent, *Last Call* (New York, 2010), 302–09, 316–19; *NYT*, 3/3/1929.

2. Okrent, *Last Call*, 294–309, 316–19, 332–33, 350–51.

3. Ibid., 224, 227, 315–16, 338–41, 350–51, 363–64.

4. Grace C. Root, *Women and Repeal* (New York, 1934), 3–5, 15–16, 27, 56, 61–66, 107, 114–118; *Time*, 7/18/1932; Marilyn Elizabeth Perry, "Sabin, Pauline Morton," American National Biography Online (February 2000), http://www.anb.org/articles/06/06-00142.html, accessed 1/16/2015; Ellen McKenzie Lawson, *Smugglers, Bootleggers, and Scofflaws* (Albany, 2013), 103; Roland Krebs and Percy J. Orthwein, *Making Friends is Our Business* (Chicago, 1953), 162–63.

5. Interview, MLPK, 12/10/1999.

6. Okrent, *Last Call*, 350–54; Franklin D. Roosevelt, "Campaign Address on Prohibition in Sea Girt, New Jersey," August 27, 1932," *The American President Project*, http://www.presidency.ucsb.edu/ws/?pid=88395, accessed 1/16/2015; Perry, "Sabin, Pauline Morton."

7. *BDE*, 7/11/1932.

8. Okrent, *Last Call*, 358, 373; *NYT*, 12/18/1934; Martin Heidegger Stack, "Liquid Bread: An Examination of the American Brewing Industry, 1865–1940" (PhD diss., Notre Dame University, 1998), 104, 219; U.S. Brewers Association, *Brewers Almanac 1961* (New York, 1961), 10; Krebs and Orthwein, *Making Friends is Our Business*, 177, 243; William Knoedelseder, *Bitter Brew* (New York, 2012), 41; Amy Mittelman, *Brewing Battles* (New York, 2008), 98–99.

9. Sonya Nance Rodriguez, Gladys J. Hildreth, and Joseph Mancuso, "The Dynamics of Families in Business," *Contemporary Family Therapy* 21, no. 4 (1999), 463–65; Jim Grote, "Conflicting Generations," *Family Business Review* 16, no. 2 (2003), 113–24.

10. Mittelman, *Brewing Battles*, 91, 108–09, 120–21, 126–27; F.&M. Schaefer Brewing Co. *To Commemorate Our Hundredth Year* (New York, 1942); Maureen Ogle, *Ambitious Brew* (Orlando, 2006), 230.

11. President's Special Report to the Annual 1930 Stockholders' Meeting: A Ten-Year Business Retrospect, PB-AMS, 3/11/1930, PBM#2.

12. Ibid.

13. William Piel, Memorandum, 5/19/1926, MaPP.

14. Henry Piel, letters to Marie Muessen Piel, 8/5, 8/12/1926, HPP.

15. William Piel, letter to Maria Piel, 3/9/1927, MaPP.

16. PB-AMS, 3/8/1927, PBM#2.

17. MBD-PB, 1/5/1928, PBM#2.

18. MBD-PB, 1/25, 4/14/1927, 1/5/1928, PBM#2; Sworn Statement by Arthur Piel, 2/27/1937, *In Sophie Piel*, PF-SP.

19. MBD-PB, 4/28/1928, 7/16, 7/16/1929, 3/7/1930, PBM#2.

20. President's Special Report, 3/11/1930, PBM#2.

21. Statement of President of Piel Bros. in re Purchase by Gottfried Piel, Sr. of 88 Brewery Bonds, MBD-PB, MPHC, 11/28/1934; MaPTF minutes, 12/17/1930; Memorandum of Agreement, 7/23/1929; MBD-PB, 11/29/1927, PBM#2.

22. President's Special Report, 3/11/1930, PBM#2.

23. Ibid.

24. Ibid.

25. Technical Director's Report, 3/11/1930; MBD-PB, 11/26/1929, PBM#2.

26. *Pot Pourri 1912* (Phillips Academy Andover), 38; Rudolf Alfred Piel, College Examinations, 6/1912, AA-PAA.

27. Childhood story told by Margarita Piel McCoy, daughter of Rudolf Piel, to the author, n.d.; Henry A. Yeomans, Harvard College, letters to Mrs. Piel, 11/27/1912, 3/18/1913; Harold N. Hillebrand, letter to Dean Yeomans, 2/18/1913; Dunham Jackson, letter to Mr. Yeomans, 2/19/1913; illegible, letter to Professor Yeomans, 2/20/1913; Student Folder Rudolf A. Piel (UAIII. 15.88.10), HUA.

28. William Piel, letter to Henry A. Yeomans, 3/26/1913; Hildreth & Company, letter "To whom it may concern," 6/18/1913; Student Folder Rudolf A. Piel, HUA; Rudolf Piel, letter to Maria Piel, 3/20/1913, PPP.

29. Dean Frederick P. Keppel, Columbia College, letter to Dean Henry A. Yeomans, Harvard College, 12/21/1914; Student Folder Rudolf A. Piel, HUA; interview, MPM, 10/4/2013.

30. William Piel, Ledger for Maria Piel, 182, GPP; interview, MPM, 1/14/2001.

31. Record in Columbia College, Name: Rudolf Alfred Piel, Admitted: 9/1913; *The Columbian 1917* (New York, 1916), 51; *Columbia University Alumni Register 1754–1931* (New York, 1933), 688, CUA; Rudolf A. Piel, Army Serial No. 2,593,793, Form 724-1, NYSA.

32. Technical Director's Report, 3/11/1930, PBM#2; interview, WPJ, 1/20/1997.

33. Technical Director's Report, 3/11/1930, PBM#2.

34. H. L. Mencken, "Malt Liquor," *The Evening Sun* (Baltimore), 12/1/1930, HPP.

35. MBD-PB, 10/7/1929, PBM#2.

36. MBD-PB, 10/16/1929, PBM#2.

37. MBD-PB, 4/28, 6/27/1928, PBM#2; contents of Box No. 94 in names of William Piel and Henry G. Piel, Manufacturers Safe Deposit Co.; interview, MPM, 9/9/2013.

38. Letter to Hy. G. Piel from Geo. W. Tucker, Attorney and Counselor at Law, 23–25 Beaver St., N.Y., 2/8/1930, File: Piel Bros. Hold. Co. Dividends, 1942-46, LP.

39. Trust Indenture between Maria Piel and William Piel, Henry Piel, Paul Piel, Louise Piel Lange, Rudolf Piel, Agnes Piel and Oswald Piel, Tashof and Keilin, 9/5/1930, PPP; interview WPJ, 1/20/1997.

40. Deed of Gift by Maria Piel, Tashof and Keilin, 9/5/1930; Paul Piel, letter to Rudolf Busch, 4/26/1960, PPP; Paul Piel letter to Erwin Lange, 7/25/1945, File: Hold. Co. Correspondence 1944–46, LP.

41. Certificate of Incorporation, MPHC, 8/13/1930; Minutes of First Meeting of Directors of Michael Piel Holding Corporation, 10/1/1930, MPHC Minutes, 1930–1931. Julian Tashof, letter to S&C, Esqs., Att: Mr. Jackson Gilbert, Re: Piel Bros—Possible Liquidation of MPHC and SPHC, 5/25/1962, PBR-SC.

42. MaPTF minutes, 12/17/1930; MPHC minutes, 1930–1931.

43. Benefits to Plant and Owners 1925–1931, 1/29/1932, PBM#2.

44. Plant Expansion: Memorandum #2, Report on Officers' Conference held Sept. 17 & 23, 1931, 9/24/1931, PBM#2.

45. PB-AMS, 9/30/1931; Comments on Problem #II, 9/24/1931, PBM#2.

46. MBD-PB, 6/10/1930, 3/17, 5/18/1931; To All To Whom These Presents Shall Come, 3/17/1931; PB-AMS, 5/18/1931; Certificate of Outstanding Bonds as of 5/28/1931; Secretary's Certificate, 5/28/1931, PBM#2.

47. Interview, DJP, 5/11/2002.

48. Letter from Bradford Norman, VP, Commercial National Bank and Trust Company, 9/12/1931, WPSP.

49. Private Memorandum, n.d., WPSP.

50. Expansion Budget: Piel Bros., 1931, WPSP.

51. Interview, Gerard Piel and Eleanor Jackson Piel, Lakeville, Connecticut, 12/26/1999.

52. Henry Piel, letters to Marie Muessen Piel, 9/12, 9/18, 9/19/1931, HPP; PB-AMS, 9/30/1931, PBM#2.

53. PB-AMS, 3/11/1930, 7/26/1932, PBM#2.

54. Pressinger & Wigg, Counsellors at Law, letter to William Piel, 8/11/1932; PB-AMS, 9/7/1932, PBM#2.

55. MBD-PB, 9/15/1932, PBM#2.

56. MBD-PB, 11/7/1932, PBM#2.

57. *NYT*, 3/26/1933.

58. MBD-PB, 4/3/1933, PBM#2.

59. MaPTF minutes, 2/13/1931; MPHC minutes, 3/19/1931.

60. MPHC minutes, 3/19/1931, 1930–1931.

61. MPHC minutes, 5/21/1931, 1930–1931.

62. MPHC minutes, 1/5, 1/19/1933, 1933–1934.

63. J. Tashof, letter to MPHC, 2/16/1935, FF-WCA; MPHC minutes, 1933–1934.

64. *NYT*, 3/19, 3/23/1930,

65. Louis C. Gosdorfer, Plaintiff, against Piel Brothers, defendants, Complaint, Supreme Court, Queens County, NY, 4/24/1933, MPHC minutes, 1933–1934.

66. *New York Law Journal*, 5/26/33, Justice Mitchell May on Tucker's Motion to Dismiss; MPHC minutes, 1933–1934.

67. Henry F. Homeyer and Louis C. Gosdorfer, Plaintiffs, against Piel Brothers, defendants, Motion by William Piel, Supreme Court, Queens County, NY, 8/3/1933, MPHC minutes, 1933–1934; *Homeyer v. Piel Bros.* (Sup. 1934) 240 App. Div. 1004, 268 N.Y. S. 268, in, *New York Law of Contracts* (Brooklyn, 1962), 305.

68. *BDE*, 5/8/1935.

69. Rudolf A. Piel, letter to A. M. McCoy, 10/30/1959, MPMP.

70. MBD-PB, 4/10/1933, PBM#2.

71. PB-AMS, 4/26, 5/1/1933, PBM#2.

72. Frank N. Kondolf, letter to William Piel, 5/25/1933; PB-AMS, 5/1, 4/19/1933, PBM#2; *NYT*, 8/31/1944.

73. MBD-PB, 5/1/1933, PBM#2; *NYT*, 8/31/1944.

74. MBD-PB, 5/18/1933, PBM#2.

75. Memo of Conference on Telephone with Rudolph [*sic*] Piel, 5/22/1933, attached to Elmer E. Wigg, letter to William Piel, 5/22/1933; MBD-PB, 7/29/1931, PBM#2.

76. Memo of Conference on Telephone with Rudolph [*sic*] Piel, 5/22/1933, PBM#2.

77. Interviews, MPM, 11/28/2004, 2/5/2013.

78. MBD-PB, 9/26/1933, PBM#2.

79. Maria Piel, letter to William Piel, 8/10/1933, MLKP.

80. Agnes Piel, postcards to Maria Piel, 9/16, 12/31/1931, 2/22, 8/25, 9/2, 9/20/1932, LP; Richard Pollak, *The Creation of Dr. B* (New York, 1997), 31–34; Nina Sutton, *Bettelheim* (New York, 1996), 92–99; affidavit attached to Agnes Piel Crane, letters to R. B. Shipley, 7/17/1939, 3/3/1938; interview, MLPK, 3/30/2001.

81. Paul Piel, letter to Henry Piel, 4/5/1960; Paul Piel, letter to Rudolf Busch, 4/15/1960, PPP; interviews, MPM, 3/14/2000, 2/5/2013, 10/23/2014. Shipping notices show the *S.S. Stuttgart* sailed from New York to Cherbourg on 6/15/1933. (See *NYT*, 6/14/1933.)

82. Margarita Piel, postcard to Maria Piel, 7/8/1933, LP.

83. William L. Shirer, *The Rise and Fall of the Third Reich* (New York, 1960), 150–212.

84. By the early 1930s, there were novels and sociological studies about these gangs of homeless young men in their teens and early twenties who lived, in Berlin and other major cities, by theft, thuggery, and prostitution. (See Ernest Haffner, *Blood Brothers* [New York, 2015]; Justus Ehrhardt, *Strassen ohne Ende* [Berlin, 1931]; or *NYT*, 2/14/2015). Margarita Piel McCoy, letter to author, 9/2001; Rudolf Piel, postcard to Maria Piel, 8/28/1933, LP.

85. Margarita Piel McCoy, letter to author, 9/2001.

86. Wm. Piel, Piel Bros. Tax Years Beginning 11/1/1936–1940, Sworn before me this 22nd day of May 1942, R. E. Parks, Notary Public (Kings County #33), MGP-BSU.

87. MPHC minutes, 3/19/1931.

88. F. L. Barth, Jr., Statement of Comptroller of Piel Bros. in re Purchase by Gottfried Piel, Sr., of 88 Brewery Bonds, 6/30/1933, MPHC minutes, 1933–1934.

89. Wm. Piel, Piel Bros. Tax Years Beginning 11/1/1936–1940, MGP-BSU.

90. E. W. Wigg, letter to William Piel, 1/17/1933, WPSP; MBD-PB, 10/30/1934, PBM#3; Wm. Piel, Piel Bros. Tax Years Beginning 11/1/1936–1940, MGP-BSU; *NYT*, 5/2/1935; Statement of the President of Piel Bros. in re Purchase by Gottfried Piel, Sr. of 88 Brewery Bonds, MPHC minutes, 11/28/1934, 1933–1934.

91. *BJ* 72, no. 5 (1935), 104.

92. *BDE*, 5/2/1935; *NYT*, 5/2/1935.

93. Peter Hernon and Terry Ganey, *Under the Influence* (New York: 1991), 151–54; Knoedelseder, *Bitter Brew*, 12–13; *NYT*, 4/6/1933, 4/8/1933; Ogle, *Ambitious Brew*, 197–201.

94. President's Report, MBD-PB, 2/1/1934, PBM#3; Hernon and Ganey, *Under the Influence*, 153–54; Krebs and Orthwein, *Making Friends is Our Business*, 397; Knoedelseder, *Bitter Brew*, 14; *NYT*, 4/6/1933, 4/8/1933; Ogle, *Ambitious Brew*, 198–99, 201–02.

95. MBD-PB, 6/22, 8/29, 9/26/1933; President's Special Report, 3/11/1930, PBM#2; President's Report, MBD-PB, 8/15/1934, PBM#3; *BDE*, 6/18/1933.

96. MBD-PB, 8/21/1933, PBM#2.

97. MBD-PB, 8/29/1933, PBM#2.

98. William Piel, Notice, 10/16/1933, PBM#2.

99. MBD-PB, 10/18/1933, PBM#2.

100. MBD-PB, 11/8/1933, PBM#2.

101. Ibid.

102. Agnes Piel Lyne, Advertising Department's Special Report and Advertising Budget, 7/1–12/31/1934, PBM#3.

103. "Brewer Wants Beer and Liquor Divorced," *Lowell Courier-Citizen* (Lowell, MA), 6/28/1934.

104. President's Report, MBD-PB, 12/5/1933, PBM#2.

105. MBD-PB, 12/20/1933, PBM#2.

106. MBD-PB, 3/6/1934; President's Report, 3/6/1934, PBM#3; 1933–1960, enclosure in H. O. Diesl, vice-president, Piel Bros., letter to Alfred M. McCoy, Jr., 11/9/1960, MPMP.

107. President's Report, MBD-PB, 6/19, 9/25/1934, PBM#3.

108. President's Report, MBD-PB, 4/25/1934, PBM#3.

109. Lyne, Advertising Department's Special Report, 7/1–12/31/1934; President's Report, MBD-PB, 8/15/1934, PBM#3.

110. David Halberstam, *The Powers That Be* (New York, 1979), 25.

111. *Niagara Falls Gazette*, 1/8, 12/18/1935.

112. President's Report, MBD-PB, 12/18/1934; MBD-PB, 12/18/1934, PBM#3.

113. U.S. Guarantee Company, Schedule of Employees Covered to Piel Bro's, 7/1/1934, PBM#3.

114. Technical Director to the Board of Directors, 9/25/1934; MBD-PB, 9/25, 10/30/1934; F. L. Barth, Jr., Comptroller, Special Report In re Pension to Mrs. Henry Jakoby, 10/29/1934, PBM#3.

115. MPHC minutes, 6/22/1934, PBM#3; Barry M. Horstman and Ralph Frammolino, "The Silberman Saga Rivals a TV Thriller," *Los Angeles Times*, 4/23/1989.

116. MPHC minutes, 7/3/1934, PBM#3; Paul Piel, letter to Louise Piel Lange, 10/20/1959, GPP; interview, MP, 12/9/2000.

117. Sworn Statements by William Piel and Elmer Wigg, 8/3/1938, *In the Matter of the Petition for the revocation of Letters Testamentory granted to Arthur Piel, as one of the*

Executors under the Last Will and Testament of Sophie Piel, PF-SP. Certificate of Increased Number of Directors of Piel Bros., 7/16/1934; PB-AMS, 7/17/1934; Agnes Piel, president, MPHC, Elmer Wigg, Arthur Piel, Walter Piel, Executors and Trustees, Estate of Sophie Piel, Deceased, Certificate of Increased Number of Directors of Piel Bros., 6/1934, PBM#3.

118. PB-AMS, 7/17/1934; MBD-PB, 7/17/1934, PBM#3.

119. Organization Chart adopted by Board of Directors, MBD-PB, 9/25/1934, PBM#3.

120. President's Report, MBD-PB, 5/29/1934; MBD-PB, 5/29/1934; Plant Transportation Committee Report, 6/4/1934, PBM#3.

121. President's Report, MBD-PB, 6/19/1934; MBD-PB, 9/25/1934; PBM#3.

122. MBD-PB, 10/30/1934, PBM#3.

123. Rolf Hofman, "From Ludwigsburg to Brooklyn—A Dynasty of German-Jewish Brewers," *Aufbau,* 6/21/2001, http://www.beerhistory.com/library/holdings/hofmann-rheingold.shtml, accessed 2/16/2013; MBD-PB, 10/30/1934, PBM#3.

124. MBD-PB, 10/30/1934, PBM#3.

125. 1934 Organization Meeting of Directors, 7/17/1934, PBM#3.

126. MBD-PB, 10/30/1934, PBM#3.

127. 1934 Organization Meeting of Directors, 7/17/1934, PBM#3.

128. Condensed Statements of Profit and Loss Years 1943 Through 1961, M&G Piel Securities, Inc. (formerly Piel Bros.), GPP.

129. Paul Piel, letter to Louise Piel Lange, 10/20/1959, GPP.

Chapter 8

1. Alfred D. Chandler, Jr., *The Visible Hand* (Cambridge, 1977), 9–11, 464–68; Thomas C. Cochran, *The Pabst Brewing Company* (New York, 1948), 392–94.

2. Barbara Murray, "The Succession Transition Process," *Family Business Review* 16, no. 1 (2003), 29.

3. *BJ* 76, no. 6 (1937), 32; *NYT,* 5/25/1937; Eric P. Nash, *Manhattan Skyscrapers* (New York, 1999), 71; Frank Henyick, "The Guy Francon Who Wasn't," *The Atlasphere,* 5/6/2010, http://www.theatlasphere.com/columns/100506-heynick-ely-kahn-fountainhead.ph, accessed 3/5/2013.

4. *BJ* 78, no. 1, (1938), 34–38.

5. *NYT,* 2/27/1936.

6. *NYT,* 12/22/1936; *BJ* 75, no. 1 (1936), 31; *BJ* 76, no. 2 (1937), 27; *BJ* 78, no. 1, (1938), 38; "A Brooklyn Brewery's Brothers Act Has Right Spiel for Fans of Piels," *Times Newsweekly.com* (Ridgewood, New York), 2/7/2002, www.timesnewsweekly.com/files/archives/, accessed 1/21/2015.

7. *NYT*, 8/12, 8/17/1937, 1/14/1938; Kenyon & Eckhardt, *Advertising Age*, 9/15/2003, http://adage.com/article/adage-encyclopedia/kenyon-eckhardt/98735/, accessed 3/4/2013.

8. *BJ* 77, no. 2 (1937), 72.

9. *NYT*, 11/15/1938, 8/24/1939, 3/29/1940; "Standard Brands," *Advertising Age*, 9/15/2003, http://adage.com/article/adage-encyclopedia/standard-brands/98892/, accessed 3/4/2013.

10. D. B. S. Maxwell, "Beer Cans: A Guide for the Archeologist," *Historical Archeology* 27, no. 1 (1993), 95–113.

11. "A Brooklyn Brewery's Brothers Act"; "Beer into Cans," *Fortune* 13, no. 1 (January 1936), 75–84; *BJ*, 7/15/1938; Maureen Ogle, *Ambitious Brew* (Orlando, 2006), 215–16.

12. *BDE*, 10/26/1941.

13. President's Report, MBD-PB, 12/18/1934; MBD-PB, 12/18/1934, PBM#3.

14. Ibid.; Piel Bros. 1933–1960, enclosure in H.O. Diesl, VP Piel Bros., letter to Alfred M. McCoy, Jr., 11/9/1960, Appendix I, MPMP. Schedule of Per Barrel Use of Materials Consumed for the Years 1940 and 1935 Analyzed as to Use in Various Types of Beer, Report of the Board's Special Committee in Response to the Letter from Mr. Henry G. Piel Dated 12/20/1940; PB-CM, Finance, 1/2/1941, 10/30/1941; PB-CM, Minutes, 1941.

15. President's Report, MBD-PB, 7/31, 9/25, 10/23, 11/23, 12/13/1934, PBM#3.

16. Arthur Andersen & Co., Piel Bros., Reports on Examination of Financial Statements for the Year Ended 12/31/1938, 12/31/1941, 12/31/1942; Sworn Statement by Elmer Wigg and Walter Piel, 11/16/1939, *In the Matter of the Judicial Settlement of the account of proceedings of Walter Piel and Elmer E. Wigg as executors of the last will and testament of Sophie Piel, deceased*, PF-SP.

17. Exhibit B, Sophia Piel Pinkney, Gottfried Piel, Arthur Piel, Robert Piel, letter to Elmer E. Wigg, 12/3/1936; Sworn Statement by Arthur Piel, 2/27/1937, *In Sophie Piel*, PF-SP.

18. Thomas Piel, letter to Anthony Piel, 6/20/2013; interviews, DJP, 5/11/2002, GP, 12/26/1999, MPM, 8/29/2013; David Piel, letter to Margarita McCoy, 9/22/1999, MPMP.

19. *BJ* 79, no. 1 (1938), 32; BDE, 3/16/1939; "Plans $35,000 Great Neck Home," *BDE*, n.d. [ca. 2/1938], Brooklyn Public Library; Thomas Piel, letter to Anthony Piel, 6/20/2013; interviews, DJP, 5/11/2002, GP, 12/26/1999.

20. Interviews, DJP, 5/11/2002, GP, 12/26/1999; *NYT*, 6/29/1938; Social Register Association, *Summer Social Register 1940 New York* (New York, 1940), 311; William Piel, Jr., *In the Matter of the Estate Tax upon the Estate of William Piel Deceased*, Estate Tax Nonresident Affidavit, 11/9/1956, Department of Taxation and Finance, State of New York, PB-SC.

21. Interview, MLPK, 3/29/2001. A photograph of Martha Piel's house appears in Martha Piel, postcard to Paul Piel, 9/29/1913, PPP.

22. Interviews, MLPK, 12/10/1999, 3/29/2001.

23. Report of the Board's Special Committee in Response to Letter from Mr. Henry G. Piel Dated 12/20/1940, PB-CM, Finance; interview, MLPK, 12/10/1999.

24. Maria Piel, letter to Henry Piel, 8/23/1937, MMPP; Paul Piel, postcard to Henry Piel, 4/11/1960, HPP.

25. Fred Lange, postcard to Erwin Lange, 8/1937, LP.

26. Interview, MPM, 3/13–14/2000; MPHC minutes, 5/8/1953, 4/26/1958.

27. Rudolf A. Piel, letter to A. M. McCoy, Jr., 10/30/1959, MPMP.

28. Paul Piel, letter to Rudolf Piel, 5/1/1958; Edward S. Frese, VP, Grace National Bank, letter to Alfred M. McCoy, Jr., 5/12/1958, MPMP; interview, MPM, 3/1/2013; Julian Tashof, Re: MPHC Memo, 2/25/1957, GPP.

29. Interviews, MPM, 10/20/2013; Rollo Lange, Dover-Foxcroft, Maine, 8/1/2000; *Annual Report of the Board of State Assessors, State of Maine 1938* (Waterville, 1939), 221–22; *Annual Report of the Board of State Assessors, State of Maine 1944* (Waterville, 1945), 192–93.

30. Interviews, MPM, 10/20/2013; Rollo Lange, 8/1/2000.

31. Sworn Statements by Rudolf A. Piel to Maria Piel, 7/1940, 9/5/1940, by Rudolf A. Piel to Louise Piel Lange and Erwin F. Lange, 9/5/1940, MGP-BSU.

32. Contents of Box No. 94 in names of William Piel and Henry G. Piel, Manufacturers Safe Deposit Co., WP-SC; interview, MPM, 9/9/2013.

33. After his mother's death many years later, Anthony Piel found a description of this visit to Parlin in his mother's correspondence. Interviews, Anthony Piel, Sharon, Connecticut, 6/8/2014, Portsmouth, New Hampshire, 6/13–14/2014.

34. Sworn Statements by William Piel, 4/28/1936, 8/3/1938; by Arthur Piel, 2/27/1937; Order by John Hetherinton, Justice, Surrogate's Court of the County of Queens, 11/15/1937, *In Sophie Piel*, PF-SP.

35. Sworn Statements by Robert Piel, 2/26/1937, by Gottfried Piel, Jr., 2/26/1937, by Sophia Piel Pinkney, 2/27/1937, *In Sophie Piel*, PF-SP.

36. Sworn Statements by William Piel, 8/3/1938, by Elmer E. Wigg, 7/12/1938; Exhibit A, Julius L. Goldstein, letter to William F. J. Piel, 9/24/1937, in Sworn Statement by Julius L. Goldstein, 8/12/1938; Memorandum of Petitioners Walter Piel and Elmer E. Wigg in opposition to the motion of Arthur Piel, respondent, to take the deposition before trial, and to inspect the records of Piel Bros., 5/17/1938, *In Sophie Piel*, PF-SP; Julius L. Goldstein, Plaintiff's Complaint, 12/31/1937; Delatour, Kennedy & Miller, Answer to the Complaint for Defendant, n.d. *Snediker Transportation Corporation, Plaintiff, against Piel Bros. Inc., Defendant*, Supreme Court of the State of New York, County of Kings, PF-SP; William Piel, Jr., letter to Henry Muessen, 3/18/1944, GC-SC.

37. Interview, Leonard Lazarus, attorney for the Gottfried Piel family, 9/25/1999; Sworn Statements by Arthur Piel, 2/27/1937, 4/22, 5/20/1938; Exhibit B in Sworn Statement by Arthur Piel, 2/27/1937; Sworn Statements by William Piel, 4/28/1936, 8/3/1938, by Hans Schaub, 4/23/1936, by Frank L. Barth, 4/28/1936; Walter Piel and Elmer E. Wigg,

Petition, 2/10/1937; Walter Piel and Elmer E. Wigg, Amended Petition, 4/28/1937; Max Heller General Trucking, invoice to Piel Bros., 11/15/1935 and Check No. R8031, Piel Bros., $2,027.25, To Snediker Transportation, 11/15/1935, in Sworn Statement by Elmer E. Wigg, 5/14/1938, *In Sophie Piel*; John Hetherington, Surrogate, Order, 3/24/1940, *In the Matter of the Application of Sophia Piel Pinkney for Letters of the Estate of Sophie Piel, deceased*; William F. Hagarty, Acting Presiding Justice, Order on Appeal from Order, Appellate Division of the Supreme Court of the State of New York, 10/22/1937, *In the Matter of the Judicial Settlement of the Final Account of Proceedings of Walter Piel and Elmer E. Wigg as Executors of the Last Will and Testament of Sophie Piel, deceased*, PF-SP.

38. Anthony H. Rose, "Beer," *SA* 200, no. 6 (1959), 90–100.

39. William F. Trimble, "George R. Hann, Pittsburgh Aviation Industries Corporation and Pennsylvania Air Line," in David W. Lewis, ed., *Airline Executives and Federal Regulation* (Columbus, 2000), 50–52; *BDE*, 10/29/1943.

40. *Toledo Blade*, 12/8/1977.

41. *NYT*, 1/24, 5/5/1941; *MBA* 29, no. 2 (1943), 49; *BDE*, 5/12/1948; Paul Piel, letter to Louise Piel Lange, 10/20/1959, GPP; William Piel, letter to Oliver B. Merrill, Jr., 10/1/1946; Oliver B. Merrill, Jr., letter to William Piel, 10/10/1946, GC-SC.

42. PB-CM, Marketing, 1/29/1941, PB-CM, Minutes, 1941.

43. Ibid.

44. Ibid.

45. Ibid.; Agnes Piel Lyne, Advertising Department's Special Report and Advertising Budget, 7/1–12/31/1934, PBM#3.

46. *Schenectady Gazette*, 4/22/1942.

47. Piel Bros., Reports on Examination of Financial Statements for the Year Ended 12/31/1938, 12/31/1941, 12/31/1942.

48. Report of response to letter of Mr. Henry G. Piel, 12/20/1940, PB-CM, Minutes, 1941.

49. Ibid.

50. Appendix I: Schedule of Per Barrel Use of Materials Consumed for the Years 1940 and 1935, Report of response to letter of Mr. Henry G. Piel, 12/20/1940, PB-CM, Minutes, 1941; *Niagara Falls Gazette*, 1/8, 12/18/1935; Hop Growers Union of the Czech Republic, "Hop Growing," *Czech Hops*, http://www.czhops.cz/index.php/en, accessed, 4/23/2015.

51. Inter-Office Correspondence, To: J. J. Tashof, Chairman Finance Committee, From: Comptroller, Subject: Extra Dividends and Bonuses—Year 1941, 10/24/1941; PB-CM, Finance, 10/30, 11/13/1941; PB-CM, Minutes, 1941.

52. Report of the Commission on Wartime Relocation and Internment of Civilians, *Personal Justice Denied* (Washington, DC, 1983), chapter 12, http://www.nps.gov/history/history/online_books/personal_justice_denied/index.htm, accessed 7/31/2014.

53. William Knoedelseder, *Bitter Brew* (New York, 2012), 45–47; Amy Mittelman, *Brewing Battles* (New York: 2008), 127, 133.

54. Paul Piel, letter to Erwin Lange, 12/8/1944, LP.

55. Henry J. Muessen, "Presentation to Stockholders of Piel Bros.," 1/18/1960, MPMP.

56. LeRoy D. France, "What's Happened to Beer Marketing in Metropolitan New York?" *MBA* 30, no. 4 (1943), 27–28; Muessen, "Presentation to Stockholders of Piel Bros.," 1/18/1960.

57. Muessen, "Presentation to Stockholders of Piel Bros.," 1/18/1960; France, "What's Happened to Beer Marketing in Metropolitan New York?" 27–38, 71–72; Mittelman, *Brewing Battles*, 127–29; Ogle, *Ambitious Brew*, 218–19.

58. France, "What's Happened to Beer Marketing in Metropolitan New York?" 27–38, 71–72; *MBA* 31, no. 6 (1944), 77; MBD-PB, 5/26, 8/30/1944, PBM#15.

59. Paul Piel, letters to Erwin Lange, 7/13/1944, 12/8/1944, LP.

60. MBD-PB, 2/4, 3/3/1944, PBM#15.

61. *BDE*, 4/6/1944.

62. Interview, GP, 12/26/1999.

63. Interview, MPM, 7/23/2002.

64. *TS*, 9/10, 10/18/1945; *Niagara Falls Gazette*, 3/9, 6/4, 6/15/1948, 2/8/1949.

65. MBD-PB, 10/30, 11/28, 12/29/1944, 2/1/1945, PBM#15; MPHC, Minutes, 1944; Consensus of Opinion of the Directors of Piel Bros., To the Stockholders of Michael Piel Holding Corp., the Trustees of the Maria Piel Trust Fund, 2/28/1946, MPHC, Minutes, 1946.

66. Letter from Arthur Andersen & Co. to J. Julian Tashof, 3/11/1946. File: Piel Bros. 1943–46, LP.

67. MBD-PB, 10/24/1945, PBM#15.

68. MBD-PB, 3/3, 3/31/1944, PBM#15.

69. MBD-PB, 6/5, 7/25/1945, PBM#15.

70. MBD-PB, 12/29/1944; PB-CM, Finance, MBD-PB, 2/1, 6/5/1945; MBD-PB, 11/21/1945, PBM#15; Richard H. Immerman, *The Hidden Hand* (Malden, MA, 2014), 13.

71. Rudolf Piel, letter to William Piel, 2/11/1946; Consensus of Opinion of the Directors of Piel Bros., 2/28/1945, MPHC, Minutes.

72. Consensus of Opinion of the Directors of Piel Bros., 2/28/1945.

73. Henry Piel, letters to Rudolf Piel, 2/28/1946, 3/1/1946, File: Piel Bros., 1946, LP; Erwin Lange, letter to Paul Piel, 7/18/1944; Erwin Lange, letter to MPHC directors, 3/6/1946; Henry Piel, letter to Louise Lange, 3/20/1946, File: Hold. Co. Correspondence 1944–46, LP.

74. William Piel, Memorandum, n.d.; Special Adjourned Meeting of the Board of Directors of MPHC, 3/23/1946, MPHC, Minutes.

75. Sophia Pinckney, et al., To the Stockholders of the MPHC, 5/10/1946, MPHC, Minutes.

76. Henry Piel, letter to Louise Lange, 3/26/1946, 3/28/1946; Louise Lange, letter to Henry Piel, 3/27/1946; Henry Piel, letter to Louise Lange and Rudolf Piel, 4/17/1946; Henry Piel, letter to Rudolf Piel, 4/1/1946, 4/2/1946, File: Hold. Co. Correspondence 1944–46, LP.

77. Erwin Lange, letter to Margarita Piel, 6/10/1946; Margarita Piel, letter to Erwin and Louise Lange, 6/14/1946; Louise Lange, letter to Henry Piel, 6/20/1946; Henry Piel, letter to Erwin Lange, 6/20/1946; William Piel, letter to stockholders M.P.H. Corp., 7/30/1946, File: Piel Bros. 1943–46, LP. Henry Piel, letter to Erwin Lange, 3/19/1947; William Piel, letter to Louise Lange, 6/6/1947, File: Piel Bros. 1947, LP; telephone interview MPM, 4/6/2015; H. C. Sumner, "The North Atlantic Hurricane of September 8–16, 1944," *Monthly Weather Review* 72, no. 9 (9/1944), 187–89, http://docs.lib.noaa.gov/rescue/mwr/072/mwr-072-09-0187.pdf, accessed 4/6/2015.

78. Minutes of a Regular Meeting of the Board of Directors of MPHC, 6/15/1946, Minutes MPHC.

79. William Piel, letter to Henry Piel, 3/4/1946, File: Piel Bros., 1946, LP; Henry Piel, letter to Louise Lange, 3/22/1947, File: Piel Bros., 1947, LP; Arthur Andersen, & Co., Piel Bros. Financial Statements as of December 31, 1946, GPP.

Chapter 9

1. *MBA* 47, no. 3 (1952), 34.

2. Maureen Ogle, *Ambitious Brew* (Orlando, 2006), 225–31.

3. Philip Van Munching, *Beer Blast* (New York, 1997), 22–23; Amy Mittelman, *Brewing Battles* (New York, 2008), 141–42.

4. Jay Maeder, "From Bob and Ray . . . Bert & Harry Piel," *DN*, 4/8/2002.

5. *MBA* 47, no. 3 (1952), 34; *MBA* 51, no. 3 (1954), 26.

6. Condensed Statements of Profit and Loss Years 1943 Through 1961, M&G Piel Securities, Inc. (formerly Piel Bros.), GPP; Henry Piel, letter to Louise Lange, 3/22/1947, File: Piel Bros. 1947, LP.

7. Account of Proceedings of Executors, Schedule E, 1/17/1947; Account of Proceedings of Executors-Trustees and of Deceased Trustees, Schedule D, 6/24/1952, *In the Matter of the Judicial Settlement of the Account of Proceedings of Elmer E. Wigg, Arthur Piel and Sophia P. Pinkney, Executors and Mildred Piel, as Executrix of Walter Piel, deceased Executor, under the Last Will and Testament of Sophie Piel, deceased*, PF-SP; USBC, *Current Population Reports* (Washington, DC, 1964), 3.

8. Henry Piel, letters to Louise Piel, 3/19/1947, 4/17/1947, File: Piel Bros. 1947, LP.

9. PB-AR 1948, 3/4/1949, GPP.

10. Henry Muessen, "Presentation to Stockholders of Piel Bros." 1/18/1960, MPMP.

11. "Contributions to Percent Change in Real GDP (the US 1947–1973)," Bureau of Economic Analysis, U.S. Department of Commerce, http://www.bea.gov/national/nipaweb/SelectTable.asp?Selected, accessed 6/10/2010; "Labor Force Statistics from the Current Population Survey," Bureau of Labor Statistics, U.S. Department of Labor, http://data.bls.gov/timeseries/LNU04000000?years_option=all_years&periods_option=specific_periods&periods=Annual+Data, accessed 6/3/2014; *NYT*, 1/21/2011; Mittelman, *Brewing Battles*, 140–41; Ogle, *Ambitious Brew*, 233–34.

12. *NYT*, 6/18/1949.

13. *AB* (12/1948), 34–35, 58; *BDE*, 10/15/1948; *NYT*, 10/30/1946, 3/7/1947.

14. *AB* (12/1948), 34–35, 58; *NYT*, 11/12/1948, 6/17/1949.

15. *MBA* 41, no. 4 (1949), 24, 113; *AB* (12/1948), 34; *NYT*, 6/17/1949.

16. *NYT*, 4/7, 4/8, 4/15/1949.

17. *MBA* 41, no. 4 (1949), 24, 113.

18. *MBA* 41, no. 6 (1949), 33–34; *NYT*, 4/15/1949.

19. *NYT*, 6/22/1949; "Agreement Covering the Employment of Brewers, Bottlers, Drivers, Chauffeurs, Drivers' and Chauffeurs' Helpers, Stablemen and Yardmen," 6/21/1949, 1, 19, PB-SC.

20. *NYT*, 6/17/1949; Muessen, "Presentation to Stockholders of Piel Bros.," 1/18/1960.

21. *Niagara Falls Gazette*, 7/5/1949.

22. *NYT*, 5/31, 6/28/1958; Muessen, "Presentation to Stockholders of Piel Bros.," 1/18/1960.

23. Memorandum of Agreement between Liebmann Breweries, Piel Bros. F & M Schaefer Brewing Co., and Jos. Schlitz Brewing Co. and . . . International Brotherhood of Teamsters, 7/4/1958; Agreement made between Local #1345 and Piel Bros. 7/8/1958; Arbitrator's Discussion, IBT, Chauffeurs, Warehousemen & Helpers, AFL-CIO, Local 1345 and Piel Brothers, American Arbitration Association, Case No. L-25929 NY-L 765-59, 11/27/1959; Affidavit, In the Matter of the Application of Frank Fink, individually and as President of Bottlers' & Drivers Union, Local 1345, I.B. of T., Petitioner, for an award confirming the arbitration award of Daniel Kornblum against Piel Bros., Respondent, Supreme Court of the State of New York, 6/22/1960, File: Piel Bros. Labor, S&C.

24. Brewery Workers Agreement 1954–1956 between the Employer and the International Brotherhood of Teamsters, 7/1/1954; Official Seniority List, Piels Liberty Avenue—Bottle Delivery, Local #1345—Group II, 7/1/1960, File: Piel Bros. Labor, S&C; R.E. Nicholls, personnel director, Piel Bros., letter to Charles Jones, S&C, 2/29/1952; Piel Bros. Retirement Plan, 6/25/1952, File: Piel Pension Plan, S&C.

25. Muessen, "Presentation to Stockholders of Piel Bros.," 1/18/1960; *Forbes*, 3/1/1957, 36.

26. PB-AR 1950, 3/27/1951, GPP.

27. Condensed Statements of Profit and Loss Years 1943 Through 1961, M&G Piel Securities, Inc. (formerly Piel Bros.), GPP.

28. *AB* (7/1948), 72; *BDE*, 6/19/1948; PB-AR 1948, 3/4/1949, GPP.

29. PB-AR 1950, 3/27/1951, GPP; Roland Krebs and Percy J. Orthwein, *Making Friends is Our Business* (Chicago, 1953), 375–80; Van Munching, *Beer Blast*, 24, 26; Ogle, *Ambitious Brew*, 216–17, 224–25, 230–31, 239–42; Will Anderson, *The Breweries of Brooklyn* (Croton Falls, NY, 1976), 105–08, 116–19.

30. PB-AR 1950, 1951, 3/27/1951, 4/1/1952, GPP; William Piel, Jr., Memorandum, 1/24/1956, *In the Matter of the Federal Estate Tax Liability of the Estate of William F.J. Piel, Date of Death, 4/6/1953*, PB-SC; MBD-PB, 9/25/1950, 6; MBD-PB, 12/18/1950, 6; MBD-PB, 1/22/1951, 5, FIT-SC; E. W. Loebs, president, American Brewing Company, Rochester, NY, letter to Oliver B. Merrill, 7/14/1950; letter from R. W. Sherwood, VP, Piel Bros., 8/1/1950, GC-SC.

31. PB-AR 1951, 4/1/1952, GPP; *BDE*, 12/14, 12/17/1951; *MBA* 46, no. 6 (1951), 75; *MBA* 47, no. 1 (1952), 75.

32. PB-AR, 1955, 3/13/1956, GPP; *MBA* 51, no. 3 (1954), 26.

33. *MBA* 39, no. 6 (1948), 42.

34. *Niagara Falls Gazette*, 6/19, 7/3/1950.

35. *MBA* 50, no. 1 (1953), 48; *MBA* 52, no. 1 (1954), 53.

36. *MBA* 49, no. 1 (1953), 47.

37. *MBA* 48, no. 5 (1952), 60.

38. *MBA* 52, no. 1 (1954), 53; PB-AR 1952, 3/3/1953, GPP.

39. Rich Cohen, *Sweet and Low* (New York, 2006), 112–15.

40. Ogle, *Ambitious Brew*, 229–32.

41. *BDE*, 2/28/1951.

42. *BDE*, 5/24, 6/28, 7/5, 9/27/1951.

43. U.S. Treasury Department, IRS, Alcohol Tax Unit, *Regulations No. 7 Relating to Labeling and Advertising of Malt Beverages As Amended to 6/12/1941 Under the Provisions of the Federal Alcohol Administration Act, as Amended* (Washington, DC, 1948).

44. Carroll E. Mealey, Deputy Commissioner, IRS, letter to Piel Bros., 6/4/1951, BGP-BSU.

45. Dwight E. Avis, Deputy Commissioner, IRS, letter to H.J. Muessen, 9/5/1951, MGP-BSU; *Evening Recorder* (Amsterdam, NY), 11/21/1951.

46. M. V. Odquist, Kenyon & Eckhardt, letter to Frank Dunn, FTC, 12/10/1951; M. V. Odquist, letter to Henry J. Muessen, 12/17/1951; Joseph W. Powers, Chief: Division of Investigation, Bureau of Antideceptive Practices, FTC, letter to M. V. Odquist, 5/2/1952; Dwight E. Avis, Deputy Commissioner, IRS, letter to M.V. Odquist, 5/2/1952; Dwight E. Avis, Deputy Commissioner, IRS, letters to Piel Bros., 7/9, 8/10/1952; H. J. Muessen, letter to Dwight E. Avis, 7/15/1952, MGP-BSU.

47. *The Kingston Daily Freeman* (Kingston, NY), 12/29/1952.

48. Dwight E. Avis, letter to Piel Bros., 12/19/1952; Inter-Office Correspondence, H. J. Muessen to George Davidson, Subject: Summary of Meeting with A.T.U., 1/9/1953, MGP-BSU.

49. Letter from Young & Rubicam, 1/12/1953; H. J. Muessen, letter to John L. Huntington, Assistant Deputy Commissioner, Alcohol Tax Unit, IRS, 1/19/1953, MGP-BSU.

50. Fred J. Loghran, letter to Thomas P. Hawkes, Advertising & Sales Promotion Manager, Piel Bros., 10/27/1953; H. J. Muessen, letter to Frederick J. Loghran, 10/28/1953; Memorandum for Files Re: Piel's Beer, 8/25/1953, enclosed in Allan E. Backman, letter to H. J. Muessen, 8/27/1953; Dwight E. Avis, Alcohol and Tobacco Tax Division, IRS, letter to Clinton M. Hester, Washington Counsel, U.S. Brewers Foundation, 5/22/1953, MGP-BSU.

51. *The Evening Bulletin* (Philadelphia), 7/16/1953; *Philadelphia Inquirer*, 8/7/1953.

52. *Advertising Age* 25, no. 13 (1954), 68.

53. Ibid.

54. John L. Huntington, acting director, Alcohol and Tobacco Tax Division, IRS, letter to Piel Bros., 5/13/1954, MGP-BSU.

55. Inter-Office Memo, C. E. Braren to T. P. Hawkes, Subject: Connecticut Circulation, 5/19/1954, MGP-BSU.

56. Dwight E. Davis, director, Alcohol and Tobacco Tax Division, IRS, letter to H. J. Muessen, 7/20/1954, MGP-BSU.

57. Affidavit, Henry J. Muessen, 1/30/1962, FIT-SC.

58. Interview, MP, NYC, 12/9/2000; Agnes Piel, letter to Edith Dettmers Piel, Sunday Morning, PPP.

59. Affidavit attached to Agnes Piel Crane, letter to R. B. Shipley, 7/17/1939, Chief Passport Division, Department of State, 362.1143, Crane, Agnes P., Richard Pollak Papers, University of Chicago; interview, MLPK, 3/29/2001. Agnes Piel Crane, letter to Cordell Hull, 2/17/1938; No. 49, To the Amercian Charge d'Affairs ad interirm, Vienna, 3/22/1938; No. 186, John C. Wiley, Amercian Charge d'Affairs ad interirm, Vienna, To: The Honorable Secretary of State, Subject: Welfare Patricia Crane, 4/6/1938, Folder 1, Decimal File 1930–39, Box 1681, A363.1115C+: 363.115S, RG 59 (Department of State), NARA. Bettelheim, Regina, page 3, Volume 13198, Passenger Lists for Refugee Arrivals, NARA; Richard Pollak, *The Creation of Dr. B* (New York, 1997), 54–59, 83–84.

60. John C. Wiley, American Consul General, Vienna, letter to Mrs. Agnes Piel Crane, 5/5/1938; Agnes Piel Crane, letter to Nathaniel P. Davis, Division of Foreign Service Administration, 5/7/1938; A.M. Warren, Chief, Visa Division, letters to Mrs. Agnes Piel Crane, 6/9, 11/17/1938; Wiley, telegram to Secretary of State, 6/10/1938; A.M.W., Memorandum for File, 11/3/1938; Geist, Berlin, telegram to Secretary of State, 11/26/1938; Bruno Bettelheim, letter to Mr. Warren, 5/16/1939, Folder 811.111 Bettelheim,

Bruno, Box 970 Visa Division, Individual Case Files, 1933–1940, RG 59 (Department of State), NARA; Pollak, *The Creation of Dr. B*, 80–91, 95–96; Gina Weinmann, interview by Richard Pollak, San Francisco, 4/5/1991.

61. Nina Sutton, *Bettelheim* (New York, 1996), 184–89; interview, MLPK, 3/29/2001; Gina Weinmann, interview by Richard Pollak, 4/5/1991.

62. Agnes Piel, letter to Paul Piel, 5/26/1942, PPP; *NYT*, 7/4/1990.

63. Louise Lange, letter to Paul Piel, n.d. [circa 1945–46], File: Hold. Co. Correspondence 1945–46, LP; Oswald Piel, letter to Jack Tashof, 4/15/1948; Erwin Lange, letter to Paul Piel, 9/8/1948, PPP; interview, Rollo Lange, 8/1/2000.

64. Thomas Piel, letter to Anthony Piel, 6/20/2013; Anthony Piel, email to author, 6/18/2013; "Funeral Held For Mrs. Piel," *Lakeville Journal*, 10/28/1948; *New York Herald Tribune*, 10/28/1948; William Piel, Jr., *In the Matter of the Estate Tax upon the Estate of William Piel Deceased*, Estate Tax Nonresident Affidavit, 11/9/1956, Department of Taxation and Finance, State of New York, PB-SC.

65. Interview, WPJ, 1/20/1997.

66. William Piel, "Salmon Kill Commentary: Part I. 1948 & 1949," 11/2/1948, 6/5, 6/24/1949.

67. Gerard Piel, letter to the author, 10/28/2000.

68. Piel, "Salmon Kill Commentary: Part I.," 4/22, 6/10, 6/11, 6/17, 8/4, 9/24/1949.

69. William Piel, "Salmon Kill Commentary: Part II. Anglers Away," 8/21/1949.

70. Ibid., 8/28/1949.

71. Ibid., 9/15, 9/30/1949.

72. Robert Meigs, Assistant Chief, Fishery Management Division, State of Washington, letter to Piel, 3/13/1950, in "Salmon Kill Commentary: Part II."

73. Piel, "Salmon Kill Commentary: Part II," 2/18, 4/23–25, 4/27, 4/29, 4/30, 5/8, 5/16, 5/18, 5/6–23/1950.

74. Ibid., 1/24/1952; interview, MPM, 1/27/2013; Henry Piel, letter to Louise Lange, 3/26/1946, File: Hold. Co. Correspondence 1944–56, LP.

75. Piel, "Salmon Kill Commentary: Part II," 1/24, 1/25/1952.

76. Ibid., 1/25, 1/31/1952.

77. Ibid., 2/3/1952.

78. Ibid., 2/1/1952; "Piel's Wins Cross of Honour," *Piel Periscope* (2/1952), clipping in William Piel's journal entry for 2/1/1952.

79. Piel, "Salmon Kill Commentary: Part II," 2/17, 2/18, 2/23, 2/29/1952; interview, MPM, 1/27/2013.

80. Piel, "Salmon Kill Commentary: Part II," 3/6/1952; Tony Patrus, "Clover Proves Success Here: Prize Cattle Enjoy Lush Pastureland on Piel Ranch," *The News Press* (Fort Myers, FL), 3/6/1952.

81. Piel, "Salmon Kill Commentary: Part II," 3/6/1952.

82. Ibid., 3/10/1952.

83. William Piel, Jr., letters to Mrs. Thomas Hassett, 11/19/1952; to Dr. Harry Wieler, 11/19/1952; to Reverend Mother Superior, Convent of Our Lady of Princeton, 11/19/1952, PB-SC; interview, WPJ, 1/20/1997.

84. *BDE*, 4/7/1953; *NYT*, 11/14/1952, 4/7/1953; *New York Herald Tribune*, 5/29/1951.

85. Telegrams and letters, File: Letters from Business Firms, to be answered, WP-SC.

86. William Piel, Jr., To the Probate Court for the District of Salisbury, Connecticut, 2/11/1954, WP-SC.

87. Schedule of Goods and Chattels, Michael Piel, 8/10/1915, Probate Court, Somerset County, Maine; William F. Hagarty, 10/22/1937, *In the Matter of the Judicial Settlement of the Final Account of Proceedings of Walter Piel and Elmer E. Wigg as Executors of the Last Will and Testament of Sophie Piel, deceased*, PF-SP.

88. IRS, letter to William Piel, Jr., Re.: Estate of William F.J. Piel, 5/9/1956; Charles Walker, To the Probate Court for the District of Salisbury, Connecticut, Exhibit to Schedule D; Tangible Personal Property, 2/10/1954, *In the Matter of the Estate of William Piel, Late of Salisbury, in Said District*, S&C; William Piel, Jr., To the Probate Court for the District of Salisbury, Connecticut, 2/11/1954; To the Probate Court for the District of Salisbury, Connecticut, Estate of William F. J. Piel, Late of Salisbury, in Said District, Deceased, Final Administration Account of Deceased, Schedule C, 3/15/1957; Memorandum To: Mrs. William E. Ward, et al., From: William Piel, Jr., Re: Estate of William Piel, 2/11/1954; William Piel, Jr., letter to Gerard Piel, 1/14/1954; Bill [William Piel, Jr.], letter to David Piel, 8/18/1953; David [Piel], letter to Bill [William Piel, Jr.], 8/5/1953; Estate of William Piel, 8/15/1955, WP-SC.

89. Anthony Piel, email to author, 6/18/2013.

90. "The Baron of Beer," *Time*, 7/11/1955, 82; *NYT*, 12/20/1945, 6/10, 12/19/1948, 3/18, 3/20, 9/20/1949, 3/31/1950; Dr. Hermann K. Scheyhing, Vice President and Economist, Grace National Bank of New York, "Estate of William F. J. Piel, Appraisal of Michael Piel Holding Company Stock as of 4/6/1953," PB-SC; William Knoedelseder, *Bitter Brew* (New York, 2012), 50.

91. Scheyhing, "Estate of William F. J. Piel, Appraisal of Michael Piel Holding Company Stock as of 4/6/1953," PB-SC; *NYT*, 3/20/1949.

92. *NYT*, 7/14/1953; *BDE*, 7/14/1953.

93. Interview, MLPK, 3/29/2001; *NYT*, 3/28/1991.

94. BDE, 12/9/1948; "Brewery Sales Turn Up," *Miami News*, 3/10/1958.

95. H. J. Muessen, letter to Charles E. Rood, vice president, Brooks Bank & Trust, Torringon, Connecticut, 8/20/1957, WP-SC.

96. Oliver B. Merrill, S&C, letter to Henry Muessen, 10/8/1953, File: Rubsam & Horrmann, Piel Bros., MGP-BSU; MBD-PB 7/27/53; Affidavit, Henry J. Muessen, 1/30/1962, 7, FIT-SC.

97. Piel Bros. Inter-Office Correspondence, To: Mr. Davidson, From: Mr. Archie Ignatow, Subject: Special Sales Projection, Date: 10/22/1953, MGP-BSU, enclosed in

R. E. Fisher, letter to Oliver Merrill 12/7/59; Memorandum To: Mr. McDonald, From: Mr. Gilbert, RE: Income Taxes—1954 and 1955, 9/21/1960, FIT-SC.

98. Piel Bros. Inter-Office Correspondence, To: Messrs. Muessen, Sherwood, Davidson, Riedel, Diesl, Nicholls, and Chaben, From: R. G. Moberly, Subject: Minutes of Staff Meeting, 10/28/1953, Date: 11/2/1953; H. J. Muessen, letter to August Horrmann, 12/2/1953, MGP-BSU.

99. Homer N. Chapin, vice president, Massachusetts Mutual Life Insurance Company, letter to Mr. H. J. Muessen, 10/14/1953; Piel Bros., Terms, n.d.; Agreement between Piel Bros. and August Horrmann, 11/16/1953, MGP-BSU.

100. Annex B: Rubsam & Horrmann Brewing Co, Balance Sheet as at 8/31/1953, in Oliver B. Merrill, S&C, letter to Henry J. Muessen, 11/23/1953, MGP-BSU.

101. Affidavit, Henry J. Muessen, 1/30/1962, FIT-SC.

102. *Staten Island Advance*, 12/3/1953; H. J. Muessen, To the Stockholders of Piel Bros., 12/10/1953; Thomas P. Hawkes, sales manager, Piel Bros., letter to John E. Grimm, Jr., Young & Rubicam, 12/3/1953, MGP-BSU.

103. *NYT*, 12/11/1953; *BDE*, 12/11/1953.

104. United States of America against Rubsam & Hormann Brewing Co., Order to Show Cause, Civil Action No. 13993, U.S. District Court, Eastern District of New York, 12/9/1953; United States of America against Rubsam & Hormann Brewing Co., Statement by Pauline B. Herring, Civil Action No. 13993, U.S. District Court, Eastern District of New York, 12/8/1953, MGP-BSU.

105. Henry Muessen, letter to United States Attorney, Eastern District of New York, 12/15/1953, MGP-BSU.

106. Irving Feldman, Inspector, Food and Drug Administration, letter to Robert Moberly, Piel's Inc., 2/18/1954, MGP-BSU.

107. MBD-PB, 3/8/1954, Piel's Inc. Minutes 1954–56.

108. MBD-PB, 5/3, 12/6/1954, Piel's Inc. Minutes 1954–56.

109. MBD-PB, 4/5, 6/7/1954, 2/14, 3/7, 4/11, 9/19, 10/10/1955; Piel's Inc. Minutes 1954–56.

110. PB-AR 1952, 3/3/1953; PB-AR 1954, 3/8/1955; PB-AR 1955, 3/13/1956; PB-AR 1956, 3/19/1957, GPP.

111. Sara Fishko, "Pioneers of the 'Soft Sell,' " *On the Media*, National Public Radio, 4/5/2013, http://www.onthemedia.org/2013/apr/05/pioneers-soft-sell/, accessed 4/9/2013.

112. Maeder, "From Bob and Ray . . ."; Fishko, "Pioneers of the 'Soft Sell,' "; *NYT*, 11/29/1960.

113. Maeder, "From Bob and Ray . . .".

114. Maeder, "From Bob and Ray . . ."; *NYT*, 10/21/1960.

115. Fishko, "Pioneers of the 'Soft Sell.' "

116. Maeder, "From Bob and Ray . . ."; Classic Piels Beer Commercial, http://www.youtube.com/watch?v=BtBx7AQALz0, accessed 4/10/2013; PB-AR 1956, 3/19/1957, GPP.

117. "Advertising: Spiel for Piel," *Time*, 5/21/1956, http://www.time.com/time/magazine/article/0,9171,808536,00.html, accessed 4/10/2013.

118. PB-AR 1956, 3/19/1957, GPP.

119. "The Best Advertising of 1956," *Tide*, 2/8/1957.

120. PB-AR 1956, 3/19/1957, GPP; Worth Gatewood, "The Truth About Bert and Harry," *DN*, 1/13/1957.

121. Anthony Piel, email to author, 6/18/2013.

122. J.A.T., Jr., Memorandum of Conferences at Piel Bros., 4/17–18/1957; A.N.H., Re: Memorandum of Conference at Piel Brewery on 1/8/1958, 1/13/1958, 1/13/1958, GC-SC.

123. PB-AR 1958, 3/10/1959; 1961, 3/14/1962, GPP.

124. Piel Bros., "11 mo. 1960 Volume," GC-SC.

125. Jerry Della Femina, *From Those Wonderful Folks Who Gave You Pearl Harbor* (New York, 1970), 142–43.

126. William Oscar Johnson, "Sports and Suds," *Sports Illustrated*, 8/8/1988, http://sportsillustrated.cnn.com/vault/article/magazine/MAG1067600/4/index.htm, accessed 4/22/2013.

127. Rudolf Piel, letter to William Piel, 2/11/1946, MPHC minutes; Condensed Statements of Profit and Loss Years 1943 Through 1961, M&G Piel Securities, Inc.

128. Report of Board's response to letter of Mr. Henry G. Piel, 12/20/1940, PB-CM minutes, 1941.

129. PB-AR 1961, 3/14/1962, GPP; *NYT*, 10/21/1960.

130. *NYT*, 10/21, 11/29/1960.

131. Interview, GP, 12/26/1999.

132. *NYT*, 12/1/1960.

133. Maeder, "From Bob and Ray . . .".

Chapter 10

1. Interview, GP, 12/26/1999.

2. William Piel, Ledger for Maria Piel, 97, 178–79, 273.

3. Elmer E. Wigg, letter to Arthur Piel, 6/12/1936; Anton Greiss, letters to Elmer E. Wigg, 5/29, 6/12, 7/7/1936, 1/27/1937; Elmer E. Wigg, letters to Walter Piel, 7/29, 8/5/1936; Elmer E. Wigg, letter to Sophia Piel Pinkney, 4/20/1937; Franz Busch and Rudolf Busch, notaries, Recklinghausen, letter to Elmer Wigg, 5/12/1937; William Piel, letter to Each Member of the Piel Family, Re. Piel Estate in Germany, 7/15/1937; William Piel, letter to Members of MPHC, Re. Estate in Germany, 3/17/1938; Franz Busch and Rudolf Busch, letter to Walter Piel, 1/13/1939; Hans Strauss, letters to Mrs. Walter Piel, 8/3/1948, 4/10/1957, MPP.

4. Leonard Lazarus, "Piel Property in Düsseldorf," enclosed in Leonard Lazarus, letter to Dr. Liessem, Notary, Düsseldorf, Germany, 7/28/1959; Dr. Liessem, letter to Paul Piel, 12/20/1960, GPP; Paul Piel, letters to Family, 8/19/1960, 3/28/1961, 10/25/1962, 11/26/1963; J. Julian Tashof, letter to Michael Piel Family, 5/21/1964; Paul Piel, letter to Marie-Luise Kemp, 4/22/1981, HPP; Margarita Piel McCoy, email to author, 2/22/2003; R. B. [Rudolf Busch], letters to Paul Piel, 12/13, 12/19/1957; J. Julian Tashof, letter to Paul Piel, 10/25/1962, MPMP; Paul Piel, letter to Rudolf Busch, 3/7/1975, Leonard Lazarus Papers.

5. Ballots for Directors, PB-AMS, 10/18/1944, PBM#15; Organization Meeting, MPHC, 5/27/1947, 6/5/1948, 11/19/1949; MBD-MPHC, 6/15/1946, 12/5/1951.

6. Paul Piel, letters to Erwin Lange, 7/13/1944, 12/8/1944, LP; Paul Piel, letter to Louise Piel Lange, 10/20/1959, MPMP.

7. Paul Piel, letter to Alfred M. McCoy, Jr., 10/30/1959, MPMP.

8. Annual Meeting of the Stockholders, MPHC, 5/8/1953; Organization Meeting, MPHC, 1/22/1955; MBD-MPHC, 4/26/1958; Paul Piel, letter to Rudolf Piel, 4/25/1955, MPMP.

9. Paul Piel, letter to Gerard Piel, 5/16/1955, GPP; MBD-MPHC, 4/23/1955.

10. J. Julian Tashof, letter to S&C, Att: Mr. Jackson Gilbert, Re: Piel Bros—Possible Liquidation of MPHC and SPHC, 5/25/1962, PBR-SC.

11. Paul Piel, letter to Gerard Piel, 5/16/1955, GPP.

12. David J. Piel, *Piel Bros & the Piels: Family Anecdotes told by David J. Piel* (Carson City, NV, 2001), "Grandmother Sets a Date"; Thomas Piel, letter to Anthony Piel, 6/20/2013; Mark Piel, letter to Paul and Edith Piel, 6/8/1955, PPP; Maria Piel, Certificate of Death, Division of Vital Statistics, Department of Health, Commonwealth of Pennyslvania, Primary Dist. No. 4631-427, 2/28/1956.

13. Interviews, MPM, 9/9/2013, 10/5/2013.

14. Interview, GP, 12/26/1999; "Institute of Notre-Dame de Namur," *The Catholic Encyclopedia* (New York, 1913).

15. Last Will of Maria Piel, 10/27/1925, In the Estate of Maria Piel, Deceased of the Township of Abington, No. 6068, Orphans Court of Montgomery County, Pennsylvania.

16. Schedule of Distribution in Accordance with Adjudication of Alfred L. Taxis, Jr., President Judge filed 11/17/1959; The first and final account of Paul Michael Piel, executor, 11/2/1959, In the Estate of Maria Piel; interview, Olga Lange, 3/30/2001; *Annual Report of the Board of State Assessors of the State of Maine 1954*, 231.

17. When I attended Columbia University from 1964–68, I lived for three years in Alpha Delta Phi fraternity at 526 West 114th Street; and when my grandfather Rudolf studied there from 1913–17, he lived for two years at Phi Kappa Sigma fraternity five doors down at 536 West 114 Street. (See *Columbia Spectator*, 2/3/1919.)

18. R.A. Piel, letter to Mrs. Gertrude Biermann, MPHC, 12/14/1959, MPMP.

19. Piel Bros. 1933–1960, enclosure in H.O. Diesl, VP Piel Bros., letter to Alfred M. McCoy, Jr., 11/9/1960, MPMP; PB-AR 1956, 3/19/1957, GPP.

20. Leonard Sloane, "Most Big Brewers Follow Trend to Mergers, Multi-Plant Operations, *Wall Street Journal*, 2/13/1957.

21. PB-AR 12/31/1958, 3/10/1959; New Administration Building, n.d., GPP.

22. Paul Piel, letter to Alfred M. McCoy, Jr., 5/21/1959, enclosing Ely Jacques Kahn, letter to Piel Bros., 5/8/1959, MPMP.

23. J. Julian Tashof, letter to Frederick Lange, 4/21/1959, MPMP.

24. Paul Piel, letter to MPHC Stockholders, 5/28/1959, MPMP.

25. Louise Piel Lange, letter to Rudolf Piel, 5/23/1959, GPP.

26. Paul Piel, letter to Louise Piel Lange, 6/7/1959, GPP.

27. Paul Piel, letter to Louise Piel Lange, 9/22/1959, GPP.

28. Paul Piel, letter to Louise Piel Lange, 10/20/1959, GPP.

29. Ibid.

30. Paul Piel, letter to Gerard Piel, 10/24/1959, GPP.

31. Paul Piel, letter to Alfred M. McCoy, Jr., 10/30/1959, GPP.

32. Rudolf Piel, letter to Alfred M. McCoy, Jr., 10/30/1959, MPMP.

33. Leonard Lazarus, letter to Paul Piel, 12/7/1959; Leonard Lazarus and Paul Piel, letter to Members of the Michael Piel and Gottfried Piel families, 12/8/1959; Paul Piel, letter to Rudolf Piel, 12/9/1959, MPMP.

34. Henry J. Muessen, "Presentation to Stockholders of Piel Bros.," 1/18/1960, MPMP.

35. Ibid.; "Hoffa Addresses Local 1345," *1345 Case: Official Publication of the Bottler-Drivers Local 1345* 3, no. 1 (1960), 1, PB-SC.

36. Louise Piel Lange, letter to Rudolf Piel, 5/23/1959; Gerard Piel, letter to Ambassador Richard C. Patterson, Waldorf Tower, NY, 5/9/1961, GPP; Anthony H. Rose, "Beer," *SA* 200, no. 6 (1959), 90–100.

37. Henry Muessen, letter to Henry Piel, 9/18/1960, GPP.

38. Henry Muessen, letter to Piel Bros. Board of Directors, 9/19/1960, GPP.

39. Henry Piel, letter to Paul Piel, 9/23/1960, HPP.

40. H. Michael Piel, letter to Agnes Piel Mueller, 12/3/1960, GPP; *BDE*, 2/8/1954.

41. Henry O. Diesel, VP Piel Bros., letter to Alfred M. McCoy, Jr., 11/9/1960, MPMP.

42. Investment Research Department, Shields & Company, "Anheuser-Busch, Inc.," 11/1960, enclosed in Louise Piel Lange, letter to Gerard Piel, 11/22/1960, GPP.

43. Frederick Lange, letter to Paul Piel, 11/12/1960, HPP.

44. Paul Piel, letter to Frederick Lange, 11/28/1960, HPP.

45. Mike Piel, letter to Henry J. Muessen, 12/16/1960; Henry J. Muessen, letter to Mike Piel, 12/30/1960; Henry J. Muessen, letter to Henry Piel, 1/23/1961, HPP.

46. Henry Muessen, letter to Piel Bros. Stockholders, 8/29/1961, MPMP.

47. *NYT*, 8/31/1961; PB-AR 1961, 3/14/1962, GPP.

48. PB-AR 1961, 3/14/1962; Condensed Statements of Profit and Loss Years 1943 Through 1961, GPP.

49. PB-AR 1961, 3/14/1962, GPP.

50. O. B. Merrill, Memordandum to: Messrs. McDonald, Piel, 4/20/1962, PBR-SC.

51. H. J. M. [Henry J. Muessen], Memorandum Re Negotiations, enclosed in letter to J. Julian Tashof, 6/4/1962, MPMP.

52. Paul Piel, letter to Henry Piel, 7/7/1962, MPMP.

53. Drewrys Limited U.S.A., Inc., General Outline of Proposed Terms of the Senior Notes, 8/28/1962, PBR-SC.

54. J. Julian Tashof, letters to Paul Piel, 7/24, 8/9/1962, GPP; H.O. Diesel, VP Piel Bros., letter to Alfred M. McCoy, Jr., 8/23/1962; MBD-MPHC, 8/22/1962; *NYT*, 12/31/1995; "Agreement between Piel Bros. as Seller & Drewrys Limited as Purchaser," Proof of 8/24/1962, 8–46, PB-AMS.

55. MBD-MPHC, 8/22/1962.

56. Memorandum from Mr. Bikales, RE: Piel Bros. Sale of Assets-Adjustment of Purchase Price, 10/5/1962, PBR-SC.

57. Hon. Edward G. Baker, Justice, Order, In the Matter of the Petition of Kings Country Trust Company as Trustee under a Deed of Trust executed by Piel Bros. on the 30th day of March, 1898, for an Order dispensing with the production of a certain mortgage and the discharge thereof, Index No. 14869/1962, Supreme Court of the State of New York, County of Kings, 10/3/1962, PBR-SC.

58. *NYT*, 3/31/1998; Maureen Ogle, *Ambitious Brew* (Orlando, 2006), 244–45.

59. *NYT*, 9/5/1962, 5/2/1963, 3/28/1991.

60. *NYT*, 10/16/1962, 2/25/1964; "Bert and Harry–Phase Two," *You Tube*, https://www.youtube.com/watch?v=lgVBJF170kw, accessed 1/16/2015.

61. *NYT*, 11/7/1962; H. J. Muessen, letter to Stockholders, 10/1/1962, MPMP.

62. H. J. Muessen, letter to Stockholders, 10/1/1963; Paul Piel, letter to Alfred M. McCoy, Jr., 10/27/1962, MPMP.

63. Henry Piel, letter to Paul Piel, 10/9/1962, GPP.

64. Louise Piel Lange, letter to Paul Piel, 10/16/1962, GPP.

65. MBD-PB, 12/1/1914, PBM#1. Paul Piel, letter to Louise Piel Lange, 11/6/1962, GPP.

66. Ibid.

67. Matthew P. Fink, *The Rise of Mutual Funds* (New York, 2008), 58, 63; Investment Company Institute, "2004 Investment Company Fact Book," chapters 1, 2, http://www.icifactbook.org/fb_ch2.html#investor, accessed 6/30/2014.

68. Paul Piel, letter to Louise Piel Lange, 11/6/1962, GPP; "Hermann K. Scheyhing," *The Hour* (Norwalk, CT), 6/9/1993.

69. Arthur Andersen & Co., M&G Piel Securities Inc. (formerly Piel Bros.), Balance Sheet as of 10/1/1962 Together with Auditor's Opinion, 11/7/1962; MBD-MPHC, 11/26/1962; handwritten note from P.[aul] to Gerard Piel on reverse side of thermofax copy of Consultant Agreement between M&G Piel Securities and Henry Muessen, 3/1/1963, GPP.

70. MBD-MGPS, 12/12/1962.

71. MBD-MGPS, 12/14/1963, 4/4/1964; Consultant Agreement, M. &. G. Piel Securities and Henry J. Muessen, 3/1/1963.

72. MBD-MGPS, 12/15/1965.

73. MBD-MGPS, 3/30/1965.

74. MBD-MGPS, 6/17, 9/25, 12/15/1965, GPP.

75. Memorandum Re. Conference on 4/24/1963 Concerning Federal Income Taxes of M. &. G. Piel Securities, Inc., enclosed in MBD-MGPS, 4/26/1963; *NYT*, 6/10/1999.

76. MBD-MGPS, 6/17/1965; J. Julian Tashof, letter to Paul Piel, 8/2/1966; Martin A. Stoll, S&C, letter to Commissioner of Internal Revenue, 8/5/1966, AWMP.

77. MBD-MGPS, 12/8/1966; Leonard Lazarus, letter to Paul Piel, 4/14/1964, GC-SC.

78. *Schenectady Gazette*, 2/25/1964.

79. *Utica Daily Press*, 3/11/1964.

80. *Schenectady Gazette*, 4/28/1964.

81. *Kingston Daily Freeman*, (Kingston, NY), 10/23/1964.

82. R. J. Schaefer, "Foreword," in Will Anderson, *The Breweries of Brooklyn* (Croton Falls, NY, 1976), 7.

83. *NYT*, 4/15/1972, 1/30, 5/11, 9/21/1973, 12/18/1974; "A Brooklyn Brewery's Brothers Act Has Right Spiel for Fans of Piels," *Times Newsweekly.com* (Ridgewood, New York), 2/7/2002, www.timesnewsweekly.com/files/archives/, accessed 1/21/2015; William Knoedelseder, *Bitter Brew* (New York, 2012), 115–16; Amy Mittelman, *Brewing Battles* (New York, 2008), 155–56.

84. Anderson, *The Breweries of Brooklyn*, 92.

85. *NYT*, 1/1, 1/16, 1/17/1976, 6/2/1996; Edwin G. Burrows and Mike Wallace, *Gotham* (New York, 1999), 53.

86. *NYT*, 1/23, 1/24, 1/29/1976, 6/2/1996.

87. William Couper, *History of the Engineering, Construction and Equipment of the Pennsylvania Railroad Company's New York Terminal and Approaches* (New York, 1912), 7–16; *NYT*, 9/9/1906.

88. *NYT*, 11/23/2004; "1950 Beer Sales of Brewing Companies," *MBA* 45, no. 3 (1951), 34; *MBA* 51, no. 3 (1954), 26.

89. Walter Thabit, *How East New York Became a Ghetto* (New York, 2003), 7–19, 37–39, 44–51.

90. Jonathan Mahler, "The Darkest Night," *NYT Magazine*, 10/5/2003, 76–82; Brian Merlis and Riccardo Gomes, *Brooklyn's Bushwick and East Williamsburg Communities* (New York, 2012), 296–99.

91. Margaret Latimer, "Brooklyn," in Kenneth T. Jackson, ed., *The Encyclopedia of New York City* (New Haven, 2010), 171; Jonathan Peters, "The Economic Impacts of the Brooklyn Waterfront," in *The Waterfront: A Brooklyn Model for Preservation and Change* (New York, 2011), 8, 16; Department of Transportation, New Jersey, *Portway Extensions*

Concept Development Study: Final Report (September 2003), VI-1–VI-9, http://www.state.nj.us/transportation/freight/portway/FR_Section_6.pdf, accessed May 24, 2015.

92. *NYT*, 6/29/2003; Merlis and Gomes, *Brooklyn's Bushwick and East Williamsburg Communities*, 299–303.

93. Peters, "The Economic Impacts of the Brooklyn Waterfront," 15; Gabrielle Wright, "Bushwick 'Revival' brings New Facts, Rent Hikes and Rapid Change," *Pavement Pieces*, 3/2/2013, http://pavementpieces.com/bushwicks-revival-brings-new-faces-rent-hikes-and-rapid-change/, accessed 9/2/2014; *NYT*, 5/10/2015.

94. Winifred Curran, "In Defense of Old Industrial Spaces," *International Journal of Urban and Regional Research* 34, no. 4 (2010), 871–85; Winifred Curran and Trina Hamilton, "Just Green Enough," *Local Environment* 17, no. 9 (2012), 1027–42.

95. "History of Schaefer Beer," http://www.schaefer-beer.com/history/default.aspx, accessed 4/24/2013; "Piels Beer," *Wikipedia*, http://en.wikipedia.org/wiki/Piels_Beer, accessed 4/23/2013; "Piels-Pabst Brewing Company," *Beer Advocate*, http://www.beeradvocate.com/beer/profile/447/5259/, accessed 12/13/2014; Mittelman, *Brewing Battles*, 267.

96. Bill Chappell, "U.S. Moves to Halt AB InBev's Purchase of Grupo Modelo," *Planet Money*, NPR, 1/31/2013, http://www.npr.org/blogs/thetwo-way/2013/01/31/170758928/u-s-moves-to-halt-ab-inbevs-purchase-of-grupo-modelo; Caitlin Kenney, "Beer Map," *Planet Money*, NPR, 2/19/2013, http://www.npr.org/blogs/money/2013/02/19/172323211/beer-map-two-giant-brewers-210-brandsKenney; Bill Chappell, "Court Approves Anheuser-Busch InBev Deal to Buy Grupo Modelo," *Planet Money*, NPR, 4/23/2013, http://www.npr.org/blogs/thetwo-way/2013/04/23/178614285/court-approves-anheuser-busch-inbev-deal-to-buy-grupo-modelo, all accessed 4/29/2013; *NYT*, 7/14/2008, 10/13, 12/19/2013; Steve Pearlstein, "Beer Merger would Worsen Existing Duopoly by AB InBev, SABMiller," *WP*, 2/2/2013; *NYT*, 9/17/2015; "Beer giants to join forces," *Wisconsin State Journal*, 10/14/2015.

97. "Budweiser-Anheuser Busch," *Beeradvocate*, http://www.beeradvocate.com/beer/profile/29/65/m; "Miller Lite," *Beeradvocate*, http://www.beeradvocate.com/beer/profile/105/332/, both accessed 6/23/2014.

98. *NYT*, 10/13/2013, 5/27/2014; Steve Hindy, *The Craft Beer Revolution* (New York, 2014), 1, 209.

99. Tom Acitelli, *The Audacity of Hops* (Chicago, 2013), xii–xv, 4–5; Hindy, *The Craft Beer Revolution*, 5–16, 20–25, 27–30, 43; Ogle, *Ambitious Brew*, 266–76.

100. Acitelli, *The Audacity of Hops*, 150–52, 156–59; Hindy, *The Craft Beer Revolution*, 89; Steve Hindy and Tom Potter, *Beer School* (New York, 2005), 9–11, 24–28, 33–34, 56–57, 64–67, 79, 158–59, 183.

101. *NYT*, 6/2/1996, 5/25/2014; Hindy and Potter, *Beer School*, vii–ix, 159–65, 178–83, 196–97; Acitelli, *The Audacity of Hops*, 157–58, 201–04; Hindy, *The Craft Beer Revolution*, 85–88, 235.

102. Craft Beer Sales by State, Brewers Association, https://www.brewersassociation. org/statistics/by-state/, accessed 5/5/2015; *NYT*, 5/25/2014; Acitelli, *The Audacity of Hops*, 157, 168–69; Hindy, *The Craft Beer Revolution*, 67–69, 235.

103. *NYT*, 10/18/2013; Barry Adams, "Beer Sales Jump 15 Percent," *Wisconsin State Journal*, 7/30/2013.

104. "Craft Brewing Facts," Brewers Association, http://www.brewersassociation.org/ pages/business-tools/craft-brewing-statistics/facts, accessed 4/24/2013; Tali Arbel, "Build a craft brewery, urban revival will come," *USA Today*, 7/6/2013, http://www.usatoday. com/story/money/business/2013/07/05/in-urban-revival-beer-creates-small-business-hubs/2487625/, accessed 9/2/2014.

Chapter 11

1. Margarita Piel McCoy, Biographical Questionnaire: Piel Family History, n.d., MPMP.

2. Barbara Murray, "The Succession Transition Process," *Family Business Review* 16, no. 1 (2003), 17–20.

3. Loretto Scott was the daughter of Edward H. Scott, brother of Sir Richard William Scott who served as Secretary of State for Canada in 1874–78 and 1896–1908 (See W. Steward Wallace, ed., *Macmillan Dictionary of Canadian Biography* [Toronto, 1978], 753; *The Citizen* [Ottawa] 11/6/1907; *The Evening Citizen* [Ottawa], 4/24, 4/26/1913; *Lakeville Journal*, 10/28/1948); *BJ* 79, no. 1 (1938), 32; *BDE*, 3/16/1939; "Plans $35,000 Great Neck Home," *BDE*, n.d. [ca.2/1938]; Social Register Association, "Summer Social Register 1940 New York," *Social Register* (New York, 1940), 311.

4. *NYT*, 12/28/1971; interviews, DJP, 5/11/2002, GP, 12/26/1999. For example, family friend William C. Cannon, though senior partner in the Davis Polk law firm and member of the Union Club, was never admitted to the *Social Register*, possibly because he was a practicing Catholic.

5. Anthony Piel, email to author, 6/18/2013; interview, WPJ, 1/20/1997.

6. *NYT*, 7/17/1933, 4/4, 5/30/1937, 3/18/1973, 4/10/1977; interview, DJP, 5/11/2002.

7. "Brown, Alexander," "Brown, George," "Brown, George S.," *The National Cyclopedia of American Biography, Vol. I* (New York, 1898), 474–75; Clarence S. Day, Jr., *Decennial Record of the Class of 1896, Yale College* (New York, 1907), 237; "Business: Brown Harriman," *Time*, 12/22/1930, http://www.time.com/time/magazine/ article/0,9171,740853,00.html, accessed 5/3/2013; *NYT*, 10/25/1916, 6/29/1938; interview, MLPK, 3/30/2001.

8. Interviews, GP, 12/26/1999, DJP, 5/11/2002; Thomas Piel, letter to Anthony Piel, 6/20/2013; Anthony Piel, email to author, 6/18/2013; *NYT*, 9/11/1933, 6/16/1934; Yale

University, *Obituary Record of Yale Graduates 1924–1925* (New Haven, 1925), 1503; *Social Register, New York, 1931, Vol. XLV, No. 1* (New York, 1930), 125; *NYT*, 1/17, 2/5/1938, 12/22/1946.

9. William Ferdinand Piel, Jr., Class of 1932, A.B. Degree, Princeton University, Transcript; *Nassau Herald* (Princeton, 1932), 328, SGM-PU; William Piel, Jr., Transcript, Harvard Law School; Gerard Piel, letter to author, 12/10/2000; interview, WPJ, 1/20/1997.

10. *NYT*, 5/1/1979, 9/25/1998; William Piel, Jr. and Martha Moore, *Lamplighters* (New York, 1981), 184–89; Marquis, *Who's Who in America 1999, Vol. 2 L–Z* (New Providence, NJ, 1999), 3509; interview, GP, 12/26/1999; *Princeton Alumni Weekly*, 11/17/1980, SGM-PU; interview WPJ, 1/20/1997.

11. Ibid.; *United States v. Morgan*, Civ. A. NO. 43-757, 118 F.Supp. 621 (1953), *United States v. Morgan, et al.*, United States District Court, S. D. NY, 10/14/1953, http://www.leagle.com/decision/1953739118FSupp621_16323, accessed 11/11/2013.

12. Interview, GP, 12/26/1999; "The Reminiscences of Gerard Piel" (OHRO-CU, 1984), 9–30; *NYT*, 9/7/2004; Gerard J. Piel, Transcript, '31–'32, '32–'33, Andover Academy; Charles Forbes, headmaster, Phillips Academy, letters to William Piel, 2/10, 3/25/1933; William Piel, letter to Gerard Piel, 2/21/1933; Gerard Piel, letter to G. Grenville Benedict, Phillips Academy, 12/30/1957, AA-PAA.

13. Gerard Joseph Piel, Certificate by Claude M. Fuess, principal, Phillips Academy, 5/21/1933; Certificate of Honorable Dismissal, Harvard College; Armin V. St. George, Report on Candidate Gerard Joseph Piel, 5/5/1933; Report of Scholastic Aptitude Test of Final Candidate, Gerard Joseph Piel, 6/24/1933, HUA.

14. Bruce V. Lewenstein, "Magazine Publishing and Popular Science After World War II," *American Journalism* 6, no. 4 (1989), 219–20; interview, GP, 12/26/1999; "The Reminiscences of Gerard Piel," 9–30; Gerard Joseph Piel, Transcript, Harvard College, 6/19/1937, HUA.

15. Gerard Piel, "The Formation of Parti Socialist (S.F.I.O): The Domestication of the French Socialists" (Department of History, 1937), 19, 30, 37, 48, 51, 89–90, 96, 121–22, Harvard College Library, Thesis Collection.

16. *1933 Pot Pourri* (Phillips Academy Andover, 1933), 52, AA-PAA; Classes of 1936 and 1937, Application Blank for the Houses, Gerard Joseph Piel, 4/15/1936; Henry Fellowships Application Form, 1936–37, Gerard Piel, 12/15/1936; *1937 Harvard Class Annual* (Cambridge, 1937), 172, 265, HUA; interview GP, 12/26/1999; *NYT*, 9/7/2004; Gerard Piel, *The Age of Science* (New York, 2001), xii–xiii.

17. "The Reminiscences of Gerard Piel," 42–44, 71–72.

18. *NYT*, 4/16/1963, 12/21/1966; "The Reminiscences of Gerard Piel," 58–60; Lewenstein, "Magazine Publishing and Popular Science After World War II," 220.

19. Interview, GP, 12/26/1999; "The Reminiscences of Gerard Piel," 63–66; Piel, *The Age of Science*, xvi–xvii.

20. Interview, GP, 12/26/1999; "The Reminiscences of Gerard Piel," 65–70; G.H. Dieke, *Robert Williams Wood 1868–1955* (Washington, DC, 1993), 50–51; Piel, *The Age of Science,* xvi–xix.

21. Interview GP, 12/26/1999; "The Reminiscences of Gerard Piel," 70, 131–35; Alan Brinkley, *The Publisher* (New York, 2010), 304–05.

22. Lewenstein, "Magazine Publishing and Popular Science After World War II," 219–27.

23. Interview, GP, 12/26/1999; Piel, *The Age of Science,* xiv.

24. "The Reminiscences of Gerard Piel," 136–44, 531; *NYT,* 9/27/1989.

25. *NYT,* 4/16/1963, 12/21/1966, 7/4/1986; "The Reminiscences of Gerard Piel," 157–58; Lewenstein, "Magazine Publishing and Popular Science After World War II," 227–28.

26. "The Reminiscences of Gerard Piel," 165–68, 174–86, 225–26, 231, 609.

27. Subject: PIEL, Gerard (aka: "Jerry" Piel), rewrite of EX-884 3/15/1967, 12/14/1967, CIA FOIA, http://www.foia.cia.gov/browse_docs_full.asp, accessed 10/30/2008.

28. *NYT,* 4/1/1950; Wendy Swanberg, "The Forgotten Censorship of *Scientific American* in 1950," History Division, Association for Education in Journalism and Mass Communication, Chicago, 8/2008, 1–15; Peter J. Kuznick, "Prophets of Doom or Voices of Sanity?" *Journal of Genocide Research* 9, no. 3 (2007), 421.

29. Swanberg, "The Forgotten Censorship of *SA* in 1950," 1–15; Jospeph T. Klapper and Charles Y. Glock, "Trial By Newspaper," *SA* 180, no. 2 (1949), 16–21; *NYT,* 7/21/1949; Daniel Patrick Monihan, *Secrecy* (New Haven, 1998), 65; "The Reminiscences of Gerard Piel," 640–42.

30. Louis N. Ridenour, "The Hydrogen Bomb," *SA* 182, no. 3 (1950), 11–15.

31. Hans A. Bethe, "The Hydrogen Bomb II," *SA* 182, no. 4 (1950), 18–23; *NYT,* 3/8/2005; interview, GP, 12/26/1999.

32. Interview, GP, 12/26/1999; "The Reminiscences of Gerard Piel," 198, 613–17.

33. Interview, GP, 12/26/1999; "The Reminiscences of Gerard Piel," 209–10.

34. *NYT,* 4/1/1950. Gerard's account is corroborated by AEC documents. See, letters from Morse Salisbury to William Borden, 4/20/1950 and Shelby Thompson to William Borden, 4/26/1950, Folder: Bethe, Hans, Box 4/5, RG 128, NARA.

35. *NYT,* 4/1, 4/22, 5/7/1950; "The Reminiscences of Gerard Piel," 208–10.

36. Subject: PIEL, Gerard (aka: "Jerry" Piel), rewrite of EX-884 3/15/1967, 12/14/1967, CIA FOIA; Rich Calder, "Miriam Moskowitz Fights to Clear Name Despite Spy Conviction," *New York Post,* 8/12/2014, http://nypost.com/2014/08/12/miriam-moskowitz-fights-to-clear-name-despite-spy-conviction/, accessed 12/13/2014.

37. "The Reminiscences of Gerard Piel," 194–95; "Science and the Citizen," *SA* 184, no. 5 (1951), 33–34.

38. "The Reminiscences of Gerard Piel," 270–72. Indicating Leon Svirsky probably testified at a closed-door executive session, the only record of his appearance is a payment

for "May 11, 1 day . . . Transportation from Ossining, N.Y., to Washington, D.C., and return amount $40.50," which was "for attendance as a witness before the subcommittee of the Committee on the Judiciary investigating the administration, operation, and enforcement of the Internal Security Act of 1950." (See U.S. Senate, Secretary of the Senate, 83d Congress, 2d Session, *Report of the Secretary of the Senate from 7/1/1952, to 1/2/1953 and from 1/3/1953, to 6/30/1953* [Washington, DC, 1953], 598.)

39. "The Reminiscences of Gerard Piel," 256–59, 264–67; Cabell Phillips, "Why They Join the Wallace Crusade," *NYT Magazine*, 5/23/1948, 12, 24–30; U.S. Senate, Committee on the Judiciary, Subcommittee To Investigate the Administration of the Internal Security Act and Other Internal Security Laws, 83rd Congress, 2d Session, *Interlocking Subversion in Government Departments. Part 20: "Army Information and Education"* (Washington, DC, 1954), 1498–1506.

40. "The Reminiscences of Gerard Piel," 272–76.

41. Ibid., 226, 272–76; *NYT*, 5/2/1942; 10/21/1972.

42. Anthony Piel, email to author, 6/18/2013; Piel and Moore, *Lamplighters*, 188.

43. "The Reminiscences of Gerard Piel," Index, 289–91, 657–69.

44. "The Reminiscences of Gerard Piel," 289–91, 657–69.

45. *NYT*, 5/1/1955, 10/2/1957, 9/17/1958, 6/2/1961, 3/14, 6/6, 10/13/1962, 5/10/1963, 11/8/1965, 12/21, 11/9/1966, 12/16, 12/23/1967, 9/24/1969; Marquis, *Who's Who in America 1999, Vol. 2*, 3508–09; "Graduating Seniors Attend Class Day Before Receiving Degrees Tomorrow," *Columbia Daily Spectator*, 6/4/1962.

46. Jean Murray, principal, City and Country School, letter to Delmar Leighton, Harvard University, 2/24/1958; Richard H. Ullman, Senior Tutor in Lowell House, reference letter for Samuel Piel, n.d., HUA; *NYT*, 6/17/1984, 9/7/2004; Bonnie Azab Powell, "One Tough Case" (2009), University of California, http://www.law.berkeley.edu/5464.htm, accessed 11/13/2013.

47. Jessie Jean Marsh, "Reception Honors Newlywed Piels," *Los Angeles Times*, 6/29/1955; *Pot Pourri 1977* (Phillips Academy Andover), 265; Eleanor J. Piel, Phillips Academy Andover, Transcript, 6/1977, AA-PAA.

48. Agnes Piel Crane, letter to A.M. Warren, 7/26/1938, Folder 811.111 Bettelheim, Bruno, Box 970 Visa Division, Individual Case Files, 1933–1940, RG 59 (Department of State), NARA; Nina Sutton, *Bettelheim* (New York, 1996), 187.

49. His various accounts of the Patsy story can be found in Bruno Bettelheim, *A Home for the Heart* (New York, 1974), 12; David Dempsey, "Bruno Bettelheim is Dr. No," *NYT Magazine*, 1/11/1970, 109; Bruno Bettelheim, *A Good Enough Parent* (New York, 1987), 199–201; Daniel Karlin, director, *Last Meeting with Bruno Bettelheim* (La Sept Fach TV-BBS Productions, 1974), broadcast on KQED, San Francisco, 3/22/1989; David James Fisher, "Last Thoughts on Therapy: Bruno Bettelheim," *Society* 28, no. 3 (1991), 68.

50. Richard Pollak, *The Creation of Dr. B* (New York, 1997), 110–11, 127–33; interviews, MLPK, 3/30/2001, MPM, Silver Lake, Vermont, 6/27/2000. Gina Weinmann,

Patsy's primary caregiver in Vienna and then Bruno Bettelheim's wife, said: "Bruno was lying when he said for three months she [Patsy] didn't say a word; the George Washington story is nonsense; she talked right from the beginning." (Gina Weinmann, interview by Richard Pollak, San Francisco, 4/5/1991.) In 2000, Margarita Piel McCoy wrote her cousin and contemporary Patsy: "Do you remember, when we were little girls, playing in the garden behind Uncle Paul's house in Greenwich Village . . . ? I do, and those were happy memories for me." (Margarita P. McCoy, letter to Patricia Lyne, 5/1/2000, MPMP.)

51. Bruno Bettelheim and Morris Janowitz, "Prejudice," *SA* 183, no. 4 (1950), 11–13; Bruno Bettelheim, "Schizophrenic Art," *SA* 186, no. 4 (1952), 30–34; Bruno Bettelheim, "Joey: A 'Mechanical Boy,'" *SA* 200, no. 3 (1959), 116–27. Emily Nussbaum, "Defending Dr. B," *NYT Book Review*, 11/24/2002, 16.

52. Interviews, GP, 12/6/2002; Eleanor Jackson Piel, MGPS-AM, Kennebunkport, Maine, 6/13/2009; "Mrs. Fritz Mueller," *Harlem Valley Times*, 1/13/1983.

53. Interviews, GP, 12/6/2002; Eleanor Jackson Piel, MGPS-AM, Kennebunkport, Maine, 6/13/2009; MLPK, 3/29/2001; Doreen Bibro (nurse who worked for Agnes Piel Mueller during the last five years of her life), NYC, 9/27/2002; Lizbeth Halliday Piel, MGPS-AM, Portsmouth, New Hampshire, 6/25/2004; Anthony Piel, email to author, 11/3/2014.

54. Gerard Piel, *Harvard Class of 1937* (Cambridge, 1962), 852–54; Monica Amarelo, "Gerard Piel, Former Publisher of *Scientific American*, Dies at Age 89," News Release, American Association for Advancement of Science, 9/8/2004, http://www.aaas.org/news/releases/2004/0908piel.shtml, accessed 5/8/2013.

55. *NYT*, 4/16/1963.

56. Chester I. Barnard, "Does the Atomic Explosion in Russia Require the U.S. to Modify Its Position in Regard to International Control of Atomic Energy?" *SA* 181, no. 5 (1949), 11–13; James R. Newman, "Two Discussions of Thermonuclear War," *SA* 204, no. 3 (1961), 197–204; P.M.S. Blackett, "Steps Toward Disarmament," *SA* 206, no. 4 (1962), 45–53; "The Reminiscences of Gerard Piel," 191–93, 294–95, 371–72, 610–11.

57. Gerard Piel, "The Illusion of Civil Defense," *Bulletin of the Atomic Scientists* 17, no. 2 (1962), 2–8.

58. *NYT*, 11/19/1961, 2/18/2013.

59. Philip Morrison and Paul F. Walker, "A New Strategy for Military Spending," *SA* 239, no. 4 (1978), 48–61; Herbert Scoville, Jr., "The Limitation of Offensive Weapons," *SA* 224, no. 1 (1971), 15–25; Herbert Scoville, Jr., "Submarines and National Security," *SA* 226, no. 6 (1972), 15–27; Herbert Scoville, Jr., "The SALT Negotiations," *SA* 237, no. 2 (1977), 24–31; *NYT*, 7/31/1985; "The Reminiscences of Gerard Piel," 647–48.

60. Subject: PIEL, Gerard (aka: "Jerry" Piel), rewrite of EX-884 3/15/1967, 112/14/1967, CIA FOIA; Van Gosse, *Where the Boys Are* (New York, 1993), 150–52.

61. Gerard Piel, letter to author, with enclosed photo of Eleanor and Gerard dancing at the White House, 8/13/2002; *NYT*, 11/30/1965, 9/10/1999.

62. *NYT*, 12/12/1966; "The Reminiscences of Gerard Piel," 424–25; Wassily W. Leontief, "Input-Output Economics," *SA* 185, no. 4 (1951), 15–21.

63. *NYT*, 12/13/1966, 9/29/1968, 9/28/1977, 7/27/1979; Jerry Mander, George Dippel, and Howard Gossage, *The Great International Paper Airplane Book* (New York, 1967); "The Reminiscences of Gerard Piel," 430–31, 604–05.

64. *NYT*, 9/29/1968.

65. *NYT*, 8/6/1964, 10/4/1976, 7/27/1979, 6/4/1984; interview, GP, 12/26/1999; "The Reminiscences of Gerard Piel," 401, 492–94; Piel, *The Age of Science*, xix–xx.

66. Interview, GP, 12/26/1999; "The Reminiscences of Gerard Piel," 533–34.

67. "The Reminiscences of Gerard Piel," 508–10, 517–18, 541–42.

68. *NYT*, 5/22/1984; interview, GP, 12/26/1999; "The Reminiscences of Gerard Piel," 532–34, 541–44.

69. Interview, GP, 12/26/1999; "The Reminiscences of Gerard Piel," 546; Gerard Piel, *Harvard Class of 1937* (Cambridge, 1987), 537–38; *NYT*, 5/27/1987.

70. *NYT*, 3/29/1986, 7/4/1986, 5/27/1987; interview, GP, 12/26/1999; "The Reminiscences of Gerard Piel," 552–72.

71. Interview, GP, 12/26/1999; "The Reminiscences of Gerard Piel," 569–75.

72. "The Reminiscences of Gerard Piel," 584–85.

73. Gerard Piel, "Natural Philosophy in the Constitution," *Science* 233, no. 4768 (1986), 1056–60; "The Reminiscences of Gerard Piel," 621–22, 629–30.

74. Colonel Jacob Ruppert, Jr. lived at 1120 Fifth Avenue, directly across 93rd Street from Gerard Piel's penthouse apartment at 1115 Fifth Avenue. But Ruppert also owned $30 million worth of real estate, largely in Manhattan, making it possible that Gerard's penthouse had once been Ruppert's ballroom. (See *NYT*, 1/14/1939.) United Nations, *Earth Summit Agenda 21* (New York, 1993); Peter Jamison, "Fears of Agenda 21 Go Mainstream in the Republican Party Platform," *Tampa Bay Times*, 8/30/2012; International Council for Local Environmental Initiatives (ICLEI), "How ICLEI Can Help Your Local Government," http://www.icleiusa.org/about-iclei, accessed 6/22/2013; Scott Paradise, "Summary Report on the Technology and Culture Seminar at MIT 1992–3," http://web.mit.edu/tac/docs/reports/annual-92-93.pdf, accessed 6/22/2013.

75. Piel, *The Age of Science*; Loren Graham, " 'The Age of Science': Back Issues," *NYT*, 11/11/2001.

76. *NYT*, 9/7/1994; "The Reminiscences of Gerard Piel," 570, 578–90; Paul McDougall, "Painful Evolution for Scientific American," *Folio* 23, no. 16 (10/1/1994), 16.

77. Gerard Piel, letter to Michael L. Piel, 4/30/2000, MPMP.

78. Transcripts for Gerard Piel, Elmar V. Piel, H. Michael Piel, Frederick Lange, and Alfred M. McCoy, Jr., AA-PAA; James C. Graham, Phillips Academy (Andover, MA), letter to Louise Lange, 3/24/1936, LP.

79. Interviews, MPM, 3/31/2002, MLPK, 12/8/2000; Hubert Michael Piel, Piel Family's Historical Biographies, n.d., MPMP.

80. *Princeton Alumni Weekly*, 4/18/1977, SGM-PU; *NYT*, 3/27, 10/30/1949; interview, MLPK, 12/8/2000; Katahdin, Breeds of Livestock, Oklahoma State University, http://www.ansi.okstate.edu/breeds/sheep/katahdin/, accessed 11/12/2013.

81. West Point Association of Graduates, "Alfred M. McCoy, Jr. 1944," http://apps.westpointaog.org/Memorials/Article/14033/, accessed 7/8/2014.

82. *SA* 291, no. 5 (2004), 32.

83. Murray, "The Succession Transition Process," 18, 24–30.

84. Dennis T. Jaffe and Sam H. Lane, "Sustaining a Family Dynasty," *Family Business Review* 17, no. 1 (2004), 82.

85. *Pot Pourri 1936* (Phillips Academy Andover), 53; Frederick Lange, College Examinations, 6/1936, AA-PAA; Frederick Lange, "Electric Power Generation and Distribution in the JN District, Maine" (B.S. Thesis, Department of Electrical Engineering, MIT, 1940); *Harvard Class of 1913* (Cambridge, 1963), 379.

86. MBD-MGPS, 10/5/1963, 6/20/1966, MPMP; Gerard Piel, letter to Paul Piel, 12/10/1963, GPP

87. Paul Piel, letter to Erwin Lange, 2/28/1965, MPMP.

88. *NYT*, 10/19/2014; Jacqueline Leavitt, "The History, Status, and Concerns of Woman Planners," *Signs* 5, no. 3 (1980), 226–30; American Planning Association, "National Planning Awards 2005," https://www.planning.org/awards/2005/, accessed 6/21/2014.

89. J. Julian Tashof, letter to MPHC, 1/21/1965, GPP; MBD-MGPS, 12/19/1972, MPMP; Interviews, MPM, 12/21/2013, 12/6/2013.

90. Interview, MPM, 6/8/2015.

91. Interview, MPM, 12/6/2013.

92. Ibid.

93. Henry Muessen, letters to Margarita Piel McCoy, 6/25, 8/18/1975, 6/26/1976, MPMP.

94. Margarita Piel McCoy, letter to author, 9/2001.

95. MBD-MGPS, 6/24/1977, 6/29/1979, MPMP; Margarita Piel McCoy, letter to author, 9/2001.

96. Uncle Paul [Piel], letters to Peggy [Margarita Piel McCoy], 4/17, 5/27/1978, MPMP; Margarita Piel McCoy, letter to author, 9/2001.

97. Interview, MPM, 12/6/2013; MGPS-AM, 6/27/1980, MPMP.

98. MBD-MGPS, 4/11/1980; MGPS-AM, Investment Committee, 6/27/1980, MPMP. Gottfried Piel, Sr., his wife Sophie, and most of their children were buried in a family plot at Woodlawn Cemetery, Bronx, NY. (Peter W. Dawson, letter to E. H. Smith, Sales Manager, Woodlawn Cemetery, 7/8/1948, attached to Walter Piel, Piel Family's Historical Biographies, n.d., MPMP).

99. Interview, MPM, 12/6/2013.

100. Ibid.; Gerard Piel, letter to John Piel, 12/19/1978; Dr. John Piel, letter to Margarita Piel McCoy, 6/19/1979; Margarita Piel McCoy, letter to Daniel Piel, 11/26/1983, MPMP.

101. Interview, MPM, 12/6/2013; Margarita Piel McCoy, letter to Frederick Lange, 4/6/1979; Frederick Lange, letter to Margarita Piel McCoy, 6/4/1979; Margarita Piel McCoy, letter to Marie-Luise Piel Kemp, 6/29/1986; Margarita Piel McCoy, letter to Frederick Lange, 8/5/1986, MPMP.

102. MGPS-AM, 6/24/1983, MPMP.

103. MBD-MGPS, 12/7/1984; Margarita Piel McCoy, letter to stockholders, 6/1985, MPMP.

104. MGPS-AM, Investment Committee, 3/22/1985, MPMP.

105. Margarita Piel McCoy, letter to author, 9/2001; Louise Piel Lange, letter to Paul Piel, 4/12/1978, PPP.

106. Margarita Piel McCoy, letter to author, 9/2001; interview, MLPK, 3/29/2001.

107. Ibid.; Bjorn Lange, "Ruth H. Lange," n.d., MPMP.

108. MGPS-AM, Investment Committee, 12/9/1983; Frederick Lange, letter to Margarita Piel McCoy, 8/27/1984, MPMP; interview, MPM, 12/20/2013.

109. MGPS-AM, 6/21/1985, 6/15/1991; MBD-MGPS, 12/6/1985, 9/29/1989; Henry J. Muessen, letter to Gerard Piel, 6/21/1985; Margarita Piel McCoy, letter to Gerard Piel, 8/29/1985; Martin A. Rothenberg, letter to J. G. Salomone, 10/21/1985; Henry J. Muessen, letter to Eleanor Jackson Piel, 12/21/1985, MPMP; *NYT*, 3/28/1991.

110. Wendy Kaufman, "Women Still Largely Absent From Corporate Boards," *NPR*, 12/10/2013, http://www.npr.org/2013/12/10/249862083/women-still-largely-absent-from-corporate-boards, accessed 9/3/2014; MBD-MGPS, 6/15/1984; Abigail L. Lange, letter to stockholders, MGPS Annual Report 2006 (2007), MPMP.

111. For laudatory profiles of Eleanor Jackson Piel's work as a civil liberties lawyer, see *NYT*, 9/3/1999 and 9/10/1999. In 2005, the American Planning Association awarded Margarita Piel McCoy the "National Women in Planning Award" for "making important contributions to planning education in California and throughout the country." (See American Planning Association, "National Planning Awards 2005," https://www.planning.org/awards/2005/, accessed 6/21/2014.)

112. MGPS-AM, 6/21/1985; MBD-MGPS, 3/21/1986; Margarita Piel McCoy, letters to stockholders, 6/1987, 6/1988; Margarita Piel McCoy, letter to Marie-Luise Piel Kemp, 7/31/1986, MPMP; *NYT*, 9/3, 9/10/1999.

113. MGPS-AM, 6/20/1987; MBD-MGPS, 3/25/1988, MPMP.

114. Frederick Lange, letters to Margarita Piel McCoy, 3/19, 9/11/1988, 1/3/1989, MPMP.

115. MBD-MGPS, 3/25/1988, 9/29/1989, 6/16, 9/21/1990, 3/26/1992; MGPS-AM, 6/24, 12/11/1989, 6/20/1992, MPMP; interview, MPM, 12/20/2013.

116. *NYT*, 7/16/1987; MBD-MGPS, 12/12/1988, 11/9/1994; MGPS-AM, Investment Committee, 9/20/1991, 9/30, 12/2/1994; MGPS-AM, 6/4/1994; Margarita Piel McCoy, letter to Leonard Lazarus and J. G. Salomone, 6/28/1994; investment manager review, 9/29–30/1994, MPMP; interview, MPM, 6/8/2015.

117. Harvey M. Ross, Fahnstock Asset Management, MGPS Shareholders Meeting, 12/5/2014; MGPS shareholders list, 6/14/2014, MGPS-AM.

118. MGPS Annual Report 2013, 5/2014.

119. MBD-MGPS, 9/19/2014.

120. Several of these dinners at the home of Gerard and Eleanor Piel (1115 Fifth Avenue, NYC), were held on 12/8/2000, 12/7/2001, and 12/6/2002. Gerard Piel, letter to Margarita McCoy, 4/29/2000, MPMP.

121. Interview, GP, NYC, 12/6/2002; Christopher Harris, "Too Much of a Good Thing," *The Citizen* (Ottawa), 5/13/1985; Mike Loomis Piel, Biographical Questionaire: Piel Family History, n.d.; Gerard Piel, letters to Margarita McCoy, 9/12/2000, 7/12/2000; Michael L. Piel, letter to Gerard Piel, 5/4/2000, MPMP.

122. *NYT*, 9/7/2004; *SA* 291, no. 5 (2004), 32.

123. MBD-MGPS, 10/1/2004.

124. Interviews, MPM and Margarita Candace Ground, 12/6/14.

125. Interviews, MPM, 3/29/2004, Eleanor Jackson Piel, NYC, 10/1/2004; personal notes from MGPS Quarterly Meeting, 10/1/2004; MBD-MGPS, 10/1/2004; Jonathan Piel, email to Jerry Salomone, 7/17/2004; Jerry Salomone, email to Jonathan Piel, 9/28/2004.

126. Personal notes taken at MGPS Quarterly Meeting, 10/1/2004.

127. Conversation with Bia Piel, NYC, 10/27/2004.

128. *NYT*, 5/16/2015.

129. As an example of a surprising finding, the sister of New York's Catholic Cardinal John J. O'Connor (1984–2000), who served as the Vatican's aggressive defender of official dogma, discovered during work on her family tree that their mother was the daughter of a Jewish rabbi. (See *NYT*, 5/4/2000, 6/11/2014.)

130. John Seabrook, "The Tree of Me," *TNY*, 3/26/2001, 58; Virginia Herrernan, "Ancestral Allure," *NYT*, 1/13/2008.

131. Interview, Gunter Lutz, father of the clinic's current head Dr. Jörg Lutz and son-in-law of Dr. Hans Heermann, son of Dr. Josef Heermann, Heermann Hof, Herne, 6/15/2004; Christian Heermann, "Familie Heermann Östrich" (Jesteburg, 9/4/2005); Markus Grenz, "Essener Arztfamilie hat seit 125 Jahren eine HNO-Praxis," *Westdeutsche Allgemeine Zeitung* (Essen), 12/26/2013, http://www.derwesten.de/staedte/essen/essener-arztfamilie-hat-seit-125-jahren-eine-hno-praxis-id8810094.html, accessed 3/2/2014. The Heermann lineage of Ear-Nose-Throat medical specialists includes Josef (b. 1862), Hans (b. 1900), Otto (b. 1911), Joaquim (b. 1930), Peter (b. 1941), Ralf (b. 1965), and Jörg Lutz (b. 1966).

132. Gregory Clark, "Your Ancestors, Your Fate," *NYT*, 2/23/2014.

Bibliography

Archives and Collections

Barnard College Archives
Benson Ford Research Center, Dearborn, Michigan
Book of Conveyances, City Registers Office, New York, NY
Books of Conveyances for New York County, City Registers Office, New York, NY
Columbia University Archives
Columbia University Libraries
Department of Health, City of New York
Department of Human Services, State of Maine
Department of Taxes and Assessments, City of New York
Green-Wood Cemetery, Brooklyn, NY
Harvard University Archives
Holmes County Clerk's Office, Millersburg, Ohio
Municipal Archives, New York, NY
New York Country Registers Office, New York, NY
New York State Archives, Albany, NY
Oral History Research Office, Columbia University
Orphans Court of Chester County, Pennsylvania
Orphans Court of Montgomery County, Pennsylvania
Phillips Academy Andover Archive
Probate Court, Somerset County, Maine
Seeley G. Mudd Manuscript Library, Princeton University
Stadtarchiv Zürich, Switzerland
Sullivan & Cromwell, New York, NY
Supreme Court, New York, NY
Surrogate's Court, County of New York
Surrogate's Court, County of Orange, NY
Surrogate's Court, Queens County, NY
Universitat Zürich, Switzerland

Universitatsarchiv Leipzig, Germany
U.S. National Archives and Records Administration
Wheaton College Archives

Articles

Amarelo, Monica. "Gerard Piel, Former Publisher of *Scientific American*, Dies at Age 89." News Release, American Association for Advancement of Science, September 8, 2004. http://www.aaas.org/news/releases/2004/0908piel.shtml. Accessed May 8, 2013.

Arbel, Tali. "Build a Craft Brewery, Urban Revival Will Come." *USA Today*, July 6, 2013. http://www.usatoday.com/story/money/business/2013/07/05/in-urban-revival-beer-creates-small-business-hubs/2487625/. Accessed September 2, 2014.

Barnard, Chester I. "Does the Atomic Explosion in Russia Require the U.S. to Modify Its Position in Regard to International Control of Atomic Energy?" *Scientific American* 181, no. 5 (1949): 11–13.

Bass, Frank. "U.S. Ethnic Mix Boasts German Accent Amid Surge of Hispanics." *Bloomberg*, March 5, 2012. http://www.bloomberg.com/news/2012-03-06/u-s-ethnic-mix-boasts-german-accent-amid-surge-of-hispanics.html. Accessed May 11, 2014.

"Beautiful 'Lake Parlin' for Sale." *Town & Country* 77, no. 3782 (1920): 4.

"Beer into Cans." *Fortune* 13, no. 1 (January 1936): 75–84.

"The Best Advertising of 1956." *Tide*, February 8, 1957.

Bethe, Hans A. "The Hydrogen Bomb II." *Scientific American* 182, no. 4 (1950): 18–23.

Bettelheim, Bruno. "Joey: A 'Mechanical Boy'." *Scientific American* 200, no. 3 (1959): 116–27.

———. "Schizophrenic Art." *Scientific American* 186, no. 4 (1952): 30–34.

———, and Morris Janowitz. "Prejudice." *Scientific American* 183, no. 4 (1950): 11–13.

Blackett, P. M. S. "Steps Toward Disarmament." *Scientific American* 206, no. 4 (1962): 45–53.

"Bowery Saturday Night." *Harpers' Monthly*, April 1871, 673–80.

Brewers Association. "Craft Beer Sales by State." https://www.brewersassociation.org/statistics/by-state/. Accessed May 5, 2015.

"Budweiser-Anheuser Busch." *BeerAdvocate*. http://www.beeradvocate.com/beer/profile/29/65/m. Accessed June 23, 2014.

"Business: Brown Harriman." *Time*, December 22, 1930. http://www.time.com/time/magazine/article/0,9171,740853,00.html. Accessed May 3, 2013.

Campbell, Kenneth. "Major General Ralph H. Van Deman." *American Intelligence Journal* 8 (Summer 1987): 13–19.

Curran, Winifred. "In Defense of Old Industrial Spaces." *International Journal of Urban and Regional Research* 34, no. 4 (2010): 871–85.

————, and Trina Hamilton. "Just Green Enough." *Local Environment* 17, no. 9 (2012): 1027–42.

Dempsey, David. "Bruno Bettelheim is Dr. No." *New York Times Magazine*, January 11, 1970, 22.

"Dr. Friedrich Lange." *Zentralblatt für Chirurgie* 52 (1927).

"The ex–Heifitz Stradivari, 1731." *The Strad* 69, no. 828 (1959): 430.

"Festscrift Karl Heescheler zur Vollendung seines siebzigsten Alterjares." *Beiblatt zur Vierteljarsschrift der Naturforschenden Gesellschaft in Zürich* 83, no. 30 (1938).

Fisher, David James. "Last Thoughts on Therapy: Bruno Bettelheim." *Society* 28, no. 3 (1991): 61–69.

Gatewood, Worth. "The Truth About Bert and Harry." *Daily News* (New York), January 13, 1957.

Gordon, Michael A. "The Labor Boycott in New York City, 1880–1886." *Labor History* 16, no. 2 (1975): 184–229.

Grenz, Markus. "Essener Arztfamilie hat seit 125 Jahren eine HNO-Praxis." *Westdeutsche Allgemeine Zeitung* (Essen), December 26, 2013. http://www.derwesten.de/staedte/essen/essener-arztfamilie-hat-seit-125-jahren-eine-hno-praxis-id8810094.html. Accessed March 2, 2014.

Gross, Daniel A. "The U.S. Confiscated Half a Billion Dollars in Private Property During WWI." *Smithsonian*, July 28, 2014. http://www.smithsonianmag.com/history/us-confiscated-half-billion-dollars-private-property-during-wwi-180952144/?no-ist. Accessed May 8, 2015.

Grote, Jim. "Conflicting Generations." *Family Business Review* 16, no. 2 (2003): 113–24.

Henyick, Frank. "The Guy Francon Who Wasn't." *The Atlasphere*, May 6, 2010. http://www.theatlasphere.com/columns/100506-heynick-ely-kahn-fountainhead.ph. Accessed March 5, 2013.

"Historic Guitar Makers of the Madrid School." Zavaleta's, La Casa de Guitarras, Tucson, AZ. http://zavaletas-guitarras.com/content/index.cfm?action=view&ContentID=65. Accessed March 3, 2012.

"History of Schaefer Beer." http://www.schaefer-beer.com/history/default.aspx. Accessed April 24, 2013.

Hofman, Rolf. "From Ludwigsburg to Brooklyn—A Dynasty of German-Jewish Brewers." *Aufbau*, June 21, 2001. http://www.beerhistory.com/library/holdings/hofmann-rheingold.shtml. Accessed February 16, 2013.

Hop Growers Union of the Czech Republic. "Hop Growing." *Czech Hops*. http://www.czhops.cz/index.php/en. Accessed April 23, 2015.

"Institute of Notre-Dame de Namur." In *The Catholic Encyclopedia*. New York, 1913. https://en.wikisource.org/wiki/Catholic_Encyclopedia_%281913%29/Congregations_of_Notre_Dame. Accessed April 22, 2013.

Investment Company Institute. "2004 Investment Company Fact Book." http://www.icifactbook.org/fb_ch2.html#investor. Accessed June 30, 2014.

"Jacob Frederick Wittemann." *American Bottler* 35, no. 10 (October 15, 1915): 60.

Jaffe, Dennis T., and Sam H. Lane. "Sustaining a Family Dynasty." *Family Business Review* 17, no. 1 (2004): 81–98.

Jankowski, Ben. "The Bushwick Pilsners." *Brewing Techniques* 2, no. 1 (1994).

Johnson, Courtney. "'Alliance Imperialism' and Anglo-American Power after 1898." In Alfred W. McCoy et al., eds. *Endless Empire,* 112–35. Madison, WI, 2012.

Johnson, William Oscar. "Sports and Suds." *Sports Illustrated,* August 8, 1988. http://sportsillustrated.cnn.com/vault/article/magazine/MAG1067600/4/index.htm. Accessed April 22, 2013.

Klapper, Joseph T., and Charles Y. Glock. "Trial By Newspaper." *Scientific American* 180, no. 2 (1949): 16–21.

Kuznick, Peter J. "Prophets of Doom or Voices of Sanity?" *Journal of Genocide Research* 9, no. 3 (2007): 411–41.

"Łąkorek: Secesyjny dwór Friedricha Lange." ["Łąkorek: The Art Nouveau Mansion of Friedrich Lange."] *Moje Mazury,* July 23, 2013. http://mojemazury.pl/164777, Lakorek-Secesyjny-dwor-Friedricha-Lange.html#axzz3G2EeqG6i. Accessed October 12, 2014.

Lange, Mathilde M. "On the Regeneration and Finer Structure of the Arms of Cephalopods." *Journal of Experimental Zoology* 31, no. 1 (1920): 1–57.

Larner, Robert J. "Ownership and Control in the 200 Largest Nonfinancial Corporations, 1929 and 1963." *The American Economic Review* 56, no. 4 (1966): 777–87.

Latimer, Margaret. "Brooklyn." In Kenneth T. Jackson, ed., *The Encyclopedia of New York City,* 171. New Haven, CT, 2010.

Leavitt, Jacqueline. "The History, Status, and Concerns of Woman Planners." *Signs* 5, no. 3 (1980): 226–30.

Leontief, Wassily W. "Input-Output Economics." *Scientific American* 185, no. 4 (1951): 15–21.

Lewenstein, Bruce V. "Magazine Publishing and Popular Science After World War II." *American Journalism* 6, no. 4 (1989): 218–34.

McDougall, Paul. "Painful Evolution for Scientific American." *Folio,* October 1, 1994.

Maeder, Jay. "From Bob and Ray . . . Bert & Harry Piel." *Daily News* (New York), April 8, 2002.

Mahler, Jonathan. "The Darkest Night." *New York Times Magazine,* October 5, 2003, 76–82.

May, Alan. "Vannie Higgins: Brooklyn's Last Irish Boss." *Crime Magazine,* October 14, 2009. http://crimemagazine.com/vannie-higgins-brooklyns-last-irish-boss. Accessed December 16, 2012.

———. "Waxey Goldon's Half Century of Crime." *Crime Magazine,* October 14, 2009. http://crimemagazine.com/waxey-gordon's-half-century-crime. Accessed December 5, 2012.

Maxwell, D. B. S. "Beer Cans: A Guide for the Archeologist." *Historical Archeology* 27, no. 1 (1993): 95–113.

McCoy, Alfred W. "Rent Seeking Families and the Philippine State." In Alfred W. McCoy, ed., *An Anarchy of Families*, 429–536. Madison, WI, 2009.

Melnick, Joseph L. "Current Status of Poliovirus Infections." *Clinical Microbiology Reviews* 9, no. 3 (1996): 293–300.

Mencken, H. L. "Malt Liquor." *The Evening Sun* (Baltimore), December 1, 1930.

"Miller Lite." *BeerAdvocate*. http://www.beeradvocate.com/beer/profile/105/332/. Accessed June 23, 2014.

Morrison, Philip, and Paul F. Walker. "A New Strategy for Military Spending." *Scientific American* 239, no. 4 (1978): 48–61.

Muller, Joann. "VW is Already the World's Leading Automaker." *Forbes*, April 18, 2013. http://www.forbes.com/sites/joannmuller/2013/04/18/vw-is-already-the-worlds-leading-automaker/. Accessed April 29, 2015.

Murray, Barbara. "The Succession Transition Process." *Family Business Review* 16, no. 1 (2003): 17–33.

Musto, David F. "The Adams Family." *Proceedings of the Massachusetts Historical Society* 93 (1981): 40–58.

———. "The Youth of John Quincy Adams." *Proceedings of the American Philosophical Society* 113, no. 4 (1969): 269–82.

Münsterberg, Hugo. "The Germans at School." *Popular Science Monthly*, 79 (1911): 602–14.

Newman, James R. "Two Discussions of Thermonuclear War." *Scientific American* 204, no. 3 (1961): 197–204.

Nussbaum, Emily. "Defending Dr. B." *New York Times Book Review*, November 24, 2002, 16.

Paradise, Scott. "Summary Report on the Technology and Culture Seminar at MIT 1992 –3." http://web.mit.edu/tac/docs/reports/annual-92-93.pdf. Accessed June 22, 2013.

Perry, Marilyn Elizabeth. "Sabin, Pauline Morton." *American National Biography Online*, February 2000. http://www.anb.org/articles/06/06-00142.html. Accessed January 16, 2015.

Peters, John P. "Suppression of the 'Raines Law Hotels.'" *Annals of the American Academy of Political and Social Science* 32 (1908): 556–66.

Piel Bros. "An Open Letter To the Medical Profession." *American Journal of Surgery* 29, no. 12 (1915): 472.

Piel, Gerard. "The Illusion of Civil Defense." *Bulletin of the Atomic Scientists* 17, no. 2 (1962): 2–8.

———. "Natural Philosophy in the Constitution." *Science* 233, no. 4768 (1986): 1056–60.

"Piel, Michael." *The Cyclopedia of American Biography, Vol. VIII*, 403. New York, 1918.

"Piels Beer." *Wikipedia*. http://en.wikipedia.org/wiki/Piels_Beer. Accessed April 23, 2013.

"Piels-Pabst Brewing Company." *BeerAdvocate.* http://www.beeradvocate.com/beer/profile/447/5259/. Accessed December 13, 2014.

Popkin, Jeremy D. "Historians on the Autobiographical Frontier." *The American Historical Review* 104, no. 3 (1999): 725–48.

Powell, Bonnie Azab. "One Tough Case." University of California–Berkeley School of Law, 2009. http://www.law.berkeley.edu/5464.htm. Accessed November 13, 2013.

Princeton Alumni Weekly, April 18, 1977. Seeley G. Mudd Manuscript Library, Princeton University.

Princeton Alumni Weekly, November 17, 1980. Seeley G. Mudd Manuscript Library, Princeton University.

Ridenour, Louis N. "The Hydrogen Bomb." *Scientific American* 182, no. 3 (1950): 11–15.

Rodriguez, Sonya Nance, Gladys J. Hildreth, and Joseph Mancuso. "The Dynamics of Families in Business." *Contemporary Family Therapy* 21, no. 4 (December 1999): 453–68.

Rose, Anthony H. "Beer." *Scientific American* 200, no. 6 (1959): 90–100.

"Science and the Citizen." *Scientific American* 184, no. 5 (1951): 33–34.

Scoville, Herbert, Jr. "The Limitation of Offensive Weapons." *Scientific American* 224, no. 1 (1971): 15–25.

———. "The SALT Negotiations." *Scientific American* 237, no. 2 (1977): 24–31.

———. "Submarines and National Security." *Scientific American* 226, no. 6 (1972): 15–27.

Schaefer, R. J. "Foreword." In Will Anderson, *The Breweries of Brooklyn,* 7. Croton Falls, NY, 1976.

"Schreiner, Bernard Francis." In Georgina Pell Curtis and Benedict Elder, eds., *The American Catholic Who's Who 1946 and 1947 (Two Years) Vol. 7,* 396. Grosse Pointe, MI, 1948.

Seabrook, John. "The Tree of Me." *New Yorker,* March 26, 2001, 58.

Segal, Richard M. "Shirt Sleeves to Shirt Sleeves in Three Generations." *Corp!* July 1, 2008. http://www.corpmagazine.com/special-interests/family-business/itemid/28/shirt-sleeves-to-shirt-sleeves-in-three-generations. Accessed April 26, 2013.

Steege, Rudolf. "XXXV. Bekannte Personlichkeiten aus dem Kreise Neumark. 1. Dr. ju. h.c. Regimontanus et Dr. med. Friedrich Lange—Lonkorrek." In *Heimatbuch für den Kreis Neumark in Westpreußen bis 1941 Kreis Löbau,* 311–15. Selbstverlag des Heimatkreises Neumark, 1979.

Sumner, H. C. "The North Atlantic Hurricane of September 8–16, 1944." *Monthly Weather Review* 72, no. 9 (September 1944): 187–89. http://docs.lib.noaa.gov/rescue/mwr/072/mwr-072-09-0187.pdf. Accessed April 6, 2015.

Trimble, William F. "George R. Hann, Pittsburgh Aviation Industries Corporation and Pennsylvania Air Line." In David W. Lewis, ed., *Airline Executives and Federal Regulation,* 50–52. Columbus, OH, 2000.

Tritsch, Shane. "Tremors in the Empire." *Chicago Magazine*, December 2002. http://www. chicagomag.com/Chicago-Magazine/December-2002/Tremors-in-the-Empire/. Accessed April 28, 2014.

Warner, Michael. "The Kaiser Sows Destruction: Protecting the Homeland the First Time Around." Central Intelligence Agency Library. https://www.cia.gov/library/center-for-the-study-of-intelligence/csi-publications/csi-studies/studies/vol46no1/article02.html. Accessed October 28, 2013.

Wright, Gabrielle. "Bushwick 'Revival' brings New Facts, Rent Hikes and Rapid Change." *Pavement Pieces*, March 2, 2013. http://pavementpieces.com/bushwicks-revival-brings-new-faces-rent-hikes-and-rapid-change/. Accessed September 2, 2014.

"Yale, Frankie." *Encyclopedia Britannica*. http://www.britannica.com/EBchecked/topic/651367/Frankie-Yale. Accessed December 16, 2012.

Younger, G. A. "Class History." In *The Senior Year Book of the Class of Nineteen Hundred and Five* (Columbia College), 63. New York, 1905.

Books

The 1918 Yearbook of the United States Brewers Association. New York, 1919.

1937 Harvard Class Annual. Cambridge, 1937.

Acitelli, Tom. *The Audacity of Hops*. Chicago, 2013.

Allen, Thomas B. *Tories*. New York, 2010.

Anderson, Will. *The Breweries of Brooklyn*. Croton Falls (NY), 1976.

Anti-Saloon League. *The National German American Alliance and its Allies—Pro-German Brewers and Liquor Dealers*. Westerville (OH), 1918.

Arrighi, Giovanni. *The Long Twentieth Century*. London, 1994.

Ball, Edward. *The Sweet Hell Inside*. New York, 2001.

Barnard College. *Directory of the Associate Alumni 1893–1934*. New York, 1934.

Baughman, James L. *Henry R. Luce and the Rise of the American News Media*. Baltimore, 2001.

Bennett, Robert J. *Entrepreneurship, Small Business, and Public Policy*. London, 2014.

Bettelheim, Bruno. *A Good Enough Parent*. New York, 1987.

———. *A Home for the Heart*. New York, 1974.

Block, Alan. *East Side West Side*. New Brunswick, 1983.

Bonsor, N. R. P. *North Atlantic Seaway, Vol. 2*. Jersey, Channel Islands, 1978.

Brenner, Marie. *House of Dreams*. New York, 1988.

Brinkley, Alan. *The Publisher*. New York, 2010.

Bromley, George W., and Walter S. *Atlas of the City of Brooklyn*. Philadelphia, 1893.

The Brooklyn City and Business Directory. Brooklyn, 1870.

The Brooklyn City Directory, Vol. LXXXVIII. Brooklyn, 1912.

Brooklyn Daily Eagle Almanac 1890, Vol. V. Brooklyn, 1890.

Brooklyn Daily Eagle Almanac 1897. Brooklyn, 1898.

Brooklyn Daily Eagle Almanac 1910. Brooklyn, 1910.

The Brooklyn Directory. Brooklyn, 1883.

The Brooklyn Directory. Brooklyn, 1884.

Brown, Roscoe C. E., and Ray B. Smith. *Political and Governmental History of the State of New York, Vol. III.* Syracuse (NY), 1922.

Burrows, Edwin G., and Mike Wallace. *Gotham.* New York, 1999.

Calhoon, Robert M. *The Loyalists in Revolutionary America.* New York, 1973.

Carnegie, Andrew. *Triumphant Democracy or Fifty Years' March of the Republic.* New York, 1886.

Catalogue of Officers and Graduates of Columbia University. New York, 1910.

Catalogue of Officers and Graduates of Columbia University, XVI Edition. New York, 1916.

Chandler, Alfred D., Jr., *The Visible Hand.* Cambridge (MA), 1977.

Chandler, David Leon. *The Binghams of Louisville.* New York, 1989.

Cochran, Thomas C. *The Pabst Brewing Company.* New York, 1948.

Cohen, Rich. *Sweet and Low.* New York, 2006.

———. *Tough Jews.* New York, 1999.

Cole, Phyllis. *Mary Moody Emerson and the Origins of Transcendentalism.* New York, 1998.

Cole, Wayne S. *An Interpretive History of American Foreign Relations.* Belmont (CA), 1974.

Columbia University Alumni Register 1754–1931. New York, 1933.

———. *One Hundred and Sixtieth Annual Commencement.* New York, 1914.

The Columbian Nineteen Hundred and Five. New York, 1905.

The Columbian Nineteen Hundred and Six. New York, 1906.

Couper, William. *History of the Engineering, Construction and Equipment of the Pennsylvania Railroad Company's New York Terminal and Approaches.* New York, 1912.

Crimm, Ana Carolina Castillo. *De León.* Austin, 2003.

Day, Clarence S., Jr., *Decennial Record of the Class of 1896, Yale College.* New York, 1907.

Dieke, G. H. *Robert Williams Wood 1868–1955.* Washington (DC) 1993.

Directory of Living Alumni of Princeton University. Princeton (NJ), 1917.

Downey, Patrick. *Gangster City.* Fort Lee (NJ), 2004.

Ehret, George. *Twenty-Five Years of Brewing.* New York, 1891.

Ehrhardt, Justus. *Strassen ohne Ende [Roads without End].* Berlin, 1931.

F. & M. Schaefer Brewing Co. *To Commemorate Our Hundredth Year.* New York, 1942.

Femina, Jerry Della. *From Those Wonderful Folks Who Gave You Pearl Harbor.* New York, 1970.

Fink, Matthew P. *The Rise of Mutual Funds*. New York, 2008.

Foyster, Elizabeth. *Marital Violence*. Cambridge (UK), 2005.

Galbraith, John Kenneth. *The Affluent Society*. New York, 1998.

Glazier, Ira A., and P. William Filby, eds. *Germans to America, Vol. 3*. Wilmington (DE), 1988.

———. *Germans to America, Vol. 44*. Wilmington (DE), 1995.

Gole, Henry G. *Exposing the Third Reich*. Lexington (KY), 2013.

Gosse, Van. *Where the Boys Are*. New York, 1993.

Goyens, Tom. *Beer and Revolution*. Urbana (IL), 2007.

Grubb, Farley. *German Immigration and Servitude in America, 1709–1914*. London, 2011.

Gullace, Nicoletta. *The Blood of Our Sons*. London, 2002.

Haffner, Ernest. *Blood Brothers*. New York, 2015.

Halberstam, David. *The Powers That Be*. New York, 1979.

Hartley, L.P. *The Go-Between*. London, 1953.

Harvard Class Album Volume XXIV. Cambridge (MA), 1913.

Harvard Class of 1913: Fiftieth Anniversary Report. Cambridge (MA), 1963.

Harvard College Class of 1911: Decennial Report, June 1921. Boston, 1921.

Harvard College Class of 1911. Cambridge (MA), 1936.

Herbst, Henry, and Don Roussin. *St. Louis Brews*. St. Louis, 2009.

Hernon, Peter, and Terry Ganey. *Under the Influence*. New York, 1991.

Higham, John. *Hanging Together*. New Haven (CT), 2001.

Hilferding, Rudolf. *Finance Capital*. London, 1981.

Hindy, Steve. *The Craft Beer Revolution*. New York, 2014.

———, and Tom Potter. *Beer School*. New York, 2005.

Homberger, Eric. *The Historical Atlas of New York City*. New York, 1994.

Hough, Emerson. *The Web*. Chicago, 1919.

Howard, Jane. *Margaret Mead*. New York, 1984.

Immerman, Richard H. *The Hidden Hand*. Malden (MA), 2014.

Jackson, Kenneth T., ed. *The Encyclopedia of New York City*. New Haven (CT), 2010.

Jackson, Richard S. *Houses of the Berkshires*. New York, 2011.

Jasanoff, Maya. *Liberty's Exiles*. New York, 2011.

The Jayhawker Yearbook. Lawrence (KS), 1922.

Jones, John P., and Paul M. Hollister. *The German Secret Service in America, 1914–1918*. Boston, 1918.

Jordan, David M. *FDR, Dewey and the Election of 1944*. Bloomington (IN), 2011.

Kaiser, Harvey H. *Great Camps of the Adirondacks*. Boston, 2003.

Kazal, Russell A. *Becoming Old Stock*. Princeton (NJ), 2004.

Kelly, Robert J. *Encyclopedia of Organized Crime in the United States*. Westport (CT), 2000.

Kerr, K. Austin. *Organized for Prohibition*. New Haven (CT), 1985.

Khaldun, Ibn. *An Arab Philosophy of History*. Princeton (NJ), 1987.

Knoedelseder, William. *Bitter Brew.* New York, 2012.

Krebs, Roland, and Percy J. Orthwein. *Making Friends is Our Business.* Chicago, 1953.

Krippner, Greta R. *Capitalizing on Crisis.* Cambridge (MA), 2012.

Kyvig, David E. *Repealing National Prohibition.* Kent, 2000.

Lain's Brooklyn and Long Island Business Directory 1892. Brooklyn, 1892.

Landes, David S. *The Unbound Prometheus.* Cambridge (UK), 1969.

Langson, Wm. J. *Trade and Commerce of Milwaukee.* Milwaukee, 1902.

Lawson, Ellen McKenzie. *Smugglers, Bootleggers, and Scofflaws.* Albany (NY), 2013.

Lerner, Michael A. *Dry Manhattan.* Cambridge (MA), 2007.

Manchester, William. *The Arms of Krupp.* New York, 2003.

Mander, Jerry, George Dippel, and Howard Gossage. *The Great International Paper Airplane Book.* New York, 1967.

Marquis. *Who's Who in America 1999, Vol. 2 L–Z.* New Providence (RI), 1999.

Mead, Margaret. *Blackberry Winter.* New York, 1972.

Merlis, Brian, and Riccardo Gomes. *Brooklyn's East New York and Cypress Hill Communities.* New York, 2010.

———, and Riccardo Gomes. *Brooklyn's Bushwick and East Williamsburg Communities.* New York, 2012.

Mintz, Steven, and Susan Kellogg. *Domestic Revolutions.* New York, 1988.

Mittelman, Amy. *Brewing Battles.* New York, 2008.

Monihan, Daniel Patrick. *Secrecy.* New Haven (CT), 1998.

The Mortarboard, Vol. 26. New York, 1920.

Moyer, David G. *American Breweries of the Past.* Bloomington (IN), 2009.

Nash, Eric P. *Manhattan Skyscrapers.* New York, 1999.

The Nassau Herald. Princeton (NJ), 1913.

The Nassau Herald. Princeton (NJ), 1932.

The National Cyclopedia of American Biography, Vol. I. New York, 1898.

New York University Bulletin VII, no. 1 (1907).

Newton, C. B., ed. *General Catalogue of Graduates and Former Students Lawrenceville School.* Lawrenceville (NJ), 1910.

Ogle, Maureen. *Ambitious Brew.* Orlando, 2006.

Okrent, Daniel. *Last Call.* New York, 2010.

Oldsey, Bernard, ed. *British Novelists, 1930–1959, Vol. Fifteen.* Detroit, 1983.

One Hundred Years of Brewing. Chicago, 1903.

Osofsky, Gilbert. *Harlem.* Chicago, 1996.

Owens, Carole. *The Berkshire Cottages.* Stockbridge (MA), 1984.

Perry, Ralph Barton. *The Plattsburgh Movement.* New York, 1921.

The Phi Gamma Delta. Indianapolis, 1907.

Phillips Academy Andover. *Pot Pourri 1906.* Andover (MA), 1906.

————. *Pot Pourri 1912*. Andover (MA), 1912.

————. *Pot Pourri 1933*. Andover (MA), 1933.

————. *Pot Pourri 1936*. Andover (MA), 1936.

————. *Pot Pourri 1977*. Andover (MA), 1977.

Piel, David J. *Piel Bros & the Piels*. Carson City (NV), 2001.

Piel, Gerard. *The Age of Science*. New York, 2001.

————. *Harvard Class of 1937*. Cambridge (MA), 1987.

Piel, William, Jr., and Martha Moore. *Lamplighters*. New York, 1981.

Polk, William R. *Polk's Folly*. New York, 2001.

Polk's New York City Directory (Boroughs of Queens and Richmond 1933–1934). New York, 1934.

Pollak, Richard. *The Creation of Dr. B*. New York, 1997.

Poly Prep. *Polyglot 1901*. Brooklyn, 1901.

Powys, John Cowper. *Autobiography*. New York, 1934.

Pure Products, Vol. III. New York, 1907.

Raab, Selwyn. *Five Families*. New York, 2005.

Rayback, Joseph G. *A History of American Labor*. New York, 1966.

Richards, David L. *Poland Spring*. Lebanon (NH), 2005.

Rippley, La Verne. *The German Americans*. Lanham (MD), 1984.

Root, Grace C. *Women and Repeal*. New York, 1934.

Sanborn Map Company. *Insurance Maps of Brooklyn, New York, Vol. Eight*. New York, 1887.

————. *Insurance Maps of Brooklyn, City of New York, Vol. 16*. New York, 1928.

————. *Insurance Maps, Borough of Brooklyn, City of New York*. New York, 1904.

————. *Insurance Maps, Borough of Brooklyn, Vol. Eight*. New York, 1908.

Schlüter, Hermann. *The Brewing Industry and the Brewing Workers' Movement in America*. Cincinnati, 1910.

Schneider, Dorothee. *Trade Unions and Community*. Urbana (IL), 1994.

Seaholm, J. E., and T. E. Graham. *Soil Survey of Holmes Country, Ohio*. Washington (DC), 1998.

The Senior Year Book of the Class of Nineteen Hundred and Five (Columbia College). New York, 1905.

Shirer, William L. *The Rise and Fall of the Third Reich*. New York, 1960.

Siebel, Dr. John E., and Anton Schwarz. *History of the Brewing Industry and Brewing Science in America*. Chicago, 1933.

Sifakis, Carl. *The Mafia Encyclopedia*. New York, 2005.

Sismondo, Christine. *America Walks into a Bar*. New York, 2011.

Social Register, New York, 1917, Vol. XXXI, no. 1. New York, 1916.

Social Register, New York, 1931, Vol. XLV, no. 1. New York, 1930.

Social Register, New York. New York, 1940.

Stiles, Henry R., ed. *The Civil, Political, Professional and Ecclesiastical History and Commercial and Industrial Record of the County of Kings and the City of Brooklyn, N.Y. from 1688 to 1884, Vols. I & II.* New York, 1884.

Sutton, Nina. *Bettelheim.* New York, 1996.

Thabit, Walter. *How East New York Became a Ghetto.* New York, 2003.

Thompson, Walter. *Federal Centralization.* New York, 1923.

The Trow Co-partnership and Corporation Directory of the Boroughs of Manhattan and the Bronx. New York, 1910.

Trow's New York City Directory Vol. XCVIII. New York, 1885.

Trow's New York City Directory Vol. CVIII. New York, 1895.

Turkus, Burton B., and Sid Feder. *Murder, Inc.* New York, 1951.

Ullitz, Hugo. *Atlas of the Borough of Brooklyn, City of New York, Vol. 4.* Brooklyn, 1905.

U.S. Brewers Association. *Brewers Almanac 1961.* New York, 1961.

Van Munching, Philip. *Beer Blast.* New York, 1997.

Wallace, W. Steward, ed. *Macmillan Dictionary of Canadian Biography.* Toronto, 1978.

Weeks, Morris, Jr. *Beer and Brewing in America.* New York, 1953.

Wittke, Carl Frederick. *Refugees of Revolution.* Philadelphia, 1952.

Yale University. *Obituary Record of Yale Graduates 1924–1925.* New Haven (CT), 1925.

Government Documents (County and State)

40 Georgia Avenue, Block 3701; 303/313 Liberty Avenue, Block 3684; 104–116 Georgia Avenue, Block 3685; and 129 Georgia Avenue, Block 3702. Book of Conveyances, City Registers Office. Borough Hall, 210 Joralemon St., Brooklyn, NY.

148 Riverside Drive, Grantor: Gottfried & Sophie Piel, Grantee: Eva Bennett, December 16, 1919, Liber 3116, 397. Book of Conveyances for New York County, City Registers Office, New York County. 66 John St., 13th fl., New York, NY 10038.

245 West 72nd Street, Grantor: Maria Piel, Grantee: Max Carnot, Alfred Timen, May 14, 1921, Liber 3209, 471. Book of Conveyances for New York County, City Registers Office, New York County. 66 John St., 13th fl., New York, NY 10038.

Annual Record of the Assessed Valuation of Real Estate. 26th Ward Vol. 5, Blocks 284 to 361, 1891 to 1894. Municipal Archives, 31 Chambers Street, New York, NY.

———. Borough of Brooklyn, Ward 26, Vol. 3, 1886 to 1887. Municipal Archives, 31 Chambers Street, New York, NY.

———. Brooklyn County, 26th Ward, Blocks 284 to 361, 1894 to 1898. Municipal Archives, 31 Chambers Street, New York, NY.

Annual Report of the Board of State Assessors of the State of Maine 1938. Waterville (ME), 1939.

Annual Report of the Board of State Assessors of the State of Maine 1944. Waterville (ME), 1945.

Annual Report of the Board of State Assessors of the State of Maine 1954. Waterville (ME), 1955.

Annual Report of the Board of State Assessors of the State of Maine 1960. Waterville (ME), 1961.

Annual Report of the Board of State Assessors of the State of Maine 1968. Waterville (ME), 1969.

Department of Transportation, New Jersey. *Portway Extensions Concept Development Study: Final Report,* September 2003. http://www.state.nj.us/transportation/freight/portway/FR_Section_6.pdf. Accessed May 24, 2015.

Grantor Williams Bellew, Grantee Michael Piel, Liber 15, 494, December 1, 1899. Book of Conveyances, City Registers Office. Borough Hall, 210 Joralemon St., Brooklyn, NY.

Homeyer v. Piel Bros. (Sup. 1934) 240 App. Div. 1004, 268 N.Y. S. 268. In *New York Law of Contracts.* Brooklyn, 1962.

Indenture between Frank Tilford and Maria Piel, May 5, 1903, Liber 93, 266–67. New York Country Registers Office, Room 205, 31 Chambers Street, New York, NY.

Indenture between Gottfried Piel and Wilhelm Piel parties of the first part, and Michael Piel party of the second part, February 18, 1884, Liber 1542, 327–28. Kings County Register's Office.

Indenture between William W. Hall and Emily Parker Hall and Gottfried Piel, March 4, 1898, Liber 60, 259. New York Country Registers Office, Room 205, 31 Chambers Street, New York, NY.

Permit No. 187, Plan No. 682, Detailed Statement of Specifications for Brick Buildings, Submitted: April 14, 1898. Department of Buildings, 210 Joralemon St., 8th fl., Brooklyn, NY.

Permit No. 1044, Inspector's Memorandum of Application for Brick Buildings, Approved: March 13, 1912. Department of Buildings, 210 Joralemon St., 8th fl., Brooklyn, NY.

Probate File of Sophie Piel, File #260-1937. Queens County Surrogate's Court, Queens, NY.

Statement, July 10, 1930, 245 W. 72nd Street, Block 1164, Lot B, Record, Office of Housing Preservations and Development, Division of Housing, Department of Buildings, 3280 Broadway, New York, NY.

Government Documents (U.S.)

Alcohol Tax Unit, Internal Revenue Service, U.S. Treasury Department. *Regulations No. 7 Relating to Labeling and Advertising of Malt Beverages as Amended to June 12,*

1941 Under the Provisions of the Federal Alcohol Administration Act, as Amended. Washington (DC), 1948.

Bureau of Economic Analysis, U.S. Department of Commerce. "Contributions to Percent Change in Real GDP (the US 1947–1973)." http://www.bea.gov/national/nipaweb/ SelectTable.asp?Selected. Accessed June 10, 2010.

Bureau of Labor Statistics, U.S. Department of Labor. "Labor Force Statistics from the Current Population Survey." http://data.bls.gov/timeseries/LNU04000000?years_option=all_ years&periods_option=specific_periods&periods=Annual+Data. Accessed June 3, 2014.

Busciolano, R. *Water-Table and Potentiometric-Surface Altitudes of the Upper Glacial, Magothy, and Lloyd Aquifers on Long Island, New York, in March–April 2000, with a Summary of Hydrogeologic Conditions.* New York, 2002. http://www.archive.org/ stream/gov.uscourts.f1.281/281.f1_djvu.txt. Accessed June 19, 2012.

Misut, Paul E., and Jack Monti, Jr. *Simulation of Ground-Water Flow and Pumpage in Kings and Queens Counties, Long Island New York.* Coram (NY), 1999.

Peters, Jonathan. "The Economic Impacts of the Brooklyn Waterfront." In *The Waterfront: A Brooklyn Model for Preservation and Change.* New York, 2011.

Piel v. Day, U.S. Supreme Court Transcript of Record with Supporting Pleadings. Making of Modern Law: U.S. Supreme Court Records and Briefs, 1832–1978. Farmington Hills (MI), 2011.

"Piel Bros. v. Day." *The Federal Reporter, Vol. 278.* St. Paul (MN), 1922.

Report of the Commission on Wartime Relocation and Internment of Civilians. *Personal Justice Denied.* Washington (DC), 1983.

Roosevelt, Franklin D. "Campaign Address on Prohibition in Sea Girt, New Jersey," August 27, 1932. *The American President Project.* http://www.presidency.ucsb.edu/ ws/?pid=88395. Accessed January 16, 2015.

U.S. Department of State. *Register of the Department of State.* Washington (DC), 1917.

———. *Register of the Department of State.* Washington (DC), 1919.

U.S. Library of Congress. *Thomas.* http://thomas.loc.gov/home/thomas.php. Accessed June 10, 2010.

U.S. Senate, 65th Congress, 2d Session, Subcommittee on the Judiciary. *National German American Alliance.* Washington (DC), 1918.

U.S. Senate, 66th Congress, 1st Session, Subcommittee on the Judiciary. *Brewing and Liquor Interests and German and Bolshevik Propaganda. Report and Hearings, Vol. 1.* Washington (DC), 1919.

U.S. Senate, Committee on the Judiciary, Subcommittee To Investigate the Administration of the Internal Security Act and Other Internal Security Laws, 83rd Congress, 2d Session. *Interlocking Subversion in Government Departments. Part 20: "Army Information and Education."* Washington (DC), 1954.

U.S. Senate, Secretary of the Senate, 83d Congress, 2d Session. *Report of the Secretary of the Senate from July 1, 1952, to January 2, 1953 and from January 3, 1953, to June 30, 1953.* Washington (DC), 1953.

U.S. Supreme Court. *James Everard's Breweries v. Day*, 265 U.S. 545 (1924). *FindLaw*. http://caselaw.lp.findlaw.com/scripts/getcase.pl?court=us&vol=265&invol=545. Accessed June 20, 2012.

U.S. Supreme Court. *Piel Bros. Appellant, against, Ralph A. Day, Appellees*, October 9, 1922.

United States v. Two Soaking Units and Various Other Articles, Claim of Excelsior Brewery, Inc. et al. No. 2554, District Court, E. D. New York, *44 F.2d 650 (1930)*, October 20, 1930. http://www.leagle.com/xmlResult.aspx?xmldoc=193069444F2d650_1489. xml&docbase=CSLWAR1-1950-1985. Accessed December 10, 2012.

Wilson, Woodrow. "Address to Congress Requesting a Declaration of War Against Germany," April 2, 1917. Miller Center, University of Virginia. http://millercenter. org/president/wilson/speeches/speech-4722. Accessed January 25, 2015.

Miscellaneous Sources

American Planning Association. "National Planning Awards 2005." https://www.planning. org/awards/2005/. Accessed June 21, 2014.

"History Now and Then." The Historic Bevo Mill. http://thebevomill.com/history-and-now/. Accessed February 3, 2014.

"Hof Waning." http://www.hof-waning.de/der-hof/veranstaltungen/. Accessed January 17, 2015.

"Scholz Garten, Politics and History." August Scholz. http://www.scholzgarten.net/politics. htm. Accessed February 3, 2014.

Swanberg, Wendy. "The Forgotten Censorship of *Scientific American* in 1950." History Division, Association for Education in Journalism and Mass Communication, 1–15. Chicago, August 2008.

Radio Broadcasts, Documentary Films, and Television Advertisements

Bert and Harry-Phase Two. YouTube. https://www.youtube.com/watch?v=lgVBJF170kw. Accessed January 16, 2015.

Chappell, Bill. "U.S. Moves to Halt AB InBev's Purchase of Grupo Modelo." *Planet Money*, National Public Radio, January 31, 2013. http://www.npr.org/blogs/thetwo-way/2013/01/31/170758928/u-s-moves-to-halt-ab-inbevs-purchase-of-grupo-modelo. Accessed April 29, 2013.

———. "Court Approves Anheuser-Busch InBev Deal to Buy Grupo Modelo." *Planet Money*, National Public Radio, April 23, 2013. http://www.npr.org/blogs/thetwo-way/2013/04/23/178614285/court-approves-anheuser-busch-inbev-deal-to-buy-grupo-modelo. Accessed April 29, 2013.

Fishko, Sara. "Pioneers of the 'Soft Sell.'" *On the Media*, National Public Radio, April 5, 2013. http://www.onthemedia.org/2013/apr/05/pioneers-soft-sell/. Accessed April 9, 2013.

Kaufman, Wendy. "Women Still Largely Absent From Corporate Boards." *Morning Edition*, National Public Radio, December 10, 2013. http://www.npr.org/2013/12/10/249862083/women-still-largely-absent-from-corporate-boards. Accessed September 3, 2014.

Kenney, Caitlin. "Beer Map: Two Giant Brewers, 210 Brands." *Planet Money*, National Public Radio, February 19, 2013. http://www.npr.org/blogs/money/2013/02/19/172323211/beer-map-two-giant-brewers-210-brands. Accessed April 29, 2013.

Last Meeting with Bruno Bettelheim. Directed by Daniel Karlin. La Sept Fach TV-BBS Productions, 1974. (Broadcast on KQED, San Francisco, March 22, 1989.)

Newspapers and Mass Media

Advertising Age
American Brewer
American Brewers' Review
BeerAdvocate
Beer Facts
Bloomberg
Brewers Journal
Brooklyn Daily Eagle
Brooklyn Times
Chicago Magazine
The Citizen (Ottawa, ON)
Columbia Alumni News
Columbia Daily Spectator
Corp!
County Courier (Central Valley, NY)
Daily News (New York)
The Evening Bulletin (Philadelphia)
The Evening Citizen (Ottawa, ON)
Evening Recorder (Amsterdam, NY)
Evening Telegram (New York)
Folio
Forbes
Fortune
Harlem Valley Times (Amenia, NY)

Harpers' Monthly
Herald Tribune (New York)
The Hour (Norwalk, CT)
The Kingston Daily Freeman (Kingston, NY)
Lakeville Journal (Lakeville, CT)
Los Angeles Times
Lowell Courier-Citizen (Lowell, MA)
Miami News
Modern Brewery Age
Morning Edition
Morning Telegraph (New York)
The News Press (Fort Myers, FL)
New York Daily Tribune
New York Post
New York Times
New York Tribune
New Yorker
New-Yorker Staats-Zeitung
Niagara Falls Gazette (Niagara Falls, NY)
Philadelphia Inquirer
The Pittsburg Press
Planet Money
Portland Evening Express (Portland, ME)
Princeton Alumni Weekly
Printers' Ink
The Providence Sunday Journal
Ridgewood Times (Ridgewood, NY)
Rochester Democrat and Chronicle
Schenectady Gazette
Scientific American
Smithsonian
Sonntagsblatt Staats-Zeitung und Herold (New York)
The Spy Glass
St. Louis Post Dispatch
Staten Island Advance
Straits Times (Singapore)
The Sun (New York)
Sunday Record (Middletown, NY)
Tampa Bay Times
Time

Times Newsweekly.com (Ridgewood, NY)
Toledo Blade
The Villager (New York)
Wall Street Journal
Washington Post
Wheaton College Newsletter (Norton, MA)
The Wheaton News (Norton, MA)
Wisconsin State Journal (Madison, WI)

Oral History Interviews

Kemp, Marie-Luise Piel. Interviews. New York, NY, and Dover-Foxcroft, ME. December 10, 1999; March 24, December 8, 2000; and March 30, 2001.

Lange, Olga. Interview. Dover-Foxcroft, ME. March 30, 2001.

Lange, Rollo. Interview. Dover-Foxcroft, ME. August 1, 2000.

Lazarus, Leonard. Interview. New York, NY. September 25, 1999.

McCoy, Margarita Piel. Interviews. New York, NY, and La Habra Heights, CA, 1997–2015.

Oral History Research Office, Columbia University. "The Reminiscences of George J. Joyce," 1962.

———. "The Reminiscences of Solomon A. Klein," 1962.

———. "The Reminiscences of John J. Lynch," 1962.

———. "The Reminiscences of William O'Dwyer," 1965.

———. "The Reminiscences of Gerard Piel," 1984.

Piel, Anthony. Interviews. Sharon, CT, and Portsmouth, NH. June 8, 13–14, 2014.

Piel, David J. Interview. Lenox, MA. May 11, 2002.

Piel, Eleanor Jackson. Interview. Lakeville, CT. December 16, 1999.

Piel, Gerard. Interview. Lakeville, CT. December 16, 1999.

Piel, Mark. Interview. New York, NY. December 9, 2000.

Piel, Thomas. Interview. Sherman, CT. June 20, 2013.

Piel, William, Jr. Interview. Sherman, CT. January 20, 1997.

Pollak, Richard. Interview. New York, NY. December 8, 2000.

Weinmann, Gina. Interview by Richard Pollak. San Francisco, CA. April 5, 1991.

Theses and Dissertations

Lange, Frederick. "Electric Power Generation and Distribution in the JN District, Maine." Bachelor of Science thesis, Massachusetts Institute of Technology, 1940.

Lange, Mathilde M. "On the Regeneration and Finer Structure of the Arms of the Cephalopods." Doctoral dissertation, Universitat Zürich, 1920.

Piel, Gerard. "The Formation of Parti Socialist (S.F.I.O.): The Domestication of the French Socialists." Bachelor of Arts thesis, Harvard University, 1937.

Piel, William F. J. "The Introduction of the Middle Class Tragedy into German Literature." Bachelor of Arts thesis, Columbia University, 1905.

Stack, Martin Heidegger. "Liquid Bread: An Examination of the American Brewing Industry, 1865–1940." Doctoral dissertation, Notre Dame University, 1998.

M&G Piel Securities, Inc.

Annual Reports, 1962 to 2015.

Arthur Andersen & Co., M&G Piel Securities Financial Statements, 1963 to 1972.

Brooklyn Storage Unit Papers.

M&G Piel Securities, Inc. Common Stock Class B (1967–1974).

———. Common Stock Class B: 76–125 (1971–1979).

Ross, Harvey M. Fahnstock Asset Management, Annual Shareholders Meeting, 1994 to 2015.

———. Fahnstock Asset Management, Quarterly Meeting, 1994 to 2015.

Stock Certificates, Book 1980–1983.

Stock Certificates, Book 1983–1993.

Stock Certificates, Book 1993–1996.

Michael Piel Holding Company

Annual Meeting of Stockholders. Minutes, March 1943 to November 1962.

Meeting of the Board of Directors. Minutes, September 1930 to March 1931.

———. Minutes, January 1933 to December 1934.

———. Minutes, January 1945 to April 1958.

———. Minutes, April 1955 to December 1962.

Piel Bros. Brewery

Agreement between Piel Bros. as Seller & Drewrys Limited as Purchaser. Proof of August 24, 1962. Piel Bros. Minutes, Annual Stockholders Meetings (1956–1962).

Annual Report, 1948.

Annual Report, 1950.

Annual Report, 1951.

Annual Report, 1952.

Annual Report to Stockholders for the Year Ending December 31, 1955.

Annual Report to Stockholders for the Year Ending December 31, 1956.

Annual Report to Stockholders for the Year Ending December 31, 1958.

Annual Report to Stockholders for the Year Ending December 31, 1961.

Arthur Andersen & Co., Piel Bros. Financial Statements, 1944–1962.

First Three Months Report–1957.

First Nine Months Report–1957.

First Six Months Report–1958.

First Nine Months Report–1959.

Muessen, Henry J. "Presentation to Stockholders of Piel Bros." January 18, 1960.

Piel Bros. Minutes of Committee Meetings, 1941.

Piel Bros. Minutes. Meeting of the Board of Directors, Book No. 1 (March 1898 to December 1926).

———. Meeting of the Board of Directors, Book No. 2 (January 1927 to December 1933).

———. Meeting of the Board of Directors, Book No. 3 (January 1934 to December 1934).

———. Meeting of the Board of Directors, Book No. 15 (January 1944 to December 1945).

———. Meeting of the Board of Directors (March 1954 to March 1956).

———. Annual Stockholders Meeting (1956–1962).

Piel Bros. Stock Certificate Books.

Piel Bros. Stock Certificates (1898–1915).

Piel, William. "Memorandum on a Decade of the Beer Business (1910 to incl. 1919 in Piel Bros' Career)." February 24, 1920. Piel Bros. Minutes, Book No. 1.

———. "President's Special Report to the Annual 1930 Stockholders' Meeting: A Ten-Year Business Retrospect." March 11, 1930. Piel Bros. Minutes, Book No. 2.

Rubsam and Horrmann Brewing Co. Minutes, Board of Directors (December 1953 to February 1954).

Piel Family and Related Papers

Heermann, Christian. "Familie Heermann Östrich." Jesteberg, September 4, 2005.

———. "Der Heermann-Hof in Östrich unter der adligen Familie der Freiherren von Romberg." Jesteburg, March 20, 2009.

———. "Zur Geschichte des Heermanns Hofes." Jesteburg, June 26, 2000.

Lange, Bjorn. "Ruth H. Lange," n.d.

Lange, Louise Piel, "Legacy to the Piel Clan," 1978.

Lange Papers. Lake Parlin, ME.

McCoy, Alfred W. Papers. Madison, WI.

McCoy, Margarita Piel. Papers. La Habra Heights, CA, and Madison, WI.

Kemp, Marie-Luise. Papers. Dover-Foxcroft, ME.

Lazarus, Leonard. Papers. New York, NY.

Piel, Gerard. Papers. New York, NY.

———. Papers, Piel Bros., M&G Piel. Madison, WI.

Piel, Henry. Papers. Dover-Foxcroft, ME.

Piel, Maria. Papers. Dover-Foxcroft, ME.

Piel, Marie Muessen. Papers. Dover-Foxcroft, ME.

Piel, Mildred. Papers. Madison, WI.

Piel, Oswald. Trunk. Thomas Kemp Farm, Dover-Foxcroft, ME.

Piel, Paul. Papers. Grafton, VT.

Piel, William, Sr. Papers. New York, NY.

Piel, William, Sr. "Dozen or Sixteen Lines." Translation from *Iliad*, Book A, 192–218. December 24, 1900.

———. "An Impromptu Sketch Book of the Summer of 1905."

———. Ledger (1910–1915).

———. Ledger, Account of Michael Piel (1898–1901).

———. Ledger for Maria Piel (1902–1915).

———. Ledger, Mortgages Owned by Michael Piel (1905–1916).

———. Ledger, Receipts of Maria Piel (1918–1924).

———. "The Parlinad, 1915–16."

———. "Salmon Kill Commentary: The Complete Angler: Part I. 1948 & 1949."

———. "Salmon Kill Commentary: The Incomplete Angler: Anglers Away. Part II. 1949 & 1950."

———. "Salmon Kill Commentary: The Incomplete Angler: Part II. Anglers Away. January 1952–March 1952."

———. "Territorial Expansion. Shall We Maintain Our Hold on the Philippines?" April 6, 1900.

———. "To Win the People's Cooperation with the 18th Amendment." March 10, 1924.

———. "Valedictory for Class of 1901." June 7, 1901.

Pollak, Richard. Papers. University of Chicago.

Sullivan & Cromwell. Piel Bros. files. New York, NY.

Index

Note: Page numbers in *italics* indicate illustrations, maps, and tables.

automobiles: Buick Roadmaster, 259, 307; Gottfried's company related to, 92, 123, 161, 188; horseless carriage, 71; increased number in Maine, 80; luxury touring cars, 77; Pierce Arrow, 203

Ave atque vale (Hail and farewell, Catullus), 258, 350

Avis, Dwight, 253–54

Bacardi, Luis, 162–63

Bachrach Studio (NY), 312

Ballantine & Sons (Newark, NJ): distribution of, 301; low-calorie beer of, 291; national brewers' competition for, 250–51; near beer of, 158; in NY market, 243, 248–49; ranking among brewers, 235

Baltimore *Evening Sun*, 190–91

Banker's Life Insurance Co. (Miami), 298

Bank of East New York, 56

Barmann Brewery (Kingston, NY), 177

Barnard, Chester I., 327

Barnard College, 168

Baruch, Bernard (financier), 317

baseball, 44, 186, 232

Baxter, Anne (actress), 231, 277

Baxter, Kenneth S., 231, 277

Beare, Arthur, 76

Beare, John, 76

Bear Stearns (firm, NY), 194

Beck, James M., 173

beer: 2.75 percent alcohol, 146–47; 3.2 percent alcohol, 196, 205–8; brief history, 14–15; "bum beer," 263, 266, *266*, 275, 285–86, 295; imports cut in WWI, 95; Justice's alcohol percentage metric for, 151; low-sugar and low-calorie versions, 252–54, 289–91; medicinal, 172–74; seasonal

and specialty brews, 89–90, 93–96. *See also* labels; national beer brands; production; Prohibition; quality; regional beer brands

specific varieties: Dortmunder, 86, 90, 94, 94–95, 220, 233; *Extracto de Malta* (export to Cuba), 157; Extra-Premium Pielsner, 232; Kapuziner, 90, 94, 95; Light Beer, 236, 259, 263; Light Brew (near beer), *155*; Muenchener, 90, 95; Muenchener Speciell-Bräu, 95; Piel Ale, 100; Pilsner (Pielsner, Pilsener), 90, 94, 95, 233; "Service Brew," 95, 99; Special Light Dortmunder, 220; Wuerzburger, 95. *See also* German-style lager beer; Kovar; near beer

"beer barons," 7, 33, 148, 186

Beer Cases, 172–73

beer coasters, 210, *210*, *237*, *268*

beer consumption: cool summer's impact on, 271–72; decline in 1914–35, 185; decline in 1950s, 243–44, 281; expanded in U.S., 33–34, 56; by glass, bottle, barrel for, *159*; increased (1970s), 299–300; post-Prohibition surge in, 209–10; shift from keg or by-the-glass to bottle sales, 89–90; shipping possibilities and, 89–90, 93; WWII increases, 234

Beer Drivers' Union No. 29, 47

Beer Facts (Piel's newsletter), 42

beer gardens, 25, 39–40, 42. *See also* Piel Bros. beer garden and banquet hall

"Beer of Broadway Fame" (Piel Bros. slogan), 236–37, *237*, 248, 252

Bennett, Charles G., 52

Bennett's casino (NY), 50

Berckmans, Bruce, 231–32, 233, 263

Berlin, Irving (composer), 167

"Bert and Harry" television commercials: development of, 267–68; image of, *268*; popularity of, 244, 252, 268–69; post–company sale return of, 294; sales slump despite, 269, *270*, 271–72, 281, 289; "soft sell" strategy of, 7, 267; termination of campaign, 272–73

Bethe, Hans A. (physicist), 319, 320

Bettelheim, Bruno, 201, 256, 325–26, 421–22n50

Bettelheim, Gina, 201, 255–56, 325

Bevo (Anheuser-Busch near beer), 98, 99, 158

Bevo Inn & Summer Garden (St. Louis, MO), 40

Bingham family, 10

Bird, Mary (later, Piel), 321

"The Birth of Venus" (Vichi), 72–73

Blackett, P. M. S., 327

Blatz Beer (Milwaukee, WI), 248–49

Block & Zirkle (firm, NY), 200

Bloomberg, Michael (mayor), 305

Bloomer Girl (show), 237

Boas, Franz (anthropologist), 190, 204

Bohack Stores (NY), 157, 182

Bohemian Hall & Beer Garden (Astoria, Queens, NY), 40

Bohr, Niels (physicist), 318

Bolshevism, 138, 139, 150

Bomb Squad (NY), 150

Bonnano, Joseph, Sr. ("Joe"), 176

bootleggers and gangsters: government's failure to counter, 156, 157–58, 173; Mafia connections of, 176, 178, 180; opportunities and profits of, 176–78; Piels threatened by, 154–55, 175, 179–80; Prohibition's fostering of, 183–85; real beer sold by, 156, 157,

181, 187, 190–91; violence among, 178–80. *See also* speakeasies

Boss, Conrad, 206

Boston "Pops" beer garden, 40

bottles and bottling: campaigns to collect, 235–36; Crown Cork capping machine for, 64; direct sales utilizing, 43–44; Goulding bottle-washing machine, 61; increased sales of, 89, 187, 262; metal caps for, 61, 235; plant for, 63, 281–82; plant improvements for, 187–88; "stubby" bottles, 220; tinted bottles introduced, 15; Torchiani pitching machines for packaging, 64. *See also* cans; labels

Bottling Brewers Protective Association of Greater New York, 148

Boulevard Brewery (Brooklyn, NY), 35

Brace, Donald (publisher), 87

Brandeis University, 324

Brayman, Nan, 318

brewers: anti-Prohibition campaigns of, 102–3; artisan ethos revived, 303–5; bankruptcy of, 51; boycott of Piels beer draught sales, 86, *88*, 88–90, 94; number surviving after Prohibition, 185, 193; Prohibition's impact on, 154–55; as scapegoats in and after WWI, 145; subversive in WWI, 149–50; union negotiations of, 101, 160; William's warning to, 96, 101–2. *See also* brewing industry; *and specific breweries*

Brewers' Association (brewery owners), 46

Brewers Board of Trade (NY), 247–48

Brewers' Exchange, 46–47

Brewers Journal, 205, 219

Brewers' Row (Brooklyn, NY): craft beer warehouse on, 304; demise of,

300–302; industry centered in, 35–37; neighborhoods near, 176. *See also* Bushwick

Brewers' Union No. 1, 48

Brewers' Union No. 64, 47, 48

brewery workers: bowling alleys for, 219; hours and conditions, 45, 101; increased wages and decreased hours, 249; killed in fire, 45–46; lack of insurance, 211; lockout of, 46, 48; number and appearance in 1900, 63–64; origins of, 101; pension plan for, 249; Prohibition-era negotiations with, 160; radicalism among, 246; strikes and boycotts of, 46–47; war bonds purchased by, 146, 234. *See also* labor union organizing

Brewery Workmen's Union of New York, 46

brewing industry: adjustments and expansions in WWII, 234–37; advertising wars in, 251–54; barrels produced in New York area, 25, 33–34; brand names in, 230–31, 244; brief history, 14–15; capitalization and globalization of, 15–16, 56; closed distribution system in (brewery to saloon), 23, 37, 39, 43, 49, 88; consolidation and demise of New York's, 299–302, 303, 304; craft brands ascent in, 303–5; danger of spoilage in, 230; innovations and efficiency in, 61; nationwide output by brewery after Prohibition, 185; post-Prohibition growth, 221; production increases in, 13–14, 23–24, 33–34, 56; Prohibition raids on, 173–75, 177–78; rankings in, 235, 243, *246*, 269–70; regional brewers

vs. national brands, 7–8, 10–11, 59, 89, 198–99, 207–8, 243–44; strikes in, 45–48, 247–50, 281; Wall Street's willingness to lend to, 238; WWI grain allocation for, 146–47. *See also* national beer brands; Piel Bros.; regional beer brands; technological innovations; *and specific breweries*

Brisbane, Arthur, 149

Bronfman family, 10, 355–56n14

Bronx: beer sales in, 92, 231; poverty in (South Bronx), 301–2; "registered hotels" in, 51; taxi driving in (South Bronx), 337

Brooklyn: barrels of beer produced in, 33–34; brewer-saloon ties in, 23; end of brewing in, 300–302; gangsters in 1920s, 154, 175–80; gentrification in, 302; German population and growth of breweries in, 25, 34–35; Piel Bros. found in, 14, 23; Prospect Heights homes in, 71; "registered hotels" in, 51; transportation connections of, 23; water supply of, 36. *See also* Brewers' Row; *and specific breweries*

Brooklyn Brewery (NY), 304–5

Brooklyn Bridge, 23, 38, 42, 93, 299

Brooklyn Daily Eagle: Gerard's work for, 314; Piels' advertisements in, 43–44; "Walks about the City" column, 41–42

topics covered: brewing in Brooklyn, 34, 35; Gosdorfer's lawsuit, 198; Gottfried Piel, 205; Kaiser's goals, 116; Lanzer Brewery, 37; Piel Bros., 23, 39, 42, 57; William Piel, 261

Brooklyn Directory (Lain), 34

Brooklyn Dodgers stadium (earlier, Brooklyn Bridegrooms), 44

transport, 37; national brands focused on, 7, 37, 61, 185; Percherons and wagons for, 42; restrictions on, 235–36; Rubsam & Horrmann purchase to help, 264–65; sales slump in, 269, *270*, 271–72; savings in shift to cans, 220; shipping outsourced, 213; Shipping Sales Department created, 89; of short-season drinks, 100–101; wholesale distributorships in major cities, 96. *See also* beer gardens; saloons and taverns; transportation

dividends. *See* finances; stockholders

Dortmund, Westphalia, breweries, 28

Dortmunder Union Brewery (Germany), 90

Downey, Roundsman, 50

Draeger, Fred J., 286, 288, 289

Drewrys Ltd. (South Bend, IN): acquired by Associated Brewing, 300; advertising of, 294; ale of (label), *293*; debentures held by Piel family, 296, 297–98; Hampden-Harvard Brewing subsidiary of, 293–94, 300; Piel Bros. sale to, 291–93

Droege, Ernst, 82

DuPont (corporation), 11

du Pont, Pierre (financier), 183

Duprés, Philippe, 268–69

Durkheim, Émile (sociologist), 314

Eastern Shipyard (Greenport, Long Island, NY), 121

East New York: African American migration to, 301; founding and growth, 37–39; gangsters in 1920s, 154, 175–80. *See also* Brooklyn; Lanzer Brewery; Piel Bros.

East New York Land Company, 37

East New York Laterne (newspaper), 39

East New York Savings Bank, 38

Eberstadt, Ferdinand (financier), 238

economic transformation: consolidation in, 10–12, 185, 217–18, 245–46, 281, 298–302, 303, 304; contextualization of, 17–18; finance capital in, 15–16, 61, 63, 281; regional brewers vs. national brands in, 7–8, 10–11, 59, 89, 198–99, 207–8, 243–44. *See also* managerial revolution; modernization; technological innovations

The Economist, 331

economy: environmental protection and growth in, 332; panic of 1837 in, 37; post-WWII growth, 247; post-WWII recessionary tendencies perceived in, 245–46; recession of 1907 in, 86; sanctions against German aliens and German Americans, 115; stock market plunge (1987), 342; WWII controls, 235–36. *See also* Depression era; economic transformation

education: assimilation via, 67–69; books at home, 72, 73; importance of, 310, 312–13

Edward and John Burke v. Blair (1924), 172–73

Ehret, George, Sr., 46, 49, 88, 115, 149. *See also* Hell Gate Brewery

Ehret Brewery (Manhattan, NY), 7, 33, 34, 40, 158

Eichenkranz singers, 44

Einstein, Albert, 318, 320

Eisenberg Malt Factory (Germany), 90

Elliott, Bob (comedian), 267

Emergency Agricultural Appropriation Act (1918), 152–53

Equitable Life Assurance (NY), 238–40, 241

ethnicity, individuals defined by, 308. *See also* assimilation; forced ethnic assimilation; German American identity

Evangelical German Church, 39

Evening Express (ME), 117

Evening Telegram (NY), 94–95, 102

Exner, Marie, 106

Fahnstock Corporation (NY), 342–43

Fair Play for Cuba Committee, 327–28

Falstaff Brewing Corp. (St. Louis, MO), 281, 288

Families in Business (Harvard University), 12

family: genealogical tracing of, xvi–xvii, 10, 20, 355n13; writing history of, 5–6, 17–21

family business: case study of, 12–14, 18; competing visions in, 198–99; corporate consolidation trend in, 10–12; cousins vs. siblings in, 338–40; cycle of, 8–10, 13, 310, 331; decline of artisan-based, 347; generational transitions in, 9–10, 91–93, 160–61, 182, 309, 338–40, 341–43; number of siblings in, 77; as oxymoron, 347; reflections on, 346–50; reputation of, 265–66; *Scientific American* as, 329–31, 332–33; as social formation, 262–63; solidarity in Prohibition, 154–55, 185–86, 191; succession transition in, 217–18. *See also* corporate board; incorporation; M&G Piel Securities; Piel Bros.

Family Business Review, 356n20

family business therapists, 12–13

family trees, xvi–xvii, 10, 20

Famo (near beer, Schlitz), 158

Farley, James (politician), 180

Farm Bureau, 240

FBI (Federal Bureau of Investigation): Gerard Piel and *Scientific American* surveilled by, 318–19, 321–22, 327–28; Robert Piel investigated by, 122–23; security checks for federal employees, 322–24; tips about Erwin Lange, 131, 135; vigilante surveillance reported to, 119–20

FDA (U.S. Food and Drug Administration), 265

Federal Brewing Company (Brooklyn, NY), *62*

Federal Employee Loyalty Program, 322–24

federal government: failure to enforce Prohibition, 156, 157–58, 173; Piels' challenge concerning medicinal beer, 171, 172–73; Prohibition raids on breweries, 173–75, 177–78. *See also* security apparatus; surveillance; taxation; *and specific agencies and departments*

Femina, Jerry Della, 271

Feng Yi, 329

Field, Marshall (retail executive), 317

finance capital, 15–16, 61, 63, 281

finances (Piel Bros.): amounts borrowed, 55–56, 59, 161, 188–89; brewery's value, 44–45; capitalization at time of incorporation, 57, 63, 64, 85–86; consolidation of, 298–99; effects of brewers' boycott of draught sales, 86, *88*, 88–90, 94; Gottfried's bankruptcy and, 161, 188–89, 204–5; gross sales (by 1900), 59; growth vs. dividends tensions, 221–23; increased sales and profits, 65–69, 85–86; investment by Sophie Piel, 41, 52, 56; modern management of, 217–18, 230–32;

new sales strategies, 93–95; Parlin estate costs, 106–7; plunging profits and, 287–88, 291; production, income, profit/loss, and dividends (1933–1961), *290*; salaries and dividends in interwar years, 213–15; salaries of executives, 65, 92, 163, 195, 199, 213–14, 232, 239, 261–62, 295, 330; sales by glass, bottle, barrel for, *159*; strikes' impact on, 249–50; turnaround in 1925, 181–82. *See also* advertisements and marketing; corporate expansion; M&G Piel Securities; stockholders

plant and production: bottling plant improvement, 187–88; efficiencies undertaken, 158, 160; expansion, 39; Lanzer property purchase, 23, 55; new administration building and bottling plant, 281–82; new machinery and production facilities, 39; sale of Piel Bros., 291–96; technological innovations, 61, 64; working capital vs. needed equipment purchases, 207

Prohibition era: declining revenues in, 181; effects of, 97–98; increased profits after, 171; losses in, 160; near beer and soft drink sales, 100, 151–52, 155; problems after, 188–91; renovations after, 193–94

Firestone family, 183
Fischer, Stephen M., 322, 330
Flagship Brewery (Staten Island, NY), 305
Flanagan, Dennis, 317, 318, 322, 329, 330–31
Flegenheimer, Arthur ("Dutch Schultz"), 179
Florida: Piels beer sales in, 89; Rudolf living in, 259–61, *260*

forced ethnic assimilation: contextualization of, 17–18; process of, 6; reflections on WWI and effects of, 143–45; state security's role in, 16–17; in WWI, 114–15. *See also* security apparatus; surveillance
Ford, Bacon & Davis (firm), 158
Ford, Roland, 135
Ford Motor Company, 313
Forest, Joseph, 107
Forest Hills Inn (Queens, NY), 197
Forest Hills National Bank (NY), 196–97
Forman, Carolyn, 339
Forsythe, R. M., 122
Fort Pitt pilsner (Pittsburgh, PA), 252
Fortune magazine, 314
The Fountainhead (Rand), 219
Francesco, Selma de, 106
Franco-Prussian War (1870–1871), 26, 28, 40, 116
fraternities, 68, 79, 413n17
Freud, Anna, 201
Freud, Sigmund, 168
Frias, George de, 137
Friedrich Wilhelm, Crown Prince of Germany, 117
Fuchs, Klaus (physicist), 318
The Future of Piel Bros. (brochure), 238
F. X. Matt Brewing (Utica, NY), 304, 305

Galbraith, John Kenneth (economist), 11, 12, 13
Gambrinus (brewing's patron saint), 44
gangsters. *See* bootleggers and gangsters
Garvin, Edwin L., 172
Gatewood, Worth, 269
Gehrder Freeundschafts Bund (cultural group, NY), 91
genealogy. *See* family

General Electric, 11, 218, 313

General Motors, 11, 218

Gentlement Prefer Blondes (show), 252

George Polk Award, 324

Georgia Avenue: beer foam covering, 97; brewery on, 37, 39, 45, 64

German American Alliance, 102

German American Civic Ball (NY), 117

German American identity: complexities of, 222–24; cultural clash in, 228; evidenced in household goods, 72–74, *73*; loyalty to Germany, 114, 116–19, *118*, 127, 169–70; maintained by immigrants and descendants, 116, 307–8; stigmatized and erased, 16–17, 114–15, 144; WWI repression of, 144, 145–46; of WWI spy, 128–29. *See also* assimilation; beer gardens; forced ethnic assimilation

German Americans: assumed assimilation in WWII, 234; attacks on, during WWI, 145–46; beer consumption of, 33–34; charity and ball of, 117; concerns about conscripting, 120–21; doctorates of, 67; funerals of, 91; president's warning to, 119; WWI surveillance of, 114–15, 143–45

German Charity Bazaar, 117

German immigrants: "48ers" wave of, 129; attacks on, during WWI, 145–46; brewing industry role of, 14–15; community organizations of, 38–39; economic sanctions against, 115; German lager beer introduced to U.S. by, 32–33; as largest ethnic group in U.S., 16–17; migration to U.S., 24–25; WWI surveillance of, 114–15, 143–45. *See also* German American identity; Piel family

German language: in 1930s, 204; Paul's fluency in, 276–77, 278, 307; in WWI period, 144, 145, 149

German-style lager beer: advertisements of, 43–44, 89; brewing process for, 35, 285–86, *286–87*; Brooklyn breweries for, 34–35; introduced to U.S., 32–33; palatibility of chilled, 34. *See also* beer

Germany: agents and spies of, 136–37; agricultural workers in, *28*, 28–29; alleged conspiracies in post-WWI, 139, 140; all-malt beer of (Munich), 36; antipathy toward, 210; compulsory military service in, 26, 28; education in, 67; failed 1848 revolution in, 129, 143; Heermanns' Westphalian homestead in, *28*, 29, 31, 169–70, *340*, 341; Henry's brewmaster training in, 90–91; inflation and privation in post-WWI, *170*, 170–71, 202; Lange family's connections to, 128–33; letters for Piels from (WWI), 117–19; Maria and Michael's marriage reportedly in, 29–30; Maria and Michael's visits to, 66, 225–26; Maria's continued support for, 114, 116–19, *118*, 127, 169–71; Mathilde Lange in legal limbo in, 133, 382n89; Piels beer praised in, 85; Piels' Mörsenbroich farm near Düsseldorf, 26, 28, 31–32, 66, 276–77; propaganda of, 115–16; violin dealers in, 74–76; WWI economy and rationing in, 133, 134. *See also* German American identity; German immigrants; Nazi Germany; World War I; World War II

Getchell, J. Stirling (advertising executive), 314–15

Heermann family *(continued)*
support for, 169–71; Rudolf and
family's visit to, 202
Heifer International, 333
Heifitz, Jascha (violinist), 75, 76, 164, 165,
190
Hell Gate Brewery (Manhattan, NY), 33,
34, 36, 186. *See also* Ehret, George,
Sr.
Hell Gate Bridge, 93
The Herald (North Dakota), 314
Hescheler, Karl, 138
Hess, Albert, 202
Higgins, Charles ("Vannie"), 176
High Button Shoes (show), 237
"High Time" (newssheet), 322
Hilferding, Rudolf (economist), 14
Hilliard, Charles C., 122
Hindenberg, Paul von (general), 118
Hindy, Steve, 304–5
Hitler, Adolf, 202–4, 226, 234. *See also*
Nazi Germany
Hitler Youth, 202–3
Hobson, Richmond (politician), 103
Hoffa, James, ("Jimmy," labor leader),
285
"Hof Waning" (Herne, Germany), 29
Hollister, Dorothy T., 124
Hollister, Mrs. George Trowbridge, 121
Hollister, Katherine A., 124
Holtz, Agnes (later, Heermann), 29
Holtzbrinck group, 331, 332–33
Hong Kong & Shanghai Bank, 342
Hoover, Herbert, 184
Hoover, J. Edgar, 319
hops: amounts used, 36, 147; cost savings
in purchase, 213, 233; imported
from Bavaria, 39, 210; imported
from Europe, 94; imported from
Munich, 224; imported from Saazer

(Czechoslovakia), advertised, *94,*
95, 100, 233; as key ingredient, 34,
35, 43, 48; in production process,
286–87; in Prohibition, 191
Horatio Hall (ship), 79
Horn, Thomas L., 122, 124
Horrmann, August, 264
horses: agricultural work, 29, 227; Amish
use of, 163; beer wagons, 35, 49, 63,
64, 206, 236; Clydesdales, 206; killed
in auto crash, 77; Percherons, 42, 49;
on summer estate, 78, 82, 107, 110;
trolleys, 38
hotels: law's exemption of alcohol sales
by, 51; Piels contracts with, 89, 96,
160, 198
House Un-American Activities Committee
(HUAC), 318, 319, 320, 321–22, 323
Hövel, Walter, 223
Howard, John C., 120
Hoyt, Philip D., 123
HUAC (House Un-American Activities
Committee), 318, 319, 320, 321–22,
323
Huber-Hittleman Brewery (Brooklyn,
NY), 304
Hull, Cordell, 255
hydrogen bombs, 319–21. *See also* nuclear
weapons

The Iliad (Homer), translations of, 87
immigrants. *See* German immigrants
InBev (multinational conglomerate), 15,
303
incorporation (1898): capitalization at
time of, 57, 63, 64, 85–86; context,
summarized, 52–53; documentation
increased after, 19–20; economic
context of, 59; effects of, 60;
financial context of, 55–59; inventory

completed for, 63–64; process of, 57–58; stock certificate issued, 58, *58*
industrialization: deskilling in, 46–47; investments and innovations in, 13–14; managerial revolution and capitalization in, 15–16, 56. *See also* technological innovations
Ingersoll, Ralph (publisher), 315
Institute of Policy Studies (DC), 328
Institut International d'Alimentation (Belgium), 259, 263
Interbrew (Belgium), 303
Internal Revenue Service (IRS): alcohol advertising rules of, 253–54; consolidation of finances and, 298; limits on advertisements, 236. *See also* taxation
"intoxicating," not defined, 151, 156. *See also* Prohibition
Italy, Stazione Zoologica in, 131, 141

Jackson, Eleanor. *See* Piel, Eleanor Jackson
Jacob Hoffman Brewery (Manhattan, NY), 151
Jacob Ruppert Brewery. *See* Ruppert Brewery
Jacob Schmidt Brewing (St. Paul, MN), 300
Jakoby, Henry, 211
James Everard's Breweries v. Day (1924), 172–73
Japanese-American Claims Act (1948), 145
Jaurès, Jean (politician), 314
Jay Treaty (1795), 145
Jenner, William E., 322
Jennings & Russell (firm, NY), 103
Jermyn, Edmund B., Jr., 122
John Friedrich (firm, NY), 75
Johns, Jasper (artist), 326

Journal of Experimental Zoology, 138
J. Stirling Getchell (firm, NY), 314–15
J. Walter Thompson (firm, NY), 98, 100, 160

Kahn, Ely Jacques (architect), 87, 219, 238, 281–82
Kahn, Herman (futurist), 327
Kaiser, Henry J. (entrepreneur), 316, 317, 321
Kaiser Alexander First Grenadier Guard Regiment, 26, 28
Kazal, Russell A., 17
Keeler, William ("Wee Willie," baseball fielder), 44
Keller-Deffner, William, 75
Kelly, Walt (cartoonist), 294
Kemp, Marie-Luise Piel (1914–2012): European travels of, 223–24; found photo of, 2, 6; on gangsters, 179; Maine home of, 341; M&G Piel Securities role of, 341, 342; at Michael Piel trust meeting, 278; on Patsy, 325; on prohibition agents, 175; Prohibition repeal efforts of, 184; summer activities, 110
Kennedy, John F., 328
Kennedy, Robert, 328
Kennedy, William ("Brickyard," pitcher), 44
Kennedy, William (author), 153
Kent, Rockwell (painter), 87
Kent, William P., 133–35, 136
Kenyon & Eckhardt (firm, NY), 220, 252
Khaldun, Ibn, 9, 13
Kheel, Theodore W. (arbitrator), 247
Killbuck Cider & Vinegar Co. (OH), 163–64, 165
Kings (Excelsior) Brewery (Brooklyn, NY), 177–78

Mitchell, Harry W., 52

modernization: consolidation in, 185, 217–18; critique of management and, 232–34; efficiencies in, 61, 158, 160, 181–82, 190, 193–94, 218–19; expansion linked to, 40–42, 43, 44–45, 56, 60–61; professional management in, 186–87; stalled, 275; tensions inherent in family business and, 8–9

Mohn family (publisher), 355–56n14

Mondadori (Italian publisher), 329

Monroe (NY) Peace Council, *142*, 142–43

Morgenthau, Henry, Sr. (diplomat), 131

The Morningside (Columbia University), 87

Mörsenbroich farm (near Düsseldorf), 26, 28, 31–32, 66, 276–77

The Mortarboard (Barnard College), 168

Moskowitz, Miriam, 321

Mueller, Agnes. *See* Piel, Agnes (1897–1983)

Mueller, Fritz, 326

Muessen, Henry J.: assistance for Margarita, 337; background of, 262–63; "Bert and Harry" ads of, 271; on brewing in WWII, 235; death, 341; Drewrys board seat of, 293, 295, 298; executive potential of, 231; expansion goals of, 250, 294; illness, 338; keg types and, 214; low-calorie beer campaign of, 289–91; on low sugar content, 253; M&G Piel Securities role of, 335, 338; on new bottling plant, 282; Paul's support for, 277, 283, 289, 295–96; on Piel Bros. decline, 284–85; as Piel Bros. president, 262; plant survey and financing under, 238; on product

problems, 286, 289; response to quality crisis and concerns, 289–91; Rubsam & Horrmann purchase by, 263–67; sale negotiations of, 287–88, 291–93

Muessen, Marie. *See* Piel, Marie Muessen

Mullan-Gage Act (NY), 171–72, 174

Mullen, Pearl, 321

Müller, Marga Piel, 224, 277

"Murder, Inc.," 179

music: Amati violin, 280; beer gardens, 39–40; Beethoven banned, 145; events at Piels, 44; funerals, 91; Paul's Transposition Piano, 167; room furnishings for, 72, 73; singing while fishing, 82; Stradivarius violin, 73, 74–76, 164, 165, 190; summer estate, 79, 83

Musto, David, 19

National Association of Cereal Beverage Manufacturers, 148

national beer brands: advertising by, 209, 281; ambitions to become, 194–95, 198–201; control of production by, 300; emergence of, 7, 37, 41, 61, 207; expansion into NY market, 248–49, 250–51, 262; growth and consolidation of, 185, 217, 245–46, 281; managerial revolution and capitalization of, 13–15; Piels in context of, 223, 284; reduced to two conglomerates, 15, 245; regional brewers vs., 7–8, 10–11, 59, 89, 198–99, 207–8, 243–44; repeal welcomed by, 206; success of, 33

National German American Alliance, 149

National Grocery, 158

household and personal goods, 67, 71, 72–74, 73; income and genteel lifestyle, 65–67, 76–77; loyalty to Germany, 114, 116–19; loyalty to U.S., 114–15; marriage, 29–30; migration to U.S., 24–25, 30–31, 32; retirement, 59, 65; significance of, 7; statuary of, 344; stories about, 3, 341; Stradivarius of, 73, 74–76; summer estate and activities, 76–79, 81; travels of, 66, 74

business: brewery expertise and innovations, 14, 25–26, 41–42, 52, 63–65; debt to Gottfried, 57, 59–60, 365n23; as principal in Piel Bros., 55–57; tensions with Gottfried, 55, 57; as vice-president of company board, 59; William hired by, 87

Piel, Michael ("Mike," 1935–2002), 258, 276–77, 333, 344

Piel, Oswald (1900–1989): board maneuvers of, 241; chicken hatchery work of, 163; dairy farm of, 165–66, 222; death, 341; honored at board meeting, 342; Loretto's disdain for, 222; Louise's breach with, 256; Maria's cash gift to, 162; on postwar expansion and loan, 240; summer activities, 106, 110; travels of, 341

Piel, Otto (1887–1932), 70; birth, 69; family role, 106; illness and later death, 166–67, 326; Maria's bequest and gift to, 162, 279

Piel, Paul (1889–1984), 70; Agnes's attachment to, 168–69; Agnes's breach with, 255–56; birth, 69; death, 341; education, 68, 333; European travels of, 116, 131, 167; family role of, 105; as family's liaison to Maria, 278–80; family tree compiled by, 20; on fight

against Germans (WWII), 235; fluent in German language, 276–77, 278, 307; Gerard's relationship with, 326; German relations' invitation to, 118; home, 167–68, 171; Lake Parlin as hotel and, 164; later years, 339–40; lifestyle, 275–76; Maria's cash gift to, 162, 167–68; marriage, 167; Otto's care by, 166; philosophical interests of, 107, 108; plans to study in Europe, 67; remembered, 307–8; summer activities, 82, 106, 110, 111; WWI service, 112, 121

business: advertising image by, 210; APL investigation, 125; on dividends, 214; as family manager, 276–80; Gosdorfer's lawsuit and, 197; Louise's suggestions condemned by, 282–84, 285; on marketing, 231; M&G Piel Securities role of, 297, 335, 337–39, 338; as Michael Piel Trust president, 192, 230, 275, 277–78; on Michael's debt to Gottfried, 59, 365n23; Michael's German properties sold by, 276–77; MID investigation and surveillance of, 125–26, 127, 128; modernization under, 230; on postwar expansion and loan, 240; sale suggestion and, 287–89; yeast culture station overseen by, 207, 219. See also corporate board, Paul's tenure

Piel, Rita (later, Brown, 1913–98), 312

Piel, Robert (1890–1952), 68, 121–24, 222, 229, 338

Piel, Roland (1902–1926), 106, 110, 164–65, 166, 280

Piel, Rudolf (1892–1961), 70; birth, 69; breach with family, 227–28; death, 240–41; education, 68, 189, 190, 203; engineering apprenticeship, 189–90;

as chief operating officer, 91; on cider beverage development, 100; on corporate board, 90, 160–61; economies implemented, 160; familial and financial pressures in Prohibition, 162, 163, 164–65, 166, 171; family members ousted by, 223–30; family resistance to and scrutiny of, 195–96; gangsters' murder attempt on, 180; groomed to manage brewery, 86–87; on "independence and quality" credo, 85; Maria's request for repayment, 200–201; medicinal beer legislation tested by, 172–73; on Michael's debt to Gottfried, 59, 365n23; Michael's German properties and, 276; modernization under, 230; on near beer and soft drink development and marketing, 96–100, 151, 181–82, 191; reforms of, 217–18; response to prohibition agents, 174–75; on sales strategies, 94; on saloon problem, 103; sibling alliances against, 186; Specialty Brews campaign of, 95–96; survival strategy in Prohibition, 155–56, 157, 161–62, 186–88; on temperance threat, 96, 101–2, 147–48; on 3.2 percent alcohol beer, 206. *See also* corporate board, William's tenure

Piel, William, Jr. ("Bill," 1909–98): assistance for Gerard in McCarthy era, 322, 323; career, 309, 313, 334; divorce, 228, education, 312–13; father's later years and, 257, 258; last visit to Maria, 278; marriage, 312; on Prohibition, 154; on Rudolf, 190; on saloons, 50; stories about, 344; WWII service and medal of, 313

Piel Bros. (brewery): Bier Stube of, 64,

97, 98, 219–20; bulk draught sales records broken, 206–7; as case study, 12–14, 18; children's return to (late 1920s), 171; Cross of Honor award for, 259, 263; industrial accidents at, 232–33; million-barrel mark reached, 243; organizational schematic of, *212*; production by barrels (1880–1960), *208*; ranking among brewers, 235, 243, *246*, 269–70; Staten Island plant purchased by, 263–67, *266*, 285–86, 294. *See also* advertisements and marketing; corporate board; distribution and shipping; finances; incorporation; Lanzer Brewery; legal issues and cases; production

beginning years: assets in starting, 25–26; context of, 32–37; direct sales of, 25, 39, 42, 43–45, 50; founding (1883), 14; growth, 7, 23–24; "independence and quality" credo of, 85–86; inventory of (1898), 63–64; layout of, 45, 63–65, 361–62n63; location of, 35, 37; model brewery facilities, 63–65; national reach, 96; property originally purchased, 23, 33, 37–38, *38*, 55, 64; prosperity despite challenges, 52–53; shift from local to regional status, 59, 89; surge in sales, 65; targeted for takeover, 61; union boycott of, 48; valuation of, 45

early corporate years: brewers' boycott of draught sales of, 86, *88*, 88–90, 94; expansion and modernization, 40 42, 43, 44–45, 56, 60–61; phases in management, 186, 217–18; slogan changed, 146; Trommer's Brewery purchased, 251; William's and Henry's roles and salaries at, 92. *See also* corporate board

Piel Bros. (brewery) *(continued)*
  Prohibition, before, during, and after:
    competing visions for, 198–99;
    efficiencies and renovations, 158, 160,
    181–82, 190, 193–94; expansion for
    3.2 percent alcohol beer production,
    196, 205–8; family's solidarity in,
    154–55, 185–86, 191; gangsters'
    threats against, 154, 175–80; law
    enforcement's targetting of and raids
    on, 173–75; medicinal beer permit
    of, 172; near beer and soft drink
    development, 151–52 (*see also* near
    beer); post-Prohibition mortgage on
    plant, 189; post-Prohibition sales
    surge, 209–10; repeal preparations by,
    205, *206*, 206–8; seasonal and special
    brews of, 89–90, 93–96; survival in
    Prohibition, 154–56, 158–71, 185–86.
    See also Prohibition
  sale of company (Piel Bros., Inc.):
    attempt to take the firm public,
    194–95; description of, 15, 291–96;
    mismanagement in late 1950s,
    281–85; modernization stalled, 275;
    Muessen's attempt to sale or merge,
    287–88; status after, 299–300
Piel Bros. beer garden and banquet hall:
    closure of, 64, 90; cooling facility on
    former space of, 250; declining sales
    at, 89; as destination family resort,
    25, 43–44; loan for building, 55–56;
    popularity and success of, 39, 53;
    Sabbath day sales at, 48; size and
    layout, 42, 63, 64; Sunday business
    of, 50–51
Piel Bros. v. Day (1921), 172–73
Piel family: autobiographical project
    of history of, 18–19; as case study,
    12–14, 18; commercial fable of, 299;

dividends and dispersal of, 215;
    documentation available, 19–20;
    finding work outside the brewery,
    162–71; fourth generation's view of
    story, 307–8; genealogical chart, xvi–
    xvii; generational transitions in, 9–10,
    91–93, 160–61, 182, 309, 338–40,
    341–43; growth vs. dividends issue,
    222–23; hierarchy created among
    children, 77, 277–78; interviews
    and perspectives on, 20–21; lessons
    of, 348–50; questions raised by, 21;
    resistance to temperance, 48–52;
    resistance to unions, 45–48; shared
    summer experiences in, 79–83, 104–
    12; significance of, 6–10, 17; themes
    in, 17–18; WWI's impact on, 112,
    114–15, 119–25, 143–45. *See also* Piel
    third generation
Piel Poultry Farm (MA), 227–28, 240
"Piel's Light Beer of Broadway Fame"
    (jingle), 237
Piel System of Roof Construction, 167
Piel third generation: city careers, 310–16;
    in cold war witch-hunt, 319–22;
    commercial benchmarks, 328–30;
    divisions healed by, 310; family
    matters and concerns of, 324–26;
    finances of, 308–9; genealogical
    chart of, xvi–xvii; launching
    Scientific American, 316–19; lives of,
    summarized, 308–10; Loyalty Board
    case of, 16, 322–24; success of, 326–
    28; transition of, 298–99. See also
    specific third-generation individuals
Pilsen Brewing Company (Chicago, IL),
    103
Pitkin, John R., 37
Pittsburgh Beer War, 247
plea bargains, 172

polio outbreak (1916), 109–10

politics: alcohol regulation by state, 171–72; ASL vs. brewers and, 102–3; Bolshevism, brewing, and German propaganda linked in, 149–50; Democratic Party and, 49–50, 52, 244; incidents related to, 44; Prohibition repeal issue in, 184–85, 196; Republican Party and, 184, 332

Polytechnic Preparatory School (Brooklyn, NY), 68, 86

Potter, Tom, 304–5

poultry business, 226–28, 240

Powys, John Cowper (writer), 167

Princeton University, 68, 122, 124, 166, 312, 338

Pritzker family, 10, 355–56n14

production (Piel Bros.): for army, 236; by barrels (1880–1960), *208*; brewing process, 35, 285–86, *286–87*; cooling facility built, 250; copper vats developed, 34; difficulties unrecognized, 288; equipment purchases critiqued, 232–33; expansion for 3.2 percent alcohol, 196, 205–8; increases in, 13–14, 23–24, 33–34, 49–50, 56, 245–46; industrial accidents in, 232–33; mass-production level, 230–31; million-barrel mark reached, 243; modernization and efficiency improvements of, 39, 218–19; monthly capacity of plant, 209; pasteurization in, 14, 15, 42, 61, 220, 285; post-Prohibition plateau of, 221; production, income, profit/loss, and dividends statistics (1933–1961), *290*; rebound despite boycott, 94; strikes' impact on, 249–50; water supply for, 35. *See also* bottles and bottling;

corporate expansion; distribution and shipping; hops; malt; refrigeration; technological innovations; yeast

professional management (Piel Bros.): case study of, 12–14, 18; divisions muted by, 214–15; modernization strategy in, 186–87; Paul's defense of, 282–84; Piels shift to, 211–15, 217–18. *See also* corporate board; corporate expansion; finances; managerial revolution

Prohibition: beginning of (1920), 152, 154–56; brewers that survived, 185, 193; campaigns against, 102–3, 183–85; as catalyst for gangster organizing, 154, 175–80; challenge to federal government during, 171–73; constitutional amendment (18th) for, 115, 147, 149–50, 151, 156; enforcement pressure in, 173–75; failure to enforce, 156, 157–58, 173; intensified pressure for, 145–48; intimations of, 150–52; local and state initiatives of, 97–98, 100, 102, 103 (*see also* South); low-alcohol beer developed in anticipation of, 96–99; managerial revolution coinciding with, 15; repeal of (21st amendment), 171, 183, 185, 196, 206, 217; repeal preparations by brewers, 205–8; surge in beer sales after, 209–10; survival in, 154–56, 158–71, 185–86; as threat to brewers, 96, 101–2, 147–48; wartime patriotism underlying, 112, 115, 150–52. *See also* bootleggers and gangsters; near beer; speakeasies; temperance movement; Volstead Act

Prohibition Party, 48

prostitution, 51

Psalm 127 (biblical reference), 32

Pullman Sleeping Car Company, 198

yeast: Christian Schmidt strain of, 36; culture station for, 97, 207; fermentation process, 32–33, 175; imported from Westphalia, 210; problems with, 286; propagation apparatus for, 95; pure culture type, 61; studies of, 91; supervisor of, 219

Ye Waverly Inn (Greenwich Village), 167
Young & Rubicam (firm, NY), 253, 267–68, 272, 294. *See also* "Bert and Harry" television commercials
YouTube, 268–69

Ziegfield Follies (musical), 236
Zurich University, 136, 138